Library of Congress Cataloging-in-Publication Data

Peak, Kenneth J.
    Policing America: challenges and best practices/Kenneth J. Peak—6th ed.
        p. cm.
    ISBN 0-13-159803-1
    1. Police—United States. 2. Law enforcement—United States.   I. Title
    HV8141.P33 2009
    363.20973—dc22

                                    2007050068

Editor in Chief: *Vernon Anthony*
Senior Acquisitions Editor: *Tim Peyton*
Development Editor: *Elisa Rogers*
Editorial Assistant: *Alicia Kelly*
Production Coordinator: *Janet Bolton*
Project Manager: *Holly Shufeldt*
Art Director: *Diane Ernsberger*
Cover Designer: *Ali Mohrman*
Cover photo: *Superstock*
Senior Operations Supervisor: *Pat Tonneman*
Director of Marketing: *David Gesell*
Executive Marketing Manager: *Adam Kloza*
Marketing Assistant: *Alicia Dysert*

This book was set in AGaramond by Laserwords. It was printed and bound by Edwards Brothers. The cover was printed by Phoenix Color Corp.

Pearson Education Ltd., London
Pearson Education Singapore, Pte. Ltd.
Pearson Education Canada, Inc.
Pearson Education—Japan
Pearson Education Australia PTY, Limited

Pearson Education North Asia, Ltd., Hong Kong
Pearson Educación de Mexico, S.A. de C.V.
Pearson Education Malaysia, Pte. Ltd.
Pearson Education, Upper Saddle River, New Jersey

10 9 8 7 6 5 4 3 2

ISBN-13: 978-0-13-159803-4
ISBN-10:   0-13-159803-1

POLICING AMERICA
CHALLENGES AND BEST PRACTICES

SIXTH EDITION

KENNETH J. PEAK
University of Nevada, Reno

PEARSON

Prentice
Hall

Upper Saddle River, New Jersey
Columbus, Ohio

This book is dedicated to the members of my immediate and extended family who daily do the work described in this book—Undersheriff Dan Peak, Officer Oliver Miller III, Lieutenant Darin and Deputy Heather Balaam, and FBI Special Agent Alan Peak—and to their spouses and parents, who worry. Be safe.

—K. J. P.

BRIEF CONTENTS

CONTENTS

    The Problem   443
    Specific Police Responses   444

APPENDIX II   CAREER INFORMATION   447
               First Things First: Preparation for Job Hunting   447
               Helpful Dose of Reality   448
                   Careers in Local Policing   449
                   Careers with State Agencies   449
                   Careers in Federal Law Enforcement   450

               NOTES   451
               INDEX   485

This sixth edition of *Policing America,* like its predecessors, benefits from the author's many (thirty-eight) years of combined practical and academic experience, which includes holding two positions as a police chief executive officer. Its chapters therefore contain a real-world flavor not found in most policing textbooks and reflect the changing times in which we live and the tremendous challenges facing federal, state, and local agents and officers every day. Though considerably different in its content from the five preceding editions, this edition continues to represent my best attempt to allow the reader, to the fullest extent possible, to experience the sensation of wearing a police uniform by providing a highly practical, comprehensive view of the world of policing.

NEW POLICING DIRECTIONS IN THIS SIXTH EDITION

In addition to dozens of new case studies of "what works" and updated materials throughout, the following are substantively new additions to this revised edition:

Assessment of anomie	Chapter 3
Contract and consolidated police services	Chapter 3
Police-media relations: The Beltway Snipers Case	Chapter 3
Police training officer (PTO) program	Chapter 4
Assessment centers	Chapter 4
Suicide by cop	Chapter 5
Combined DNA Index Systems (CODIS) and postconviction testing	Chapter 7
Use-of-force continuum	Chapter 9
Contagious shooting	Chapter 9
Duty of care and failure to protect	Chapter 10
National Incident Management System (NIMS)	Chapter 11
Meth labs, open-air drug markets, raves, and gang initiatives	Chapter 11
New border problems and initiatives	Chapter 12
Youth violence, bullying, and underage drinking	Chapter 12
Robotics	Chapter 14
Principles of predictions and futures research	Chapter 15
"What Works": Police Problem-Oriented Approaches to Community Problems	Appendix I

CHAPTER CONTENTS

The book's new subtitle—*Challenges and Best Practices*—is indicative of this edition's stronger emphasis on what the police are doing to address the many crime problems and issues that plague America. And nowhere is this new emphasis more obvious than in Appendix I, where three problems—child pornography on the Internet, identity theft, and street racing—are discussed as well as methods being used by the police to deal with them. The specter of terrorism and our resulting emphasis on homeland security also loom large throughout this edition, as well as what the police are doing to prevent—and react to—any future attacks.

As indicated above, this sixth edition includes several beneficial changes in its organization and content. First, the book's fifteen chapters are now divided into five parts, which better organize and cluster the overall content. In addition, two chapters, Chapters 11 and 12, are new to this edition; both are oriented toward specific crime problems (terrorism, gangs, and drugs in Chapter 11; illegal immigration, the Mafia, hate crimes, and youth crimes in Chapter 12) as well as what the police are doing to confront those challenges. Finally, policing at the local (municipal and county) level has been removed from Chapter 2 and is now a separate chapter, Chapter 3.

New materials have also been added throughout and include those on the reorganized federal law enforcement structure; state and local (municipal police and county sheriff) departments; technologies in use or in development; recent major court decisions affecting the police; the National Incident Management System for addressing terrorism; new programs for addressing and mediating peace with gangs; assessment centers; suicide by cop; the new police training officer (PTO) concept; a greatly expanded section on civil liability; and recent areas of concern with and scrutiny of forensic laboratories and DNA databases. Furthermore, this edition continues to provide updated information and coverage of such topics as the patrol function, community policing and problem solving, investigations, accountability, civil liability, and the future of policing. More than thirty exhibits are also disseminated throughout the book to help explicate the materials. Seven of those exhibits provide information about policing in other countries that is related to the chapters in which they appear; because crime is an international problem, it is increasingly important to understand how the police function in foreign venues. Chapter 2 includes an exhibit discussing the International Criminal Police Organization, or Interpol. In addition, there are five Practitioner's Perspectives, short essays written by selected individuals with expertise in selected areas of policing, scattered throughout the book.

There are several pedagogical attributes as well. To help make this textbook more reader-friendly, each chapter begins with learning objectives and an introduction. Each key term is boldface in the chapter, and a list of the key terms is found at the end of each chapter. There are also review questions, independent student activities, and related Web sites at the end of each chapter. I recommend that you examine the review questions after reading each chapter to get a feel for how well you understand the chapter's contents. The independent activities and recommended Web sites are intended to enhance your understanding of the applied aspects of policing. Other instructional aids include the Practitioner's Perspectives, tables and figures, and exhibits with recent news items.

The two appendices are instructive as well, and maintain the book's theme of examining solutions to problems of crime and disorder. The first, entitled "What Works": Police Problem-Oriented Approaches to Community Problems, contains three case studies of crime and disorder and demonstrates what police are doing to address child pornography on the Internet, identity theft, and street racing. The second appendix provides law enforcement career information and includes some realistic, matter-of-fact information that job hunters should know about federal, state, and local agencies. Finally, a detailed index at the end of the book makes it easy for you to find information on specific topics quickly.

From its beginning through the final chapter, this book provides a penetrating view of what is certainly one of the most difficult and challenging occupations in America: policing.

CHAPTER ORGANIZATION

In Part I, the foci are the foundations and evolution of policing. This part now has what I term a "funneling effect." Chapter 1 takes a broad view, tracing the history of policing, from its beginning in England to its migration and origin in the United States, and its three eras in this country; included is a discussion of the three generations of community policing and problem solving. Chapter 2 takes a wholly domestic view and examines the organization and administration of federal and state law enforcement agencies to protect their respective borders, particularly in the post-9/11 era of homeland defense. The dual roles of state agencies—those of general police duties as well as state bureaus of investigation—are also discussed. Chapter 3 continues this funneling effect, examining the status, organization, and administration of local agencies such as municipal police departments and sheriff's offices, including profiles of both and comparisons with each other. Also discussed are definitions of organizations; organizational communication; functions of police executive officers, middle managers, and supervisors; influence of politics; and agency accreditation. Finally, Chapter 4 is even smaller in scope, examining how the process works that is generally used to transform an individual citizen into a trained, ready-to-serve police officer through the police subculture. Included are the hiring and training processes and the roles, functions, and styles of policing in our society.

Part II generally looks at policing from various occupational perspectives. It opens with Chapter 5, which explores the very important function of patrolling and includes the purposes and nature of patrol; the dangers encountered; the variations in patrol work by shift, beat, and assignment; the discretionary authority of officers; and the traditional traffic function. Chapter 6 focuses on a form of policing that is being embraced by thousands of police agencies across the United States and around the world, community-oriented policing and problem solving (COPPS), and Chapter 7 focuses on criminal investigation, including the highly progressive fields of forensic science and criminalistics.

In Part III, we look at the various means by which police authority is constrained, how officers are to be ethically grounded, and how they may be disciplined when they use inappropriate methods. Chapter 8 looks at the rule of law, court decisions, and constitutional enactments that direct and constrain police actions; the focus here is on the Bill of Rights in the Constitution, particularly the Fourth, Fifth, and Sixth Amendments. Chapter 9 looks at police accountability and includes the issues of police ethics, use of force, corruption, and discipline. Police civil liability is then examined in Chapter 10, which is greatly expanded and updated and includes various areas in which officers may be liable and citizens may seek legal redress.

Part IV contains three chapters that collectively address a number of special population, problems, and challenges faced by the police. Chapter 11 looks at the major problems and methods connected with terrorism (including the National Incident Management System, bioterrorism, and the USA PATRIOT Act), gangs (including graffiti, types of programs, and mediating of peace), and drugs (including methamphetamine, open-air markets, and raves). Chapter 12 considers crime problems posed by and methods for dealing with immigrants (including several new border initiatives), the Mafia, hate offenses, and youth violence (including school violence and bullying, gun violence, and other problems). Chapter 13 describes a number of trends (labor relations, women and minorities in policing, and private security/policing) and issues (stress, higher education for officers, and the problem of homelessness).

In Part V, Chapter 14 examines contemporary police technology, including new technologies for dealing with old crime problems and the myriad uses of computers, electronics, and imaging and communications systems. The development and use of less-lethal weapons, innovations in firearms training, and other new technologies are also discussed. Chapter 15 looks at the future of policing, with emphasis on new technologies that could dramatically affect police operations and training.

Finally, as noted earlier, the appendices continue the book's overarching theme of "best practices." Appendix I looks at three contemporary problems of crime and disorder (listed above) and the solutions attempted by the police, and Appendix II provides information concerning careers in law enforcement at all levels. The book's index serves as its ending point.

As noted earlier, greater emphasis is placed in this sixth edition on the more serious problems that today's police are facing and the methods that the police are employing to address them.

SUPPLEMENTS

Instructor Resource Center

Register today at www.prenhall.com to access instructor resources digitally.

To access supplementary materials online, instructors need to request an instructor access code. Go to **www.pearsonhighered.com/irc** where you can register for an instructor access code. Within 48 hours after registering you will receive a confirming e-mail including an instructor access code. Once you have received your code, go to the site and log on for full instructions on downloading the materials you wish to use.

This text is accompanied by an Instructor's Manual with Test Bank, TestGen, PowerPoints, Test Item File for WebCT, Test Item File for Blackboard/Course Compass, and a Companion Web site (www.Prenhall.com/peak <http://www.prenhall.com/peak>).

ACKNOWLEDGMENTS ◀••••••••••••••••••

This edition, like its five predecessors, is the result of the professional assistance of several practitioners and publishing people at Prentice Hall. First, I continue to benefit from my friendships and professional associations with Tim Peyton, executive editor; Elisa Rogers, associate editor; and Janet Bolton, project manager. I also wish to acknowledge the invaluable assistance of the following reviewers: Rodney Brewer, University of Louisville; Jim Golden, University of Arkansas–Little Rock; David R. Graff, Kent State University–Tuscarawas; Larry Karson, University of Houston–Downtown; Matthew Morgan, Indiana State University; Joe Morris, Northwestern State University; and Peter L. Sanzen, Hudson Valley Community College. Their reviews of this sixth edition resulted in many beneficial changes.

KENNETH J. PEAK

Ken Peak's career as a practitioner and educator in law enforcement and criminal justice spans more than thirty-five years, including nearly eight years as a police chief executive and beat officer. He is currently a full professor and former chairman of the Department of Criminal Justice, University of Nevada, Reno, where he was named teacher of the year by the university's honor society. He entered municipal policing in Kansas in 1970 and subsequently held positions as a nine-county criminal justice planner in Kansas; director of a four-state Technical Assistance Institute for the Law Enforcement Assistance Administration; director of university police at Pittsburg State University in Kansas; acting director of public safety at the University of Nevada, Reno; and assistant professor of criminal justice at Wichita State University. He has authored or coauthored twenty other textbooks, including *Justice Administration: Police, Courts, and Corrections Management* (5th ed.); *Community Policing and Problem Solving: Strategies and Practices* (5th ed., with Ronald W. Glensor); *Police Supervision and Management: In an Era of Community Policing* (2nd ed., with Ronald W. Glensor and Larry K. Gaines); *Women in Law Enforcement Careers: A Guide for Preparing and Succeeding* (with V. Lord); and *Policing Communities: Understanding Crime and Solving Problems* (an anthology, with R. Glensor and M. Correia). He has also published two historical books—*Kansas Temperance: Much Ado about Booze, 1870–1920* (with P. Peak) and *Kansas Bootleggers* (with Patrick G. O'Brien)—as well as more than fifty journal articles and book chapters. He has served as chairman of the Police Section of the Academy of Criminal Justice Sciences and as president of the Western and Pacific Association of Criminal Justice Educators. His teaching interests include policing, administration, victimology, and comparative justice systems. He received two gubernatorial appointments to statewide criminal justice committees while residing in Kansas and holds a doctorate from the University of Kansas.

PART I

FOUNDATIONS

DEVELOPMENT OF LAW ENFORCEMENT ORGANIZATIONS AND POLICE OFFICERS

This part's four chapters look at the foundations of policing while also taking a "funneling" approach, going from the larger joint foreign and domestic origins of policing in Chapter 1 to the smaller individual officer focus in Chapter 4. Chapter 1 discusses the historical development of the police in England and its migration to the United States, where it has now survived three eras. Chapter 2 takes a domestic approach, looking at how U.S. federal and state agencies are organized and function to protect their respective borders, particularly in the post-9/11 era of homeland defense. Chapter 3 continues this funneling effect with a view and comparisons of local (municipal police and county sheriff) agencies' functions in society. Finally, Chapter 4, as noted above, is even smaller in scope, examining how the individual citizen is transformed into a police officer through the police subculture and the hiring, training, and socialization processes.

1

HISTORICAL DEVELOPMENT

COMING TO AMERICA

Nature proukit them to begin some litil police, for some of them began to plant trees, some to daut beasties, some gathrid the fruitis.
—*Quote from a Scottish document 1549*

The farther back you can look, the farther forward you are likely to see.
—*Winston Churchill*

LEARNING OBJECTIVES

AS A RESULT OF READING THIS CHAPTER, THE STUDENT WILL:

– UNDERSTAND THE MAJOR POLICE-RELATED OFFICES AND THEIR FUNCTIONS DURING THE EARLY ENGLISH AND COLONIAL PERIODS

– KNOW THE LEGACIES OF COLONIAL POLICING THAT REMAINED INTACT AFTER THE AMERICAN REVOLUTION

– COMPREHEND THE THREE PRIMARY ERAS OF POLICING AND THE MAIN CHARACTERISTICS OF EACH

– BE ABLE TO LIST THE THREE EARLY ISSUES OF AMERICAN POLICING AND TO DESCRIBE THEIR PRESENT STATUS

– UNDERSTAND THE UNIQUE CHARACTERISTICS OF LAW ENFORCEMENT AS IT EXISTED IN THE WILD WEST

– BE AWARE OF THE DEFINITIONS AND ADVANTAGES OF THE POLITICAL AND PROFESSIONAL ERAS OF POLICING

– UNDERSTAND WHAT LED TO THE DEVELOPMENT OF THE COMMUNITY-ORIENTED POLICING AND PROBLEM-SOLVING (COPPS) ERA AND SOME OF ITS MAIN FEATURES

– BE ABLE TO EXPLAIN HOW TODAY POLICING HAS COME FULL CIRCLE, RETURNING TO ITS ORIGINS

– BE AWARE OF THE THREE GENERATIONS OF COMMUNITY-ORIENTED POLICING AND PROBLEM SOLVING

INTRODUCTION

To understand contemporary policing in America, it is necessary to understand its antecedents; we will gain a better understanding of this history by looking at its three eras. The police, it has been said, are "to a great extent, the prisoners of the past. Day-to-day practices are influenced by deeply ingrained traditions."[1] Another reason for analyzing historical developments and trends is that several discrete legacies have been transmitted to modern police agencies. In view of the significant historical impact on modern policing, it is necessary to turn back the clock to about A.D. 900.

Therefore, we begin with a brief history of the evolution of four primary criminal justice officers—sheriff, constable, coroner, and justice of the peace—from early England to the twentieth century in America. We then examine policing from its early beginnings in England to the American colonial period, when volunteers watched over their "human flock." The concepts of patrol, crime prevention, authority, professionalism, and discretion can be traced to the colonial period. We move on to the adoption of full-time policing in American cities (in what is termed the political era, with its predominant issues, political influences, and other problems) and on the western frontier. Then we consider the reform era, or the movement to professionalize the police by removing them from politics (and, at the same time, the citizenry) and casting them as crime fighters. Next, we discuss the movement away from the professional model into the community era, centering on the influence of the President's Crime Commission; this portion of the chapter also briefly considers community-oriented policing and problem solving (COPPS, discussed thoroughly in Chapter 6), including its three eras. A chapter summary, key terms, review questions, independent student activities, and related Web sites conclude the chapter.

ENGLISH AND COLONIAL OFFICERS OF THE LAW

All four of the primary criminal justice officials of early England—the sheriff, constable, coroner, and justice of the peace—either still exist or existed until recently in the United States. Accordingly, it is important to have a basic understanding of these offices, including their early functions in England and, later, in America. Following is a brief discussion of each.

Sheriff

The word **sheriff** is derived from the term *shire reeve*—*shire* meaning "county" and *reeve* meaning "agent of the king." The shire reeve appeared in England before the Norman conquest of 1066. His job was to maintain law and order in the tithings. (Tithings are discussed further in the next section.) The office survives in England, but since the nineteenth century, the sheriff has had no police powers. When the office began, however, the sheriff exercised the powers of a virtual viceroy in his county. He assisted the king in fiscal, military, and judicial affairs and was referred to as the "king's steward," but the sheriff was never a popular officer in England. As men could buy their appointment from the Crown, the office was often held by nonresidents of the county who seemed intent only upon fattening their purses and abusing the public. In addition, English sheriffs were often charged with being lazy in the pursuit of criminals. Indeed, by the late thirteenth century, sheriffs were forbidden to act as justices. The position of coroner was created to act as a monitor over the sheriff. Thereafter, the status and responsibility of the position began to diminish. Coroners were locally elected officials, and their existence prompted the public to seek similar selection and control over sheriffs. In response, just before his death, Edward I granted to the counties the right to select their sheriffs. With the subsequent appearance of the justice of the peace, the sheriff's office declined in power even further. At the present time in England, a sheriff's only duties are to act as officer of the court, summon juries, and enforce civil judgments.[2]

The first sheriffs in America appeared in the early colonial period. By contrast to the status of the office in England, control over sheriffs has rested with the county electorate since 1886. Today, the American sheriff remains the basic source of rural crime control. When the office appeared in the colonies, it was little changed from the English model. However, the power of appointment was originally vested in the governor, and the sheriff's duties included apprehending criminals, caring for prisoners, executing civil process, conducting elections, and collecting taxes. In keeping with English tradition, and fearing oppression and extortion by the sheriff, colonists generally limited the sheriff's term of office; sometimes the term was as short as a single year. The duties of collecting taxes and conducting elections alone accorded the sheriffs tremendous power and influence.[3]

In the late nineteenth century, the sheriff became a popular figure in the legendary Wild West (discussed later in this chapter). The frontier sheriffs often used the concept of *posse comitatus,* an important part of the criminal justice machine that allowed the sheriff to deputize common citizens to assist in the capture of outlaws, among other tasks. The use of the posse declined after 1900 because the enlistment of untrained people did not meet the requirements of a more complex society. Overall, by the turn of the twentieth century, the powers and duties of the sheriff in America had changed very little in status or function. In fact, the office has not changed much today; the sheriff continues to enjoy the authorization to use police powers.

Constable

Like the sheriff, the **constable** can be traced back to Anglo-Saxon times. The office began during the reign of Edward I, when every parish or township had a constable. As the county militia turned more and more to matters of defense, the constable alone pursued felons—hence the ancient custom of citizens raising a loud "hue and cry" and joining in pursuit of criminals lapsed into disuse. During the Middle Ages, there was as yet no high degree of specialization. The constable had a variety of duties, including collecting taxes, supervising highways, and serving as magistrate. The office soon became subject to election and was conferred upon local men of prominence. However, the creation of the office of justice of the peace around 1200 quickly changed this trend forever; soon the constable was limited to making arrests only with warrants issued by a justice of the peace.

As a result, the office, deprived of social and civic prestige, was no longer attractive. It carried no salary, and the duties were often dangerous. Additionally, there was heavy attrition in the office, so its term was limited to one year in an attempt to attract officeholders. Patrick Colquhoun, a London magistrate and noted police author, disposed of the parish constables altogether, and in 1856 Parliament completely discarded the office.[4]

The office of constable experienced a similar process of disintegration in the colonies. As elected officials, American constables had a variety of duties similar to those of their counterparts in England. However, the American constables, usually two in each town, were given control over the night watch. By the 1930s, state constitutions in twenty-one states provided for the office of constable, but constables still received no pay in the early part of the twentieth century, and like their British colleagues, they enjoyed little prestige or popularity after the early 1900s. The position fell into disfavor

A leatherhead and his sentry box. Called leatherheads because of their distinctive leather helmets, the constable watch patrolled the city from scattered sentry boxes in the early decades of the 1800s. They wore helmets for protection against falling debris from fires, a constant danger in cities with many wooden buildings.

(Courtesy NYPD Photo Unit)

largely because most constables were untrained and were believed to be wholly inadequate as officials of the law.[5]

Coroner

The office of **coroner** is more difficult to describe. It has been used to fulfill many different roles throughout its history and has steadily changed over the centuries. There is no agreement concerning the date when the coroner first appeared in England, but there is general consensus that the office was functioning by the end of the twelfth century. The reason is that both the Crown and the property holders were anxious to increase the prestige of this office at the expense of the sheriff. From the beginning, the coroner was elected; his duties included oversight of the interests of the Crown, not only in criminal matters but in fiscal matters as well. In felony cases, the coroner could conduct a preliminary hearing, and the sheriff often came to the coroner's court to preside over the coroner's jury. The coroner's inquest provided another means of power and prestige. The inquest determined the cause of death and the party responsible for it. Initially, coroners were given no compensation, yet they were elected for life. Soon, however, it became apparent that officials holding this office were unhappy with the burdensome tasks and the absence of compensation. Therefore, they were given the right to charge fees for their work.[6]

As was true of sheriffs and constables, at first the office of the coroner in America was only slightly different than what it had been in England. The office was slow in gaining recognition in America, as many of the coroners' duties were already being performed by the sheriffs and justices of the peace. By 1933, the coroner was recognized as a separate office in two-thirds of the states. Tenure was generally limited to two years. By then, however, the office had been stripped of many of its original functions, especially its fiscal roles. Today, in many states, the coroner legally serves as sheriff when the elected sheriff is disabled or disqualified. However, since the early part of the twentieth century, the coroner has basically performed a single function: determining the causes of all deaths by violence or under suspicious circumstances. The coroner or his or her assistant is expected to determine the causes and effects of wounds, lesions, contusions, fractures, poisons, and more. The coroner's inquest resembles a grand jury at which the coroner serves as a kind of presiding magistrate. If the inquest determines that the deceased came to his or her death through criminal means, the coroner may issue a warrant for the arrest of the accused party.[7]

The primary debate regarding the office of coroner has centered on the qualifications needed to hold the office. Many states have traditionally allowed laypeople, as opposed to physicians, to be coroners. Thus people of all backgrounds—ranging from butchers to musicians—have occupied this powerful office. America still clings to the old English philosophy that the chief qualifications for the position of coroner are "the possession of tact, sound discretion, practical sense, sympathy, quick perception and a knowledge of human nature."[8]

Justice of the Peace

The **justice of the peace (JP)** can be traced back as far as 1195 in England. By 1264 the *custos pacis,* or conservator of the peace, nominated by the king for each county, presided over criminal trials. Soon, in recognition of its new status, the term *custos* was dropped and *justice* substituted for it. Early JPs were wealthy landholders. They allowed constables to make arrests by issuing them warrants. Over time, this practice removed power from constables and sheriffs. The duties of JPs eventually included the granting of bail to felons, which led to corruption and criticism as the justices bailed people who clearly should not have been released into the community. By the sixteenth century, the office came under criticism again because of the caliber of the people holding it. Officeholders were often referred to as "boobies" and "scum of the earth."[9] The only qualification necessary was being a wealthy landowner who was able to buy his way into office.

By the early twentieth century, England had abolished the property-holding requirement, and many of the medieval functions of the JP's office were removed. Thereafter, the office possessed extensive but strictly criminal jurisdiction, with no jurisdiction whatsoever in civil cases. This contrasts with the American system, which gives JPs limited jurisdiction in both criminal and civil cases. Interestingly, even today relatively few English JPs have been trained in the law.

The JP's office in the colonies was a distinct change from the position as it existed in England. JPs were elected to office and given jurisdiction in both civil and criminal cases. By 1930, the office had constitutional status in all of the states. JPs have long been allowed to collect fees for their services. For example, in the 1930s the JP typically received 10¢ for administering an oath, 50¢ for preparing information, 50¢ for issuing a warrant for arrest, $1 per day for attendance in court, 25¢ for issuing a subpoena, and 5¢ for filing each paper required by law. As in England, it is typically not necessary to hold a law degree or to have pursued legal studies in order to be a JP in the United States. Thus tradespeople and laborers have long held the position, and American JPs come from all walks of life. In the past, they held court in their saddle shops, kitchens, and flour mills.[10]

Perhaps the most colorful justice of the peace was Roy Bean, popularized in the movies as the sole peace officer in a 35,000-square-mile area west of the Pecos River, near Langtry, Texas. Bean was known to hold court in his shack, where signs hung on the front porch proclaimed, "Justice Roy Bean, Notary Public," "Law West of the Pecos," and "Beer Saloon." Cold beer and the law undoubtedly shared many quarters on the western frontier.

A familiar complaint about modern-day JPs has been that they often operate in collusion with police officers, who set up speed traps to collect and share the fines. Indeed, many JPs have been known to complain when the police bring them too few cases, or none at all, or when the police take their "business" to other JPs, thereby reducing their incomes. This reputation, coupled with the complaints about their qualifications, has caused the office of JP to be ridiculed. JPs are today what they perhaps were intended to be—lay and inexpert upholders of the law. On the whole, the office has declined from dignity to obscurity and ridicule. As one observer noted, this loss of prestige can never be recovered.[11]

Justice of the Peace Roy Bean, Langtry, Texas, about 1900.

(Library of Congress, Prints & Photographs Division, Historic American Buildings Survey or Historic American Engineering Record, Reproduction Number HABS TEX, 233-LANG, 1-1)

THE OLD ENGLISH SYSTEM OF POLICING

Like much of the American criminal justice system, modern American policing can be traced directly to its English heritage. Ideas concerning community policing, crime prevention, the posse, constables, and sheriffs were developed from English policing. Beginning about A.D. 900, the role of law enforcement was placed in the hands of common citizens. Each citizen was responsible for aiding neighbors who might be victimized by outlaws.[12] No formal mechanism existed with which to police the villages, and the informal voluntary model that developed was referred to as "kin police."[13] Slowly this model developed into a more formalized community-based system.

After the Norman conquest of 1066, a community-based system called "frankpledge" was established. This system required that every male above the age of twelve form a group with nine of his neighbors. This group, called a "tithing," was sworn to help protect fellow citizens and to apprehend and deliver to justice any of its members who committed a crime. Tithingmen were not paid salaries for their work, and they were required to perform certain duties under penalty of law.[14] Ten tithings were grouped into a hundred, directed by a constable who was appointed by a nobleman. The constable was the first police official with law enforcement responsibility greater than simply protecting his neighbors. As the tithings were grouped into hundreds, the hundreds were grouped into shires, which are similar to today's counties.

By the late sixteenth century, however, wealthier merchants and farmers became reluctant to take their turn in the rotating job of constable. The office was still unpaid, and the duties were numerous. Wealthier men paid the less fortunate to serve in their place until there came a point at which no one but the otherwise unemployable would serve as constable. Thus from about 1689 on, the demise of the once-powerful office was swift. All who could afford to pay their way out of service as constable to King George I did so. Daniel Defoe, the noted author, spoke for many when he wrote in 1714 that the office of constable represented "an unsupportable hardship; it takes up so much of a man's time that his own affairs are frequently totally neglected, too often to his ruin."[15]

Another cause of the decline of the old system, as mentioned earlier, was the corruption of the JPs. Following the Glorious Revolution in 1688, many families whose members had once filled the office became disaffected with the Crown and began to refuse the position. Soon, the people who did become JPs were inspired primarily by the office's potential for profit. The unsavory magistrates became known as the "justices of mean degree," and the "trading justice" of the first half of the eighteenth century emerged in a criminal justice system where anything was possible for a fee.

The potential for corruption in this system is obvious. The JP was rewarded in proportion to the number of people he convicted, so extortion was rampant. Ingenious criminals were able to exploit this state of affairs to great advantage. One such criminal was Jonathan Wild, who, for seven years before his execution in 1725, obtained single-handed control over most of London's criminals. Wild's system was simple: After ordering his men to commit a burglary, he would meet the victim and courteously offer to return the stolen goods for a commission. Wild was so successful in fencing stolen property that he found it necessary to transport his booty to warehouses abroad. That he could have operated such a business for so long is a testimony to the corrupt nature of the magistrates of the "trading justice" period.[16]

This early English system, in large measure voluntary and informal, continued with some success well into the eighteenth century. By 1800, however, the collapse of its two primary offices and the growth of large cities, crime, and civil disobedience required that the system be changed. The British Parliament was soon forced to consider and adopt a more dependable system.

Policing in Colonial America

The first colonists transplanted the English policing system, with all of its virtues and faults, to seventeenth- and eighteenth-century America. Most of the time, the colonies were free of crime as the settlers busied themselves carving out a farm and a living. Occasionally colonists ran afoul of the law by violating or neglecting some moral obligation. They then found themselves in court for working on the Sabbath, cursing in public, failing to pen animals properly, or begetting children out of wedlock. Only two "crime waves" of note occurred during the seventeenth century, both in Massachusetts. In one case, between 1656 and 1665, Quakers who dared challenge the religion of the Puritan colony were whipped, banished, and, in three instances, hanged. The second "crime wave" involved witchcraft. Several alleged witches were hanged in 1692 in Salem; dozens more languished in prison before the hysteria abated.[17]

Once colonists settled into villages, including Boston (1630), Charleston (1680), and Philadelphia (1682), local ordinances provided for the appointment of constables, whose duties were much like those of their English predecessors. County governments, again drawing on English precedent, appointed sheriffs as well. The county sheriff, appointed by a governor, became the most important law enforcement official, particularly when the colonies were small and rural. The sheriff apprehended criminals, served subpoenas, appeared in court, and collected taxes. The sheriff was also paid a fixed amount for each task performed; the more taxes he collected, for example, the higher his pay.[18]

Criminal acts were so infrequent as to be largely ignored; in fact, law enforcement was given low priority. Service as a constable or watchman was obligatory, and for a few years citizens did not seem to mind this duty. But as towns grew and the task of enforcing the laws became more difficult and time-consuming, the colonists, like their English counterparts, began to evade the duty when possible. The "watch-and-ward" responsibility of citizens became more of a comical "snooze-and-snore" system. In Boston, the citizens were so evasive about performing police services that in 1650 the government threatened citizens who refused to serve with heavy fines. New Amsterdam's Dutch officials introduced a paid watch in 1658, and Boston tried the concept in 1663, but the expense quickly forced both cities to discontinue the practice.[19] Apparently, paid policing might have been a good substitute for halfhearted voluntary service, but only if the citizens did not have to pay for it.

Unfortunately for these eighteenth-century colonists, their refusal to provide a dependable voluntary policing system came at a time when economic, population, and crime growth required a reliable police force. But the most reliable citizens continued to refuse the duty, and watchmen were hardly able to stay awake at night. The citizen-participation model of policing was breaking down, and something had to be done, especially in the larger colonies. Philadelphia devised a plan, enacted into law, that restructured the way the watch was performed. City officials hoped that it would solve the problem of enforcing the laws. The law empowered officials, called "wardens," to hire as many watchmen as needed; the powers of the watch were increased; and the legislature levied a tax to pay for it. Instead of requiring all males to participate, only male citizens interested in making money needed to join the watch. Philadelphia's plan was moderately successful, and other cities were soon inspired to follow its example and offer tax-supported wages for watches.[20]

From the middle to the late eighteenth century, massive social and political unrest caused police problems to increase even more. From 1754 to 1763, the French and Indian War disrupted colonial society. When the war ended, a major depression impoverished many citizens. That depression ended with the American Revolution. In 1783, after the revolution ended, another depression struck; this one lasted until about 1790. Property and street crime continued to flourish, and the constabulary and the watches were unable to cope with it. Soon it became evident that, like the English, the American people needed a more dependable, formal system of policing.

Legacies of the Colonial Period

As uncomplicated and sedate as colonial law enforcement seems, especially when compared to contemporary police problems, the colonial period is very important to the history of policing because many of the basic ideas that influence modern policing were developed during that era. Specifically, the colonial period transmitted three legacies to contemporary policing.[21]

First, as just discussed, the colonists committed themselves to local (as opposed to centralized) policing. Second, the colonists reinforced that commitment by creating a theory of government called **republicanism**. Republicanism asserted that power can be divided, and it relied on local interests to promote the general welfare. Police chiefs and sheriffs might believe that they alone know how to address crime and disorder, but under republicanism, neighborhood groups and local interest blocs have input with respect to crime-control policy. Republicanism thus established the controversial political framework within which the police would develop during the next two hundred years.[22]

Finally, the colonial period witnessed the onset of the theory of crime prevention. This legacy would alter the shape of policing after 1800 and would eventually lead to the emergence of modern police agencies. The population of England doubled between 1700 and 1800. Parliament, however, did nothing to solve the problems that arose from social change. Each municipality or county, therefore, was left to solve its problems in piecemeal fashion. After 1750, practically every English city increased the number of watchmen and constables, hoping to address the problem of crime and disorder but not giving any thought to whether this ancient system of policing still worked. However, the cities did adopt paid, rather than voluntary, watches.[23]

London probably suffered the most from this general inattention to social problems; awash in crime, whole districts had become criminal haunts that no watchmen visited and no honest citizens frequented. Thieves became very bold, robbing their victims in broad daylight on busy streets. In the face of this situation, English officials still continued to prefer the existing policing arrangements over any new ideas. However, three men—Henry Fielding, his half brother John Fielding, and Patrick Colquhoun—began to experiment with possible solutions. And although their efforts would have no major effect in the short term in England, they laid the foundation on which later reformers would build new ideas.

Henry Fielding's acute interest in, and knowledge of, policing led to his 1748 appointment as chief magistrate of Bow Street in London. He soon became one of England's most acclaimed theorists in the area of crime and punishment. Fielding's primary argument was that the severity of the English penal code, which provided for the death penalty for a large number of offenses including the theft of a handkerchief, did not work in controlling criminals. He believed the country should reform the criminal code to deal more with the origins of crime. In 1750, Fielding made the pursuit of criminals more systematic by creating a small group of "thief takers." Victims of crime paid handsome rewards for the capture of their assailants, so these volunteers stood to profit nicely by pursuing criminals.[24]

When Henry Fielding died in 1754, John Fielding succeeded him as Bow Street magistrate. By 1785, his thief takers had evolved into the Bow Street Runners—some of the most famous policemen in English history. While the Fieldings were considering how to create a police force that could deal with changing English society, horrible punishments and incompetent policing continued throughout England.

Patrick Colquhoun was a wealthy man who was sincerely interested in improving social conditions in England. In 1792, Colquhoun was appointed London magistrate,

Henry Fielding.

(Library of Congress)

and for the next quarter of a century he focused on police reform. Like the Fieldings, he wrote lengthy treatises on the police, and he soon established himself as an authority on police reform. Colquhoun believed that government could, and should, regulate people's behavior. This notion contradicted tradition and even constitutional ideals, undermining the old principle that the residents of local communities, through voluntary watchmen and constables, should police the conduct of their neighbors. Colquhoun also endorsed three ideas originally set forth by the Fieldings: (1) The police should have an intelligence service for gathering information about offenders; (2) a register of known criminals and unlawful groups should be maintained; and (3) a police gazette should be published to assist in the apprehension of criminals and to promote the moral education of the public by publicizing punishments such as whipping, the pillory, and public execution. To justify these reforms, Colquhoun estimated that, in 1800, London had ten thousand thieves, prostitutes, and other criminals who stole goods valued at more than a half million pounds from the riverside docks alone.[25]

Colquhoun also believed that policing should maintain the public order, prevent and detect crime, and correct bad manners and morals. He did not agree with the centuries-old notion that watchmen—who, after all, were amateurs—could adequately police the communities. Thus Colquhoun favored a system of paid professional police officers who would be recruited and maintained by a centralized governmental authority. Colquhoun believed that potential criminals could be identified before they did their unlawful deeds.[26] Thus began the notion of proactive policing—that is, preventing the crime before it occurs. Colquhoun died before his proposals were adopted, and as the eighteenth century ended in England and America, the structure of policing was largely unchanged. However, both nations had experienced the inadequacies of the older form of policing. Although new ideas had emerged, loyalties to the old system of policing would remain for some time.

POLICE REFORM IN ENGLAND AND AMERICA, 1829–1860

Two powerful trends in England and America brought about changes in policing in both countries in the early and mid-nineteenth century. The first was urbanization, and the second was industrialization. These developments generally increased the standard of living for both Americans and western Europeans. Suddenly, factories needed sober, dependable people who could be trusted with machines. To create a reliable workforce, factory owners began advocating temperance. Although many workers resented this attempt at social control and reform, clearly a new age, a new way of thinking, had begun. Crime also increased during this period. Thus social change, crime, and unrest made the old system of policing obsolete. A new policing system was needed, one that could deal effectively with criminals, maintain order, and prevent crime.[27]

In England, after the end of the Napoleonic Wars in 1815, workers protested against new machines, food riots, and an ongoing increase in crime. The British army, traditionally used to disperse rioters, was becoming less effective as people began resisting its commands. In 1822, England's ruling party, the Tories, moved to consider new alternatives. The prime minister appointed Sir Robert Peel to establish a police force to combat the problems. Peel, a wealthy member of Parliament who was familiar with the reforms suggested by the Fieldings and Colquhoun, found that many English people objected to the idea of a professional police force, thinking it a possible restraint on their liberty. They also feared a stronger police organization because the criminal law was already quite harsh, as it had been for many years. By the early nineteenth century, there were 223 crimes in England for which a person could be hanged. Because of these two obstacles, Peel's efforts to gain support for full-time, paid police officers failed for seven years.[28]

Peel finally succeeded in 1829. He had established a base of support in Parliament and had focused on reforming only the metropolitan police of London rather than trying to create policing for the entire country. Peel submitted a bill to Parliament. This bill, which was very vague about details, was called "An Act for Improving the Police in and Near the Metropolis." Parliament passed the Metropolitan Police Act of 1829. The General Instructions of the new force stressed its preventive nature, saying that "the principal object to be attained is 'the prevention of crime.' The security of person and property will thus be better effected, than by the detection and punishment of the offender after he has succeeded in committing the crime."[29] The act called on the home secretary to appoint two police commissioners to command the new organization. These two men were to recruit "a sufficient number of fit and able men" as constables.[30] Peel chose a former

Sir Robert Peel.

(Library of Congress)

military colonel, Charles Rowan, as one commissioner, and a barrister (attorney), Richard Mayne, as the other. Both turned out to be excellent choices. They divided London into seventeen divisions, using crime data as the primary basis for creating the boundaries. Each division had a commander called a "superintendent"; each superintendent had a force of 4 inspectors, 16 sergeants, and 165 constables. Thus London's Metropolitan Police immediately consisted of nearly 3,000 officers. The commissioners decided to put their constables in a uniform (a blue coat, blue pants, and a black top hat) and to arm them with a short baton (known as a "truncheon") and a rattle for raising an alarm. Each constable was to wear his own identifying number on his collar, where it could be easily seen.[31]

Interestingly, the London police (nicknamed "bobbies" after Sir Robert Peel) quickly met with tremendous public hostility. Wealthy people resented their very existence and became particularly incensed at their attempts to control the movements of their horse-drawn coaches. Several aristocrats ordered their coachmen to whip the officers or simply drive over them. Juries and judges refused to punish those who assaulted the police. Defendants acquitted by a hostile judge would often sue the officer for false arrest.

Policing London's streets in the early 1830s proved to be a very dangerous and lonely business. The two commissioners, Rowan and Mayne, fearing that public hostility might kill off the police force, moved to counter it. The bobbies were continually told to be respectful yet firm when dealing with the public. Citizens were invited to lodge complaints if their officers were truly unprofessional. This policy of creating public support gradually worked; as the police became more moderate in their conduct, public hostility also declined.[32]

Peel, too, proved to be very farsighted and keenly aware of the needs of both a professional police force and the public that would be asked to maintain it. Indeed, Peel

A "Peeler," c. 1829. "Peeler,"
"Robert," and "Bobby" were all early
names for a police officer, the latter
remaining as a nickname today.

(Courtesy NYPD Photo Unit)

saw that the poor quality of policing contributed to social disorder. Accordingly, he drafted several guidelines for the force, many of which focused on community relations. He wrote that the power of the police to fulfill their duties depended on public approval of their actions; that as public cooperation increased, the need for physical force by the police would decrease; that officers needed to display absolutely impartial service to law; and that force should be employed by the police only when attempts at persuasion and warning had failed, and then they should use only the minimal degree of force possible. Peel's remark that "the police are the public, and the public are the police" emphasized his belief that the police are first and foremost members of the larger society.[33]

Peel's attempts to appease the public were necessary; during the first three years of his reform effort, he encountered strong opposition. He was denounced as a potential dictator, the *London Times* urged revolt, and *Blackwood's* magazine referred to the bobbies as "general spies" and "finished tools of corruption." A secret national group, the Blue Devils and the Raw Lobsters, was organized to combat the police. During this initial five-year period, Peel endured the largest police turnover rate in history. Estimates vary widely, but this is thought to be fairly accurate: 1,341 constables resigned from London's Metropolitan Police from 1829 to 1834; that's roughly half of the constables on the force. The pay of three shillings a day was meager, and probably few of the officers ever considered the position as a career. In fact, many of the men, who had been laborers, took jobs as bobbies to tide them over during the "stress of weather," waiting until the inclement weather passed and they could resume their trades.[34] Peel drafted what have become known as "Peel's principles of policing." Most, if not all, are relevant to today's police community:

1. The police must be stable, efficient, and organized along military lines.
2. The police must be under governmental control.
3. The absence of crime will best prove the efficiency of the police.
4. The distribution of crime news is absolutely essential.
5. The deployment of police strength by both time and area is essential.
6. No quality is more indispensable to a policeman than a perfect command of temper; a quiet, determined manner has more effect than violent action.
7. Good appearance commands respect.
8. The securing and training of proper persons are at the root of efficiency.
9. Public security demands that every police officer be given a number.
10. Police headquarters should be centrally located and easily accessible to the people.
11. Policemen should be hired on a probationary basis.
12. Police records are necessary to the correct distribution of police strength.[35]

London's "experiment" in full-time policing did not bring about the instant expansion of the model across England. It would take many years for other English communities to replace their stubborn reliance on the watchman system.

POLICING COMES TO THE UNITED STATES: THE POLITICAL ERA, 1840S TO 1930S

The English experiment with policing was not going unnoticed in the United States. Americans had been observing Peel's successful experiment with the bobbies on the patrol beat. However, industrialization and social upheaval had not reached the proportions here that they had in England, so there was not the same urgent need for full-time policing. Yet by the 1840s, when industrialization began in earnest in America, U.S. officials began to watch the police reform movement in England more closely.

Eventually, of course, policing would become entrenched in America and evolve through three full eras: political, reform, and community. To gain a better understanding of these three eras, an overview of each is provided in Table 1-1.

Imitating Peel

When the movement to improve policing did begin in America in the 1840s, it occurred in New York City. (Philadelphia, with a private bequest of $33,000, actually began a paid daytime police force in 1833; however, it was disbanded three years later.) The police reform movement had actually begun in New York in 1836, when the mayor advocated a new police organization that could deal with civil disorder. The city council denied the mayor's request, saying that the doctrine of republicanism prevented it and that, instead, citizens should simply aid one another in combating crime.

Efforts at police reform thus stayed dormant until 1841, when a highly publicized murder case resurrected the issue, showing again the incompetence of the officers under

TABLE 1-1

The Three Eras of Policing

	POLITICAL ERA (1840s TO 1930s)	REFORM ERA (1930s TO 1980s)	COMMUNITY ERA (1980s TO PRESENT)
Authorization	Politics and law	Law and professionalism	Community support (political), law, and professionalism
Function	Broad social services	Crime control	Broad provision of services
Organizational design	Decentralized	Centralized and classical	Decentralized using task forces and matrices
Relationship to community	Intimate	Professional and remote	Intimate
Tactics and technology	Foot patrol	Preventive patrol and rapid response to calls	Foot patrol, problem solving, and public relations
Outcome	Citizen and political satisfaction	Crime control	Quality of life and citizen satisfaction

Source: Adapted from George L. Kelling and Mark H. Moore, *The Evolving Strategies of Policing* (Washington, DC: U.S. Department of Justice, National Institute of Justice Perspectives on Policing, November 1988).

the old system of policing. Mary Cecilia Rogers left her New York home one day and disappeared; three days later; her body was discovered in the Hudson River. The public and newspapers clamored for the police to solve the crime. The police appeared unwilling to investigate until an adequate reward was offered.[36] Edgar Allan Poe's 1850 short story "The Mystery of Marie Roget" was based on this case. The Rogers case and the police response did more to encourage police reorganization than all of the previous cries for change. Thus began the **political era of policing**.

In 1844, the New York State legislature passed a law establishing a full-time preventive police force for New York City. However, this new body came into being in a very different form than in Europe. The American version, as begun in New York City, was deliberately placed under the control of the city government and city politicians. The American plan required that each ward in the city be a separate patrol district, unlike the European model, which divided the districts along the lines of criminal activity. The process for selecting officers was also different. The mayor chose the recruits from a list of names submitted by the aldermen and tax assessors of each ward; the mayor then submitted his choices to the city council for approval. This system adhered to the principles of republicanism and resulted in most of the power over the police going to the ward aldermen, who were seldom concerned about selecting the best people for the job. Instead, the system allowed and even encouraged political patronage and rewards for friends.[37]

The law also provided for the hiring of eight hundred officers—not nearly enough to cover the city—and for the hiring of a chief of police, who had no power to hire officers, assign them to duties, or fire them. Furthermore, the law did not require the officers to wear uniforms; instead, they were to carry a badge or other emblem for identification. Citizens would be hard-pressed to recognize an officer when they needed one. As a result of the law, New York's officers would be patrolling a beat around the clock, and pay scales were high enough to attract good applicants. At the same time, the position of constable was dissolved. Overall, these were important reforms over the old system and provided the basis for continued improvements that the public supported.[38]

It did not take long for other cities to adopt the general model of the New York City police force. New Orleans and Cincinnati adopted plans for a new police force in 1852, Boston and Philadelphia followed in 1854, Chicago in 1855, and Baltimore and Newark in 1857.[39] By 1880, virtually every major American city had a police force based on Peel's model.

Early Issues and New Traditions

Three important issues confronted these early American police officers as they took to the streets between 1845 and 1869: whether the police should be in uniform, whether they should be armed, and whether they should use force.

The issue of a police uniform was important for several reasons. First, the lack of a uniform negated one of the basic principles of crime prevention—that police officers be visible. Crime victims wanted to find a police officer in a hurry. Further, uniforms would make it difficult for officers to avoid their duties, since it would strip them of their anonymity. Interestingly, police officers themselves tended to prefer not to wear a uniform. They contended that the uniform would hinder their work because criminals would recognize them and flee and that the uniform was demeaning and would destroy their sense of manliness and democracy. One officer went so far as to argue that the sun reflecting off his badge would warn criminals of his approach; another officer hired an attorney and threatened to sue if he were compelled to don a uniform. To remedy the problem, New York City officials took advantage of the fact that their officers served four-year terms of office; when those terms expired in 1853, the city's police commissioners announced they would not rehire any officer who refused to wear a uniform. Thus New York became the first American city with a uniformed police force. In 1860, it was followed by Philadelphia, where there was also strong police objection to the policy. In Boston (1858) and Chicago (1861), police accepted the adoption of uniforms more easily.[40]

A more serious issue confronting politicians and the new police officers was the carrying of arms. At stake was the personal safety of the officers and the citizens they served. Nearly everyone viewed an armed police force with considerable suspicion. However, after some surprisingly calm objections by members of the public, who noted that the London police had no need to bear arms, it was agreed that an armed police force was unavoidable. Of course, America had a long tradition that citizens had the right—sometimes even the duty—to own firearms. And armed only with nightsticks, the new police could hardly withstand attacks by armed assailants. The public allowed officers to carry arms simply because there was no alternative, which was a significant change in American policing and a major point of departure from the English model. Practically from the first day, then, the American police have been much more open to the idea of carrying weapons.[41]

Eventually the use of force, the third issue, would become necessary and commonplace for American officers. Indeed, the uncertainty about whether an offender was armed perpetuated the need for an officer to rely on physical prowess for survival on the streets. The issue of use of force will be discussed further in Chapter 9.

Attempts at Reform in Difficult Times

By 1850, American police officers still faced a difficult task. In addition to maintaining order and coping with vice and crime, they would, soon after putting on the uniform, be separated from their old associates and viewed with suspicion by most citizens. With few exceptions, the work was steady, and layoffs were uncommon. The nature of the work and the possibility of a retirement pension tied officers closely to their jobs and their colleagues. By 1850, there was a surplus of unskilled labor, particularly in the major eastern cities. The desire for economic security was reason enough for many able-bodied men to try to enter police service. New York City, for example, paid its police officers about twice as much as unskilled laborers could earn. Police departments had about twice as many applicants as positions. The system of political patronage prevailed in most cities, even after civil service laws attempted to introduce merit systems for hiring police.[42]

In New York, the police reform board was headed by Theodore Roosevelt, who sought applications for the department from residents in upstate areas. When these officers, later called "bushwhackers," were appointed, they were criticized by disgruntled Tammanyites (corrupt New York City politicians) who favored the political patronage system. The Tammanyites complained that the bushwhackers "could not find their way to a single station house."[43] Roosevelt's approach violated the American tradition of hiring local boys for local jobs. In England, meanwhile, police officials purposely sought applicants from outside the London area, believing that it was advantageous to hire young men who were not wise to the local ways or involved with local people.[44]

Citizens saw these new uniformed anomalies as people who wanted to spoil their fun or close their saloons on Sunday. In addition to police officers' geographic and social isolation, they became isolated in other ways, most of which still prevail today. For example, from the onset of professional American policing, there was little or no lateral movement from one department to another; the officer typically spent his entire career in one city, unable to transfer seniority or knowledge for use in a promotion in another city. Consequently, police departments soon became very inbred; new blood entered only at the lowest level. Tradition became the most important determinant of police behavior: A major teaching tool was the endless string of war stories the recruit heard, and the emphasis in most departments was on doing things as they had always been done. Innovation was frowned upon, and the veterans impressed on the rookies the reasons why things had to remain the same.[45]

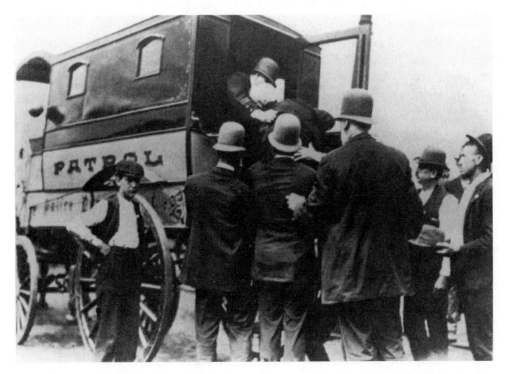

An example of a horse-drawn paddy wagon in use in many cities at the turn of the twentieth century.

(Reprinted from The Blue and the Brass: American Policing 1890–1910, 1976. Copyright held by the International Association of Chiefs of Police, 515 North Washington Street, Alexandria, VA 22314 USA. Further reproduction without express written permission from IACP is strictly prohibited.)

The police officers of the late nineteenth century kept busy with riots, strikes, parades, and fires. These events often made for hostile interaction between citizens and the police. Labor disputes often meant long hours of extra duty for the officers, for which no extra pay was received. This, coupled with the fact that the police did not engage in collective bargaining, resulted in the police having little empathy or identification with strikers or strikebreakers. Therefore the use of the baton to put down riots, known as the "baton charge," was not uncommon. On New York's Lower East Side—where labor conflict was frequent—Jewish spokespeople called the police "Black Hundreds" in memory of conditions in czarist Russia.[46]

During the late nineteenth century, large cities gradually became more orderly places. The number of riots dropped. In the post–Civil War period, however, ethnic group conflict sometimes resulted in individual and group acts of violence and disorder. Hatred of Catholics and Irish Protestants led to the killing and wounding of over one hundred people in large eastern cities. Still, American cities were more orderly in 1900 than they had been in 1850. The possibility of violence involving labor disputes remained, and race riots increased in number and intensity after 1900, but daily urban life became more predictable and controlled. American cities absorbed millions of newcomers after 1900 without the social strains that attended the Irish immigration of the 1830s to 1850s.[47]

Increased Politics and Corruption

A more developed urban life also promoted order. Work groups and social clusters provided a sense of integration and belonging. Immigrants established benefit societies, churches, synagogues, and social clubs. At the same time, the police had acquired experience in dealing with potential sources of violence. Police in northern and western cities reflected the times. Irish-Americans constituted a heavy proportion of the police departments by the 1890s; they made up more than one-fourth of the New York police force as early as the 1850s. Huge proportions of Irish officers were also found in Boston, Chicago, Cleveland, and San Francisco.[48]

Ethnic and religious disputes were found in many police departments. In Cleveland, for example, Catholics and Masons distrusted one another, while in New York, the Irish officers controlled many hirings and promotions. And there were still strong political influences at work. George Walling, a New York Police Department superintendent for eleven years, lamented after his retirement that he had largely been just a figurehead. Politics were played to such an extent that even nonranking patrol officers used political backers to obtain promotions, desired assignments, and transfers.

Police corruption also surfaced at this time. Corrupt officers wanted beats close to the gamblers, saloonkeepers, madams, and pimps—people who could not operate if the officers were "untouchable" or "100 percent coppers."[49] Political pull for corrupt officers could work for or against them; the officer who incurred the wrath of his superiors could be transferred to the outposts, where he would have no chance for financial advancement.

While police departments often had strong rivalries and political and religious factions, the officers banded together against outside attack. In New York, officers routinely committed perjury to protect one another against civilian complaints. An early form of "internal affairs" thus developed in the 1890s: the "shoofly," a plainclothes officer who checked on the performance of the patrol officers. When Theodore Roosevelt served as police commissioner in New York, he frequently made clandestine trips to the beats to check his officers; any malingerers found in the saloons were summoned to headquarters in the morning.[50]

Meanwhile, on the American Frontier...

While large cities in the East were struggling to overcome social problems and establish preventive police forces, the western half of America was anything but passive. Many historians believe that the true character of Americans developed on the frontier. Rugged individualism, independence, and simplicity of manners and behavior lent dignity to American life.

Most Americans are fascinated by this period of police history, a time when heroic marshals had gunfights in Dodge City and other wild cowboy towns. But this period is also riddled with exaggerated legends and half-truths. During the second half of the nineteenth century, the absence of government created a confusing variety of forms of policing in the West. Large parts of the West were under federal control, some had been organized into states, and still others were under Native American control, at least on paper. Law enforcement was performed largely by federal marshals and their deputies. Once a state was created within a territory, its state legislature had the power to attempt to deal with crime by appointing county sheriffs. Otherwise, there was no uniform method for attempting to control the problems of the West.

When the people left the wagon trains and their relatively law-abiding ways, they attempted to live together in communities. Many different ethnic groups—Anglo-Americans, Mexicans, Chinese, Native Americans, freed blacks, Australians, Scandinavians, and others—competed for often scarce resources and fought one another violently, often with mob attacks. Economic conflicts were frequent between cattlemen and sheepherders, and they often led to major range wars. There was constant labor strife in the mines. The bitterness of slavery remained, and many men with firearms skills learned during the Civil War turned to outlawry after leaving the service. (Jesse James was one such person.) In spite of these difficulties, westerners did manage to establish peace by relying on a combination of four groups who assumed responsibility for law enforcement: private citizens, U.S. marshals, businessmen, and town police officers.[51]

Private citizens usually helped to enforce the law by joining a posse or making individual efforts. Such was the case with the infamous Dalton Gang in Coffeyville, Kansas. The five gang members attempted to rob a bank in Coffeyville in 1892. However, private citizens, seeing what was occurring, armed themselves and shot at the Daltons as they attempted to escape, killing four of the five. Another example of citizen policing was the formation of vigilante committees. Between 1849 and 1902, there were 210 vigilante movements in the United States, most of them in California.[52] While throughout history many vigilante groups have practiced "informal justice" by illegally taking the law into their

WHAT SCIENCE HAS DONE FOR THE POLICE

CHIEF FRANCIS O'NEILL, CHICAGO, 1903

The watchman of a century ago with his lantern and staff who called out the passing hours in stentorian tones during the night is now but a tradition. He has been succeeded by a uniformed constabulary and police who carry arms and operate under semi-military discipline. The introduction of electricity as a means of communication between stations was the first notable advance in the improvement of police methods. I remember the time when the manipulation of the dial telegraph by the station keeper while sending messages excited the greatest wonder and admiration. The adoption of the Morse system of telegraphy was a long step forward and proved of great advantage. In 1876, all desk sergeants were required to take up the immediate study of the Morse system of telegraphy. Scarcely one-fourth of them became proficient before modern science, advancing in leaps and bounds, brought forth that still more modern miracle—the telephone. Less than one-quarter century ago the policeman on post had no aid from science in communicating with his station or in securing assistance in case of need. When required by duty to care for the sick and injured or to remove a dead body, an appeal to the owner of some suitable vehicle was his only resource. These were desperate times for policemen in a hostile country with unpaved streets. The patrol wagon and signal service have effected a revolution in police methods. The forward stride from the lanterned night watch, with staff, to the uniformed and disciplined police officer of the present, equipped with telegraph, telephone, signal service, and the Bertillon system of identification,* is indeed an interesting one to contemplate.

*Alphonse Bertillon (1853–1914) developed a system for criminal identification based on precise measurements of the human body. The system was used in Paris in 1882 and was officially adopted for all of France in 1888.
Source: Proceedings of the International Chiefs of Police, tenth annual convention, May 12–14, 1903, p. 67.

own hands, breaking the law with violence and force, they also performed valuable work by ridding their communities of dangerous criminals.

Federal marshals were created by congressional legislation in 1789. As marshals began to appear on the frontier, the vigilantes tended to disappear. The marshals enforced federal laws, so they had no jurisdiction over matters not involving a federal offense. They could act only in cases involving theft of mail, crimes against railroad property, murder on federal lands (much of the West was federal property for many decades), and a few other crimes. Their primary responsibility was in civil matters arising from federal court decisions. Federal marshals obtained their office through political appointment; therefore they did not need any prior experience and were politically indebted. Initially, they received no salary but were instead compensated with fees and rewards. Because chasing outlaws did not pay as much as serving civil process papers, the marshals tended to prefer the more lucrative, less dangerous task of serving court paperwork. Congress saw the folly in this system and, in 1896, enacted legislation providing regular salaries for marshals.[53]

When a territory became a state, the primary law enforcement functions usually fell to local sheriffs and marshals. Train robbers such as Jesse James and the Dalton Gang were among the most famous outlaws to violate federal laws. Many train robbers became

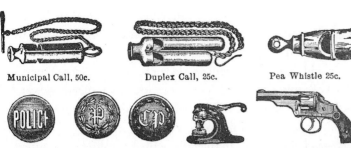

Early-twentieth-century police equipment.

(Courtesy NYPD Photo Unit)

Municipal Call, 50c.   Duplex Call, 25c.   Pea Whistle 25c.

Buttons—Coat, per doz., 65c.; per gross, $5.00; Vest, per doz., 45c; per gross, $2.50.
Seals, old style press, $2; Nickel-plated pocket seal, $2.50; Handy Pocket seal $2.00.
Revolvers and Holsters, Riot Guns, all styles and sizes. WRITE FOR PRICES.

Cell Pails, Cedar, Porcelain lined. $2.50; Bulls-Eye Oil Lamps, regulation, solid brass
nickeled, $3.50; brass, $3; Japanned. $2; Metal Wreaths, gilt or German Silver, 15c;
numbers 5c. each; wired on wreaths. 5c. extra each wreath; Bean's Hard Glove, $2.
made of Sole Leather, neatly covered, easily carried in place of Club or Billet,

TOWER'S PATENT DOUBLE LOCK HANDCUFFS AND LEG IRONS

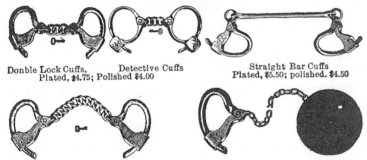

Double Lock Cuffs,   Detective Cuffs   Straight Bar Cuffs
Plated, $4.75; Polished $4.00   Plated, $5.50; polished. $4.50

Double Lock Legirons, plated, $7; polished, $6; Single Legiron, with ball and chain,
12-lbs., $5; 15-$5.25; 18-$5.50; 22-$5.75; 25-$6; 28-$6.25; 32-$6.50; 40-$6.75; 50-$7. If you
wish a pair of Legirons instead of a single Legiron, add $3.00 to above prices,

Leininger's Shackle (Oregon Boot,)   Giant Cuffs,   Cuffs for three hands,
11-lbs. $9.00; 15-lbs. $9.50. $6.00   Plated, $7; polished. $6
Extra Handcuff and Legiron Keys, 25 cents each.

legendary for having the courage to steal from the despised railroad owners. What is often overlooked in the tales of these legendary outlaws is their often total disregard for the safety and lives of their victims. To combat these criminals, federal marshals found their hideouts, and railroad companies and other businesses often offered rewards for information leading to their capture. Occasionally, as in the case of Jesse James and the Daltons, the marshals' work was done for them—outlaws were often killed by friends (usually for a reward) or by private citizens.[54]

Gunfights in the West actually occurred very rarely; few individuals on either side of the law actually welcomed stand-up gunfights. It was infinitely more sensible to find cover from which to have a shootout. Further, handguns were not the preferred weapon— a double-barreled shotgun could do far more damage than a handgun at close range. Local law enforcement occurred as people settled into communities. Town meetings were held where a government was established and local officials were elected. Sheriffs quickly became important officials, but they spent more time collecting taxes, inspecting cattle brands, maintaining jails, and serving civil papers than they did actually dealing with outlaws. In addition, with the growing use of U.S. marshals to uphold the law (some of the more storied ones being Wyatt Earp, "Wild Bill" Hickok, and William "Bat" Masterson), most people were inclined to be law-abiding.[55]

Only forty-five violent deaths from all causes can be found in western cow towns from 1870 to 1885, when they were thriving. This low figure reflects the real nature of the cow towns. Businessmen had a vested interest in preventing crime from occurring and in not hiring a trigger-happy sheriff or marshal. They tended to avoid hiring individuals like John Slaughter, sheriff of Cochise County, Arizona, who never brought a prisoner back alive for eight years. Too much violence ruined a town's reputation and harmed the local economy.[56]

The Entrenchment of Political Influence

Partly because of their closeness to politicians, police during the early twentieth century began providing a wide array of services to citizens. Many police departments were involved in the prevention of crime and the maintenance of order as well as a variety of social services. In some cities, they operated soup lines, helped find lost children, and found jobs and temporary lodging in station houses for newly arrived immigrants.[57] Police organizations were typically quite decentralized, with cities being divided into precincts and run like small-scale departments, hiring, firing, managing, and assigning personnel as necessary. Officers were often recruited from the same ethnic stock as the dominant groups in the neighborhoods and lived in the beats they patrolled, and they were allowed considerable discretion in handling their individual beats. Detectives operated from a caseload of "persons" rather than offenses, relying on their charges to inform on other criminals.[58]

The strength of the local political influence over the police was that officers were integrated into neighborhoods. This strategy proved useful; it helped contain riots, and the police helped immigrants establish themselves in communities and find jobs. There were weaknesses as well: The intimacy with the community, closeness to politicians, and decentralized organizational structure (and its inability to provide supervision of officers) also led to police corruption. The close identification of police with neighborhoods also resulted in discrimination against strangers, especially ethnic and racial minorities. Police officers often ruled their beats with the "end of their nightsticks" and practiced "curbside justice."[59] The lack of organizational control over officers also caused some inefficiencies and disorganization; thus the image of the bungling Keystone Kops was widespread.

THE REFORM ERA: 1930S TO 1980S

Attempts to Thwart Political Patronage

During the early nineteenth century, reformers sought to reject political involvement by the police, and civil service systems were created to eliminate patronage and ward influences in hiring and firing police officers. In some cities, officers were not permitted to live in the same beat they patrolled in order to isolate them as completely as possible from political influences. Police departments became one of the most autonomous agencies in urban government.[60] However, policing also became a matter viewed as best left to the discretion of police executives. Police organizations became law enforcement agencies with the sole goal of controlling crime. Any noncrime activities they were required to do were considered "social work." The **reform era of policing** (also termed "the professional era of policing") would soon be in full bloom.

The scientific theory of administration was adopted, as advocated by Frederick Taylor during the early twentieth century. Taylor first studied the work process, breaking down jobs to their basic steps and emphasizing time and motion studies, all with the goal of maximizing production. From this emphasis on production and unity of control flowed the notion that police officers were best managed by a hierarchical pyramid of control. Police leaders routinized and standardized police work; officers were to enforce laws and make arrests whenever they could. Discretion was limited as much as possible. When special problems arose, special units (for example, vice, juvenile, drugs, tactical) were created rather than assign problems to patrol officers.

The Era of August Vollmer

The policing career of **August Vollmer** has been established as one of the most important periods in the development of police professionalism (see Exhibit 1-1). In April 1905 at age twenty-nine, Vollmer became the town marshal in Berkeley, California. At that time, policing had become a major issue all across America. Big-city police departments had become notorious for their corruption, and politics rather than professional principles dominated most police departments.[61]

Vollmer commanded a force of only three deputies; his first act as town marshal was to request an increase in his force from three to twelve deputies in order to form day and night patrols. Obtaining that, he soon won national publicity for being the first chief to order his men to patrol on bicycles. Time checks he had run demonstrated that officers on bicycles would be able to respond three times more quickly to calls than men on foot possibly could. His confidence growing, Vollmer next persuaded the Berkeley City Council to purchase a system of red lights. The lights, hung at each street intersection, served as an emergency notification system for police officers—the first such signal system in the country.[62]

In 1906, Vollmer, curious about the methods criminals used to commit their crimes, began to question the suspects he arrested. He found that nearly all criminals used their own peculiar method of operation, or **modus operandi**. In 1907, following an apparent

EXHIBIT 1-1

The Crib of Modern Law Enforcement

A Chronology of August Vollmer and the Berkeley Police Department

1905	Vollmer is elected Berkeley town marshal. Town trustees appoint six police officers at a salary of $70 per month.
1906	Trustees create detective rank. Vollmer initiates a red light signal system to reach beat officers from headquarters; telephones are installed in boxes. A police records system is created.
1908	Two motorcycles are added to the department. Vollmer begins a police school.
1909	Vollmer is appointed Berkeley chief of police under a new charter form of government. Trustees approve the appointment of a Bertillon expert and the purchase of fingerprinting equipment. A modus operandi file is created, modeled on the British system.
1911	All patrol officers are using bicycles.
1914	Three privately owned autos are authorized for patrol use.
1915	A central office is established for police reports.
1916	Vollmer urges Congress to establish a national fingerprint bureau (later created by the FBI in Washington, D.C.), begins annual lectures on police procedures, and persuades biochemist Albert Schneider to install and direct a crime laboratory at headquarters.

1917	Vollmer has the first completely motorized force; officers furnish their own automobiles. Vollmer recruits college students for part-time police jobs. He begins consulting with police and reorganizing departments around the country.
1918	Entrance examinations are initiated to measure the mental, physical, and emotional fitness of recruits; a part-time police psychiatrist is employed.
1919	Vollmer begins testing delinquents and using psychology to anticipate criminal behavior. He implements a juvenile program to reduce child delinquency.
1921	Vollmer guides the development of the first lie detector and begins developing radio communications between patrol cars, handwriting analysis, and use of business machine equipment (a Hollerith tabulator).

Following his retirement from active law enforcement in 1932, Vollmer traveled around the world to study police methods. He continued serving as professor of police administration at the University of California, Berkeley, until 1938, and authored or coauthored four books on police and crime from 1935 to 1949. He died in Berkeley in 1955.

suicide case that Vollmer suspected of being murder, Vollmer sought the advice of a professor of biology at the University of California. He became convinced of the value of scientific knowledge in criminal investigation.[63]

Vollmer's most daring innovation came in 1908: the idea of a police school. The first formal training program for police officers in the country drew on the expertise of university professors as well as police officers. The school included courses on police methods and procedures, fingerprinting, first aid, criminal law, anthropometry, photography, public health, and sanitation. In 1917, the curriculum was expanded from one to three years.[64]

In 1916, Vollmer persuaded a professor of pharmacology and bacteriology to become a full-time criminalist in charge of the department's criminal investigation laboratory. By 1917, Vollmer had his entire patrol force operating out of automobiles; it was the first completely mobile patrol force in the country. And in 1918, to improve the quality of police

August Vollmer as town marshal, police chief, and criminalist.

(Courtesy Samuel G. Chapman)

recruits in his department, he began to hire college students as part-time officers and to administer a set of intelligence, psychiatric, and neurological tests to all applicants. Out of this group of "college cops" came several outstanding and influential police leaders, including O. W. Wilson, who served as police chief in Wichita and Chicago and as the first dean of the school of criminology at the University of California. Then, in 1921, in addition to experimenting with the lie detector, two of Vollmer's officers installed a crystal set and earphones in a Model T touring car, thus creating the first radio car.

These and other innovations at Berkeley had begun to attract attention from municipal police departments across the nation, including Los Angeles, which persuaded Vollmer to serve a short term as chief of police beginning in August 1923. Gambling, the illicit sale of liquor (Prohibition was then in effect), and police corruption were major problems in Los Angeles. Vollmer hired ex-criminals to gather intelligence information on the criminal network. He also promoted honest officers, required three thousand patrol officers to take an intelligence test, and, using those tests, reassigned personnel.[65] He was already unpopular with crooks and corrupt politicians, and these personnel actions made Vollmer very unpopular within the department as well. When he returned to Berkeley in 1924, he had made many enemies, and his attempts at reform had met with too much opposition to have any lasting effect. It would not be until the 1950s, under Chief William Parker, that the Los Angeles Police Department (LAPD) would become a leader in this reform era of policing.[66]

Vollmer, although a leading proponent of police professionalism, also advocated the idea that the police should function as social workers. He believed the police should do more than merely arrest offenders; they should also seek to prevent crime by "saving" offenders.[67] He suggested that police work closely with existing social welfare agencies, inform voters about overcrowded schools, and support the expansion of recreational facilities, community social centers, and antidelinquency agencies. Basically, he was suggesting that the police play an active part in the life of the community. These views were very prescient; today, his ideas are being implemented in the contemporary movement toward **community policing** and problem-oriented policing (discussed in Chapter 6). Yet the major thrust of police professionalization had been to insulate the police from politics. This contradiction illustrated one of the fundamental ambiguities of the whole notion of professionalism.[68]

In the late 1920s, Vollmer was appointed the first professor of police administration in the country at the University of Chicago. Upon returning to Berkeley in 1931, he received a similar appointment at the University of California, a position he held concurrently with the office of chief of police until his retirement from the force in 1932. He continued to serve as a university professor until 1938.[69]

The Crime Fighter Image

The 1930s marked an important turning point in the history of police reform. O. W. Wilson emerged as the leading authority on police administration, the police role was redefined, and the crime fighter image gained popularity.

Wilson, who learned from J. Edgar Hoover's transformation of the Federal Bureau of Investigation (FBI) into a highly prestigious agency, became the principal architect of the police reform strategy.[70] Hoover, appointed FBI director in 1924, had raised the eligibility and training standards of recruits and had developed an incorruptible crime-fighting organization. Municipal police found Hoover's path a compelling one.

Professionalism came to mean a combination of managerial efficiency and technological sophistication and an emphasis on crime fighting. The social work aspects of the policing movement fell into almost total eclipse. In sum, under the professional model of policing, officers were to remain in their "rolling fortresses," going from one call to the next with all due haste. As Mark Moore and George Kelling observed, "In professionalizing crime fighting…citizens on whom so much used to depend [were] removed from the fight."[71]

The Wickersham Commission

Another important development in policing, one that was strongly influenced by August Vollmer, was the creation of the **Wickersham Commission**. President Coolidge had appointed the first National Crime Commission in 1925, in an admission that crime control had become a national problem. This commission was criticized for working neither through the states nor with professionals in criminal justice, psychiatry, social work, or the like. Nevertheless, coming on the heels of World War I, the crime commission took advantage of FBI Director J. Edgar Hoover's popular "war on crime" slogan to enlist public support. Political leaders and police officials also loudly proclaimed the "war on crime" concept; it continued the push for police professionalism.

Coolidge's successor, President Herbert Hoover, became concerned about the lax enforcement of Prohibition, which took effect in 1920. It was common knowledge that an alarming number of American police chiefs and sheriffs were accepting bribes in exchange for overlooking moonshiners; other types of police corruption were occurring as well.

Hoover replaced the National Crime Commission with the National Commission on Law Observance and Enforcement—popularly known as the **Wickersham Commission** after its chairman, former U.S. Attorney General George W. Wickersham. This presidential commission completed the first national study of crime and criminal justice, issuing fourteen reports. Two of those reports, the "Report on Lawlessness in Law Enforcement" and the "Report on Police," represented a call by the national government for increased police professionalism.

The "Report on Police" was written in part by August Vollmer, and his imprint on this and other reports is evident. The second report, the "Report on Lawlessness in Law Enforcement," concerned itself with police misconduct and has received the greatest public attention, both then and today. The report indicated that the use of third-degree interrogation methods of suspects by the police (including the infliction of physical or mental pain to extract confessions) was widespread in America. This report, through its recommendations, mapped out a path of professionalism in policing for the next two generations. The Wickersham Commission recommended, for example, that the corrupting influence of politics should be removed from policing. Police chief executives should be selected on merit, and patrol officers should be tested and should meet minimal physical standards. Police salaries, working conditions, and benefits should be decent, the commission stated, and there should be adequate training for both preservice and in-service officers. The commission also called for the use of policewomen (in cases involving juveniles and females), crime-prevention units, and bureaus of criminal investigation.

Many of these recommendations represented what progressive police reformers had been wanting for the previous forty years; unfortunately, President Hoover and his administration could do little more than report the Wickersham Commission's recommendations before leaving office. Franklin Roosevelt's administration provided the funding and leadership necessary for implementing Wickersham's suggestions in the states.

Police as the "Thin Blue Line": William H. Parker

The movement to transform the police into professional crime fighters found perhaps its staunchest champion in **William H. Parker**, who began as a patrol officer with the LAPD in 1927. Parker used his law degree to advance his career, and by 1934 he was LAPD's trial prosecutor and an assistant to the chief.[72]

Parker became police chief in 1950. Following an uproar over charges of police brutality in 1951, he conducted an extensive investigation that resulted in the dismissal or punishment of over forty officers. Following this incident, he launched a campaign to transform the LAPD. His greatest success, typical of the new professionalism, came in administrative reorganization. The command structure was simplified as Parker aggressively sought ways to free every possible officer for duty on the streets, including forcing the county sheriff's office to guard prisoners and adopting one-person patrol cars. Parker also made the rigorous selection and training of personnel a major characteristic of the LAPD. Higher standards of physical fitness, intelligence, and scholastic achievement weeded out many applicants, while others failed the psychiatric examinations.

Once accepted, recruits attended a thirteen-week academy that included a rigorous physical program, rigid discipline, and intensive study. Parker thus molded an image of a tough, competent, polite, and effective crime fighter by controlling recruitment. During the 1950s, this image made the LAPD the model for reform across the nation; thus the 1950s marked a turning point in the history of professionalism.[73]

But Parker's impact on the police shows the very real limitations of the professional style of policing. Parker conceived of the police as a "thin blue line," protecting society from barbarism and Communist subversion. He viewed urban society as a jungle, needing the restraining hand of the police; only the law and law enforcement saved society from the horrors of anarchy. The police had to enforce the law without fear or favor. Parker opposed any restrictions on police methods. The law, he believed, should give the police wide latitude to use wiretaps and to conduct search and seizure. For him, the Bill of Rights was not absolute but relative. Any conflict between effective police operation and individual rights should be resolved in favor of the police, he believed, and the rights of society took precedence over the rights of the individual. He thought that evidence obtained illegally should still be admitted in court and that the police could not do their jobs if the courts and other civilians were continually second-guessing them.

Basically, Parker believed that some "wicked men with evil hearts" preyed on society and that the police must protect society from attack by them. But Parker's brand of professional police performance lacked total public support. Voters often supported political machines that controlled and manipulated the police in anything but a professional manner; the public demanded a police department that was subject to political influence and manipulation and then condemned the force for its crookedness. The professional police officer was in the uncomfortable position of offering a service that society required for its very survival but that many people did not want at all.[74]

Still, Parker's influence over police administration has not perished altogether. And to the extent that his influence remains today, it may hinder the spread of the concepts of community policing and problem-oriented policing, which are discussed more thoroughly in Chapter 6.

A RETREAT FROM THE PROFESSIONAL MODEL

Coming Full Circle to Peel: The President's Crime Commission

The 1960s were a time of explosion and turbulence. Inner-city residents rioted in several major cities, protestors denounced military involvement in Vietnam, and assassins ended the lives of President John F. Kennedy and Dr. Martin Luther King Jr. The country was witnessing tremendous upheaval, and incidents like the so-called police riot at the 1968 Democratic National Convention in Chicago raised many questions about the police and their function and role.

To this point, there had been few inquiries concerning police functions and methods[75] for two reasons. First was a tendency on the part of the police to resist outside scrutiny. Functioning in a bureaucratic environment, they, like other bureaucrats, were sensitive to outside research. Many police administrators perceived a threat to their career and to the image of the organization, as well as a concern about the legitimacy of the research itself. There was a natural reluctance to invite trouble. Second, few people in policing perceived a need to challenge traditional methods of operation. The "if it ain't broke, don't fix it" attitude prevailed, particularly among old-school administrators. Some ideas were etched in stone, such as the belief that more police personnel and vehicles equaled more patrolling and, therefore, less crime, a quicker response rate, and a happier citizenry. A corollary belief is that the more officers riding in the patrol car, the better. The methods and effectiveness of detectives and their investigative techniques were not even open to debate. As Herman Goldstein has stated, however, "Crises stimulate progress. The police came under enormous pressure in the late 1960s and early 1970s, confronted with concern about crime, civil rights demonstrations, racial conflicts, riots and political protests."[76]

As noted in Table 1-2, five national commissions attempted to examine police methods and practices during the 1960s and 1970s, each viewing them from different perspectives. Of particular note was a commission whose findings are still widely cited today and that provided the impetus to return the police to the community: the President's Commission on Law Enforcement and the Administration of Justice. Termed the **President's Crime Commission**, this body was charged by President Lyndon Johnson to find solutions to America's internal crime problems, including the root causes of crime, the workings of the justice system, and the hostile, antagonistic relations between the police and civilians. Among the commission's recommendations for the police were hiring more minority members as officers to improve police-community relations, upgrading the quality of police officers through better-educated officers, promoting to supervisory positions college-educated individuals, screening applicants more rigorously, and providing intensive preservice training for new recruits. It was believed that a higher caliber of recruits would raise police service delivery, promote tranquility within the community, and relegate police corruption to a thing of the past.[77]

TABLE 1-2

National Commissions That Studied Police Practices

Five national studies looked into police practices during the 1960s and 1970s, each with a different focus:

- The President's Commission on Law Enforcement and the Administration of Justice (1967)
- The National Advisory Commission on Civil Disorders (1968)
- The National Commission on the Causes and Prevention of Violence (1968)
- The President's Commission on Campus Unrest (1970)
- The National Advisory Commission on Criminal Justice Standards and Goals (1973)

The President's Crime Commission brought policing full circle, restating several of the same principles that were laid out by Sir Robert Peel in 1829: that the police should be close to the public, that poor quality of policing contributed to social disorder, and that the police should focus on community relations. Thus by 1970, there had been what was termed a systematic demolition of the assumptions underlying the **professional era of policing**.[78] Few authorities on policing today could endorse the basic approaches to police management that were propounded by O. W. Wilson or William Parker. We now know much that was still unknown by the staff of the President's Crime Commission in 1967. For example, as will be seen in Chapter 5, we have learned that adding more police or intensifying patrol coverage does not reduce crime and that neither faster response time nor additional detectives will improve clearance rates.

THE COMMUNITY ERA: 1980s TO PRESENT

In the early 1970s, it was suggested that the performance of patrol officers would improve by redesigning their job based on motivators.[79] This suggestion later evolved into a concept known as **team policing**, which sought to restructure police departments, improve police-community relations, enhance police officer morale, and facilitate change within the police organization. Its primary element was a decentralized neighborhood focus for the delivery of police services. Officers were to be generalists, trained to investigate crimes and basically attend to all of the problems in their area; a team of officers would be assigned to a particular neighborhood and would be responsible for all police services in that area.

In the end, however, team policing failed for several reasons. Most of the experiments were poorly planned and hastily implemented, resulting in street officers who did not understand what they were supposed to do. Many mid-management personnel felt threatened by team policing and did not support the experiment.

There were other developments for the police during the late 1970s and early 1980s. Foot patrol became more popular, and many jurisdictions (such as Newark, New Jersey; Boston; and Flint, Michigan) even demanded it. In Newark, an evaluation found that officers on foot patrol were easily seen by residents, produced a significant increase in the level of satisfaction with police service, led to a significant reduction of perceived crime problems, and resulted in a significant increase in the perceived level of neighborhood safety.[80]

These findings and others discussed later shattered several long-held myths about measures of police effectiveness. In addition, research conducted during the 1970s suggested that information could help police improve their ability to deal with crime. These studies, along with studies of foot patrol and fear reduction, created new opportunities for police to understand the increasing concerns of citizens' groups about problems (gangs, prostitutes) and to work with citizens to do something about them. Police discovered that when they asked citizens about their priorities, citizens appreciated their asking and often provided useful information.

Simultaneously, the problem-oriented approach to policing was being tested in Madison, Wisconsin; Baltimore County, Maryland; and Newport News, Virginia.

Studies there found that police officers have the capacity to do problem solving successfully and can work well with citizens and other agencies. Also, citizens seemed to appreciate working with police. Moreover, this approach gave officers more autonomy to analyze the underlying causes of problems and to find creative solutions. Crime control remained an important function, but equal emphasis was given to prevention.

In sum, following are some of the factors that set the stage for the emergence of the **community era of policing**:

- Narrowing of the police mission to crime fighting
- Increased cultural diversity in our society
- Detachment of patrol officers in patrol vehicles
- Increased violence in our society
- Scientific view of management, stressing efficiency more than effectiveness, quantitative policing more than qualitative policing
- Downturn in the economy and, subsequently, a "do more with less" philosophy toward the police
- Increased dependence on high-technology equipment rather than contact with the public
- Emphasis on organizational change, including decentralization and greater officer discretion
- Isolation of police administration from community and officer input
- Concern about police violation of the civil rights of minorities
- Yearning for personalization of government services
- Burgeoning attempts by the police to adequately reach the community through crime prevention, team policing, and police-community relations

Most of these elements contain a common theme: the isolation of the police from the public.

COPPS is now recognized as being on the cutting edge of what is new in policing.[81] Indeed, the Violent Crime Control and Law Enforcement Act of 1994 authorized $8.8 billion over six years to create the Office of Community Oriented Policing Services (COPS) within the U.S. Department of Justice, to add one hundred thousand more police officers to communities across the country, and to create thirty-one regional community policing institutes (RCPIs) to provide training and technical assistance for implementation and technology throughout the nation (educating police personnel on the proper approach to implementing the strategies and the technologies that are available for enhancing COPPS, discussed in Chapter 14).

The Three Generations of COPPS

COPPS is the established paradigm of contemporary policing, both at home and abroad; it enjoys a large degree of public acceptance.[82] According to Willard M. Oliver, it has now moved through three generations: innovation, diffusion, and institutionalization.[83]

The first generation of COPPS, *innovation*, spans the period from 1979 through 1986. It began with the seminal work of Herman Goldstein concerning needed improvement of policing[84] and with the "broken windows" theory of James Q. Wilson and George L. Kelling.[85] Early trials of community policing during this period—called "experiments," "test sites," and "demonstration projects"—were usually restricted to larger metropolitan cities. The style of policing that was employed was predominantly narrow in focus, such as foot patrols, problem-solving methods, or community substations. These small-scale experiments provided a source of innovative ideas for others to consider.

The second generation, *diffusion,* covers the period from 1987 through 1994. The concepts and philosophy of community policing and problem solving spread rapidly among police agencies through various forms of communication within the police subculture. Community policing was adopted quickly during this period. In 1985, slightly more than three hundred police agencies employed some form of community policing,[86] whereas by 1994 it had spread to more than eight thousand agencies.[87] The practice of community policing during this generation was still generally limited to large- and medium-sized cities, and the strategies normally targeted drugs and fear of crime issues while improving police-community relations. Much more emphasis was placed on evaluating outcomes through the use of appropriate research methodologies.

The third generation, *institutionalization,* began in 1995 and continues to the present. Today we see widespread implementation of community policing and problem solving across the United States. Nearly 7 in 10 (68 percent) of the nation's 17,000 local police agencies, employing 90 percent of all officers, have adopted this strategy.[88] This generation has seen COPPS become deeply entrenched within the political process, funded by federal grant money through the Violent Crime Control and Law Enforcement Act of 1994. Community policing today has extended to such programs as youth firearm violence, gangs, and domestic violence, while extending into geomapping software and crime prevention through environmental designs.

SUMMARY

This chapter has presented the evolution of policing through its three eras, and some of the individuals, events, and national commissions that were instrumental in taking policing through those eras. It has also shown how the history of policing may be said to have come full circle to its roots, wherein it was intended to operate with the consent and assistance of the public. Policing is now attempting to throw off the shackles of tradition and become more community oriented.

This historical overview also reveals that many of today's policing issues and problems (most or all of which are discussed in subsequent chapters) actually began surfacing many centuries ago: graft and corruption, negative community relations, police use of force, public unrest and rioting, general police accountability, the struggle to establish the proper roles and functions of the police, the police subculture, and the tendency to withdraw from the public, cling to tradition, and be inbred. All in all, however, it would seem the police learned well their lessons from history, as these problems do not pervade the nation's 17,000 agencies or their 800,000 officers. As we will see, the community era is spreading and thriving in today's police world.

KEY TERMS

August Vollmer
community era of policing
community policing
constable
coroner
justice of the peace (JP)
modus operandi
political era of policing
President's Crime Commission
professional era of policing
reform era of policing
republicanism
sheriff
team policing
Wickersham Commission
William H. Parker

REVIEW QUESTIONS

1. What were the major police-related offices and their functions during the early English and colonial periods?

2. What legacies of colonial policing remained intact after the American Revolution?

3. List the three early issues of American policing, and describe their present status.

4. What unique characteristics of law enforcement existed in the Wild West? What myths concerning early western law enforcement continue today?

5. What were some of the major characteristics of the political and reform eras of policing?

6. What led to the development of the contemporary community-oriented policing and problem-solving era, and what are some of its main features?

7. How can it be said that policing has come full circle, returning to its origins?

8. What are the three generations of community-oriented policing and problem solving?

INDEPENDENT STUDENT ACTIVITIES

1. Interview retired or long-time police officers about the kinds of changes they have witnessed in policing from their earliest years in the field to the present.

2. Through these interviews and your own independent research of police operations of the past, explore the ways in which the traditional model of policing differs from today's community policing and problem solving.

3. Looking at some of the early police offices described in this chapter (such as constable, coroner, and justice of the police), determine through interviews and research whether such positions ever existed in your home jurisdiction, and if they did, what their duties and functions were.

RELATED WEB SITES

Library of Congress
http://loc.gov/library

National Archive of Criminal Justice Data
http://www.icpsr.unmich.edu/NACJD/index.html

Office of Community Oriented Policing Services (COPS)
http://www.usdoj.gov/cops

FEDERAL AND STATE AGENCIES

PROTECTING OUR BORDERS

Islamic governments have never and will never be established through peaceful solutions and cooperative councils. They are established as they always have been...by pen and gun...by word and bullet...by tongue and teeth.
—Terrorist manual

LEARNING OBJECTIVES

AS A RESULT OF READING THIS CHAPTER, THE STUDENT WILL:

– BE AWARE OF THE MAJOR ORGANIZATIONS THAT COMPOSE THE DEPARTMENT OF HOMELAND SECURITY AND THEIR PRIMARY FUNCTIONS

– KNOW THE MAJOR FUNCTIONS OF THE FOUR PRIMARY LAW ENFORCEMENT AGENCIES WITHIN THE DEPARTMENT OF JUSTICE AS WELL AS TWO RELATED ORGANIZATIONS, THE CENTRAL INTELLIGENCE AGENCY AND THE INTERNAL REVENUE SERVICE

– KNOW WHERE AND HOW FEDERAL AGENTS ARE TRAINED

– UNDERSTAND THE PURPOSES OF THE UNIFORM CRIME REPORTS AND THE NATIONAL CRIME INFORMATION CENTER

– KNOW THE PRIMARY DUTIES AND TITLES OF STATE BUREAUS OF INVESTIGATION AS WELL AS STATE AGENCIES PERFORMING GENERAL LAW ENFORCEMENT FUNCTIONS

INTRODUCTION

Perhaps more than any other chapter in this textbook, this chapter reflects the impact of the events of September 11, 2001, when foreign terrorists attacked us on our own soil. No segment of our society was altered more than our nation's police organizations, particularly the **federal law enforcement agencies** (local police agencies are discussed in Chapter 3).

Therefore, this chapter examines how our law enforcement agencies are now structured and how they function, particularly during this time when our nation's very existence depends on the ability to be proactive to prevent more terrorist attacks.

The chapter begins with an examination of the Department of Homeland Security (DHS). It looks at the roles and functions of its five **directorates** and their organizations, including the U.S. Secret Service. Next is a discussion of the retooled U.S. Department of Justice and its four primary law enforcement organizations: the Federal Bureau of Investigation (FBI); the Bureau of Alcohol, Tobacco, Firearms, and Explosives (ATF); the Drug Enforcement Administration (DEA); and the U.S. Marshals Service (USMS) (included in this chapter is an exhibit describing the role and functions of the International Criminal Police Organization, or Interpol). Then the chapter reviews the functions of three related organizations: the Central Intelligence Agency (CIA), the Criminal Investigation Division of the Internal Revenue Service (IRS), and the Federal Law Enforcement Training Center (FLETC). Next is an overview of state agencies. A chapter summary, key terms, review questions, independent student activities, and related Web sites conclude the chapter.

In a related vein, note that Appendix II at the book's end provides information for those wishing to pursue a career in federal, state, or local law enforcement agencies. The general problem of terrorism is discussed in Chapter 11, which also includes new federal legislation that gives the CIA and other federal agencies greater authority in combating terrorism: the Military Commissions Act of 2006.

An overhead view of Ground Zero on 9/11.

(Courtesy U.S. Customs and Border Protection, photographer James Tourtellotte)

FEDERAL AGENCIES

This section describes the major law enforcement arms of the federal government, most of which are found within DHS and the Department of Justice. Table 2-1 shows the

TABLE 2-1

Gender and Race or Ethnicity of Federal Officers with Arrest and Firearm Authority

Agency	Number of Officers	Female	PERCENT OF FULL-TIME FEDERAL OFFICERS WITH ARREST AND FIREARM AUTHORITY Racial/Ethnic Minority Total Minority	American Indian	Black or African American	Asian or Pacific Islander	Hispanic or Latino, Any Race	Other Race
U.S. Customs and Border Protection	28,200	15.3%	46.8%	0.6%	5.0%	4.2%	36.9%	0.0%
Federal Bureau of Prisons	15,361	13.3	39.7	1.3	24.2	1.5	12.7	0.0
Federal Bureau of Investigation	12,414	18.5	17.2	0.4	5.8	3.6	7.4	0.0
U.S. Immigration and Customs Enforcement	10,691	13.7	33.9	0.6	8.6	2.7	22.0	0.0
U.S. Secret Service	4,780	10.5	19.6	0.6	11.2	2.6	5.2	0.0
Drug Enforcement Administration	4,500	8.9	19.4	0.4	7.6	2.5	8.9	0.0
Administrative Office of the U.S. Courts	4,166	44.2	32.2	0.5	15.3	1.6	14.1	0.6
U.S. Marshals Service	3,233	10.2	20.0	0.7	7.3	2.3	9.6	0.1
U.S. Postal Inspection Service	2,999	19.6	36.4	0.5	21.6	4.7	9.6	0.0
Internal Revenue Service, Criminal Investigation	2,791	30.0	24.0	0.8	10.2	4.5	8.1	0.4
Veterans Health Administration	2,474	6.9	40.1	0.9	26.8	2.5	10.0	0.0
Bureau of Alcohol, Tobacco, Firearms & Explosives	2,398	13.3	19.9	1.1	9.3	2.1	7.5	0.0
National Park Service— Ranger Division	1,547	18.2	10.3	2.1	2.5	2.4	3.0	0.3
U.S. Capitol Police	1,535	18.8	34.7	0.3	28.9	1.2	4.2	0.0
Bureau of Diplomatic Security, Diplomatic Security Service	825	11.8	20.0	0.7	9.7	3.4	5.5	0.7
U.S. Fish and Wildlife Service	713	8.7	13.6	3.5	1.7	1.4	7.0	0.0
National Park Service— U.S. Park Police	612	11.4	18.8	0.0	10.9	2.8	5.1	0.0
USDA Forest Service	604	17.5	17.4	6.5	3.3	1.3	6.3	0.0

Note: Table includes employees in U.S. territories.

Source: U.S. Department of Justice, Bureau of Justice Statistics, *Federal Law Enforcement Officers, 2004* (Washington, DC: Author, 2006), p. 6.

number of full-time federal agents employed in federal agencies employing five hundred or more sworn personnel, by gender and race/ethnicity.

Department of Homeland Security (DHS)

To combat terrorism in the aftermath of September 11, the **Department of Homeland Security (DHS)** was formed by H. R. 5005, the Homeland Security Act of 2002. DHS was activated in January 2003 and immediately put 180,000 new federal employees to work and committed $32 billion in 2003 toward safeguarding the nation, developing vaccines to protect against biological or chemical threats, training and equipping first responders (local police, firefighters, and medical personnel), and funding science and technology projects to counter the use of biological weapons and assess vulnerabilities. Since 2003, more than $100 billion has been appropriated by the federal government to support homeland security. Figure 2-1 shows the organizational structure of DHS.[1]

Following are brief descriptions of the major organizations that currently compose DHS[2]:

- The Directorate for Preparedness works with state, local, and private-sector partners to identify threats, determine vulnerabilities, and target resources where risk is greatest, thereby safeguarding our borders, seaports, bridges, and highways as well as critical information systems.
- The Science and Technology Directorate is the primary research and development arm of the department. It provides federal, state, and local officials with the technology and capabilities to protect the homeland.
- The Management Directorate is responsible for department budgets and appropriations, expenditure of funds, accounting and finance, procurement, human resources, information technology systems, facilities and equipment, and identification and tracking of performance measurements.
- The Office of Policy Directorate is the primary policy formulation and coordination component for DHS. It provides a centralized and coordinated focus to the development of departmentwide long-range planning to protect the United States.
- The Federal Emergency Management Agency (FEMA) Directorate prepares the nation for hazards, manages federal response and recovery efforts following any national incident, and administers the National Flood Insurance Program.
- The Customs and Border Protection (CBP), as shown in Table 2-1, has the greatest number of sworn personnel of all federal agencies. CBP is responsible for protecting our nation's borders in order to prevent terrorists and terrorist weapons from entering the United States while facilitating the flow of legitimate trade and travel. On a typical day the CBP will process more than 1,100,000 passengers and pedestrians, execute more than 60 arrests at ports of entry, and seize an average of 2,187 pounds of narcotics in 65 seizures at its 317 ports of entry. The CBP protects nearly 7,000 miles of border with Canada and Mexico and 95,000 miles of shoreline.[3] Figure 2-2 shows the organizational structure of CBP.
- The Immigration and Customs Enforcement (ICE), the largest investigative arm of DHS, is responsible for identifying and shutting down vulnerabilities both in the nation's borders and in economic, transportation, and infrastructure security. ICE employees work in offices nationally and around the world. The four main branches

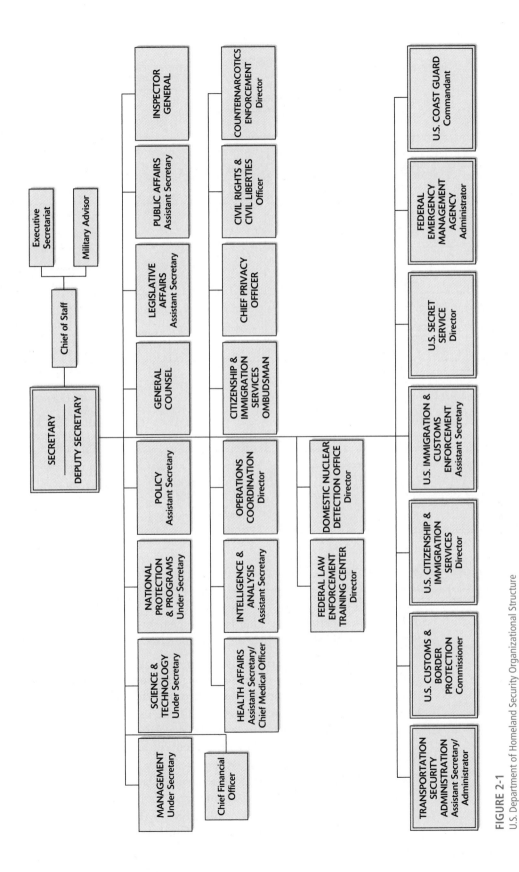

FIGURE 2-1

U.S. Department of Homeland Security Organizational Structure

Source: Department of Homeland Security Web site, http://www.dhs.gov/xlibrary/assets/DHS_OrgChart.pdf (accessed April 12, 2007).

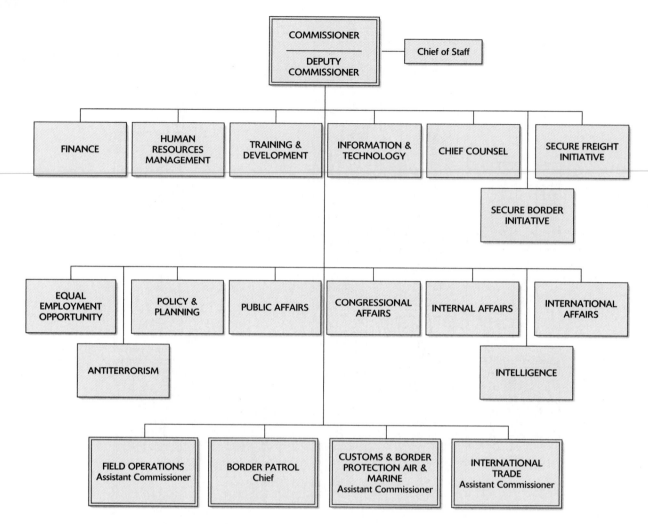

FIGURE 2-2
U.S. Customs and Border Protection Organizational Structure

Source: U.S. Customs and Border Protection Web site, http://www.cbp.gov/linkhandler/cgov/toolbox/about/organization/orgcha1.ctt/orgcha1.pdf (accessed April 12, 2007).

of ICE work together with other law enforcement and intelligence entities to keep the United States secure. There are four branches:

1. The Office of Investigations investigates a wide range of domestic and international activities arising from the movements of people and goods that violate immigration and customs laws and threaten national security.

2. The Office of Detention and Removal Operations is responsible for public safety and national security by ensuring the departure from the United States of all illegal aliens through the fair enforcement of the nation's immigration laws.

3. The Federal Protective Service is responsible for policing, securing, and ensuring a safe environment in which federal agencies can conduct their business at more than 8,800 federal facilities nationwide.

4. The Office of Intelligence is responsible for the collection, analysis, and dissemination of strategic and tactical intelligence data for use by ICE and DHS.[4]

CBP agents make an enforcement stop of an airplane.

(Courtesy U.S. Customs and Border Protection, photographer James Tourtellotte)

- The Office of Intelligence and Analysis is responsible for using information and intelligence from multiple sources to identify and assess current and future threats to the United States.
- The Office of Operations Coordination is responsible for monitoring the security of the United States on a daily basis and coordinating activities within the department and with governors, DHS advisors, law enforcement partners, and critical infrastructure operators in all 50 states and more than 50 major urban areas nationwide.
- The Domestic Nuclear Detection Office works to enhance the nuclear detection efforts of federal, state, territorial, tribal, and local governments and the private sector and to ensure a coordinated response to such threats.
- The Transportation Security Administration (TSA) protects the nation's transportation systems. TSA has 43,000 security officers, inspectors, directors, air marshals, and managers. They protect the nation's transportations systems, ensuring that people can travel safely. TSA screens people at airports, inspects rail cars, patrols subways with law enforcement partners, and perform a variety of other functions using federal air marshals, flight deck officers, canine and explosives detection personnel, and armed security officers.[5]
- The Federal Law Enforcement Training Center (FLETC) provides career-long training to law enforcement professionals to help them fulfill their responsibilities safely and proficiently. FLETC serves as an interagency law enforcement training organization

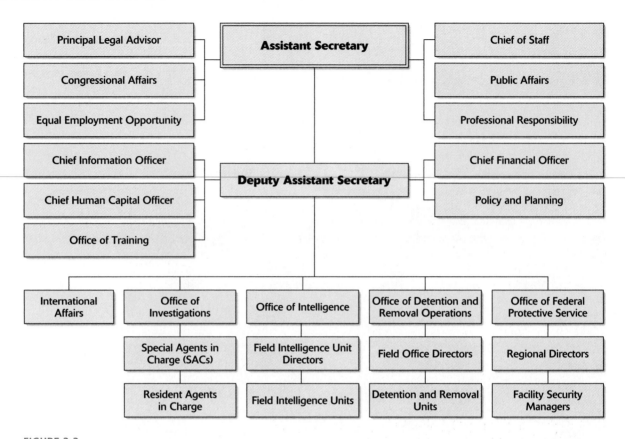

FIGURE 2-3

U.S. Immigration and Customs Enforcement Organizational Structure

Source: Department of Homeland Security Web site, http://www.dhs.gov/xlibrary/assets/DHS_OrgChart.pdf (accessed April 12, 2007).

for more than 80 federal agencies; provides services to state, local, and international law enforcement agencies; and graduates approximately 25,000 students per year. The center is headquartered at Glynco, Georgia.[6]

- The Citizenship and Immigration Services is responsible for the administration of immigration and naturalization adjudication functions and the establishment of immigration services policies and priorities.

- The Coast Guard protects the public, the environment, and U.S. economic interests in the nation's ports, on its waterways, along the coast, on international waters, or in any maritime region as required to support national security.

- The Secret Service protects the president and other high-level officials and investigates counterfeiting and other financial crimes, including financial institution fraud, identity theft, computer fraud, and computer-based attacks on our nation's financial, banking, and telecommunications infrastructure. The Secret Service's Uniformed Division protects the White House complex and the vice president's residence as well as foreign embassies and missions in the Washington, D.C., area. The Secret Service has agents assigned to approximately 125 offices located in cities throughout the United States and in select foreign cities.[7] See Exhibit 2-1 for information on Interpol.

EXHIBIT 2-1

Interpol

The U.S. Department of Justice and the attorney general serve as this nation's contact with the International Criminal Police Organization (Interpol), which is the oldest, the best-known, and probably the only truly international crime-fighting organization. Interpol is charged with capturing criminals who seek to keep one country or continent ahead of the long arm of the law. Many crimes are conducted on an international scale, such as drug trafficking, bank fraud, money laundering, and counterfeiting, for which the crooks may escape detection for years while they enjoy their profits. Interpol agents do not patrol the globe, nor do they make arrests or engage in shootouts. They are basically intelligence gatherers who have helped many nations work together in attacking international crime since 1923.[1]

Lyon, France, serves as the headquarters for Interpol's crime-fighting tasks. One cardinal rule is observed—Interpol deals only with common criminals; it does not become involved with political, racial, or religious matters. Today 186 member countries constitute Interpol.

U.S. participation in Interpol began in 1938 when Congress, under 22 U.S.C. 263a, authorized the attorney general to accept membership in the organization on behalf of the federal government.[2] Today drugs and organized crime, financial and high-tech crime, fugitives, public safety and terrorism, and trafficking in human beings are Interpol's five high-priority crime areas.[3]

Interpol has a basic three-step formula for offenses that all nations must follow for success: pass laws specifying the offense is a crime; prosecute offenders and cooperate in other countries' prosecutions; and furnish Interpol with and exchange information about crime and its perpetrators. This formula could reverse the trend that is forecast for the world at present: an increasing capability by criminals for violence and destruction. The following crimes, because they are recognized as crimes by other countries, are covered by almost all U.S. treaties of extradition: murder, rape, bigamy, arson, robbery, burglary, forgery, counterfeiting, embezzlement, larceny, fraud, perjury, and kidnapping.[4]

1. INTERPOL, "About INTERPOL," http://www.interpol.int/public/icpo/default.asp (accessed November 1, 2007).
2. John J. Imhoff and Stephen P. Cutler, "Interpol: Extending Law Enforcement's Reach around the World," *FBI Law Enforcement Bulletin*, December 1998, pp. 10–17. Also see Interpol, http://www.interpol.int.
3. Interpol, "About Interpol," www.interpol.int/public/icpo/default.asp (accessed November 2, 2007).
4. Michael Fooner, *Interpol: Issues in World Crime and International Criminal Justice* (New York: Plenum Press, 1989), p. 179.

Department of Justice

The **Department of Justice** is headed by the attorney general, who is appointed by the president and approved by the Senate. The president also appoints the attorney general's assistants and the U.S. attorneys for each of the judicial districts. The U.S. attorneys in each judicial district control and supervise all federal criminal prosecutions and represent the government in legal suits in which it is a party. These attorneys may appoint committees to investigate other governmental agencies or offices when questions of wrongdoing are raised or when possible violations of federal law are suspected or detected.

The Department of Justice is the official legal arm of the government of the United States. Within this department are several law enforcement organizations that investigate violations of federal laws (Figure 2-4). We will discuss the FBI, the AFT, the DEA, and the USMS. (The Community Oriented Policing Services will be discussed in Chapter 6.)

FEDERAL BUREAU OF INVESTIGATION (FBI)

Beginnings.   The FBI was created and funded through the Department of Justice Appropriation Act of 1908. The FBI was first known as the Bureau of Investigation. With

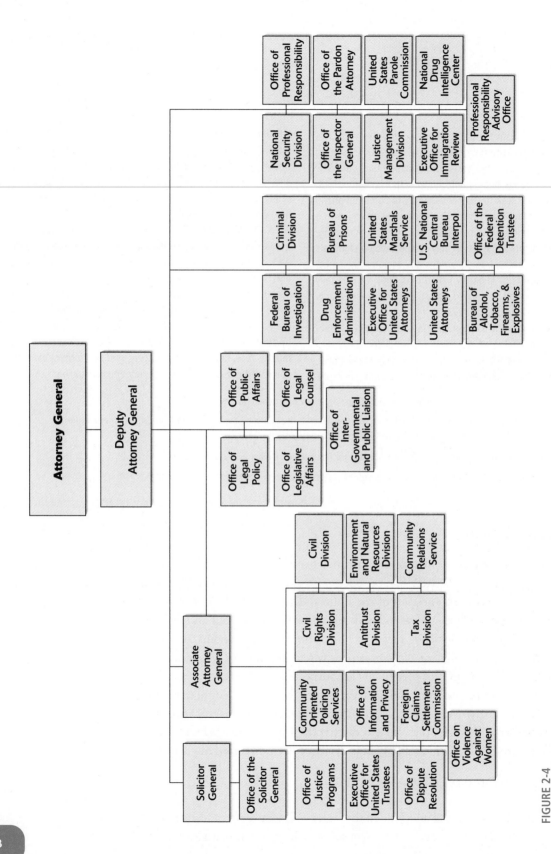

FIGURE 2-4

U.S. Department of Justice Organizational Structure

Source: U.S. Department of Justice Web site, http://www.usdoj.gov/dojorg.htm (accessed April 12, 2007).

thirty-five agents, it originally had no specific duties other than the "prosecution of crimes," focusing on bankruptcy fraud, antitrust crimes, neutrality violations, and crimes on Native-American reservations. Espionage and sabotage incidents during World War I, coupled with charges of political corruption reaching into the Department of Justice and the bureau itself, prompted angry demands for drastic changes.[8]

A new era was begun for the FBI in 1924 with the appointment of J. Edgar Hoover as director; he served in that capacity until his death in 1972. Hoover was determined that the organization would become a career service in which appointments would be made strictly on personal qualifications and abilities, and promotions would be based on merit. Special agents were college graduates, with degrees in law or accounting preferred. A rigorous course of training had to be completed, and agents had to be available for assignment wherever their services might be needed. Hoover coordinated the development of the Uniform Crime Reporting system, and during his tenure in office many notorious criminals, such as Bonnie Parker, Clyde Barrow, and John Dillinger, were tracked and captured or killed. The building housing the FBI Headquarters in Washington, D.C., bears his name.[9]

The bureau's Identification Division was created on July 1, 1924, and its laboratory opened in 1932. Then, in 1933, all of the bureau's functions were consolidated and transferred to a Division of Investigation, which became the Federal Bureau of Investigation on March 22, 1935.

Contemporary Priorities and Roles.   Today the FBI has fifty-six field offices and approximately four hundred resident agencies and more than fifty foreign liaison posts called legal attaches. About 18,000 nonsworn employees perform professional, administrative, technical, or other functions in support of the 12,400 sworn special agents shown in Table 2-1. The national priorities of the

J. Edgar Hoover.

(Courtesy Federal Bureau of Investigation)

FBI have been modified in major fashion since September 11, 2001. Today these are the agency's top three priority areas[10]:

1. To protect the United States from terrorist attack
2. To protect the United States against foreign intelligence operations and espionage
3. To protect the United States against cyber-based attacks and high-technology crimes

Beyond these top priorities, others include combating public corruption, transnational and national criminal organizations, white-collar crime, and significant violent crime and protecting civil rights.[11]

These priorities have certainly changed since the twin towers fell in New York City; before September 11, the FBI focused on merely "catching bad guys and putting them behind bars." Sweeping structural and philosophical changes have come as well, transforming an investigative agency into an intelligence-gathering service. And the FBI has been successful in its new role, identifying "sleeper cells" of terrorists in the United States and disrupting al Qaeda operations in places such as Michigan and New York. Ultimately, the bureau will have 1,200 special agents and analysts assigned to counterterrorism work, coordinating all terrorism investigations as well as sifting and analyzing strands of information. About 22,000 new computers and a new $596 million software package have been added to the FBI field offices to aid agents in doing complex searches, e-mailing color photos of suspects, and searching for trends. This upgrade includes a 40-million-page database of evidence dating back to the 1993 bombing of the World Trade Center, documents seized from Afghanistan, and 2 million pages of cable traffic.[12]

Recently, the FBI was given new powers to aid its reform efforts to battle terrorism. The bureau can now monitor Internet sites, libraries, churches, and political organizations. In addition, under revamped guidelines, agents can attend public meetings for the purpose of preventing terrorism.[13] The bureau also participates with local police in dozens of task forces nationwide that target fugitives and violent gangs.

But counterterrorism still constitutes only a fraction of the bureau's workload; the FBI also continues to investigate bank robberies, white-collar crimes, and organized crime and drug syndicates—staples of the agency's workload for a long time—while it combats radical Islamic fundamentalism and global terrorism with a workforce in which just 1 percent of the FBI's 12,200 agents have any familiarity with the Arabic language.[14]

Ancillary Investigative, Training, and Reporting Services. Today the FBI's laboratory examines blood, hair, firearms, paint, handwriting, typewriters, and other types of evidence. Highly specialized techniques are now utilized—at no charge to **state police** and local police agencies—for analysis of DNA, explosives, hairs and fibers, tool marks, drugs, plastics, and bloodstains.

Another feature of the bureau is its National Academy, which graduated its first class in 1935. Today thousands of local police managers from across the country have received training at the National Academy in Quantico, Virginia, which has twenty-one buildings on 385 acres. The FBI also provides extensive professional training to national supervisory-level police officers at the National Academy. (More information on local police training is provided in Chapter 4.)

A very successful function of the FBI, inaugurated in 1950, is its "Ten Most Wanted Fugitives" list, which over the years has contained many notable fugitives. As of 2000, the bureau had caught about 460 top ten fugitives; the Internet has helped to invigorate the program, with the "Ten Most Wanted" Web page receiving about 25 million hits per month.[15]

The FBI also operates the **National Crime Information Center (NCIC)**, through which millions of records relating to stolen property and missing persons and fugitives are instantaneously available to local, state, and federal authorities across the United States and Canada. In a related vein, one of the FBI's several annual publications is the **Uniform Crime Reports (UCR)**, which include crime data reported from more than fifteen thousand state and local police agencies concerning twenty-nine types of offenses: eight Part I, or index, offenses (criminal homicide, forcible rape, robbery, aggravated assault, burglary, larceny-theft, motor vehicle theft, and arson) and twenty-one Part II offenses. The UCR also includes a so-called crime clock, shown in Figure 2-5.

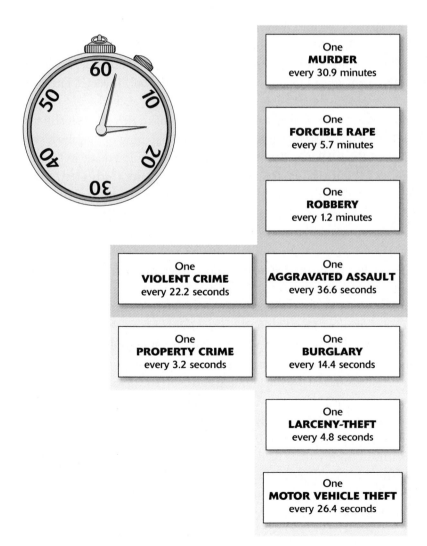

One
MURDER
every 30.9 minutes

One
FORCIBLE RAPE
every 5.7 minutes

One
ROBBERY
every 1.2 minutes

One
VIOLENT CRIME
every 22.2 seconds

One
AGGRAVATED ASSAULT
every 36.6 seconds

One
PROPERTY CRIME
every 3.2 seconds

One
BURGLARY
every 14.4 seconds

One
LARCENY-THEFT
every 4.8 seconds

One
MOTOR VEHICLE THEFT
every 26.4 seconds

FIGURE 2-5
UCR Crime Clock

Source: United States Department of Justice, Federal Bureau of Investigation, Crime in the United States, 2006, *http://www.fbi.gov/ucr/cius2006/about/crime_clock.html (accessed November 1, 2007).*

There are several shortcomings in the UCR data, however. First, many crime victims do not report their victimization to the police; the local police, therefore, are unaware of these "hidden" offenses. Also, the entire reporting system is voluntary, and there is no penalty for police agencies that do not report to the FBI. Furthermore, the reporting system is not uniform, so crimes may be reported incorrectly or inaccurately. At best, the UCR has limitations and must be used cautiously.

A large amount of information concerning the FBI's application and hiring process—including its minimum requirements and the kinds of knowledge, skills, and abilities it now seeks for its new special agents—is available on the agency's Web site. Figure 2-6 depicts the FBI's organizational structure.

BUREAU OF ALCOHOL, TOBACCO, FIREARMS, AND EXPLOSIVES (ATF) The ATF originated as a unit within the IRS in 1862, when certain alcohol and tobacco tax statutes were created. The next year, Congress authorized the hiring of three "detectives" to aid in the prevention, detection, and punishment of tax evaders. Originally called the Alcohol, Tobacco, Tax Unit, it eventually became the Alcohol, Tobacco, and Firearms Division within the IRS. In 1972, it became the Bureau of Alcohol, Tobacco, and Firearms, under the direct control of the Treasury Department; in January 2003, it was moved to the Justice Department and renamed the Bureau of Alcohol, Tobacco, Firearms, and Explosives.[16]

Like the FBI and several other federal agencies, the ATF has a rich and colorful history, much of which has involved capturing bootleggers and disposing of illegal whiskey stills during Prohibition.[17] From 1920 to 1933, congressional legislation made it illegal to manufacture, possess, or sell intoxicating liquors in the United States (with a few exceptions). Still, America was awash with liquor. History is replete with accounts of violations of Prohibition laws; much has been written and portrayed in movies of that era, when the moonshiners tried to outsmart and outrun the law.[18] Speakeasies (secret bars) proliferated across America to satisfy the American yearning for liquor. This era bolstered the popularity of such G-men as Eliot Ness; the 1960s television program *The Untouchables* was inspired by his career.

The ATF administers the U.S. Criminal Code provisions concerning alcohol and tobacco smuggling and diversion. The ATF is also responsible for enforcing all the federal laws relating to firearms, explosives, and arson; it works with federal, state, and local law enforcement organizations and seeks to battle terrorism, prevent crime, conduct fair and effective industry regulation, and provide training and expertise to federal, state, local, and international law enforcement partners. The Homeland Security Act of 2002 transferred these enforcement activities of the ATF, along with certain other functions, to the Department of Justice from the Department of the Treasury. ATF's sworn and nonsworn personnel work primarily in twenty-three field divisions across the fifty states, with offices as well in Guam, the Virgin Islands, Puerto Rico, Mexico, Canada, Colombia, and France.[19]

Each year the ATF initiates approximately 30,000 firearms investigations, resulting in more than 6,000 defendants being convicted of firearms-related offenses.[20] It also

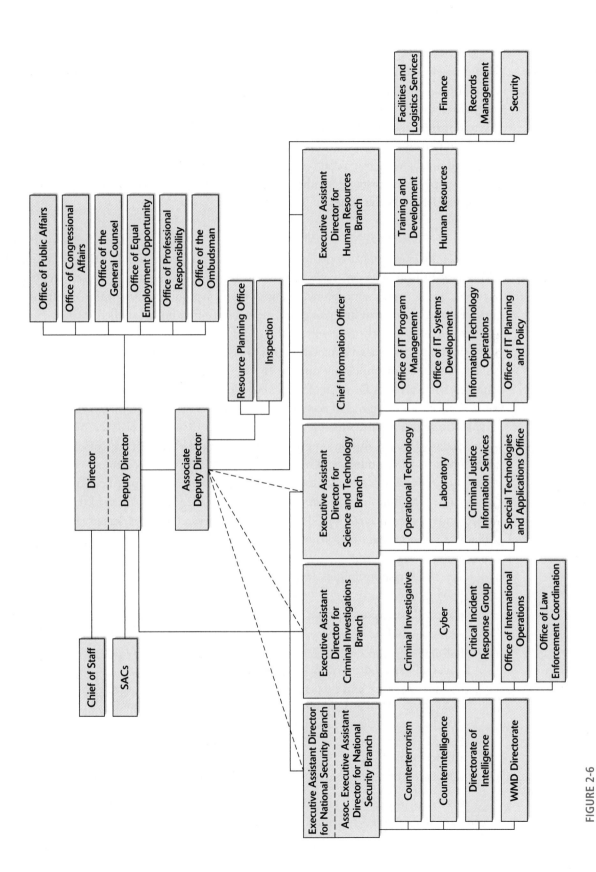

FIGURE 2-6
Federal Bureau of Investigation Organizational Structure

Source: Federal Bureau of Investigation Web site, http://www.fbi.gov/aboutus/todaysfbi/orgchart.htm (accessed April 12, 2007).

investigates nearly 400 bombings, 750 incidents involving recovered explosives or explosive devices, and more than 60 thefts of explosives[21]; performs about 15,000 firearms-
related inspections; and completes more than 2,700 explosives-compliance and 5,000
explosives-application inspections.[22] The ATF also maintains a Bomb and Arson Tracking
System, which allows local, state, and other federal agencies to share information about
bomb and arson cases[23]; 4 National Response Teams of highly trained agents that can be
deployed to major explosion and fire scenes in the United States; an International Response
Team that provides assistance in other countries; 32 explosives-detection canine teams; and
3 national laboratory facilities.[24]

DRUG ENFORCEMENT ADMINISTRATION (DEA)   The DEA began with the
passage of the Harrison Narcotic Act, signed into law on December 17, 1914, by President
Woodrow Wilson. The act made it unlawful for any "nonregistered" person to possess
heroin, cocaine, opium, morphine, or any of their by-products. Drug enforcement began
in 1915, and during that first year, agents seized forty-four pounds of heroin and achieved
106 convictions (mostly the result of illicit activities of physicians).[25]

In the 1920s, federal narcotics agents focused on organized gangs of Chinese immigrants suspected of importing opium. In 1920, the Volstead Act ("Prohibition") was
enacted; the Narcotics Division of the Prohibition Unit of the Revenue Bureau consisted
of 170 agents working out of seventeen offices around the country. New authority was
granted to agents by the Narcotic Drugs Import and Export Act of 1922.

Today's DEA is also an outgrowth of the former Bureau of Narcotics, which was
established in 1930 under the direct control of the Treasury Department. In 1968, the
Bureau of Narcotics was transferred from the Treasury to the Department of Justice and
was renamed the Bureau of Narcotics and Dangerous Drugs. In 1973, the DEA was established under a plan that combined the functions of several agencies. In January 1982, the
DEA was given primary responsibility for drug and narcotics enforcement, sharing this
jurisdiction with the FBI.

The major responsibilities of the DEA's 4,400 agents, under the U.S. Code, include
the following[26]:

- Development of an overall federal drug-enforcement strategy, including programs, planning, and evaluation
- Full investigation of and preparation for the prosecution of suspects for violations under all federal drug-trafficking laws
- Full investigation and preparation for the prosecution of suspects connected with illicit drugs seized at U.S. ports of entry and international borders
- Conduct of all relations with drug-enforcement officials of foreign governments
- Full coordination and cooperation with state and local police officials on joint drug-enforcement efforts
- Regulation of the legal manufacture of drugs and other controlled substances

Overseas, the DEA maintains seventy-one offices in fifty foreign countries.[27]
Figure 2-7 depicts DEA's various programs and operations.

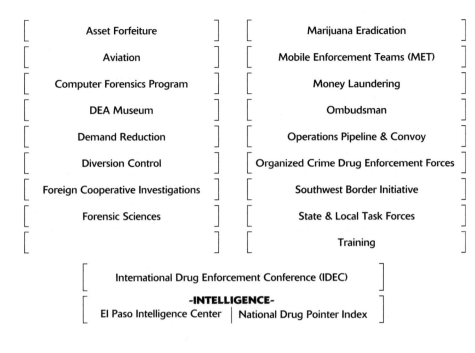

FIGURE 2-7
U.S. Drug Enforcement Administration Programs and Operations

Source: U.S. Drug Enforcement Administration Web site, http://www.usdoj.gov/dea/programs/progs.htm (accessed April 12, 2007).

U.S. MARSHALS SERVICE (USMS)   The USMS is one of the oldest federal law enforcement agencies, established under the Judiciary Act of 1789; George Washington appointed thirteen marshals, one for each of the original thirteen states. The USMS formally assumed the responsibility for the apprehension of federal fugitives in 1979. Today it has about 2,650 officers with arrest powers. Each district headquarters office is managed by a politically appointed U.S. marshal and a chief deputy U.S. marshal, who direct a staff of supervisors, investigators, deputy marshals, and administrative personnel. As in the so-called Wild West, the backbone of the USMS today is the deputy U.S. marshals, who pursue and arrest DEA fugitives—suspects wanted for federal drug violations—and escaped federal prisoners and who provide a secure environment for the federal courts and judges.[28]

Virtually every federal law enforcement initiative involves the USMS. Its agents produce prisoners for trial; protect the courts, judges, attorneys, and witnesses; track and arrest fugitives; and manage and dispose of seized drug assets.

In 1971, the USMS created the Special Operations Group (SOG), consisting of a well-trained elite group of deputy marshals. The group provides support in priority or dangerous situations, such as the movement of a large group of high-risk prisoners, and at trials involving alleged drug traffickers or members of subversive groups.

Another important function of the USMS is the operation of the Witness Protection Program. Federal witnesses are sometimes threatened by defendants or their associates (for example, they sometimes testify against organized crime figures). If certain criteria are met, the USMS will provide a complete change of identity for witnesses and their families, including new Social Security numbers, residences, and employment. This protection program was established in 1970.

Other Federal Agencies

CENTRAL INTELLIGENCE AGENCY (CIA)   Although not a law enforcement agency, the CIA is of significant importance at the federal level to the nation's security and warrants a brief discussion. The National Security Act of 1947 established the National Security Council, which in 1949 created a subordinate organization, the CIA. Considered the most clandestine government service, the CIA participates in undercover and covert operations around the world for the purposes of managing crises and providing intelligence during the conduct of war.[29] See Exhibit 2-2 for a discussion of police and security in another part of the world—China.

To accomplish its mission, the CIA engages in research and development and deploys high technology for intelligence purposes. After the terrorist attacks in this country, the CIA created special centers to address such issues as counterterrorism, counterintelligence, international organized crime and narcotics trafficking, and arms control intelligence.[30]

The CIA is an independent agency responsible to the president through its director. The agency recently recruited applicants in weekly news magazines and its Web site for employees in its National Clandestine Service, where employees can have "a career

EXHIBIT 2-2

Comparative Closeup

Police Role and Accountability in China

The police role and functions have been transformed in China—a nation with 1.3 billion people and 3.7 million square miles of territory—in order to deal with the country's changing social and economic environment. The key to the success of the strategies rests with the police's ability to keep tight control over the population through the household registration system and extensive surveillance. Every citizen must register his or her residence in a locality with the police; neighborhood committees are established in all neighborhoods. This system has the advantage of enabling officers to keep close contact with community residents and to keep a tight surveillance on every neighborhood. No strangers can enter a neighborhood without being noticed immediately and reported promptly to the police.[1] Although this system would be considered quite intrusive to Americans, the system does allow the police to monitor large city populations and criminals, especially gangs. Community policing (examined in Chapter 6) has also worked well in China; to combat the current rise in crime, the government advocates an overall strategy known as "compre-

hensive management"—the mobilization of all possible social forces to strengthen public security and prevent crime.[2]

Police accountability is a matter of concern in China, however. The Chinese police in general enjoy a positive image in the eyes of the public; one national survey showed that 70 percent of the public expressed confidence that if they reported personal victimization to the police, their complaints would be addressed.[3] The Chinese police, however, are not immune from misconduct, and there have been increasing numbers of reported cases of police corruption, abuse of power, and infringement of citizens' rights. The public law also established an internal police supervisory system, however, providing that higher-level police agencies must oversee and inspect the legality of law enforcement activities of lower-level police agencies. The law also established an internal supervisory system within each police bureau; a committee has the authority to receive and investigate complaints against officers and to impose disciplinary sanctions against them as necessary.

1. Yue Ma, "The Police Law 1995: Organization, Functions, Powers, and Accountability of the Chinese Police," *Policing: An International Journal of Police Strategy and Management* 20 (1997): 113–35.

2. Ibid., p. 132.

3. X. Wang, "Preliminary Analysis of Current Situation of Chinese Young People's Feeling of Safety," *Public Security Studies* 4 (1991): 115–26.

with unmatched opportunities and extraordinary experiences."[31] Applicants must have a bachelor's degree (with a preferred grade-point average of 3.0 or higher) and an interest in international affairs and national security, impeccable integrity, strong interpersonal skills, and excellent written and oral skills. Individuals who are hired with critical language skills can qualify for a hiring bonus of up to $35,000.[32]

INTERNAL REVENUE SERVICE (IRS)   The IRS has as its main function the monitoring and collection of federal income taxes from American individuals and businesses. Since 1919, the IRS has had a Criminal Investigation (CI) Division employing "accountants with a badge." The CI Division investigates possible criminal violations of income tax laws and recommends appropriate criminal prosecution whenever warranted.[33]

The first chief of the Special Intelligence Unit, Inspector Elmer I. Irey, gained notoriety by participating in investigations that included income tax evasion charges against organized crime kingpin Alphonse ("Al") Capone and the kidnapping of Charles Lindbergh's baby in 1932.[34] Since then, the list of celebrated, prosecuted CI "clients" has been impressive and includes federal judges, prominent politicians, and athletes. Indeed, today there is a much greater appreciation for what a financial investigator can do for almost any type of criminal investigation.[35]

IRS agents are armed; the U.S. Code authorizes them to execute search warrants, make arrests without warrants for tax-related offenses, and seize property related to violations of the tax laws. Agents engage in money-laundering investigations under Title 18 of the U.S. Code and investigate for tax and currency violations any individuals who organize, direct, and finance high-level criminal enterprises.[36]

The CI Division enforces nearly all of the provisions of the Bank Secrecy Act, requiring financial institutions or individuals to report certain domestic and foreign currency transactions to the federal government. The CI also enforces the wagering tax laws and conducts investigations related to the pornography industry. Another important area of the division is the Questionable Refund Program, which attempts to detect and stop fictitious claims for tax refunds.

FEDERAL LAW ENFORCEMENT TRAINING CENTER (FLETC)   **The Federal Law Enforcement Training Center (FLETC)**, which was established in 1970 and remains part of the Treasury Department, offers law enforcement training for personnel from many federal agencies. In 1975, the center was located in Glynco, Georgia, where it occupies a 1,500-acre campus with state-of-the-art classrooms and provides training for about seventy-five U.S. federal law enforcement organizations.[37] Other domestic campuses are located in Artesia, New Mexico, and Charleston, South Carolina; a fourth training facility is being built in Maryland.

Like most of the federal agencies discussed in this chapter, FLETC has been struggling to meet new demands placed on it since the September 11 attacks. A significant surge in hiring by federal agencies (particularly in the new Federal Air Marshal Service and Transportation Security Administration) resulted in an influx of a large number of law enforcement personnel at FLETC's campuses around the country.

TABLE 2-2

Other Federal Agencies Employing 500 or More Full-Time Officers with Authority to Carry Firearms and Make Arrests

AGENCY	FULL-TIME OFFICERS
Administrative Office of the U.S. Courts	4,126
U.S. Postal Inspection Service	2,976
Veterans Health Administration	2,423
National Park Service	2,148
U.S. Capitol Police	1,535
Bureau of Diplomatic Security, Diplomatic Security Service	825
U.S. Fish and Wildlife Service, Division of Law Enforcement	708
U.S. Forest Service, Law Enforcement & Investigations	600

Source: U.S. Department of Justice, Bureau of Justice Statistics, *Federal Law Enforcement Officers, 2004* (Washington, DC: Author, July 2006), p. 2.

In the fiscal year preceding the terrorist attacks, more than 21,000 students spent over 101,000 student weeks of training at FLETC's campuses; in the fiscal year following the attacks, more than 28,000 students spent about 157,000 weeks in training at these campuses. This latter figure represented a 72 percent increase in weeks of training since fiscal year 1999.[38]

To help address the demands placed on FLETC, its budget of about $146 million includes 754 full-time staff members.

Table 2-2 shows a number of federal law enforcement agencies not discussed above, whose employees have the authority to carry firearms and to make arrests.

STATE AGENCIES

Two Types of Organizations

When discussing state agencies, it is important to distinguish between state police organizations, which we will primarily be discussing below and which are general law enforcement agencies engaged in patrol and related functions, and **state bureaus of investigation (SBIs)**, which are the state's equivalent to the FBI. The SBIs investigate all manner of cases assigned to them by their state's laws and usually report to the state's attorney general. They are plainclothes agencies that usually investigate both criminal and civil cases involving the state and/or multiple jurisdictions. They also provide technical support to local agencies in the form of laboratory or record services and may assist in investigating more serious crimes (e.g., homicide). State bureaus of investigations normally exist either independently or within a Department of Public Safety (which is an umbrella agency coordinating and/or controlling the various state-level law enforcement agencies) or within the state police force.[39]

Agency Titles

The most prevalent title for state police organizations having general law enforcement functions is evenly split between two types: 21 (42.9 percent) of the 49 states having these agencies use the title State Police, and 21 (42.9 percent) use either State or Highway Patrol. Next in frequency of use is the designation Department of Public Safety, used in 4 (8.2 percent); Highway Safety Patrol, in 3 (6.1 percent) is fourth; and the title State Troopers is only used in Alaska.[40]

State Police Organizations

Today there are about 58,000 full-time sworn personnel in the forty-nine state law enforcement agencies (Hawaii has no state agency).[41] As noted above, state police agencies perform general law enforcement duties. Given that the public typically views state troopers while they patrol and enforce traffic laws on state highways, they actually perform a surprising variety of nontraffic functions. As an example, although the Missouri State Highway Patrol (MSHP) states on its Web site that its troopers provide assistance to motorists and "investigate highway traffic crashes and other roadway emergencies," it also states that "other responsibilities include assisting local peace officers upon request, investigating crimes, and enforcing criminal laws."[42] Figure 2-8 shows the MSHP organizational structure.

Other examples of nontraffic functions of state police include special operations and special units, with 42 of the 49 state agencies (85.7 percent) having sworn personnel assigned to special weapons and tactics (SWAT) teams, 35 (71.4 percent) having personnel in search and rescue assignments, 36 (73.5 percent) assigning personnel either full-time or part-time to special drug units, and 37 (75.5 percent) having personnel assigned either full-time or part-time to multiagency drug task forces. Some state personnel are also assigned to court-related functions: 37 (75.5 percent) of the 49 state agencies use personnel for executing warrants, and 6 (12.2 percent) have personnel assigned to court security.[43]

Another unexpected area (again, given that these personnel are typically seen while patrolling in their automobiles) concerns the variety of modes of patrolling. Of the 49 state law enforcement agencies, 14 (28.9 percent) deploy bicycle patrols, 9 (18.4 percent) maintain foot patrols, 9 (18.4 percent) have marine patrols, and 25 (51.0 percent) use motorcycle patrols.[44]

Data Collection

Another area that has become important for the state police is data collection for the purpose of identifying, reducing, and preventing any bias-based policing (discussed in Chapter 9). Of the nation's 49 state law enforcement agencies whose primary duties include highway patrol, 29 (59.2 percent) require their traffic patrol officers to record motorists' race or ethnicity during traffic stops. In addition, 12 of these 29 (41.4 percent)

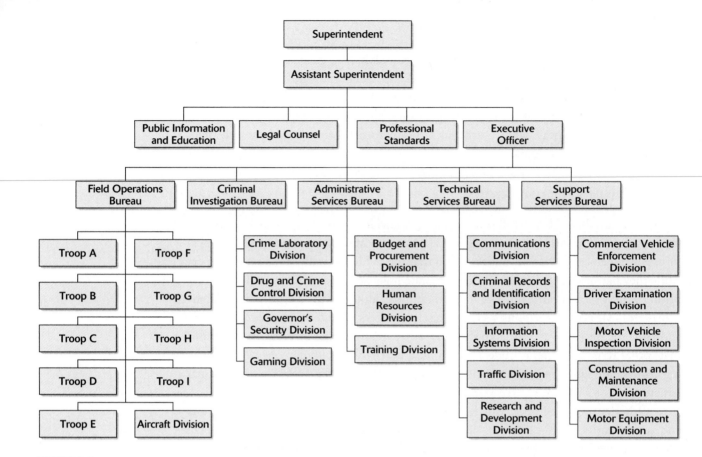

FIGURE 2-8
Missouri State Highway Patrol Organizational Structure

Source: Missouri State Highway Patrol Web site, http://www.mshp.dps.missouri.gov/MSHPWeb/Publications/Brochures/AnnualReport2005.pdf (accessed April 12, 2007).

state agencies also require specialized units (such as investigative units) to collect race or ethnicity data; 22 states (44.9 percent) require officers to record race or ethnicity data for all officer-initiated stops and 7 for more limited circumstances.[45]

SUMMARY

Although modern policing in the United States is still based on the nineteenth-century British model of the Metropolitan Police of London, a tremendous amount of specialization has evolved in today's sphere of policing, especially among federal, state, and (as will be seen in Chapter 3) local agencies. Policing has developed into a highly organized discipline with many branches and narrow fields of jurisdiction and responsibility. This has happened not so much because of needs being demonstrated by formal research but because of the necessity of keeping abreast of activities of sophisticated criminals and would-be terrorists who would violate the peace and dignity of people in many different ways.

Specifically, this chapter described the major federal law enforcement agencies of the new Department of Homeland Security, the Department of Justice, and other federal agencies and provided an overview of state police agencies. Perhaps what was most evident is how the law enforcement agencies of the federal government have re-tooled to meet today's challenge of terrorism.

It is clear that now, more than any other time in this nation's history, "business as usual" cannot be the order of the day. Our federal and state law enforcement agencies must take a more farsighted approach to their work while learning new methods for preventing and responding to potential terrorist attacks. This chapter has demonstrated that law enforcement agencies must be—and are being—flexible as the need arises.

KEY TERMS

Department of Homeland Security (DHS)
Department of Justice
directorate
federal law enforcement agency
Federal Law Enforcement Training Center (FLETC)
National Crime Information Center (NCIC)
state bureau of investigation (SBI)
state police
Uniform Crime Reports (UCR)

REVIEW QUESTIONS

1. What are the major component agencies of DHS and their primary functions?
2. What are the major functions of the four agencies of the Department of Justice that are described in this chapter?
3. Where and how are federal agents trained?
4. What functions do the CIA and the IRS perform?
5. What are the primary differences between federal and state law enforcement agencies?

INDEPENDENT STUDENT ACTIVITIES

1. Select a federal or state law enforcement agency in your area in which you have a particular interest. Using information obtained from this chapter and the agency's Web site, determine its origin, jurisdiction, mission, and functions. Also try to learn about its salaries, benefits, overall working conditions, budget, policies and procedures, recruitment and training, and so forth.

2. Try to determine what kinds of measures the agency has taken for homeland defense, any specialized training that has been provided to personnel (first responder and otherwise) in the event of a terrorist attack or other critical incident, and how the agency will cooperate with other agencies.

RELATED WEB SITES

Bureau of Alcohol, Tobacco, Firearms, and Explosives
http://www.atf.gov

Bureau of Customs and Border Protection
http://www.cbp.gov

Bureau of Immigration and Customs Enforcement
http://www.customs.gov

Bureau of Justice Assistance
http://www.ncjrs.org

Bureau of Justice Statistics
http://www.ojp.usdoj.bjs

Department of Homeland Security
http://www.dhs.gov/dhspublic

Department of Justice
http://www.usdoj.gov

Drug Enforcement Administration
http://www.dea.gov

Federal Bureau of Investigation
http://www.fbi.gov

Interpol
http://www.interpol.int

National Commission on Terrorist Attacks upon the United States (also known as the 9-11 Commission)
http://www.gpoaccess.gov/911

Office of International Criminal Justice
http://www.oicj.org

United Nations Crime and Justice Information Network
http://www.ifs.univie.ac.at/,uncjin/uncjin.html

United Nations Online Crime and Justice Clearinghouse
http://www.unojust.org

U.S. Customs and Border Protection
http://www.cbp.gov

U.S. Marshals Service
http://www.usdoj.gov/marshals

U.S. Secret Service
http://www.ustreas.gov/usss/protection/shtml

CHAPTER 3

POLICE IN SOCIETY

ORGANIZATION AND ADMINISTRATION OF MUNICIPAL AND COUNTY AGENCIES

The superior leader gets things done
With very little motion.
He imparts instruction not through many words
But through a few deeds.
When [actions] succeed he takes no credit.
And because he takes no credit
Credit never leaves him.
—*Lao-Tzu*

Uneasy lies the head that wears the crown.
—*Shakespeare, Henry IV*

LEARNING OBJECTIVES

AS A RESULT OF READING THIS CHAPTER, THE STUDENT WILL:

- BE ABLE TO DIAGRAM AND EXPLAIN THE ELEMENTS OF THE BASIC ORGANIZATIONAL STRUCTURE OF A POLICE AGENCY

- DESCRIBE THE BASIC ELEMENTS OF THE COMMUNICATIONS PROCESS, INCLUDING UPWARD, DOWNWARD, HORIZONTAL, AND GRAPEVINE COMMUNICATION

- UNDERSTAND WHAT IS MEANT BY SPAN OF CONTROL AND UNITY OF COMMAND

- KNOW THE DEFINITION AND USES OF POLICIES AND PROCEDURES

- BE ABLE TO DISTINGUISH BETWEEN MUNICIPAL POLICE DEPARTMENTS AND COUNTY SHERIFF'S OFFICES IN TERMS OF OPERATION; SCREENING, HIRING, AND TRAINING PROCESSES; POLICIES AND PROCEDURES; AND TECHNOLOGIES

- BE AWARE OF THE MAJOR ROLES OF POLICE EXECUTIVES, USING THE MINTZBERG MODEL OF CHIEF EXECUTIVE OFFICERS

- KNOW THE ROLES AND FUNCTIONS OF CONTEMPORARY CHIEFS OF POLICE AND COUNTY SHERIFFS

- UNDERSTAND THE EXTENT TO WHICH POLICE CHIEFS ARE CONNECTED TO THEIR COMMUNITIES

- BE ABLE TO DISCUSS THE ROLES AND FUNCTIONS OF MID-LEVEL MANAGERS AND FIRST-LINE SUPERVISORS

- UNDERSTAND HOW NEW YORK CITY'S COMPSTAT PROCESS FUNCTIONS

- COMPREHEND THE HISTORICAL RELATIONSHIP AND MAJOR PROBLEMS BETWEEN THE POLICE AND POLITICIANS

- APPRECIATE AND UNDERSTAND THE RATIONALE FOR THE POLICE MAINTAINING GOOD MEDIA RELATIONS

- UNDERSTAND HOW POLICE SERVICES MAY BE CONTRACTED, CONSOLIDATED, AND CIVILIANIZED

- BE ABLE TO EXPLAIN THE PROCESS FOR AND BENEFITS OF ACCREDITATION OF POLICE AGENCIES

INTRODUCTION

Chapter 2 examined how federal agencies have changed their mission and priorities since 9/11; certainly local law enforcement agencies received a mandate to cooperate, coordinate, and communicate. Furthermore, Hurricane Katrina hitting the Gulf Coast in late August 2005 also demonstrated that, in addition to crime fighting, local police departments and sheriff's offices must plan for exigencies involving acts of nature. In the wake of the hurricane, it became woefully clear that such groundwork had not been laid in preparation for what is literally the worst-case scenario.

This chapter examines two major aspects of local policing: organization and administration. After first looking at organizations and bureaucracies generally, we discuss organizational communication, including that which occurs within police organizations. Next we examine police agencies as organizations, including their structure, command principles, and use of policies and procedures; then we compare municipal police departments and county sheriff's offices in terms of their operations, policies and procedures, equipment, screening and testing of new recruits, and technologies. Also included in this chapter is a review of the functions and community connectedness (using a study of anomie) of the municipal police chief and the county sheriff. Following that, we use a management model to better understand the general functions of police administrators in their interpersonal, informational, and decision-maker roles and include a short illustration of good police administration: the Compstat process in New York City. We then briefly consider the roles and functions of middle managers and examine more thoroughly the complex role of first-line supervisors. Next we address the tenuous historical relationship between police administrators and politicians and look at the important area of police-media relations. Following that are descriptions of how agencies may contract, consolidate, and civilianize their services. Then we consider how police agencies may become accredited and the advantages of doing so. A chapter summary, key terms, review questions, independent student activities, and related Web sites conclude the chapter.

It should be noted that other important, related aspects about local police officers—women and minorities, higher education, stress, and collective bargaining—are discussed in Chapter 13.

ORGANIZATIONS AND THE POLICE

What Are Organizations?

It is no surprise that one of the most widely read and long-running cartoon strips is that of "Dilbert," Scott Adams's mouthless engineer who is surrounded by downtrodden workers, inconsiderate bosses, and a dysfunctional organization. Unfortunately, many people in our society identify with Dilbert: One survey found that more than 70 percent of U.S. workers experience stress at work because of red tape, unnecessary rules, poor communication with management, and other causes.[1] But it does not have to be so, as we will see in this chapter.

Organizations are entities of two or more people who cooperate to accomplish an objective. In that sense, undoubtedly the first organizations were primitive hunting parties. Organization and a high degree of cooperation were required to bring down large animals. Organizations were also used to build pyramids and other monuments.[2] *Organization* can be defined as arranging and utilizing resources of personnel and materiel in such a way as to attain specified objectives.

Every organization is unique. Larry Gaines, Mittie Southerland, and John Angell provided an excellent analogy that helps us understand organizations:

> Organization corresponds to the bones which structure or give form to the body. Imagine that the fingers were a single mass of bone rather than four separate fingers and a thumb made up of bones. The mass of bones could not, because of its structure, play musical instruments, hold a pencil, or grip a baseball bat. A police department's organization is analogous. It must be structured properly if it is to be effective in fulfilling its many diverse goals. Organization may not be important in a police department consisting of three officers, but it is extremely important in [larger] cities.[3]

As Gaines, Southerland, and Angell also noted, the development of an organization should be done with careful evaluation or the agency may become unable to respond efficiently to community needs. For example, the implementation of too many specialized units in a police agency (such as community relations, crime analysis, or media relations units) may leave too few people to do the general grassroots work of the organization. (As a rule of thumb, at least 55 percent of all sworn police personnel should be assigned to patrol.[4])

Formal organizational structures, which spell out areas of responsibility, lines of communication, and the chain of command, are discussed later in this chapter.

Organizations as Bureaucracies

Organizations can be **bureaucracies**. Large organizations are more complex than smaller ones, with much more specialization, a more hierarchical structure, and a more authoritarian style of command.[5] Bureaucracies share several traits: People perform many different tasks while working toward a common goal, specialized tasks are placed in separate departments or bureaus with a hierarchical structure and a division of labor between personnel, and there is a clear **chain of command** through which information flows upward and commands flow downward. To ensure consistency and uniformity, there is normally an abundance of written rules for the performance of duties. Career paths up through the organization allow employees to progress in an orderly fashion.[6]

ORGANIZATIONAL COMMUNICATION

Definitions and Characteristics

Communication is one of the most important dynamics of an organization. Indeed, a major role of today's administrators and other leaders is that of communication. Managers of all types of organizations spend an overwhelming amount of their time engaged in the process of—and coping with problems in—communication.

Today we communicate via electronic mail, Web sites, facsimile machines, video camcorders, cellular telephones, satellite dishes, and other high-tech means. We converse orally, in written letters and memos, through our body language, via television and radio programs, and through newspapers and meetings. Even private thoughts—which take place four times faster than the spoken word—are communication. Every waking hour our minds are full of ideas and thoughts; psychologists say that nearly one hundred thousand thoughts pass through our minds every day, conveyed by a multitude of media.[7] Communication becomes exceedingly important and sensitive in nature in a police organization because of the nature of the information that is processed by officers—who often see people when they are at their worst and when they are in their most embarrassing and compromising situations. To "communicate" what is known about these kinds of behaviors could be devastating to the parties concerned.

Studies have long shown that communication is the primary problem in administration, however, and lack of communication is the primary complaint of employees about their immediate supervisors.[8] Managers are in the communications business. The following has been said about communication:

> Of all skills needed to be an effective manager/leader/supervisor, skill in communicating is the most vital. In fact, more than 50 percent of a [criminal justice] manager's time is spent communicating. **First-line supervisors** usually spend about 15 percent of their time with superiors, 50 percent of their time with subordinates, and 35 percent with other managers and duties. These estimates emphasize the importance of communications in everyday . . . operations.[9]

Several elements constitute the communications process: encoding, transmission, medium, reception, decoding, and feedback.[10] Following are brief descriptions of these elements:

Encoding. To convey an experience or idea to someone, we translate, or encode, that experience into symbols. We use words or other verbal behaviors and gestures or other nonverbal behaviors to convey the experience or idea.

Transmission. This element involves the translation of the encoded symbols into some behavior that another person can observe. The actual articulation (moving our lips, tongue, and so on) of the symbol into verbal or nonverbal observable behavior is transmission.

Medium. Communication must be conveyed through some channel, or medium. Media for communication may include our sight, hearing, taste, touch, or smell. Some other media are the television, the telephone, paper and pencil, and the radio. The choice of the medium is very important; for example, a message that is transmitted via a formal letter from the chief executive officer will carry more weight than if the same message is conveyed via a secretary's memo.

Reception. The stimuli, the verbal and nonverbal symbols, reach the senses of the receiver and are conveyed to the brain for interpretation.

Decoding. The individual who receives the stimuli develops some meaning for the verbal and nonverbal symbols and decodes the stimuli. These symbols are translated into some concept or experience of the receiver.

Feedback. When the receiver decodes the transmitted symbols, he or she usually provides some response, or feedback, to the sender. If someone appears puzzled, we repeat the message or we encode the concept differently and transmit some different symbols to express the same concept. Feedback acts as a guide or steering device and lets us know whether the receiver has interpreted our symbols as we intended.

Communication within Police Organizations

Communication within police organizations may be downward, upward, or horizontal. There are five types of downward communication within such an organization[11]:

1. *Job instruction.* Communication relating to the performance of a certain task.
2. *Job rationale.* Communication relating a certain task to organizational tasks.
3. *Procedures and practice.* Communication about organizational policies, procedures, rules, and regulations.
4. *Feedback.* Communication about how an individual performs an assigned task.
5. *Indoctrination.* Communication designed to motivate the employee.

Upward communication in a police organization may encounter several obstacles. First, the physical distance between superior and subordinate impedes upward communication. Communication is often difficult and infrequent when superiors are isolated. In large police organizations, the administration may be located in headquarters that are removed from the operations personnel. The complexity of the organization may also cause prolonged delays in communication. For example, if a patrol officer observes a problem that needs to be taken to the highest level, normally this information must first be taken to the sergeant and then to the lieutenant, the captain, the deputy chief or the chief, and so on. At each level, the superiors reflect on the problem, put their own interpretation on it (possibly including how the problem might affect them professionally or even personally), and may even dilute or distort the problem. Thus delays in communication are inherent in a bureaucracy.

Horizontal communication thrives in an organization when formal communication channels are not open.[12] The disadvantage of horizontal communication is that it is much easier and more natural to achieve than vertical communication; therefore it often replaces vertical channels. Horizontal channels are usually of an informal nature, including the grapevine, which is discussed next. The advantage is that horizontal communication is essential if the subsystems within a police organization are to function in an effective and coordinated manner. Horizontal communication among peers may also provide emotional and social bonds that build morale and feelings of teamwork among employees.

The Grapevine

Something "heard through the grapevine" is a rumor from an anonymous source. The expression "grapevine telegraph" is also sometimes used, referring to the speed with which rumors spread. Rumors are another type of communication, and police agencies certainly have their share of scuttlebutt. Departments even establish rumor control centers during major riots. Compounding the usual barriers to communication is the fact that policing is a twenty-four-hour, seven-day occupation, so rumors are easily carried from one shift to the next.

The grapevine's most effective characteristics are that it is fast, it operates mostly at the place of work, and it supplements regular formal communication. On the positive side, it can be a tool management can use to get a feel for employees' attitudes, to spread useful information, and to help employees vent their frustrations. The grapevine, however, can also carry untruths and be malicious. Without a doubt, the grapevine is a force for administrators to reckon with every day.

Written Communication

Within complex organizations, confidence is generally placed in the written word. It establishes a permanent record, but transmitting information in this way does not necessarily ensure that the message will be clear to the receiver, despite the writer's best efforts. This may be due in large measure to shortcomings in the writer's skills. Nonetheless, police organizations rely heavily on written communication, as evidenced by the proliferation of written directives and reports found in most of these agencies.

In the same vein, written communication is also preferred as a medium for dealing with citizens or groups outside the police agency. This means of communication provides the greatest protection against the growing number of legal actions taken against agencies by activists, citizens, and interest groups. In recent years, e-mail has also proliferated as a communications medium in criminal justice organizations. E-mail can provide an easy-to-use and almost instantaneous communication through a computer—in upward, downward, or horizontal directions. For all its advantages, however, e-mail messages can lack security and be ambiguous not only with respect to the meaning of the contents but also with regard to what they represent. Are such messages, in fact, mail that should be given the full weight of an office letter or memo, or should they be treated more as offhand comments?[13]

Barriers to Effective Communication

In addition to the inaccurate nature of the grapevine and the preponderance of poor writing skills, several other potential barriers to effective communication exist. Some people, for example, are not good listeners. Unfortunately, listening is one of the most neglected and least understood of the communication arts.[14] We allow other things to obstruct our communication, including time, too little or too much information, the tendency to say what we think others want to hear, the failure to select the best word, prejudices, and strained sender-receiver relationships.[15] Also, subordinates do not always have the same "big picture" viewpoint that superiors possess and may not communicate well with more fluent and persuasive superiors.

POLICE AGENCIES AS ORGANIZATIONS

Chain of Command

The administration of most police organizations is based on a traditional pyramidal, quasi-military organizational structure that contains the elements of an organization and a bureaucracy. First, these agencies are organized into a number of specialized units. Figure 3-1 shows the hierarchy of managers within the typical police organization and the inverse relationship between rank and numbers of personnel; in other words, as rank increases, the number of people who occupy that rank decreases. Some larger agencies have additional ranks, such as corporal and major, but this can lead to concerns about becoming too top-heavy. The rank hierarchy allows an organization to designate authority and responsibility at each level and to maintain a chain of command.

Administrators (chiefs and assistant chiefs), mid-level managers (captains and lieutenants), and first-line supervisors (sergeants) ensure that these units work together toward a common goal. If each unit worked independently, fragmentation, conflict, and competition would result, subverting the goals and purposes of the entire organization. Police agencies consist of people who interact within the organization and with external groups, and they exist to serve the public.

Police departments are different from most other kinds of organizations for the simple reason that policing is significantly different from most other kinds of work. A special organizational structure has evolved to help carry out the complex responsibilities of policing. The highly decentralized nature and the varying size of American police departments, however, compel police agencies to vary in organization.

Organizational Structure

Every police agency, no matter what its size, has an **organizational structure**, which is often prominently displayed for all to see in the agency's facility. Even a community with only a town marshal has an organizational structure, although the structure will be very

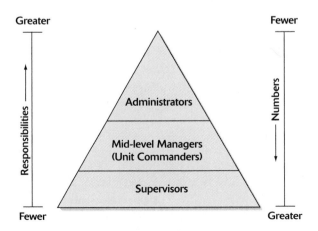

FIGURE 3-1
Hierarchy of Managers within the Typical Police Organization

Source: Larry K. Gaines, Mittie D. Southerland, John E. Angell, and John L. Worrall, Police Administration *(New York: McGraw-Hill, 2003), p. 11. Used with permission.*

horizontal, with the marshal performing all of the functions displayed in Figure 3-2, the basic organizational chart for a small agency.[16]

Operations, or line, personnel are engaged in active police functions in the field. They may be subdivided into primary and secondary operations elements. The patrol function—often called the backbone of policing—is the primary operational element because of its major responsibility for policing. (The patrol function is examined in Chapter 5.) In most small police agencies, patrol forces are responsible for all operational activities: providing routine patrols, conducting traffic and criminal investigations, making arrests, and functioning as generalists.[17] The investigative and youth functions are the secondary operations elements. (We discuss the investigative function thoroughly in Chapter 7, juvenile rights in Chapter 8, and youth crimes in Chapter 12.)

The support (or nonline) functions and activities can become quite numerous, especially in a large agency. These functions fall into two broad categories: staff (or administrative) services and auxiliary (or technical) services. The staff services usually involve personnel and include such matters as recruitment, training, promotion, planning and research, community relations, and public information services. Auxiliary services are the kinds of functions that civilians rarely see. They include jail management, property and evidence, crime laboratory services, communications processes, and records and identification. Many career opportunities exist for those who are interested in police-related work but who cannot or do not want to be a field officer.

Obviously, the larger the agency, the greater the need for specialization and the more vertical the organizational chart will become. With greater specialization come the need and opportunity for officers to be assigned to different tasks, often rotating from one assignment to another after a fixed interval. For example, in a medium-sized department serving a community of one hundred thousand or more, it would be possible for a police officer with ten years of police experience to have been a dog handler, a motorcycle officer, a detective, and a traffic officer while simultaneously holding a slot on the special weapons or hostage negotiations team.

The organizational structure of the Chicago, Illinois, Police Department (CPD) is shown in Figure 3-3. The city of Chicago has a population of about 2.8 million,[18]

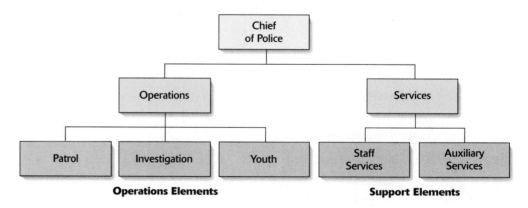

FIGURE 3-2
A Basic Police Organizational Structure

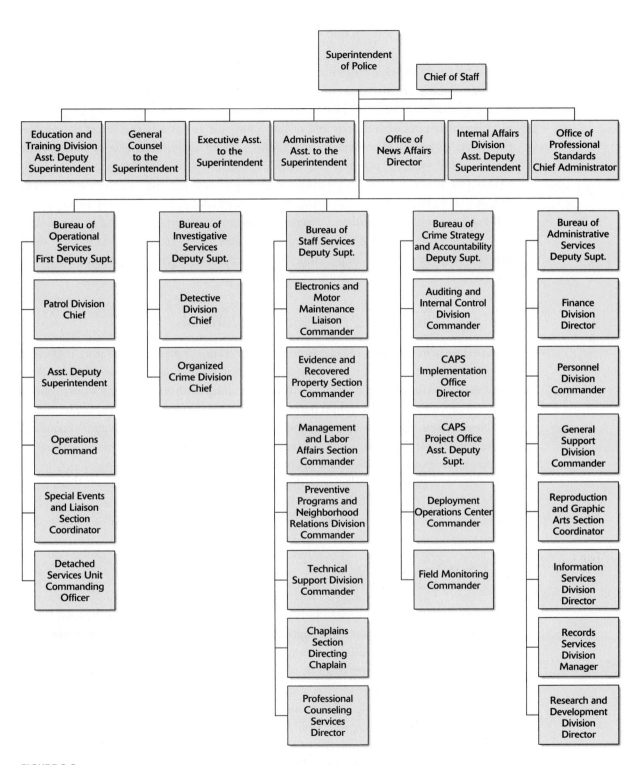

FIGURE 3-3

Organizational Structure for the Chicago Police Department

Source: Chicago, Illinois, Police Department, Annual Report 2005 Year in Review, *http://egov.cityofchicago.org/webportal/COCWebPortal/ COC_EDITORIAL/04AR.pdf, p. 38 (accessed April 14, 2007).*

and the CPD has nearly 16,000 sworn officers and a budget of a little more than $1 billion.[19]

This organizational structure provides an excellent illustration of the various components of police organizations while also functionally providing several major functions: (1) It apportions the workload among members and units according to a logical plan; (2) it ensures that lines of authority and responsibility are as definite and direct as possible; (3) it specifies a unity of command throughout, so there is no question about which orders should be followed; (4) it assigns responsibility and authority, and if responsibility is delegated, the delegator is held responsible; and (5) it coordinates the efforts of members so that all will work harmoniously to accomplish the mission.[20] In sum, this structure establishes the chain of command and determines lines of communication and responsibility.

In addition to these generally well-known and visible areas of specialization, there are other lesser known areas of policing, such as community crime prevention, child abuse, drug education, and missing children units.[21]

Unity of Command and Span of Control

A related principle is unity of command, an organizational principle dictating that every officer should report to one and only one superior (following the chain of command) until that superior officer is relieved. Ambiguity about authority can and does occur in police organizations—who should handle calls, who is in charge at a crime scene, and so on. Nevertheless, the unity-of-command principle ensures that multiple and/or conflicting orders are not issued to the same officer by several supervisors. It is important that all officers know and follow the chain of command at critical incidents.

The term *span of control* refers to the number of subordinates one individual can effectively supervise. The limit is small; it is normally three to five at the top level of the organization and is often broader at the lower levels.[22] The tendency in modern police operations is to have supervisors spread too thinly.

Organizational Policies and Procedures

It has been said that a well-written policy and procedure manual serves as the foundation of a professional law enforcement agency.[23] In policing, **policies and procedures** and **rules and regulations** are also important for defining role expectations for officers. Police leaders rely on these directives to guide officers' behavior and performance. Because police agencies are intended to be service oriented in nature, they must work within specific well-defined guidelines designed to ensure that all officers conform consistently to behavior that will enhance public protection.[24]

This tendency for organizations to promulgate policies and procedures as well as rules and regulations has been caused by three contemporary developments. First is the requirement for administrative due process in employee disciplinary matters, encouraged by federal court rulings, police officer bill of rights legislation, and labor contracts. Another development is the threat of civil litigation. Lawsuits against local governments and their criminal justice agencies and administrators have become commonplace; written guide-lines by law enforcement agencies prohibiting certain acts provide a hedge against successful civil litigation.[25] Finally, a third stimulus is the trend toward the accreditation of police agencies (discussed below). Agencies that either are pursuing accreditation or have become accredited must follow policies and practice procedures.[26]

Policies are quite general and serve basically as guides to thinking rather than action. Policies reflect the purpose and philosophy of the organization and help interpret them for the officers. An example of a policy might be that everyone found to be driving while under the influence of drugs or alcohol must be arrested or that all juveniles who are to be detained must be taken to a specified facility.

Procedures are more detailed than policies and provide the preferred methods for handling matters pertaining to investigation, patrol, booking, radio transmissions, filing of reports, roll call, use of force, arrest, sick leave, evidence handling, promotion, and many other elements of the job. Most police agencies are awash in procedures. Methods for accomplishing certain tasks are also found in myriad city or county administrative regulations and police agency general orders (such as when a new federal court decision relating to search and seizure is announced or a new state or local law regarding the use of force takes effect).

Rules and regulations are specific guidelines that leave little or no latitude for individual discretion. Some examples are requirements that police officers not smoke in public, that they check the operation of their vehicle and equipment before going on patrol, that they not consume alcoholic beverages within a specified number of hours before going on duty, or that they arrive in court or at roll call early. Rules and regulations are not always popular, especially if they are perceived as unfair or unrelated to the job. Nonetheless, it is the supervisor's responsibility to ensure that officers perform these tasks with the same degree of professional demeanor as they do other job duties.

LOCAL AGENCIES

Police Departments and Sheriff's Offices: A Comparison

Today Sir Robert Peel (discussed in Chapter 1) would be amazed because there are about 17,000 general-purpose **municipal police departments** and county sheriff's departments in the United States.[27] These agencies are composed of about 452,000 sworn full-time municipal police officers[28] and 174,000 sworn full-time sheriff's deputies.[29] Of those, about 11.3 percent of municipal police officers are women,[30] which is close to the figure for sheriff's personnel (12.9 percent are women).[31] Furthermore, 23.6 percent of police are racial and ethnic minorities,[32] while 18.8 percent of sheriff's personnel are racial and ethnic minorities.[33]

As shown in Table 3-1, police departments and sheriff's offices are engaged in a variety of operations, which entail different forms of patrol, special units, assignments, and jail functions. Although both **municipal police and county sheriff's departments** have general police responsibilities (for example, traffic enforcement, accident investigation,

TABLE 3-1

Operations of Police Departments and Sheriff's Offices

	Foot Patrol	Bicycle Patrol	Motor-cycle Patrol	Horse Patrol	Special Drug Unit	Court Security	Transport of Prisoners	Serving of Civil Process	Jail Operations	SWAT Opera-tions	Search and Rescue Operations
Police departments	59%	38	14	2	18	27	32	18	9	25	21
Sheriff's offices	25%	39	11	5	36	94	89	98	76	43	56

Source: Adapted from U.S. Department of Justice, Bureau of Justice Statistics, *Local Police Departments, 2003* (Washington, DC: Author, 2006), p. iii;
U.S. Department of Justice, Bureau of Justice Statistics, *Sheriff's Offices, 2003* (Washington, DC: Author, 2006), p. iii.

patrol, first response to incidents, criminal investigation) and employ a variety of means for patrolling in their jurisdictions, the table shows that sheriff's offices have far greater responsibilities for providing court security, transporting prisoners, serving civil process (for example, divorce papers, eviction notices), and operating local jails than do police agencies. Also, both engage in special weapons and tactics (SWAT) and search and rescue operations, although the latter occur to a much greater extent, probably due to the more rural nature of the typical sheriff's office jurisdiction.[34]

Table 3-2 reveals the kinds of policies and procedures that exist in both types of organizations. There is very little difference except that more sheriff's offices have policies

About three-fourths of all sheriff's offices operate a jail.

(Courtesy Washoe County, Nevada, Sheriff's Office)

TABLE 3-2

Policies and Procedures of Police Departments and Sheriff's Offices

	Use of Force	Appearance and Conduct	Handling of Juveniles	Pursuit Driving	Collecting of Racial Profiling Data	Strip Searches	Handling of Citizen Complaints	Plan for Terrorist Attack
Police departments	95%	94	84	94	62	60	87	39
Sheriff's offices	97%	93	83	95	63	81	82	48

Source: Adapted from U.S. Department of Justice, Bureau of Justice Statistics, *Local Police Departments, 2003* (Washington, DC: Author, 2006), p. iii; U.S. Department of Justice, Bureau of Justice Statistics, *Sheriff's Offices, 2003* (Washington, DC: Author, 2006), p. iii.

and procedures for conducting strip searches of persons booked into jail. This is probably due to the fact that a much higher percentage of sheriff's offices operate a local jail (as shown in Table 3-1).

The methods used for screening and testing new officers, and the length of their initial training, are displayed in Table 3-3. A considerably higher percentage of police agencies use physical agility tests, perform psychological evaluations, and provide educational incentive pay to officers and that municipal police officers receive about fifty-five additional hours of initial (academy and field) training.

Table 3-4 provides information concerning the kinds of equipment that these agencies authorize or require their personnel to carry. The .40-caliber semiautomatic pistol is most frequently authorized, followed by a nearly equal number of agencies that authorize a .45-caliber and a 9 mm. Dogs appear to be used for general police duties at a much higher level by sheriff's offices.

In Table 3-5 are shown the various purposes for which computers are being used. It is clear that computers are being utilized in a large number of agencies. What is also

TABLE 3-3

Screening, Testing, and Training of New Recruits

	Medical Exam	Drug Test	Physical Agility Test	Psycho-logical Evaluation	Credit Check	Person-ality Inventory	Written Aptitude Test	Requirement of Two-Year Degree	Educational Incentive Pay	Required Academy and Field Training Hours
Police departments	85%	73	50	67	55	26	43	9	32	954
Sheriff's offices	76%	68	38	50	48	21	37	5	20	899

Source: Adapted from U.S. Department of Justice, Bureau of Justice Statistics, *Local Police Departments, 2003* (Washington, DC: Author, 2006), p. iii; U.S. Department of Justice, Bureau of Justice Statistics, *Sheriff's Offices, 2003* (Washington, DC: Author, 2006), p. iii.

TABLE 3-4

Equipment Used by Police Departments and Sheriff's Offices

	Authorized .40-Caliber	Authorized 9mm	Authorized .45-Caliber	Required Body Armor	Supplied Body Armor	Batons	Stun Guns or Tasers	Pepper Spray	Video Cameras	Dogs
Police departments	62%	34	34	71	83	95	23	98	60	29
Sheriff's offices	62%	33	35	70	88	92	30	96	66	55

Source: Adapted from U.S. Department of Justice, Bureau of Justice Statistics, Local Police Departments, 2003 (Washington, DC: Author, 2006), p. iii; U.S. Department of Justice, Bureau of Justice Statistics, Sheriff's Offices, 2003 (Washington, DC: Author, 2006), p. iii.

TABLE 3-5

Uses of Computers by Police Departments and Sheriff's Offices

	Records	Criminal Investigation	Dispatch	Crime Analysis	Traffic Stop Data	Crime Mapping	Hot Spot ID
Police departments	69%	50	33	32	46	19	11
Sheriff's offices	67%	51	50	26	34	14	7

Source: Adapted from U.S. Department of Justice, Bureau of Justice Statistics, Local Police Departments, 2003 (Washington, DC: Author, 2006), p. iii; U.S. Department of Justice, Bureau of Justice Statistics, Sheriff's Offices, 2003 (Washington, DC: Author, 2006), p. iii.

shown, however, is that many more agencies could be using computers for crime mapping and for identifying hot spots (discussed in Chapter 6); perhaps the costs involved in acquiring these computer capabilities are still prohibitive for many agencies.

In a related vein, Table 3-6 shows the kinds of special technologies that the agencies employ. Again, it is clear that advanced technologies, including infrared (thermal) imaging equipment, tire deflation spikes, and various forms of digital equipment, are being introduced into police and sheriff's departments.

TABLE 3-6

Special Technologies Used by Police Departments and Sheriff's Offices

	Infrared (Thermal) Images	Tire Deflation Spikes	Digitized Mug Shots	Digitized Suspect Composites	Digitized Finger-prints	Digitized Facial Recognition
Police departments	23%	31	48	20	26	4
Sheriff's offices	35%	48	74	25	48	6

Source: Adapted from U.S. Department of Justice, Bureau of Justice Statistics, Local Police Departments, 2003 (Washington, DC: Author, 2006), p. iii; U.S. Department of Justice, Bureau of Justice Statistics, Sheriff's Offices, 2003 (Washington, DC: Author, 2006), p. iii.

TABLE 3-7

Community Policing in Police Departments and Sheriff's Offices

	Assess New Officers' COPPS Skills	Train New Officers in COPPS	Assign Officers to COPPS Projects	Upgrade Technology for COPPS
Police departments	27%	31	58	21
Sheriff's offices	23%	27	18	17

Source: Adapted from U.S. Department of Justice, Bureau of Justice Statistics, *Local Police Departments, 2003* (Washington, DC: Author, 2006), p. iii; U.S. Department of Justice, Bureau of Justice Statistics, *Sheriff's Offices, 2003* (Washington, DC: Author, 2006), p. iii.

Finally, Table 3-7 demonstrates municipal police and county sheriff's activities in community policing, including the extent to which these agencies assess, train, and assign personnel and use technologies in this strategy. It is clear that community-oriented policing and problem solving (COPPS) has established a foothold in local police and sheriff's departments.

Executive Officers: Chiefs of Police and Sheriffs

Having analyzed police organizations, we now look at the two primary chief executive officers: the police chief (also known as the police superintendent, commissioner, or director) and the county sheriff. After looking at the qualifications for and functions of these positions, we consider their roles in more detail with the Mintzberg model of chief executive officers.

The chief or sheriff of a ten-person agency faces many of the same problems and expectations as his or her big-city counterpart. The difference between managing large and small departments is a matter of scale. Executives of large departments face a larger volume of many of the same problems that executives of small departments face. The leader of a small department must not only deal with all these managerial concerns but in many cases must also perform the duties of a working officer.

Furthermore, the police manager's style must be flexible. Management style is always contingent on the situation and the people being managed.[35] The police manager would behave one way at the scene of a hostage situation and another way at the scene of a shoplifting. A less experienced employee will require a more authoritarian style of management than a more experienced employee.

CHIEFS OF POLICE

Qualifications, Selection, and Tenure.   The required qualifications for the position of **chief of police** vary widely, depending on the size of the agency and the region of the country. Smaller agencies, especially those in rural areas, may not have any minimum educational requirement for the job. Large agencies, on the other hand, may require college education plus several years of progressively responsible police management experience.[36]

Although it is certainly cheaper to select a police chief from within the organization than to recruit an outsider, the value of doing so is open to debate. There are obvious advantages and disadvantages to both practices. One study of police chiefs promoted from within and hired from outside in the West found significant differences in only one area: educational attainment. The outsiders were more highly educated, but the two groups did not differ in other areas, including background, attitudes, salary, tenure in current position or in policing, and size of agency, community, or current budget.[37] Some states have made it nearly impossible for nonresidents to be hired as police chiefs. For example, California has mandated that the chief be a graduate of its full Peace Officers Standards and Training (POST) academy; New Jersey and New York also encourage "homegrown" chiefs.[38]

A survey by the Police Executive Research Forum (PERF) of 358 police chiefs in larger jurisdictions (fifty thousand or more residents) found that these chiefs were more educated than ever before (87 percent held a bachelor's degree and 47 percent had a master's degree) and were more likely to have been chosen from outside the agencies they head. Even so, most chiefs spent less than five years in the position.[39]

To obtain the most capable people for executive positions in policing—and to avoid personnel, liability, and other kinds of problems that can arise from poor personnel choices—many agencies have adopted the assessment center method (discussed in Chapter 4), an elaborate yet efficacious means of hiring and promoting personnel. Although more costly and time-consuming than conventional testing methods (for example, candidates' resumes are examined and oral interviews are held), the assessment center method is well worth the extra investment. Money invested at the early stages of hiring or promotion can save untold dollars and problems for many years to come. The process may include interviews; psychological tests; management tasks; group discussions; simulations of interviews with subordinates, the public, and the news media; fact-finding exercises; oral presentation exercises; and written communications exercises.[40]

Job security for police chiefs ranges from full civil service protection in a small percentage of agencies to appointment and removal at the discretion of the mayor or city manager. There is a growing trend for a fixed term of office, such as a 4- or 5-year contract. Traditionally, however, the tenure of police chiefs has been short. A federal study in the mid-1970s found that the average term in office by chiefs of police was 5.4 years.[41] Another study by PERF a decade later found the average to be practically unchanged: 5.5 years. That figure has not changed in more recent times.[42] Those who are appointed from within the agency tend to have longer tenure than those appointed from outside. This lack of job tenure has several negative consequences, including the difficulty of long-range planning, the possible negative effect of frequently having new policies and administrative styles, the inability of the short-term chief to develop a political power base and local influence, and the time and expense involved in hiring a new chief.

Anomie.   **Anomie** is related to the breaking down of an individual's sense of attachment to society and to others. An anomic individual feels that community leaders are indifferent to his or her needs, that the social order is unpredictable, that he or she cannot count on anyone for support, and that life itself is meaningless.[43] Hays et al.,[44] using a scale developed by Srole in 1956,[45] examined whether or not police chiefs are high or low in their level of anomie. They found that the latter is the case; the majority of the 1,500 police chiefs in their study did not appear to experience severe levels of social distancing from their fellow human beings. This is important because police chiefs must be well connected with their communities, subordinates, municipal leaders, and significant others. As leaders of policing organizations, chiefs must be well integrated into their communities, and this research found that this appeared to be the case. In a very real sense, the position of police chief is a networking type of job, and chiefs must be well integrated with a variety of people. A severely anomic police chief could have disastrous effects on a municipality.[46]

SHERIFFS

Nature of Position.   As discussed in Chapter 1, the position of **sheriff** has a long tradition. Sheriffs today tend to be elected; thus most candidates are aligned with a political party, and it is possible that the only qualification a person brings to the office is the ability to get votes.

In some areas of the country, the sheriff's term of office is limited to 2 years, and the sheriff is prohibited from serving successive terms. In most counties, however, the sheriff has a 4-year term and can be reelected. Sheriffs enjoy no guarantee of tenure in office, although a federal study found that sheriffs (who average 6.7 years in office) had longer tenure in office than police chiefs.[47] The politicization of the office of sheriff can obviously result in both high turnover rates of personnel who do not have civil service protection and a lack of long-range (strategic) planning.

Also, largely due to the political nature of the office, sheriffs tend to be older, are less likely to have been promoted through the ranks of the agency, have less specialized training, and are less likely to be college graduates compared to police chiefs. Research has also found that sheriffs in small agencies have more difficulty with organizational problems (field activities and budget management, for example), whereas sheriffs in large agencies find dealing with local officials and using planning and evaluation to be more troublesome.

Functions.   Because of the diversity of sheriff's offices throughout the country, it is difficult to describe a "typical" sheriff's department; the offices run the gamut from the traditional, highly political, limited-service office to the modern, fairly nonpolitical, full-service police organization.[48] It is possible, however, to list functions commonly associated with the sheriff's office:

- Maintaining and operating the county correctional institutions
- Serving civil processes (protective orders, liens, evictions, garnishments, and attachments) and performing other civil duties, such as extradition and transportation of prisoners
- Collecting certain taxes and conducting real estate sales (usually for nonpayment of taxes) for the county
- Performing routine order-maintenance duties by enforcing state statutes and county ordinances, arresting offenders, and performing traffic and criminal investigations
- Serving as bailiff of the courts

Other general duties vary from one region to another.

Next we continue to discuss the roles of police chiefs and sheriffs but in a different manner, using the Mintzberg model of chief executive officers.

MINTZBERG MODEL OF CHIEF EXECUTIVE OFFICERS

What do contemporary police executives really do? Ronald Lynch described in simple terms their primary tasks:

> They listen, talk, write, confer, think, decide—about men, money, materials, methods, facilities—in order to plan, organize, direct, coordinate, and control their research service, production, public relations, employee relations, and all other activities so that they may more effectively serve the citizens to whom they are responsible.[49]

A police executive actually has many roles. Some chief executive officers (CEOs) openly endorse and subscribe to the philosophy of Henry Mintzberg, who described a set of behaviors and tasks of CEOs in any organization.[50] Following is an overview of the roles of the police agency CEO—that is, the chief of police or sheriff—using the **Mintzberg model** and its interpersonal, informational, and decision-maker roles as an analytic framework.

Interpersonal Role

First we will consider the interpersonal role, which includes figurehead, leadership, and liaison duties. As a figurehead, the CEO performs various ceremonial functions. Examples include riding in parades and attending other civic events; speaking before school and university classes and civic organizations; meeting with visiting officials and dignitaries; attending academy graduations and swearing-in ceremonies and some weddings and funerals; and visiting injured officers in the hospital. Like the mayor who cuts ribbons and kisses babies, the CEO performs these duties simply because of his or her position within the organization; the duties come with being a figurehead. While police chiefs and sheriffs cannot realistically be expected to commit to every committee meeting, speaking engagement, and other events to which they are invited, they are obligated from a professional standpoint to attend as many as they can.

The leadership function requires the CEO to motivate and coordinate workers while resolving different goals and needs within the department and the community. A chief or sheriff may have to urge the governing board to enact a code or ordinance that, whether popular or not, is in the best interest of the jurisdiction. For example, a police chief recently led a drive to pass an ordinance that prohibited parking by university students in residential neighborhoods surrounding the campus, which was a highly unpopular undertaking, but the chief pursued it because of the hardships suffered by the area residents. CEOs also provide leadership in such matters as bond issues (to raise money for more officers or new buildings) and should advise the governing body on the effects of proposed ordinances.

The role as liaison is performed when the CEO of a police organization interacts with other organizations and coordinates workflows. It is not uncommon for police executives from one geographic area—the police chief, the sheriff, the ranking officer of the local highway patrol office, the district attorney, the campus police chief—to meet informally each month to discuss common problems and strategies. Also, the chief executives serve as liaisons between their agencies and others in forming regional police councils, narcotics units, crime labs, dispatching centers, and so forth. They also meet with representatives of the courts, the juvenile system, and other criminal justice agencies.

Informational Role

The second major role of a CEO under the Mintzberg model is the informational role, which involves the CEO in monitoring/inspecting and disseminating information and acting as spokesperson. In the monitoring/inspecting function, the CEO constantly looks at the workings of the department to ensure that things are operating smoothly (or as smoothly as a police agency can be expected to run). This function is often referred to as "roaming the ship," and many CEOs who have isolated themselves from their personnel and from the daily operations of the agency can speak from sad experience of the need to be alert and to create a presence. Many police executives use daily staff meetings to discuss any information about the past twenty-four hours that might affect the department.

The disseminating tasks involve getting information to members of the department. This may include memorandums, special orders, general orders, and policies. The spokesperson function is related but is more focused on getting information to the news media. This is another very difficult task for the chief executive; news organizations are in a competitive field in which scoops and deadlines and the public's right to know are all-important. Still, the media must understand those occasions when a criminal investigation can be seriously affected by premature or overblown coverage. We discuss police-media relations in more detail below.

Decision-Maker Role

Finally, as a decision maker, the CEO of a police organization serves as an entrepreneur, a disturbance handler, a resource allocator, and a negotiator. As entrepreneur, the CEO must sell ideas to the governing board or the department. Ideas might include new computers or a new communications system, a policing strategy (such as COPPS), or different work methods, all of which are intended to improve the organization. Sometimes there is a blending of roles, as when several police executives band together (functioning as liaisons) and go to the state attorney general and the legislature to lobby (in an entrepreneurial capacity) for new crime-fighting laws.

As a disturbance handler, the executive's tasks range from the minor (perhaps resolving trivial disputes between staff members) to the major (such as handling riots or muggings in a local park or cleaning up the city's downtown). Sometimes the intradepartmental disputes can reach major proportions; for example, if the patrol commander tells the street officers to arrest more public drunks, it might create a severe strain on the jail division commander's resources, causing enmity between the two commanders and forcing the chief executive to intervene.

As a resource allocator, the CEO must be able to say no to subordinates. However, subordinates should not be faulted for trying to obtain more resources or for trying to improve their unit as best they can. The CEO must have a clear idea of the budget and what the priorities are and must listen to citizen complaints and act accordingly. For example, ongoing complaints of motorists speeding in a specific area will result in a shifting of patrol resources to that area or neighborhood.

As a negotiator, the police manager resolves employee grievances and sits as a member of the negotiating team for labor relations. A survey by PERF found that seven out of ten municipal police departments with more than seventy-five employees have some form of union representation.[51]

Collective bargaining puts the CEO in a difficult position. As a member of management, the CEO is often compelled to argue against salaries and benefits that would assist the rank and file. As mentioned earlier, however, as long as a limited supply of funds is available to the jurisdiction, managers will have to draw the line at some point and say no to subordinates. Again, the collective-bargaining unit and individual officers cannot be faulted for trying to improve salaries, benefits, and working conditions, but sometimes these associations go outside the boundary of reasonableness and reach an impasse or deadlock in contract negotiations with management. These situations can become uncomfortable and even disastrous, leading to work stoppages, work speedups, work slowdowns, or other such tactics (discussed further in Chapter 13).

Example of Mintzberg in Action: NYPD's Compstat

New York City's **Compstat** process is a relatively new approach to crime analysis and prevention. It employs several aspects of the Mintzberg model of chief executive officers, including the interpersonal, informational, and decision-maker roles and several of their subcategories.

Because of the massive size and bureaucracy of the New York Police Department (NYPD), New York City is probably the last city in which one would expect to find a major innovation in police administration and operations—one that has been described as having the "potential to become the dominant mode of policing in America."[52] But that situation changed with the election of Mayor Rudolph Giuliani in November 1993 and his appointment of Police Commissioner William Bratton in January 1994.

Before 1993, the city's daily crime statistics were almost useless for crime analysis: At least two months' time was required for commanders to even obtain the figures. Meanwhile, crime was at a very high level, and the NYPD, by its own admission, had gotten out of the habit of being held accountable for the crime problem. Bratton established three clear-cut goals for the NYPD: Reduce crime significantly, reduce the fear of crime, and work on improving the quality of life.[53] What quickly evolved in the NYPD was a computer file to compare statistics—hence the acronym *Compstat.*

Computerization changed everything in the NYPD, enabling the organization to change from being reactive to being proactive and goal specific. A four-step process became the essence of Compstat: (1) collecting information in a timely and accurate manner, (2) using effective tactics to respond to problems, (3) deploying personnel and resources rapidly, and (4) following up and assessing relentlessly. With these four steps, Compstat enables the NYPD to pinpoint and analyze crime patterns almost instantly and to respond in the most appropriate manner. A side benefit is that with Compstat, the organization is able to identify emerging leaders from deep within its ranks.[54]

Compstat is best known for its semiweekly high-stress 7:00 A.M. brainstorming sessions at police headquarters, where field commanders are grilled about crime in their areas. The results have been impressive: From 1993 to 1996, New York City experienced the most dramatic decline in crime in the nation. As an example, according to Federal Bureau of Information (FBI) statistics, New York accounted for 61 percent of the nationwide decline in felonies during the first six months of 1995. The most unanticipated result of Compstat was that the decline in crime occurred in every police precinct in the city, debunking the theory that police can only displace crime from one area to another.[55] Because of these successes, by late 1996 the National Institute of Justice was attempting to replicate Compstat in two other jurisdictions. According to one observer, "Compstat and the re-engineered NYPD are pointing the way to a new perspective on community policing, and demonstrating that a community orientation is not incompatible with aggressive, focused law enforcement."[56]

MIDDLE MANAGERS: CAPTAINS AND LIEUTENANTS

Few police administration books discuss the **middle managers** of a police department: captains and lieutenants. This is unfortunate because they are too numerous and too powerful within police organizations to ignore. Opinions vary about these mid-management personnel, however, as will be seen later.

Normally, captains and lieutenants are commissioned officers, with the position of captain second in rank to the executive managers. Captains have authority over all officers of the agency below the chief or sheriff and are responsible only to them. Lieutenants are in charge of sergeants and all officers and report to captains. Captains and lieutenants may perform the following functions[57]:

- Inspecting assigned operations
- Reviewing and making recommendations on reports
- Helping to develop plans
- Preparing work schedules
- Overseeing records and equipment
- Overseeing recovered or confiscated property
- Enforcing all laws and orders

Too often middle managers become glorified paper pushers, especially in the present climate of myriad reports, budgets, grants, and so on. Police agencies should take a hard look at what managerial services are essential and whether lieutenants are needed to perform such services. Recently some communities, such as Kansas City, Missouri, eliminated the rank of lieutenant, finding that this move had no negative consequences and some positive effects.[58]

Obviously, when a multilayered bureaucracy is created, a feudal kingdom and several fiefdoms will occupy the building. As Richard Holden observed, however, "If feudalism was so practical, it would not have died out in the Middle Ages."[59] It is important to remember that the two crucial elements to organizational effectiveness are top administrators

POLICE INGENUITY AND ENTREPRENEURSHIP

DENNIS D. RICHARDS

The 30-odd miles of California shore loosely known as Malibu arguably make up one of the most famous stretches of beach in the world. The Malibu coast is also part of the more than 240 square miles policed by the Malibu Station of the Los Angeles County Sheriff's Department. The public beaches generated great seasonal surges of transient populations. Predictably, the police problems of the nearby expensive real estate were exacerbated by the summer influx. Patrol officers, driving conventional vehicles, made what reasonable observations they could from highways or parking lots and ventured onto the sand only in response to a call for service. Soon, however, the question arose as to how best to provide an increased police presence. I was asked to study the feasibility of routine beach patrol at Malibu and, if practicable, to suggest a proposal.

The first patrol vehicle under consideration was a three-wheel all-terrain vehicle known as an ATC. The ATC, equipped with soft oversized tires, was light and maneuverable enough to travel over both dry sand and the wet areas where tides rendered previous patrol activities marginal. However, the ATC was unable to transport prisoners, was underpowered, was unable to carry extra equipment in a secure manner, and needed significant renovation to carry and power a police radio. Traditional four-wheel-drive vehicles also couldn't provide services: Visibility of objects on the ground was poor, making it somewhat tricky for an officer to drive through a crowd of sunbathers without running over someone; they were comparatively heavy and tended to bog down; finally, beachgoers found these vehicles offensive because of their tank-like military appearance.

I then discovered that the lifeguards were experimenting with dune buggies and were extremely enthusiastic regarding their performance. I tested one and was convinced that a dune buggy was the best mode of patrol, but the department's executives also had to be convinced of its efficacy. I borrowed a lifeguard's buggy, positioned it on a scenic stretch of beach, and photographed it with a uniformed deputy standing on either side. A department staff artist used this photograph as a basis for conceptual drawings, changing the bright lifeguard yellow to black and white and overlaying the department's radio car logo on the buggy's nose. The artist also attached a traditional light bar and siren to the crash bar and, in various drawings, dressed the deputies in a softer image, wearing shorts, polo shirts, stripped-down duty belts, and baseball caps.

Armed with these visual aids, we made our presentation. The concept captured the administration's imagination, and the dune buggy beach patrol was approved. The patrol was launched with considerable fanfare from the media. The sheriff personally chauffeured members of the press along Malibu Beach in a patrol buggy, and more importantly, the stubby little cars were an instant hit with the public, which found them more amusing than threatening. Beachgoers frequently flagged them down and asked to be photographed with the vehicles. The positive public relations achieved by this operation were one of its most valuable aspects.

Dennis D. Richards served as deputy, sergeant, and lieutenant with the Los Angeles County Sheriff's Office [LACSO] from 1965 to 1986.

and operational personnel. Middle management can pose a threat to the agency by acting as a barrier between these two primary elements. Research has shown an inverse relationship between the size of the hierarchy in an organization and its effectiveness.[60] Normally, the closer the administrator is to the operations, the more effective the agency.

First-Line Supervisors

At some point during the career of a patrol officer who has acquired the minimum years of experience, he or she has the opportunity to test for promotion to **first-line supervisor**, or sergeant. Competition for this position is quite keen in most departments. To compete well, officers are often advised to rotate into different agency assignments to gain exposure to a variety of both police functions and supervisors before testing for the sergeant's position. The promotional system, then, favors not only those officers who are skilled at test taking but also those who have experience outside the patrol division.[61]

The supervisor's role, put simply, is to get his or her subordinates to do their very best. This task involves a host of activities, including communicating, motivating, mediating, mentoring, leading, team building, training, developing, appraising, counseling, and disciplining. As a result, no other rank in the police hierarchy exerts more direct influence over the working environment, morale, and performance of employees.

Adding to the complexity of the supervisor's role is the fact that the supervisor is generally in his or her first leadership position. A new supervisor must learn how to exercise command and be responsible for the behavior of several other employees. Long-standing relationships are put under stress when one party suddenly has official authority over former equals. Expectations of leniency or preferential treatment may have to be dealt with.

Getting that first promotion.

(Courtesy Sparks, Nevada, Police Department)

The supervisor is caught in the middle, working with rank-and-file employees—labor—on the one hand and middle or upper management on the other. While it is management's job to squeeze as much productivity out of workers as possible, labor's motivation often seems to be to avoid work as much as possible. Supervisors find themselves right in the middle of this contest.

Ten Tasks

For all of these reasons, the first-line supervisor has one of the most complex roles in the organization. If the supervisor fails to make sure that employees perform correctly, the unit will not be very successful, causing difficulties for mid-level managers and administrators. Ten tasks are most important for sergeants and are listed in order of their importance[62]:

1. Supervising subordinate officers in the performance of their duties (including such tasks as maintaining inventory of equipment, training subordinates, preparing monthly activity reports, scheduling vacation leave)
2. Disseminating information to subordinates
3. Ensuring that general and special orders are followed
4. Observing subordinates in handling calls and other duties (including securing major crime scenes)
5. Reviewing and approving various departmental reports
6. Listening to problems voiced by officers
7. Answering backup calls
8. Keeping superiors apprised of ongoing situations
9. Providing direct supervision for potential high-risk calls or situations
10. Interpreting policies and informing subordinates

Types of Supervisors

Four distinct types of first-line supervisors have been identified: traditional, innovative, supportive, and active.[63] These types of supervisors can be found in any police department, depending on the individual's experiences on the job, his or her training, and the department's organizational climate.

The *traditional* supervisor is law enforcement oriented. These supervisors expect their subordinates to produce high levels of measurable activities such as traffic citations and arrests, to respond efficiently to calls for service, and to accurately complete reports and other paperwork. Traditional supervisors provide officers with a substantial amount of instruction and oversight, and they tend to place greater emphasis on punishment than rewards. They see their primary role as controlling subordinates and often have morale and motivational problems with their officers.

The *innovative* supervisor is most closely associated with community policing. Innovative supervisors may be the opposite of traditional supervisors. They do not generally place a great deal of emphasis on citations or arrests, and they depend more on developing relationships with subordinates than on using power to control or motivate them. Innovative supervisors usually are good mentors, tending to coach rather than order. They are open to new ideas and innovations, with the ultimate goal of developing officers so that they can solve problems and have good relations with citizens.

The third type of supervisor is the *supportive* supervisor, who (like the innovative supervisor) is concerned with developing good relations with subordinates. The primary difference is that supportive supervisors are concerned with protecting officers from what they view as unfair management practices, seeing themselves as a buffer between management and officers. They attempt to develop strong work teams and motivate officers by inspiring them. Their shortcoming is that they tend to see themselves as "one of the troops" and sometimes fail to emphasize departmental goals and responsibilities.

The final category of supervisor is the *active* supervisor. These supervisors tend to be active in the field: They sometimes act like police officers, but with stripes or rank (not afraid to "get their hands dirty"), and they often become involved with field situations rather than supervising them. They are able to develop good relations with subordinates because they are perceived as being hardworking and competent. Their shortcoming is that by being overly involved in some field situations, they may not give their subordinates the opportunity to develop.

Overall, the most effective form of supervision may be the active supervisor. Subordinates working for active supervisors perform better in a number of areas, including problem solving and community policing. Active supervisors are able to develop a more productive work unit because they lead by example.

POLICE AND POLITICS

Good Politics, Bad Politics

As we saw in Chapter 1, the history of policing is so replete with politics that it even experienced a political "era." Still, this is an aspect of policing that is often overlooked, and it has had both good and bad elements. Political influence can range from major beneficial policy, personnel, and budgetary decisions to the overzealous city manager or city council member who wants to micromanage the police department and even appears unexpectedly at night at a crime scene (overheard on his or her police scanner) to "help" the officers.

Norm Stamper, former chief of police in Seattle, Washington, described the relationship between politics and policing very well:

Everything about policing is ultimately political. Who gets which office: political. Which services are cut when there's a budget freeze: political. Who gets hired, fired, promoted: political, political, political. The challenge. . .is to make sure the politics of picking and promoting people is as fair as possible. And as mindful of the *greater good* of the organization and of the community as possible. I hire my brother-in-law's cousin, a certifiable doofus, because he's got a bass boat I wouldn't mind borrowing—bad politics. I promote a drinking buddy—bad politics. I pick an individual because he or she will add value to the organization and will serve the community honorably— good politics.[64]

Political Exploitation of the Police

Politics is the art or science of government. One definition of policing is very similar to that of politics: "the internal control and regulation of a political unit [such as a state or community] through exercise of governmental powers."[65] Both words derive from the Greek terms for "citizen" and "citizenship," and *police* also comes from the Greek word for "city": *polis*.

Historically, police departments in the United States have been political bodies, extensions of the municipal political authority.[66] Because of the close relationship between police departments and the political leadership of the community, political power has often been abused. From the beginning of the twentieth century, when the journalist Lincoln Steffens exposed corruption in American cities, to more recent times, when police scandals have rocked departments in New York City, Chicago, and Miami, politics has been shown to be entwined in the relationships that often bind criminals and police officers. Partisan politics has often been the cause of police corruption.[67]

Even in the nineteenth century, police forces were not autonomous; political figures outside the departments began to make key decisions regarding promotions, assignments, and disciplinary matters. For their own part, police officers often sought promotions, soft jobs, or particular beats. Some officers wanted a beat close to their homes; corrupt officers wanted a beat with many saloons and brothels to raise their income. In the late nineteenth century, promotion depended on political influence and money, and some officers had to borrow the means for career advancement. Impartial police administration was the last thing politicians in large cities wanted—their interests were best served by a policing system that was easily manipulated.[68]

Police Executive Relations and Expectations

The chief of police is generally considered to be one of the most influential and prestigious people in local government. However, much of the power of the office has eroded because of the high attrition rate, the increased power of local personnel departments, and the strong influence of police unions. Furthermore, mayors, city managers and administrators, members of the agency, citizens, special-interest groups, and the media all have differing, often conflicting, expectations of the role of chief of police.

The mayor or city manager is likely to believe that the chief of police should be an enlightened administrator whose responsibility is to promote departmental efficiency, reduce crime, improve service, and so on. Other mayors and managers will appreciate the chief who simply "keeps the lid on" and manages to keep the morale high and the number of citizen complaints low.[69] However, the mayor or city manager may also properly expect the chief to be part of the city management team, communicate city management's policies to police personnel, establish agency goals and objectives, select and effectively manage people, and be a responsible steward of the budget.[70]

The relationship between the police chief and the mayor is difficult to articulate. However, several points are indispensable in the relationship. First, the mayor is boss; indeed, the mayor possesses the legal or political power to fire or force the police chief out of office almost at whim. Second, the mayor has the responsibility for assuring the public that the police are doing the best they can with available resources. Third, the police executive, if chosen on merit, has considerable knowledge about the problems of the community and a wide array of possible solutions, expertise that will serve city hall well and the mayor should come to rely on the chief's pragmatism and take-charge approach as well. Finally, the mayor must give the chief the authority to run his or her department day to day; without this autonomy, perhaps guided by the mayor's input, the chief's authority will be eroded.[71]

Members of the police agency may have different expectations of the chief executive. They may be less concerned with cost-effectiveness and more concerned with good salaries, benefits, and equipment. The officers expect the chief to be their advocate, backing them up when necessary and representing the agency well in dealings with judges and prosecutors who may be indifferent or hostile to their interests. Citizens, for their part, expect the chief of police to provide efficient and cost-effective police services while keeping crime and tax rates down and eliminating corruption and illegal use of force.

Special-interest groups expect the chief to advocate desirable policy positions; for example, Mothers Against Drunk Driving (MADD) insists on strong police measures combating driving under the influence. Finally, the media expect the chief to cooperate fully with their efforts to obtain fast and complete crime information.

POLICE-MEDIA RELATIONS

The topic of **media relations** with respect to police was mentioned briefly above in the discussion of the Mintzberg model of chief executive officers. However, due to its importance, here we discuss it in greater detail.

As the saying goes, "Perception is reality." While there are not nearly as many police programs on television today as in the past—such as the 1970s, when 42 police programs premiered[72]—certainly the manner in which the police are depicted in film and television has a strong influence on how the police are viewed by society. Not only do people identify with the struggle between good and evil that is conducted by the actors in such programs (and they especially like private eyes, who can be more "flexible" in their adherence to the rule of law), but they also apparently find the quirks and idiosyncrasies of title figures such as *McCloud* (Dennis Weaver), *Columbo* (Peter Falk), and *Kojak* (Telly Savales) to be as endearing as the investigations they were conducting.[73]

As mentioned earlier, news dissemination is a delicate undertaking for the police chief executive officer. News organizations, especially the television and print media, are highly competitive businesses that seek to obtain the most complete news in the shortest amount of time, which often translates to wider viewership and therefore greater advertising revenues for them. From one perspective, the media must appreciate that a criminal investigation can be seriously compromised by premature or excessive coverage. From another perspective, the public has a legitimate right to know what is occurring in the community, especially matters relating to crime. Therefore, the prudent police executive attempts to have an open and professional relationship with the media in which each side knows and understands its responsibilities. It is therefore of the utmost importance that either the chief executive or his or her designee—a trained public information officer (PIO)—know how to perform public speaking as well as what kind and how much information he or she should divulge to media outlets. (*Note:* In a related vein, while it has not become a widespread problem, at least one state supreme court has held a police PIO liable for statements made in a news release, telling a reporter that a defendant operated an illegal gambling operation; the court ruled there was no reasonable basis for making such injurious statements.[74])

Unfortunately, many police executives (a good number who involuntarily left office) can speak of the results of failing to develop an appropriate relationship with the media. The author is aware of one former police chief in a medium-sized western city who sported a bumper sticker on his vehicle stating "I don't trust the liberal media." This action obviously did not endear him to the local newspaper, nor did it help him in editorials and articles when an issue concerning his involvement in a sexual harassment allegation became public. This chief obviously did not recognize the power of the pen; as one person put it, "Don't argue with someone who buys his ink by the barrel!"

An example of positive police-media relations is the performance of former Montgomery County, Maryland, Police Chief Charles Moose during the 2002 Beltway Snipers case (see Exhibit 3-1).

EXHIBIT 3-1

Police-Media Relations: The Beltway Snipers Case

An example of the relationship that can develop between the police and the media is the Washington, D.C.–area sniper investigation of late 2002. The media were used to communicate with the snipers—who eventually were captured after the suspects' photographs and a vehicle description were broadcast. For twenty-three days in October 2002, a two-person sniper team terrorized the Washington, D.C., and central Virginia regions. This case would ultimately involve fourteen shootings and ten deaths, and its investigation included more than twenty local, two state, and at least ten federal law enforcement agencies. It was clearly one of the largest and most complex multijurisdictional investigations ever. First, the chief refused to engage in speculation, thereby defusing all of the "what if" scenarios posed by copy-hungry reporters. Second, media briefings were conducted on a regular basis; this was an important bit of media relations and control in the sense of minimizing coverage based on commentary by the army

of "experts" who can surface during such an event. Finally, this high degree of access enabled the police to build public trust rather than have reporters engage in further (and often damaging) speculation as the case progressed. Reliable information flow is crucial to the success of such a major investigation: The ability to collect, analyze, and disseminate tips, leads, intelligence, and criminal histories can mean the difference between a quick apprehension and a prolonged frustrating effort. It was crucial that effective communication was maintained with residents, government leaders, and the media. Police executives also kept their patrol officers informed of all pertinent and current information about the investigation and provided them with a list of questions to ask when talking to residents or conducting field interviews. The lessons learned from this case will serve as an important blueprint for similarly situated law enforcement executives in the future.

Sources: Adapted from Gerard R. Murphy and Chuck Wexler, *Managing a Multi-jurisdictional Case: Lessons Learned from the Sniper Investigation* (Washington, DC: Police Executive Research Forum, October 2004), p. 39; Richard B. Weinblatt, "The Police and the Press," http://www.policeone.com/media-relations/articles/118445/ (accessed January 4, 2007); and Patrick Collins, "Handling the Media: The Lessons of Some Moose-terpiece Theater," *Law Enforcement News*, November 30, 2002, p. 1.

WAYS TO STRETCH RESOURCES: CONTRACT AND CONSOLIDATED POLICING AND CIVILIANIZATION

The United States has many small police agencies; in fact, of the estimated seventeen thousand local police departments, nearly half (45.5 percent) employ fewer than ten sworn personnel; three-fourths employ twenty-five or fewer sworn personnel.[75] Many communities that are small in size find it extremely difficult (if not impossible) to maintain a 24/7 police or sheriff's department—particularly one that is trained and staffed well enough to provide a full range of policing services. Therefore, several approaches have been developed by agencies facing staffing and funding shortages for reducing and/or sharing the costs of full enforcement operations: contracting, consolidating, and civilianizing services.

These concepts are not of recent origin. Indeed, as early as 1973 a major presidential commission on criminal justice—the National Advisory Commission on Criminal Justice Standards and Goals—recommended the following:

> At a minimum, police agencies that employ fewer than 10 sworn employees should consolidate for improved efficiency and effectiveness. If the most effective and efficient police service can be provided through mutual agreement or joint participation with other criminal justice agencies, the governmental entity or the police agency immediately should enter into the appropriate agreement or joint operation.[76]

Next, we discuss the means by which this can be—and is being—done.

Contract and Consolidated Policing

There are two primary means by which police agencies can be unified. The first and simplest is **contract policing**. Smaller communities, either incorporated or unincorporated, can contract their police services with another larger agency. For example, the Los Angeles Sheriff's Department contracts with forty separate cities to provide police service.[77] This approach is attractive if a jurisdiction finds itself unable to afford the full spectrum of policing expenditures; it might enter into a contractual agreement with another agency to share these expenses. Contract policing is, in effect, *partial* consolidation, with a unit of government maintaining its own police agency but contracting with another jurisdiction for services it could not afford. Some examples of contracted services include personnel wages and benefits, patrol vehicle and maintenance costs, uniforms, dispatchers, communications equipment, jails, forensic laboratories, mobile crime-scene units, consolidated narcotics units, and even airplanes for extradition of arrestees. Pooling their human and technological resources can typically result in better services while avoiding duplication of those services and normally does so at less expense.

Another means of unifying agencies and possibly achieving cost savings is through **consolidated policing**, which is the merging of two or more city and/or county governments into a single policing entity. Two jurisdictions can be completely combined into a single agency, with its sworn personnel enforcing a single set of statutes or ordinances, wearing the same uniform, driving the same type of patrol vehicle, and so on. Again, the advantage is in avoiding duplication of services (for example, by having the ability to purchase equipment in larger volume), which leads to economy of scale. As a caveat, however, the initial cost of implementing consolidation can be high. In some states, the enabling legislation requires that when two or more agencies combine their operations, the best salary and benefits packages that already existed be brought into the newly consolidated organization. This so-called cherry picking can obviously be quite expensive, especially in the initial stages of consolidation when the new consolidated agency may also be top-heavy with administrative personnel. Cost savings to be realized through consolidation, therefore, may not be realized for many years (if ever), depending on how the agency is structured, how the enabling legislation is written, and so on.

Civilianization

Most citizen calls for police service do not involve a crime or require a sworn officer to enforce the laws. For that reason, many agencies are increasingly using **civilianization** for a lot of functions performed traditionally by sworn personnel. This has worked particularly well for such aspects of policing as dispatching, crime analysis (forensics), crime-scene investigation, report taking, and even supplemental patrol duties. And as with contract and consolidated police services, doing so can be much more cost-effective by using nonsworn personnel, thus freeing sworn officers for critical police work. This is especially important when many agencies today are being tasked to do more with less.

In fact, the use of civilians has become so widespread that an area of controversy has arisen surrounding their use: How civilianized should the department become? Police unions are becoming increasingly wary of management's outsourcing of traditional police tasks to civilians, viewing the latter as potential threats to their livelihood. Therefore, as civilianization becomes more widespread, police chief executives must be mindful of the potential for friction and poor officer morale because no one—citizens, sworn officers, or civilian personnel—will benefit by losing a healthy and productive work environment. Where they exist, the unions should be included in any planning and discussion of civilianization and should help to fashion a plan that benefits the agency in ways that will be received well by the rank and file.[78]

AGENCY ACCREDITATION

In 1979, the **accreditation** of police agencies began slowly with the creation of the **Commission on Accreditation for Law Enforcement Agencies (CALEA),** located in Fairfax, Virginia. CALEA is a nonprofit organization that has developed and administers 459 voluntary standards for law enforcement agencies to meet. These standards cover the roles and responsibilities of the agency: organization and administration; law enforcement, traffic, and operational support; prisoner- and court-related services; and auxiliary and technical services. Accreditation, a voluntary process, is quite expensive, both in actual dollars and in human resources, and it often takes a year to eighteen months for an agency to prepare for the assessment.[79] Today there are nearly six hundred agencies accredited or recognized in one of CALEA's various programs, with several hundred others working toward their first award.[80]

Once an agency believes it is ready to be accredited, an application is filed and the agency receives a self-evaluation questionnaire to determine its current status. If the self-evaluation indicates that the agency is ready to attempt accreditation, an on-site team appointed by CALEA conducts an assessment and writes a report on its findings. After becoming accredited, the agency must apply for reaccreditation after five years.[81]

Several unanticipated consequences of the accreditation process have emerged. A number of states have formed coalitions to assist police agencies in the process of accreditation. Also, some departments report decreased insurance costs as a result of accreditation. Finally, the national transition to COPPS (discussed more fully in Chapter 6) has not been lost on CALEA. Today the accreditation self-assessment process provides many opportunities to institutionalize community policing. Not only do the accreditation standards help weave community policing into an agency's internal fabric, they also provide a way to integrate such objectives into external service delivery[82]:

- Enhancing the role and authority of patrol officers
- Improving analysis and information management
- Managing calls for service

In comparing accredited and nonaccredited police agencies, Kimberly McCabe and Robin Fajardo found that accredited police agencies (1) provided more training for their officers and required higher minimum educational requirements for new officers, (2) were nearly twice as likely to require drug testing for sworn applicants, and (3) were more likely to operate special units for the enforcement of drug laws and laws against child abuse.[83] Notwithstanding the rigorous standards that must be met in order for agencies to become accredited, McCabe and Fajardo found that there were no differences in accredited versus nonaccredited agencies in terms of starting salaries or annual budgets, officer demographics (for example, race and sex of the officers), or officers' use of body armor. (Because many researchers view accreditation as a means of reducing liability insurance, it was expected that officers in accredited agencies would be required to wear protective body armor.[84])

SUMMARY

This chapter has discussed local (municipal and county) police agencies as organizations and bureaucracies and has explored organizational communication and the roles and functions of police executives, middle managers, and first-line supervisors. A management model was employed to clarify the general roles and functions of police administrators; included was a brief illustration of good police administration—the Compstat process in

New York City (which is believed by many observers to be the dominant mode of policing in the future). Also addressed was the relationship between the police and politics and how it permeates the field. Contract and consolidated policing and civilianization as well as agency accreditation were also examined.

In the past, particularly during the political era of policing, many administrators, managers and supervisors, and officers were hired and attained their level of leadership responsibility through political favoritism. This hiring and promoting of unqualified personnel contributed heavily to the massive growth of employee labor unions. This chapter has demonstrated that today's challenges are too complex and dangerous to leave personnel administration and hiring to chance. Today, to be an effective administrator, the individual must not only know about policing but must also learn all he or she can about the most valuable asset—people. Upon acquiring these human skills, the technical, conceptual, and other necessary skills of the job must follow, lest the new leader walk off the gangplank and then sink in an ocean of "alligators." Poor administration and management skills can and do lead to serious problems of ethics, civil liability, and accountability, as will be seen in later chapters.

KEY TERMS

accreditation
anomie
bureaucracy
chain of command
chief of police
civilianization
Commission on Accreditation for Law Enforcement Agencies (CALEA)
communication
Compstat
consolidated policing
contract policing
first-line supervisor
media relations
middle manager
Mintzberg model
municipal police department
organization
organizational structure
policies and procedures
rules and regulations
sheriff's office

REVIEW QUESTIONS

1. What are the elements—and purposes—of the basic organizational structure of a police agency? Diagram these basic elements.

2. What are the processes of upward, downward, horizontal, and grapevine communication, and how do these processes apply to a police organization?

3. What are the primary differences between municipal police departments and sheriff's offices in terms of their operations, policies and procedures, and use of technologies?

4. What are the roles of the police executive under the Mintzberg model of chief executive officers?

5. How would you define and explain the uses of span of control, policies, and procedures?

6. How do the roles and functions differ for contemporary chiefs of police and county sheriffs?

7. What are the roles and functions of mid-level managers and first-line supervisors?

8. How does New York City's Compstat process function?

9. What is the historical relationship between the police and politicians, and what have been some major problems?

10. What is the rationale for the police maintaining good media relations, and what kinds of good practices provide this?

11. How do contract, consolidated, and civilianized police services operate, and what are their advantages?

12. How does a police organization become accredited, and what is the process for doing so?

INDEPENDENT STUDENT ACTIVITIES

1. Select a law enforcement agency (municipal police department or sheriff's office) in your area. Using information obtained from this chapter and the agency's Web site or interviews, determine what its history is as well as how it operates with respect to jurisdiction, mission, and functions. (You might also see how the agency compares with information provided in Tables 3-1 through 3-7.) Also look at its organizational structure, salary and benefits packages, policies and procedures, and recruitment and training processes. Try to determine what measures the agency has taken for homeland defense, any specialized training that has been provided to personnel in the event of a terrorist attack or other critical incident, how the agency will cooperate with other agencies, and so on. Determine, to the extent possible, the priorities, budgets, management philosophies, and major contemporary challenges and problems that confront police executives in your area.

2. Examine the contemporary nature of the police chief's and sheriff's duties in your area. Determine what qualifications the police chiefs and sheriffs possessed in order to attain their present positions, and learn the kinds of tasks they perform that comport with the Mintzberg model of chief executives.

3. Interview a first-line supervisor to better ascertain why the roles and functions of that position are considered to be among the most complex in the police hierarchy.

4. Ascertain whether or not your local police agency uses something similar to Compstat for collecting crime information, responding to problems, deploying personnel and resources rapidly, and following up and assessing outcomes. If not, is there a crime-analysis unit that does something similar? If so, what methods does it use?

5. Try to assess the extent of good police-media relations in your community (perhaps you can do so by examining editorials and letters to the editor or having discussions with news reporters).

6. Inquire of local agencies the extent to which they are sharing resources, that is, contracting, consolidating, and civilianizing services.

7. Is a police agency in your area accredited? If so, find out what the organization had to do in order to become accredited as well as the costs and benefits of doing so.

RELATED WEB SITES

Commission on the Accreditation of Law Enforcement Agencies
http://www.calea.org

International Association of Chiefs of Police
http://www.theiacp.org

National Sheriffs Association
http://www.sheriffs.org

Police Executive Research Forum
http://www.policeforum.org

CHAPTER

4

FROM CITIZEN TO OFFICER

PREPARING FOR THE STREET

I think the necessity of being ready increases. Look to it.
—*Abraham Lincoln*

Learn how to be a policeman, because that cannot be improvised.
—*Pope John XXIII*

LEARNING OBJECTIVES

AS A RESULT OF READING THIS CHAPTER, THE STUDENT WILL:

- UNDERSTAND SOME OF THE PROBLEMS CONFRONTING TODAY'S POLICE RECRUITERS AND SOME UNIQUE MEASURES BEING TRIED TO OBTAIN A VIABLE APPLICANT POOL

- BE ABLE TO EXPLAIN THE GENERAL HIRING PROCESS AND TYPES OF TESTS AND EXAMINATIONS THAT ARE USED TO HIRE AND TRAIN POLICE OFFICERS

- UNDERSTAND THE ASSESSMENT CENTER CONCEPT AND ITS FUNCTIONS FOR HIRING AND PROMOTING THE BEST PERSONNEL

- KNOW THE KINDS OF SKILLS AND KNOWLEDGE THAT ARE IMPARTED TO POLICE TRAINEES DURING THEIR ACADEMY TRAINING AND THE TYPICAL SUBJECTS THAT ARE FOUND IN A POLICE ACADEMY CURRICULUM

- UNDERSTAND THE METHODS AND PURPOSES OF BOTH THE FTO AND PTO PROGRAMS

- BE AWARE OF WHAT IS MEANT BY THE TERM *WORKING PERSONALITY* AND HOW IT IS DEVELOPED AND FUNCTIONS

- BE ABLE TO DEFINE POLICE CYNICISM AND EXPLAIN HOW IT OPERATES

- BE ABLE TO DELINEATE THE IDEAL TRAITS OF POLICE OFFICERS

- KNOW WHY THE CRIME FIGHTER IMAGE IS THE GREATEST OBSTACLE IN ACCEPTING A REALISTIC VIEW OF THE POLICE ROLE

- BE ABLE TO DESCRIBE THE PRIMARY FUNCTIONS AND STYLES OF POLICING

99

INTRODUCTION

This chapter **generally** describes how an officer's career begins and, to a large extent, how his or her occupational personality is formed. Studying the subculture of the police helps us define the "cop's world" and the officer's role in it; this subculture shapes the officer's attitudes, values, and beliefs.

The idea of a police subculture was first proposed by William Westley in his 1950 study of the Gary, Indiana, Police Department, where he found, among many other things, a high degree of group cohesion, secrecy, and violence.[1] It is now widely accepted that the police develop traditions, skills, and attitudes that are unique to their occupation because of their duties and responsibilities.[2]

We begin at the threshold, looking at some of the methods, challenges, and problems connected with the recruitment of qualified individuals. Then we track the typical police applicant's progression through the various types of tests that may be employed—written, psychological, physical, oral, character, and medical screening—and discuss the assessment center.

Then we examine formal police training at the academy, where the initiation of the officer-to-be into the police subculture commences in earnest. The chapter discusses types of academies and their general curriculum as well as examining some of the informal learning that takes place there. We then look at postacademy training—the field training officer concept. Following that is a look at how officers adopt their working personality: formal and informal rules, customs, and beliefs of the occupation. This portion of the chapter includes an assessment of the traits that make a good officer. Finally, we examine the roles, functions, and styles of policing. It is important to define and understand how these aspects of policing may differ and conflict; even though in these difficult times it is easy to believe that our society has a unified view of the purposes and operations of its police agencies, there actually can be a good deal of disagreement in these areas.

A chapter summary, key terms, review questions, independent student activities, and related Web sites conclude the chapter.

FIRST THINGS FIRST: RECRUITING QUALIFIED APPLICANTS

Wanted: Those Who Walk on Water

Recruiting that results in an adequate pool of applicants is an extremely important facet of the police hiring process. August Vollmer stated:

> [Law enforcement candidates should] have the wisdom of Solomon, the courage of David, the patience of Job and leadership of Moses, the kindness of the Good Samaritan, the diplomacy of Lincoln, the tolerance of the Carpenter of Nazareth, and, finally, an intimate knowledge of every branch of the natural, biological and social sciences.[3]

Many people believe that the police officer has the most difficult job in America. Police officers are solitary workers, spending most of their time on the job unsupervised.

Also, people who are hired today will become the supervisors of the future. For all of these reasons, police agencies must attempt to attract the best individuals possible.

Police applicants typically come from lower-middle-class or working-class backgrounds;[4] they generally have a high school education and a history of employment. They also tend; at the application stage, to be enthusiastic, idealistic, uninformed about the reality of police work, and very different from the stereotype of the police officer as authoritarian, suspicious, and insensitive.[5]

Some studies indicate that police applicants are primarily motivated by the need for job security.[6] Other researchers have found that both males and females listed the same six factors—desire to help people, job security, crime fighting, job excitement, prestige, and a lifetime interest—as strong positive influences in their career choices.[7] Joel Lefkowitz concluded that police candidates were lower than average in their desire to do autonomous work,[8] and other studies have indicated that applicants tend to favor a more directive leadership style. Such findings are not unusual, given that most police agencies are highly structured and paramilitary in nature. Studies do not establish that police candidates fit the stereotypes of harsh, controlling people who wish to dominate others. Leadership, or the ability to take charge of situations, is a desirable attribute, however. Some researchers have found that the typical police applicant is very similar to the average college student.[9]

Bruce Carpenter and Susan Raza, using the Minnesota Multiphasic Personality Inventory (MMPI), found that police applicants differed from the general population in several important ways.[10] Police applicants, they learned, are somewhat more psychologically healthy, are generally less depressed and anxious, and are more assertive and interested in making and maintaining social contacts. Furthermore, few police aspirants have emotional difficulties, and they have a greater tendency to present a good impression of themselves than the general population does. They are a more homogeneous group.

Female police applicants tend to be more assertive and nonconforming and to have a higher energy level than male applicants; they are also less likely to identify with traditional sex roles than male applicants. Older police applicants tend to be less satisfied, have more physical complaints, and are more likely to develop physical symptoms under stress than younger applicants. Applicants to large city police forces are generally less likely to have physical complaints and have a higher energy level than applicants to small or medium-sized agencies. (This is probably explained by the fact that applicants in large cities are significantly younger.[11]) Some departments are under a mandate to recruit special groups of people, such as women, African-Americans, and Hispanics; several cities have also recruited homosexuals.

What psychological qualities should agencies seek? According to psychologist Lawrence Wrightsman,[12] it is important that police applicants be incorruptible and have high moral character. They should be well adjusted, able to carry out the hazardous and stressful tasks of policing without "cracking up," and thick-skinned enough to operate without defensiveness. They should have a genuine interest in people and a compassionate sense of the innate dignity of others. Applicants should also be free of emotional reactions, they should not be impulsive or overly aggressive, and they should be able to exercise restraint. This is especially important given their active role in crime detection.

Finally, they need logical skills to assist in their investigative work. An interesting example of some of the logical skills needed for police work is provided by Al Seedman, former chief of detectives in the New York Police Department (NYPD):

> In the woods just outside of town they found the skeleton of a man who'd been dead for three months or so. I asked whether this skeleton showed signs of any dental work. But the local cops said no, although the skeleton had crummy teeth. No dental work at all. Now, if he'd been wealthy, he could have afforded to have his teeth fixed. If he'd been poor, welfare would have paid. If he was a union member, their medical plan would have covered it. So this fellow was probably working at a low-paying non-unionized job, but making enough to keep off public assistance. Also, since he didn't match up to any family's missing-person report, he was probably single, living alone in an apartment or hotel. His landlord never reported him missing, either, so most likely he was also behind on his rent and the landlord probably figured he had just skipped. But even if he had escaped his landlord, he would never have escaped the tax man. The rest was simple. I told these cops to wait until the year is up. Then they can go to the IRS and get a printout of all single males making less than $10,000 a year but more than the welfare ceiling who paid withholding tax in the first three quarters but not in the fourth. Chances are the name of their skeleton will be on that printout.[13]

Other desirable traits of entry-level officers are discussed later in this chapter.

Recruiting Problems and Successes

Whether one blames the national economy, higher educational requirements, or noncompetitive wages and benefits, police and sheriff's department officials in virtually every region of the country agree that the generous pool of applicants from which they once sought qualified candidates is becoming increasingly shallow.[14] In fact, the National Association of Police Organizations (NAPO) recently named recruitment one of the top problems facing police agencies.[15]

The state of the economy can also have a strong influence on recruitment. The recent boom in California's economy caused problems for recruiters in that state's police agencies. With the unemployment rate running below 5 percent, police departments found it hard to compete with the private sector, despite offering relatively high pay, full benefits, and generous retirement plans. The Los Angeles Police Department (LAPD) saw its applications decline by about half in three years.[16] Chicago, which tested 25,000 applicants in 1993, had only 1,900 testees in the year 2000.

The requirement that applicants possess college credits is believed to make recruitment problems more acute. Several agencies that now require two years of college credits believe that this standard has reduced their applicant pool significantly. (The benefits of higher education for police officers are discussed in Chapter 13.) At the same time, a Census Bureau report put the average salary of a nonsupervisory police officer at $34,700; this compares to the average $40,546 that a technical support worker can expect to make and the average $51,351 that managers or executives earn. According to NAPO, add to that the media attention given to corrupt officers, police shootings, and department scandals, and it may be understandable why people are shying away from police careers. To counter this declining interest, departments are accentuating the occupation's positive aspects: solid insurance, excellent retirement plans, long vacations, and opportunities to advance.[17]

Recruiting and retaining women in police service remain particularly problematic. Gender bias (reflected in the absence of women being hired and promoted to policy-making positions) and sexual harassment concerns prevent many women from applying and cause many female officers to leave, and quickly: About 60 percent of female officers who leave their agency do so during their second to fifth years on the job.[18] (Problems associated with bringing women into policing—and retaining them—are discussed more fully in Chapter 13.)

But some agencies have successfully addressed the recruitment dilemma. For example, the New York State Police (NYSP) recently swore in its largest class in thirty years. Using an academic survey developed by a high-ranking trooper with a doctorate, the agency asked people what would make them consider joining the state police. (Their answer: job enrichment or more interesting work.) The survey also revealed that the two factors playing a key role in a person's decision to enter police work were the ability to help others and the opportunity to serve the community—two factors that the NYSP stresses in its mission and values statements and in its recruitment drives. Also emphasized in recruitment literature and television announcements is how female troopers can balance family and career as well as the various specialized jobs—foreign language proficiency or scuba diving, for example—that are available within the NYSP. The organization enlisted the entire force as recruiters and sought applicants at nontraditional locations, such as women's road races and health clubs.[19]

Other methods employed by police agencies in their attempts to develop a bigger pool of applicants include seeking applicants far from home (for example, Los Angeles recruits in Chicago, and Chicago recruits in Wisconsin), having downloadable application forms on the Web, lowering the minimum age from twenty-two to twenty-one, and allowing some applicants to substitute work experience for college credits.[20] See Exhibit 4-1 for police recruiting issues in Ireland.

TESTING: THE HURDLE PROCESS FOR NEW PERSONNEL

Even though a person meets the minimum qualifications for being a police officer (age, education, no disqualifying criminal record), much work still remains to be done before he or she is ready to be put to work as a police officer. The new recruit must successfully complete what is known as the **hurdle process**. In this section, we consider some kinds of tests that are used to weed out undesirable candidates.

Tables 4-1 and 4-2 show the kinds of tests and background checks that are used in selecting new officer recruits. Both tables are broken down by agency size, from under 2,500

EXHIBIT 4-1

Comparative Closeup

Recruiting Officers in Northern Ireland

Since 1922, it has been the task of the Northern Ireland police force—the Police Service of Northern Ireland (PSNI; formerly the Royal Ulster Constabulary, or RUC)—to combat acts of terrorism and other forms of criminal activity. Although terrorist acts have declined in recent years, in the past members of the PSNI viewed themselves as fighting a terrorist war while locked between two extremist groups and having to guard against many acts of terrorism directed against themselves as well as civilians.

Many officers have been attacked by people living in Ireland who want the nation to be British, and some officers have had their cars bombed or homes burned. Notwithstanding this uniquely dangerous situation, the PSNI has been recognized by police experts and terrorists alike as one of the world's most experienced and best police forces.

With about 8,000 personnel (7,300 of whom are full-time and 870 are part-time sworn officers), the department adheres to high standards of professionalism and behavior. According to the "Police Recruitment Regulations 2001," the current practice is for 50 percent of the officers who are hired to be Catholic and 50 percent non-Catholic; minimum qualifications include being a British subject or a Commonwealth or Republic of Ireland citizen, being 18 to 52 years of age and in good physical and mental health, possessing certain skills or competencies to carry out the duties of a police officer, and not having specified criminal convictions. The PSNI is very supportive of the community policing philosophy (discussed in Chapter 6). Indeed, recently the PSNI won several prestigious awards, including the United Kingdom's top award for community policing achievement.

Sources: Adapted from Paul K. Clare , "The Royal Ulster Constabulary: Northern Ireland's Beleaguered Police Force," *Criminal Justice International* 3 (May–June 1987): 3–6 and United Kingdom, Statutory Rules of Northern Ireland, "Police Recruitment Regulations, 2001," http://www.hmso.gov.uk/sr/sr2001/20010140.htm (accessed August 26, 2004).

TABLE 4-1

Interviews, Tests, and Examinations Used in Selection of New Officer Recruits in Local Police Departments, by Size of Population Served

Population Served	INTERVIEWS, TESTS, AND EXAMINATIONS USED TO SELECT NEW OFFICER RECRUITS									
	Personal Interview	Medical Exam	Drug Test	Psychological Evaluation	Physical Agility Test	Written Aptitude Test	Personality Inventory	Polygraph Exam	Voice Stress Analyzer	Second-Language Ability Test
All sizes	98%	85%	73%	67%	50%	43%	26%	25%	4%	1%
1,000,000 or more	94%	100%	100%	100%	94%	81%	56%	81%	0%	0%
500,000–999,999	100	100	95	100	86	84	48	64	11	11
250,000–499,999	95	93	98	98	93	83	51	78	10	2
100,000–249,999	95	97	86	95	88	82	50	77	11	1
50,000–99,999	99	97	90	97	83	80	47	57	7	3
25,000–49,999	99	99	88	96	76	76	45	47	12	2
10,000–24,999	99	98	88	89	71	72	40	42	6	1
2,500–9,999	99	91	74	71	52	48	26	25	3	–
Under 2,500	98	73	63	47	31	20	16	11	2	–

Note: List of selection methods is not intended to be exhaustive.
—indicates less than 0.5%.

Source: U.S. Department of Justice, Bureau of Justice Statistics, *Local Police Departments, 2003* (Washington, DC: Author, May 2006), p. 8.

TABLE 4-2

Background Checks Used in Selection of New Officer Recruits in Local Police Departments, by Size of Population Served

	BACKGROUND CHECKS USED TO SELECT NEW OFFICER RECRUITS				
Population Served	Criminal Record Check	Background Investigation	Driving Record Check	Credit History Check	Volunteer Service Check
All sizes	99%	98%	96%	55%	8%
1,000,000 or more	100%	100%	100%	81%	0%
500,000–999,999	100	100	100	89	19
250,000–499,999	100	100	98	88	7
100,000–249,999	100	99	98	88	12
50,000–99,999	99	100	99	87	8
25,000–49,999	100	100	99	83	11
10,000–24,999	99	99	99	76	8
2,500–9,999	99	98	99	55	9
Under 2,500	98	97	92	39	6

Note: List of selection methods is not intended to be exhaustive.

Source: U.S. Department of Justice, Bureau of Justice Statistics, *Local Police Departments, 2003* (Washington, DC: Author, May 2006), p. 8.

to more than 1 million. A May 2006 study by the federal Bureau of Justice Statistics (see Tables 4-1 and 4-2) found that nearly all local police agencies (99 percent) use criminal record checks, background investigations (98 percent), and driving record checks (96 percent) to screen applicants. Personal interviews (98 percent), psychological evaluations (67 percent), written aptitude tests (43 percent), physical agility tests (50 percent), personality inventory (26 percent), drug tests (73 percent), and medical exam (85 percent) are also commonly used.[21]

Certainly not all types of tests shown in Figure 4-1 are employed by all of the seventeen thousand police agencies in America, nor are these tests necessarily given in the sequence shown. Under affirmative action laws and court decisions, a burden rests with police administrators to demonstrate that the tests used are job related. The hiring sequence shown in Figure 4-1, called the "multiple hurdle procedure,"[22] may take longer than three months to complete, depending on the number and types of tests used and the ease of scheduling and performing them.

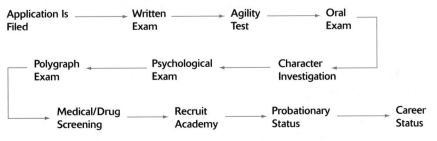

FIGURE 4-1
Major Elements of the Police Hiring Process

Written Examinations: General Knowledge and Psychological Tests

Measures of general intelligence and reading skills are the best means a police agency can use for predicting who will do well in the police academy.[23] Of course, any such test must be reliable and valid. To achieve reliability and validity, many (if not most) police agencies purchase and use "canned" test instruments—those prepared by professional individuals or companies.

Larger police departments and state police agencies use four types of written tests: cognitive tests (measuring aptitudes in verbal skills and mathematics, reasoning, and related perceptual abilities), personality tests (predominantly the MMPI), interest inventories (the Strong-Campbell, the Kuder, and the Minnesota Interest tests), and biographical data inventories.[24]

Over time, research findings have been mixed concerning the implications of written examinations. For example, a 1962 study of deputy sheriffs found that candidates with written test scores above the ninety-seventh percentile were most apt to be successful in their careers.[25] However, a study of the Tucson, Arizona, Police Department determined that the IQ scores of officers who dropped out of the force were significantly higher than those of a norm group. The study concluded that one can be too bright to be a cop, unless an alternate career development program can be developed to challenge and use highly intelligent people.[26] Of course, there is much more to police work than reading skills.

General intelligence tests are often administered and scored by the civil service or the central personnel office. Most frequently, those who fail the entrance examination (that is, they do not make the minimum score, which is usually set at 70 percent) will go on to other careers, although most jurisdictions allow for a retest after a specified period of time. The names of those who pass are forwarded to the police agency for any further in-house testing and screening.[27]

Another form of written examination for police applicants is the psychological screening test. There are two major concerns in using such tests to screen out applicants: stability and suitability. Candidates must be carefully screened in order to exclude those who are emotionally unstable, overly aggressive, or suffering from some personality disorder. The two primary tests of suitability of police candidates are the MMPI and the California Personality Inventory (CPI).[28] Stability is a major legal concern. If an officer commits a serious, harmful, and inappropriate act, the question of his or her stability will be raised, and the police agency may be asked to provide documentation about why the officer was deemed stable at the time of employment. It has been found that 2 to 5 percent of the police applicant pool may be eliminated due to severe emotional or mental problems.[29]

Physical Agility Test

Entry-level physical examinations range from a minimally acceptable number of push-ups to timed running and jumping tests to tests of strength and agility, such as dragging weights, pushing cars, leaping over six-foot walls, walking on horizontal ladders,

Physical agility is an important part of the police recruitment and training process.

(Courtesy Washoe County, Nevada, Sheriff's Office)

crawling through tunnels, and negotiating monkey bars. The problem is that very few of these activities are actually performed by police officers on the job.

The challenge for police executives, and an area of lawsuit vulnerability, is selecting a truly job-related physical agility test. Police agencies must determine the nature and extent of physical work performed by police officers and use that information to develop an instrument to measure applicants' ability to perform that work. One such test is based on the theory that police officers must perform three basic physical functions: getting to the problem (possibly needing to run, climb, vault, and so forth), resolving the problem (perhaps needing to fight or wrestle with an offender), and removing the problem (often requiring that the officer carry heavy weights). To establish the testing protocol for a given jurisdiction, the officers fill out written forms concerning the kinds of physical work that they performed each workday for one month. Information from the forms is then analyzed by computer and used to develop a physical agility test that accurately measures the recruit's ability to do the kinds of work performed by police officers in that specific locale.[30] If challenged in court, agencies using such tests can show that they test for the actual job requirements of their jurisdiction and do not discriminate on the basis of gender, race, height, age, and physical condition.

Personal Interview

As noted in Table 4-1, the personal interview is used by 98 percent of all police agencies as part of the selection process.[31] Candidates appear individually before one or more boards that are composed of members of the police agency and often the community. Candidates may also be asked to participate in a clinical interview with a psychologist; studies have indicated that the clinical interview complements the written psychological test.[32]

The purpose of the interview is to assess aspects of the candidate that cannot be measured on other tests, such as appearance, ability to communicate and reason (often using situational questions), and general poise and bearing. The interview is not normally well suited for judging character, dependability, initiative, or other such factors.

A primary advantage of the interview is that evaluators can ask applicants to explain how they would behave and use force in given situations because any number of possible scenarios exist. Following are five examples of the kinds of situations that might be posed to police applicants to see how well they think on their feet, develop appropriate responses, and prioritize their actions:

1. You are dispatched to a neighborhood park to check out a young man who is acting strangely. Upon arrival, you see the youth standing near a group of children playing on a merry-go-round. He is holding a .22-caliber rifle. What is your next action?

2. You are in the men's locker room at the end of your shift. You hear another male officer talking about a female officer's body. What do you do?

3. You are at home watching a football game on a weekend. Your neighbor comes to your door and frantically claims that his door has been kicked in and that he believes someone is inside. What do you do? What if the neighbor tells you that his daughter is upstairs in his house? How would you proceed?

4. You are in a downtown area making an arrest. A crowd gathers and you begin to hear comments about "police harassment." Soon the crowd becomes angry. How do you react?

5. You and another officer are responding to a burglary call at an office building. While searching the scene, you observe the other officer remove an expensive fountain pen from the top of a desk and put it in his pocket. What do you do?

Character Investigation

As indicated earlier, nearly all local police departments use background checks or character investigations—probably the most important element of the selection process. If done properly, the character investigation will also be one of the most time-consuming and costly elements of the process.

Character is one of the most subjective yet most important factors an applicant brings to the job, and it cannot be measured with data and interviews. A character investigation involves talking to the candidate's past and current friends, coworkers, teachers, neighbors, and employers. The applicant should be informed that references will be checked and that in the course of reviewing them, the investigation may spread to other references and others who are known to the applicant. No expense should be spared in talking with anyone who has personal knowledge of the candidate and can provide crucial information; if the job is done properly, the investigator will not only have a complete knowledge of the person's character but will also know where any skeletons may be buried in the applicant's background.

Polygraph Examination

As shown in Table 4-1, 25 percent of the nation's police agencies—including 77 percent of those that serve populations of 100,000 or more—conducted polygraph examinations as part of their selection process.[33] These agencies are willing to devote the extra resources necessary to help them determine that their applicants are honest and to secure higher-quality employees.

A survey of the benefits of polygraph examinations for police applicants by Richard Arther, director of the National Center of Lie Detection, supported the need for the polygraph for police recruitment[34]:

- An applicant for a police position in Lower Merion, Pennsylvania, came to that agency highly recommended by a police lieutenant and his employer at a home for blind, retarded children. During the polygraph examination, however, the applicant admitted to at least fifty instances of sexually abusing the children under his care.
- An applicant with the Wichita, Kansas, Police Department admitted to the polygraphist that he had been involved in many burglaries. The detective division was able to clear eight unsolved crimes as a result of the applicant's confession.
- A police officer in one California police department applied for employment in the Salinas, California, Police Department. He appeared to be a model police officer, was in excellent physical condition, and was familiar with state codes. His previous experience made him a potentially ideal candidate. However, during the polygraph exam, he admitted to having committed over a dozen burglaries while on duty and to having used his patrol car to haul away the stolen property. He also admitted to planting stolen narcotics on innocent suspects in order to make arrests and to having had sexual intercourse with girls as young as sixteen in his patrol car.
- An applicant for the San Diego Sheriff's Department admitted to that agency's polygraphist that on weekends he would go from bar to bar pretending to be drunk. He would then seek out people to pick fights with, since he could only have an erection and orgasm while inflicting pain on others. In addition to these sadistic tendencies, he also admitted that he got rid of his frustrations by savagely beating "niggers, Chicanos, and long-haired pukes who cause all the trouble."

These are but a few examples of how the investment of time and money for polygraph examinations can spare the public and police agencies a tremendous amount of trouble and expense later on. It is doubtful that few (if any) of these behaviors would have surfaced during the course of a personal interview or a background investigation. Polygraph testing is discussed in greater detail in Chapter 7 in connection with criminal investigations.

Medical Examination and Drug Screening

Someone once said that some police medical examinations are often of the "Can you hear thunder/see lightning?" variety—meaning that they are cursory at best. It is also widely believed that policing is only for those young people who are in peak physical condition. Whether these statements are facetious or not, it is certainly true that policing is no place for the physically unfit. Such officers would be a hazard not only to themselves but also to their coworkers. The job, with its stress, shift work, many hours of inactivity during patrol time, and other factors, can be physically debilitating even for veteran officers, especially those who fail to exercise and eat properly, so police administrators certainly do not want applicants who are unfit. The Federal Bureau of Investigation (FBI), for example, will not consider applicants whose weight exceeds the norm for their height and body type. Unfit personnel are thought to have lower energy levels, to give less attention to duty, and to take more sick days. Early retirement and disability often result, as well as increased operating expenses for replacing ill officers and hiring and training new permanent replacements.

More and more often, police agencies, like private-sector businesses, the military, and other sensitive government agencies, are compelling prospective employees to submit to a drug test. Substance abuse remains a very real problem in the workplace, resulting in poor productivity, lowered agency morale, and increased accidents and injuries.

Assessment Center

Recently, the use of an **assessment center** has become more popular with police agencies. While used by many departments for promotional testing and for hiring a chief executive, some agencies also use this method for hiring new personnel. An assessment center may include interviews; psychological tests; in-basket exercises; management tasks; group discussions; role-playing exercises, such as simulations of critical incidents or interviews with subordinates, the public, and news media; fact-finding exercises; oral presentation exercises; and written communication exercises. Behaviors and skills that are important to the successful performance of the position are identified and possibly weighted, and each candidate is evaluated on his or her ability to perform them.

Individual and group role-playing provides a hands-on atmosphere during the selection process. For example, candidates may be required to perform in simulated police-community problems (such as having candidates conduct a "meeting" to hear concerns of local minority groups), react to a major incident (such as a simulated shooting or riot situation), hold a news briefing, or participate in other such exercises. They may be given an in-basket situation, for example, assuming the role of the new chief or captain who

Role-playing scenarios are very effective for training academy recruits to handle difficult situations.

(Courtesy City of NYPD Photo Unit)

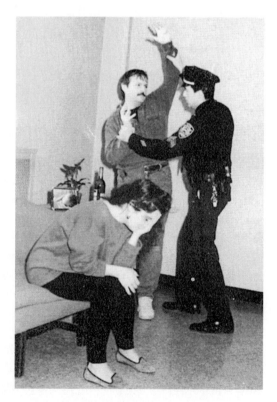

receives an abundance of paperwork, policies, and problems to be prioritized and dealt with in a prescribed amount of time. To evaluate candidates' writing abilities, they may be given a specified amount of time (30 minutes, for example) to develop a new use-of-force policy for a hypothetical or real police agency, allowing raters to assess candidates' written communication skills and their understanding of the technical side of police work, as well as the ways they think and build a case.

During each exercise, several assessors or raters analyze each candidate's performance and record some type of quantitative or qualitative evaluation score, which is then turned over to the hiring or promoting authority. Raters are typically selected who have held and now supervise the position for which candidates are testing. For example, if the assessment center is used to hire new officers, it would minimally be best that sergeants serve as raters (for promotion to sergeant, lieutenants should be raters, and so on).

Assessment centers are obviously more difficult logistically to conduct and are normally more labor-intensive and costly than traditional (mere interviewing) procedures, but they are well worth the extra investment. Monies invested at the early stages of a hiring or promotional process can help the agency to make the best hiring decisions and save untold problems for years to come.

FORMAL ENTRY INTO POLICING: ACADEMY TRAINING

Types of Academies

Today, with the concern for employing well-trained officers and avoiding civil liability lawsuits, **academy training** is regarded as a vital part of the hiring process, or as W. Clinton Terry puts it, as "another filter through which the candidate must successfully pass."[35] The recruit academy marks a major point in the career of officers-to-be; for many police agencies, academy training provides the bulk of the formal training that officers will acquire during their career. The academy also plays a significant role in shaping the officer's attitudes and is the beginning point for the officer's occupational socialization.

With in-house police academies, the department is authorized by some certifying body to train its own officers; there are also state and regional academies. Some police academies are operated by community colleges and universities. In a relatively new concept, civilians attend police academies at their own cost, hoping to gain employment as a free agent with a police agency after graduating and becoming formally certified. This preservice model is becoming more and more popular; police administrators are realizing tremendous savings by not paying salaries, registration fees, living expenses, and other costs that normally accrue while their employees receive academy training.

As shown in Table 4-3, the length of required academy recruit training varies tremendously by size of jurisdiction. The overall average is about 600 hours in the academy plus about 300 hours of field training, but the range is from about 1,000 hours in cities of 1 million population or more (and about 500 hours of field training) to less than 600 hours in cities of less than 2,500 (with about 200 hours of field training). Many metropolitan police agencies, some federal organizations (such as the FBI), and many state agencies

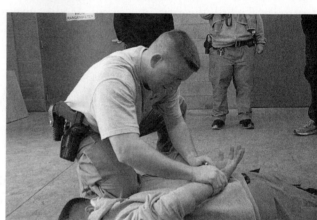

Police academy recruits engage in a variety of training activities.

(Courtesy City of NYPD Photo Unit [top left]; R. Brand [top right]; and Washoe County, Nevada, Sheriff's Office)

operate their own basic training academies, while several federal agencies send their personnel to the Federal Law Enforcement Training Center in Glynco, Georgia.

Curriculum: Current Status and Ongoing Need for Revision

Recruit training curricula vary from state to state, but most are heavily weighted toward the technical aspects of police work. Typically, today's basic recruit academy provides training in the following general areas: the criminal justice system, the law, human values and problems, patrol and investigation procedures, police proficiency (including armed and unarmed defense, riot and prisoner control, physical conditioning, and driver training), and administration (including departmental rules and regulations, policies, and organization).[36] More specifically, the modern training academy environment includes presentations about diverse cultural groups, dispute resolution, victim and witness assistance, field sobriety

TABLE 4-3

Training Requirements for New Officer Recruits in Local Police Departments, by Size of Population Served

| | AVERAGE NUMBER OF HOURS REQUIRED | | | | | |
| | Academy | | | Field | | |
Population Served	Total	State-Mandated	Other Required	Total	State-Mandated	Other Required
All sizes	628	588	40	326	147	179
1,000,000 or more	1,016	689	327	513	153	360
500,000–999,999	920	588	332	561	104	456
250,000–499,999	950	620	330	652	200	452
100,000–249,999	815	642	173	624	253	371
50,000–99,999	721	657	64	598	268	330
25,000–49,999	702	657	46	527	210	317
10,000–24,999	672	642	30	442	164	279
2,500–9,999	630	597	32	314	151	162
Under 2,500	577	542	35	199	106	93

Note: Average number of training hours excludes departments not requiring training.

Source: U.S. Department of Justice, Bureau of Justice Statistics, *Local Police Departments, 2003* (Washington, DC: Author, May 2006), p. 9.

tests, and use of computers. Modern recruits can expect to learn about proper radio procedures, recognition and management of stress, courtroom demeanor, and accurate report writing. Training may also be provided on such diverse topics as organized crime, state alcoholic beverage control, and wildlife and game laws.

John Broderick contended that there are essentially three types of police academies: the stress academy (or plebe system), the technical training model, and the college system.[37] The stress academy has been described as "a cross between Paris Island marine boot camp and college."[38]

Stress academies are intended to emphasize physical, mental, and emotional activities that transform the recruit into a disciplined police officer. Typically, many recruits drop out or lose their self-esteem.[39]

The technical training model, adopted by many departments, is like advanced military training in that it teaches useful operational skills and the use of equipment. The graduate of this program has technical competence. Officers who graduate are good at report writing, can cite many of the laws they are to enforce, know the radio code, have qualified with their weapons, and are able to testify in court. Critics of this model, however, contend that it requires only that recruits be receptive to the "pour it in with a funnel" approach of instructors and be able to recite what has been taught.

The third type of academy training often occurs in a college setting and stresses professionalism. The college system of academy training, which recognizes that recruits are

A recruit is sprayed with oleocapsicum. Officers often must learn from personal experience the effects of less-lethal weapons they will be carrying.

(Courtesy U.S. Customs and Border Protection, photographer Gerald L. Nino)

intelligent and capable of reasoning and decision making, has gotten a good deal of attention in recent years. Less emphasis is put on stress, discipline, and technical training; more focus is placed on discussion and problem analysis.

Studies indicate that upon entry into the academy, recruits are normally confident and believe that their success is all but guaranteed. John Van Maanen wrote that this level of confidence is not always justified:

> The individual usually feels upon swearing allegiance to the department, city, state and nation that "he's finally made it." However, the department instantaneously and somewhat rudely informs him that until he has served his probationary period he may be severed from the membership rolls at any time without warning, explanation or appeal. It is perhaps ironic that in a period of a few minutes, a person's position vis-a-vis the organization can be altered so dramatically.[40]

An analysis of the curricula of basic training academies in thirty states by David Bradford and Joan Pynes revealed that little has changed since 1986. Less than 3 percent of basic training academy time is spent in the cognitive and decision-making domain; the remaining time is spent in task-oriented activities. The exception is the Commonwealth of Massachusetts, which recently revised its basic curriculum so that now nearly all of its training is cognitive. According to the Massachusetts Criminal Justice Training Council, the objective of the cognitive training is to get the officer to "understand how to speak to, reason with, and listen to people and learn to use communication skills to manage a wide range of problematic situations. Physical tactics and tools, though readily available, are secondary to the primary response of communication."[41]

Bradford and Pynes assert that community-oriented policing and problem solving (COPPS, discussed in Chapter 6) requires the utilization of extensive cognitive and reasoning aptitudes and effective interpersonal skills and judgment. However, their examination of current basic training curricula found that problem solving and interpersonal skills development are low priorities of administrators and training directors.[42] Bradford and Pynes conclude that there is a lack of congruence between the curriculum taught in many police academies and the job responsibilities of COPPS officers; given the rapid spread of the COPPS approach, as well as the availability of related textbooks, they ask, "Why, then, are training academy curricula not changing?"[43]

New Demeanor and Uniform

As academy training begins, recruits adopt a new identity and a system of discipline in which they learn to take orders and not to question authority. They learn that loyalty to fellow officers, a professional demeanor and bearing, and respect for authority are highly valued in this occupation. The classroom teaches the recruit how to approach situations. Outside the classroom, as recruits share war stories discussed with academy staff, they informally transmit the proper attitudes to one another. Thus the recruits begin to form a collective understanding of policing and how they are supposed to function, and they gradually develop a common language and demeanor. Many people also believe that the police develop a swagger, a confident, authoritarian way of walking and presenting themselves. This is the beginning of the police officer's **working personality**.[44]

Recruits may wear a uniform for the first time during academy training, which is typically an awe-inspiring experience for them. The uniform sets them apart from society at large and conveys a sense of authority and responsibility to the recruit and to the public. "Image is everything," according to a popular saying, and the choice of agency uniform can go a long way toward setting the image and tone of the department. Police uniforms come in various colors, styles, and fabrics. Some agencies even have their officers wearing blue jeans or shorts and T-shirts (for beach patrol, for example).

The belt is one of the most important components of the patrol uniform and is certainly one of the heaviest. It often exceeds twenty pounds when laden with weapon, cuffs, baton, radio, flashlight, extra ammunition, chemical weapons, and so on. The uniform hat comes in several styles and is probably the piece of equipment that most readily identifies the officer and the department's image; each type of hat makes a certain statement to the public about the officer and his or her authority. The officer's badge also conveys a tremendous sense of authority. The most popular are customized shields, incorporating everything from the state motto and seal to symbols that convey the agency's image and philosophy. When designing its badge, a police department considers its tradition and history as well as those of the community.[45]

Suspicion: The "Sixth Sense"

Police recruits are taught to nurture a **"sixth sense"**: suspicion. A suspicious nature is as important to the street officer as a fine touch is to a surgeon. The officer should not only be able to visually recognize but also be able to physically sense when something is wrong or out of the ordinary. A Chicago Police Department bulletin stated:

> Actions, dress, [and] location of a person often classify him as suspicious in the mind of a police officer. Men loitering near schools, public toilets, playgrounds and swimming pools may be sex perverts. Men loitering near…any business at closing time may be robbery suspects. Men or youths walking along looking into cars may be car thieves or looking for something to steal. Persons showing evidence of recent injury, or whose clothing is disheveled, may be victims or participants in an assault or strong-arm robbery.[46]

Officers are trained to be observant, to develop an intimate knowledge of the territory and people, and to "notice the normal….Only then can [they] decide what persons or cars under what circumstances warrant the appellation 'suspicious.'"[47] They must recognize when someone or something needs to be checked out. The following observations often warrant a field investigation[48]:

- People who do not "belong" where they are observed
- Automobiles that do not "look right" (such as dirty cars with clean license plates or a vehicle with plates attached with wire or in another unusual fashion)
- Businesses that are open at odd hours or that are not operating according to routine or custom
- People who exhibit exaggerated unconcern over contact with the officer or who are visibly "rattled" when near the officer
- Solicitors or peddlers who are in a residential neighborhood
- Lone males who sit in cars near a shopping center or near a school paying unusual attention to women or children
- Persons who are hitchhikers
- Persons who wear a coat on a hot day

The academy also teaches neophyte officers that their major tool is their body; like mountain climbers, acrobats, or athletes, their body is an essential tool for the performance of their trade. The gun and nightstick initially fascinate the recruits, but until they are adequately trained, officers using them would be more a menace to society than a protector. Proper handling and safety measures are drilled into the recruits—the message is unequivocal that recruits will not be trusted with these potentially lethal weapons until they become proficient in their use. The new officers must be taught to measure their capacity to do the job, to assess carefully the physical capabilities of people they confront on the street, and to determine whether someone can be subdued without assistance or the risk of injury if a physical altercation should develop.[49]

The officers are also told, however, that they cannot approach every situation with the holster unsnapped or baton raised or twirling; they must demonstrate poise and not be eager to use force. It is constantly instilled in them that the days of the club-swinging cop are gone. Thus, knowing that the body is a tool, the recruits are taught how to unobtrusively position themselves, whether at a vehicle stop or while engaged in a discussion on the street, in order to gain a physical advantage should trouble arise. They are taught when to use force and when to relent, to always keep control of the situation, and to feel that they would emerge victorious should force be required. Thus, in addition to weapons training, they may be given some weaponless defense training, including some holds that can be applied to subjects to bring them into compliance.

Recruits are taught some aspects of human nature and are encouraged not to be prejudicial in their actions or speech. They learn to deal with criminal suspects, offenders, victims, and witnesses and to be suspicious of "eyewitness" accounts. (For example, twenty-five "witnesses" claimed that they helped carry Abraham Lincoln from Ford Theater into the little house where he died; eight different people said they held his head, and eighty-four people said they were in the room that night.[50])

Recruits often participate in hands-on training, practicing their new techniques in the field in simulated situations. Quite possibly the ultimate in hands-on training occurs at the Hogan's Alley complex at the FBI Academy in Quantico, Virginia, which opened in 1987 and covers almost thirty-five acres. This facility combines training, office, and classroom space on one site, increasing training effectiveness. Hogan's Alley (the name given many early-twentieth-century training facilities, apparently after an old comic strip about mischievous Irish kids) resembles a fully developed urban area. The set includes a business area and a residential street with townhouses and apartments. The use of movie-set techniques gives the illusion of depth and space. All furnishings—including a fleet of cars, furniture, desks, and even a pool table—were forfeited by convicted criminals. Federal agents are trained in the practical skills of crime-scene investigation and photography, surveillance techniques, arrest mechanics, and investigative skills. Trainees participate in paintball gunfights with persons role-playing criminals.

Other methods of police training that are currently used include **computer-based training (CBT)**, electronic bulletin boards, satellite training and teleconferencing, online computer forums, and correspondence courses. With computer costs declining, CBT is becoming increasingly popular and has been shown to be very effective. As CBT simulates real-life situations through the use of computer-modeled problems, it closely duplicates the way we think. One study found that police officers who learned about the exclusionary rule (discussed in Chapter 8) through CBT understood the material significantly better than the non-CBT control group.[51]

Virtual reality is another available (although very costly) form of police training. Trainees wear a head-mounted device that restricts their vision to two monitors and projects a computer-generated three-dimensional illusion that engulfs the senses of sight, sound, and touch. Virtual reality may one day be commonly used for training police officers in such areas as pursuit driving, firearms training, critical-incident management, and crime-scene processing.

Finally, graduation day arrives, and the academy experience becomes a rite of passage. Graduation also means new uniforms, associates, and responsibilities and a raise in pay and status. As Arthur Niederhoffer observed, for many officers academy graduation is a worthy substitute for a college education. But "the very next morning the graduate is rudely dumped into a strange precinct where he must prove himself."[52]

The FBI's Hogan's Alley.

(Courtesy Federal Bureau of Investigation)

POSTACADEMY FIELD TRAINING

Field Training Officer (FTO) Program

Once the recruits leave the academy, their knowledge of and acceptance into the police subculture are not yet complete. Another very important part of this acquisition process is being assigned to a veteran officer for initial field instruction and observation in what is sometimes called a **field training officer (FTO) program**. The oldest formal FTO program began in the San Jose, California, Police Department in 1972.[53] This training program provides recruits with an opportunity to make the transition from the academy to the streets under the protective arm of a veteran officer. Recruits are on probationary status, normally ranging from six months to one year; they understand that they may be immediately terminated if their overall performance is unsatisfactory during that period. Figure 4-2 is a flowchart of the San Jose FTO program.

Most FTO programs consist of four identifiable phases: an introductory phase (the recruit learns agency policies and local laws), the training and evaluation phases (the recruit is introduced to more complicated tasks that patrol officers confront), and a final phase (the FTO acts strictly as an observer and evaluator while the recruit performs all the functions of a patrol officer).[54] The National Institute of Justice (NIJ), surveying nearly six hundred police agencies, found that 64 percent had an FTO program and that such programs had reduced the number of civil liability suits filed against their officers and against standardized training programs.[55] The length of time rookies are assigned to FTOs will vary; a formal FTO program might require close supervision for a range of one to twelve weeks.

Although some police officers end their formal training with the conclusion of academy and field training, most police officers receive in-service training throughout their careers. Most states require a minimum number of hours of in-service training for police officers, and many departments exceed the minimum requirement. News items, court decisions, and other relevant information can be covered at roll call before the beginning of each shift. Short courses ranging from a few hours to several weeks are available for in-service officers through several means such as videos and nationally televised training programs.

With the ever-changing laws and methods of policing and the constant specter of liability, such ongoing training is essential—police officers must keep abreast of current changes in their field. As Roger Dunham and Geoffrey Alpert put it, "Whether an officer is overweight or out of shape, a poor shot, uses poor judgment, or is too socialized into the police subculture to provide good community policing, in-service training can be used to restore the officer's skills or to improve his attitude."[56]

Police Training Officer (PTO) Program

There is another new approach to training new officers that is slowly gaining traction across the nation; as with the FTO program discussed above, it is multifaceted and is an in-depth method: the **police training officer (PTO) program**. A PTO program seeks to take the traditional FTO program to a higher level, one that embraces new officers and evaluates them on their understanding and application of community-oriented policing and problem solving (COPPS, discussed in Chapter 6).

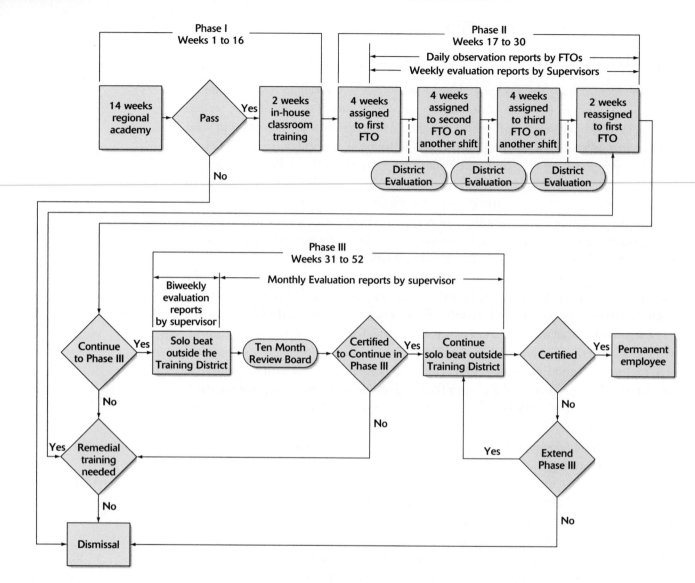

FIGURE 4-2

Flowchart for the Field Training Officer (FTO) Program for the San Jose, California, Police Department

Source: M. S. McCampbell, Field Training for Police Agencies: The State of the Art *(Washington, DC: U.S. Department of Justice, National Institute of Justice, 1987), pp. 4–6.*

With a half million dollars in federal assistance, training needs were assessed and a new PTO program was recently initiated in the Reno, Nevada, Police Department and at five other national sites. Its theoretical underpinnings include adult and problem-based learning. The PTO program covers two primary training areas: substantive topics (the most common policing activities) and core competencies (the required common skills which officers engage in and which are required in the daily performance of their duties). New officers must successfully pass fifteen core competencies, specific skills, knowledge, and abilities that have been identified as essential for good policing. There is a learning

A Problem-Based
Learning Manual
for Training and Evaluating
Police Trainees

pto
manual

The federal Office of Community Oriented Policing Services publishes a manual on the PTO approach for training new police officers.

(Courtesy U.S. Department of Justice, Office of Community Oriented Policing Services)

matrix that serves as a guide for trainees and trainers during the training period and that demonstrates the interrelationships between the daily policing activities and core competencies during the eight phases of the PTO program.[57]

New Technology

New technology in the training function includes software known as ADORE (for Automated Daily Observation Report and Evaluation). FTOs in several agencies now field-testing the software find that it saves them time because they do not have to write reports for each recruit by hand. ADORE, which can be accessed through either a laptop or a Palm Pilot, allows FTOs to take computerized notes while watching trainees at work; it also reduces paperwork by allowing trainers to easily compile numbers for evaluating performance in dozens of categories. The software is credited with reducing FTO burnout, which is often a part of the paper-intensive evaluation process.[58]

Another new form of technology for police training that is being tested involves pursuit simulation. The training simulator is thought to be an effective means of determining how and when a vehicle pursuit should be halted. In one scenario, trainees in a simulated pursuit swerve around computerized images of a transit bus, a produce truck, a minivan, and a child on a skateboard before the chased vehicle enters a school zone, where the officer should end the hot pursuit. These simulated pursuits also allow supervisors to see how well trainees conduct themselves in accordance with their agency's pursuit policy, which is often several pages long.[59]

WORKING PERSONALITY: HAVING THE "RIGHT STUFF"

Development and Use of a Police Personality

Since William Westley first wrote about the police subculture in 1950, the notion of a police personality has become a popular area of study. In 1966, Jerome Skolnick[60] described what he termed the *working personality* of the police. He determined that the police role contained two important variables: danger and authority. Danger is a constant feature of police work. Police officers, constantly facing potential violence, are warned at the academy to be cautious and are told many war stories of officers shot and killed at domestic disturbances or traffic stops. Consequently, they develop a "perceptual shorthand," Skolnick said, that they use to identify certain kinds of people as "symbolic assailants"—individuals whom the officer has come to recognize as potentially violent based on their gestures, language, and attire.

The police, as Skolnick stated, represent authority, but unlike doctors, ministers, and the like, they must establish their authority. The symbols of that authority—the gun, the badge, and the baton—assist them, but officers' behavior and confidence are more important in social situations. As William Westley said, an officer "expects rage from the underprivileged and the criminal but understanding from the middle classes: the professionals, the merchants and the white-collar workers. They, however, define him as a servant, not as a colleague, and the rejection is hard to take."[61] Thus officers cannot even depend on their symbols and position of authority in dealing with the public; they are often confused when the public does not automatically observe and accept their authority.

Considerable research has compared the personality characteristics of the police with those of the general public,[62] and a number of differences have been discovered. One study found the average officer to be more intelligent, assertive, dependable, straightforward, and conscientious than civilians.[63] Other researchers who recently studied state traffic officers and deputy sheriffs using the MMPI and CPI scales reported that the officers scored high on the values of achievement, strong work ethic, ambition, leadership potential, and organizational skills.[64] Studies have also found conservatism and a high degree of cynicism among officers, although those traits are found to be present in much of the society at large. The late LAPD Chief William Parker asserted that police were "conservative, ultraconservative, and very right wing."[65]

Niederhoffer reported his classic study of **police cynicism** in 1967, using the NYPD as the site of a longitudinal study.[66] He found that although typical recruits begin their career without a trace of cynicism, police cynicism spikes most dramatically immediately after they leave the basic academy. This is probably because they confront the reality of the streets—the pain and criminality of society—and perhaps lose friends. Cynical veteran peers frequently reinforce the worst aspects of the job. In the period of about two to six years of service, the cynicism level continues to increase, but at a slower rate. The recruit has begun to adapt to the occupation and the people to be dealt with every day. At about mid-career (about eight to thirteen years of service), the cynicism level actually begins to decline, possibly because the officer has accepted the job and has been promoted, earns a decent salary and benefits, and realizes that he or she is about halfway to retirement. Toward the end of the career, the degree of cynicism levels off; for many officers, this is a period of coasting toward retirement.

A police officer's view of humanity may become distorted and cynical because many of the people the police deal with are offenders. They see what they feel are miscarriages of justice, such as improper or lenient court decisions, perjury on the witness stand, plea bargaining (where defendants are allowed to plead guilty to less serious offenses than charged or to fewer counts than charged, and observe fellow officers who do not live up to their code of ethics. Cynicism does have a protective feature, however: It can help to make the officer callous, allowing him or her to observe things that would sicken or horrify the average citizen without becoming mentally debilitated.

John Broderick[67] presented another view of the working personality of the police. He believed that there are actually four types of police personalities: enforcers, idealists, realists, and optimists. Enforcers are officers who believe that the job of the police consists primarily of keeping their beats clean, making good arrests, and sometimes helping people. These officers have sympathy for vagrants, the elderly, the working poor, and others whom they see as basically good people. However, drug users, cop haters, and others frustrate the efforts of enforcers to make them "good," which makes the enforcers very unhappy. Thus they have high job dissatisfaction and an attitude of resentment, feeling that a lot of people are hostile toward them.

Idealists, according to Broderick, are officers who put high value on individual rights and due process. They also believe that it is their duty to keep the peace, protect citizens from criminals, and generally preserve the social order. As a group with a high percentage of college graduates, their commitment to the job is the lowest of the four groups, and they are less likely to recommend the job to a son or daughter.

Realists place relatively little emphasis on either social order or individual rights, Broderick says. They seem less frustrated, having found a way to come to terms with a difficult job. For them, the reality of the job consists of manila envelopes and properly completed forms. Realists see many problems in policing, such as special privileges given to politicians. Reality is not warm bodies to be dealt with but rather the paperwork that the bodies leave behind. They work well in the ordered, predictable environment of a police records room.

Broderick's last group, the optimists, also places a relatively high value on individual rights. Like idealists, they see their job as people oriented instead of crime oriented. They see policing as providing opportunities to help people; they view the television version of policing as totally unrealistic and find it rewarding to spend the majority of their time in service activities. Optimists have the lowest amount of job resentment, are committed to the job, and would choose policing as a career all over again. They enjoy the mental challenge of problem solving.

What Traits Make a Good Cop?

It is not too difficult to identify a bad cop through his or her unethical or criminal behavior. It is probably more difficult for the average person to identify the **traits of good officers**. How can a quantitative measure assess the work of police? Is it possible to judge the quality of an officer's work? These are challenging questions for police supervisors.

A major obstacle to assessing police performance rests with the nature of police work generally and the variation in the kinds of work performed by different shifts. The police role varies according to whether the officer is assigned to the day shift, evening (swing) shift, or night (graveyard) shift. (See Chapter 5 for a description of how police work varies by shift.)

Dennis Nowicki[68] acknowledged that while certain characteristics form the foundation of a police officer—honesty, ethics, and moral character—no scientific formula can be used to create a highly effective officer. However, he compiled twelve qualities that he believes are imperative for entry-level police officers:

1. *Enthusiasm.* Believing in what one is doing and going about even routine duties with a certain vigor that is almost contagious.
2. *Good communications skills.* Having highly developed speaking and listening skills and interacting equally well with a wealthy person or someone lower on the socioeconomic ladder.
3. *Good judgment.* Having wisdom and the ability to make good analytic decisions based on an understanding of the problem.
4. *Sense of humor.* Being able to laugh and smile in order to help oneself cope with regular exposure to human pain and suffering.
5. *Creativity.* Using creative techniques to place oneself in the mind of the criminal and accomplish legal arrests.
6. *Self-motivation.* Making things happen, proactively solving difficult cases, and creating one's own luck.
7. *Knowing the job and the system.* Understanding the role of a police officer and the intricacies of the justice system, knowing what the administration requires, and using both formal and informal channels to be effective.

8. *Ego.* Believing one is a good officer and having the self-confidence that enables one to solve difficult crimes.

9. *Courage.* Being able to meet physical and psychological challenges, thinking clearly during times of high stress, admitting when one is wrong, and standing up for what is right.

10. *Discretion.* Enforcing the spirit of the law (not the letter of the law), giving people a break, showing empathy, and not being hard-nosed, hardheaded, or hard-hearted.

11. *Tenacity.* Staying focused, seeing challenges rather than obstacles, and viewing failure not as a setback but as an experience.

12. *Thirst for knowledge.* Being aware of new laws and court decisions and always learning (from the classroom but also via informal discussions with other officers).

ROLES, FUNCTIONS, AND STYLES OF POLICING

Definition and Knowledge of the Police Role

Why do the police exist? What are they supposed to do? Often these questions are given oversimplified answers such as "They enforce the law" or "They 'serve and protect.' "[69]

But policing is much more complex. As Herman Goldstein put it, "Anyone attempting to construct a workable definition of the police role will typically come away with old images shattered and with a newfound appreciation for the intricacies of police work."[70] Even with all of the movies and television series depicting police in action, most Americans probably still do not have an accurate idea of what the police really do. This confusion is quite understandable because the police are called on to perform an almost countless number of tasks. Police are even used as prosecutors in some states, such as New Hampshire.

Who defines the police role? There are several groups and individuals who do[71]:

- Private citizens influence the nature of the police role through their contacts with the police, by participation in COPPS groups (discussed in Chapter 6), and through the election of public officials who set policy and appoint police administrators.

- Legislative bodies influence the role of the police by enacting statutes, both those that govern the police and those that the police use to govern others. In addition, legislative bodies determine police department budgets.

- The courts actively police the police by handing down decisions that regulate police conduct.

- Executives such as city managers and prosecutors help to define the police role by determining the types of cooperative agreements and evidence necessary for a prosecutable case.

- Police officers themselves define their roles by choosing to intervene in some incidents while ignoring others.

One of the greatest obstacles to understanding the American police is the crime fighter image. Many people believe that the role of the police is confined to law enforcement: the prevention and detection of crime and the apprehension of criminals. This is not an accurate view of contemporary policing.[72] It does not describe what the police do on a daily basis.

First, only about 20 percent of the police officer's typical day is devoted to fighting crime per se.[73] As Jerome Skolnick and David Bayley point out, the crimes that terrify Americans the most—robbery, rape, burglary, and homicide—are rarely encountered by police on patrol: "Only 'Dirty Harry' has his lunch disturbed by a bank robbery in progress. Patrol officers individually make few important arrests. The 'good collar' is a rare event. Cops spend most of their time passively patrolling and providing emergency services."[74]

The crime fighter image persists, although it is extremely harmful to the public and individual officers.[75] The public suffers from this image because it gives rise to unrealistic expectations about the ability of the police to catch criminals. The image harms individual officers, who believe that rewards and promotions are tied only to success in capturing criminals. Also, many individuals enter policing expecting it to be exciting and rewarding, as depicted on television and in the movies. Later they learn that much of their time is spent with boring, mundane tasks that are anything but glamorous, that much of the work is trivial, and that paperwork is seldom stimulating.

Role Conflicts

Role conflicts may develop with officers and their departments. A family disturbance is a good example. Assume that Jane Smith reports to the police that her husband, John, is assaulting her. Police officers must respond to the disturbance, and the law empowers them to intervene, to enforce the law, and to maintain order. For the combatants, it is a very trying experience, not only because their family is dysfunctional but also because the police have been summoned to their home. Veteran officers might view the domestic call as trivial and inconvenient, leaving the scene as quickly as possible to go perform "real" police duties.

By the same token, the role of the police is often in the eye of the beholder. For example, the domestic argument just described might best seem to fit the category of maintaining order. However, if the responding officers are trained in crisis intervention or if they refer the couple to counseling, they are providing a social service. On the other hand, if John is found to have assaulted Jane, it is likely a criminal matter. If the police make an arrest or even just assist Jane in swearing out a warrant, the matter becomes a law enforcement issue. The category to which this incident is assigned will vary greatly from agency to agency, officer to officer, and researcher to researcher, making it difficult to draw any solid conclusions about the police role.

Still, it is important to be as explicit as possible about the police role for several reasons. First, we can recruit and select competent police personnel only when we have a clear vision of what the police are supposed to accomplish. Second, evaluation for retention and promotion is useful only to the extent that we evaluate in terms of what the police are supposed to do. Third, budgetary decisions should be based on an accurate analysis of police roles. Fourth, efficiency and effectiveness in police organizations depend on accurate task descriptions. Finally, public cooperation with the police depends on developing reasonable expectations of the roles of the police and the public.[76]

The police must identify those crimes on which police resources should be concentrated, focusing on the crimes that generate the most public fear and economic loss. The chief executive should have written policies to ensure that the police mission and the objectives used to achieve that mission are maintained by the police department. In other words, it is not enough for the police to "maintain order" or "provide justice." A police department may use many methods to maintain order and provide justice. In China or Saudi Arabia, those methods would be far different from those generally employed in the United States. But would "justice" result? In America, the police must maintain order without resorting to extralegal means or violating human rights.

Policing Functions and Styles

Officers may be said to perform four basic **policing functions**: (1) enforcing the laws, (2) performing services (such as maintaining or assisting animal-control units, reporting burned-out street lights or damaged traffic signs, delivering death messages, checking the welfare of people in their homes, delivering blood), (3) preventing crime (patrolling, providing the public with information on crime prevention), and (4) protecting the innocent (by investigating crimes, police are systematically removing innocent people from consideration as crime suspects).

James Q. Wilson[77] looked at the functions of the police differently, determining that the police perform two basic functions: maintaining order (peacekeeping) and enforcing the law. Maintaining order constitutes most of the activities of the police; as noted earlier, less than 20 percent of the calls answered by police are directly related to crime control or law enforcement. Much of an officer's time is spent with such service activities as traffic control and routine patrol. Indeed, in some cases the police deliberately avoid enforcing the law in an attempt to maintain order. For example, if the police know of a busy street where many drivers speed, they may desist from setting up a speed trap during rush hours so as not to impede the flow of traffic and possibly cause accidents.

Enforcing the law means upholding the statutes, but this is not as simple and straightforward a function as it might seem. First, the police are really not very good at performing the law enforcement function; they have not traditionally been successful at preventing crime or providing long-term solutions to neighborhood disorder (although the relatively new community-policing and problem-solving concepts are addressing this shortcoming). Second, there are several types of crime—such as white-collar crime—with which the local police seldom deal. Third, the police, representing only about 2.3 officers per 1,000 population in the United States, cannot effectively control the public alone. Finally, the police are successful in solving only a fraction of the property and personal crimes that occur.[78]

Wilson also maintained that there are three distinctive **policing styles**[79]:

1. *Watchman style.* The watchman style involves the officer as a "neighbor." Here, officers act as if order maintenance (rather than law enforcement) is their primary function. The emphasis is on using the law as a means of maintaining order rather than regulating conduct through arrests. Police ignore many common minor violations, such as traffic and juvenile offenses. These violations and so-called victimless crimes, such as gambling and prostitution, are tolerated and will often be handled informally. Thus the individual officer has wide latitude concerning whether to enforce the letter or the spirit of the law; the emphasis is on using the law to give people what

they "deserve." It assumes that some people, such as juveniles, are occasionally going to "act up."

2. *Legalistic style.* A legalistic style casts the officer as a "soldier." This style takes a much harsher view of law violations: Police officers issue large numbers of traffic citations, detain a high volume of juvenile offenders, and act vigorously against illicit activities, and large numbers of other kinds of arrests occur as well. Chief administrators want high arrest and ticketing rates not only because violators should be punished but also because it reduces the opportunity for their officers to engage in corrupt behavior. This style of policing assumes that the purpose of the law is to punish.

3. *Service style.* The service style views the officer as a "teacher." This style falls in between the watchman and legalistic styles. The police take seriously all requests for either law enforcement or order maintenance (unlike in the watchman-style department) but are less likely to respond by making an arrest or otherwise imposing formal sanctions. Police officers see their primary responsibility as protecting public order against the minor and occasional threats posed by unruly teenagers and "outsiders" (tramps, derelicts, out-of-town visitors). The citizenry expects its service-style officers to display the same qualities as its department store salespeople: They should be courteous, neat, and deferential. The police will frequently use informal sanctions instead of making arrests.

Which Role, Function, and Style Are Typically Employed?

As we have seen, the role, function, and style of the police will differ by time and place. They will also be fluid within the agency, changing with the times, the political climate, and the problems of the day. Most police agencies do not determine which problems they address; rather, they respond to the problems that citizens believe are important, and the police agencies depend on the goals set by the community, the chief executive, and the individual officers. Sometimes roles, functions, and styles overlap, but most of the time they are distinct.

SUMMARY

We began this chapter with a look at the officer's world and an explanation of how private citizens are socialized into their role as police officers and prepared for working the street; an emphasis was placed on viewing these officers as individuals rather than in the aggregate, as is often the case. The reader has seen how people are recruited, tested, and trained for their role as police officers through a series of "hurdles"; during this process they are transformed psychologically, physically, and emotionally to become competent and to function in the very challenging world of the police.

We have established that a working personality develops in police officers. Both formal training and peer relations are instructive and helpful in teaching the novice officer how to act, think, and view certain elements of the job. Unfortunately, it was shown that danger, suspicion, constantly witnessing of the seedy side of humanity, and other factors also tend to inculcate in police officers another common trait: cynicism.

This chapter also examined the roles, functions, and styles of the local police in America. More than a century and a half after the adoption of the early British model of policing (discussed in Chapter 1), there is still widespread disagreement, conflict, and debate concerning what we truly want our police to do, represent, and become.

The hiring process described in this chapter is certainly the ideal rather than the real. Probably few of the seventeen thousand American police agencies compel their applicants to successfully complete the entire battery of tests and screening examinations described here, nor do all departments have the inclination or resources to engage in a full-fledged FTO or PTO program that would monitor and further train new recruits. It is also doubtful that formal education requirements are being elevated for or acquired by police at the rate of the society at large. Yet the present recruitment and training process seems to work well overall, except in those instances where a jurisdiction, sorely needing personnel, engages in rapid hiring and can easily bring substandard people into the field.

KEY TERMS

academy training
assessment center
computer-based training (CBT)
field training officer (FTO) program
hurdle process
police cynicism
police training officer (PTO) program
policing functions
policing styles
recruiting
"sixth sense"
traits of good officers
working personality

REVIEW QUESTIONS

1. What are some of the problems confronting today's police recruiters and some of the unique measures they use to obtain a viable applicant pool?

2. What is generally the hiring process of new police officers and the kinds of tests that are commonly given to applicants?

3. Which kinds of skills and knowledge are imparted to police trainees during their academy training, and what are the typical subjects that are taught in a police academy curriculum?

4. What are the methods and purposes of the FTO and PTO programs?

5. What is meant by the term *working personality,* how was the concept developed, and what is its function?

6. What is police cynicism, and how does it operate?

7. Review the ideal traits of police officers.

8. Explain why the crime fighter image is the greatest obstacle in accepting a realistic view of the police role.

9. What are the primary functions and styles of policing?

INDEPENDENT STUDENT ACTIVITIES

1. Visit your city or county human resources office to learn about police recruitment and hiring methods, including the desired qualities of candidates, the various kinds of tests given, and the length of academy training.

2. Interview local police officers to learn about their socialization into the police subculture, including the academy experience, their adjustment to being "set apart" from society by wearing a police uniform, their development of a "sixth sense," and their general development of a working personality.

3. Ask local police executives whether they believe that police officers should possess a college degree (and why or why not). Learn about any educational incentive programs that local agencies offer. Ask the interviewees what constitutes a "good" police officer.

4. Meet with female and minority officers to learn of the unique challenges they encountered upon entering law enforcement.

RELATED WEB SITES

Equal Employment Opportunity Commission
http://www.eeoc.gov

National Association of Police Organizations
http://www.napo.org

National Law Enforcement Trainers Association
http://www.nleta.com

PART II

POLICING AS WORK
PATROLLING, PROBLEM SOLVING, DETECTING

This part shows the various forms of police work. First, Chapter 5 considers methods employed and dangers confronted while on patrol. Next, in Chapter 6, we review the philosophy and strategies—and indeed the current era—of contemporary policing: community-oriented policing and problem solving. Then in Chapter 7, we look at the rapidly developing field of criminal investigation, including its history, the various methods and activities, and the role of investigative personnel.

ON PATROL

METHODS AND MENACES

The nature of police work is often eight hours of boredom interrupted by five minutes of terror. Nothing is "routine" because you never know if you're going to be involved with Miss America driving her kids around or a convicted felon with a gun.
—*A western U.S. police lieutenant, after a fellow officer was recently shot in the head (the officer survived)*

The wicked flee when no man pursueth, but the righteous are bold as a lion.
—*Inscription on the National Law Enforcement Officers Memorial in Washington, D.C., from Proverbs 28:1*

LEARNING OBJECTIVES

AS A RESULT OF READING THIS CHAPTER, THE STUDENT WILL:

- UNDERSTAND THE GENERAL NATURE OF PATROL, INCLUDING HOW THE PATROL FUNCTION IS AFFECTED BY THE OFFICER'S SHIFT ASSIGNMENT AND THE NATURE OF THE BEAT TO WHICH HE OR SHE IS ASSIGNED

- BE AWARE OF SOME OF THE HAZARDS THAT ARE INHERENT IN POLICE WORK AND PATROL FUNCTIONS, AND KNOW THE NEWLY ENACTED PIECE OF LEGISLATION THAT ALLOWS RETIRED OFFICERS TO CARRY THEIR WEAPONS

- KNOW HOW THE PATROL VEHICLE HAS EVOLVED AND IS USED TODAY

- BE ABLE TO LIST SEVERAL OF THE MAJOR STUDIES AND FINDINGS OF THE PATROL FUNCTION

- BE ABLE TO DEFINE WHAT IS MEANT BY POLICE DISCRETION, AND UNDERSTAND SOME OF ITS ADVANTAGES AND DISADVANTAGES AS WELL AS THE FACTORS THAT CAN ENTER INTO THE OFFICER'S DECISION-MAKING PROCESS

- KNOW THE NATURE AND IMPORTANCE OF THE TRAFFIC FUNCTION IN PATROL WORK

INTRODUCTION

The patrol function has long been viewed as the backbone of policing, the most important and visible part of police work. It is the primary means by which the police fulfill their mission. Patrol officers are the eyes and ears of the police organization, the worker bees of community policing and problem solving, the initial responders and protectors of the crime scene, and typically the first police representative whom citizens meet. All other specialized units either directly or indirectly support the patrol function. Patrol is where the art of policing is learned, citizens go to lodge concerns and complaints, and needs of the community are met. Significantly, all police chiefs, sheriffs, and other high-ranking personnel began their careers as patrol officers.

Indeed, this chapter serves as a prologue to many different kinds of police activities described in later chapters, all of which branch off from the patrol function. Because patrol duties normally involve 60 to 70 percent of a police agency's workforce, this task has been a topic of considerable interest and analysis.

In addition to the patrol function, the work of policing also revolves around the discretionary use of authority. Patrol officers possess a wide range of options as they go about the business of patrolling, including whether or not to stop and question or cite someone, to arrest, to use force, or to shoot. From the relatively innocuous traffic stop to the use of lethal force, many choices are involved, including some with serious consequences.

This chapter begins by describing the culture of the beat; included are sections concerning the purposes and nature of patrol, patrol work as a function of shift and beat assignment, and the extent and kinds of violence and occupational hazards that may be confronted while officers are on patrol. Then we consider an often overlooked yet extremely important tool for patrol: the patrol vehicle. Next is an overview of what research has revealed concerning the patrol function. Following that is an examination of the discretionary use of police authority, a review of the factors and political considerations that can enter into an officer's decision-making process, and the advantages and disadvantages of such discretionary authority. After an examination of another function that is closely related to patrol—traffic—the chapter concludes with a summary, key terms, review questions, independent student activities, and related Web sites.

Two closely related topics that are at the heart of the patrol function are discussed in later chapters: community-oriented policing and problem solving (Chapter 6) and the tools and high technology used by patrol officers in the performance of their duties, including less-lethal weapons (Chapter 14).

PATROL AS WORK: CULTURE OF THE BEAT

Purposes and Nature of Patrol

In Chapter 4, we discussed the role and functions of the police, including the four basic tasks of policing: preventing crime, enforcing the laws, protecting the innocent, and providing services. In this section, we expand that discussion by looking at the **beat culture**, or some of the methods and problems that are connected with the **patrol function**.

Police work has certainly changed since 1910, when Leonard Fuld observed that "the policeman's life is a lazy life in as much as his time is spent doing nothing."[1] Today there is a myriad of duties for the patrol officer to perform, and danger is a constant adversary.

When not handling calls for service, today's officers frequently engage in problem-solving activities (see Chapter 6) and in random preventive patrol, hoping to deter crime with a police presence. There are several forms of preventive patrol, including automobile, foot, bicycle, horse, motorcycle, marine, helicopter, and even snowmobile patrols. During all of these, the officer is alert for activities and people who seem out of the ordinary. The traditional method of **deployment** of patrol officers should take into account the where and when of crime, attempting to distribute available personnel at the places and the times of day and days of week when trouble and crime seem to occur with greatest frequency. Unfortunately, many departments still deploy their patrol officers in their jurisdictions by using convenient beat dividers, such as streets or bodies of water, instead of analyzing when and where crime and other disturbances are taking place.

Patrol officers also attempt to effect good relations with the people on their beat, realizing that they cannot apprehend criminals or even maintain a quiet sector without public assistance. In many ways, the success of the entire police agency depends on the skill and work of the patrol officers. For example, upon arriving at a crime scene, they must protect and collect evidence, treat and interview victims, locate and interview suspects and witnesses, and make important discretionary decisions such as whether to arrest someone and even perhaps whether to use their weapons.

The American Bar Association offered the following major purposes of police patrol[2]:

- To deter crime by maintaining a visible police presence
- To maintain public order
- To enable the police department to respond quickly to law violations or other emergencies
- To identify and apprehend law violators
- To aid individuals and care for those who cannot help themselves
- To facilitate the movement of traffic and people
- To create a sense of security in the community

Officers must become very knowledgeable about their **beat assignments**: They must be familiar with such details as where the doors and windows of buildings are, where the alleys are, where smaller businesses are located, and how the residential areas they patrol are laid out. Officers must learn what is normal on their beats and thus be able to discern people or things that are abnormal; in short, they should develop a kind of sixth sense that is grounded on suspicion—an awareness of something bad, wrong, harmful, without solid evidence. This is often termed "JDLR" (things "just don't look right").

Patrol officers may also develop certain informal rules pertaining to their beats. For example, they may adopt the belief that "after midnight, these alleys belong to me." In other words, an officer may take the position that any person who is observed in "his" or "her" alley after midnight must be checked out—especially if that person is wearing dark clothing or is acting in a furtive or surreptitious manner.

Several authors have described, often in colorful but realistic terms, the kinds of situations encountered by officers on patrol. For example, as W. Clinton Terry III put it:

> Patrol officers respond to calls about overflowing sewers, reports of attempted suicides, domestic disputes, fights between neighbors, barking dogs and quarrelsome cats, reports of people banging their heads against brick walls until

they are bloody, requests to check people out who have seemingly passed out in public parks, requests for more police protection from elderly ladies afraid of entering their residence, and requests for information and general assistance of every sort.[3]

A former police chief described patrol duties as follows:

Cops on the street hurry from call to call, bound to their crackling radios, which offer no relief—especially on summer weekend nights. That is the time when the [city] throbs with noise, booze, violence, drugs, illness, blaring TVs, and human misery. The cops jump from crisis to crisis, rarely having time to do more than tamp one down sufficiently and leave for the next. Gaps of boredom and inactivity fill the interims, although there aren't many of these in the hot months.[4]

Indeed, patrolling officers will encounter all manner of things while engaged in routine patrol—things they discover as well as problems phoned in by citizens. They are assigned "attempt to locate" calls (usually involving missing persons, ranging from juveniles who have not returned home on time to elderly people who have wandered away from nursing homes); "attempt to contact" and "be on the lookout" calls (requested by an out-of-town individual who needs police to try to locate someone in order to deliver a message, for example); and "check the welfare of" calls (involving a person who has not been seen or heard from for some time).

One type of call is said to have broken the back of many police agencies: nonemergency calls to 911. Several hundred thousand 911 calls are made each day across the nation—and 90 percent of them are for nonemergencies. Departments must find ways to free patrol officers from what has been called the "tyranny of 911": nonstop calls that send officers bouncing from one nonemergency call for service to the next. (The author witnessed one such call to a 911 dispatcher in the Midwest. The caller was reporting a goat standing on

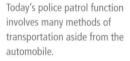

Today's police patrol function involves many methods of transportation aside from the automobile.

(Courtesy Fort Lauderdale, Florida, Police Department)

the front porch.) Indeed, the range of "emergencies" 911 callers report boggles the mind: Some people call because they want to know when the National Football League game begins that day, some people want to know the weather report, and some want help to exorcise the alien who entered their kitchen through the refrigerator's electrical cord. Nonemergency 911 calls leave officers little time for community-oriented policing and problem-solving (COPPS) activities.[5] Exhibit 5-1 describes the complex nature of a patrol officer's work.

Activities during Occasional Hours of Boredom

As indicated earlier, contrary to the image that is portrayed on television, some (or even much) of the time officers devote to patrolling consists of gaps of inactivity. During those periods of time (particularly on the graveyard shift, when even late-night people and partygoers submit to fatigue and go home to sleep), patrol officers engage in a variety of activities to pass the time:

- They create "private places" for themselves—fire stations, hospitals, and other places where they can wash up, have a cup of coffee, make a phone call, or simply relax for a few moments.
- They engage in police-related activities, such as completing reports, checking license plates of vehicles that are parked at motels (to locate stolen vehicles or wanted persons), or meeting with other officers. Other more relaxing activities might include exercising in the station house workout room.
- Even while engaged in routine patrol, the officer is often encouraged during recruit training to make good use of this slack time by engaging in "what if" mental exercises: "What if an armed robbery occurred at (location)? How would I get there most rapidly? What would I do after arrival? Where would I find available cover?" Of course, officers can concoct any number of scenarios and types of calls for service to keep themselves mentally honed and ready to respond in the most efficacious manner.
- An often overlooked part of policing is that patrol officers must also spend a lot of time—especially during the earlier part of their careers—memorizing many things: the "Ten Code," for example, and the numbering systems of streets and highways within their jurisdiction. (Indeed, new recruits can and do "wash out" during the field training phase of their careers because of their inability to read an in-car map of the city, thus preventing them from arriving at their destination promptly.)

Exhibit 5-2 provides a comparative view of a venue where police do in fact have very little to do: Saudi Arabia.

Patrol Work as a Function of Shift Assignment

Although the following analysis does not apply to all jurisdictions, the nature of patrol work is very closely related to the officer's particular **shift assignment**. Following are general descriptions of the nature of work on each of the three daily shifts.

Officers working the day shift (approximately 8 A.M. to 4 P.M.) probably have the greatest contact with citizens and provide **traffic control**. Officers may start their day by watching school crossings and unsnarling traffic jams. Speeding and traffic accidents are more common as people hurry to work in the morning. Officers also participate in school and civic

EXHIBIT 5-1

Police Patrol: A Job Description

This behavioral analysis of a patrol officer's job provides one of the few empirical descriptions of the complex and varied demands of patrol work. Based on extensive field observations, the findings are reported as a list of the attributes that are required for successful performance in the field. Although completed over three decades ago, the findings appear to conform well to the patrol activities of today. The researchers concluded that patrol officers must do the following:

1. Endure long periods of monotony in routine patrol, yet react quickly (almost instantaneously) and effectively to problem situations observed on the street or to orders issued by the radio dispatcher.

2. Gain knowledge of the patrol area, not only of its physical characteristics but also of its normal routine of events and the usual behavior patterns of its residents.

3. Exhibit initiative, problem-solving capacity, effective judgment, and imagination in coping with the numerous complex situations they are called on to face, such as a family disturbance, a potential suicide, a robbery in progress, an accident, or a disaster.

4. Make prompt and effective decisions, sometimes in life-and-death situations, and be able to size up a situation quickly and take appropriate action.

5. Demonstrate mature judgment (for example, when deciding whether an arrest is warranted by the circumstances or whether a warning is sufficient or when facing a situation in which the use of force may be needed).

6. Demonstrate critical awareness in discerning signs of out-of-the-ordinary conditions or circumstances that indicate trouble or a crime in progress.

7. Exhibit a number of complex psychomotor skills, such as driving a vehicle in normal and emergency situations; firing a weapon accurately under extremely varied conditions; maintaining agility, endurance, and strength; and showing facility in self-defense and apprehension (for example, taking a person into custody with a minimum of force).

8. Perform the communication and record-keeping functions of the job, including oral reports, formal case reports, and departmental and court forms.

9. Have the facility to act effectively in extremely divergent interpersonal situations. Police officers constantly confront people who are violating the law, ranging from curfew violators to felons. They constantly confront people who are in trouble or who are victims of crimes. At the same time, officers must relate to law-abiding citizens such as businesspeople, residents, school officials, visitors on their beat. Their interpersonal relations must range up and down a continuum defined by friendliness and persuasion on one end and by firmness and force on the other.

10. Endure verbal and physical abuse from citizens and offenders (as when placing a person under arrest or facing day-in and day-out race prejudice) while using only necessary force in the performance of their job.

11. Exhibit a self-assured professional presence and a self-confident manner when dealing with offenders, the public, and the courts.

12. Be capable of restoring equilibrium to social groups (for example, restoring order in a family fight, in a disagreement between neighbors, or in a clash between rival youth groups).

13. Be skillful in questioning suspected offenders, victims, and witnesses of crimes.

14. Take charge of situations, such as a crime or accident scene, yet not unduly alienate participants or bystanders.

15. Be flexible enough to work under loose supervision in most day-to-day patrol activities and also under direct supervision in situations where large numbers of officers are required.

16. Tolerate stress in a multitude of forms, such as meeting the violent behavior of a mob, coping with the pressures of a high-speed chase or a weapon being fired, or assisting a woman bearing a child.

17. Exhibit personal courage in the face of dangerous situations that may result in serious injury or death.

18. Maintain objectivity while dealing with a host of special-interest groups, ranging from relatives of offenders to members of the press.

19. Maintain a balanced perspective in the face of constant exposure to the worst side of human nature.

20. Exhibit a high level of personal integrity and ethical conduct (for example, refraining from accepting bribes or favors and providing impartial law enforcement).

Source: Adapted from M. E. Baehr, J. E. Furcon, and E. C. Froemel, *Psychological Assessment of Patrolman Qualifications in Relation to Field Performance* (Washington, DC: Department of Justice, 1968), pp. 11–3 to 11–5.

EXHIBIT 5-2

Comparative Closeup

Little to Do on Patrol: Saudi Arabia

The police in Saudi Arabia assist with enforcing the very cruel (by Western standards) Islamic law, which is governed by the Koran (see Exhibit 8-2 in Chapter 8), including the so-called chop-chops, which are conducted in many cities and with greater frequency in the Justice Square in Riyadh on Fridays. Believing that public beheadings and amputations deter other prospective offenders, people in the vicinity of the square are encouraged by the police to witness these events. When a thief's right hand is cut off in public, a string is tied to the middle finger and the hand is hung from a hook high on a streetlight in Justice Square for all to see. Because there is a near total absence on Saudi Arabia's streets of gangs, drive-by shootings, purse snatchings, and contraband, the police patrol the streets in Chevrolets, BMWs, and Volvos, looking for minor infractions of the law.[1]

Owing to the aforementioned harsh criminal code, there is little for the Saudi police to do in terms of crime prevention or investigation.

The religious police—the Mutawin— patrol and stroll in their white cotton robes and sandals and look, as one writer observed, like "desert nomads who have stumbled unexpectedly into the 20th century."[2] They look for people who are improperly dressed or women who have a loose strand of hair falling across their face or who need to adjust their tarhas (head coverings). Around-the-clock patrols ensure that shops are closed in time for daily prayers and that only married couples are sitting in family sections of restaurants. The patrols often follow persons suspected of being involved in what is deemed immoral behavior, such as drug use, homosexuality, gambling, and begging. Teams of religious police will also destroy home satellite dishes, which bring uncensored Western television broadcasts into Saudi homes.[3]

1. Personal communication with a former American residing in Saudi Arabia, July 27, 1994.
2. Chris Hedges, "Everywhere in Saudi Arabia, Islam Is Watching," *New York Times*, January 6, 1993, p. A
3. Ibid.

presentations and other such programs. Most errands and nonpolice duties assigned to the police are performed by day shift officers, such as unlocking parking lots, escorting people, delivering agendas to city council members, transporting evidence to court, and seeing that maintenance is performed on patrol vehicles. Day shift officers are more likely to be summoned to such major crimes as armed robberies and bomb threats. This shift often has lulls, as most people are at work or in school. Usually, the officers with the most seniority work the day shift.

Officers of the swing, or evening, shift (4 P.M. to 12 A.M.) come on duty in time to untangle evening traffic jams and respond to a variety of complaints from the public. Youths are out of school, and shops are beginning to close; as darkness falls, officers must begin checking commercial doors and windows on their beat (new officers are amazed at the frequency with which businesspeople leave their buildings unsecured). Warm weather brings increased drinking and partying, along with noise complaints. Domestic disturbances begin to occur, and the action at bars and nightclubs is beginning to pick up—soon fights will break out. Many major events, such as athletic events and concerts, occur in the evenings, so officers often perform crowd and traffic control duties. Toward the end of the shift, fast-food restaurants and other businesses begin complaining about loitering and littering by teenagers. Arrests are much more frequent than during the day shift, and officers must attempt to take one last look at the businesses on the beat before ending their shift to ensure that none have been burglarized during the evening and night hours. That done, arrest and incident reports must be completed before officers may leave the station house for home.

The night shift (12 A.M. to 8 A.M.), known throughout history as the graveyard shift, is an entirely different world. Because of its adverse effects on the officers' sleeping and eating habits, this shift is usually worked by newer officers (who also must work most weekends and holidays because of low seniority), but only long enough for the officers to build enough seniority to transfer to another shift. Few officers actually like the shift enough to want to devote much of their career working it. (Many agencies also have shift rotation, transferring their officers from one shift to another at fixed intervals.)

Officers on this shift come on duty fresh and ready for action. From about midnight to 3 A.M., the night shift is quite busy as bars and taverns close. Traffic is relatively heavy for several hours and then normally drops off to a trickle. The "night people" begin to come out—those who sleep in the daytime and prowl at night, including the burglars. The nightly cat-and-mouse game begins between the cops and the robbers. Night shift officers come to know who these people are and what vehicles they drive, what crimes they prefer, what their habits are, and where they hang out. Night shift officers spend much of the night patrolling alleys and businesses, working their spotlight as they seek signs of suspicious activity such as open doors and windows in businesses or signs of unlawful entry. They also watch the residential areas, performing courtesy checks of homes in general and with greater scrutiny when people are away on vacation and have asked the police for a periodic check of their property.

Such patrol work is inevitably eerie in nature. Officers typically work alone under cover of darkness, often without hope of rapid backup units, although where possible, greater attention is given to providing backup to night shift officers, even during traffic stops. The police never know who or what awaits them around the next dark corner. The protective shroud of darkness given to the offenders makes the night shift officers more wary. As mentioned earlier, after midnight, graveyard officers view alleys as theirs alone; anyone violating the peace of "their" alleys—especially one of the known "night people" or anyone wearing dark clothing or engaging in other suspicious activity—should be prepared to explain his or her actions and presence. Such individuals may also be compelled to undergo a stop-and-frisk (pat-down) search.

Once the alleys and buildings have been checked, the officers begin rechecking them, avoiding any routine pattern that burglars may discern. Some burglars can tell which beats are "open"—that is, wide open for burglarizing—by observing which patrol vehicles are parked at the station or at restaurants; therefore, officers should vary their patrol routine each night. At two or three in the morning, boredom can set in. Some officers welcome this change of pace, while others loathe it and look for ways to fight the monotony of the "dog watch." For them, the occasional high-speed chase may bring a welcome adrenaline rush, as does a crime in progress. Other means of staying alert include meeting and chatting with other officers who are also bored with patrol and stopping for coffee. But these officers must be mentally prepared for action; they know that while this is normally a quiet shift after the initial activity, when something does occur on the night shift, it is often a major incident or crime.

Influence of an Assigned Beat

Just as the work of the patrol officer is influenced by his or her shift assignment, the nature of that work is determined by the beat assignment. Each beat has its own personality, which may be quite different from other contiguous beats in terms of its structure and demographic character, as seen in the following hypothetical examples:

- Beat A contains a university with many large crowds that attend athletic and concert events; it also contains a number of taverns and bars where students congregate, resulting in an occasional need for police presence. A large hospital is located in this sector. Residents here are predominantly middle class. A large number of shopping malls and retail businesses occupy the area. The crime rate is quite low here, as are the numbers of calls for service. The university commands a considerable amount of officer overtime for major events as well as general officer attention for parking problems. During university homecoming week and other major events, officers in this beat will be going from call to call while officers assigned to other beats may find themselves completely bored. One portion of the beat contains several bars that attract working-class individuals and generate several calls for service each week due to fights, traffic problems, and so forth.
- Beat B is almost totally residential in nature and is composed of the "old money" people of the community: upper- and upper-middle-class people who "encourage" routine patrols by the police. Some of the community's banks, retail businesses, and industrial complexes are also located in this area. Most people have their homes wired for security, either to a private security firm or to the local police department. The crime rate and calls for service are relatively low in this beat, but there is a large amount of territory to patrol, and a major thoroughfare runs along the beat's perimeter, generating some serious traffic accidents.
- Beat C is composed primarily of blue-collar working-class people. It generates a low to medium number of calls for service relative to the other beats, and much of its geographic area is consumed by a small airport and a large public park with a baseball diamond/golf course complex.
- Beat D is the worst in the city in terms of quality of life, residents' income levels, and police problems. Though smaller in size than the other beats, it generates a very high number of calls for service. It contains a large number of residents living on the margins of the economy, lower-income housing complexes, taverns, barely surviving retail businesses, older mobile home parks and motels, and a major railroad switching yard. Officers are constantly driving from call to call, especially during summer weekend nights. At night, officers who are engaged in calls for service—even traffic stops—are given backup by fellow officers whenever possible.

Of course, even the normal ebb and flow of beat activity is greatly altered when a critical incident occurs; for example, an act of nature (such as a tornado, an earthquake, or a fire) or a major criminal event (such as a bank robbery or a kidnapping) can wreak havoc on a beat that is normally the most placid in nature.

Three "cops' rules" are part of the beat culture[6]:

1. Don't get involved in another officer's sector; "butt out" unless asked to come to a beat to assist. Each officer is accountable for his or her territory, and each officer must live with the consequences of decisions that pertain to his or her beat.

2. Don't leave work for the next duty shift; take care of such practical matters as putting gas in the patrol car and taking all necessary complaints before leaving the station house.

3. Hold up your end of the work: don't slack off.

WHERE DANGER LURKS: OCCUPATIONAL HAZARDS OF PATROL

At Peril Everywhere

Certainly policing everywhere is potentially a very dangerous job, and the felonious murder of even one police officer is a tragedy. There is one country, however, where felonious killings of police officers is astronomical in comparison with other venues; that venue is Iraq, where 12,000 police officers were killed during the 4-year period from 2003 to 2006 (see Exhibit 5-3).[7] To put this carnage into statistical perspective (and assuming that nearly all of the Iraqi police killings were felonious in nature, due to suicide bombs and improvised explosive devices, or IEDs), we might compare Iraq's police killings with those of the United States, where a total of 220 police officers were murdered during the same time frame. At the current U.S. rate, it would take about *55* years for as many American police officers to be murdered as were killed in 4 years in Iraq.[8] This comparison shows how utterly widespread police killings have recently been in Iraq.

Next we look in greater detail at the killing of police officers in the United States.

Officers Killed in the United States

Although several occupations—commercial fishing, logging, and piloting airplanes in particular—have workers dying at much higher rates than policing,[9] police officers' lives are still rife with **occupational hazards**. They never know if the citizen they are about to confront is armed, is high on drugs or alcohol, or plans to engage in a relatively recent phenomenon known as "suicide by cop" (discussed below). They may also be killed by noncriminal means. For example, during 2006, forty-eight police officers lost their lives feloniously in the line of duty (Exhibit 5-4 provides a profile of those officers, in terms of personal characteristics and some of the circumstances involved), and sixty-six died as the result of accidents and other causes in the line of duty.[10] Although the number of officers killed annually has generally declined since 2001, this is still a dangerous nation, and today's police officer would be very unwise to go on patrol without wearing body armor, although wearing body armor is certainly no guarantee that he or she will survive a shooting. Table 5-1 provides a longitudinal profile (five-year averages and ten-year averages) of the victim officers who were feloniously killed, as well as the circumstances, from 1987 to 2006.

An area in which better efforts must be made for officer safety is traffic accidents, where 73 of the 151 officers killed in 2006 were in traffic fatalities—a 16 percent increase over 2005. Experts fear (but it has not been proven) that a contributing factor may be that more officers are driving without seatbelts in order to have quicker access to their sidearms in the event someone begins shooting at them. However, traffic accidents alone may explain a good proportion

EXHIBIT 5-3

Comparative Closeup
The World's Most Dangerous Venue—Iraq

Undoubtedly, the most dangerous international venue in which to be in policing today is Iraq. This carnage is, of course, a result of the country's rampant terrorist acts. Following are but a few examples of the attacks upon Iraqi police—attacks that are all too commonplace there but that would bring shock and horror to Americans if committed but once in the United States:

- In December 2006, 12 Iraqi police officers were killed by a suicide bomber and explosions in one weekend in Baghdad.[1]
- In November 2005, 6 Iraqi police officers were killed and 12 others wounded in a gun battle at a checkpoint north of Baghdad. At least 40 gunmen in three vehicles began shooting at the checkpoint near Baquba; the battle continued for about 30 minutes.[2]
- In September 2004, a suicide attacker detonated a car bomb outside the Iraqi police academy in Kirkuk as hundreds of trainees and civilians were leaving, killing 20 and wounding 36.[3]
- In February 2004, insurgents using rocket-propelled grenades, machine guns, and mortars staged a brazen daylight attack on a Fallujah police station, freeing dozens of prisoners in a battle that killed 23 people and wounded 37.[4]
- A truck bomb also exploded at a police station south of Baghdad as dozens of would-be police recruits lined up to apply for jobs, killing at least 54 people and wounding 60 others.[5]

Indeed, the high number of Iraqi police deaths prompted several members of a U.S. House Select Committee on Intelligence to pay tribute in Baghdad to these murdered officers[6] and forced the officers themselves to discontinue wearing their blue uniform shirts, because insurgents shot people wearing such clothes.[7] The Iraqi police—poorly trained and badly equipped—knew that without U.S. military backing they would be hard-pressed to keep basic order, much less do battle with well-armed guerrillas.[8] Many were former instruments of the Saddam government, when decades of pent-up anger over repression, torture, and death found voice in tens of thousands of Iraqis.[9] These officers quickly became targets of convenience for those opposed to the U.S. occupation of the country, because the Iraqi people viewed them as collaborators with American soldiers (who did in fact train these officers) and knew their faces and where they lived.[10]

The Iraqi officers' duties are varied: At times they clashed almost daily with demonstrators, often armed only with a "rusting pair of binoculars, an AK-47, and a half magazine of bullets," to guard the country's vast borders.[11] They were also expected to control the widespread vice—prostitution, pornographic adult cinemas, drug abuse—that has pervaded Baghdad and other cities since Saddam's fall. This dismal situation was compounded by police corruption, civilian looting, and chaotic traffic problems with which the police found themselves involved while having little in the way of key equipment, such as radios, vehicles, uniforms, or computers, all for a notoriously low pay of $20 per month.[12]

1. Lauren Frayer, "12,000 Iraqi Police Killed Since 2003," Associated Press, December 25, 2006.
2. "Officials: Iraqi Police Killed in Checkpoint Battle," www.cnn.com/2005/WORLD/meast/11/04/iraq.main/ (accessed October 2, 2006).
3. Yehia Barzanji, "Bomb at Iraqi Police Station Kills 20," *Army Times,* September 4, 2004, http://www.armytimes.com/story.php (accessed September 7, 2004).
4. Anthony Shadid, "Insurgents Storm Iraq Police Station, 23 Die in Fighting," *Washington Post,* February 15, 2004, p. 1A.
5. CBS News, "Timeline," http://911research.wtc7.net/cache/post911/attacks/iraq/cbc_timeline.html" (accessed January 3, 2007).
6. "Lawmakers Honor Slain Iraqi Officers," Associated Press, *Reno Gazette-Journal,* February 17, 2004.
7. Alex Berenson, "Arms and Aims: The Art of War vs. the Craft of Occupation," *New York Times,* November 2, 2003, p. D1.
8. Ibid.
9. Joel Brinkley, "The Struggle for Iraq: Violence, Revenge Drives String of Killings in Basra," *New York Times,* November 1, 2003, p. A6.
10. Dan Murphy, "Iraqi Police in the Crosshairs of Anti-U.S. Forces," *Christian Science Monitor,* 95(222) October 10, 2003, p. 7.
11. Joshua Hammer, "Holding the Line," *Newsweek,* February 16, 2004, p. 32.
12. Christine Caryl, "Iraqi Vice," *Newsweek,* December 22, 2003, p. 38.

EXHIBIT 5-4

Officers Killed in the United States: A Profile

According to the Federal Bureau of Investigation, the 48 officers who were feloniously killed in 2006 compose the following profile:

- They were about 38 years old.
- They had worked in law enforcement for about 11 years.
- They were assigned to patrol (27).

- They were murdered with firearms (46); of these, 36 were slain with handguns.
- They were wearing body armor (26).
- They were disproportionately employed in the South (22).

Source: Adapted from the Federal Bureau of Investigation, Uniform Crime Reports, *Law Enforcement Officers Killed and Assaulted 2006,* http://www.fbi.gov /ucr/killed/2006/feloniouslykilled.html (accessed November 7, 2007).

of the fatalities; over the past thirty years, the number of officers killed in traffic crashes has jumped by 40 percent while the number shot to death has declined by about the same amount.[11]

Suicide by Cop

DEFINITIONS   A type of incident that certainly poses serious potential for danger to the police is **suicide by cop**, which is defined as "an act motivated in whole or in part by the offender's desire to commit suicide that results in a justifiable homicide by a law enforcement officer."[12]

Presently, the extent of the suicide by cop phenomenon remains unknown for two reasons:

1. Lack of both a clear definition and established reporting procedures
2. Immediate removal of suicide attempts from the criminal process and placement within the mental health arena, causing the police investigation to cease and preventing an agency from identifying a potential threat to its officers

TABLE 5-1

Law Enforcement Officers Feloniously Killed, Profile of Victim Officer, Averages, 1987–2006

Average	2006	5-Year Average		10-Year Average	
		1997–2001	2002–2006	1987–1996	1997–2006
Age	38	36	38	36	37
Years of service	11	10	11	10	10
Height	5'11"	5'11"	5'11"	5'11"	5'11"
Weight[1]	203	198	200	—	199

[1]Prior to 1995, data on weight were not collected.

Note: The 72 deaths that resulted from the events of September 11, 2001, are not included in this table.

Source: Federal Bureau of Investigation.

The patrol function often takes officers to places that are "brutish" and dangerous.

(Courtesy Washoe County, Nevada, Sheriff's Office)

Although it is difficult to measure, one study by a medical organization of deputy-involved shootings in the Los Angeles County, California, Sheriff's Department found that suicide by cop incidents accounted for 11 percent of all deputy-involved shootings and 13 percent of all deputy-involved justifiable homicides. The report concluded that suicide by cop constitutes an actual form of suicide.[13]

CASE STUDY   While each case of suicide by cop is different, following is an example of how such an incident might occur:

An officer is dispatched to an apartment building in response to a woman yelling for help. Upon arriving at the location, the officer observes a woman standing on the front steps. The officer is waved inside, and as she enters the apartment, she hears a man yelling and then sees him standing in the kitchen area. When the male observes the female officer, he produces a large butcher knife and holds the blade of the knife firmly against his stomach with both hands; he appears highly intoxicated, agitated, and angry. The officer draws her service weapon and orders the man to put down the knife. The offender responds by stating, "[Expletive] you, kill me!" The officer attempts to talk with the offender, who responds by turning around and slicing himself severely on his forearm, bleeding profusely. The officer repeatedly asks him to drop the knife. The offender begins to advance toward the officer and telling her to shoot him while still ignoring her commands to drop the knife. From a distance of approximately 12 feet, he raises the knife in a threatening manner and charges the officer; she fires her weapon, striking him in the chest and hand, killing him.[14]

TWO-TIERED INVESTIGATION   At minimum, to establish what happened and to track the incidents of suicide by cop, it is recommended that the following two investigative steps ensue when such an incident appears to have occurred: reporting procedure and classifying procedure.

Reporting Procedure.   The reporting officer should list in detail in the initial offense report the specific elements observed at the scene:

- Statements made by the offender, including the names of any witnesses to the statements
- Type(s) of weapon possessed by the offender
- Offender's specific actions that resulted in the use of deadly force
- Offender's conduct that the officer deemed bizarre or inappropriate
- Circumstances indicating that the offender's motivation may have been suicide

A trained individual or unit must then sift carefully through the facts and circumstances, using stringent criteria to determine if the incident probably was motivated by the offender's *will* to commit suicide, noting items such as the following:

- Notes or recent correspondence, such as e-mails and other computer files, left at the scene or any other place the offender frequented
- Detailed verbatim statements from family members, friends, and associates
- Forensic evidence pertinent to the investigation (if the offender used a firearm, whether it was loaded with proper ammunition and capable of firing ammunition)
- Personal history of the offender, including medical and psychiatric information, credit reports, insurance policies, employment records, history of significant relationships, prior suicides of family members, and prior attempted suicides (particularly attempts that involved confrontations with law enforcement officers)
- Criminal history, including sentencing information, presentence reports, psychiatric evaluations, and prison records

As an example, the follow-up investigation of the above case study would reveal the following:

- The offender possessed a weapon capable of inflicting serious bodily injury or death.
- He used the weapon to seriously injure himself and attacked the officer with the weapon.
- During the attack, he demanded that the officer kill him.

Following those findings, there should also be a classifying procedure.

Classifying Procedure.   An officer or unit with expertise in the use of deadly force incidents renders the final determination of whether a suicide by cop incident has occurred, focusing on the subject's motivation. The classification should include indicators that can help establish motivations and behavior patterns of the offender, for later tabulation and analysis.[15] The investigation of the above case study would thus demonstrate that the elements of a suicide by cop event were present, so the case would be classified as such.

Arms and Armor for Duty

Jerome Skolnick and David Bayley describe how officers prepare to face the beat's dangers on their tour of duty:

> Policing in the United States is very much like going to war. Three times a day in countless locker rooms, large men and a growing number of women carefully arm and armor themselves for the day's events. They begin by strapping on [body armor]. Then they pick up a wide, heavy, black leather belt and hang around it the tools of their trade: gun, mace, handcuffs, bullets. When it is fully loaded they swing the belt around their hips with the same practiced motion of the gunfighter in Western movies, slugging it down and buckling it in front. Inspecting themselves in a full-length mirror, officers thread their night sticks into a metal ring on the side of their belt.[16]

As John Crank states, "This is not a picture of American youth dressing for public servitude. These are warriors going to battle, the New Centurions, as Wambaugh calls them. In their dress and demeanor lies the future of American policing."[17] As Crank also observes, police recognize many citizens for what they are: "Dangerous, unpredictable, violent, savagely cunning...in a world of capable and talented reptilian, mammalian...predators."[18]

This depiction of the people officers confront on the beat may seem overly contrived, exaggerated, or brusque. Most patrol officers with any length of service, however, can attest to the fact that there are certain members of our society who, as one officer put it, are "irretrievable predators that just get off...on people's pain and on people's crying and begging and pleading. They don't have any sense of morality, [and] they don't have any sense of right and wrong."[19] During their careers, most patrol officers are verbally threatened by such individuals; they take the great majority of such threats with a grain of salt. Occasionally, however, the "irretrievable predator" who possesses no sense of morality will issue such a threat, which the officer will (and must) take quite seriously. This is a very disconcerting part of the job.

The importance of patrol officers providing backup to one another—especially during the hours of darkness—cannot be overstated, as shown by Anthony Bouza:

> The sense of "us vs. them" that develops between cops and the outside world forges a bond between cops whose strength is fabled. It is widened by the dependence cops have on each other for safety and backup. The response to help is a cop's life-line. An "assist police officer" is every cop's first priority. The ultimate betrayal is for one cop to fail to back up another.[20]

In this same vein, patrol officers quickly come to know whom they can count on when everything "hits the fan"—which officers will race to assist another officer at a barroom brawl, a felony in progress, and so on—and which will not.

H.R. 218

A relatively new legislative enactment, the **Law Enforcement Officers Safety Act of 2004 (H.R. 218)**, exempts qualified police officers from state laws prohibiting the carrying of concealed weapons and allows retired officers having at least fifteen years of service to carry a firearm.[21] The purpose of the act, its supporters state, is to afford these retired officers "protection of themselves, their families and our nation's communities." Retired officers who carry weapons under this law do not possess any police powers or immunities in other states, however, and are personally responsible for checking and understanding the laws of any jurisdictions they visit while armed.[22]

AN IMPORTANT BEAT ICON: THE PATROL VEHICLE

Sanctuary and Place for Vital Gear

Long before the *Blues Brothers* movie provided notoriety for police vehicles (the main characters adopted as their "Blues Mobile" a retired 1974 Dodge Monoco police car with a powerful 440-cubic-inch engine), vehicles used by the police for patrolling and chasing offenders were being viewed with some degree of awe by most Americans. Conversely, the **patrol vehicle** is perhaps the most underappreciated and ignored aspect of police work—by both scholars and officers themselves. The patrol vehicle warrants greater attention because it is not only a place where officers on patrol spend a great deal of their time but also their sanctuary. It contains the myriad vital tools for accomplishing their work and to a great extent represents their authority.

The patrol vehicle is generally safe and comfortable, containing several essential accoutrements (a radio, spotlight, and weapons such as a shotgun or rifle) that contribute to the officer's safety. It is a mobile haven, providing comfort from the extreme weather conditions that often exist in much of the nation, as well as against humans who would hurt the officer. Because the officer's world can be cruel and dangerous (an average of sixty police officers have been feloniously killed each year in this millennium),[23] the patrol car affords him or her access to the tools of defense. The vehicle is also a safe place to deposit combative prisoners for transport, and many models are constructed to be hosed out in case a prisoner vomits or urinates in the vehicle.

Vital tools can also be stored in or mounted on the vehicle, which serves as a virtual office: the radio (for summoning assistance), warning lights and siren, defensive weapons (for example, a shotgun or other firearm as well as a Taser, baton, or other less-lethal tool), possibly an onboard computer and video recorder, flares, cameras and other evidence-gathering equipment. On the graveyard shift, the spotlight can be the officer's greatest asset.

Finally, the police vehicle is a rolling symbol of authority. For this reason, few people enjoy seeing a police vehicle appear in their rearview mirror; for some, it is a prelude to being issued a traffic citation or, worse, being taken to jail. Still, it can be stated that since the first police car appeared, citizens have been fascinated with the speed and imposing appearance of these automobiles.

Evolution of the Patrol Vehicle

At one time or another, police departments have placed decals and emergency equipment on all sorts of cars. In 1950, Ford Motor Company introduced the first "police package"— a vehicle with a 110-horsepower (hp) engine, heavy-duty suspension components, a larger radiator, extra transmission and power steering cooling, a larger battery, and a more powerful electrical system. Soon Buick produced a police package as well, and the early 1960s saw the Dodge Dart following suit. The late 1960s brought Plymouth's twin offerings, the Belvedere and the Fury, and Dodge introduced its 440 CI Magnum engine, with 375 hp.[24]

In the early 1970s, the AMC Matador was widely used, but durability problems caused it to reign for only a few years. The energy crisis of the mid-1970s brought the Chevrolet Nova 9C1, which was developed through a collaboration between Chevrolet, the Los Angeles County Sheriff's Office, and *Motor Trend* magazine. It and the highly recognizable Dodge Monaco dominated the market in the late 1970s.[25]

The drive for fuel efficiency and stricter emissions standards continued into the 1980s, which has been termed the "Dark Ages" of police vehicle history.[26] The creation of the underpowered Dodge R-body police package and the Aries K were the result; with a mere 84-hp engine, the Aries required 17 seconds to reach 60 mph. The only bright spot of this decade was the California Highway Patrol's unveiling of the 157-hp Ford Mustang GT pursuit vehicle, which was used in thirty-five states by 1991.[27]

During the early 1990s, both Dodge and Chrysler announced that they were dropping out of the police car market, shocking police departments everywhere and leaving only the Chevrolet Caprice and the Ford Crown Victoria as heavy-duty models.[28] In the late 1990s and continuing into the early 2000s, the Crown Victoria assumed the mantle as the nation's most popular police cruiser, with three-fourths of the market. The Crown Victoria came under a cloud, however, because of fires that killed as many as eleven officers when their cars were struck at the rear, causing the fuel tanks to explode. Over several years' time, a recall, many lawsuits and investigations, and a task force created by Ford were initiated because of the problem.[29]

Recently, two long-standing police vehicle models have announced their intention to increase their presence in the policing world. In mid-2006, DaimlerChrysler offered the police a 340-hp Hemi engine in its Dodge Charger R/T police package. Chevrolet offers its front-wheel-drive 200-hp Impala; indeed, it has been rumored that the New York Police Department plans to eventually convert its entire patrol fleet to Impalas.[30]

Today's Accoutrements

Henry Ford would be amazed with today's police cruisers, in which high technology and utility still trump luxury. In addition to the traditional beefed-up engines, heavy suspension, and upgraded electrical systems, some also contain several features that mean a lot to the officers on patrol. For example, some new models come with plates in the driver's seatback to protect against assault from the rear, cutouts in the driver's seat for a holster, extra-long safety belts, reinforced front steel beams and higher-rated tires for high-speed pursuits, a voice-recognition system for accessing onboard computers, a camera mounted in the overhead light bar with output to a laptop computer, an aircraft-style "blue box" accident data recorder, and crush-resistant bumpers.[31]

In sum, it is clear that the value of the patrol vehicle cannot be overstated in terms of helping the police to fulfill their mission to serve and protect. In addition, the vehicle will continue to become even more important to officers and citizens alike as new technological advances are included in its design and functionality.

Patrolling on Two Wheels—The Segway

It is hardly intimidating to see a police officer checking the beat on his or her patrol vehicle at twelve miles per hour, but more than eighty U.S. police departments—as well as officers on college campuses, at airports, and in other venues—are now doing so on their Segways. Launched in 2001, the battery-powered Segway provides officers with more mobility than a bicycle and the ability to negotiate large crowds quickly and easily; it also saves gas and is proving to be very public-friendly. Models come equipped with a siren, saddle bags to carry forms and other materials, and even an alarm that allows officers to park the machine while tending to business without fear of its being stolen.[32]

Input from patrol officers is often used to create the console setup. Here, microphones are placed on the passenger side, at an angle and height that are easy for the officer to reach.

(Courtesy Woodcrest Vehicle Center)

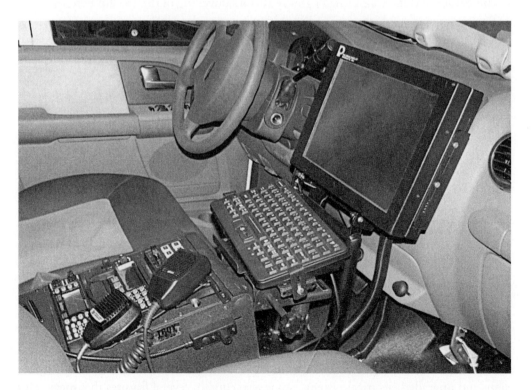

STUDIES OF THE PATROL FUNCTION

Because of the vast resources devoted to the patrol function and a desire to make patrolling more productive and pleasant for officers, many patrol studies have been conducted. Several have uncovered deficiencies and exposed myths about preventive patrol. These studies have helped us understand how the professional policing model put up walls between the public and the police, whom many people began to view as an occupying force.[33] As the Police Foundation said, "Isolated in their rolling fortresses, police seem[ed] unable to communicate with the citizens they presumably served."[34]

The best-known study of patrol efficiency, the **Kansas City Preventive Patrol Experiment**, was conducted in Kansas City, Missouri, in 1973, by George Kelling and a research team at the Police Foundation. The researchers divided the city into fifteen beats, which were then categorized into five groups of three matched beats each. Each group consisted of neighborhoods that were similar in terms of population, crime characteristics, and calls for police services. Patrolling techniques used in the three beats varied: There was no preventive patrol in one beat (police only responded to calls for service), there was increased patrol activity in another (two or three times the usual amount of patrolling), and there was the usual level of service in the third. Citizens were interviewed and crime rates were measured during the year the experiment was conducted. This experiment challenged several traditional assumptions about routine police patrol. The study found that the deterrent effect of policing was not weakened by the elimination of routine patrolling. Citizens' fear of crime and their attitudes toward the police were not affected, nor was the ability of the police to respond to calls.

The Kansas City Preventive Patrol Experiment (depicted in Figure 5-1) indicated that the old sacrosanct patrol methods were subject to question. As one of the study's authors

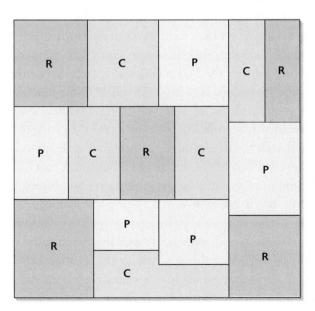

FIGURE 5-1

Schematic Representation of Fifteen-Beat Area, Kansas City Preventive Patrol Experiment

Source: George L. Kelling, Tony Pate, Duane Dieckman, and Charles E. Brown, The Kansas City Preventive Patrol Experiment: Final Report *(Washington, DC: Police Foundation, 1974), p. 9. Used with permission of the Police Foundation.*

P = proactive
C = control
R = reactive

stated, "[It showed] that the traditional assumptions of 'Give me more cars and more money and we'll get there faster and fight crime' is probably not a very viable argument."[35]

In the mid-1970s, it was suggested that the performance of patrol officers would improve by redesigning the job based on motivators rather than by attempting to change the individual officer selected for the job (by such means as increasing education requirements).[36] This suggestion later evolved into a concept known as "team policing," which differed from conventional patrol in several areas. Officers were divided into small teams that were assigned permanently to small geographic areas or neighborhoods. Officers were to be generalists, trained to investigate crimes and to attend to all the problems in their area. Communication and coordination between team members and the community were to be maximized; team involvement in administrative decision making was emphasized as well. This concept, later abandoned by many departments (apparently because of its strain on resources), was the beginning of the 1980s movement to return to community-oriented policing.

Two more attempts to increase patrol productivity, generally referred to as "directed patrol," occurred in 1975. The New Haven, Connecticut, Police Department used computer data of crime locations and times to set up deterrent runs (D-runs) to instruct officers on how to patrol. For example, the officer might be told to patrol around a certain block slowly, park, walk, get back in the car, and cruise down another street. A D-run took up to an hour, with each officer doing two or three of them per shift. Support for patrol officers was generally low, and the program did not reduce crime but rather displaced it. After a year, the experiment quietly died.[37] Wilmington, Delaware, instituted a split-force program, whereby three-fourths of the 250 patrol officers were assigned to a basic patrol unit to answer prioritized calls. The remaining officers were assigned to the structured unit and were deployed in high-crime areas, usually in plainclothes, to perform surveillances, stakeouts, and other tactical assignments. An evaluation of the project found that police productivity increased 20 percent and crime decreased 18 percent in the program's first year.[38]

In the late 1970s, a renewed interest in foot patrol—in keeping with Peel's view that police officers should walk the beat—compelled the Police Foundation to evaluate the effectiveness of foot patrol in selected New Jersey cities between 1977 and 1979. It was found that, for the most part, crime levels were not affected by foot patrol, but it did have a significant effect on the attitudes of area residents. Specifically, residents felt safer, thinking that the severity of crimes in their neighborhoods had diminished. Furthermore, evaluations of the Neighborhood Foot Patrol Program in Flint, Michigan, in 1985 found that foot officers had a higher level of job satisfaction[39] and felt safer on the job than motor officers.[40]

Other studies have illuminated the patrol function as well. A long-standing assumption was that as police response time increased, the ability to arrest perpetrators proportionately decreased. Thus, conventional wisdom held, more police were needed on patrol in order to get to the crime scene more quickly and catch the criminals. In 1977, a study examined police response time in Kansas City, Missouri, finding that response time was unrelated to the probability of making an arrest or locating a witness. Furthermore, neither dispatch nor travel time was strongly associated with citizen satisfaction. The time it takes to report a crime, the study found, is the major determining factor of whether an on-scene arrest takes place and whether witnesses are located.[41] It has also been found that two-person patrol cars are no more effective than one-person cars in reducing crime or catching criminals. Furthermore, injuries to police officers are not more likely to occur in one-person cars. Finally, most officers on patrol do not stumble across felony crimes in progress.[42]

While these studies should not be viewed as conclusive—different results could be obtained in different communities—they do demonstrate that old police methods should be viewed very cautiously. Many police executives have had to rethink the sacred cows of patrol functions.

DISCRETIONARY USE OF POLICE AUTHORITY

Myth of Full Enforcement

The municipal police chief or county sheriff is asked during a civic club luncheon speech which laws are and are not enforced by his or her agency. The official response will inevitably be that *all* of the laws are enforced equally, all of the time. Yet the chief or sheriff knows that full enforcement of the laws is a myth—that there are neither the resources nor the desire to enforce them all, nor are all laws enforced impartially. It is neither prudent nor politically wise to list the offenses for which the police treat some offenders more harshly or more leniently or when they look the other way (and *non*enforcement of laws is a form of discretion). There are legal concerns as well. For example, releasing some offenders (for example, to get information about other crimes or because of a good excuse) cannot be the official policy of the agency; however, the chief or sheriff cannot broadcast that fact to the public.

Indeed, it has been stated that the "single most astonishing fact of police behavior is the extent to which police do *not* enforce the law when they have every legal right to do so."[43] As an example, police scholar George Kelling described a Newark, New Jersey, street cop with whom he spent many hours walking a beat:

> As he saw his job, he was to keep an eye on strangers, and make certain that the disreputable regulars observed some informal but widely understood rules. Drunks and addicts could sit on the stoops, but could not lie down. People could drink on side streets, but not at the main intersection. Bottles had to be in paper bags. Talking to, bothering or begging from people waiting at the bus stop was strictly forbidden. Persons who broke the informal rules, especially [the latter], were arrested for vagrancy. Noisy teenagers were told to keep quiet.[44]

This quote points out the inextricable link between the patrol function and **discretionary use of police authority**: We cannot have one without the other.

Attempts to Define Discretion

Scholarly knowledge about the way police make decisions is limited. What is known, however, is that when police observe something of a suspicious or illegal nature, two important decisions must be made: (1) whether to intervene in the situation and (2) how to intervene.

The kind, number, and possible combination of interventions are virtually limitless. What kinds of decisions are available for an officer who makes a routine traffic stop? David Bayley and Egon Bittner observed long ago that officers have as many as 10 actions to select from at the initial stop (for example, order the driver out of the car), 7 strategies appropriate during the stop (such as a roadside sobriety test), and 11 exit strategies (for instance, releasing the driver with a warning), representing a total of 770 different combinations of actions that might be taken![45]

Criminal law has two sides—the formality and the reality. The formality is found in the statute books and opinions of appellate courts; the reality is found in the practices of enforcement officers. In some circumstances, the choice of action to be taken is relatively easy, such as arresting a bank robbery suspect, but in other situations, such as quelling a dispute between neighbors, the choice is more difficult. Drinking in the park is a crime according to many local ordinances, but quietly drinking at a family picnic without disturbing others is not a crime according to the reality of the law because officers uniformly refuse to enforce the ordinance in such circumstances. When the formality and the reality differ, the reality prevails.[46]

These examples demonstrate why the use of discretion is one of the major challenges facing U.S. police today. Our system tends to treat people as individuals: One person who commits a robbery is not the same as another person who commits a robbery because our system takes into account why and how a person committed a crime (his or her intent, or *mens rea*). Under our judicial process, when one person shoots another, a variety of possible outcomes can occur. The most important decisions take place on the streets, day or night, generally without the opportunity for the officer to consult with others or to carefully consider all the facts.

Determinants of Officer Discretion

Ours is supposed to be a government of laws, not of people. That axiom is simply a myth—at least in the manner in which the law is applied. Official discretion pervades all levels and most agencies of government. The discretionary power of the police is awesome. Kenneth Culp Davis, an authority on police discretion, writes, "The police are among the most important policy makers of our entire society. And they make far more discretionary determinations in individual cases than does any other class of administrators; I know of no close second."[47]

What determines whether the officer will take a stern approach (enforcing the letter of the law with an arrest) or will be lenient (issuing a verbal warning or some other outcome short of arrest)? Several variables enter into the officer's decision:

1. The *law* is indeed a factor in discretionary use of police authority. For example, many state statutes and loal ordinances now mandate that the police arrest for certain suspected offenses, such as driving under the influence or committing domestic violence.

2. The *officer's attitude* can also be a factor. First, some officers are more willing to empathize with offenders who feel they deserve a break than others. Also, as Carl

Klockars and Stephen Mastrofski observed, although violators frequently offer what they feel are very good reasons for the officer to overlook their offense, "every police officer knows that, if doing so will allow them to escape punishment, most people are prepared to lie through their teeth."[48] What also makes situations awkward is that the officer cannot comfortably acknowledge the real reasons for denying a citizen's appeal for discretion. Imagine a police officer saying to a traffic violator, "The city depends on traffic fines for revenue," "Sorry, I don't like people like you," "Sorry, I don't think your excuse is good enough," or "Sorry, but I don't believe you."[49] Furthermore, police officers, being human, can bring to work either a happy or an unhappy disposition. If, on the same day as reporting for duty, the officer received an IRS notice saying back taxes were owed, had a nasty spat with a significant other, and was bitten while picking up the family pet shortly before leaving for work, he or she might naturally be more inclined to enforce the letter of the law rather than dispense leniency. Personal views toward specific types of crimes also play a role; for example, perhaps the officer is fed up with juvenile crimes that have been occurring of late and thus will not give any leniency to youths he or she confronts who are involved in even minor crimes.

3. Another major consideration in the officer's choice among various options is the *citizen's attitude*. If the offender is rude and condescending, denies having done anything wrong, or uses some of the standard clichés that are almost guaranteed to rankle the officer—such as "You don't know who I am" (someone who is obviously very important in the community), "I'll have your job," "I know the chief of police," "I'm a taxpayer, and I pay your salary"—the probable outcome is obvious. On the other hand, the person who is honest with the officer, avoids attempts at intimidation and sarcasm, and does not try to "beat the rap" may fare better.

Several studies have found that not only a citizen's demeanor but also his or her social class, sex, age, and race influence the decisions made by patrol officers.[50] This possible discrimination on the part of officers points out that the police—like other citizens—are subject to stereotypes and biases that will affect their behavior.

Pros, Cons, and Politics of Discretionary Authority

Several ironies are connected with the way in which the police apply discretion. First is the inverse relationship between the officers' rank and the amount of discretion that is available. In other words, as the rank of the officer increases, the amount of discretion that he or she can employ normally decreases. The street officer makes discretionary decisions all the time, decisions about whether to arrest, shoot, and so forth. But the chief of police, who does very little actual police work, may be very constrained by department, union, affirmative action, or governing board guidelines and policies. Furthermore, the chief of police knows that there are neither the resources nor the desire to enforce all the laws that are broken.

Finally, the issue of police discretion is shrouded in controversy. There are several arguments both for and against discretion. Advantages include that it allows the officer to treat different situations in accordance with humanitarian and practical goals. For example, an officer pulls over a speeding motorist, only to learn that the car is en route to the hospital with a woman who is about to deliver a baby. While the agitated driver is endangering everyone in the vehicle as well as other motorists on the roadway, discretion allows the officer to be compassionate and empathetic, giving the car a safe escort to the hospital rather than issuing a citation for speeding. In short, discretionary use of authority allows the police to employ a philosophy of justice tempered with mercy.

Conversely, discretion can also carry the specter of partiality—the ability of officers to treat different people differently for committing essentially the same offense. Critics of discretion also argue that such wide latitude in decision making may serve as a breeding ground for police corruption; for example, an officer may be offered a bribe to overlook an offense. And as Lawrence Sherman observed, another problem is that the police do not know the consequences of their discretionary decisions. He contrasted the police with artisans and navigators who receive feedback on the effects of their decisions. The police, however, have failed to create a feedback information system that tells them what happens after they leave a call or even after they make an arrest. Thus police lack knowledge about the effects of their discretionary actions on suspects, victims, witnesses, and potential criminals.[51]

Certain aspects of policing will never be completely free of discretion, however; to a large extent, the work of a police officer is unsupervised and unsupervisable. As the police strive to achieve professionalism, they will remember that discretion is a key element of a profession.

Police discretion is also part of the American political process.[52] As Kenneth Culp Davis observed, a major contributing factor to police discretion is that state legislative commands are ambiguous. Legislatures speak with three voices: (1) They enact state statutes that seemingly require full enforcement of the laws, (2) they provide only enough resources for limited enforcement of them, and (3) they consent to such limited enforcement.[53] Some observers have even questioned the legality and morality of police discretion.[54] It might also be added that the statute books are often treated as society's "trash bins." A particular behavior is viewed negatively, so a law is passed against it, and the police are stuck with the dilemma of having to enforce or ignore what may be an overly broad or unpopular law.

There are other aspects of politics in police discretion. For example, several state and local governments restricted police use of deadly force long before the Supreme Court did away with the common law "fleeing felon" doctrine in *Tennessee* v. *Garner* (1985).[55]

A RELATED FUNCTION: TRAFFIC

A major figure in policing in the mid-1900s, O. W. Wilson, reportedly said that "the police traffic function overshadows every other function." That may be an overstatement today, but a strong link still exists between the patrol function and **traffic control**. Traffic stops account for about half (52 percent) of the contact Americans have with the police.[56] Therefore, the importance of a seemingly trivial traffic stop cannot be overstated because the manner in which the officer conducts the stop may in large measure determine the citizen's view of the police for many years to come.

The traffic function is a major part of the police role.

(Courtesy Washoe County, Nevada, Sheriff's Department)

Note that in this section our focus is on the police traffic function alone. In Chapter 9, which deals generally with police accountability, we extend this discussion to include accusations of racial bias that can flow from traffic stops that subsequently involve searches of citizens.

Enforcement of Traffic Laws: Triumph and Trouble

A 2006 report by the Federal Bureau of Justice Statistics stated that there are 193 million drivers in the United States and that each year about 16.8 million, or 8.7 percent, of those who are over age sixteen will be stopped each year by the police. Although total drivers are evenly divided between males and females, males (60.8 percent) are stopped by police at a much higher rate than females (39.2 percent); furthermore, young drivers (ages sixteen to twenty-four) are more likely to be stopped by the police (26 percent of the total). About six in ten persons who are stopped are ticketed for a violation.[57] Table 5-2 shows the characteristics of drivers stopped by police compared to characteristics of all drivers in the United States, by gender, age, and race.

Police endeavor to reduce traffic deaths and injuries through the enforcement of traffic laws, and on its face, this is a noble undertaking. But this is a very delicate area of contact between citizens and their police. Indeed, citizens may have their one and only contact with a police officer because of some traffic-related matter; therefore, the extent to which the officer displays a professional demeanor—and the attitude and demeanor projected by the citizen—may well have long-term effects for both and carry long-term significance for both community policing (which relies heavily on community teamwork)

TABLE 5-2

Characteristics of Drivers Stopped by Police Compared to Characteristics of Drivers in the United States: Gender, Age, and Race/Hispanic Origin

Demographic Characteristic	DRIVERS STOPPED BY POLICE IN 2002		DRIVERS IN THE UNITED STATES	
	Number	Percent	Number	Percent
Total	16,783,467	100.0%	192,687,190	100.0%
Gender				
Male	10,210,452	60.8%	96,291,891	50.0%
Female	6,573,016	39.2	96,387,512	50.0
Age				
16–19	1,653,563	9.9%	12,125,184	6.3%
20–24	2,707,711	16.1	17,301,693	9.0
25–29	1,999,671	11.9	16,268,499	8.4
30–34	1,765,379	10.5	18,303,679	9.5
35–39	1,976,042	11.8	19,890,322	10.3
40–44	1,737,807	10.4	21,720,402	11.3
45–49	1,497,266	8.9	19,868,465	10.3
50–54	1,214,760	7.2	17,018,579	8.8
55–59	859,629	5.1	13,609,756	7.1
60–64	599,061	3.6	10,324,572	5.4
65–69	313,104	1.9	8,317,154	4.3
70–74	208,994	1.2	7,028,204	3.6
75 or older	250,480	1.5	10,867,718	5.6
Age				
16–24	4,361,274	26.0%	29,434,855	15.3%
25 or older	12,422,193	74.0	163,245,009	84.7
Race/Hispanic origin				
White	12,842,254	76.5%	146,779,643	76.2%
Black	1,852,086	11.0	20,260,621	10.5
Hispanic	1,595,872	9.5	18,619,405	9.7
Other race	493,256	2.9	7,000,729	3.6

Note: Detail may not add to total due to estimation procedures.

Source: U.S. Department of Justice, Bureau of Justice Statistics, *Characteristics of Drivers Stopped by the Police* (Washington, DC: Author, June 2006), p. 2.

and public relations. More than a few bond issues to hire new officers, purchase new equipment, or build a new police station house have been defeated at the ballot box because of ill will created by the police traffic function.

There are differing levels of traffic enforcement. Some departments are relatively lenient, but others have initiated ticket quotas, and some jurisdictions pressure their officers to have a "ticket blizzard" to generate revenue. Aside from often being rankled by having to pay a fine, many citizens also believe the police should be engaged in other, "more important" functions ("Why aren't you out catching bank robbers?"). Therefore, traffic stops can be a major source of friction between police officers and citizens, and strict traffic enforcement policies can negatively impact police-community relations.[58] Furthermore, because of a process known as "extinction"—people forgetting about the traffic citation they received and the need to obey traffic laws—the long- and even short-term deterrent effects of handing out traffic citations have been called into question.[59]

Despite citizen disgruntlement with traffic enforcement, traffic stops and citations generally remain an integral part of police work. Police administrators find such work to be easily verifiable evidence that their officers are working.[60] Traffic enforcement has even gone high tech with the advent of the traffic camera, which has been nicknamed "the photocop." Traffic cameras, either mounted on a mobile tripod or permanently fixed on a pole, emit a narrow beam of radar that triggers a flash camera when the targeted vehicle is exceeding the speed limit by a certain amount, usually ten miles per hour.

Police in Berkeley, California, have applied a new twist to the traffic function. Drivers who are "caught" driving safely and courteously are stopped and issued coupons good for movies or free nonalcoholic beverages at a local cafe. This Good Driver Recognition Program, which began with officers' donations, now receives city funding.[61]

Traffic Collision Investigation

Patrol officers have long been required to investigate traffic accidents. (*Note:* The long-used term "traffic accident" is increasingly being replaced with *traffic collision* because "accident" implies that the crash was unintended, but with the increase in road rage incidents and other uses of motor vehicles as weapons, "collision" can include both intended and unintended crashes.) In this era of accountability and litigation, and due to the vast amount of damage done to people and property each year as a result of traffic accidents, it is essential that officers understand this process of investigation and cite the guilty party—not only from a law enforcement standpoint but also in the event that the matter is taken to civil court. Until officers receive formal training in this complex field, they are in a very precarious position.

In addition to basic traffic accident investigation (TAI) training normally provided at the police academy, several agencies offer good in-service courses, and Northwestern University has a renowned TAI program. The process of analyzing road and damage evidence, estimating speeds, reconstructing what occurred and why, issuing citations properly, drawing a diagram of the scene, and explaining what happened in court is too important to be left to untrained officers. The public demands skilled accident investigations.

Pursuit of the "Phantom" Driver

One of the traffic-related areas in which the police enjoy wide public support is their efforts to identify, apprehend, and convict the hit-and-run (or "phantom") driver. No one thinks highly of these drivers (who are often intoxicated) who collide with another vehicle or person and leave the scene. This matter is more of a criminal investigation than an accident investigation for the police. In some states, the killing of a human being by someone driving under the influence (DUI) is a felony. Physical evidence and witness statements must be collected in the same fashion as in a conventional criminal investigation; paint samples and automobile parts left at the scene are sent to crime laboratories for examination. The problem for the police is that unless the driver of the vehicle is identified—by physical evidence, an eyewitness, or a confession—the case can be lost. If the phantom vehicle is located, the owner can simply tell the police that his or her vehicle was stolen or on loan. Thus, the police often must resort to psychology to get a confession by convincing the suspect that incriminating evidence exists.

Chapter 14, dealing with police technology, contains information on the use of the Global Positioning System (GPS) for investigating traffic accidents.

SUMMARY

This chapter has examined several issues related to the patrol function, which can be fairly stated as being the essence of policing. It discussed the purposes and nature of patrol; the influence of an officer's shift, beat, and vehicle; some hazards of this function; the discretionary authority of patrol officers; and the traffic function. The latter, an often unpopular task, nevertheless occupies a major place in the police milieu.

It was demonstrated that the patrol function is truly the backbone of policing, the primary means by which the police fulfill their mission. As noted earlier, patrol officers do the work of community policing and problem solving, and they are the eyes and ears of the police organization. Patrol is the beginning point for all other specialized and administrative assignments, where citizens go to lodge concerns and complaints and where the needs of the community are met.

Because of the importance of patrol, research has tried to determine what works on patrol, and research findings on the patrol function were also presented—clearly it concerns more than just "driving around." Perhaps we have not yet reached the point of understanding how to best deploy patrol officers to their maximum effect, but research is demonstrating that some patrolling methods, which for decades were felt to be "tried and true," are myths and do not work. Ongoing research on the patrol function is needed. The fundamental—and seemingly simple—police task of seeing and being seen is indeed complicated and challenging. Knowledge of patrol utilization and effectiveness becomes more crucial because research has shown the crime-solving ability of detectives to be overrated. We have also seen that the street cop performs a variety of duties while using wide discretion in deciding how to handle problems.

In essence, this chapter has attempted to put readers in the patrol officer's position by giving them a sense of what's involved in that profession.

KEY TERMS

beat assignment
beat culture
deployment
discretionary use of police authority
Kansas City Preventive Patrol Experiment
Law Enforcement Officers Safety Act of 2004 (H.R. 218)
occupational hazard
patrol function
patrol vehicle
shift assignment
suicide by cop
traffic control

REVIEW QUESTIONS

1. How is the patrol function affected by the officer's shift assignment and the nature of the beat to which he or she is assigned?

2. What are some of the occupational hazards that are inherent in beat patrol? What does H.R. 218 permit?

3. What is meant by suicide by cop, and what is the two-step investigative process that needs to take place to determine when it has occurred and to analyze the phenomenon?

4. What are some of the major findings of studies of the patrol function? (Emphasize in your answer the Kansas City Preventive Patrol Experiment.)

5. What is meant by discretionary use of police authority, and what are some of its advantages, disadvantages, and factors that enter into the officer's decision-making process?

6. Why is the traffic function important in patrol work, and how can it bring about bad citizen-police relations?

7. Why is the patrol vehicle so important in the lives and duties of patrol officers?

INDEPENDENT STUDENT ACTIVITIES

1. If possible, participate in a ride-along program with local police officers. Try to determine the primary differences in police work from shift to shift and from officer to officer; the extent of the emphasis on the traffic function; and the recognition of, and potential for,

danger while on duty. Observe the patrol methods that the officers use, the manner in which the patrol vehicle is equipped (including the officers' own tools brought to the vehicle), and the various lethal and less-lethal weapons they carry.

2. Examine the use of police discretion in a local law enforcement agency. Which offenses allow officers little or no discretionary use of authority? Which offenses provide the greatest amount of freedom in terms of options? What do officers see as the advantages and disadvantages of this discretion?

RELATED WEB SITES

COPNET (links to law enforcement agencies nationwide)
http://police.sas.ab.ca

Northwestern University Traffic Institute
http://server.traffic.northwestern.edu

Police Executive Research Forum
http://www.policeforum.org

Police Foundation
pfinfo@policefoundation.org

U.S. Department of Justice, Federal Bureau of Investigation, *Crime in the United States: Uniform Crime Reports*
http://www.fbi.gov/ucr/killed/2006/feloniouslykilled.html

COMMUNITY-ORIENTED POLICING AND PROBLEM SOLVING

ADDRESSING CRIME AND DISORDER

If people are informed, they will do the right thing. It's when they are not informed that they become hostages to prejudice.
—*Charlayne Hunter-Gault*

Well done, good and faithful servant! You have been faithful with a few things; I will put you in charge of many things.
—*Matthew 25:21*

LEARNING OBJECTIVES

AS A RESULT OF READING THIS CHAPTER, THE STUDENT WILL:

- BE ABLE TO DEFINE COMMUNITY-ORIENTED POLICING AND PROBLEM SOLVING (COPPS) AND TO DESCRIBE HOW THIS CONCEPT DIFFERS FROM TRADITIONAL POLICING

- KNOW AND UNDERSTAND THE FOUR PARTS OF THE SARA PROBLEM-SOLVING PROCESS FOR POLICE

- BE ABLE TO DESCRIBE SOME IMPORTANT CONSIDERATIONS FOR IMPLEMENTING AND EVALUATING COPPS INITIATIVES

- KNOW WHAT IS MEANT BY CRIME PREVENTION, AND BE ABLE TO DESCRIBE HOW IT RELATES TO COMMUNITY POLICING AND PROBLEM SOLVING

- BE ABLE TO SUMMARIZE SOME MEANS BY WHICH COPPS CAN ADDRESS NEIGHBORHOOD DISORDER, DOMESTIC VIOLENCE, AND JUVENILE PROBLEMS (AFTER READING THE CASE STUDIES IN THE CHAPTER)

- UNDERSTAND THE ROLE OF THE PATROL OFFICER UNDER COPPS

INTRODUCTION

This is a uniquely challenging time to be entering police work. As mentioned in Chapter 1, a strategy that runs counter to the professional model of policing is spreading across the country: community-oriented policing and problem solving (COPPS). This chapter examines the rationale for and methods of that strategy, which represents a return to the philosophy and practices of policing of the early nineteenth century.

For the past several decades, the dominant police strategy emphasized motorized patrol, rapid response time, and retrospective investigation of crimes. Those strategies have some merit for police operations, but they were not designed to address root community problems but were instead designed to detect crime and apprehend criminals— hence the image of the "crime fighter" cop. Current wisdom holds that the police cannot unilaterally attack the burgeoning crime, drug, and gang problems that beset our society, draining our federal, state, and local resources. Communities must police themselves. We also understand that it is time now for new police methods and measures of effectiveness.

This chapter begins by examining community-oriented policing (COP), and then it reviews a more recent development, which extends COP by using the community to address crime and disorder: problem-oriented policing (POP). Included is an overview of the scanning, analysis, response, assessment (SARA) problem-solving process. Following that, we look at how these two interrelated and complementary concepts work to engage the community in crime fighting through what has been termed *community-oriented policing and problem solving (COPPS)*. We review how COPPS should be implemented and evaluated and how it relates to two elements of crime prevention: environmental design and repeat victimization. Next are two case studies of problem-solving efforts by police in Charlotte-Mecklenburg, North Carolina, and Tulsa, Oklahoma. A chapter summary, key terms, review questions, independent student activities, and related Web sites conclude the chapter.

BASIC PRINCIPLES OF COMMUNITY POLICING

Redefined Role

There is a growing awareness that the community can and must play a vital role in problem solving and crime fighting. A fundamental aspect of **community-oriented policing (COP)** has always been that the public must be engaged in the fight against crime and disorder. And as we noted in Chapter 1, Robert Peel emphasized in the 1820s in his principles of policing that the police and community should work together.[1]

In the early 1980s, the notion of community policing emerged as the dominant model for thinking about policing. It was designed to reunite the police with the community.[2] No single program describes community policing. Community policing has been applied in various forms by police agencies in the United States and abroad and differs according to community needs, local politics, and available resources.

COP is much more than a police-community relations program; it attempts to address crime control through a working partnership with the community. Community institutions such as families, schools, and neighborhood and merchants' associations are seen as key partners with the police in creating safer, more secure communities. The views of community members have greater status under community policing than under the traditional policing model.[3]

Citizen input is crucial to the police for crime detection and prevention.

(Courtesy Hayward, California, Police Department)

COP is a long-term process that involves fundamental institutional change. This concept redefines the role of the officer on the street from crime fighter to problem solver and neighborhood ombudsman. It forces a cultural transformation of the entire department, including a decentralized organizational structure and changes in recruiting, training, awards systems, evaluations, and promotions. This philosophy also requires officers to break away from the binds of incident-driven policing and to seek proactive and creative resolution to the problems of crime and disorder.

The major points at which COP departs from traditional policing are shown in Table 6-1.

Community Building in New Station House Design and Amenities

Even traditional monolithic police station houses are being changed in terms of design and amenities in some jurisdictions in order to better engage in community building. Generally, the public areas of most station houses are very stark, cold, unfriendly places. As is true for trips for the dentist, few people go to their police station voluntarily, but some jurisdictions are hoping to change that.

In the Los Angeles Police Department (LAPD) West Valley Station, in Reseda, California, residents will find ATMs in the light-filled lobby, kitchen-equipped meeting rooms for public use, and even an inviting outdoor courtyard with barbecue facilities. Gone from such "second-generation" station houses are the small windows that were located

TABLE 6-1

Traditional versus Community Policing: Questions and Answers

QUESTION	TRADITIONAL POLICING	COMMUNITY POLICING
Who are the police?	A government agency principally responsible for law enforcement.	The police are the public, and the public are the police: The police officers are those who are paid to give full-time attention to the duties of every citizen.
What is the relationship of the police force to other public-service departments?	Priorities often conflict.	The police are one department among many responsible for improving the quality of life.
What is the role of the police?	To focus on solving crimes.	To take a broader problem-solving approach.
How is police efficiency measured?	By detection and arrest rates.	By the absence of crime and disorder.
What are the highest priorities?	Crimes that are high value (e.g., bank robberies) and those involving violence.	Whatever problems disturb the community most.
What, specifically, do police deal with?	Incidents.	Citizens' problems and concerns.
What determines the effectiveness of police?	Response times.	Public cooperation.
What view do police take of service calls?	Deal with them only if there is no real police work to do.	View them as a vital function and a great opportunity.
What is police professionalism?	Responding swiftly and effectively to serious crime.	Keeping close to the community.
What kind of intelligence is most important?	Crime intelligence (study of particular crimes or series of crimes).	Criminal intelligence (information about the activities of individuals or groups).
What is the essential nature of police accountability?	Highly centralized; governed by rules, regulations, and policy directives; accountable to the law.	Emphasis on local accountability to community needs.
What is the role of headquarters?	To provide the necessary rules and policy directives.	To preach organizational values.
What is the role of the press liaison department?	To keep the "heat" off operational officers so they can get on with the job.	To coordinate an essential channel of communication with the community.
How do the police regard prosecutions?	As an important goal.	As one tool among many.

Source: Malcolm K. Sparrow, Department of Justice, National Institute of Justice, "Implementing Community Policing" (Washington, DC: U.S. Government Printing Office, November 1988), pp. 8–9.

high off the ground to deter drive-by shootings but which made the buildings look like bunkers and armed camps. Such police stations also typically offer more areas that are open to the public (such as cafeterias where officers and civilians can eat together), bigger lobbies where people can comfortably sit, and community rooms where people can hold meetings and training sessions.[4]

LAPD's West Valley ("second-generation") Station House.

(Courtesy LAPD; used with permission)

MAJOR STEP FORWARD: PROBLEM-ORIENTED POLICING

Problem solving is not new—police officers have always tried to solve problems. The difference is that in the past, officers received little guidance, support, or technology from police administrators for dealing with problems, so the routine application of problem-solving techniques is new. It is premised on two facts: that problem solving can be applied by officers throughout the agency as part of their daily work and that routine problem-solving efforts can be effective in reducing or resolving problems.

Problem-oriented policing (POP) was grounded on different principles than COP, but they are complementary. POP is a strategy that puts the COP philosophy into practice because it advocates that police examine the underlying causes of recurring incidents of crime and disorder. The problem-solving process helps officers identify problems, analyze them completely, develop response strategies, and assess the results.

Herman Goldstein is considered by many to be the principal architect of POP. Goldstein coined the term "problem-oriented policing" in 1979 out of frustration with the dominant model for improving police operations: "More attention [was] being focused on how quickly officers responded to a call than on what they did when they got to their destination."[5]

Goldstein argued for a radical change in the direction of efforts to improve policing. The first step in POP is to move beyond just handling incidents and recognize that incidents are often overt symptoms of problems. It requires that officers take a more in-depth interest in incidents by acquainting themselves with some of the conditions and factors that cause them. The expanded role of police officers under POP is discussed later.

POP has at its nucleus a four-stage problem-solving process known as **scanning, analysis, response, assessment (SARA)**.[6]

Scanning: Problem Identification

Scanning involves problem identification. As a first step, officers should identify problems on their beats and look for a pattern, or persistent repeat incidents. At this juncture, the question might well be asked, "What is a problem?" *Problem* may be defined as a group of two or more incidents that are similar in one or more respects, causing harm and, therefore, being of concern to the police and the public. Incidents may be similar in various ways:

- *Behaviors.* People's behaviors are the most frequent indicator and include activities such as drug sales, robberies, thefts, and graffiti.
- *Locations.* Problems may occur in area hot spots, such as in downtown areas, in housing complexes plagued by burglaries, and in parks in which gangs commit crimes.
- *People.* Both repeat offenders and repeat victims account for a high proportion of crime.
- *Time.* Incidents may be similar in terms of the season, the day of the week, or the hour of the day; examples include rush hours, bar closing times, and tourist seasons.
- *Events.* Crimes may peak during events such as university spring break, rallies, and gatherings.

There does not appear to be any inherent limit on the types of problems patrol officers can face because all types of problems are candidates for problem solving.

Numerous resources are available to the police to help them identify problems, including calls for service (CFS) data, especially repeat calls from the same location or a series of similar incidents. Other ways include citizen complaints, census data, data from other government agencies, newspaper and media coverage of community issues, officer observations, and community surveys.

The primary purpose of scanning is to conduct a preliminary inquiry to determine whether a problem really exists and whether further analysis is needed. During this stage, priorities should be established if multiple problems exist, and a specific officer or team of officers should be assigned to handle the problem. Scanning initiates the problem-solving process.

Analysis: Heart of Problem Solving

The second stage, analysis, is the heart of the problem-solving process. Crime analysis has been defined as "a set of systematic, analytical processes providing timely and pertinent information to assist operational and administrative personnel."[7]

Effective tailor-made responses cannot be developed unless people know what is causing the problem. Thus the purpose of analysis is to learn as much as possible about a problem in order to identify its causes. Complete analysis includes identifying the seriousness of the problem, knowing all the individuals or groups involved and affected, listing all the causes of the problem, and assessing current responses and their effectiveness.

Over time, several methods have been developed for analyzing crime and disorder. We examine some of them now: the problem-analysis triangle; the use of crime mapping and offense reports, the analysis of CFS; and the use of community surveys.

PROBLEM-ANALYSIS TRIANGLE.   One tool that may be used for analyzing problems is the **problem-analysis triangle**, which helps officers visualize the problem and understand the relationship between the three elements of the triangle (see Figure 6-1). Additionally, it suggests where more information is needed and helps with crime control and prevention. Generally, three elements must be present before a crime or harmful behavior—a problem— can occur: an offender (someone who is motivated to commit harmful behavior), a victim (a desirable and vulnerable target), and a location (although the victim and offender are not always in the same place at the same time; we discuss locations later). If these three elements show up over and over again in patterns of recurring problems, removing one of these elements can stop the pattern and prevent future harm.[8]

MAPPING AND OFFENSE REPORTS   Computerized crime mapping (discussed in greater detail in Chapter 14) also assists with crime analysis. Mapping combines geographic information from global positioning satellites with crime statistics gathered by the department's computer-aided dispatching (CAD) system and demographic data provided by private companies or the U.S. Census Bureau.

Police offense reports can also be useful, analyzed for suspect characteristics, *modi operandi* (MOs), victim characteristics, and many other factors. Offense reports are also a potential source of information about high-crime areas and addresses, since they capture exact descriptions of locations. In a typical department, however, patrol officers may write official reports on only about 25 to 30 percent of all calls to which they respond. Another limitation is that there may be a considerable lag between when the officer files a report and when the analysis is complete.[9]

FIGURE 6-1
Problem-Analysis Triangle

Source: Department of Justice, Bureau of Justice Assistance, Comprehensive Gang Initiative: Operations Manual for Implementing Local Gang Prevention and Control Programs *(Draft, October 1993), p. 3.*

Once disorder begins to descend on a location, crime soon follows—and the police will become involved.

(Courtesy Reno, Nevada, Police Department)

Computer software now exists for COPPS to assist with profiling beats and demographics, finding patterns of problems, helping plan daily officer activities, balancing beat and officer workloads, and identifying current levels of performance. Such software can scan through hundreds of millions of pieces of data for patterns, trends, or clusters in beats and neighborhoods while ranking and reranking problems. In the field, the officer simply highlights the neighborhood, beat, or grid under consideration and then selects the problem or problems to be worked on from a menu on the computer.

CFS ANALYSIS With the advent of CAD systems, a more reliable source of data on CFS has become available. CAD systems, containing information on all types of CFS, add to information provided by offense reports, yielding a more extensive account of what the public reports to the police.[10] The data captured by CAD systems can be sorted to reveal hot spots of crime and disturbances—specific locations from which an unusual number of calls to the police are made.

A study in Minneapolis on hot spots analyzed nearly 324,000 CFS for a one-year period over all 115,000 addresses and intersections. The results showed relatively few hot spots accounting for the majority of calls to the police[11]:

- In all the calls, 50 percent came from 3 percent of the locations.
- All robbery calls came from 2.2 percent of the locations.
- All rape calls came from 1.2 percent of the locations.
- All auto thefts came from 2.7 percent of the locations.

Many police agencies have the capability to use CAD data for repeat-call analysis (which is related to repeat victimization, discussed later). The repeat-call locations identified in this way can become targets of directed patrol efforts, including problem solving. For example, a precinct may receive printouts of the top twenty-five CFS areas to review for problem-solving assignments. In Houston, the police and Hispanic citizens were concerned about violence at cantinas (bars). Through repeat-call analysis, police learned that only 3 percent of the cantinas in the city were responsible for 40 percent of the violence. The data narrowed the scope of the problem and enabled a special liquor-control unit to better target its efforts.[12]

Repeat alarm calls are another example of how CAD data can be used to support patrol officer problem solving. In fact, when an experiment began in Baltimore County, Maryland, some commanders preferred that officers start with alarm projects. Data documenting repeat alarm calls by address were readily available, and commanders anticipated that solving alarm problems would be relatively simple and would bring considerable benefits compared to the investment of time.[13]

COMMUNITY SURVEYS   Not to be overlooked in crime analysis is the use of community surveys to analyze problems. For example, an officer may canvass all the business proprietors in shopping centers on his or her beat. In Baltimore, an officer telephoned business owners to update the police department's after-hours business contact files. Although the officer did not conduct a formal survey, he used this task to inquire about problems the owners might want to bring to police attention.

Citizen surveys provide the police with valuable information about citizen concerns and police performance.

(Courtesy Reno, Nevada, Police Department)

On a larger scale, a team of officers may survey residents of a housing complex or neighborhood known to have particular crime problems. The survey could assist in determining residents' priority concerns, acquiring information about hot spots, and learning more about residents' expectations of police.[14] Residents are also more likely to keep the police abreast of future problems when patrol officers leave their cards and encourage residents to contact them directly.

Many police agencies now provide citizens with crime analysis information via the Internet. As an example, Exhibit 6-1 shows the home page of the Tempe, Arizona, Police Department's Crime Analysis Unit.

Response: Formulation of Tailor-Made Strategies

After a problem has been clearly defined and analyzed, the officer confronts the ultimate challenge in POP: the search for the most effective way of dealing with it. The response may be quite simple (such as reprogramming a public telephone at a convenience store where drug dealers conduct their "business" so that it only makes outgoing calls) or quite involved (for example, screening and evicting some tenants from a housing complex; cleaning up a neighborhood that is overcome with graffiti, debris, and junk cars; taking legal action to create a curfew; or condemning and razing a drug house).[15] A number of examples of responses are provided in the two COPPS case studies discussed later.

This stage of the SARA process focuses on developing and implementing responses to the problem. Before entering this stage, the police agency must overcome the temptation to implement a response prematurely and must be certain that it has thoroughly analyzed the problem; attempts to fix problems quickly are rarely effective in the long term.

Assessment: Evaluation of Overall Effectiveness

Finally, in the assessment stage, officers evaluate the effectiveness of their responses. A number of measures have traditionally been used by police agencies and community members to assess effectiveness. These include numbers of arrests; levels of reported crime; response times; clearance rates; citizen complaints; and various workload indicators, such as CFS and the number of field interviews conducted.[16] Several of these measures may be helpful in assessing the impact of a problem-solving effort.

A number of nontraditional measures will also shed light on whether a problem has been reduced or eliminated[17]:

- Reduced instances of repeat victimization
- Decreases in related crimes or incidents
- Neighborhood indicators, including increased profits for businesses in the target area, increased usage of the area, increased property values, less loitering and truancy, and fewer abandoned cars

EXHIBIT 6-1

The Home Page of the Tempe, Arizona, Police Department's Crime Analysis Unit

ABOUT CRIME ANALYSIS

Historically, the causes and origins of crime have been the subject of investigation by varied disciplines. Following are some factors known to affect the volume and type of crime occurring from place to place:

- Population density and degree of urbanization with size locality and its surrounding area
- Variations in composition of the population, particularly youth concentration
- Stability of population with respect to residents' mobility, commuting patterns, and transience
- Modes of transportation and highway system
- Economic conditions, including median income, poverty level, and job availability
- Cultural factors and educational, recreational, and religious characteristics
- Family conditions with respect to divorce and family cohesiveness
- Climate
- Effective strength of law enforcement agencies
- Administrative and investigative emphases of law enforcement
- Policies of other components of the criminal justice system (for example, prosecutorial, judicial, correctional, and probational)
- Citizens' attitudes toward crime
- Crime-reporting practices of the citizenry

DEFINITION OF CRIME ANALYSIS

A set of systematic, analytical processes directed at providing timely and pertinent information relative to crime patterns and trend correlations to assist the operational and administrative personnel in planning the deployment of resources for the prevention and suppression of criminal activities, aiding the investigative process, and increasing apprehensions and the clearance of cases. Within this context, Crime Analysis supports a number of department functions including patrol deployment, special operations and tactical units, investigations, planning and research, crime prevention, and administrative services (budgeting and program plan ning). [Steven Gottlieb et al., 1994, "Crime Analysis: From First Report to Final Arrest"]

Source: Tempe, Arizona, Police Department

TYPES OF CRIME ANALYSIS

Tactical. Provides information used to assist operations personnel (patrol and investigative officers) in identifying specific and immediate crime trends, patterns, series, sprees, and hot spots; investigating leads; and clearing cases. Analysis includes associating criminal activity by method of the crime, time, date, location, suspect, vehicle, and other types of information.

    Strategic. Is concerned with long-range problems and projections of long-term increases or decreases in crime (crime trends). Strategic analysis also includes the preparation of crime statistical summaries, resource acquisition, and allocation studies.

    Administrative. Focuses on provision of economic, geographic, or social information to administration.

CRIME ANALYSIS PERSONNEL

The Tempe Police Department's Crime Analysis Unit consists of three full-time crime analysts and a full-time crime analysis clerk. The Tempe Police Department's Crime Analysis Unit performs all three types of crime analysis: tactical, strategic, and administrative.

INTERESTING STATISTICS

- The population of Tempe was 165,890 in 2006.
- There were a total of 128,818 citizen-generated calls for service in 2006 (a 0.5% decrease from 2005).
- The most common type of citizen-generated call for service is the "suspicious activity" call. These calls account for approximately 10.5% of the total number of citizen-generated calls for service.
- Approximately one police report is generated for every four calls for service (these are not necessarily criminal reports).
- In 2006 Tempe's crime rate was 82.9 Part I crimes per 1,000 persons.

    To develop tailored responses, problem solvers should review their findings about the three sides of the crime triangle—victims, offenders, and locations—and develop creative solutions that will address at least two sides of the triangle. It is also important to remember that the key to developing tailored responses is making sure that the responses are very focused and directly linked to the findings from the analysis phase of the project.

    Responses may be wide ranging and often require arrests, referral to social service agencies, or changes in ordinances. Note that apprehension is not always the most effective solution.

- Increased citizen satisfaction regarding the handling of the problem, determined through surveys, interviews, focus groups, electronic bulletin boards, and so on
- Reduced citizen fear related to the problem

Assessment is obviously key in the SARA process; knowing that we must assess the effectiveness of our efforts emphasizes the importance of documentation and baseline measurement. Supervisors can help officers assess the effectiveness of their efforts.

Exhibit 6-2 provides an example of the SARA process in action in Oakland, California.

COLLABORATIVE APPROACH: BASIC PRINCIPLES OF COPPS

The two concepts of COPPS are separate but complementary notions that can work together. Both COP and POP share some important characteristics: (1) decentralization (to encourage officer initiative and the effective use of local knowledge), (2) geographically defined rather than functionally defined subordinate units (to encourage the development of local knowledge), and (3) close interactions with local communities (to facilitate responsiveness to, and cooperation with, the community).[18] The following definition accurately captures the essence of this concept:

> Community-Oriented Policing and Problem Solving (COPPS) is a proactive philosophy that promotes solving problems that are criminal, affect our quality of life, or increase our fear of crime, as well as other community issues. COPPS involves identifying, analyzing, and addressing community problems at their source.[19]

For COPPS to succeed, the following measures are required[20]:

- Conducting accurate community needs assessments
- Mobilizing all appropriate players to collect data and brainstorm strategies
- Determining appropriate resource allocations and creating new resources where necessary
- Developing and implementing innovative, collaborative, comprehensive programs to address underlying causes and causal factors
- Evaluating programs and modifying approaches as needed

IMPLEMENTATION OF COPPS

Since COPPS came into being, most police executives have implemented the strategy throughout the entire agency. Some executives, however, have attempted to introduce the concept in a small unit or an experimental district,[21] often in a specific geographic area of the jurisdiction.

It is strongly argued that a departmentwide implementation of COPPS be used. When COPPS is established as a distinct unit within patrol rather than departmentwide,

EXHIBIT 6-2

A Winning Example: The Oakland Airport Motel Program

The Oakland Police Department (OPD) addressed a serious motel problem near its local airport. For the following efforts, the OPD won the coveted Herman Goldstein Award for Excellence in Problem-Oriented Policing, conferred at the annual International Problem Oriented Policing Conference:

- *Scanning.* Located along a major gateway to the city of Oakland, the Oakland Airport Motel is situated within a commercial area comprising lodging, restaurants, and fast-food outlets; it is also situated about two miles from Oakland's professional baseball, football, and basketball franchises. A complainant informed an Oakland officer that while working at the motel for several weeks, prostitutes soliciting sex had approached him nightly, that prostitutes "had the run of the place," and that there were loud parties and disturbances each night around the clock, junked vehicles littering the parking lot, and the smell of marijuana coming through his window nightly as well.

- *Analysis.* After consulting with city zoning and attorney offices concerning applicable laws, an officer reviewed the property owner information and determined that a large corporation owned the motel, there was not a policy of limiting the duration of guest stays, and a disproportionately high number of narcotics arrests had occurred over the previous two years. The officer made a site visit, photographing and documenting his observations and interviewing tenants and motel staff. He noted that a corner of the motel parking lot was used as a freelance and illegal auto repair business, that rooms were routinely rented to minors, and that prostitution activity was rampant. A review of police incidents over three years revealed that the motel had an astounding 900 percent higher number of police incidents than comparable area lodging facilities.

- *Response.* A response plan was developed. Phase One involved working with the motel manager to clean up the property and to deal with problem tenants. A policy was implemented to restrict renting rooms to persons age twenty-one or older, to evict problem tenants in a timely manner, to monitor the parking lot to prevent junked vehicles from being dumped there, and to fire employees caught renting out rooms "under the table" and using their passkeys. Corporate officials balked at several of these initiatives, however, so the officer sent a drug nuisance

abatement notification letter to the motel. Police surveillance revealed that motel security guards were not taking affirmative steps to keep nuisances out of the parking lot, and frequent prostitution and open drug transactions continued to occur. An undercover officer rented rooms at the motel; on two occasions, motel managers changed the room lock and took the undercover officer's property left in the rooms so as to double-rent the rooms. Given this lack of improvement, Phase Two involved meeting with the motel's corporate officials. A document was prepared covering the criminal activity at the motel over a three-year period; descriptions and photographs of the prostitution and violent crimes occurring at the site; and the legal consequences and costs of not complying with relevant legal, health, and safety codes. It was requested that the motel be closed for 90 days to improve the physical aspects and to retrain motel staff in their proper duties and that the corporate officials post a $250,000 performance bond and repay OPD for investigative costs. Corporate officials promised swift change; again, however, there was little improvement in the conditions at the motel after two weeks had passed. Phase Three of the project was then launched: preparation of lawsuits and negotiations. Police continued surveillance of activities at the motel, and a drug nuisance abatement lawsuit was prepared for filing and sent to the chief executive officer at his home in France. Finally, after seven hours of negotiations, corporate officials agreed to post the performance bond and to pay the city $35,000 in fees and expenses incurred to date. Furthermore, barbed wire was installed along all fence lines to discourage fence climbing, area lighting was upgraded, room rates were increased by 50 percent to improve its clientele, room rentals for more than 30 days were prohibited, foot and vehicle traffic was stopped for identification by security guards, a "no-rent" list was developed for banned guests, cleaning and painting of the property was accomplished, rigorous background checks were performed on new employs, and problem employs were terminated.

- *Assessment.* Seven months after these activities were launched, calls for service to the motel dropped by 59 percent. Two years later, there had been only one call for police service. Overall crime and nuisance activity were also on par with the other five adjacent motels.

Source: Adapted from "The Oakland Airport Motel Program: Eliminating Criminal and Nuisance Behavior at a Motel," in U.S. Department of Justice, National Institute of Justice, *Best Practices in Problem-Oriented Policing: Winners of the 1999 Herman Goldstein Award for Excellence in Problem-Oriented Policing* (Oakland, CA: Oakland Police Department, 2003), pp. 1–7.

the introduction of this "special unit" seems to exacerbate the conflict between community policing's reform agenda and the more traditional outlook and hierarchical structure of the agency. A perception of elitism is created—a perception that is ironic because COPPS is meant to close the gap between patrol and special units and to empower and value the rank-and-file patrol officer as the most important functionary of police work.

The key lesson from research in **implementation**, however, is that there is no golden rule or any universal method to ensure the successful adoption of COPPS. Two general propositions are important, however, for implementing the concept: the role of the rank-and-file officer and the role of the environment (or "social ecology") where COPPS is to be implemented.[22] The social ecology of COPPS includes both the internal/organizational and external/societal environments.

Moving an agency from the reactive, incident-driven mode to COPPS is a complex endeavor, often requiring a complete change in the culture of the police organization. Four principal components of implementation profoundly affect the way agencies do business: leadership and administration, human resources, field operations, and external relations.[23] These factors are discussed next.

Leadership and Administration

It is essential that the chief executive communicate the idea that COPPS is department-wide in scope. To get the whole agency involved, the chief executive must adopt four practices as part of the implementation plan[24]:

1. Communicate to all department members the vital role of COPPS in serving the public. They must understand why handling problems is more effective than just handling incidents.
2. Provide incentives to all department members to engage in COPPS. This includes a new and different personnel evaluation and reward system as well as positive encouragement.
3. Reduce the barriers to COPPS that can occur. Procedures, time allocation, and policies all need to be closely examined.
4. Show officers how to address problems. Training is a key element of COPPS implementation. The executive must also set guidelines for innovation. Officers must know they have the latitude to innovate.

Human Resources

With regard to human resources, middle managers (captains and lieutenants) and first-line supervisors (sergeants) also play a crucial role in planning and implementing COPPS and in encouraging their officers to be innovative, take risks, and be creative.[25] First-line supervisors and senior patrol officers seem to generate the greatest resistance to community policing, largely because they have long-standing working styles cultivated from years of traditional police work and because these officers can feel disenfranchised by a management system that takes the best and brightest out of patrol and (they often believe) leaves them behind.

Field Operations

Furthermore, the mechanisms that motivate, challenge, reward, and correct employees' behaviors in the field must be compatible with the principles of COPPS. These include recruiting, selection, training, performance evaluation, promotion, honors and awards, and discipline, all of which should be reviewed to ensure that they promote and support the tenets of COPPS. First, recruiting literature should reflect the principles of COPPS. A job-task analysis identifying the new knowledge, skills, and abilities should be conducted and become a part of the testing process for entry-level employees. COPPS should also be integrated into academy training, field-training programs, and in-service training. Performance evaluations and reward systems should reflect new job descriptions and officers' application of their COPPS training. Finally, promotion systems should be expanded from their usual focus on tactical decision making, should include knowledge of the research on community policing, and should test an officer's ability to apply problem solving to various crime and neighborhood problems.

External Relations

Collaborative responses to neighborhood crime and disorder are essential to the success of COPPS. This requires new relationships and the sharing of information and resources between the police and the community, local government agencies, service providers, and businesses. The media provide an excellent means for police to educate the community about COPPS and crime and disorder.

Political support is another essential consideration when implementing COPPS. The political environment varies considerably, say, with the strong mayor and council-manager forms of government. These and other rapidly changing political environments make the implementation of COPPS more difficult—especially when we add to the mix the at-will employment of most police executives.

BROADER ROLE FOR THE STREET OFFICER

A major departure of POP from the conventional style lies with POP's view of the line officer, who is given much more discretion and decision-making ability and is trusted with a much broader array of responsibilities.

POP values "thinking" officers, urging that they take the initiative in trying to deal more effectively with problems in the areas they serve. This concept effectively uses the potential of college-educated officers, "who have been smothered in the atmosphere of traditional policing."[26] It also gives officers a new sense of identity and self-respect; they are more challenged and have opportunities to follow through on individual cases—to analyze and solve problems—which will give them greater job satisfaction. Using patrol officers in this manner allows the agency to provide sufficient challenge for both those who are better educated and those who remain patrol officers throughout their entire career.[27]

Under POP, officers continue to handle calls, but they also do much more. They combine the information gathered in their responses to incidents with information obtained from other sources to get a clearer picture of the problem. They then address the underlying conditions. If they are successful in ameliorating these conditions, fewer incidents may occur, and those that do occur may be less serious; the incidents may even cease. At the very least, information about the problem can help police design more effective ways of responding to each incident. Police administrators ought to be recruiting people as police officers who can "serve as mediators, as dispensers of information, and as community organizers."[28]

Exhibit 6-3 provides information on community policing in another location: Japan.

EXHIBIT 6-3

Comparative Closeup
Community Policing in Japan

Japan possesses the oldest and best-established community policing system in the world. Japan initiated its system immediately after World War II out of a combination of traditional culture and American democratic ideals. Four elements are at the core of this philosophy: (1) community-based crime prevention, (2) reorientation of patrol activities to emphasize nonemergency servicing, (3) increased accountability to the public, and (4) decentralization of command.[1]

Each of Japan's 47 prefectures has its own autonomous police force, and together they employ about 220,000 officers—on densely populated islands totaling about 144,000 square miles and 150 million people.[2] The officers deal face-to-face with citizens daily and, therefore, have become a part of the community rather than being separated from the people in a vehicle. Also, Japanese neighborhood crime-prevention associations have generally given Japanese culture a much closer relationship between people and their neighbors.

Japanese police place heavy emphasis on order maintenance and crime prevention, aiding the community to resolve problems that could lead to disorder. Counseling services are part of every Japanese police station, provided by an experienced older officer and ranging from family disputes to questions about contracts and indebtedness. Trained in dispute resolution, the police are able to provide a helpful informal conciliation.[3]

The urban police officer in Japan visits neighborhood households and does police business in what is termed the koban.[4] A koban may be found every few blocks, and there are about 15,000 kobans across the country—8,000 of which have officers who actually live inside. Police officers generally stand watch at the doorway of the koban or at nearby traffic intersections to help minimize crimes and traffic accidents, direct traffic, and make arrests when necessary. The Japanese police try to keep the number of people for which a koban is responsible to less than 12,000 and the area to less than four-tenths of a square mile.[5]

1. Jerome H. Skolnick and David H. Bayley, *Community Policing: Issues and Practices around the World* (Washington, DC: National Institute of Justice, 1988).

2. Richard J. Terrill, *World Criminal Justice Systems: A Survey,* 5th ed. (Cincinnati, OH: Anderson, 2003), pp. 378–380.

3. David H. Bayley, *Forces of Order: Police Behavior in Japan and the United States* (Berkeley: University of California Press, 1991), p. 87

4. *Community Police Activities of Japan* (Tokyo: National Police Agency of Japan, 1992), pp. 2, 9.

5. David H. Bayley, *A Model of Community Policing: The Singapore Story* (Washington, DC: U.S. Department of Justice, National Institute of Justice, 1989), p. 8.

DID IT SUCCEED? EVALUATING COPPS

Rigorous **evaluation** is an essential component of the COPPS initiative. Until rigorous evaluations are completed, there will be no clear verdict about whether the COPPS approach made a difference in controlling crime and disorder. An evaluation will also help to determine whether a crime-prevention initiative has achieved such goals as reducing crime and the fear of crime, has raised the community's quality of life, and is worthy of continued funding.

Evaluating the outcomes of problem-solving projects is not the same as the assessment stage of the SARA problem-solving process. Evaluation is the more overarching concept and involves large projects—surveys, performance evaluations, and so on. Broken down into simplified steps, evaluation asks some or all of the following questions[29]:

- What is the problem? (Define it by such measures as community indicators, police data, and public surveys.)
- How does the project intend to address the problem? (Look at the project's goal statements.)
- What does the project do to resolve the problem? (Look at the project's objectives.)
- How does the project carry out its objectives? (Look, for example, at collaborative efforts among the police, other governmental agencies, and private businesses.)
- What impact (over time) does the prevention project have on the problem? (For example, over a specified time period, reported crimes increased or decreased by what percentage?)

The evaluative criteria employed in the professional policing model, such as crime rates, clearance rates, and response times, have been problematic when applied to the professional model itself and are even less appropriate for the COPPS model. These measures do not gauge the effect of crime-prevention efforts. A decrease in the reliance on these quantitative measures of police success is also important because communities differ in the services they desire, depending on their particular characteristics.[30]

Several criteria can assist in assessing the success of a COPPS effort. An effective COPPS strategy has a positive impact on reducing neighborhood crime, allays citizen fear of crime, and enhances the quality of life in the community.[31] Assessing the effectiveness of COPPS efforts includes determining whether problems have indeed been solved and how well the managers and patrol officers have used community partnerships.

COPPS evaluations can include outcome measures and impact measures. Outcome measures might include the following[32]:

- *Control of crime.* Compare, for example, the present rates of serious and violent crimes with those of an earlier time period. Included in this category are behavioral changes, such as the increased use of a once drug-infested park or a greater number of students attending drug-education programs.
- *Citizen satisfaction with police services and decrease in their fear of crime.* Satisfaction is measured with basic survey techniques (discussed later). Content analysis of media portrayals of police work, analysis of letters from citizens, and analysis of citizen complaints can also be used to evaluate citizen satisfaction with police services.

Outcome measures can also reflect environmental changes (such as number of street lights installed, traffic patterns altered, graffiti removed).

Impact measures describe and monitor changes in community indicators (such as community efforts to prevent or deal with crime and violence, community perception of quality of life, level of business, and other activity in the area).[33]

CRIME PREVENTION

An important corollary of COPPS—and a critical and rapidly developing concept that all police officers should understand—is crime prevention. It stands to reason that it is preferable as well as much less expensive (in terms of both financial and human resources) to prevent a crime from occurring in the first place rather than to try to solve the offense and arrest, prosecute, and possibly incarcerate the offender. A focus on crime prevention shifts a police organization's purpose. Once the question becomes "How can we prevent the next crisis?" all kinds of approaches become possible.[34]

Crime prevention once consisted primarily of exhorting people to "lock it or lose it" and giving advice to citizens about door locks and window bars for their homes and businesses. It typically was (and often still is) an add-on program for the police agency, which normally included a few officers who were trained to go to citizens' homes and perform security surveys or to speak publicly on the subject of target hardening. Times are rapidly changing in this regard.

Crime prevention and COPPS are close companions, attempting to define the problem, identify the contributing causes, seek out the proper people or agencies to assist in identifying potential solutions, and work as a group to implement the solution. The problem drives the solution.[35] At its heart, COPPS is about preventing crime.

Next we briefly discuss two important aspects of crime prevention—crime prevention through environmental design and repeat victimization—and briefly mention a drug-prevention program.

Crime Prevention through Environmental Design

Crime prevention through environmental design (CPTED) is defined as the "proper design and effective use of the environment that can lead to a reduction in the fear and incidence of crime, and an improvement in the quality of life."[36] At its core are three principles that support problem-solving approaches to crime[37]:

1. *Natural access control.* Employ elements such as doors, shrubs, fences, and gates to deny access to a crime target and to create a perception among offenders that there is a risk in selecting the target.
2. *Natural surveillance.* Place windows, lighting, and landscaping properly to increase the ability to observe intruders as well as regular users, allowing observers to challenge inappropriate behavior or to report it to the police or to the property owner.
3. *Territorial reinforcement.* Use elements such as sidewalks, landscaping, and porches to distinguish between public and private areas and to help users exhibit signs of ownership that send hands-off messages to would-be offenders.

Five types of information are needed for CPTED planning[38]:

1. *Crime-analysis information.* Crime mapping, police crime data, incident reports, and victim and offender statistics are all included.
2. *Demographics.* Statistics about residents, such as age, race, gender, income, and income sources, are used.
3. *Land use information.* Zoning information (such as residential, commercial, industrial, school, and park zones) as well as occupancy data for each zone is analyzed.
4. *Observations.* Information includes observations of parking procedures, maintenance, and residents' reactions to crime.
5. *Resident information.* Resident crime surveys and interviews with police and security officers are assessed.

Repeat Victimization

Our society—including the police—gives far greater attention to criminal offenders than to crime victims. Just as at the zoo, where there always seem to be more spectators around the lions and tigers than around wildebeests and antelope, more attention is focused on the predators than on their prey. However, an evolving body of research in Great Britain suggests that crime victims should be placed on the national agenda. In the United States—where POP has spread across the country—patterns of **repeat victimization (RV)** have not been examined or assimilated into problem solving. Police officers in the United States would benefit from this developing body of knowledge, which can play a major role in crime prevention and analysis.

The premise underlying RV is that if the police want to know where a crime will occur next, they should look at where it happened last. RV is not new; police officers have always been aware that the same people and places are victimized again and again. What is new, however, are attempts abroad to incorporate RV knowledge into formal crime-prevention efforts.

One in three burglaries reported in the United States is a repeat burglary of a household. Furthermore, a 48 percent RV rate was found for sexual incidents (including grabbing, touching, and assault), 43 percent for assaults and threats, and 23 percent for vehicle vandalism.[39] A study of white-collar crime indicated that the same people are victims of fraud and embezzlement time and time again[40] and that banks that have been robbed also have high rates of RV.[41] These data show that providing crime-prevention assistance to potential victims is not only morally justifiable in most instances but also an efficient and practical way of allocating limited police resources.

Why would a burglar return to burgle the same household again? One could argue that, for several reasons, the burglar would be stupid not to return: Temporary repairs to a burgled home will make a subsequent burglary easier, the burglar is familiar with the physical layout and surroundings of the property, the burglar knows what items of value were left behind at the prior burglary, and the burglar also knows that items that were taken at an earlier burglary are likely to have been replaced through insurance policies.

RV is arguably the best single predictor routinely available to the police in the absence of specific intelligence information. A small number of victims accounts for a disproportionate number of victimizations.[42]

Drug Abuse Resistance and Education

A related attempt to prevent crime should be discussed briefly: the well-known Drug Abuse Resistance and Education (DARE) program. The program, launched in 1983 and now administered by police in 80 percent of schools, has not fared well among researchers. Over the past decade, studies have repeatedly shown that the $226 million program has little effect on keeping kids from abusing drugs. Indeed, the mayor of Salt Lake City recently halted the city's budget for DARE, declaring it "a complete waste of money, a fraud on the American people."[43] One of its key flaws, researchers allege, has been that students are taught that all drugs are equally dangerous; when students find that this is not true, the DARE message is undercut.[44]

Now DARE officials are admitting that the program needs a new direction. Officials are revamping the program, reducing the lecturing role of local officers and involving kids in a more active way. A new curriculum is being developed for use in some schools that will show brain scans after drug use to demonstrate the harm, shift officers into more of a coaching role, and have kids engage in role-playing about peer pressure.[45]

COPPS CASE STUDIES

Following are two excellent case studies of COPPS efforts using the SARA model. The first is in Charlotte-Mecklenburg, North Carolina,[46] and the second in Tulsa, Oklahoma.[47] In each case, instead of merely showing up at a crime scene, taking offense reports, and leaving the scene, the police employed a variety of responses to combat crime and disorder.

Addressing Domestic Violence in Charlotte-Mecklenburg

SCANNING   For several years, the Charlotte-Mecklenburg, North Carolina, Police Department (CMPD) had made domestic assaults a priority and had worked to analyze those cases, intervene, and reduce the occurrence of domestic violence in the community. Then an officer working a particularly serious domestic case became concerned about the overall number of domestic assaults in his patrol district in a year's time: 305 domestic assaults, or 30 percent of the total assaults. Many of these assaults involved the same individuals but at different locations in the county; rather than a repeat-call location being the hot spot for crime, he surmised that tracking *participants* might be a better indicator of future violence.

ANALYSIS   A much more thorough analysis of domestic assault reports showed that the average victim had filed nine previous police reports, most involving the same suspect but sometimes crossing police district boundaries. Many of the prior reports were for other indicator crimes, such as trespassing, threatening, and stalking. Most repeat-call locations were domestic situations. It became clear that it was best to regard the victim and suspect as the hot spots instead of a fixed geographic location.

RESPONSE   Officers developed a tailored response plan for each repeat offense case, including zero tolerance of criminal behavior by the suspect and assistance from other criminal justice and social services agencies. A Police Watch Program was implemented in which systematic zone checks of both the victim's residence and workplace were made when appropriate. A Domestic Violence Hotline voice-mail system was also initiated, which victims could use to report miscellaneous incidents involving the suspect. Officers developed detailed case files and created a separate database with victim and offender background data. The database tracked victims and offenders as moving hot spots from one address to another and across patrol district boundaries.

ASSESSMENT   Repeat calls for service were reduced by 98.9 percent at seven target locations. Domestic assaults decreased 7 percent in this targeted patrol district while increasing 29 percent in the rest of the city. Only 14.8 percent of domestic violence victims in the project reported repeat victimization, as opposed to a benchmark figure of 35 percent. No internal affairs complaints were generated by officer contacts with suspects.

Ameliorating Juvenile Problems in Tulsa

SCANNING   North Tulsa experienced consistently higher crime rates than the rest of the city. Nearly half of the violent crimes that were reported occurred in this section of the city—a depressed low-income area lacking adequate services. The Tulsa Housing Authority was established to support the city's low-income public housing. In an attempt to determine the nature of the crime problem in North Tulsa, a special management team of Tulsa police officials conducted a study and decided to concentrate on five public-housing complexes where high crime rates and blatant street dealing existed.

ANALYSIS   A residential survey conducted by patrol officers revealed that 86 percent of the occupants lived in households headed by single females. Officers in the target area noticed large groups of school-age youth in the housing complexes who appeared to be selling drugs during school hours. A comparison of the dropout and suspension rates in North Tulsa schools with those in other areas of the city determined that the city's northernmost high school, serving most of the high school–age youth in the five complexes, had the highest suspension (4.4 percent) and dropout (10 percent) rates of any school in the city. It also reported the highest number of pregnant teenagers in the school system. Few of the juveniles observed in the complexes had legitimate jobs, and most of them appeared to be attracted to drug dealing by the easy money.

Supervisors at Uniform Division North placed volunteers into two-officer foot teams, assigned to the complexes on eight-hour tours. The teams established a rapport with residents and assured them that police were present to ensure their safety. Within a month, officers verified juvenile involvement in drug trafficking. A strategy was needed to provide programs to deter youth from selling or using drugs.

RESPONSE   Officers S. and N., assigned to foot patrol at one of the complexes, believed that the youth needed programs that would improve their self-esteem, teach them values, and impart decision-making skills. Because 86 percent of the boys came from homes without fathers, the officers started a Boy Scout troop in the complex for boys between eleven and seventeen years of age to provide positive role models for them. Officer N., a qualified Boy Scout leader, and Officer S. began meeting with the boys on Saturdays in a vacant apartment.

Officers J. and E. also organized a Boy Scout troop. In addition, they started a group that worked to raise money for needy residents and police-sponsored youth activities. Officer J. spoke at civic group meetings and local churches throughout the city to solicit donations and increase awareness of the needs of young people on the city's north side. Volunteers came from the churches and the civic groups where Officer J. spoke.

Officers B. and F., foot patrol officers at another complex, developed plans for unemployed young people. Officer B. organized a group called the Young Ladies Awareness Group, which hosted guest speakers who taught different job-related skills each week. Programs instructed young women how to dress for job interviews and employment; role-playing officers demonstrated proper conduct during interviews. The women were also instructed in résumé writing and makeup, hair care, and personal hygiene. Officer F. worked with a government program that sponsored sessions on setting goals and building self-esteem to prepare young people to enter job-training programs. Officer F. also helped area youth apply for birth certificates and arranged for volunteers from the Oklahoma Highway Patrol and a local school to help teach driver's education. Officers even provided funds for young people who were unable to pay the fees to obtain birth certificates or driver's licenses. Officers F. and B. also tried to explain the value of an education and persuade youth in their complex to return to school. Unfortunately, parents too often appeared unconcerned when their children missed classes.

The foot patrol officers became involved in a day camp project conducted at "the Ranch," a 20-acre northside property that the police had confiscated from a convicted drug dealer. The project used the property for a day camp for disadvantaged youth recruited from the target projects. Tulsa's mayor and chief of police came to the Ranch to meet with the youth, as did psychologists, teachers, ministers, and celebrities. Guests tried to convey the value of productive and drug-free lives, among other ethical values.

To combat dropout and suspension problems, a program called Adopt a School had police officers patrol the schools during classes, not to make arrests but rather to establish rapport with the students. The program was intended to reduce the likelihood of student involvement in illegal activities.

ASSESSMENT   The police noted a decline in street sales of illegal drugs in the five target complexes. Youth reacted positively to the officers' efforts to help them, and the programs seemed to deter them from drug involvement. The police department continued to address the problems of poor youth in North Tulsa. Foot patrol officers met with the Task Force for Drug Free Public Housing to inform the different city, county, and statewide officials of the needs of youth in public housing. Other social services agencies began working with the police department, establishing satellite offices on the north side of the city, scheduling programs, and requesting police support in their efforts.

SUMMARY

This chapter examined the basic principles and strategies of the current community era—the era in which policing now resides (as noted in Chapter 1). It examined community policing and problem solving (COPPS), which is the best strategy for addressing neighborhood crime and disorder now and in the future. Blending the two concepts of community policing and problem-oriented policing results in a better, more comprehensive, and long-term approach to providing quality police service, combining the emphasis on forming a police-community partnership to fight crime with the use of the SARA problem-solving process. It was shown that two very important components of this philosophy are the expanded role of the street officer and the focus on crime analysis.

The associated strategy of crime prevention, including crime prevention through environmental design (CPTED) and repeat victimization (RV), is equally important. It is clear that the field of crime prevention has "matured" from its earlier forms, originally involving strategic placement of rocks by early cave dwellers and more recently having to do primarily with target hardening one's home with better locks. This chapter has shown their various elements as well as the results of research efforts concerning what good can occur when measures are taken to prevent crimes.

The overarching theme is that the police realize that they alone cannot prevent or address crime and disorder and that a partnership with the community is essential if the physical and social problems that plague communities are to be reduced or eliminated.

KEY TERMS

community-oriented policing (COP)
crime prevention through environmental design (CPTED)
evaluation
implementation
problem-analysis triangle
repeat victimization (RV)
scanning, analysis, response, assessment (SARA)

REVIEW QUESTIONS

1. How would you define community policing, and what are some of the major ways this concept differs from traditional policing?

2. What are the four parts of the SARA problem-solving process?

3. Why are the implementation and evaluation phases of COPPS so critical?

4. What is meant by crime prevention, and how does it relate to COPPS?

5. What do the case studies demonstrate in terms of what COPPS can do with domestic violence and juvenile problems?

INDEPENDENT STUDENT ACTIVITIES

1. Determine whether the COPPS strategy has been adopted by agencies in your local area. If it has, how does COPPS differ in terms of agency philosophy and methods from the traditional professional model of policing?

2. Using information provided in this chapter concerning the SARA problem-solving process, perform a problem-solving exercise with a particularly crime-ridden neighborhood, beat, or area of your jurisdiction.

RELATED WEB SITES

Community Policing Consortium
http://www.communitypolicing.org

National Crime Prevention Council
http://www.ncpc.org

Office of Community Oriented Policing Services (COPS)
http://www.usdoj.gov/cops

CHAPTER 7

CRIMINAL INVESTIGATION

THE SCIENCE OF DETECTION

And the Lord said unto Cain, Where is thy brother Abel?
[The first recorded instance of a criminal interrogation]
And he said, I know not; am I my brother's keeper?
[The first recorded instance of perjury]
And He said, what hast thou done? The voice of thy brother's blood crieth unto me
from the ground. [The first recorded instance of criminal evidence]
—Genesis 4:9–10

Murder though it hath no tongue will speak.
—Shakespeare, Hamlet, *Act II, Scene 2*

LEARNING OBJECTIVES

AS A RESULT OF READING THIS CHAPTER, THE STUDENT WILL:

– BE ABLE TO DISTINGUISH BETWEEN *FORENSIC SCIENCE* AND *CRIMINALISTICS*

– UNDERSTAND THE ORIGINS OF CRIMINALISTICS

– BE ABLE TO COMPARE ANTHROPOMETRY AND DACTYLOGRAPHY

– UNDERSTAND HOW AUGUST VOLLMER AND OTHERS CONTRIBUTED TO THE DEVELOPMENT OF CRIMINAL INVESTIGATION TECHNIQUES

– KNOW THE KINDS OF QUALITIES THAT DETECTIVES NEED TO POSSESS

– BE ABLE TO EXPLAIN THE BASIC FUNCTIONS OF THE POLYGRAPH AND ITS LEGAL STATUS IN THE COURTS

– UNDERSTAND HOW DNA ANALYSIS OPERATES AS WELL AS ITS FUTURE OUTLOOK, BOTH LEGALLY AND SCIENTIFICALLY

– KNOW WHAT IS MEANT BY FORENSIC ENTOMOLOGY AND ITS ADVANTAGES IN CRIMINAL INVESTIGATION

– COMPREHEND HOW DOGS ARE BEING TRAINED TO ASSIST IN INVESTIGATIONS

– UNDERSTAND HOW STALKING AND CYBERCRIMES ARE INVESTIGATED

– KNOW THE PURPOSE AND OPERATION OF A COLD CASE SQUAD

INTRODUCTION

The challenges involved with investigating crimes may well be characterized by a quote from Ludwig Wittgenstein: "How hard I find it to see what is right in front of my eyes!"[1] Investigating crimes has indeed become a complicated art as well as a science, as will be seen in this chapter.

The art of sleuthing has long fascinated the American public. Certainly the expanding uses of DNA in the news; such television series as *CSI: Crime Scene Investigation*; and books and movies describing real-life serial killers such as the "Zodiac," "BTK," the "Green River Killer," and the "Night Stalker" have done much to capture the public's fascination with criminal investigation and forensic science in the twenty-first century. This interest in sleuthing is not a recent phenomenon, however; for decades, Americans have feasted on the exploits of dozens of fictional masterminds, including Sherlock Holmes, Agatha Christie's Hercule Poirot, Clint Eastwood's portrayal of Detective "Dirty Harry" Callahan, and Peter Falk's Columbo, to name a few.

In reality, investigative work is largely misunderstood, often boring, and generally overrated; it results in arrests only a fraction of the time; and it relies strongly on the assistance of witnesses and even some luck. Nonetheless, the related fields of forensic science and criminalistics are the most rapidly developing areas of policing—and probably in all of criminal justice. This is an exciting time to be in the investigative or forensic disciplines.

This chapter begins by defining forensic science and criminalistics and by looking at their origins; included is a brief discussion of crime scenes. Then we discuss the evolution of criminal investigation, emphasizing the identification of people and firearms. Next we analyze the application of forensic science within the larger context of the criminal justice system, followed by a review of the qualities detectives should have.

We also consider undercover police work, briefly touch on the use of polygraph testing, and examine DNA analysis. We then look at behavioral science applications in investigations, including criminal profiling as well as psychics and hypnosis. Finally we examine some recent investigative developments and problems in the field, including forensic entomology, the increasing use of dogs in investigations, the investigation of stalkers and "cybercrooks," the handling of cold cases, and the recent concern with and oversight of forensic laboratories. A chapter summary, key terms, review questions, independent student activities, and related Web sites conclude the chapter.

Note that a large number of textbooks are available that cover in depth the many topics that exist within the broad area of criminal investigation. Several of them are listed in the Notes section at the end of the book, and the reader is encouraged to seek them out for further, more in-depth inquiry.

SCOPE OF FORENSIC SCIENCE AND CRIMINALISTICS

Definitions of Terms

The terms **forensic science** and **criminalistics** are often used interchangeably. Forensic science is the broader term and is that part of science used to answer legal questions. It is the examination, evaluation, and explanation of physical evidence in law. Forensic science encompasses pathology, toxicology, physical anthropology, odontology (development of dental structure and dental diseases), psychiatry, questioned documents, ballistics, tool work comparison, and serology (reactions and properties of serums), among other fields.[2] Criminalistics is one branch of forensic science; it deals with the study of physical evidence related to crime. From such a study, a crime may be reconstructed (see Exhibit 7-1).

Criminalistics is interdisciplinary, drawing on mathematics, physics, chemistry, biology, anthropology, and many other scientific fields.[3] Dr. Paul Kirk, a leader in the criminalistics movement in this country, once remarked: "Criminalistics is an occupation that has all of the responsibilities of medicine, the intricacy of the law, and the universality of science."[4] Criminalistics has occasionally reached plateaus, but on the whole it is a dynamic and progressive discipline.

EXHIBIT 7-1

Making His Bones: Famed Sculptor Is a Secret Weapon in Missing-Person Cases

He's a sculptor of international renown, but to those in law enforcement, Philadelphia artist Frank Bender is a secret weapon capable of re-creating from just the bones a face so uncannily like that of its owner that he is credited with helping investigators around the country solve their most stubborn missing-person cases....

Bender has done 28 sculptures for police. Each takes approximately one month, and he charges $1,700—the amount he says agencies are willing to pay. In his most recent case, he was asked to help identify a man whose decapitated and dismembered body was found in two burn barrels last summer in the Pocono Mountains of Pennsylvania....

Bender, 61, is also a founding member of the Vidocq Society, an organization of 82 individuals who, upon request, will put their considerable forensic expertise to work on tough investigations....

When constructing his sculptures, Bender works with a chart that gives tissue thickness for 21 points of the face, depending on a victim's age, race and ethnicity. But it is the skull that is the "road map of the face," abetted by a healthy dose of Bender's own intuition....

Among his most famous re-creations was that of John List, an accountant who murdered his mother, wife, and three children in their New Jersey home in 1971 [and] then disappeared. Working with a profiler, Bender was able to come up with a clay bust that was shown on "America's Most Wanted." List was captured a few days after the program aired in 1989.

Another was Anna Mary Duval, a 62-year-old Phoenix woman who had been shot three times in the head. Years later, mobster John Martini was convicted of her murder.

Bender also does age reconstructions, some of which have led to the capture of drug traffickers and gangsters....

And it was Bender's pastel-and-charcoal renderings, along with busts, of Robert Nauss, a convicted killer and former head of the Warlocks motorcycle gang, and Hans Vorhauer, a methamphetamine manufacturer with a genius IQ, that helped investigators find the pair after they broke out of a Maryland prison in the mid-1980s.

Source: "Making His Bones: Famed Sculptor Is a Secret Weapon in Missing-Person Cases," *Law Enforcement News,* April 15, 2003, p. 4. John Jay College of Criminal Justice, CUNY, 899 Tenth Avenue, New York, NY 10019.

Basically, the analysis of physical evidence is concerned with identifying traces of evidence, reconstructing criminal acts, and establishing a common origin of samples of evidence. Peter DeForest and colleagues described the types of information that physical evidence can provide[5]:

- *Information on the **corpus delicti** (or body of the crime).* Physical evidence, such as tool marks, a broken door or window, a ransacked home, missing valuables in a burglary, a victim's blood, a weapon, or clothing torn in an assault, shows that a crime was committed.

- *Information on the **modus operandi** (or method of operation).* Physical evidence points to the means used by the criminal to gain entry, the tools used in the crime, the types of items taken, and other signs, such as urine left at the scene, an accelerant used at an arson scene, and the way crimes are committed. Many well-known criminals have left their "calling card" at their crimes, in terms of either what they did to their victims or what the physical condition of the crime scene was.

- *Linking of a suspect with a victim.* One of the most important linkages, particularly with violent crimes, is the connection to the suspect. This can include hair, blood, clothing fibers, and cosmetics that may be transferred from the victim to the perpetrator. Items found in a suspect's possession, such as bullets or a bloody knife, can also be linked to a victim.

- *Linking of a person to a crime scene.* Also a common and significant type of linkage, this includes fingerprints, glove prints, blood, semen, hairs, fibers, soil, bullets, cartridge cases, tool marks, footprints or shoe prints, tire tracks, and objects that belonged to the criminal. Stolen property is the most obvious example.

- *Disproving or supporting of a witness's testimony.* Evidence can indicate whether or not a person's version of events is true. An example is a driver whose car matches the description of a hit-and-run vehicle. If blood is found on the underside of the car and the driver claims that he hit a dog, tests on the blood can determine whether the blood is from an animal or from a human.

- *Identification of a suspect.* One of the best forms of evidence for identifying a suspect is fingerprints, which prove "individualization." Without a doubt, that person was at the crime scene.

A Word about Crime Scenes

On the subject of **crime scenes**, we will not go into detail concerning the roles of patrol officers, crime-scene technicians, and investigators at crime scenes; however, it should be emphasized that the protection of the crime scene and all evidence contained therein is of utmost importance for these personnel if the scene is to be properly preserved and evidence collected and analyzed. It is critical that at the moment they arrive, responding personnel are trained to (1) describe vehicles (make, model, color, condition, license plate number) and individuals (height, weight, race, age, clothing, sex, distinguishing features), including their direction of travel from first observation; (2) assess the scene for officer safety (downed power lines, animals, biohazards, chemicals, weapons); (3) watch for violent persons and attend to any emergency medical needs; and (4) prevent any unauthorized persons from entering the scene. A very good resource for crime-scene investigation,

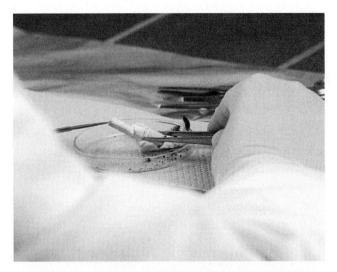
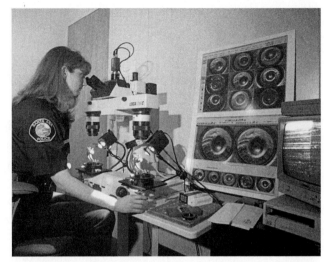
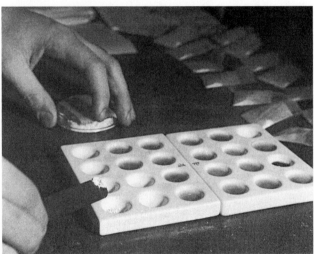
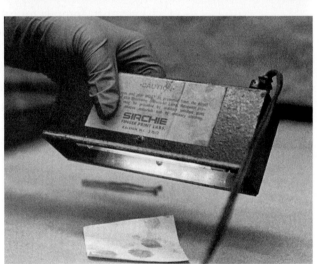

Technology is rapidly advancing in forensic laboratories. Shown here are lab technicians using an automated fingerprinting system, looking into a compound comparison microscope (used to compare items such as fibers and hairs), doing a drug analysis, and performing a ballistics test.

(© Markus Matzel/Peter Arnold, Inc. [top left]; © Spencer Grant [top right]; Getty Images, Inc. [bottom left]; and © Mikael Karlsson/arrestingimages.com [bottom right])

published by the National Institute of Justice, is titled *Crime Scene Investigation: A Reference for Law Enforcement Training.*[6]

ORIGINS OF CRIMINALISTICS

The study of criminalistics began in Europe. The first major book describing the application of scientific disciplines to criminal investigations was written in 1893 by Hans Gross, a public prosecutor and later a judge from Graz, Austria.[7] Translated into English in 1906, the book remains a highly respected work in the field. Two prominent aspects of criminalistics, personal identification and firearms analysis, are covered next, followed by a discussion of individual contributions, investigative techniques, and state and federal developments in the field.

Personal Identification: Anthropometry and Dactylography

ANTHROPOMETRY   Historically there have been two major systems for personal identification of criminals: anthropometry and **dactylography**. The former did not survive long; the latter, better known as fingerprint identification, is widely used throughout the world today.

Anthropometry was developed by Alphonse Bertillon (1853–1914) in 1882. The **Bertillon system**, the first attempt at criminal identification that was thought to be reliable and accurate, was based on the theory that human beings differ from each other in the exact measurements of their bodies and that the sum of these measurements yields a characteristic formula for each individual.[8]

Bertillon performed menial tasks in 1879 for the Paris Police Department, filing cards that described criminals so vaguely as to have little meaning—"stature: average… face: ordinary."[9] He began comparing photographs of criminals and taking measurements of those who had been arrested, and eventually he concluded that if eleven physical measurements of a person were taken, the chances of finding another person with the same eleven measurements were 4,191,304 to 1.[10] Bertillon's report of his findings to his superiors was treated as a "joke," however[11]; but in 1883 his "joke" was given worldwide attention when it was implemented on an experimental basis and Bertillon correctly made his first criminal identification.[12]

Around the start of the twentieth century, many countries abandoned anthropometry, or the **Bertillon system**, adopting the simpler and more reliable system of fingerprint identification.[13] Still, Bertillon's pioneering work in personal identification has earned him a place in history, and today he is considered the "father of criminal investigation."[14]

DACTYLOGRAPHY   Dactylography was first used in 1900 in England as a system of criminal identification; however, fingerprints have a long legal and scientific history. In the first century, a Roman lawyer named Quintilianus introduced a bloody fingerprint at trial, successfully defending a child accused of murdering his father.[15] In 1684 in England, Dr. Nehemiah Grew first called attention to the system of pores and ridges in the hands and feet; in 1823, John Perkinje named nine standard types of fingerprint patterns and outlined a broad method of classification.[16] Despite these developments, fingerprinting would not emerge as a prominent means of criminal identification for another seventy-five years.

Beginning in 1858, William Herschel, a British official in India, requested the palm prints and fingerprints of those with whom he did business, and eventually he came to believe that they were individualistic; in 1877, however, his superiors told Herschel that his idea was insane, so he never pursued his theory.[17] In 1888, Sir Francis Galton (1822–1911) became interested in criminal investigation and contacted Herschel, who unselfishly turned over all of his files in the hope that Galton could apply fingerprinting

A police officer taking Bertillon measurements.

(Courtesy St. Louis, Missouri, Police Department)

to practical police uses.[18] In 1892, Galton published the first definitive book on dacty-lography, *Finger Prints*, in which he presented statistical proof of the uniqueness of fin-gerprints and of their applications.[19] In Argentina two years later, Juan Vucetich outlined his method of fingerprint classification. A disciple of Vucetich's, Inspector Alvarez, obtained the first American criminal conviction based on fingerprints in 1892 when they helped convict a woman who beat her two sons to death.[20]

The major breakthrough for fingerprints was made by Edward Henry (1850–1931), who developed a fingerprint-classification system in 1897 that was adopted throughout British India. In 1901, Henry published his *Classification and Use of Finger Prints* and was appointed assistant police commissioner of London, rising to the post of commissioner two years later.[21]

The Jones Case. In 1904, Detective Sergeant Joseph Faurot of New York City was sent to England to study fingerprints. Upon his return to New York, Faurot was told by his superiors to forget such scientific nonsense, and he was transferred to a walking beat. In 1906, Faurot arrested a man who was creeping out of a suite at the Waldorf-Astoria Hotel; the man claimed to be a respected citizen named James Jones, but Faurot sent the man's fingerprints to Scotland Yard and learned that "James Jones" was actually Daniel Nolan, who had twelve prior convictions for hotel thefts. Nolan confessed to several thefts in the

Waldorf-Astoria and was sent to prison for seven years. Publicity surrounding this case greatly advanced the credibility of fingerprinting in America.[22]

The West Case. An even more important incident that furthered the use of fingerprints in America occurred in 1903 when Will West arrived at the federal penitentiary in Leavenworth, Kansas. While West was being processed into the institution, a staff member said that a photograph was already on file for him, along with Bertillon measurements. West denied ever having been in Leavenworth. A comparison of fingerprints showed that despite nearly identical physical appearance and Bertillon measurements, the identification card on file belonged to a William West who had been in Leavenworth since 1901. The incident served to establish the superiority of fingerprints over anthropometry as a system of personal identification.

Firearms Identification

Firearms are perennially the leading instrument of death for Americans, used in about two-thirds of the nation's seventeen thousand homicide deaths each year.[23] Furthermore, the Centers for Disease Control recently found in an eight-year study that 93 percent of all firearms-related deaths involve the intentional use of guns.[24] The frequency of shootings in this country has made firearms identification very important.

The "West Brothers" case.

(Courtesy Federal Bureau of Investigation)

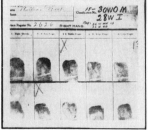

In 1835, Henry Goddard made the first successful attempt to identify a murderer from a bullet recovered from the body of a victim. Goddard noticed that the bullet had a distinctive slight gouge on it and seized a bullet mold with a corresponding gouge at the home of a suspect; the defendant confessed.[25] In 1889, a Professor Lacassagne removed a bullet from a corpse in France, finding seven grooves made as the bullet passed through the barrel of a gun; Lacassagne identified the gun that could have left seven grooves. With this evidence, a man was convicted of the murder.[26] Then, in 1898, a German chemist named Paul Jeserich compared a bullet taken from the body of a man murdered near Berlin with one from the defendant's revolver, later testifying that the defendant's revolver fired the fatal bullet.[27] In 1913, Professor Balthazard published a major article on firearms identification, noting that the firing pin, breechblock, extractor, and ejector all leave marks on cartridges and that these markings vary among different types of weapons. Little progress was then made in this area due to the intervention of World War I.

Chicago witnessed the St. Valentine's Day Massacre in 1929. A special grand jury inquiring into the matter noted that there were no facilities for analyzing the numerous bullets and cartridge cases that had been strewn about. As a result, several influential jury members raised funds to establish a permanent crime laboratory. Colonel Calvin Goddard (1858–1946) was appointed director of the lab, which was established at Northwestern University Law School.[28] Goddard is the person most responsible for raising the status of firearms identification to a science and for perfecting the bullet comparison microscope.[29]

Firearms identification goes beyond comparing a bullet found in the victim and a test bullet fired from the defendant's weapon. It also includes identifying types of ammunition, designing firearms, restoring obliterated serial numbers on weapons, and estimating the distance between a gun's muzzle and a victim when the weapon was fired.[30]

Contributions of August Vollmer and Others

August Vollmer's contributions to the development of criminalistics and investigative techniques were considerable. In 1907, as police chief of Berkeley, California, he enlisted the services of a University of California chemistry professor named Loeb to identify a suspected poison during a murder investigation. Vollmer instituted a formal training program to ensure that his officers properly collected and preserved criminal evidence. Vollmer called on scientists on campus on several other occasions, and his support helped John Larson produce the first workable polygraph in 1921.

Vollmer also established the first full forensic laboratory in Los Angeles in 1923; the concept soon spread to other cities, including Sacramento (a state laboratory), San Francisco, and San Diego. Because Vollmer's subsequent efforts to establish a relationship between his police department and the university led other scientists to get involved in forensic science, eventually courses in forensics were offered as part of the biochemistry curriculum at the University of California at Berkeley,[31] with many graduates of that program becoming criminalists.

Other early major contributors included Albert Osborn, who in 1910 wrote *Questioned Documents,* a definitive work; Edmond Locard, who maintained a central interest in locating microscopic evidence; and Leone Lattes, who in 1915 developed a blood-typing procedure from dried blood, a key event in serology.[32]

Evolving Investigative Techniques in America

Following the advent of private police in America in the mid-1840s (most notably Pinkerton's National Detective Agency, discussed in Chapter 13), the concept of plainclothes officers spread in America. By 1845, New York City had eight hundred such officers, and in 1857 the department was authorized to appoint twenty patrol officers as "detectives."[33] In November 1857, the New York Police Department (NYPD) established a rogues' gallery—photographs of known offenders arranged by criminal specialty and offender height, and by June 1858, it had over seven hundred photographs for detectives to study for future recognition.[34] Several offenders grimaced, puffed their cheeks, rolled their eyes, and otherwise tried to distort their features to lessen the chance of later recognition.[35]

To assist its detectives, in 1884 Chicago established the nation's first municipal Criminal Investigation Bureau[36]; the Atlanta Police Department's Detective Bureau was organized in 1885.[37] In 1886, Thomas Byrnes, chief detective of New York City, published *Professional Criminals in America,* which included pictures, descriptions, and methods of all criminals known to him.[38] To supplement the rogues' gallery, Byrnes instituted the Mulberry Street Morning Parade. Daily at 9 A.M., all criminals arrested in the past twenty-four hours were marched before his detectives, who were expected to take notes and to recognize the criminals later.[39] (In 1894, however, Byrnes was forced to leave the department after growing wealthy by tolerating gambling dens and brothels.[40])

State and Federal Developments

From its earliest days, the federal government employed investigators to detect revenue violations, but their responsibilities were narrow and their numbers few.[41] In 1865, Congress created the U.S. Secret Service to combat counterfeiting. In 1903—two years after the assassination of President McKinley—the guarding of the president was made a permanent Secret Service responsibility.[42] In 1905, the California Bureau of Criminal Identification was established to share information about criminal activity; that same year, the state of Pennsylvania created the Pennsylvania State Police, one of whose functions was to provide local police with assistance in investigations, a tradition that continues today.[43]

The forerunner of what was to become the Federal Bureau of Investigation (FBI) (discussed in Chapter 2) was created in 1908. In 1924, J. Edgar Hoover assumed leadership of the Bureau of Investigation; eleven years later, Congress enacted legislation giving the FBI its present designation. Under Hoover, who understood the importance and uses of information, records, and publicity, the FBI became known for investigative efficiency. In 1932, the FBI established a crime laboratory and made its services free—they remain free of charge today to state and local police. In 1935, it opened its National Academy, providing training courses for state and local police as well as federal officers. And in 1967, the National Crime Information Center (NCIC) was made operational by the FBI, providing data on wanted persons and stolen property in all fifty states. These developments gave the FBI considerable influence over policing in America; Hoover and the FBI vastly improved policing practices in this country, keeping crime statistics and assisting investigations.[44]

FORENSIC SCIENCE AND THE CRIMINAL JUSTICE SYSTEM

Investigative Stages and Activities

The police (more specifically, investigators and criminalists) operate on the age-old theory that there is no such thing as a perfect crime: Criminals either leave a bit of themselves (such as a hair or clothing fiber) at the crime scene or take a piece of the crime scene away with them. Thus it is the job of the police and the crime lab to unify their efforts and to find that incriminating piece of evidence, which they can use in conjunction with other pieces of evidence to determine "whodunit" and to bring the guilty party to justice.

In the apprehension process, when a crime is reported or discovered, police officers respond, conduct a search for the offender (it may be a "hot" crime-scene search where the offender is likely present, a "warm" search in the general vicinity, or a "cold" investigative search), and check out suspects. If the search is successful, evidence for charging the suspect is assembled, and the suspect is apprehended.[45] Cases not solved in the initial phase of the apprehension process are assigned either to an investigative specialist or, in smaller police agencies, to an experienced uniformed officer who functions as a part-time investigator. According to Paul Weston and Kenneth Wells, what follows are the basic **investigative stages**[46]:

Preliminary investigation. The work of the preliminary investigation is crucial, involving the first police officer at the scene. Duties to be completed include establishing whether a crime has been committed; securing from any witnesses a description of the perpetrator and his or her vehicle; locating and interviewing the victim and all witnesses; protecting the crime scene (and searching for and collecting all items of possible physical evidence); determining how the crime was committed and what the resulting injuries were, as well as the nature of property taken; recording in field notes and sketches all data about the crime; and arranging for photographs of the crime scene.

Continuing investigation. The next stage, which begins when preliminary work is done, includes conducting follow-up interviews; developing a theory of the crime; analyzing the significance of information and evidence; continuing the search for witnesses; beginning to contact crime lab technicians and assessing their analyses of the evidence; conducting surveillances, interrogations, and polygraph tests, as appropriate; and preparing the case for the prosecutor.

Reconstruction of the crime. The investigator seeks a rational theory of the crime. Most often, inductive reasoning is used: The collected information and evidence are carefully analyzed to develop a theory. Often, a rational theory of a crime is developed with some assistance from the careless criminal. *Verbrecherpech,* or "criminal's bad luck," is an unconscious act of self-betrayal. One of the major traits of criminals is vanity; their belief in their own cleverness, not chance, is the key factor in their leaving a vital clue. Investigators look for mistakes.

Focus of the investigation. When the last stage is reached, all investigative efforts are directed toward proving that one suspect (perhaps with accomplices) is guilty of the crime. This decision is based on the investigator's analysis of the connections between the crime, the investigation, and the habits and attitudes of the suspect.

Arrest and Case Preparation

A lawful arrest brings the investigation into even greater focus and provides the police with several investigative opportunities. The person arrested can be searched and booked at the police station, and fingerprints are taken for positive identification and possible future use. Evidence may be found at these stages. The prisoner may wish to talk to the police. Here, the officer must obviously know and understand the laws of arrest and search and seizure as well as the laws of evidence (especially the "chain of custody"). Any evidence found during the arrest must be collected, marked, transported, and preserved as carefully as that found at a crime scene.

"Case preparation is organization."[47] For an investigation to succeed at trial, all reports, documents, and exhibits must be arrayed in an orderly manner. This package must then be forwarded to the prosecutor. At this point, the investigator never injects personal opinions or conclusions into the case. The identification of the accused leads to an array of witnesses and physical evidence. The *corpus delicti* of the crime has been established, and the combination of "what happened" and "who did it" has occurred, at least in the mind of the investigator. The investigator must also prepare for the almost inevitable negative evidence that must be countered at trial, where the accused may contend that he or she did not commit the crime. (He or she may try to attack the investigative work, use an alibi, or get the evidence suppressed.) The defendant may offer an affirmative defense, admitting that he or she committed the acts charged but claiming that he or she was coerced, acted in self-defense, was legally insane, and so forth. Or the defendant may attack the *corpus delicti,* contending that no crime was committed or that there was no intent present.[48]

In the prosecutor's office, the case is reviewed, assigned for further investigation, and (if warranted) prepared for trial. Conferences with the investigator and witnesses are usually held. The prosecutor may waive prosecution if the case appears to be too weak to result in a conviction; if the accused will inform on other (usually more serious) offenders; if a plea bargain is more attractive than a trial; or if there are mitigating circumstances in the case (such as emotional disturbance).

An investigation is successful when the crime being investigated is solved and the case closed. Often a case is considered cleared even if no arrest has been made, as when the offender dies, the case is found to be a murder-suicide, the victim refuses to cooperate with the police or prosecutor, or the offender has left the jurisdiction and the cost of extradition is not justified.[49]

DETECTIVES: QUALITIES, MYTHS, AND ATTRIBUTES

The **detective** function is now well established within the police community. A survey by the RAND Corporation revealed that every city with a population of more than 250,000, along with 90 percent of the smaller cities, has officers specifically assigned to investigative duties.[50]

Several myths surround police detectives, who are often portrayed in movies as rugged, confident (sometimes overbearing), independent, streetwise individualists who bask in glory, are rewarded with big arrests, and are adorned by beautiful women. Detective work carries a strong appeal for many patrol officers, young and veteran alike. In reality, detective work is seldom glamorous or exciting. Investigators, like their bureaucratic cousins, often wade in paperwork and spend many hours on the telephone. Furthermore, studies have not been kind to detectives, showing that their vaunted productivity is overrated. Not all cases have a good or even a 50-50 chance of being cleared by an arrest. Indeed, in a study of over 150 large police departments, a RAND research team learned that only about 20 percent of their crimes could have been solved by detective work.[51] Another study, involving the Kansas City, Missouri, Police Department, found that fewer than 50 percent of all reported crimes received more than a minimal half hour's investigation by detectives. In many of these cases, detectives merely reported the facts discovered by the patrol officers during the preliminary investigations.[52]

Yet the importance and role of detectives should not be understated. Detectives know that a criminal is more than a criminal. As Weston and Wells said:

> John, Jane and Richard are not just burglar, prostitute and killer. John is a hostile burglar and is willing to enter a premises that might be occupied. Jane is a prostitute who wants a little more than pay for services rendered and is suspected of working with a robbery gang and enticing her customers to secluded areas. Richard is an accidental, a person who, in a fit of rage, killed the girl who rejected him.[53]

To be successful, the investigator must possess four personal attributes to enhance the detection of crime: an unusual capability for observation and recall; an extensive knowledge of the law, rules of evidence, scientific aids, and laboratory services; a powerful imagination; and a working knowledge of social psychology.[54] Successful detectives (and even patrol officers) also appear to empathize with the suspect; if a detective can appear to understand why a criminal did what he or she did ("You robbed that store because your kids were hungry, right?"), a rapport is often established that results in the suspect's telling the officer his or her life history—including how and why he or she committed the crime in question. Perhaps first and foremost, however, detectives need logical skills, the ability to exercise deductive reasoning, to assist in their investigative work. (An interesting example of the logical skills needed for police work was provided by Al Seedman, former chief of detectives for the New York Police Department, in Chapter 4.)

Homicide investigation is the most important and challenging work performed by detectives.

(Courtesy NYPD Photo Unit)

OFFICERS WHO "DISAPPEAR": WORKING UNDERCOVER

Undercover work is a highly sought-after and valued type of investigative police work. Undercover work can be defined as the assignment of police officers to investigative roles in which they adopt fictitious civilian identities for a sustained period of time in order to uncover criminal activities that are not usually reported to police.[55] (For more about undercover work, see the Practitioner's Perspective by former FBI special agent George Togliatti in Chapter 12.)

Undercover police operations have increased greatly since the 1970s, owing largely to expanded drug investigations. The selection process typically is intense and very competitive. Since only a few officers are actually selected for undercover assignments, these officers enjoy a professional mystique, in large measure because of wide discretionary and procedural latitude in their roles, minimal departmental supervision, ability to exercise greater personal initiative, and higher degree of professional autonomy than regular patrol officers.[56]

Problems with the Role

The conditions of undercover work, however, may lessen officer accountability and lower adherence to procedural due process and confidence in the rule of law.[57] One of the most important requirements is the ability to cultivate informants for information on illegal activities and for contacts with active criminals. Deals and bargains must be struck and honored. Therefore close association with criminals—both the informants and the targeted offenders—heightens the challenges of the undercover role considerably. Undercover officers must sustain a deceptive front over extended periods of time, thereby facing increased risk of stress-induced illness, physical harm, and corruption. One study determined that the greater the number of undercover assignments undertaken, the more drug, alcohol, and disciplinary problems federal officers had during their careers.[58]

Undercover agents can experience profound changes in their value systems, often resulting in an overidentification with criminals and a questioning of certain criminal statutes they are sworn to enforce.[59] These isolated assignments may also involve a separation of self, disrupting or interfering with officers' family relationships and activities and perhaps even leading to a loss of identity and the adoption of a criminal persona as they distance themselves from a conventional lifestyle.[60] Author Gary Marx cites one instance:

> A good example of this is the case of a Northern California police officer who participated in a "deep cover" operation for eighteen months, riding with the Hell's Angels. He was responsible for a very large number of arrests, including previously almost untouchable higher-level drug dealers. But this was at the cost of heavy drug use, alcoholism, brawling, the break-up of his family, an inability to fit back into routine police work, resignation from the force, several bank robberies, and a prison term.[61]

Return to Patrol Duties

Ending an undercover assignment, and then returning to patrol duty, is an awkward experience for many officers, who experience difficulty in adjusting to the everyday routine of traditional police work. These officers may suffer from such emotional problems as anxiety, loneliness, and suspiciousness, and they may experience marital problems. Officers will quickly have less autonomy and diminished initiative in job performance; they are no longer working in a tight-knit unit with expanded freedom and control and no longer feel as though they are behind enemy lines in the battle against crime, where their work experiences are intense and inherently dangerous. The return to routine patrol may be analogous to coming down from an emotional high, and officers in this position may feel depressed and lethargic.[62]

USES OF THE POLYGRAPH

Discussed in Chapter 4 in terms of its use in police recruiting and hiring, the polygraph has also been used by the police in the investigation of serious crimes since at least the early 1900s. The modern polygraph is a briefcase-sized device or computerized model that records changes in skin resistance (perspiration), blood pressure, pulse rate, and breathing. Activity in each of these physiological measurements is monitored and recorded on a paper chart.[63]

The polygraph, commonly referred to as a lie detector, cannot actually detect when a lie is told; therefore, the **polygraph examination** is an inferential process in which "lying" is inferred from comparisons of the aforementioned physiological responses to questions that are asked during polygraph testing. In police work, the two major uses of polygraph testing are specific issue testing and preemployment screening. In specific issue testing, the polygraph is used to investigate whether a particular person is responsible for or involved in the commission of a specific offense. The use of the polygraph for preemployment screening is very controversial and is, in fact, illegal in some jurisdictions. When used, however, polygraph testing can help to verify information collected during traditional background investigations and to uncover information not otherwise available. Studies show that polygraph procedures may yield an accuracy of about 90 percent.[64]

The commonly held belief that polygraph examination results are not admitted into evidence in court is untrue. Some courts admit polygraph evidence even over the objection of counsel; in other jurisdictions, polygraph results are admitted by stipulation. At the federal level, there is no single standard governing admissibility. It is also common for prosecutors to use polygraph results to decide which charges to file, if any, and defense attorneys rely on polygraph testing to plan their defense and to negotiate pleas. Some judges also use polygraph results in sentencing decisions.[65]

DNA ANALYSIS

Discovery and Types of Analyses

Although O. J. Simpson's criminal trial in 1995 brought DNA testing to the attention of most Americans and heightened their interest in it, more recent cases involving the innocence of inmates across the country have caused DNA to be front and center in the news. Indeed, in April 2007 it was reported that the two hundredth person—a former Army cook who spent nearly twenty-five years in prison for a rape he did not commit—was exonerated by DNA evidence (the tenth exoneration since January 2002).[66]

DNA (deoxyribonucleic acid) is the basic building code for all the human body's chromosomes and is the same for each cell of an individual's body, including skin, organs, and all body fluids.[67] Developed in England in 1984 by Alec Jeffreys, forensic DNA is culled either from a tiny blood sample taken from a fingertip (the FBI's preferred method) or from a swab of the inside of the mouth.[68] Forensic science consultant Richard Saferstein, former chief forensic scientist of the New Jersey State Police, states that portions of the DNA structure are as unique to each individual as fingerprints and that inside each of the 60 trillion cells in the human body are strands of genetic material—chromosomes. Arranged along the chromosomes, like beads on a thread, are nearly 100,000 genes, which are the fundamental unit of heredity. They instruct the body cells to make proteins that determine everything from hair color to susceptibility to diseases. Each gene is actually composed of DNA specifically designed to carry out a single body function. Scientists have determined that DNA is the substance by which genetic instructions are passed from one generation to the next.[69]

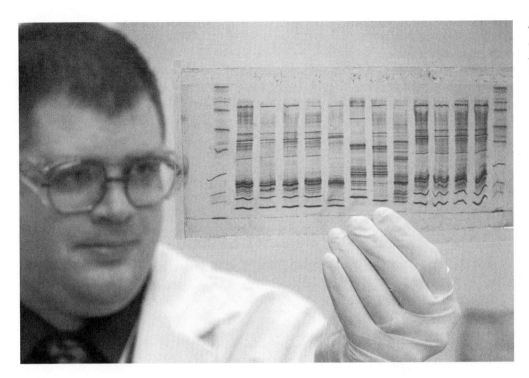

A chemist reads a DNA profile.

(Courtesy U.S. Customs and Border Protection, photographer James Tourtellotte)

DNA profiling, also called genetic fingerprinting or DNA typing, has shown much promise in helping investigators to solve crimes and to ensure that those guilty of crimes are convicted in court by the examination of DNA samples from a body fluid to determine whether they came from a particular subject. For example, semen on a rape victim's jeans can be positively or negatively compared with a suspect's semen. DNA is thus powerful evidence. Indeed, Howard Safir, former New York police commissioner, described DNA typing as the primary tool for the police in reducing crime in the twenty-first century. A further testimonial of DNA's promise in investigations was provided by Elizabeth Devine, former supervising criminalist of the Los Angeles County Sheriff's Department:

> The power of what we can look for and analyze now is incredible. It's like magic. Every day we discover evidence where we never thought it would be. You almost can't do anything without leaving some DNA around. DNA takes longer than fingerprints to analyze, but you get a really big bang for your buck.[70]

The DNA Analysis Unit of the FBI Laboratory analyzes body fluids and body fluid stains recovered as evidence in violent crimes. Examinations include the identification and characterization of blood, semen, saliva, and other body fluids using traditional serological techniques and related biochemical analysis. Once the stain is identified, it is characterized by DNA analysis using what is termed "restriction fragment length polymorphism (RFLP)," which uses highly dangerous radioactive material to produce a DNA image on an X-ray film. Polymerase chain reaction–short tandem repeat (PCR-STR), a second identification method, has several advantages: It requires only a pin-sized sample rather than the dime-sized sample needed for RFLP; if the sample is broken down by exposure to heat, light, or humidity, it can still be analyzed; only two days are needed for laboratory analysis, compared to eight weeks for RFLP; and the DNA process can be automated, greatly reducing the possibility of human error.[71] The unit also uses mitochondrial DNA (MtDNA)—a tiny ring-shaped molecule that is much smaller than the more familiar nuclear DNA—that can be extracted from hair and bones when little else remains of a body. This technique was involved in solving the Green River Killer case in Washington State (see Exhibit 7-2) and was recently used in the high-profile case involving Scott Peterson, who was convicted in November 2004 of drowning his pregnant wife, Lacy, in Modesto, California.

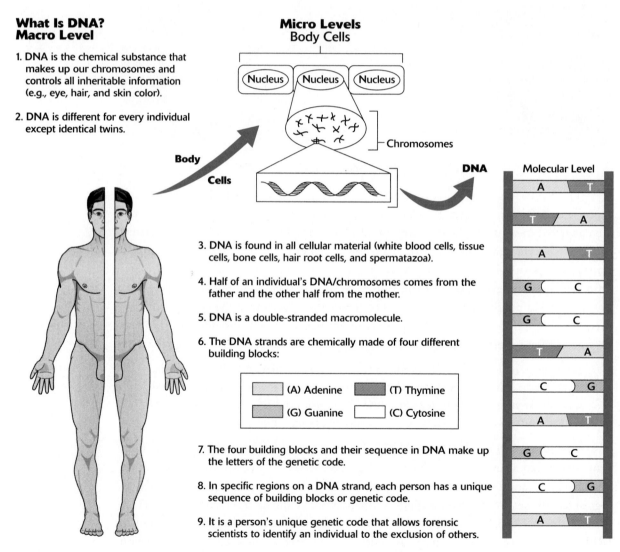

FIGURE 7-1
What is DNA?

Source: Federal Bureau of Investigation, Laboratory Division.

EXHIBIT 7-2

DNA and the Green River Killer

For nearly two decades, evidence from crimes committed by Washington State's Green River Killer—three tiny swabs of semen recovered from the decomposing bodies of prostitutes—sat in a sheriff's office evidence locker in Seattle. Until recently, technicians could not identify suspects using such small DNA samples. In 2001, however, the specimens, along with saliva and blood taken from three possible suspects, were sent to the state crime lab for advanced DNA testing. In November 2003, Gary Ridgway, a fifty-four-year-old truck painter, confessed to forty-eight strangulation murders, ending a nearly twenty-year investigation and making him the serial killer convicted of the most murders in U.S. history. Mitochondrial DNA, which attempts to match DNA found outside the nucleus of cells, was used to match bones in this case.

Source: Adapted from Andrew Murr, "Reeling in a Monster," *Newsweek,* November 17, 2003, p. 44; and Tracy Johnson, "Listed as Green River Victim, Family Learns Truth: Girl Is Dead," *Seattle Post-Intelligencer,* http://seattlepi.nwsource.com/local/gree03/shtml (accessed January 8, 2004).

CODIS

Another recent DNA innovation is the **Combined DNA Index System (CODIS).** CODIS contains DNA profiles obtained from subjects convicted of homicide, sexual assault, and other serious felonies. Investigators are able to search and compare evidence from their individual cases against the system's extensive national file of DNA genetic markers.[72] CODIS provides software and support services so that state and local laboratories can establish databases of convicted offenders, unsolved crime scenes, and missing persons. It allows these forensic laboratories to exchange and compare DNA profiles electronically, thereby linking serial violent crimes, especially sexual assaults, to each other and identifying suspects by matching DNA from crime scenes to convicted offenders.[73]

Postconviction Testing

A major issue in the DNA field involves postconviction testing. Because the speed and accuracy of testing have improved and because there are stories of convicted people who were exonerated because of DNA tests, many inmates now want to be tested if there is any evidence from which DNA can be extracted. They have everything to gain and nothing to lose.

Each state has its own set of procedural rules for postconviction relief that set the grounds on which a new trial is available and the threshold that must be met in order to merit a new trial. In most states, the rules of criminal procedure require new evidence to be brought before the court within six months of the conviction. This potentially excludes offenders who were convicted before DNA testing was available but for whom such testing may now provide important evidence relevant to their case. The potential for DNA to exonerate as well as convict offenders has led to specific state statutes to allow for postconviction DNA testing under certain circumstances, even after the convicted person has exhausted all of his or her appeals. The motions allowed and the processes being created under these new laws allow judges broader authority to order or admit DNA evidence in such cases. To date, thirty-one states have laws in place to provide for motions for post-conviction DNA testing.[74]

A Wider Net: New Law Expands DNA Gathering

In early 2007, the U.S. Department of Justice finalized guidelines for allowing the collection of DNA from most people arrested or detained by federal authorities, a vast expansion that will include hundreds of thousands of illegal immigrants each year. The new forensic DNA sampling was authorized by Congress in the January 2006 renewal of the Violence against Women Act, and it permits DNA collection from anyone under arrest by federal authorities and from illegal immigrants detained by federal agents. The new law, with its strong support from crime victims' organizations and some women's groups, was sponsored by U.S. senators from Texas and Arizona (13 percent of illegal immigrants detained in Arizona in 2006 had criminal records).[75]

Border Patrol and immigration agents detained more than 1.2 million immigrants in 2006, the majority of them at the border with Mexico. FBI officials estimate an increase in DNA collection ranging from 250,000 to as many as 1 million samples per year, whereas the FBI laboratory currently receives about 96,000 samples a year. Only seven states now collect DNA from suspects when they are arrested; of those, only two states are authorized by their laws to send those samples to the federal database.[76]

BEHAVIORAL SCIENCE IN CRIMINAL INVESTIGATION

Criminal Profiling

The **criminal profiling** of serial killers has captured the public's fancy more than any other investigative technique used by the police. The success of profiling depends on the profiler's ability to draw on investigative experience, training in forensic and behavioral science, and empirically developed information about the characteristics of known offenders. It is more art than science. The focus of the analysis is the behavior of the perpetrator while at the crime scene.[77]

There are various types of investigative profiles. Drug-courier profiles have been developed from collections of observable characteristics that experienced investigators believe indicate a person who is carrying drugs. Other types of profiles include loss-control specialists' profiles of shoplifters as well as threat assessments, such as the Secret Service's profiles of potential presidential assassins. Criminal profiling of violent offenders, however, is the area for which the most descriptive information has been collected and analyzed and the most extensive training programs have been developed.[78] Unfortunately, most people associate criminal profiling with the psychic profiler on television's *The Profiler* or with Agent Starling in the film *The Silence of the Lambs*—both of which are inaccurate portrayals.[79]

Profiling is not a new discovery; indeed, Sir Arthur Conan Doyle's fictional character Sherlock Holmes often engaged in profiling. For example, in "A Study in Scarlet," published in 1887, Holmes congratulated himself on the accuracy of his psychological profile: "It is seldom that any man, unless he is very full-blooded, breaks out in this way through emotion, so I hazarded the opinion that the criminal was probably a robust and ruddy-faced man. Events proved that I had judged correctly."[80] Profiling was used by a psychiatrist to study Adolph Hitler during World War II and to predict how he might react to defeat.[81]

Psychological profiling, while not an exact science, is obviously of assistance to investigators; however, it does not replace sound investigative procedures. Profiling works in harmony with the search for physical evidence. Victims play an important role in the development of a profile, as they can provide the investigator with the offender's exact conversation. Other items needed for a complete profile include photographs of the crime scene and any victims, autopsy information, and complete reports of the incident, including the weapon used. From this body of information the profiler looks for motive.[82]

Serial murderers—killers who are driven by a compulsion to murder again and again—are also profiled. Many psychologists believe that serial murderers fulfill violent sexual fantasies they have had since childhood. They satisfy their sexual needs by thinking about their killings, but when the satisfaction wears off, they kill again. Most serial murderers, the FBI has learned, are solitary males; an alarming number are doctors, dentists, or other health-care professionals. Almost one-third are ex-convicts and former mental patients. Many, like Kenneth Bianchi, the Los Angeles Hillside Strangler, are attracted to policing. (Bianchi, who was working as a security guard when he was finally caught in Washington State, often wore a police uniform during his crimes.) Serial killers seem normal, and they principally attack lone women, children, older people, homeless people, hitchhikers, and prostitutes.[83]

Another psychology-related investigative tool is psycholinguistics, which provides an understanding of those who use criminal coercion as well as strategies for dealing with threats. The 1932 kidnapping case of Charles Lindbergh's infant son (perpetrated by a German-born illegal alien, whose notes revealed his background and ethnicity) marked the beginning of this investigative method. Concentrating on evidence obtained from a message, spoken or written, the psycholinguistic technique microscopically analyzes the threats or messages for clues to the origins, background, and psychology of the maker. Every sentence, syllable, phrase, word, and comma is computer-scanned. A "threat dictionary" containing more than 350 categories and 15 million words is consulted; these "signature" words and phrases are then used to identify possible suspects.[84]

Clearly, profiling can be useful in criminal inquiries in several ways: focusing the investigation on more likely types of offenders, suggesting proactive strategies, suggesting trial strategies, and preventing violent crimes. From 1984 to 1991, the FBI trained thirty-three state and local police investigators in the profiling process. The program required twelve months of intensive training and hands-on profiling experience and consisted of an academic phase and an application phase.[85]

Psychics and Hypnosis

Psychics are also brought in from time to time, usually as a last resort when an investigation has stalled and no solution is imminent. Psychics are believed to possess extrasensory perception (ESP) or paranormal powers. National interest was focused on parapsychology—the discipline dealing with ESP, clairvoyance, and so forth—with the publicity accompanying the solving of three sex murders of youths in South Gate, California, in 1978. After two fruitless years of investigation, police resorted to the services of a local psychic, who helped an artist sketch a drawing of a face that had appeared to the psychic in a vision. With this information, police apprehended a suspect. However, Martin Reiser, a prominent Los Angeles Police department (LAPD) psychologist, has studied the use of psychics and has found no support for the "contention that psychics can provide significant information leading to the solution of major crimes."[86]

In the early 1970s, policing turned to hypnosis as an investigative tool. A number of police practitioners were trained in how to place witnesses, victims, arresting officers, and even investigators in a hypnotic state.[87] Hypnosis has been used to help people recall license plate numbers, names, places, or details of an incident. Although a trend toward acceptance of hypnosis by appellate courts began to develop in the early and mid-1970s, a 1976 California ruling reflected current skepticism with the technique. Hypnosis was used in a murder case to secure details of the suspect's identity and to obtain his conviction.[88] Following this case, the courts, increasingly concerned with the suggestibility of potential witnesses while under hypnosis, began rendering adverse rulings against such testimony. It then became clear to police and prosecutors that witnesses whose recall had been enhanced through hypnosis could not be put on the witness stand. Today, hypnosis is used sparingly, generally for people who would otherwise be useless as material witnesses.

Today only two states—Nevada and Texas—expressly allow such evidence. Officials in those states believe that forensic hypnotists can help otherwise frustrated investigators to solve crimes and that investigators with information obtained through hypnotism are free to either confirm, corroborate, or refute that information through the use of other evidence.[89]

RECENT DEVELOPMENTS IN FORENSIC SCIENCE AND INVESTIGATION

Technological opportunities—as well as new scientific and investigative problems—are rapidly developing for federal, state, and local police practitioners. In this section, we discuss several of them.

Forensic Entomology: "Insect Detectives"

An example of how the field of **forensic entomology** is quickly developing is the use of new "investigators": insects. Anyone involved in death investigations is aware of the connection between dead bodies and insects, especially maggots. As one forensic entomologist stated, "Insects are major players in nature's recycling effort, and in nature a corpse is simply organic matter to be recycled. Left to its own devices, nature quickly populates a corpse with a diverse community of organisms, all dedicated to reducing the body to its basic components."[90]

Until recently, most death investigators regarded insects as merely a sign of decay to be washed away rather than as potentially significant evidence. Yet the application of insect evidence to criminal investigations is not a new idea. In 1255, a Chinese "death investigator" named Sung Ts'u wrote a book titled *The Washing Away of Wrongs*. Sung tells of a murder in a Chinese village in which the victim was repeatedly slashed. The local magistrate thought the wounds might have been inflicted by a sickle and ordered all the village men to assemble, each with his own sickle. In the hot summer sun, flies were attracted to one sickle because of the residue of blood and small tissue fragments still clinging to the blade and handle. The owner of the sickle confessed.[91]

Not until several centuries later, in 1668, was the link between fly eggs and maggots discovered in the West. Before then, people did not realize that maggots hatched from the eggs flies laid on exposed meat or decomposing bodies. Unfortunately, it was not until much later, in 1855, that this discovery would be used in a forensic investigation. During a remodeling of a house outside Paris, the mummified body of an infant was discovered behind a mantelpiece. An autopsy determined that a flesh fly had exploited the body during the first year and that mites had laid their eggs on the dried corpse the following year. The logical suspects were people who were the occupants of the house in 1848—a young couple—who were subsequently arrested and convicted.[92]

In the mid-1930s, entomological evidence came to the fore in a brutal murder case. A woman saw a severed human arm while looking over a bridge spanning a small stream in Scotland. Ultimately, more than seventy pieces of two badly decomposed corpses—the wife of a local physician and her personal maid—were recovered from the area. Some maggots were discovered feeding on the decomposing body parts and were sent to the laboratory; they were identified as belonging to a type of blow fly and were thought to be between twelve and fourteen days old. For a number of reasons, suspicion fell on the physician: the entomological estimate of the time of death, the skillful manner of the dismemberment, and the fact that the doctor had been seen with a cut finger. He was convicted of both murders.[93]

Today forensic entomology can be of tremendous assistance to investigators. When a person dies, hundreds of species of insects descend on the corpse and the crime scene. Attracted by what scientists think may be a "universal death scent," common green flies, ground beetles, and other insects that thrive on flesh migrate to a corpse to lay eggs or to feast. The death of a human triggers very predictable patterns of insect activity that can be traced backward through time. There are several waves of insects, and their presence is informative. The life cycles of these creatures are so fixed and precise that they act as a natural clock to the trained eye.[94]

There is also the phenomenon of succession: As each organism feeds on a body, it changes the body; this change in turn makes the body attractive to another group of organisms, which changes the body for the next group, and so on until the body has been reduced to a skeleton. This is a predictable process.[95] This process is now being studied scientifically at the so-called Body Farm at the University of Tennessee in Knoxville—the only place in the world where corpses rot in the open air to advance human knowledge (see Exhibit 7-3). William Bass III, the Body Farm's founder, trains anthropologists and FBI agents in human decomposition. More than twenty corpses are decomposing there as maggots do their work; over the years, more than three hundred bodies have decayed at this location, some in car

EXHIBIT 7-3

A New Crime-Scene Academy

A number of assessments have found that the quality of evidence collection and identification could be improved, particularly at the local level. Now help is on the way. The Knoxville, Tennessee, Police Department is spearheading a project to create a National Forensic Academy for in-service criminalists. The 400-hour curriculum includes 180 hours of class work and 220 hours of field practicum. The academy session ends with 10 hours of testing. It covers arson, autopsy, trace evidence (including DNA and serology), mass fatalities, death investigations, cold case studies, emerging trends, fingerprinting, blood splatter, child fatality investigations, and computer forensics, among other topics. Applicants for the fourteen available slots must be first-line responders, computer literate, willing to participate in group activities, and prepared to work with human cadavers. The first academy class was held in September 2001.

Source: Adapted from "Is Your Crime-Scene Work a Crime? Help Will Soon Be on the Way," *Law Enforcement News,* March 15, 2001, p. 1. John Jay College of Criminal Justice, CUNY, 899 Tenth Avenue, New York, NY 10019.

trunks, others under water or under the earth or hung from scaffolds. The overarching goal of the study is to produce an atlas for the police that will provide a "gold standard" for decomposition—a page-by-page, color-by-color, insect-by-insect depiction of the process of human decay on a time and temperature line. The study also includes burying multiple bodies under four pads of concrete to assist the FBI's tests of its latest ground-penetrating radar.[96]

Often the strongest circumstantial evidence in a criminal prosecution is the fact that the victim and a suspect were seen together. For example, the body of a nine-year-old girl who had been missing for three weeks was found in Kenosha, Wisconsin. Insect evidence put her death at midnight twenty-one days before—the exact day she had gone to a carnival with the suspect, who was convicted.[97]

There are other uses of insects as well. A man claiming to have found his girlfriend dead was convicted of her murder when none of the usual creatures were present on the body (it was shown that the man opened the windows before the police arrived, hence the absence of insects). A Florida murderer who dropped his victim in a swamp was convicted when mayflies, only active in a swamp region a few days of the year, were found in his car radiator. In a rape case, the offender was convicted when his ski mask was found to contain larvae from caterpillars that emerged only in late summer and were known to dwell in the woods next to the rape scene. Furthermore, insects feeding on infected tissues where children's diapers were not changed or under bandages and bedsheets that were used by the elderly have often been the only evidence that neglect has occurred.[98]

Use of "Nonhuman Detectives": Dogs

Police dogs now also play an increasingly vital role in investigative work and are used around the world. In addition to their historical uses of tracking and catching criminals and for controlling crowds, because of their keen sense of smell and agility they are now being used by the police for finding drugs, explosives, and human remains. They are taught how to bark continuously when they find what they are looking for and how to chase and attack, even when they are being threatened with weapons.

The most popular breed for police work is the German shepherd. Chosen for their intelligence and highly developed senses, they also tend to be more instinctively suspicious of strangers than other breeds. However, springer spaniels and Labrador retrievers are often used for police work as well because of their natural tracking abilities.

As the threat of terrorism has increased, these specialist police dogs have become even more important to the police. Just as police work is making increasing use of new technology, so is the training police dogs receive. Police dogs are now being trained to work with cameras attached to their heads, enabling them to enter dangerous places and send pictures back to officers.[99]

Stalking Investigations

Stalking was recently described as "the crime of the 1990s."[100] California enacted the first antistalking law in 1990, following the stalking and subsequent death of Rebecca Shaeffer, the costar of the television series *My Sister Sam*. Today all but two states have their own antistalking laws (Arizona and Maine use their harassment and terrorizing statutes to combat stalking).[101]

There are four types of stalking situations:

1. *Erotomanic stalking.* The erotomanic stalker has a delusional disorder in which the victim, usually a person of higher status and opposite gender (often a celebrity or a public figure), is believed to be in love with the stalker. In fact, the victim does not know the stalker, and the stalking is usually short-lived, lasting one to four months.

2. *Love obsessional stalking.* Similar to the erotomanic stalker, the love obsessional type does not know the victim except through the media and has a psychiatric diagnosis. These stalkers usually write letters and make telephone calls in a campaign to make their existence known to the victim. This behavior lasts much longer, often exceeding ten years.

3. *Simple obsessional stalking.* In this type of incident, the simple obsessional stalker had a prior relationship with the victim (as a former spouse or employer, for example), and the stalking began after the relationship soured. The stalking usually lasts about five months. (*Note:* Stalking is most often perpetrated against current or former intimate partners, with young women between ages eighteen and twenty-nine as the primary targets; therefore, stalking is closely related to the national problem of domestic violence.[102])

4. *False victimization syndrome.* The rarest form, a person with false victimization syndrome claims that someone is stalking him or her in order to gain attention as a victim. There is no stalker, and this phenomenon is similar to Munchausen syndrome by proxy, in which people intentionally produce physical symptoms of illness in their children in order to gain attention and sympathy.[103]

Evidence collection for crimes of stalking begins with the victims. Victims should record each time they see the stalker or when any contact is made and should document specific details, such as time, place, location, and any witnesses. Messages on answering machines, faxes, letters, and computer e-mails provide useful evidence for building a case against the offender. Police agencies should also consider providing victims with a small tape recorder to facilitate the collection of this information and should encourage victims to report in a journal how the stalking has affected them and their lifestyle, to later help convince a jury of the victims' fear and trauma. Another investigative strategy is doing surveillance on suspects at times when they are likely to stalk their victims. Executing a search warrant for the suspect's personal and work computers, residence, and vehicle can prove useful in many circumstances; officers should look for spying equipment (such as binoculars and cameras), photos, and any property belonging to the victim.[104]

Investigation of Cybercrooks

Today an estimated 605 million people around the world are plugged into cyberspace, and thousands more enter the online world each day.[105] The Internet has revolutionized the way people communicate, shop, entertain themselves, learn, and conduct business. But as the saying goes, "The fleas come with the dog": This high-tech revolution in our homes and offices has opened a whole new world for the criminal element, creating a new type of criminal—the **cybercrook**. Indeed, the problem of cybercrime has become so prevalent that a new Computer Crime and Intellectual Property Section has been created in the Criminal Division of the U.S. Department of Justice; it can be accessed at www.cybercrime.gov (cyberterrorism is discussed further in Chapter 15). CyberAngels, an organization founded by a twenty-one-year-old man that assists victims of Internet crimes, receives 650 online stalking complaints every day. The Federal Trade Commission receives more than eighteen thousand Internet-related complaints each year. At least three hundred Web sites offer counterfeit drivers' licenses, law enforcement credentials, passports, Social Security cards, and military identification cards.[106]

Pornographers and pedophiles (discussed below) are also on the Web as well as other, newer types of criminals: better educated, upscale, older, and increasingly female. Computer crimes include identity theft; cyberterrorism; software piracy; industrial espionage; credit card, consumer, and stock market fraud; baby adoption scams; and embezzlement. These crimes compel the development of new investigative techniques, specialized and ongoing training for police investigators, and the employment of individuals with strong technical backgrounds. Obviously, the police must become better educated, better equipped, and more adaptable.[107]

The technical staff of many (if not most) police agencies are civilians, who are generally kept away from the operational side of the organization. They understand what computers do but not necessarily how that capability supports the operational needs of the police officer on the street. Thus the sworn officer or detective is generally unprepared for the types of criminal schemes described above. This situation must change.

We discuss liability issues concerning the handling of computer evidence in Chapter 10.

Protection of the Innocents: Crimes against Juveniles and Missing Youths

Although the number of crimes against children has been declining in America, children still have very high rates of victimization. Pedophiles and pornographers are now increasingly engaging in Internet sex crimes against minors. Some writers have estimated that about 89,000 such cases occur each year,[108] but that figure has almost certainly grown. The possession of child pornography is an element in two-thirds of all Internet sex crimes against minors.[109] Furthermore, juveniles ages twelve through seventeen constitute 23 percent of all violent crime victims, and one victim survey found that 1.38 million Americans were victims of violent crimes from birth through age seventeen; 555,000 of them were victimized violently from birth through age eleven.[110]

In addition, according to a study by the U.S. Department of Justice's Office of Juvenile Justice and Delinquency Prevention, about 1,315,000 children are missing from their caretakers each year; about 800,000 of them are reported to the authorities for the purpose of locating them. Nearly all (99.8 percent) of the children reported missing by a caretaker were located or returned home alive.[111]

Fortunately, the police have valuable resources for investigating such cases. The National Center for Missing and Exploited Children (NCMEC), for example, provides police training and other services nationwide for investigating instances where children are abducted, endangered, and sexually exploited. The NCMEC also does the following[112]:

Age-enhances photographs of children missing for two years or more
Reconstructs facial images from morgue photographs of unidentified juveniles so that posters can be made
Distributes photographs and descriptions of missing children worldwide
Maintains a free and secure lost child Web site for the police

The NCMEC was established in 1984 and is a private not-for-profit organization located in Alexandria, Virginia.

No Stone Unturned: Cold Cases

Many jurisdictions plagued by a significant number of unsolved murders, or **cold cases**, have created a cold case squad. These squads can be especially useful in locating and working with past and potential witnesses and in reviewing physical evidence to identify suspects. (See Exhibit 7-2, concerning the case of the Green River Killer.)

The most important component of cold case squads is personnel—the squads must have the right mix of investigative and supervisory talent. Squads may also use, as needed, the services of federal law enforcement agencies, medical or coroners' offices, retired personnel, criminalists or other specialists, or college or student interns. Cold cases selected for investigation are usually at least a year old and cannot be addressed by the original investigative personnel because of workload, time constraints, or the lack of viable leads. Cases are prioritized on the basis of the likelihood of an eventual solution. The highest-priority cases are those in which there is an identified homicide victim, suspects were previously named or identified through forensic methods, an arrest warrant was previously issued, significant physical evidence can be reprocessed, newly documented leads have arisen, and critical witnesses are available and willing to cooperate.[113] See Exhibit 7-4 for information on a new institute focusing on cold cases.

EXHIBIT 7-4

Looking at "Cold" Cases

At the new Institute for Cold Case Evaluation at West Virginia University, a nonprofit consulting center, law-enforcement agencies will have at their disposal a diverse array of scientists in fields ranging from anthropology to entomology, according to the institute's creator, Max Houck, a forensic anthropologist who previously worked at the FBI crime laboratory.

Each year, the number of cold cases in the nation grows by about another 6,000, on top of the 200,000 unsolved murder cases that have accumulated since 1960.

"At other agencies, they just take the last retiree, hire him back as a contractor and give him a desk and a phone because that's all they have," Houck told the Associated Press. "Then they put a stack of files in front of him...with no resources."

Houck, who teaches at the university, said the ICCE will provide departments with free or discounted services from at least two dozen scientists. It will launch a Web site as well, with a free electronic newsletter and a secure chat room for investigators. The public can browse the site, searching through cases and making donations that will help fund the center.

Source: "Case Studies," *Law Enforcement News,* November 15/30, 2003, p. 7. John Jay College of Criminal Justice, CUNY, 899 Tenth Avenue, New York, NY 10019.

Labs and Databases under Fire

Beginning in mid-2007, heightened concerns about problems in forensic laboratories as well as wider police use of DNA caused both areas to come under greater scrutiny. Next we briefly look at both areas.

Because of what were perceived as "critical problems"—including allegations of misconduct in death-penalty cases—several states were launching oversight boards to investigate misconduct in crime labs. Crime lab problems (falsified tests, misplaced evidence, scientific mistakes) have surfaced across the country in recent years, leading to lawsuits and sometimes audits in Massachusetts, Montana, Ohio, Oklahoma, West Virginia, and elsewhere. The steady stream of exonerations and scandals has raised doubts about everything from the handling of DNA evidence to overly broad conclusions from hair and blood comparisons. Discredited beliefs about how to determine arson and faulty conclusions from ballistics testing have added to the questions. An analysis of eighty-six exonerations found that forensic testing errors were the second most common factor, behind only eyewitness errors. The 2004 federal Justice for All Act requires states that accept federal funding for DNA testing to also ensure there is a government entity able to conduct independent investigations into misconduct. The law spurred the creation of oversight boards in Minnesota, Texas, and Virginia. The commissions are felt to offer an unprecedented opportunity to reexamine justice as it is handed down in the nation's courtrooms. Proponents have been hoping they can strengthen trust in the evidence relied on by police, prosecutors, and juries.[114]

Another recent controversy concerns DNA databases. Specifically, a number of state legislatures and defense groups are concerned with the growing number of police crime labs (now in at least six states) that are creating databases of DNA taken from people *not* convicted or charged during investigations and then using that DNA to match them to other crimes. Laboratories use these databases to store DNA data that are not eligible to be collected in the larger federal database, which contains only DNA from people convicted of or charged with serious crimes. Many people feel that such databases operate beyond the reach of state and federal laws, and few court rulings exist to say whether these databases are legal or whether data contained in them can be used in criminal cases.[115]

SUMMARY

This chapter has discussed the evolution of criminal investigation, including definitions of key terms, identification of people and firearms, ways investigators work within the larger context of the criminal justice system, qualities needed by detectives, undercover police work, polygraph testing, DNA analysis, profiling, recent investigative developments, and special investigations (such as stalking, cybercrooks, and cold cases).

The evolution of forensic evidence, criminalistics, and criminal investigation is the product of a successful symbiosis of science and policing. This chapter has shown the truly interdisciplinary nature of police work; we discussed not only the influence of the so-called hard sciences—computer science, chemistry, biology, and physics—but also the assistance of psychology.

Forensic science is arguably the most rapidly progressing area of criminal justice, and there is little doubt that the future holds even greater advances in this realm. This discipline has traveled a great distance, especially in laboratory processes, in DNA analysis and application, and in ever-expanding uses of the computer. The potential of the computer to assist in solving crimes is limited only by our funds and imagination. Thus policing should continue to reap the benefits of applying scientific aids to effect criminal justice for years to come.

Certainly this area of policing carries with it a high degree of fascination and mystique for the public, and rightfully so. Although policing certainly has its limitations, such as paperwork, boredom, failures, and other liabilities, there is nothing quite like using "gee whiz" investigative tools and techniques to catch bad guys—at least in the public's mind.

KEY TERMS

Bertillon system
cold case
Combined DNA Index Systems (CODIS)
corpus delicti
crime scene
criminalistics

criminal profiling
cybercrook
dactylography
detective
forensic entomology
forensic science
investigative stages
modus operandi
polygraph examination
stalking

REVIEW QUESTIONS

1. How would you distinguish between the terms *forensic science* and *criminalistics*?

2. What are the origins of criminalistics, and what are the differences between anthropometry and dactylography?

3. How did August Vollmer and other pioneers in law enforcement contribute to the development of criminal investigation techniques?

4. What qualities do detectives need and use?

5. What are the basic functions of the polygraph and its legal status in the courts?

6. How does DNA analysis operate, and what is its future outlook, both legally and scientifically?

7. What contributions has behavioral science made to criminal investigation? (Provide actual case studies.)

8. What are some fundamental uses and advantages of forensic entomology for criminal investigation?

9. What are the four types of stalking situations, and how do detectives go about addressing them?

10. How has the Internet provided new opportunities for criminals?

11. What is the purpose of a cold case squad, and how does it operate?

12. What concerns have been raised about forensic labs and DNA databases, and what is being done to address those concerns?

INDEPENDENT STUDENT ACTIVITIES

1. Tour a modern forensics laboratory (or interview a forensic examiner) to learn about the laboratory's existing capabilities, areas of service, and other related information. Also learn about how the chain of evidence is protected and how evidence is stored until trial. Ask the technicians what they see as the most rapidly developing areas of forensics.

2. Interview several detectives about the methods and technologies they use for processing a crime scene, their training and education, the primary obstacles in bringing a case to trial, the greatest challenges in their work, the methods they use for interviewing suspects, any recent changes in the investigative field, and so on.

3. Determine the method that is predominantly used to extract and examine DNA in your jurisdiction, and learn about some of the local cases in which DNA evidence has been employed.

4. Interview someone in the investigative field to learn his or her views on such controversial methods as the use of psychics and hypnosis.

RELATED WEB SITES

American Academy of Forensic Sciences
http://www.aafs.org

American Board of Criminalistics
http://www.criminalistics.com

American Society of Crime Laboratory Directors
http://www.ascld.org

Crime Mapping Research Center (CMRC)
http://www.ojp.usdoj.gov/cmrc

FBI Crime Lab
www.fbi.gov/hq/lab/labhome.htm

Forensic Science Information
http://ash.lab.rl.fws.gov

P A R T   I I I

CONSTRAINTS
RULE OF LAW, ACCOUNTABILITY, AND LIABILITY

This part examines the constraints that have been placed on the considerable power and authority possessed by the police. First, Chapter 8 reviews the rule of law, looking at the practical effects of the provisions contained in the Fourth, Fifth, and Sixth Amendments to the Bill of Rights. Next, Chapter 9 examines how the police are held accountable in the course of their work: the ethical demands under which they must function, the restraints as well as authority granted with respect to their use of force; the problem of police corruption; and the means by which officers may be disciplined. Finally, in Chapter 10 we view the legal means by which, as well as the kinds of situations for which, the public may seek redress for the transgressions of the police in order to determine whether police organizations, supervisors, and/or individual officers are civilly liable.

RULE OF LAW

EXPOUNDING THE CONSTITUTION

A government of laws, and not of men.
—*John Adams, 1774*

We must never forget that it is a constitution we are expounding.
—*John Marshall, in* McCulloch v. Maryland, *1819*

LEARNING OBJECTIVES

AS A RESULT OF READING THIS CHAPTER, THE STUDENT WILL:

- UNDERSTAND WHAT IS MEANT BY THE RULE OF LAW

- BE ABLE TO OUTLINE THE PROTECTIONS AFFORDED CITIZENS BY THE FOURTH, FIFTH, AND SIXTH AMENDMENTS

- KNOW HOW TO DEFINE AND GIVE EXAMPLES OF PROBABLE CAUSE

- BE AWARE OF THE RATIONALE FOR AND RAMIFICATIONS OF THE EXCLUSIONARY RULE

- BE ABLE TO DISTINGUISH BETWEEN ARRESTS AND SEARCHES AND SEIZURES WITH AND WITHOUT A WARRANT

- KNOW SOME SIGNIFICANT WAYS IN WHICH THE *MIRANDA* DECISION HAS BEEN ERODED

- BE ABLE TO DELINEATE THE MAJOR RIGHTS OF JUVENILES AS WELL AS THE MAJOR PHILOSOPHICAL DIF-
FERENCES IN THE LAW FOR TREATMENT OF JUVENILE AND ADULT OFFENDERS

INTRODUCTION

The Bill of Rights—the first ten amendments to the U.S. Constitution—was passed largely to protect all citizens from excessive governmental power. The police are expected to control crime within the framework of these rights; they must conduct themselves in a manner that conforms to the **rule of law** as set forth in the U.S.

Constitution, state constitutions, statutes passed by state legislatures, and the precedent of prior interpretations by the courts.

What is meant by the rule of law? This commonly used phrase was comprehensively defined in 1885 by Albert Venn Dicey in his now-classic *Introduction to the Study of the Law of the Constitution.*[1] Dicey identified three principles that together establish the rule of law:

1. Absolute supremacy or predominance of regular law as opposed to the influence of arbitrary power
2. Equality before the law or the equal subjection of all classes to the ordinary law of the land administered by the ordinary courts
3. Law of the Constitution as a consequence of the rights of individuals as defined and enforced by the courts

In other words, under the rule of law of the United States, the means are more important than the ends. A nation's democratic form of government would be of little value if the police could arrest, search, and seize its citizens and their property at will. If one considers the policing systems of some nondemocratic countries (such as those discussed in exhibits spread throughout this book), it is readily apparent that from the citizen's standpoint, legal curbs on those who enforce the law are absolutely necessary.

This chapter examines three constitutional amendments that regulate the police and prevent abuses of power: the Fourth Amendment (probable cause, exclusionary rule, arrest, search and seizure, electronic surveillance, and lineups), the Fifth Amendment (confessions, interrogation, and entrapment), and the Sixth Amendment (right to counsel and interrogation). To avoid overwhelming the reader with case titles, only better-known court cases—such as *Miranda* v. *Arizona*—are included in the body of the chapter; others are cited in the Notes section. Finally, we discuss a related yet in some ways very different area of law and procedure: the law pertaining to juvenile offenders. A chapter summary, key terms, review questions, independent student activities, and related Web sites conclude the chapter.

Because of space limitations, many Supreme Court decisions affecting police powers in this country have necessarily been omitted from this discussion. Many publications cover those decisions, however. Among them are monthly police periodicals such as the *FBI Law Enforcement Bulletin* and *The Police Chief* magazine; other sources include the *Criminal Law Reporter*, *U.S. Law Week*, and the *Supreme Court Bulletin*.

FOURTH AMENDMENT

The right of the people to be secure in their persons, papers, and effects, against unreasonable searches and seizures, shall not be violated, and no Warrants shall issue, but upon probable cause, supported by Oath or affirmation, and particularly describing the place to be searched, and the persons or things to be seized.

The **Fourth Amendment** is intended to limit overzealous behavior by the police. Its primary protection is the requirement that a neutral detached magistrate, rather than a police

Officers have a responsibility to testify in court.

(Bob Daemmrich, The Image Works)

officer, issue warrants for arrest and **search and seizure**. Crime, though a major concern to society, is balanced by the concern that officers might thrust themselves unnecessarily into our homes. The Fourth Amendment requires that the necessity for a person's right of privacy to yield to society's right to search is best decided by a neutral judicial officer, not by an agent of the police.[2]

Probable Cause

The standard for a legal arrest is **probable cause**. This important concept is elusive at best; it is often quite difficult for professors to explain and even more difficult for students to understand. One way to define *probable cause* is to say that for an officer to make an arrest, he or she must have more than a mere hunch yet less than actual knowledge that the arrestee committed the crime. I often use the following example to better explain the concept:

> At midnight, a fifty-five-year-old woman, having spent several hours at a city bar, wished to leave the bar and go to a nightclub in a rural part of the county. A man offered her a ride, but rather than driving directly to the nightclub, he drove to a remote place and parked the car. There he raped the woman and forced her to sodomize him. She fought him and later told the police she thought she had broken the temples (side pieces) of his black glasses. After the act, he drove her back to town; when she got out of the car, she saw the license plate number and thought that the hood of the car was colored red. Her account of the crime and her physical description of the rapist immediately

prompted a photograph lineup; a known rape/sodomy suspect's picture was shown to her, along with those of several other men with a similar description. She tentatively identified the suspect in the mug shot but could not be certain; the suspect's mug shot had been taken several years earlier.

With this preliminary information, two police officers (one of whom was the author) hurried to the suspect's home to question him. They did not have a warrant. Upon entering the suspect's driveway, the officers observed a beige car—with a red hood. Probable cause was beginning to build. Next the officers noted that the vehicle's license plate number matched the one given by the victim; probable cause was now growing by leaps and bounds. Then the suspect exited the house and walked toward his car; the officers observed that his eyeglasses frame was black but that the temples were gold, indicating that the black temples had probably been broken and replaced by spare gold temples. The officers now had, by any standard, adequate probable cause to lead a "reasonable and prudent" person to believe that this suspect was the culprit; the failure to arrest him would have been a gross miscarriage of justice. The suspect was thus arrested and placed in an actual lineup, where the victim identified him. This was one of those rare cases where the evidence was so compelling that the defendant pleaded guilty at his initial appearance and threw himself on the judge's mercy.

Of course, the facts of each case and the probable cause present are different; the court will examine the type and amount of probable cause that the officer had at the time of the arrest. It is important to note that a police officer cannot add to the probable cause used to make the arrest after effecting the arrest; the court will determine whether there existed sufficient probable cause to arrest the individual based on the officer's knowledge of the facts at the time of the arrest.

The Supreme Court has upheld convictions when probable cause was provided by a reliable informant,[3] when it came in an anonymous letter,[4] and when a suspect fit a Drug Enforcement Administration profile of a drug courier.[5] The Court has also held that police officers who "reasonably but mistakenly conclude that probable cause is present" are granted qualified immunity from civil action.[6]

Exclusionary Rule

The Fourth Amendment recognizes the right to privacy, but its application raises some perplexing questions. First of all, not all searches are prohibited—only those that are unreasonable. Another issue has to do with how to handle evidence that is illegally obtained. Should murderers be released, Justice Benjamin Cardozo asked, simply because "the constable blundered"?[7] The Fourth Amendment says nothing about how it is to be enforced, a problem that has stirred a good amount of debate for a number of years. Most of this debate has focused on the wisdom of, and the constitutional necessity for, the so-called **exclusionary rule**, which requires that all evidence obtained in violation of the Fourth Amendment be excluded from government's use in a criminal trial.

The exclusionary rule has an interesting history. It first appeared in the federal criminal justice system in 1914, when the Supreme Court ruled in *Weeks* v. *United States* that all illegally obtained evidence was barred from use in federal prosecutions.[8] The practice has not existed in the state systems for nearly as long, however. Relatively few states employed the rule until 1950; indeed, as of 1949, only seventeen states followed the *Weeks* doctrine. There was considerable objection both within and outside the Supreme Court about the states being able to do what was forbidden to the federal government. The ludicrous nature of this situation becomes evident in that until 1960, any evidence illegally seized by state or local police officers could be turned over to and used by federal officers in federal courts; this was known as the "silver platter doctrine."[9]

In 1926, a police officer arrested a man in a hallway for stealing an overcoat—a misdemeanor. The officer then entered the defendant's room and searched it, discovering a bag containing a blackjack. Appealing his conviction for possessing the weapon, the defendant made a motion to suppress the blackjack as evidence, as it had been obtained through a warrantless search. Justice Cardozo delivered a classic objection to the rule and considered its far-reaching effects:

> A room is searched against the law, and the body of a murdered man is found. The privacy of the home has been infringed, and the murderer goes free. On the one side is the social need that crime shall be repressed. On the other hand, the social need that the law shall not be flouted by the insolence of office. There are dangers in any choice.[10]

Justice Oliver Wendell Holmes took an opposite view of the rule in his dissenting opinion in a wiretapping case.[11] Holmes said that we must consider two desirable objects— that criminals should be detected and all available evidence used and that the government should not itself commit other crimes while gathering evidence. Holmes was repulsed by the manner in which government "dirtied" itself by engaging in snooping and wiretapping activities. In *Olmstead* v. *United States* (1928), Holmes made his classic statement, "For my part, I think it is a less evil that some criminals should escape than that the government should play an ignoble part."

The 1961 Supreme Court decision in *Mapp* v. *Ohio*[12] put an end to confusion over the admissibility of illegally seized evidence in the state courts (see Court Closeup). But the Court's decision in *Mapp* did not end the controversy surrounding the exclusionary rule: Opponents of the rule are left with the suspicion that the rule is invoked only by someone—usually a guilty person—who does not want evidence of his or her crimes to be used at trial; furthermore, they believe that the suspect's behavior has been much more reprehensible than that of the police.[13]

The Supreme Court has objected to police behavior when it "shocks the conscience," excluding evidence, for example, that was obtained by forcible extraction (by stomach pump) from a man who had swallowed two morphine capsules in the police's presence.[14]

MODIFICATIONS OF THE EXCLUSIONARY RULE   Three major decisions during the 1983–1984 term of the Supreme Court served to modify the exclusionary rule. Justice William Rehnquist established a "public safety exception" to the doctrine. In that case, the defendant was charged with criminal possession of a firearm after a rape victim

COURT CLOSEUP

Mapp v. Ohio, 367 U.S. 643 (1961)

In May 1957, three Cleveland police officers went to the home of Dolree Mapp to follow up on an informant's tip that a suspect in a recent bombing was hiding there. They also had information that a large amount of materials for operating a numbers game would be found. Upon arrival at the house, officers knocked on the door and demanded entrance, but Mapp, after telephoning her lawyer, refused them entry without a search warrant.

Three hours later, the officers again attempted to enter Mapp's home, and again she refused them entry. They then forcibly entered the home. Mapp confronted the officers, demanding to see a search warrant; an officer waved a piece of paper at her, which she grabbed and placed in her bosom. The officers struggled with Mapp to retrieve the piece of paper, at which time Mapp's attorney arrived at the scene. The attorney was not allowed to enter the house or to see his client. Mapp was forcibly taken upstairs to her bedroom, where her belongings were searched. One officer found a brown paper bag containing books that he deemed to be obscene.

Mapp was charged with possession of obscene, lewd, or lascivious materials. At the trial, the prosecution attempted to prove that the materials belonged to Mapp; the defense contended that the books were the property of a former boarder who had left his belongings behind. The jury convicted Mapp, and she was sentenced to an indefinite term in prison.

In May 1959, Mapp appealed to the Ohio Supreme Court, claiming that the obscene materials were not in her possession and that the evidence was seized illegally. The court disagreed, ruling the evidence admissible. In June 1961, the U.S. Supreme Court overturned the conviction, holding that the Fourth Amendment's prohibition against unreasonable search and seizure had been violated:

> [Because] the right to be secure against rude invasions of privacy by state officers is…constitutional in origin, we can no longer permit that right to remain an empty promise. We can no longer permit it to be revocable at the whim of any police officer who, in the name of law enforcement itself, chooses to suspend its enjoyment.

described him to the police. The officers located him in a supermarket, and upon questioning him about the weapon's whereabouts (without giving him the *Miranda* warning), they found it located behind some cartons. Rehnquist said that the case presented a situation in which concern for public safety outweighed a literal adherence to the rules. The police were justified in questioning the defendant on the grounds of "immediate necessity."[15]

Another 1984 decision announced the "inevitability of discovery exception." A ten-year-old girl was murdered and her body hidden. While transporting the suspect, detectives—who had promised the suspect's attorney that they would not question him while in transit—appealed to his sensitivities by saying it would be proper to find the body so that the girl's parents could give her a Christian burial. (This became known as the "Christian Burial Speech.") The suspect directed them to the body. In 1977, the Supreme Court ruled that the detectives had violated the defendant's rights by inducing him to incriminate himself without the presence of counsel. But the Court left open the possibility that the state could introduce evidence that the body would have been found even without the suspect's help. Using this "inevitability of discovery" opening, the Iowa courts found the defendant guilty, and in 1984 the Supreme Court upheld his conviction.[16]

Also in 1984, the Court ruled that evidence can be used even if obtained under a search warrant that is later found to be invalid. The Court held that evidence obtained by police officers acting in good faith on a reasonable reliance on a search warrant issued by a neutral magistrate could be used at trial even if the warrant was later found to be lacking in probable cause. This decision prompted a strong dissenting opinion by three justices, including William Brennan Jr., who said, "It now appears that the Court's victory over the Fourth Amendment is complete."[17]

Another ruling favorable to the police was handed down in 1988. Federal agents, observing suspicious behavior in and around a warehouse, illegally entered the building (with force and without a warrant) and observed marijuana in plain view. They left and obtained a search warrant for the building; then they returned and arrested the defendant for conspiracy to deliver illegal drugs. The Court allowed the evidence to be admitted at trial, saying that it ought not to have been excluded simply because of unrelated illegal conduct by the police. If probable cause could be established apart from their illegal activity, the Court said, evidence obtained from the search should be admitted.[18]

VIEWS ON THE EXCLUSIONARY RULE   Today there are basically two schools of thought, or models, regarding the use of illegally seized evidence. The **crime-control model** holds that the police are going to make mistakes occasionally, and the victim is entitled to sue and have his or her complaint considered by a jury. Most important, this model holds, there is no reason why the evidence should not be used against the suspect at trial, even if obtained illegally. Proponents of the **due process model**, on the other hand, believe that the only way to deal with illegally obtained evidence is to suppress it before trial. When such evidence is allowed at trial, convictions based wholly or in part on it should be reversed. The victim of an illegal seizure usually is in no financial position to sue, and departmental discipline of officers is totally ineffective as a deterrent. Thus the only way to control the illegal collection of evidence is to take the profit out of it.[19]

The current trend is clearly toward the crime-control model, which weakens the impact of the exclusionary rule. Not only do many court watchers expect the Supreme Court to continue this trend, but a large number of law-and-order citizens also favor the rule's decline. Indeed, Chief Justice Rehnquist has openly called for its removal. Acknowledging that the primary reason for the rule is to control police misconduct, Rehnquist notes that since *Mapp* was decided, redress is more easily obtainable by a defendant whose constitutional rights have been violated, given the *Bivens* decision and the long-dormant Section 1983 actions. (See Chapter 10.) Further, Rehnquist believes that modern juries can be trusted to return fair awards to injured parties, saying, "I feel morally certain that the United States is the only nation in the world in which the most relevant, most competent evidence as to the guilt or innocence of the accused is mechanically excluded because of the manner in which it may have been obtained."[20]

In summary, since the Warren Court expanded the rights of criminal defendants in the 1960s, a surge of cases to the Supreme Court has raised further questions concerning the exclusionary rule. Many observers expected the Court to overturn *Mapp*, yet the Court has not done so, apparently believing that without *Mapp*, the flagrant abuses that occurred before it could resurface.

See Exhibit 8-1 for a discussion of the exclusionary rule as it pertains to school settings.

EXHIBIT 8-1

Must Students "Shed Their Constitutional Rights at the Schoolhouse Gate"?

Rumors begin circulating among students in a high school that a senior possesses drugs and a gun in his locker. The school's principal questions the student, who denies the allegation. However, three other teachers report hearing "hallway chatter" of the same nature, so the principal conducts a search of the student's locker. She observes no gun but does find a stash of marijuana, a pipe, and other drug paraphernalia, as well as some photographs of other students engaged in drug activities. A digital camera is also found, but the principal does not look at its contents, being concerned that she might accidentally delete any photographic evidence. The principal contacts the local police and turns over the items to the responding officer. While in the principal's office, the officer turns on the digital camera and finds photographs involving child pornography. The student is charged with child pornography and drug violations. The defense argues that all evidence should be suppressed because both the principal and the officer violated the student's Fourth Amendment rights in their warrantless searches.

At issue is whether or not students in public institutions enjoy Fourth Amendment privileges and whether limits are placed on the police and school administrators regarding students' right of privacy. Even though parents transfer their authority for care and custody over their minor children to the school authorities while their children are in school, the school is an arm of government, which implicates constitutional concerns because Americans are generally protected against government's unreasonable searches and seizures.

The U.S. Supreme Court recognizes that schoolchildren have legitimate expectations of privacy while attending school, but schools also need to maintain a safe and secure learning environment. This latter interest dictates a different balancing scheme under the Fourth Amendment. Typically, prior to conducting a search, a police officer must be able to articulate that there was probable cause to believe that evidence of criminal activity exists in the place to be searched. However, where the interests of *public safety* are best served by a Fourth Amendment standard of reasonableness that stops short of probable cause, the Supreme Court has adopted such a standard. Therefore, for searches by officials in schools, the standard used is reasonable suspicion, which allows the school to achieve the goal of preserving order without invading the privacy interests of the students any more than necessary. Police officers, however, cannot automatically commence a search under the same standard applied to school authorities; officers are still held to a stricter Fourth Amendment standard because their government functions are different.

In the hypothetical case presented above, the principal's search of the student's locker was probably reasonable given the principal's reasonable suspicion. However, the police officer's warrantless search of the digital camera would be scrutinized under a different standard. A court would most likely suppress the digital photos discovered on the camera on the grounds that the officer should have secured the evidence and applied for a search warrant.

In sum, as the Court stated in 1969, students "do not shed their constitutional rights at the schoolhouse gate,"[1] and reasonableness remains the cornerstone by which the police and school officials' actions will be judged.

[1]This quote is from *Tinker v. Des Moines Independent Community School District*, 393 U.S. 503, 506, 89 S.Ct. 733 (1969).
Source: Adapted from Lucy Ann Hoover, "Getting Schooled in the Fourth Amendment," *FBI Law Enforcement Bulletin,* March 2007, pp. 22–32.

Arrests

A restriction on the right of the police to arrest is the hallmark of a free society. A basic condition of freedom is that one cannot be legally seized in an arbitrary and capricious manner at the discretion or whim of any government official. It is customary to refer to the writ of *habeas corpus*—the "Great Writ"—as the primary guarantee of personal freedom in a democracy. *Habeas corpus* is defined simply as a writ requiring an incarcerated person to be brought before a judge for an investigation of the restraint of that person's liberty. It should be noted that *habeas corpus* is the means of remedying wrongful arrest or other detention that has already occurred and that may have been illegal. The constitutional or statutory provisions for making an arrest are of crucial importance because they prevent police action that could be very harmful to the individual.[21]

ARRESTS WITH A WARRANT   It is always best for a police officer to effect an arrest with a warrant. In fact, in 1980, the Supreme Court required police officers to obtain warrants when making felony arrests, should there be time to do so—that is, when there are no **exigent circumstances**.[22] To obtain an arrest warrant, the officer or a citizen swears in an **affidavit** (as an "affiant") that he or she possesses certain knowledge that a particular person has committed an offense. For example, a private citizen tells police or the district attorney that he or she attended a party at a residence where drugs or stolen articles were present, or (as is often the case) a detective gathers physical evidence or interviews witnesses or victims and determines that probable cause exists to believe that a particular person committed a specific crime. In any case, a neutral magistrate, if he or she agrees that probable cause exists, will issue the arrest warrant. Officers will execute the warrant, taking the suspect into custody to answer the charges.

WARRANTLESS ARRESTS   An arrest without a warrant requires exigent circumstances and that the officer possess probable cause (as explained earlier in the sodomy case). Street officers rarely have the time or opportunity to effect an arrest with a warrant in hand. Although the following real-life case involves a search preceding an arrest, it will make the point. One afternoon a police officer was sent to the residence of several college students. They reported that four men left their party and that soon afterwards another guest discovered that a stereo had been taken from a car parked in the yard. A description of the men and their vehicle was given to the officer, who soon observed a vehicle and four men matching the description. The men were stopped in their vehicle, and the officer called for backup.

The law does not require that the officer ask the subjects to stay put while he speeds off to the courthouse to attempt to secure a search warrant. The doctrine of probable cause allows the officer to search the vehicle and arrest the occupants if stolen or contraband items are found (as in this case, where the stolen stereo was found under the driver's seat). Police officers encounter these kinds of situations thousands of times each day. Such searches and arrests without benefit of a warrant are legally permissible, provided the officer had probable cause (which can later be explained to a judge) for his or her actions.

COURT CASES   In 1979, the Supreme Court rendered two decisions relating to arrests. Police, the Court said, must have probable cause to take a person into custody and to the police station for **interrogation**.[23] Police may not randomly stop a single vehicle to check the driver's license and registration; there must be probable cause for stopping the driver.[24] However, in 1990, the Court ruled that the stopping of all vehicles passing through sobriety checkpoints—a form of seizure—did not violate the Constitution, although singling out individual vehicles for random stops without probable cause is not authorized.[25] Several days later, it ruled that police were not required to give drunk-driving suspects a *Miranda* warning and could videotape their responses.[26]

In related decisions in the 2003–2004 term, the Supreme Court held that police may arrest *everyone* in a vehicle in which drugs are found. A Baltimore officer, stopping a speeding car and finding cocaine in an armrest in the backseat, was told by the driver and the two passengers that none of them owned the contraband; he arrested all three. Chief Justice Rehnquist wrote that in a small space like a car, officers can reasonably infer "a common enterprise" among a driver and passengers and would have probable cause to suspect that the drugs might belong to any or all of them.[27] A few months later, the Court ruled that police may set up roadblocks to collect information from motorists about crime. Short stops, "a very few minutes at most," are not too intrusive considering the value in crime solving; police may also hand out fliers or ask drivers to volunteer information, the Court noted.[28]

Finally, since 1975, police practice has been to ensure that a person arrested without a warrant receives a "prompt" initial appearance for a probable cause determination to see if the police were justified in arresting and holding the detainee. In its 1990–1991 term, the Supreme Court said that "prompt" does not mean "immediate" and that within forty-eight hours is generally soon enough.[29]

See Exhibit 8-2 for a discussion of the rule of law in another country: Saudi Arabia.

Search and Seizure

Because of the serious nature of police invasion of private property, the Supreme Court has had to examine several issues, particularly as they relate to searches of suspects' homes. In late 2003, the Court clarified how long police must wait before breaking into a home to serve a warrant, ruling unanimously that it was constitutional for police to wait fifteen to twenty seconds before knocking down the door of a drug suspect because to wait any longer would give the suspect time to flush evidence down the toilet. (The justices refused, however, to state exactly how long is reasonable in serving warrants.)[30] However, in 1995, the Court affirmed without decision an opinion of the Pennsylvania Supreme Court that the police violated the Fourth Amendment when they broke down the door of a residence only one or two seconds after they knocked, announced their presence, and said that they had a warrant. There were no exigent circumstances present.[31] Furthermore, in *Wilson* v. *Arkansas* (1995),[32] the Court found a search invalid when police in Arkansas, armed with a search warrant after receiving an informant's tip that drugs were being sold at the defendant's home, identified themselves *as they entered* the residence, where they subsequently found drugs and paraphernalia.

EXHIBIT 8-2

"The Unkindest Cut": Islam's Rule of Law

Shakespeare certainly did not have Saudi Arabia in mind when he had Mark Antony say, following the murder of Julius Caesar, that his stabbing by Brutus, Caesar's friend and a man whom Caesar trusted most of all, was "the unkindest cut of all." But certainly the law that provides for so-called chop-chops to be used against criminals in Islamic countries, governed by the Koran, constitutes the harshest criminal code in the world.

And in no Islamic country is the interpretation of Islamic law more strict than in Saudi Arabia. To describe Saudi law is to speak of their religion, culture, and customs, all of which are bound closely together. Islam means complete submission to the will of God and to provide a well-ordered society. Alcohol is forbidden in Saudi Arabia, and possession of even small amounts of hashish or marijuana can carry a punishment of two years' imprisonment or deportation.[1]

The law of Islam (the Sharia) is the fundamental code in Saudi Arabia, and it contains three categories of crimes: *Hudud* crimes, or those against the divine or God's rights; *Quesas* and *Diyya* crimes, or those against the individual; and *Tazir* crimes, those left undetermined by religious law. For the crime of theft, even for the first offense, the penalty may be amputation of the left hand at the wrist. The penalty for slander is flogging, usually with 80 lashes, and the same penalty may be applied for consuming alcohol. The penalty for adultery is flogging 100 times. A woman who engages in adultery is subjected to flogging or burial to the waist in a pit; stoning may follow. Highway robbery is punishable by execution or crucifixion, the amputation of opposite hands and feet, or exile from the land. Transgression will be confronted by the Saudi armed forces until the foes of the imam are defeated, and apostasy carries the death penalty.[2] Public executions are commonplace in Saudi Arabia. Hundreds of worshippers, including children and women, often gather to observe these and other punishments. The crowd usually applauds after the execution, and some bystanders spit on the blood of the dead persons and curse them.[3]

1. Saudi Arabian International Schools, *An Introduction to the Kingdom of Saudi Arabia* (Riyadh, Saudi Arabia: Author, 1996), p. 17.
2. Adel Mohammed el Fikey, "Crimes and Penalties in Islamic Criminal Legislation," *CJ International* 2 (July–August 1986), p. 13.
3. Reuter, *Gulf News,* "Saudi beheadings resume after break," May 19, 1989, p. 1.

Another decision relating to the area of police conduct at a private home during a search was rendered in March 2005. Following a drive-by shooting, police in Simi Valley, California, were searching a suspected gang member's house for *evidence* of a crime—weapons, ammunition, and gang paraphernalia, in the present case—rather than for contraband. Because of the high-risk nature of the case, a special weapons team entered the home, handcuffed the four occupants, and so detained them in a garage for two to three hours. The plaintiff alleged a violation of her Fourth Amendment rights. The Supreme Court reversed, finding that her detention was permissible, nor did the Court see a distinction between detention for a search for criminal evidence and detention for a search for contraband, because her detention was based on the existence of a warrant for a residence; furthermore, her being handcuffed was reasonable because of the officers' continuing safety interests.[33]

However, the Court upheld a search (with a warrant) of a third party's property when police had probable cause to believe it contained fruits or instrumentalities of a crime (for example, a newspaper office containing photographs of a disturbance),[34] a search of a wrong apartment conducted with a warrant but with a mistaken belief that the address was correct,[35] and a warrantless search and seizure of garbage in bags outside the defendant's home.[36]

The Court has also attempted to define when a person is considered "seized," an important issue because seizure involves Fourth Amendment protections. Is a person "seized" while police are pursuing him or her? Basically, there is no rule that determines the point of seizure in all situations—the standard is whether a suspect believes his or her liberty is restrained. This is ultimately a question for a judge or jury to decide.[37] In a recent roadblock case, the Court did provide some guidance, however. Where a police roadblock resulted in the death of a speeder, the Court said roadblocks involve a "governmental termination of freedom of movement," that the victim was therefore seized under the Fourth Amendment, and that the police were liable for damages.[38]

Two decisions in the 1990–1991 Supreme Court term expanded police practices. The Court looked at a police drug-fighting technique known as "working the buses." Police board a bus at a regular stopping place, approach seated passengers, and ask permission to search their luggage for drugs. Justice O'Connor, writing for the majority, said that such a situation should be evaluated in terms of whether a person in the passenger's position would have felt free to decline the officer's request or to otherwise terminate the encounter; it was held that such police conduct does not constitute a search.[39] In a companion decision in 2002, the justices held that the police—focusing on possible terrorists as well as drug couriers—may question passengers on buses and trains and may search for evidence without informing passengers that they can refuse. Police in Florida were on a Greyhound bus, asking questions of each passenger, when two men wearing heavy clothing on a warm day consented to a search of their luggage and bodies; police found bricks of cocaine strapped to their legs. The Court said the men were not coerced into consenting and that nothing about the fact that they were seated on a bus forced them to give their **consent**.[40]

The Court also decided that no "seizure" occurs when a police officer seeks to apprehend a person through a show of authority but applies no physical force (such as in a foot pursuit). In this case, a juvenile being chased by an officer threw down an object, later determined to be crack cocaine. The Supreme Court found no seizure or actual restraint in this situation.[41] Also, it should be noted that the Court held that no individualized suspicion of misconduct was required in either of these cases.

Supreme Court decisions have authorized a warrantless seizure of blood from a defendant to obtain evidence. (This was a case of driving under the influence, the drawing of blood was done by medical personnel in a hospital, and there were exigent circumstances—the evidence would have been lost by dissipation in the body.)[42] However, when police compelled a robbery suspect to submit to surgery to remove a bullet, the Court held that such an intrusion to seize evidence was unreasonable; this case said there are limits to what police can do to solve a crime.[43]

SEARCHES AND SEIZURES WITH AND WITHOUT A WARRANT   As is the case with making an arrest, the best means by which the police can search a person or premises is with a search warrant issued by a neutral magistrate. Such a magistrate has determined, after receiving information from a sworn affiant, that probable cause exists to believe that a person possesses the fruits or instrumentalities of a crime or that they are present at a particular location. Again, as with arrest, the "luxury" of searching and seizing with a warrant is usually confined to investigative personnel, who can interview victims and witnesses and gather other available evidence and then request the warrant. Street officers rarely have the opportunity to perform such a search, as the flow of events normally requires quick action to prevent escape and to prevent evidence from being destroyed or hidden.

Five types of searches may be conducted without a warrant: (1) searches that are incidental to lawful arrest, (2) searches that are done during field interrogation (stop-and-frisk searches), (3) searches of automobiles that are carried out under special conditions, (4) seizures of evidence that is in "plain view," and (5) searches when consent is given.

Searches Incidental to Lawful Arrest.   In *United States* v. *Robinson* (1973), the defendant was arrested and taken to the police station for driving without a permit—an offense for which a full-scale arrest could be made. Robinson was taken to jail and searched, and heroin was found. He tried to suppress the evidence on the grounds that the full-scale arrest and custodial search were unreasonable for a driver's license infraction. The Supreme Court disagreed, saying that the arrest was legal and that when police assumed custody of him, they needed total control and therefore could perform a detailed inventory of his possessions: "It is the fact of the lawful arrest that establishes the authority to search and we hold that in the case of lawful custodial arrest a full search of the person is not only an exception to the warrant requirement of the Fourth Amendment, but is also a 'reasonable' search under that Amendment."[44]

The rationale for this decision was in part the possibility that the suspect might destroy evidence unless swift action was taken. But in *Chimel* v. *California* (1969), when officers without a warrant arrested an individual in one room of his house and then proceeded to search the entire three-bedroom house, including the garage, attic, and workshop, the Supreme Court said that searches incidental to lawful arrest are limited to the area within the arrestee's immediate control or that area from which he or she might obtain a weapon. Thus if the police are holding a person in one room of the house, they are not authorized to search and seize property in another part of the house, away from the arrestee's immediate physical presence.[45]

The Court approved the warrantless seizure of a lawfully arrested suspect's clothes even after a substantial time period had elapsed between the arrest and the search.[46] Another advantage given the police was the Court's allowing a warrantless in-home "protective sweep" of the area in which a suspect is arrested to reveal the presence of anyone else who might pose a danger. Such a search, if justified by the circumstances, is not a full search of the premises and may only include a cursory inspection of those spaces where a person could be hiding.[47]

Searches during Field Interrogation (Stop and Frisk).   In 1968, the U.S. Supreme Court heard a case challenging the constitutionality of on-the-spot searches and questioning

Female officer searching a person.
(Courtesy Reno, Nevada, Police Department)

by the police. The case, *Terry* v. *Ohio*, involved a suspect who was stopped and searched while apparently "casing" a store for robbery (see the Court Closeup).

The Court's dilemma in this case was whether to rule that in some circumstances the police do not need probable cause to stop and search people, and thus appear to invalidate *Mapp* v. *Ohio*, or to insist on such a high standard for action by the police that they could not function on the streets.[48] The Court held that a brief on-the-spot stop for questioning, accompanied by a superficial search (a pat-down search) of external clothing for weapons, was something less than a full-scale search and therefore could be performed with less than the traditional amount of probable cause. This case instantly became—and remains—a major tool for the police.

While *Terry* said the stop and frisk is legal under the Fourth Amendment in cases involving direct police observation, other cases have said that such a stop is legal when based on information provided by an informant[49] and when an individual is the subject of a "wanted" flier from another jurisdiction.[50] In summary, police officers are justified, both to provide for their own safety and to detect past or future crimes, in stopping and questioning people. A person may be frisked for a weapon if an officer fears for his or her life, and the officer may go through the individual's clothing if the frisk indicates the presence of a weapon. Regardless of the rationale for the stop and frisk, there will always be some argument about whether this type of search is being used frivolously or to harass individuals. However, in balancing the public's need for safety against individual rights, the

COURT CLOSEUP

Terry v. *Ohio,* 319 U.S. 1 (1968)

Cleveland Detective McFadden, a veteran of nineteen years of police service, first noticed Terry and another man at about 2:30 P.M. on the afternoon of the arrest in October 1963. McFadden testified that it appeared the men were "casing" a retail store. He observed the suspects making several trips down the street, stopping at a store window, walking about a half block, turning around and walking back again, pausing to look inside the same store window. At one point they were joined by a third party, who spoke with them and then moved on. McFadden claimed that he followed them because he believed it was his duty as a police officer to investigate the matter further.

Soon the two rejoined the third man; at that point McFadden decided the situation demanded direct action. The officer approached the subjects, identified himself, and then requested that the men identify themselves as well. When Terry said something inaudible, McFadden "spun him around so that they were facing the other two, with Terry between McFadden and the others, and patted down the outside of his clothing." In a breast pocket of Terry's overcoat, the officer felt a pistol. McFadden found another pistol on one of the other men. The two men were arrested and ultimately convicted of concealing deadly weapons. Terry appealed on the ground that the search was illegal and that the evidence should have been suppressed at trial.

The U.S. Supreme Court disagreed with Terry, holding that the police have the authority to detain a person briefly for questioning even without probable cause if they believe that the person has committed a crime or is about to commit a crime. Such detention does not constitute an arrest. The officer may also frisk a person if the officer reasonably suspects that he or she is in danger.

Court was willing to tip the scales in favor of community protection, especially where the safety of the officer was concerned.[51]

An important expansion of the *Terry* doctrine was handed down in 1993 in *Minnesota* v. *Dickerson,*[52] in which a police officer observed a man leave a notorious crack house and then try to evade the officer. The man was eventually stopped and patted down, during which time the officer felt a small lump in the man's front pocket that was suspected to be drugs. After manipulating and squeezing the lump, the officer removed it from the man's pocket; the object was crack cocaine wrapped in a cellophane container. Although the defendant's arrest and conviction were later thrown out (the Supreme Court reasoned that the search was illegal because it went beyond the limited frisk for weapons, as permitted by *Terry*), the Court also allowed such seizures in the future when officers' probable cause is established by the sense of touch.

Another case extending *Terry, Illinois* v. *Wardlow,*[53] was decided in January 2000. The Court held that a citizen's running away from the police—under certain conditions—supports reasonable suspicion to justify a search. Two Illinois police officers investigating drug transactions in an area of heavy drug activity observed Wardlow holding a bag. Upon seeing the two officers, Wardlow fled, but he was soon stopped. The officers conducted a protective pat-down and then squeezed the bag; they felt a gun and arrested Wardlow. The Court reasoned that, taken together, several factors (the stop occurred in a high-crime area;

the suspect acted in a nervous, evasive manner; and the suspect engaged in unprovoked flight upon noticing the police)[54] were sufficient to establish reasonable suspicion.

Another important Supreme Court decision in February 1997 took officer safety into account. In *Maryland* v. *Wilson,*[55] the Court held that police may order passengers out of vehicles they stop, regardless of any suspicion of wrongdoing or threat to the officers' safety. Chief Justice Rehnquist cited statistics showing officer assaults and murders during traffic stops and noted that the "weighty interest" in officer safety is present whether a vehicle occupant is a driver or a passenger. (Here, a Maryland state trooper initiated a traffic stop and ordered an apparently nervous passenger, Wilson, to exit the vehicle. While doing so, Wilson dropped a quantity of crack cocaine, for which he was arrested and convicted.)

Searches of Automobiles.   The third general circumstance allowing a warrantless search is when an officer has probable cause to believe that an automobile contains criminal evidence. The Supreme Court has traditionally distinguished searches of automobiles from searches of homes on the grounds that a car involved in a crime can be rapidly moved and its evidence irretrievably lost. The Court first established this doctrine in *Carroll* v. *United States* (1925). In this case, officers searched the vehicle of a known bootlegger without a warrant but with probable cause, finding sixty-eight bottles of illegal booze. On appeal, the Court ruled that the seizure was justified. However, *Carroll* established two rules: First, to invoke the *Carroll* doctrine, the police must have enough probable cause that if there had been enough time, a search warrant would have been issued; second, urgent circumstances must exist that require immediate action.[56]

A police officer engages in a vehicle search.

(Courtesy Federal Bureau of Investigation)

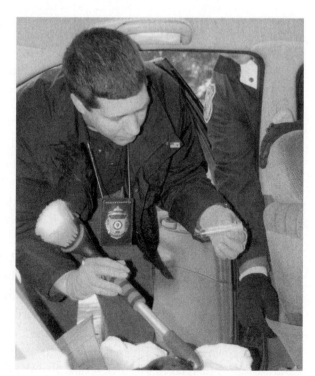

Extending the creation of the *Carroll* doctrine, however, two new questions confronted the justices: whether impounded vehicles were subject to warrantless search and whether searches could be made of vehicles stopped in routine traffic inspections. In *Preston* v. *United States* (1964), the Court ruled that once the police had made a lawful arrest and then towed the suspect's car to a different location, they could not conduct an incidental search of the vehicle. The Court reasoned that because such a search was remote in time and place from the point of arrest, it was not incidental and therefore was unreasonable.[57]

Harris v. *United States* (1968) upheld the right of police to enter an impounded vehicle following a lawful arrest in order to inventory its contents.[58] Building on this decision, the Court later upheld a warrantless search of a vehicle in custody, saying that because the police had probable cause to believe it contained evidence of a crime and could be easily moved, it made little difference whether a warrant was sought or an immediate search conducted.[59]

In 1974, the expectation of citizens to privacy in their vehicles was further diminished when the Court said an automobile has "little capacity for escaping public scrutiny [as] it travels public thoroughfares where both its occupants and its contents are in plain view."[60] This position was reinforced in 1976 when the Court said that a validly impounded car may be searched without probable cause or warrant as it is reasonable for an inventory of its contents to be made as a protection against theft or charges of theft while the car is in police custody.[61]

An automobile may be searched following the lawful search of its driver or another occupant. Following the rationale of *Chimel,* the Court ruled that the entire interior of the car, including containers, may be examined even if the items are not within the driver's reach.[62] The Court went on to say that a warrantless search of an automobile incidental to a lawful arrest, including its trunk and any packages or luggage, is permissible if there is probable cause to believe that it contains evidence of a crime.[63] The Court also authorized a protective pat-down of vehicle passenger compartments for weapons (similar to that of persons in *Terry* v. *Ohio*) after a valid stop and when officers have a reasonable belief that they may be in danger.[64] Finally, it was decided in 1987 that evidence seized by opening a closed container during a warrantless inventory search of a vehicle incidental to lawful arrest is admissible.[65]

During its 1990–1991 term, the Supreme Court extended the long arm of the law with respect to automobiles. In a May 1991 decision, the Court declared that a person's general consent to a search of the interior of an automobile justifies a search of any closed container found inside the car that might reasonably hold the object of the search; thus, an officer, after obtaining a general consent, does not need to ask permission to look inside each closed container.[66] One week later, the Court ruled that probable cause to believe that a container within a car holds contraband or evidence allows a warrantless search of that item under the automobile exception, even in the absence of probable cause extending to the entire vehicle.[67] This decision clarified the *Carroll* doctrine.

During its 1998–1999 term, the Court held that when an officer has probable cause to search a vehicle, the officer may search objects belonging to a passenger in the vehicle, provided the item the officer is looking for could reasonably be in the passenger's belongings.[68]

(Here the officer was searching an automobile for contraband and searched a passenger's purse, finding drug paraphernalia there.)

Then in January 2005, the Supreme Court decided by a 6-2 vote that a motorist has no legitimate expectation of privacy during a traffic stop for contraband hidden in a vehicle and detected by a drug-sniffing dog. In *Illinois* v. *Caballes*,[69] the defendant had been stopped for speeding; while the state trooper was issuing a citation, another trooper walked a drug-sniffing dog around the car. The dog alerted at the trunk, and after a search the troopers found marijuana, for which Caballes was arrested and convicted. The Court noted that Caballes was stopped lawfully and that the entire episode lasted less than ten minutes; also, drug-sniffing dogs only detect illegal activity (as opposed to, say, thermal-imaging devices that police once used to seek out marijuana growing in a home, which the Court said in 2001 were illegal because such devices can also detect lawful activities such as a person's taking a daily sauna or a bath).

Plain-View Searches.   The police do not have to search for items that are in plain view. If such items are believed to be fruits or instrumentalities of a crime and the police are lawfully on the premises, they may seize them. For example, if an officer has been admitted into a home with an arrest or search warrant and sees drugs and paraphernalia on a living room table, he or she may arrest the occupants on drug charges as well as the other charges. If an officer performs a traffic stop for an offense and observes drugs in the backseat of the car, he may arrest for that as well. Provided that the officer was lawfully in a particular place and that the plain-view discovery was inadvertent, the law does not require the officer to ignore contraband or other evidence of a crime that is in plain view.

The Supreme Court has said that officers are not required to immediately recognize an object in plain view as contraband before it may be seized. (For instance, an officer may see a balloon in a glove box with a white powdery substance on its tip and later determine the powder to be heroin.)[70] Furthermore, fences and the posting of "No Trespassing" signs afford no expectation of privacy and do not prevent officers from viewing open fields without a search warrant,[71] nor are police prevented from making a naked-eye aerial observation of a suspect's backyard or other curtilage (the grounds around a house or building).[72]

Two decisions in the late 1980s have further defined the plain-view doctrine. In one case, an officer found a gun under a car seat while looking for the vehicle identification number; the Court upheld the search and the resulting arrest as being a plain-view discovery.[73] However, in another similar situation, the Court disallowed an arrest when an officer, during a legal search for weapons, moved a stereo system to locate its serial number, saying that this constituted an unreasonable search and seizure.[74]

Searches with Consent.   Another permissible warrantless search involves citizens waiving their Fourth Amendment rights and consenting to a search of their persons or effects. It must be established at trial, however, that a defendant's consent was given voluntarily. In some circumstances, as with metal detectors at airports, an agent's right to search is implied.

In the leading case on consent searches, *Schneckloth* v. *Bustamonte* (1973), a police officer stopped a car for a burned-out headlight. Two other backup officers joined him.

When asked if his car could be searched, the driver consented. The officers found several stolen checks in the trunk. The driver and passenger were arrested and convicted. On appeal, the defendants argued that the evidence should have been suppressed, as they did not know they had the right to refuse the officers' request to search the car. The Supreme Court upheld their convictions, reasoning that the individuals, although poor, uneducated, and alone with three officers, could reasonably be considered capable of knowing and exercising their right to deny officers permission to search their car.[75]

However, police cannot deceive people into believing they have a search warrant when they in fact do not. For example, the police, looking for a rape suspect, announced falsely to the suspect's grandmother that they had a search warrant for her home; the evidence they found was ruled to be inadmissible.[76] A hotel clerk cannot give a valid consent to a warrantless search of the room of one of the occupants; hotel guests have a reasonable expectation of privacy, and that right cannot be waived by hotel management.[77]

Finally, the right of police to search a home when one occupant consents and the other objects was the subject of a Supreme Court decision in March 2006. There, police responded to the home of a Georgia couple following a domestic disturbance. The wife told the officers that her husband was a drug user and had drugs in their home. An officer asked the husband for permission to search the residence and was denied. The wife granted consent, however, and led the officers to a bedroom where cocaine was kept. The defendant-husband appealed on the grounds that the drugs were the product of an unlawful search, and the Supreme Court agreed on the grounds that the Fourth Amendment should not ignore the privacy rights of an individual who is present and asserting his rights.[78] Note, however, that an occupant may still give police permission to search when the other resident is absent or does not protest.

Electronic Surveillance

It was the original view of the Supreme Court, in *Olmstead* v. *United States* (1928), that wiretaps were not searches and seizures and did not violate the Fourth Amendment; this represented the old rule on wiretaps.[79] However, that decision was overruled in 1967 in *Katz* v. *United States*, which held that any form of electronic surveillance, including wiretapping, is a search and violates a reasonable expectation of privacy.[80] The case involved a public telephone booth, deemed by the Court to be a constitutionally protected area where the user has a reasonable expectation of privacy. This decision expressed the view that the Constitution protects people, not places. Thus the Court has required that warrants for electronic surveillance be based on probable cause, describe the conversations to be overheard, be for a limited period of time, name subjects to be overheard, and be terminated when the desired information is obtained.[81]

However, the Supreme Court has held that while electronic eavesdropping (that is, an informant wearing a "bug," or hidden microphone) did not violate the Fourth Amendment (a person assumes the risk that whatever he or she says may be transmitted to the police),[82] the warrantless monitoring of an electronic beeper in a private residence violated the suspect's right to privacy. A federal drug agent had placed a beeper inside a can of ether, which was being used to extract cocaine from clothing imported into the United States and had monitored its movements.[83]

Lineups

A police **lineup**, as well as other face-to-face confrontations after the accused has been arrested, is considered a critical stage of criminal proceedings; therefore, the accused has a right to have an attorney present. If counsel is not present, the evidence obtained is inadmissible.[84] However, the suspect is not entitled to the presence and advice of a lawyer before being formally charged.[85]

Lineups that are so suggestive as to make the result inevitable violate the suspect's right to due process. (In one case, the suspect was much taller than the other two people in the lineup, and he was the only person wearing a leather jacket similar to that worn by the robber. In a second lineup, the suspect was the only person who had participated in the first lineup.[86]) In short, lineups must be fair to suspects; a fair lineup guarantees no bias against the suspect.

The Supreme Court has held that a suspect may be compelled to appear before a grand jury and give voice exemplars for comparison with an actual voice recording. Appearance before a grand jury is not a search, and the giving of a voice sample is not a seizure that is protected by the Fourth Amendment.[87]

FIFTH AMENDMENT

> No person shall be held to answer for a capital, or otherwise infamous crime, unless on a presentment or indictment of a Grand Jury, except in cases arising in the land or naval forces, or in the Militia, when in actual service in time of war or public danger; nor shall any person be subject for the same offense to be twice put in jeopardy of life or limb; nor shall be compelled in any criminal case to be a witness against himself, nor be deprived of life, liberty, or property, without due process of law; nor shall private property be taken for public use, without just compensation.

A major tool used in religious persecutions in England during the sixteenth century was the oath. Ministers were called before the Court of Star Chamber (which, during much of the sixteenth and seventeenth centuries, enforced unpopular political policies and meted out severe punishments, including whipping, branding, and mutilation, without a jury trial) and questioned about their beliefs. Being men of God, they were compelled to tell the truth and admitted to their nonconformist views; for this, they were often severely punished or even executed.[88] In the 1630s, the Star Chamber and similar bodies of cruelty were disbanded by Parliament. People had become repulsed by compulsory self-incrimination; the privilege against self-incrimination was recognized in all courts when claimed by defendants or witnesses. Today, the **Fifth Amendment** clause applies not only to criminal defendants but also to any witness testifying in a civil or criminal case and anyone testifying before an administrative body, a grand jury, or a congressional committee. However, the privilege does not extend to blood samples, handwriting exemplars, and other such items that are not considered to be testimony.[89]

The right against self-incrimination is one of the most significant provisions in the Bill of Rights. Basically it states that no criminal defendant shall be compelled to take the witness stand and give evidence against himself or herself. No one can be compelled to answer any question if his or her answer can later be used to implicate or convict him or her. Some people view the defendant's "taking the Fifth" as an indication of guilt; others view this as a basic right in a democracy, wherein a defendant does not have to contribute to his or her own conviction. In either case, the impact of this amendment is felt daily by the criminal justice system.

Decisions Supporting *Miranda:* Confessions

Traditionally, the U.S. Supreme Court has excluded physically coerced confessions on the grounds that such confessions might very well be untrustworthy or unreliable in view of the duress surrounding them. As the quality of police work has improved, police use of physical means to obtain confessions has diminished. Some cases that have come before the Supreme Court involved psychological rather than physical pressure on the defendant to confess. One such case involved an accused who was questioned for eight hours by six police officers in relays and was told falsely that the job and welfare of a friend who was a rookie cop depended on his confession. He was also refused contact with his lawyer. The Court reversed his conviction, not so much on the grounds that the confession was unreliable but on the grounds that it was obtained unfairly.[90]

In the 1960s, the Supreme Court ruled in *Escobedo* v. *Illinois* (1964),[91] discussed later, and in *Miranda* v. *Arizona* (1966)[92] (see Court Closeup) that confessions made by suspects who have not been notified of their constitutional rights cannot be admitted into evidence. In these cases, the Court emphasized the importance of a defendant having the "guiding hand of counsel" present during the interrogation process.

Once a suspect has been placed under arrest, the *Miranda* warning must be given before interrogation for any offense, be it a felony or a misdemeanor. An exception is the brief routine traffic stop; however, a custodial interrogation of a suspect for driving under the influence (DUI) requires the *Miranda* warning.[93] Moreover, after an accused has invoked the right to counsel, the police may not interrogate the same suspect about a different crime.[94] Once a "Mirandized" suspect invokes his or her right to silence, interrogation must cease. The police may not readminister *Miranda* and interrogate the suspect later unless the suspect's attorney is present. If, however, the suspect initiates further conversation, any confession he or she provides is admissible.[95]

Decisions Eroding *Miranda:* Interrogations

Miranda, Escobedo, and *Mapp* combined to represent the centerpiece of the Warren Court's "due process revolution" of the 1960s. However, several decisions, including many by the Burger Court, have dealt severe blows to *Miranda*.

COURT CLOSEUP

Miranda v. *Arizona*, 384 U.S. 436 (1966)

While walking to a Phoenix, Arizona, bus stop on the night of March 2, 1963, eighteen-year-old Barbara Ann Johnson was accosted by a man who shoved her into his car, tied her hands and ankles, and drove her to the edge of the city, where he raped her. He then drove Johnson to a street near her home, letting her out of the car and asking that she pray for him.

The Phoenix police subsequently picked up Ernesto Miranda for investigation of Johnson's rape and included him in a lineup at the police station. Miranda was identified by several women; one identified him as the man who had robbed her at knifepoint a few months earlier, and Johnson thought he was the rapist.

Miranda was a twenty-three-year-old eighth-grade dropout with a police record dating back to age fourteen, and he had also served time in prison for driving a stolen car across a state line. During questioning, the police told Miranda that he had been identified by the women; Miranda then made a statement in writing that described the rape incident. He also noted that he was making the confession voluntarily and with full knowledge of his legal rights. He was soon charged with rape, kidnapping, and robbery.

At trial, Miranda's court-appointed attorney got the officers to admit that during the interrogation the defendant was not informed of his right to have counsel present and that no counsel was present. Nonetheless, Miranda's confession was admitted into evidence. He was convicted and sentenced to serve twenty to thirty years for kidnapping and rape.

On appeal, the U.S. Supreme Court ruled:

> [T]he current practice of incommunicado interrogation is at odds with one of our Nation's most cherished principles—that the individual may not be compelled to incriminate himself. Unless adequate protective devices are employed to dispel the compulsion inherent in custodial surroundings, no statement obtained from the defendant can truly be the product of free choice.

It has been held that a second interrogation session held after the suspect had initially refused to make a statement did not violate *Miranda*.[96] If a suspect waives his or her *Miranda* rights and makes voluntary statements while irrational (allegedly "following the advice of God"), those statements too are admissible.[97] The Court also decided that when a suspect waived his or her *Miranda* rights, believing the interrogation would focus on minor crimes, but the police shifted their questioning to a more serious crime, the confession was valid—there was no police deception or misrepresentation.[98] When a suspect invoked his or her right to assistance of counsel and refused to make written statements but then voluntarily gave oral statements to police, the statements were admissible (defendants have "the right to choose between speech and silence").[99] Finally, a suspect need not be given the *Miranda* warning in the exact form that it was outlined in *Miranda* v. *Arizona*. In one case, the waiver form said the suspect would have an attorney appointed "if and when you go to court." The Court held that as long as the warnings on the form reasonably convey the suspect's rights, they need not be given verbatim.[100]

In 1994, the Supreme Court ruled that after police officers obtain a valid *Miranda* waiver from a suspect, they may continue questioning him or her when he or she makes an ambiguous or equivocal request for counsel during questioning. In this case,[101] the defendant stated during an interview and after waiving his rights, "Maybe I should talk to a lawyer." The officers inquired about this statement, determined that he did not want a lawyer, and continued their questioning. When a suspect unequivocally requests counsel, all questioning must cease. However, here the Court held that when the suspect mentions an attorney, the officers need not interrupt the flow of the questioning to clarify the reference but may continue questioning until there is a clear assertion of the right to counsel, such as "I want a lawyer."

Entrapment

The due process clause of the Fifth Amendment requires "fundamental fairness"—government agents may not act in a way that is "shocking to the universal sense of justice." Thus the police may not induce or encourage a person to commit a crime that he or she would otherwise not have attempted, that is, **entrapment**.[102] This is the current test used by many courts to evaluate police behavior. Some states take a broader view than others as to what constitutes entrapment. For example, a police department in a western state had police officers impersonate homeless people. The decoys pretended to be asleep or passed out from intoxication on a public bench, and paper money visibly protruded from their pockets. Several passersby helped themselves to the money and were arrested on the spot. On appeal, the prosecution argued that a thief is a thief, the people had the intent to commit theft, and the decoy operation simply provided an opportunity for dishonest people to get caught. The state supreme court disagreed, calling the operation entrapment, adding that the situation could cause even honest people to be overcome by temptation.

However, the Supreme Court approved an undercover drug agent's provision of an essential chemical for the manufacture of illegal drugs. (The defendant, the majority said, was an "unwary criminal" who was already "predisposed" to commit the offense).[103] Nor is it entrapment when a drug agent sells drugs to a suspect, who then sells it to government agents. Government conduct in this case is shocking to civil libertarians, but the focus here is the conduct of the defendant, not the government. As long as government's conduct is not outrageous and the defendant was predisposed to crime, the arrest is valid.[104]

The Supreme Court has held that police officers "may not originate a criminal design, implant in an innocent person's mind the disposition to commit a criminal act, and then induce commission of the crime."[105]

SIXTH AMENDMENT

> In all criminal prosecutions the accused shall enjoy the right to a speedy and public trial, by an impartial jury of the State and district wherein the crime shall have been committed, which district shall have been previously ascertained by law, and to be informed of the nature and cause of the accusation; to be confronted with the witnesses against him; to have compulsory process

for obtaining witnesses in his favor; and to have the assistance of counsel for his defense.

Right to Counsel

Many people believe that the **Sixth Amendment** right of the accused to have the assistance of counsel before and at trial is the greatest right we enjoy in a democracy. Indeed, a close reading of the cases mentioned here would reveal the negative outcomes that are possible when a person—rich or poor, illiterate or educated—has no legal representation.

Over seventy years ago, in *Powell* v. *Alabama* (1932), it was established that in a capital case, when the accused is poor and illiterate, he or she enjoys the right to assistance of counsel for his or her defense and due process.[106] In *Gideon* v. *Wainwright* (1963), the Supreme Court mandated that all indigent people charged with felonies in state courts be provided counsel.[107]

Note that *Gideon* applied only to felony defendants. In 1973, *Argersinger* v. *Hamlin* extended the right to counsel to indigent people charged with misdemeanor crimes if they face the possibility of incarceration (however short the incarceration may be).[108]

Another landmark decision concerning the right to counsel is *Escobedo* v. *Illinois* (1964).[109] Danny Escobedo's brother-in-law was fatally shot in 1960; Escobedo was arrested without a warrant and questioned, but he made no statement to the police. He was released after fourteen hours of interrogation. Following police questioning of another suspect, Escobedo was again arrested and questioned at police headquarters. Escobedo's request to confer with his lawyer was denied, even after the lawyer arrived and asked to see his client. The questioning of Escobedo lasted several hours, during which time he was handcuffed and forced to remain standing. Eventually, he admitted being an accomplice to murder. Under Illinois law, an accomplice was as guilty as the person firing the fatal bullet. At no point was Escobedo advised of his rights to remain silent or to confer with his attorney.

Escobedo's conviction was ultimately reversed by the Supreme Court, based on a violation of Escobedo's Sixth Amendment right to counsel. However, the real thrust of the decision was his Fifth Amendment right not to incriminate himself; when a defendant is scared, flustered, ignorant, alone, and bewildered, he or she is often unable to effectively make use of protections granted under the Fifth Amendment without the advice of an attorney.[110] The *Miranda* decision set down two years later simply established the guidelines for the police to inform suspects of all of these rights.

What Constitutes an Interrogation?

The Supreme Court has stated that an interrogation takes place not only when police officers ask direct questions of a defendant but also when the police make remarks designed to appeal to a defendant's sympathy, religious interest, and so forth. This has been deemed soliciting information through trickery and deceit. The "Christian Burial Speech" case (discussed earlier) and *Escobedo* demonstrated that even before (and certainly after) a suspect has been formally charged, a suspect in police custody should not be interrogated without an attorney present unless he or she has waived the right to counsel.

However, the Supreme Court upheld a conviction when two police officers, in a suspect's presence, discussed the possible whereabouts of the shotgun used in a robbery and expressed concern that nearby schoolchildren might be endangered by it. Hearing this conversation, the suspect led officers to the shotgun, thereby implicating himself. On appeal, the Court said that interrogation includes words and actions intended to elicit an incriminating response from the defendant and that no such interrogation occurred here; this was a mere conversation between officers, and the evidence was admissible.[111]

In another case, the Court ruled that if the police were present at and recorded a conversation between a husband and wife (this tape was later used against the husband at trial, where he claimed insanity in the killing of his son), an interrogation did not occur. The Court believed that the police merely arranged a situation in which it was likely the suspect would make incriminating statements, so anything recorded could be used against him in court.[112]

Two cases on police interrogations were heard during the 1990–1991 Supreme Court term. First, the Court held that a defendant who is in custody and has been given the *Miranda* warning may be questioned later on a separate as-yet-uncharged offense. In this case, the defendant appeared with an attorney at a bail hearing on robbery charges. Later, while he was still in custody, the police, after reading him his rights, questioned him about a murder; the defendant agreed to discuss the murder without counsel and made incriminating statements that were used to convict him.[113] In the second case, representing a victory for the defense, the Court held that once a criminal suspect has asked for and consults with a lawyer, interrogators may not later question him without his lawyer being present.[114]

JUVENILE RIGHTS

The criminal justice system's philosophy toward juveniles is very different from its philosophy toward adults. Consequently, police officers, who are constantly dealing with juvenile offenders, must know and apply a different standard of treatment in these situations. The approach toward juvenile offenders is generally that society, through poor parenting, poverty, and so forth, is primarily responsible for their criminal behavior.

The prevailing doctrine that guides our treatment of juveniles is **parens patriae**, meaning that "the state is the ultimate parent" of the child. In effect, as long as we adequately care for and provide at least the basic amenities for our children as required under the law, they are ours to keep, but when children are physically or emotionally neglected or abused by their parents or guardians, the juvenile court and police may intervene and remove the children from that environment. Then the doctrine of **in loco parentis** takes hold, meaning that the state will act in place of the parent. The author can state from experience that there is probably no more overwhelming or awe-inspiring duty for a police officer than having to testify in juvenile court that a woman is an unfit mother and that parental ties should be legally severed. However, when a person chooses to be a negligent or abusive parent, it is clearly in everyone's best interest for the state to assume care and custody of the child.

The juvenile justice system, working through and with the police, seeks to protect the child. It seeks to rehabilitate, not punish; its procedure is generally amiable, not adversarial. That is why the term *In Re*, meaning "concerning" or "in the matter of," is commonly used in many juvenile case titles—for example, a case would be called *In Re Smith* rather than the adversarial and more formal *State* v. *Smith*. Juvenile court proceedings are generally shrouded in privacy, heard before a judge only. However, when a juvenile commits an act that is so heinous that the protective and helpful juvenile court philosophy will not work, the child may be remanded to the custody of the adult court to be tried as an adult.

Juvenile delinquency (an ambiguous term that has no widespread agreed-on meaning but has a multitude of definitions under state statutes[115]) became recognized as a national problem in the 1950s. As a result, several important decisions by the Supreme Court between 1960 and 1970 addressed the rights of juveniles. *Kent* v. *United States* (1966)[116] involved a sixteen-year-old male who was arrested in the District of Columbia for robbery, rape, and burglary. The juvenile court, without holding a formal hearing, waived the matter to a criminal court, and Kent was tried and convicted as an adult. Kent appealed, arguing that the waiver without a hearing violated his right to due process. The Supreme Court agreed.

Another landmark case extending due process to juveniles was *In Re Gault* (1967).[117] Gerald Gault was a fifteen-year-old who resided in Arizona and allegedly made obscene telephone calls. When a neighbor complained to police, Gault was arrested and eventually sent to a youth home (a previous crime, stealing a wallet, was also taken into account), to remain there until he either turned twenty-one or was paroled. Before his hearing, Gault did not receive a timely notice of charges. At his hearing, Gault had no attorney present, nor was his accuser present; no transcript was made of the proceedings, and Gault was not read his rights or told he could remain silent. Gault appealed on the grounds that all of these due process rights should have been provided. The Supreme Court reversed his conviction, declaring that these Fourteenth Amendment protections applied to juveniles as well as adults. This case remains the most significant juvenile rights decision ever rendered.

In 1970, the Supreme Court decided *In Re Winship,* which involved a twelve-year-old boy convicted in New York of larceny.[118] At trial, the court relied on the "preponderance of the evidence" standard of proof against him rather than the more demanding "beyond a reasonable doubt" standard used in adult courts. At that time, juvenile courts could apply any of three standards of proof (the third was "clear and convincing evidence"). The Court reversed Winship's conviction on the grounds that the "beyond a reasonable doubt" standard had not been used.

Other precedent-setting juvenile cases followed. In *McKeiver* v. *Pennsylvania* (1971), the Supreme Court said juveniles do not have an absolute right to trial by jury; whether or not a juvenile receives a trial by jury is left to the discretion of state and local authorities.[119] In *Breed* v. *Jones* (1975), the Court concluded that the Fifth Amendment protected juveniles from double jeopardy, or being tried twice for the same offense. (Breed had been tried both in California Juvenile Court and later in Superior Court for the same offenses.)[120]

In March 2005, the U.S. Supreme Court, in *Roper* v. *Simmons,* ruled that the Eighth and Fourteenth Amendments forbid the execution of offenders who were under the age of eighteen when their crimes were committed.[121]

SUMMARY

Our society places great importance on individual freedom, and the power of government has traditionally been feared; therefore, our Constitution, courts, and legislatures have seen fit to rein in the power of government agents through what is commonly referred to as the "rule of law," which was defined in the chapter introduction. This necessary aspect associated with having police in a democracy carries with it a responsibility for police practitioners to understand the law and—more important, perhaps—to keep abreast of the legal changes our society is constantly undergoing.

The law is dynamic, that is, it is constantly changed by the Supreme Court and other federal courts and by state courts and legislatures. It is imperative that police agencies have a formal mechanism for imparting these legal changes to their officers.

The number of successful criminal and civil lawsuits against police officers today demonstrates that the police have not always done their homework and simply do not apply the law in the manner in which the federal courts intended. Officers must understand and enforce the law properly. In this grave business of adult cops and robbers, the means are in many respects more important than the ends. The courts and the criminal justice system should expect and allow nothing less.

KEY TERMS

affidavit
consent
crime-control model
due process model
entrapment
exclusionary rule
exigent circumstance
Fifth Amendment
Fourth Amendment
in loco parentis
interrogation
lineup
parens patriae

probable cause
rule of law
search and seizure
Sixth Amendment

REVIEW QUESTIONS

1. What is meant by the rule of law?

2. What protections are afforded citizens by the Fourth, Fifth, and Sixth Amendments?

3. What is an example of probable cause?

4. From both the police and community perspectives, what are the ramifications of having and not having the exclusionary rule?

5. How would you distinguish between arrests and searches and seizures with and without a warrant, and which form is best? (Provide examples of each.)

6. In what significant ways has the *Miranda* decision been eroded, and what is its long-term outlook, given the shifting composition of judges on the Supreme Court?

7. What major legal rights exist for juveniles, and what are the major differences in philosophy and treatment between juvenile and adult offenders?

INDEPENDENT STUDENT ACTIVITIES

1. Read a primer on legal research methods, and then go to a law library and locate the following landmark U.S. Supreme Court decisions: *Miranda* v. *Arizona*, *Terry* v. *Ohio*, and *Mapp* v. *Ohio* (their case citations are given in the Notes section).

2. Have an attorney or a police officer explain the elusive concept of probable cause. Ask him or her to provide some real-life examples of this concept as it has been applied on the street.

3. Interview officers or court personnel concerning their views on the advantages and disadvantages of the exclusionary rule. Try to imagine the ramifications of a justice system in which the exclusionary rule did not exist.

4. Imagine scenarios involving different types of criminal activities in which an officer might need to search a person or a vehicle without a warrant. (For example, assume an officer stops a vehicle matching the description of one used in a robbery where a bank bag containing cash and various food items were taken. What kinds of items might the officer view in the backseat of the vehicle that would constitute probable cause and justify a warrantless search?)

RELATED WEB SITES

Administrative Office of the Courts
http://www.uscourts.gov

American Bar Association
http://www.abanet.org

Justice Information Center
http://www.ncjrs.org

U.S. Supreme Court
http://www.supremecourtus.gov

ACCOUNTABILITY

ETHICS, USE OF FORCE, CORRUPTION, AND DISCIPLINE

Our biggest problems are internal, not external. I'm a personnel manager who happens to wear a uniform. I couldn't tell you how to process a DUI arrest, but I can tell you how to investigate and discipline an officer. That's how [policing] has changed.
—*A Western U.S. deputy chief of police*

But justice is inverted when those engines of the law,
Instead of pinching vicious men, keep honest ones in awe.
—*Daniel Defoe*

LEARNING OBJECTIVES

AS A RESULT OF READING THIS CHAPTER, THE STUDENT WILL:

- UNDERSTAND WHAT IS MEANT BY POLICE ACCOUNTABILITY

- BE ABLE TO DEFINE ETHICS, INCLUDING THE PRINCIPLES OF DOUBLE EFFECT, NOBLE CAUSE CORRUPTION, THE "DIRTY HARRY PROBLEM," AND TO DELINEATE SOME OF THE UNIQUE ETHICAL PROBLEMS THAT COMMUNITY POLICING CAN POSE

- KNOW HOW PACKER'S CRIME-CONTROL MODEL AND DUE PROCESS MODEL ARE IMPLICATED IN THE MATTER OF ETHICS

- UNDERSTAND THE USES AND LIMITS OF POLICE FORCE, INCLUDING THE USE-OF-FORCE CONTINUUM

- KNOW THE TYPES OF POLICE BRUTALITY

- UNDERSTAND SOME FACTORS THAT CONTRIBUTE TO POLICE VIOLENCE

- KNOW WHAT CONSTITUTES INAPPROPRIATE USE OF FORCE BY THE POLICE

- BE ABLE TO DEFINE BIAS-BASED POLICING, AND KNOW HOW IT CAN BE ADDRESSED

- BE ABLE TO EXPLAIN HOW AND WHY POLICE CORRUPTION BEGAN AND WHAT FACTORS WITHIN BOTH THE COMMUNITY AND POLICING SEEM TO FOSTER AND MAINTAIN IT

- UNDERSTAND THE CONSTITUTIONAL LIMITATIONS THAT FEDERAL COURTS HAVE PLACED ON OFFICERS' RIGHTS AND BEHAVIORS

- KNOW THE GENERAL PROCESS THAT POLICE AGENCIES USE TO DEAL WITH CITIZEN COMPLAINTS

- KNOW SOME OF THE FACTORS USED FOR DETERMINING SANCTIONS FOR OFFICERS WHO ARE TO BE DISCIPLINED

INTRODUCTION

"Character," it might be said, "is who we are when no one is watching." Unfortunately, character cannot be trained at the police academy nor given to someone in a pill or intravenously. Character and ethical conduct, for police officers, mean they would never betray their oath of office, their public trust, or their badge. Character and ethics are *sine qua non* for the police—without those attributes, nothing else matters. These qualities constitute the foundation of their occupation and will certainly affect the officers' philosophy concerning when to use force and whether or not to engage in corruption or report other officers who do. Therefore, perhaps no general area of policing carries more controversy, concerns, problems, and questions than the aspects of policing that are discussed in this chapter concerning police accountability: ethics, use of force, corruption, and discipline.

First the subject of police ethics—its definitions, types, and problems—is examined. Incorporated in this discussion are ethical ideals, including differing views of how much latitude the police should be permitted in doing their work, as well as some ethical issues that are posed in this era of community policing and problem solving. Next we consider the equally controversial area of police use of force, and we discuss the use-of-force continuum, police shootings, and legal restrictions. In a related vein, we then look at police brutality; also discussed is the "hot button" issue of bias-based policing and other field tactics. We then consider police corruption: types and causes, problems posed by the police code of silence, and some possible solutions for dealing with it. Next is an overview of areas in which the federal courts have placed limitations on behaviors of the police by virtue of their unique role. Included here are freedom of speech, search and seizure, self-incrimination, freedom of religion, sexual misconduct, residency requirements, moonlighting, misuse of firearms, and alcohol and drug abuse. Finally, the chapter examines disciplinary policies and practices, including handling citizens' complaints and doling out sanctions. A chapter summary, key terms, review questions, independent student activities, and related Web sites conclude the chapter.

POLICE ETHICS

In a broad sense, for the police, being ethical should include holding themselves and others accountable for their actions. **Accountability**, like character and ethics, is also a significant watchword for today's police, and certainly all citizens expect their public servants to be accountable. What does accountability mean for the police? Beyond the obvious, such as having character and ethics and being good stewards of the public's trust, the term can also include the following: Police officers will treat all persons with dignity and respect and in a lawful manner; they will not use more force than necessary; they will not demonstrate bias for or against any particular group of persons; they will make every effort to ensure that all officers are well trained to meet the highest standards of professionalism; and they will maintain adequate policies, procedures, rules, regulations, General Orders, and so forth for ensuring the public's trust, which includes procedures for investigating alleged incidents of bias and unprofessional behavior. Consider the following scenario.

The police have long been criticized for a variety of reasons, as shown in this 1874 caricature of police as pigs.

(Courtesy The Granger Collection, New York)

A Scenario

Assume that the police have strong suspicions that Jones is a serial rapist, but they have not secured enough probable cause to obtain a search warrant for Jones's car and home, where evidence might be found. Officer Brown feels frustrated and, early one morning, uses a razor blade to remove the current registration decal from the license plate on Jones's car. The next day he stops Jones for operating his vehicle with an expired registration; he impounds and inventories the vehicle and finds evidence of several sexual assaults, which ultimately leads to Jones's conviction on ten counts of forcible rape and possession of burglary tools and stolen property. Brown receives accolades for the apprehension. Was Officer Brown's removal of the registration decal legal? Should Brown's actions, even if improper or illegal, be condoned for "serving the greater public good"? Did Brown use the law properly?

This hypothetical sequence of events and the accompanying questions should be kept in mind as we consider the definitions and problems of police **ethics**. Exhibit 9-1 describes some means by which a police agency's culture of integrity can be measured.

EXHIBIT 9-1

Measuring a Police Department's "Culture of Integrity"

Researchers believe they have found a quantitative method that allows police executives to assess their agency's level of resistance to corruption. A national survey of 3,235 officers in thirty police departments asked them to examine eleven common scenarios of police misconduct. The study was based on the premise that organizational and occupational culture can create an atmosphere in which corruption is not tolerated. Survey questions were designed to indicate whether officers knew the rules governing misconduct and how strongly they supported those guidelines, whether they knew the disciplinary penalties for breaking those rules and believed them to be fair, and whether they were willing to report misconduct. Respondents found some types of transgressions to be significantly less serious than others. The more serious the transgression was perceived to be, the more willing officers were to report a colleague and to believe that severe discipline was

appropriate. Four scenarios that were not considered major transgressions by officers included operating a private security business while off duty, receiving free meals, accepting free holiday gifts, and covering up a police drunk-driving accident. Indeed, a majority of respondents said they would not report a fellow officer for accepting free gifts, meals, or discounts or for having a minor traffic accident while under the influence of alcohol.

The intermediate levels of misconduct included using excessive force on a car thief following a foot pursuit, a supervisor's offering time off during holidays in exchange for a tune-up on his personal vehicle, and accepting free drinks in return for ignoring a late bar closing. Very serious forms of misconduct, as perceived by the respondents, included accepting a cash bribe, stealing money from a found wallet, and stealing a watch from a crime scene.

Source: Adapted from "How Do You Rate? The Secret to Measuring a Department's 'Culture of Integrity,'" *Law Enforcement News,* October 15, 2000, pp. 1, 6. John Jay College of Criminal Justice, CUNY, 555 W. 57th St., New York, NY 10019.

Definitions and Types of Problems

Proper ethical behavior has always been the cornerstone of policing (based on the Law Enforcement Code of Ethics, discussed below) and is what the public expects of its public servants. Ethics usually involves standards of moral conduct and what we call "conscience," the ability to recognize right from wrong and to act in ways that are good and proper; it concerns choices of good and bad actions as well as moral duties and obligations.

There are both absolute and relative ethics. Absolute ethics is a concept wherein an issue only has two sides: Something is either good or bad, black or white. The original interest in police ethics focused on such unethical behaviors as bribery, extortion, excessive force, and perjury. Few communities can tolerate the absolute unethical behavior of rogue officers; for instance, anyone would have a hard time trying to rationally defend a police officer's stealing.

Relative ethics, as demonstrated in the scenario above, can be much more complicated and can have varying shades of gray. The problem here is this: What is considered ethical behavior by one person may be deemed highly unethical by someone else. Not all police ethical issues are clear-cut. For example, communities seem willing at times to tolerate extralegal behavior by the police if there is a greater public good, especially in dealing with such problems as gangs and the homeless or with offenders like the serial rapist in our scenario.

A community's acceptance of relative ethics may send the wrong message: that there are few boundaries placed on police behaviors and that, at times, "anything goes" in the fight against crime. Giving false testimony to ensure that a public menace is "put away" or using illegal wiretapping to get evidence from an organized crime figure's telephone conversations might sometimes be viewed as "necessary" and "justified," though illegal. This viewpoint—the principle of **double effect**—holds that when one commits an act to achieve a good end, even though an inevitable but intended effect is negative, then the act might be justified. Other related catchwords for this phenomenon are **noble cause corruption** and the **"Dirty Harry problem."**[1] (The latter is based on the 1971 Warner Brothers film of the same title in which Detective Harry Callahan [Clint Eastwood] uses extralegal methods to accomplish legitimate police goals. For example, Callahan tortures a vicious kidnapper until he learns where he has hidden the victim. Such treatment might be condoned by many people because the heinous treatment of the offender is viewed as less shocking than what the offender did to his victim.)

The discussion of noble cause corruption and double effect is closely entwined with Herbert Packer's two classic models of law enforcement: crime control and due process.[2] The **crime-control model** holds that repression of criminal conduct is the most important function of the police; police efficiency with an emphasis on speed and finality, is a top priority. The **due process model**, conversely, operates under the principle that efficiency is less important than eliminating errors and that the protection of the process of law is more important than any end result of conviction. Under this model, there is a recognition that the coercive power of the state (including all the tools and resources at the disposal of the police and prosecutors) is sometimes subject to abuse and must be guarded against by due process.

Noble cause corruption is a type of wrongdoing that stems from a crime-control orientation. It is a type of means-end thinking in that the end of crime control justifies the means, even if the means are otherwise unethical or illegal. Therefore, in this view police officers may feel compelled to lie ("testilying") under oath, use physical coercion during an interrogation, ignore exculpatory evidence if they feel they have the right offender in custody, overlook criminal acts of an informant, plan or manufacture evidence, and so on. What sets apart these acts from other ethical issues is that they are done for arguably good motives.[3]

Ethics and Community Policing

With the shift to community-oriented policing and problem solving (COPPS, discussed in Chapter 6), some concerns have been raised about the increased number of ethical dilemmas that COPPS officers confront because they have greater discretion and more public interaction than other officers. Gratuities—free gifts that are supposedly given to the police without obligation—are an example of an ethical problem that can arise with more frequency under COPPS. Whether the police should receive such minor gratuities as free coffee and meals is a long-standing and controversial issue, one for which there will probably never be widespread consensus. Proponents argue that police deserve such perks and that minor gratuities are the building blocks of positive social relationships. Harmless gratuities, it is maintained, may create good feelings in the community toward police officers, and vice versa. Opponents believe, however, that the receipt of gratuities can lead to future deviance. This is the **slippery slope perspective**, which holds that the acceptance of minor gratuities begins a process wherein the recipient's integrity is gradually subverted, which eventually leads to more serious unethical conduct.[4] Given that judges, educators, and other professionals neither expect nor receive such gifts, some people (and police agencies) conclude that gratuities are unethical. As an example, after firing an officer for stealing cigars, sandwiches, magazines, and other goods from merchants, the Bradenton, Florida, Police Department established a policy prohibiting sworn personnel from accepting discounted meals from restaurant owners.[5]

The following scenario involves COPPS and gratuities:

> The sheriff's department has a long-standing policy concerning the solicitation and acceptance of gifts. A deputy has been working a problem-solving project in a strip mall area that has experienced juvenile loitering, drug use, prostitution, and vandalism after hours in the parking lot. The mall manager, Mr. Chang, believes it is his moral duty to show his appreciation to the deputy and has made arrangements for the deputy and his family to receive a 15 percent discount at every store in the mall. Knowing that the department policy requires that such offers be declined, the deputy is also aware that Chang will feel very hurt if the proffered gift is refused.[6]

A particularly strong consideration in this scenario is that the mall manager is Asian-American and might be extremely hurt if his gift was rejected. Some policy issues are also presented in this scenario. For example, in developing a rapport with a mall restaurant manager, is an officer who was formerly prohibited from accepting a free meal now free to do so? Assume that other deputies learn of Chang's new discount arrangement and go to the mall expecting to be treated similarly, resulting in complaints to the sheriff by several business owners. Certainly some people would hold this action to be unethical, given the officers' motivation (personal gain) and their exploitation of the situation.

In sum, the subject of police ethics is not simplistic in nature. We all know that officers should do right, not wrong, but the existence and use of relative ethics make this a complicated issue at best. What can be said is that police officers must be recruited and trained with ethics in mind because they will be given much freedom to become more involved in their community and given wider discretion to make important decisions when addressing neighborhood disorder.

Exhibit 9-2 shows the very important Law Enforcement Code of Ethics, which police officers are sworn to uphold; the code not only contributes to the professional image of law enforcement, but it also brings about self-respect among officers and affords feelings of mutual respect among police personnel.

EXHIBIT 9-2

Law Enforcement Code of Ethics

All law enforcement officers must be fully aware of the ethical responsibilities of their position and must strive constantly to live up to the highest possible standards of professional policing.

The International Association of Chiefs of Police believes it is important that police officers have clear advice and counsel available to assist them in performing their duties in accordance with these standards. The association has adopted the following ethical mandates as guidelines to meet these ends.

PRIMARY RESPONSIBILITIES OF A POLICE OFFICER

A police officer acts as an official representative of government who is required and trusted to work within the law. The officer's powers and duties are conferred by statute. The fundamental duties of a police officer include serving the community; safeguarding lives and property; protecting the innocent; keeping the peace; and ensuring the rights of all to liberty, equality and justice.

PERFORMANCE OF THE DUTIES OF A POLICE OFFICER

A police officer shall perform all duties impartially, without favor or affection or ill will and without regard to status, sex, race, religion, political belief or aspiration. All citizens will be treated equally with courtesy, consideration and dignity.

Officers will never allow personal feelings, animosities or friendships to influence official conduct. Laws will be enforced appropriately and courteously, and in carrying out their responsibilities, officers will strive to obtain maximum cooperation from the public. They will conduct themselves in appearance and deportment in such a manner as to inspire confidence and respect for the position of public trust they hold.

DISCRETION

A police officer will use responsibly the discretion vested in the position and exercise it within the law. The principle of reasonableness will guide the officer's determinations, and the officer will consider all surrounding circumstances in determining whether any legal action shall be taken.

Consistent and wise use of discretion, based on professional policing competence, will do much to preserve good relationships and retain the confidence of the public. There can be difficulty in choosing between conflicting courses of action. It is important to remember that a timely word of advice rather than arrest—which may be correct in appropriate circumstances—can be a more effective means of achieving a desired end.

USE OF FORCE

A police officer will never employ unnecessary force or violence and will use only such force in the discharge of duty as is reasonable in all circumstances.

Force should be used only with the greatest restraint and only after discussion, negotiation and persuasion have been found to be inappropriate or ineffective. While the use of force is occasionally unavoidable, every police officer will refrain from applying the unnecessary infliction of pain or suffering and will never engage in cruel, degrading or inhuman treatment of any person.

CONFIDENTIALITY

Whatever a police officer sees, hears or learns [that] is of a confidential nature will be kept secret unless the performance of duty or legal provision requires otherwise.

Members of the public have a right to security and privacy, and information obtained about them must not be improperly divulged.

INTEGRITY

A police officer will not engage in acts of corruption or bribery, nor will an officer condone such acts by other police officers.

The public demands that the integrity of police officers be above reproach. Police officers must, therefore, avoid any conduct that might compromise integrity and thus undercut the public confidence in a law enforcement agency. Officers will refuse to accept any gifts, presents, subscriptions, favors, gratuities or promises that could be interpreted as seeking to cause the officers? to refrain from performing official responsibilities honestly and within the law. Police officers must not receive private or special advantage from their official status. Respect from the public cannot be bought; it can only be earned and cultivated.

COOPERATION WITH OTHER OFFICERS AND AGENCIES

Police officers will cooperate with all legally authorized agencies and their representatives in the pursuit of justice.

An officer or agency may be one among many organizations that may provide law enforcement services to a jurisdiction. It is imperative that a police officer assist colleagues fully and completely with respect and consideration at all times.

PERSONAL/PROFESSIONAL CAPABILITIES

Police officers will be responsible for their own standard of professional performance and will take every reasonable opportunity to enhance and improve their level of knowledge and competence.

(continued)

Through study and experience, a police officer can acquire the high level of knowledge and competence that is essential for the efficient and effective performance of duty. The acquisition of knowledge is a never-ending process of personal and professional development that should be pursued constantly.

PRIVATE LIFE
Police officers will behave in a manner that does not bring discredit to their agencies or themselves.

A police officer's character and conduct while off duty must always be exemplary, thus maintaining a position of respect in the community in which he or she lives and serves. The officer's personal behavior must be beyond reproach.

Source: Adopted by the Executive Committee of the International Association of Chiefs of Police on October 17, 1989. Used with permission.

USE OF FORCE

A Tradition of Problems

Throughout our history, police agencies have faced allegations of brutality and corruption. In the late nineteenth century, New York Police (NYPD) Sergeant Alexander "Clubber" Williams epitomized police brutality; he spoke openly of using his nightstick to knock a man unconscious, batter him to pieces, or even kill him. Williams supposedly coined the term *tenderloin* when he commented, "I've had nothing but chuck steaks for a long time, and now I'm going to have me a little tenderloin."[7] Williams was referring to opportunities for graft in an area in New York City that was the heart of vice and nightlife, often termed Satan's Circus. This was Williams's beat, where his reputation for brutality and corruption became legendary.[8]

Although police brutality and corruption are no longer openly tolerated, a number of events have demonstrated that the problem still exists and requires the attention of police officials. Several of these events, such as the so-called police riot in 1968 during the Democratic National Convention, were discussed in Chapter 1.

Legitimate Uses of Force

Our society recognizes three legitimate and responsive forms of force: the right of self-defense, including the valid taking of another person's life in order to protect oneself from harm; the power to control those for whom one is responsible (such as a prisoner or a patient in a mental hospital); and the relatively unrestricted authority of police to use force as required. Police work is dangerous—a routine arrest may result in a violent confrontation, sometimes triggered by drugs, alcohol, or mental illness. To cope, police officers are given the unique right to use force, even deadly force, against others. There are, of course, limitations on when an officer may exercise deadly force; they are discussed later in this chapter.

Egon Bittner defined **police use of force** as the "distribution of non-negotiably coercive remedies."[9] He asserted that the duty of police intervention in matters of societal disorder "means above all making use of the authority to overpower resistance. This feature of

"Clubber" Williams.

(The Granger Collection, New York)

police work is uppermost in the minds of people who solicit police aid. Every conceivable police intervention projects the message that force may…have to be used to achieve a desired objective."[10] The exercise of force by police can take several forms, ranging from a simple verbal command to the use of lethal force. These forms of force are discussed next as continuums.

Use-of-Force Continuums

Use-of-force continuums have been evolving for over three decades and are explained from the very simple to the more elaborate. Figure 9-1 depicts a simple linear use-of-force continuum containing five escalating steps[11]:

1. *Officer presence and verbal direction.* The officer uses positive body language to set appropriate boundaries. Merely being at a scene can generally quell a potentially violent situation. Sometimes verbal direction is also used to request citizen compliance.

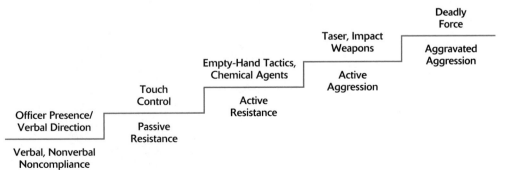

FIGURE 9-1
Linear Use-of-Force Continuum

Source: Lorie A. Fridell, "Improving Use-of-Force Policy, Policy Enforcement and Training," in Chief Concerns: Exploring the Challenges of Police Use of Force, *eds. Joshua A. Ederheimer and Lorie A. Fridell (Washington, DC: Police Executive Research Forum, April 2005), p. 48.*

2. *Touch control.* An officer can use physical contact with a citizen who displays passive resistance, such as placing his or her hand on the person's arm to request that he or she move or comply with some other request by the officer.

3. *Empty-hand tactics and chemical agents.* When active resistance is encountered, the police can use empty-hand tactics, such as weaponless defense maneuvers, and chemical agents, including pepper spray.

4. *Tasers and impact weapons.* When active aggression is displayed, the police response involves the use of a wide variety of less-lethal weapons (batons, Tasers, flashlights, and so forth) to apply increased mechanical pressure at specific points of the person's body, including nerve pathways and joints; these weapons may also be used to stun the subject. General police instruction is to use such weapons only below shoulder level.

5. *Deadly force.* Deadly force refers to an officer using a handgun, shotgun, rifle, or some other means when aggravated aggression is demonstrated by an individual who is attempting to employ deadly force against the officer or other persons.

Today, however, more departments and researchers are uncomfortable with the simplistic sequential depiction of the use-of-force continuum. They feel that police use of force is not, and cannot always be, employed in such a sequential or stair-step fashion as this continuum implies. Therefore, many agencies have adopted the *circular* use-of-force continuum that is shown in Figure 9-2. The circular model places the force options in a random order, depending on the situation.

No matter how the police agency's use-of-force continuum is displayed, however, it is essential that all sworn officers still are governed by a sound use-of-force policy, are trained well in the various kinds of use of force they may be called on to employ, and

FIGURE 9-2
Circular Use-of-Force Continuum

Source: Lorie A. Fridell, "Improving Use-of-Force Policy, Policy Enforcement and Training," in Chief Concerns: Exploring the Challenges of Police Use of Force, *eds. Joshua A. Ederheimer and Lorie A. Fridell (Washington, DC: Police Executive Research Forum, April 2005), p. 50.*

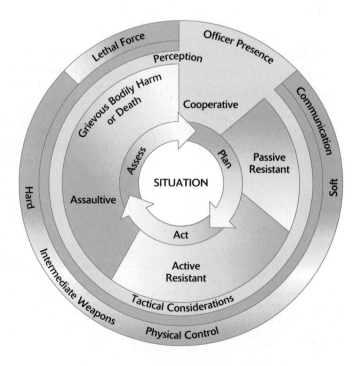

have effective mechanisms for enforcing the policy that will provide accountability for such uses of force.

Police Shootings: Conundrum and Controversy

Clearly, nothing can inflame a community and raise tensions like **police shootings**, and there has been no dearth of high-profile police shooting incidents during the early part of this millennium:

- In July 2005, more than thirty Los Angeles officers, including its SWAT team, responded to a hostage situation and were caught in a crossfire from the front and back of an auto sales lot; the nineteen-month-old daughter of the suspect was killed. The Police Commission found that there was poor communication and a breakdown in command and control during the incident and that seventeen officers needed additional training. The probe involved microscopic analysis of about 130 bullets and more than 100 casings involving thirteen firearms.[12]
- In April 2007, three NYPD officers were indicted for manslaughter and reckless endangerment for a shooting incident where they fired 50 rounds at a car of unarmed men leaving a bachelor party at a strip club; the groom died on his wedding day.[13] The incident heightened racial tensions and, for many people, brought to mind the 1999 NYPD killing of an unarmed West African, Amadou Diallo, whom officers shot as he was reaching for his wallet, firing 41 shots and striking him 19 times.

These are what are known in police parlance as **contagious shootings**—gunfire that spreads among officers who believe that they or their colleagues are facing a threat. It spreads like wildfire and often leads to an outcry from community leaders or family members. The phenomenon appears to have also happened in 2005 when eight officers fired 43 shots at an armed man in Queens, New York, killing him. In July 2005, three officers fired 26 shots at a pit bull that had bitten a chunk out of an officer's leg in a Bronx apartment building; in 1995, in the Bronx, officers fired 125 bullets during a botched robbery, with one officer firing 45 rounds.[14]

These incidents that also involve minority group members will often heighten the tension and lead to charges of racism against the entire police agency. One *Washington Post* columnist offered that "it is the police culture, more than race, that is at the crux of the problem...a mentality of brutality."[15] Such kinds of police uses of force even caused one organization, the Human Rights Watch, to state the following in a report titled *Shielded from Justice: Police Brutality and Accountability in the United States*:

> Police abuse remains one of the most serious and divisive human rights violations in the United States. The excessive use of force by police officers, including unjustified shootings, severe beatings, fatal chokings, and rough treatment, persists because overwhelming barriers to accountability make it possible for officers who commit human rights violations to escape due punishment and often to repeat their offenses.[16]

The Human Rights Watch also noted in the report that officers who repeatedly commit human rights violations tend to be a small minority but that "they are protected, routinely, by the silence of their fellow officers and by flawed systems of reporting, over-sight, and accountability; by the scarcity of meaningful information about trends in abuse; data lacking regarding the police departments' response to those incidents; and their plans or actions to prevent brutality."[17]

Paradoxically, for all their severity and inflammatory nature, the extent of police shootings is largely unknown. As the *New York Times* stated:

> We like to think we live in the information age. For all the careful accounting, however, there are two figures Americans don't have: the precise number of peo-ple killed by the police, and the number of times police use excessive force. Despite widespread public interest and a provision in the 1994 Crime Con-trol Act requiring the Attorney General to collect the data, statistics on police shootings and use of non-deadly force continue to be piecemeal products of spotty collection and are dependent on the cooperation of local police depart-ments. No comprehensive accounting for the nation's 17,000 police depart-ment exists.[18]

The *Times* suggests that this lack of accurate statistics makes it impossible to draw meaningful conclusions about deadly encounters between the police and the civilian pop-ulation and that the major reason for the vacuum is the failure of the police in many cities to keep and report accurate figures that distinguish between what the police see as "jus-tifiable" shootings—those in which the suspect posed a serious threat—and incidents where an officer may have unlawfully fired at an unarmed civilian.[19]

Notwithstanding this lack of data collection for such incidents, the U.S. Department of Justice has relatively new legal means to investigate allegations of racial bias in police departments. The law authorizing such investigations, passed in 1994 after the Rodney King beating in Los Angeles, compels police agencies to initiate safeguards against exces-sive force and racial bias (for instance, computer systems to track complaints and disci-plinary actions) to determine whether the police engaged in "a pattern and practice" of racial discrimination or brutality.[20]

Legal Restrictions

When the colonists came to this country from England, they brought with them a com-mon law principle that authorized the use of deadly force to apprehend any and all flee-ing felony suspects. As our laws and society evolved, however, it became possible for police to use deadly force against people who were at great distances from them, including peo-ple suspected of nonviolent property crimes. The justification and necessity for the fleeing-felon rule came into question.[21] Then the U.S. Supreme Court's 1985 decision in ***Tennessee v. Garner***[22] greatly curtailed the use of deadly force. The Court held that the use of deadly force to prevent the escape of all felony suspects was constitutionally unrea-sonable. It is not better, the Court reasoned, that all felony suspects die than that they escape. Where the suspect poses no immediate threat to the officer or to others, the harm resulting from failing to apprehend him or her does not justify the use of deadly force to do so. The misuse of firearms is discussed more fully later in this chapter.

Police Brutality

Many people contend that there are actually three means by which the police can be "brutal." There is the literal sense of the term, which involves the physical abuse of others. There is the verbal abuse of citizens, exemplified by slurs or epithets. Finally, for many who feel downtrodden, the police symbolize brutality because the officers represent the establishment's law, which serves to keep minority groups in their place. It is perhaps the last form of **police brutality** that is of the greatest concern for anyone who is interested in improving community relations. Because it is a philosophy or frame of mind, it is probably the most difficult to overcome.

Citizens' use of the term *police brutality* encompasses a wide range of practices, from profane and abusive language to actual physical force or violence.[23] Some would claim that there is little (if any) police brutality in today's enlightened police agencies. Others acknowledge that police brutality exists today but add that "*brutality is the prerogative of the police state. To tolerate any of it is to differ from the police state only in degree*" (emphasis in original).[24]

While no one can deny that some police officers use brutal practices, it is impossible to know with any degree of accuracy how often and to what extent these incidents occur. They are low-visibility acts, and many victims decline to report them. Although it is widely believed that brutality is a racial matter primarily involving white police and black victims, Albert Reiss found that lower-class white men were as likely to be brutalized by the police as lower-class black men.[25] What is most disturbing is that 37 percent of the instances of excessive force occurred in settings controlled by the police—station houses and patrol cars. In half the situations, a police officer did not participate but did not restrain his or her colleague, indicating that the informal police culture did not disapprove of the behavior.[26]

It is doubtful that police brutality will ever disappear forever. There are always going to be, in the words of A. C. Germann, Frank Day, and Robert Gallati, "Neanderthals" who enjoy their absolute control over others and become tyrannical in their arbitrary application of power.[27] Therefore, many people support the use of formal citizen complaint review procedures for investigating allegations of brutality and excessive use of force.

Vehicle Pursuits

In 2007 the U.S. Supreme Court issued a major decision concerning the proper amount of force the police may use during high-speed vehicle pursuits. The fundamental question was whether or not the serious danger created by the fleeing motorist justifies the use of deadly force to eliminate the threat. In other words, was the level of force used proportionate to the threat of reckless and dangerous driving? The incident involved a nineteen-year-old Georgia youth driving at speeds up to ninety miles per hour and covering nine miles in six minutes, with a deputy sheriff in pursuit; the chase ended in a violent crash that left Harris a quadriplegic. His lawyers argued that the Fourth Amendment protects against the use of excessive force, such as high-speed drivers having their cars rammed by

Scenes from the *Walker Report* of the 1968 Chicago Democratic National Convention.

police (by intentionally stopping a fleeing vehicle in such a manner, a "seizure" occurs for Fourth Amendment purposes). Conversely, the deputy's lawyers argued that such drivers pose an escalating danger to the public and must be stopped to defuse the danger (the deputy's supervisor had authorized the use of the precision immobilization technique, or PIT, where the officer uses his patrol vehicle to cause the speeder's to spin out; PIT was not used in the Harris chase, however). The Court's 8-1 opinion, authored by Justice Scalia, stated, "A police officer's attempt to terminate a dangerous high-speed car chase that threatens the lives of innocent bystanders does not violate the Fourth Amendment, even when it places the fleeing motorist at risk of serious injury or death."[28]

Bias-Based Policing and Other Field Tactics

Bias-based policing—also known as "driving while black or brown" (DWBB)—involves unequal treatment of any person on the basis of race, ethnicity, religion, gender, sexual orientation, or socioeconomic status. A 2007 study released by the Bureau of Justice Statistics found that while black, Hispanic, and white drivers are equally likely to be pulled over by the police, blacks and Hispanics are much more likely to be searched and arrested, and police are much more likely to threaten or use force against blacks and Hispanics than against whites in any encounter, whether at a traffic stop or elsewhere. The report warned that the findings do not prove that police treat people differently along racial lines and that the differences could be explained by driver conduct or other circumstances.[29] Nonetheless, traffic stops are a politically volatile issue, and such studies underscore minority groups' complaints that many stops and searches are based on race rather than on legitimate suspicions.

Some police executives defend officers' selective stopping of citizens as effective crime fighting, based not on prejudice but on probabilities, the statistical reality that certain people are disproportionately likely to commit crimes. Bernard Parks, former African-American police chief of Los Angeles, explained:

> We have an issue of violent crime against jewelry salespeople. The predominant suspects are Colombians. We don't find Mexican-Americans, or blacks, or other immigrants. It's a collection of several hundred Colombians who commit this crime. If you see six in a car in front of the Jewelry Mart, and they're waiting and watching people with briefcases, should we play the percentages and follow them? It's common sense.[30]

Still, bias-based policing has become a despised police practice in the new millennium. Profiling on the basis of race is given no public support. The best defense for the police may be summarized in two words: *collect data.* (Chapter 2 contains a discussion of what many state police agencies are doing to record racial and ethnic data for traffic stops.) Collecting traffic stop data helps chiefs and commanders to determine whether officers are stopping or searching a disproportionate number of minorities and enables them to act on this information right away. Technology—including mobile data computers and wireless handheld devices—can be used for this purpose.

EXHIBIT 9-3

Sacramento Searches for Biased Policing

In the late 1990s, the Sacramento, California, Police Department (SPD) began a study on racially biased policing. The goal was to determine the degree of intrusiveness of traffic stops and whether or not such stops were indicative of racially biased policing. Even though there were no reported complaints of such policing, the SPD recognized the importance of responding to national concern about the problem. The researchers began by collecting reports, editorials, and anecdotal information for insight into approaches taken by other agencies. Meetings were held with the community, civil rights organizations, the police union, and agency staff. Officers were invited to provide input on how to conduct the study. The SPD also invited the American Civil Liberties Union, the Mexican American Legal Defense and Education Fund, and neighborhood associations to participate.

Once the study began, officers filled out data-collection forms for each traffic stop, which included the officer's badge number, age, race, and unit assignment. The study examined data on traffic patterns and type of crimes throughout the city.

In the end, the SPD came to the conclusion that rarely could an officer identify the race of the drivers or occupants of cars before they were actually stopped. The study did find that traffic stops involving African-Americans occurred at a disproportionately higher rate than their overall population, so the study was extended for two years in order to examine whether systems existed that encouraged bias-based policing. Now, as part of its community policing program, "Police as Problem Solvers/Peacemakers Initiative," the SPD is providing technical assistance to other local police agencies interested in collecting data on biased policing.

Source: Adapted from Tammy Jones, "Sacramento Searches for Biased Policing," in *Community Links* (Washington, DC: Community Policing Consortium, February 2003), pp. 1–2.

Exhibit 9-3 shows what the Sacramento, California, Police Department has done to study and address biased policing, although no such complaints had been reported in the city.

Other police field practices, such as the following, can be sources of tension between minorities and police as well:

- *Delay in responding to calls for service.* Studies of police work have found that patrol officers sometimes delay responding to calls for service, especially in cases of family disturbances.[31] Although this delay may be justified on grounds of officer safety (that is, an officer must await backup) and while these studies did not demonstrate any pattern of racial bias, delays do not improve public perceptions of the police.

- *Verbal abuse, epithets, and other forms of disrespect.* Offensive labels for people are a regular aspect of the working language of some police officers. One study found that 75 percent of all officers used some racially offensive words, most of which were not uttered in the presence of citizens; however, police openly ridicule and belittle citizens in 5 percent of all encounters.[32] In some situations, the police use the terms as a control technique in an attempt to establish their authority.[33] Nonetheless, verbal abuse should be avoided at all times.

- *Excessive questioning and frisking of minority citizens.* Allegations of harassment by police are often raised by racial minorities who believe they have been unnecessarily subjected to field interrogations. Many officers, because they are trained to be suspicious and must often confront individuals in questionable circumstances, regard such activities as legitimate and effective crime-fighting tactics.

- *Discriminatory patterns of arrest and traffic citations.* African-Americans are arrested more often than whites relative to their numbers in the population.[34] African-American complainants request arrests more often than whites. Since most incidents are intraracial, this can result in more arrests of African-Americans.[35] Police have been found more likely to arrest both white and African-American suspects in low-income areas. Insofar as African-Americans are disproportionately represented among the poor, however, this factor is likely to result in a disproportionately high arrest rate for African-Americans.[36]

- *Excessive use of physical force.* Police have been found to use force in about 5 percent of all encounters involving offenders. In about two-thirds of the incidents involving force, its application was judged to be reasonable. White and African-American officers used excessive force at nearly the same rate. It is known that "a sizable minority of citizens experience police misconduct at one time or another."[37] The result, of course, is that many racial minorities perceive that their race is being unduly brutalized. And, to them, perception is reality.

A Related Issue: Domestic Violence

A 1996 federal law, titled the Domestic Violence Offender Gun Ban (popularly known as the **Lautenberg Amendment**), bars anyone—including police and military personnel—from carrying firearms if they have a conviction for domestic violence. Although no figures are available regarding loss of jobs, that has been the case for hundreds of police officers across the nation. In many cases, officers found to have past misdemeanor convictions have lost their jobs.[38]

No one denies that a police officer who beats a spouse or child should be fired. The ban's supporters maintain that the police must also be held accountable when they commit any type of domestic violence and that their easy access to firearms can cause a domestic argument to escalate to homicide.[39] However, critics of the law, including many politicians, police associations, and unions, argue that the law is too broad.

Assume, for example, that a police officer tells her fifteen-year-old son that he cannot leave the house and hang out with some kids she knows to be using drugs. He attempts to leave and calls her some names, so she grabs him by the arm and sits him down. Except for a bruise on his arm, he is not injured, but he calls the police, a report is filed, and she is convicted of misdemeanor assault in a trial by judge with no right to trial by jury. Because of the domestic-violence law, she loses her right to carry a gun, and thus her career is ended.[40] Because police agencies typically have no unarmed positions, the law in effect ends the careers of officers who are affected by it.

The issue is not whether abusive police officers should be fired but whether the law as it is written is effective and legal. Several state lawsuits, including lawsuits by the National Association of Police Officers (which argues that officers are being "sacrificed on the altar of political correctness"[41]), have challenged the constitutionality of the law. In August 1998, the U.S. Court of Appeals for the District of Columbia Circuit exempted police and federal law enforcement agents within its jurisdiction from the law.

POLICE CORRUPTION

History: Long-Standing "Plague"

"For as long as there have been police, there has been **police corruption**,"[42] observed Lawrence Sherman concerning the oldest and most persistent problem in American policing. To make the point, corruption has long plagued the NYPD, as determined by the Knapp Commission, which investigated police corruption there in the early 1970s.[43] Knapp's 1973 report stated that there are two primary types of corrupt police officers: the "meat-eaters" and the "grass-eaters." Meat-eaters, who probably constitute a small percentage of police officers, spend a good deal of their working hours aggressively seeking out situations that they can exploit for financial gain, including gambling, narcotics, and other lucrative enterprises. No change in attitude is likely to affect meat-eaters; their income is so large that the only way to deal with them is to get them off the force and prosecute them. Grass-eaters constitute the overwhelming majority of those officers who accept payoffs; they are not aggressive but will accept gratuities from contractors, tow-truck operators, gamblers, and the like.

The Knapp Commission also identified several factors that influence how much graft police officers receive, the most important of these being the character of the individual officer. The branch of the department and the type of assignment also affect opportunities for corruption. Typically, plainclothes officers have more varied opportunities than uniformed patrol officers, and uniformed officers located in beats with, say, several vice dens will have more opportunities for payoffs. Another factor is rank: the amount of the payoff received generally ascends proportionally with rank.

Police corruption can be defined broadly, from major forms of police wrongdoing to the pettiest forms of improper behavior. Another definition is "the misuse of authority by a police officer in a manner designed to produce personal gain for the officer or for others."[44] Police corruption is not limited to monetary gain, however. Gains may be made through the acceptance of services received, status, influence, prestige, or future support for the officer or someone else.[45]

Events like those described in Los Angeles and other cities have focused attention on the broader issue of rogue cops in police departments across the country, especially in minority neighborhoods.[46] The brazenness and viciousness of today's corrupt police officers trouble even their staunchest defenders.

Types and Causes

Several factors contribute to police corruption, among them the rapid hiring of personnel, civil service and union protections that make it difficult to fire officers,[47] and temptations from money and sex.

Two theories—the "rotten apple" theory and the "environmental" theory—have been suggested to explain police corruption. The rotten apple theory holds that corruption is the result of having a few bad apples in the barrel who probably had character defects prior to employment. The environmental theory suggests that corruption is more the result of a widespread politically corrupt environment; politically corrupt cities create an environment in which police misconduct flourishes.[48]

Police corruption takes two basic forms: external and internal. The external form includes those activities (such as gratuities and payoffs) that occur from and through police contacts with the public. Internal corruption involves the relationships among police officers within the workings of the police department; this includes payments to join the police force, to get better shifts or assignments, to receive promotions, and the like.[49]

Ellwyn Stoddard, who coined the term *blue-coat crime,* described several different forms of deviant practices among both police and citizens. In the following list, those coming first would probably elicit the least fear of prosecution, and those at the end would probably invoke major legal ramifications[50]:

- *Mooching.* Receiving free coffee, meals, liquor, groceries, laundry services, and so forth.
- *Chiseling.* Demanding free admission to entertainment or price discounts on goods and services.
- *Favoritism.* Using license tabs, window stickers, or courtesy cards to gain immunity from traffic arrest.
- *Prejudice.* Behaving less than impartially toward minority group members or others who are less likely to have influence in city hall.
- *Bribery.* Receiving payments of cash or gifts for past or future assistance in avoiding prosecution, including political payoffs for favoritism in promotions. Police officers who accept payoffs or protection money are said to be "on the pad."
- *Shakedown.* Stealing expensive items for personal use and attributing the loss to criminal activity when investigating a burglary or unlocked door.
- *Perjury.* Following the "code" that demands that officers lie to provide an alibi for fellow officers apprehended in unlawful activity.
- *Premeditated theft.* Being involved in planned burglaries that involve the use of tools or keys to gain entry or any prearranged act of unlawful acquisition of property that cannot be explained as a spur of the moment theft.

The most common and extensive form of corruption involves the receipt by police officers of small gratuities or tips. Officers may regard discounts and free services as relatively unimportant, while the payment of cash—bribery—is a very different matter.[51] Former New York Police Commissioner Patrick V. Murphy was one of those who "drew the short line," telling his officers that "except for your paycheck, there is no such thing as a clean buck."[52] Such police officials would argue that even the smallest gratuities can create an expectation of some patronage or favor in return. Retail establishments do not offer gratuities to other persons in professional positions (doctors, lawyers, educators) for performing their duties, and the argument can certainly be made that the police should be similarly viewed and treated.

Withrow and Dailey[53] offered a uniquely different viewpoint toward gratuities. They propose a "**model of circumstantial corruptibility**," stating that the exchange of a gift is influenced by two elements: the role of the giver and the role of the receiver. The role of the *giver* determines the level of corruptibility, in this model; the giver is either taking a position as a:

- *presenter*, who offers a gift voluntarily without any expectation of a return from the receiver;
- *contributor*, who furnishes something toward a result and expects something in return; or a
- *capitulator*, who involuntarily responds to the demands of the receiver.

The role of the receiver of the gift is obviously very important as well; the receiver can act as an:

- *acceptor*, who receives the gift humbly and without any residual feelings of reciprocity;
- *expector*, who looks forward to the gift and regards it as likely to happen, and will be annoyed by the absence of the gift; or
- *conqueror*, who assumes total control over the exchange and influence over the giver.

The function of the model is centered on the intersection of the giver and the receiver. For example, when the giver assumes the role of the presenter and the receiver is the acceptor, the result is a giving exchange, and corruption does not occur. However, if giver and receiver occupy other roles, corruptibility can progress to higher levels of social harm, a "hierarchy of wickedness." Bribery results when something of value is given and the giver expects something in return, while the receiver agrees to conform his behavior to the desires of the giver. It is therefore of great importance that the police consider the role of the giver as well as their own intentions when deciding whether or not to accept a gratuity. In certain circumstances, the exchange of *any* gratuity is ethical or unethical regardless of its value.

Another serious form of police corruption is related to drugs. Until the 1960s, most police corruption was associated with the protection of gambling operations, illegal liquor establishments, prostitution, and similar "victimless" activities. More recently, however, drug-related police corruption has probably surpassed those earlier forms of deviance. A typology of drug-related corruption has been developed by David Carter, who believes that the numbers of such cases "have notably increased"[54]:

> *Type I drug corruption* occurs when an officer seeks to use his or her position simply for personal gain. This type of drug corruption includes giving information to drug dealers about investigations, names of informants, planned raids, and so forth; accepting bribes from drug dealers in exchange for nonarrest, evidence tampering, or perjury; stealing drugs from the police property room for personal consumption; "seizing" drugs for personal use without arresting the person possessing the drugs; taking either the profits of drug dealers' sales or the drugs themselves for resale; and extorting money or property from drug traffickers in exchange for nonarrest or non-seizure of drugs.
>
> *Type II drug corruption* involves the officer's search for legitimate goals and may not even be universally perceived as being corrupt. Officer gain may involve organizational benefit, perhaps a form of "winning" or "revenge." Included are such actions

as giving false statements to obtain arrest or search warrants against suspected or known drug dealers, committing perjury during hearings and trials of drug dealers, planting or creating evidence against known drug dealers, using entrapment, and falsely spreading rumors that a dealer is a police informant in order to endanger that person.

See Exhibit 9-4 for a discussion of corruption in another mileau: Mexico.

Code of Silence

Patrick V. Murphy wrote that "the most difficult element to overcome in the fight against corruption in the department was the code of silence."[55] This **code of silence**—keeping quiet in the face of misconduct by other officers—has been well documented. Evidence of the fraternal bond that exists in policing was found by William Westley as early as 1970, when more than 75 percent of the officers surveyed said that they would not report another officer for taking money from a prisoner, nor would they testify against an officer accused by a prisoner.[56] (In a related vein, see Exhibit 9-1.)

EXHIBIT 9-4

Comparative Closeup
Corruption in Mexico

If one word were to be used by most Americans to historically and stereotypically describe Mexico's police and government, it would probably be corruption. Mexico's former President Vicente Fox hoped to reverse that image—and reality—by creating a new government commission to investigate past scandals, overhaul police forces top to bottom, and exert much greater effort in combating drug trafficking.[1]

The 2000 election of President Fox—a charismatic Harvard MBA—concluded the world's longest-running political dynasty by defeating the seventy-one-year reign of the National Action Party. Fox promised to carry out major social and economic reforms, root out corruption, examine Mexico's human rights record, and review its struggle against the nation's drug lords.[2] Fox's promises generally did not materialize, however, and in 2003 and 2004 thousands of people protested out of frustration with a poor economy and what was perceived as political paralysis.[3] His detractors viewed him as a do-nothing president who simply travels about the country giving daily speeches touting his administration.[4]

Still, Fox had some successes. He worked to clean up corruption and crack down on Mexico's drug trade (the police made several arrests of high-profile drug lords and tightened border security), but there remains much to accomplish, and atrocities are still reported. For example, in February 2004, thirteen Ciudad Juarez state police officers were reportedly held and questioned about drug trafficking and the murders of at least a dozen people, feeding fears that officers there were taking part in the crimes they were supposed to be fighting. In addition, the state police acknowledged that about three hundred Ciudad Juarez officers were fired from 2002 to 2004 and that hundreds of murders, including dozens of young women who were strangled and dumped in the desert outside the city, had gone unsolved.[5]

1. Elliot Blair Smith, "Fox Ready for 'Revolution of Hope,'" *USA Today,* December 1, 2000, p.1.
2. Ibid.
3. "Thousands Demonstrate against Mexican Leader," Associated Press, *Reno Gazette Journal,* November 28, 2003, p. 3A.
4. Traci Carl, "Three Years Later, Mexico Disenchanted with Vicente Fox," Associated Press, *Reno Gazette Journal,* July 13, 2003, p. 3A.
5. "13 Officers Held after Bodies Found in Mexico," Associated Press, *Reno Gazette Journal,* January 30, 2004, p. 1A.

As an example, Officer Jack Smith finds himself in a moral dilemma. He knows of another officer's misconduct; he witnessed the officer putting expensive ink pens in his pocket while securing an unlocked office supply store on the graveyard shift. If reported, the misconduct will ruin the officer, but if not reported, the behavior could eventually cause enormous harm. To outsiders, this is not a dilemma at all; the only proper path is for Smith to report the misconduct. To philosophers, the doctrines of utilitarianism (the ethic of good consequences) and deontology (the ethic of rights and duties) require that Officer Smith work to eliminate corruption. But the outsiders and the philosophers are not members of the close fraternity of police, nor do they have to depend on other officers for their own safety.

There are several arguments for and against Officer Smith's informing on his partner. Reasons for informing include the fact that the harm caused by a scandal would be outweighed by the public's knowledge that the police department is free of corruption; also, individual episodes of corruption would be brought to a halt. The officer, moreover, has a sworn duty to uphold the law. Any employee has a right to be allowed to do his or her duty, including blowing the whistle on employers or colleagues. Reasons against Officer Smith's informing include the fact that a skilled police officer is a valuable asset whose social value far outweighs the damage done by moderate corruption. Also, discretion and secrecy are obligations assumed by joining and remaining within the police fraternity; dissenters should resign rather than inform. Furthermore, it would be unjust to inflict punishment of dismissal and disgrace on an otherwise decent officer.[57]

How does one reconcile these two varying points of view? Probably the first thing to do is to realize that each view is morally defensible. A person who is in charge of investigating police corruption would no doubt be warmer toward the punitive view, while at the other extreme would be the person who would overlook such behaviors at all times. The ideal position might be in the middle—to maintain a commitment to professionalism and ethics without overreacting (for example, without insisting that officers report on their fellows every time they see someone napping or conducting personal business while on duty).

The good news is that a recent survey by the National Institute of Justice found that about 83 percent of all officers in the United States do not accept the code of silence as an essential part of the mutual trust necessary to good policing.[58]

Investigation and Prosecution

Federal powers and jurisdiction for investigating and prosecuting police corruption were significantly expanded through the Hobbs Act in 1970. (See 18 U.S.C., Section 1955.) Two important elements of this federal statute that allow the investigation of police corruption are extortion and commerce. Whenever a police officer solicits a payoff from a legitimate business owner to overlook law violations (for example, a tavern owner who was selling alcohol to minors), extortion (involving fear) occurs, and that extortion affects legitimate commerce. The Hobbs Act may be employed by the prosecutor when these two elements are present. The meaning of extortion has been expanded so that it now covers most payoff arrangements that involve public officials.[59] The only areas of police corruption that may be beyond the reach of the Hobbs Act are internal corruption and the acceptance of isolated gratuities.

The federal perjury statute (18 U.S.C. 1621) and the federal false sworn declaration statute (18 U.S.C. 1623), both enacted in 1970, have also become powerful weapons for prosecutors in investigating public corruption. Both statutes deal with false testimony under oath, and in an investigation of corruption they are pertinent at the grand jury stage.[60]

Possible Solutions

There are several other possible measures for overcoming the pernicious effects of police corruption. In addition to the obvious need for an honest and effective police administration, it is also necessary to train recruits on the need for a corruption-free department. The creation and maintenance of an internal affairs unit and the vigorous prosecution of law-breaking police officers are also critical to maintaining the integrity of officers. Finally, there should be some mechanism for rewarding the honest police officers that should minimally include protection from retaliation when they inform on crooked cops. All police officers should be given formal written guidelines on the departmental policy on soliciting and accepting gifts and gratuities. This apprises officers of the administration's view of such behavior and assists the chief executive in maintaining integrity and disciplining wayward officers. Figure 9-3 is an example of a good policy concerning gratuities.

Finally, computers can also assist with investigations of police corruption. Indeed, information that was uncovered about corruption within the Chicago Police Department was obtained through an $850 software program known as Brainmaker, an early-warning program intended to flag at-risk officers before they commit acts that could get them arrested or fired. With this type of approach, at-risk officers can be provided with counseling before serious problems occur.[61]

Exhibit 9-5 shows what one city has done, and the kind of software that it used, to create an early-warning system.

---

1. Without the express permission of the Sheriff, members shall not solicit or accept any gift, gratuity, loan, present, or fee where there is any direct or indirect connection between this solicitation or acceptance of such gift and their employment by this office.

2. Members shall not accept, either directly or indirectly, any gift, gratuity, loan, fee, or thing of value, the acceptance of which might tend to improperly influence their actions, or that of any other member, in any matter of police business, or which might tend to cast an adverse reflection on the Sheriff's Office.

3. Any unauthorized gift, gratuity, loan, fee, reward, or other thing falling into any of these categories coming into the possession of any member shall be forwarded to the member's commander, together with a written report explaining the circumstances connected therewith. The commander will decide the disposition of the gift.

FIGURE 9-3
The gratuity policy of the Washoe County, Nevada, Sheriff's Office

Source: Washoe County Sheriff's Office.

Many police agencies maintain an internal affairs division for investigating citizen complaints against officers.

(Courtesy Reno, Nevada, Police Department)

LIMITATIONS ON OFFICERS' CONSTITUTIONAL RIGHTS

Police officers are generally afforded the same rights, privileges, and immunities outlined in the U.S. Constitution for all citizens. However, by virtue of their position, they may be compelled to give up certain rights in connection with an investigation of on-duty misbehavior or illegal acts. These rights are the basis for legislation such as the Peace Officers' Bill of Rights (discussed in Chapter 13), labor agreements, and civil service and departmental rules and regulations that guide an agency's disciplinary process.

Following is a brief overview of some areas in which the federal courts have placed **limitations on officers' constitutional rights** and have held sworn officers more accountable by virtue of the higher standard required by their occupation.

Free Speech

Although the right of freedom of speech is one of the most fundamental and cherished of all American rights, the Supreme Court has indicated that "the State has interests as an employer in regulating the speech of its employees that differ significantly from those it possesses in connection with regulation of the speech of the citizenry in general."[62] Thus the state may impose restrictions on its police employees that it would not be able to impose on civilians; however, these restrictions must be reasonable. For example, a department may not prohibit "any activity, conversation, deliberation, or discussion which is derogatory to the Department," as such a rule obviously prohibits all criticism of the agency by its officers, even in private conversation.[63]

EXHIBIT 9-5

A Means of Policing the Police

A lawsuit filed recently by dozens of plaintiffs, alleging that they were roughed up by a band of Oakland, California, officers calling themselves "the Riders," was settled for $11 million and resulted in a new Personnel Information Management System (PIMS) being implemented in 2005. PIMS will document use-of-force incidents, citizen complaints, attendance, shootings, and accidents, as well as commendations, awards, and letters of appreciation. Its main purpose is to help supervisors identify trends that might indicate [when] an officer needs an intervention. Based on a Phoenix, Arizona, model, the system holds the supervisor all the way up the chain accountable for doing something and is a tremendous risk management tool; it emphasizes guiding employees, not merely disciplining them. At the extreme, it allows for getting to people before they "crash and burn, and kill somebody in a police pursuit, traffic accident, or whatever." The system refreshes itself nightly by collecting new information added that day. An Oakland police captain emphasized that a lot of use-of-force problems, incidents, or attendance issues do not make one a bad officer; an officer working in a busy area abundant with shootings will be involved in more car chases and fights and have more use-of-force incidents than one working in a less active downtown area.

Source: Jim McKay, "Policing the Police: Oakland, Calif., Tackles Police Misconduct Issues with Database," *Government Technology,* October 2004, p. 48.

Another First Amendment–related area is that of personal appearance. The Supreme Court has upheld several grooming standards for officers (regarding length of hair, sideburns, and mustaches) to make officers readily recognizable to the public and to maintain the esprit de corps within the department.[64]

Searches and Seizures

The Fourth Amendment to the U.S. Constitution protects "the right of the people to be secure in their persons, houses, papers, and effects, against unreasonable searches and seizures." The Fourth Amendment usually applies to police officers when they are at home or off duty in the same manner as it applies to all citizens. However, because of the nature of their work, police officers can be compelled to cooperate with investigations of their behavior when ordinary citizens would not. For example, regarding equipment and lockers provided by the department to the officers, the officers have no expectation of privacy that affords or merits protection.[65]

However, lower courts have established limitations on searches of employees themselves. The question of whether prison authorities have the right to search their employees arose in a 1985 Iowa case in which employees were forced to sign a consent form as a condition of hire. The court disagreed with such a broad policy, ruling that the consent form did not constitute a blanket waiver of all Fourth Amendment rights.[66] Police officers may also be forced to appear in a lineup, a clear "seizure" of their person.

Self-Incrimination

The Supreme Court has addressed questions concerning the Fifth Amendment as it applies to police officers who are under investigation. In *Garrity* v. *New Jersey,*[67] a police officer was ordered by the attorney general to answer questions or be discharged. The officer testified that information obtained as a result of his answers was later used to convict him of criminal charges. The Supreme Court held that the information obtained from the officer could not be used against him at his criminal trial because the Fifth Amendment forbids the use of coerced confessions.

However, it is proper to fire a police officer who refuses to answer questions that are related directly to the performance of his or her duties, provided that the officer has been informed that any answers may not be used later in a criminal proceeding.[68]

Religious Practices

Police work requires that personnel be available and on duty twenty-four hours a day, seven days a week. Although it is not always convenient or pleasant, shift configurations require that many officers work weekends, nights, and holidays. It is generally assumed that an officer who takes such a position agrees to work such hours and abide by other such conditions; it is usually the personnel with the least seniority on the job who must work the most undesirable shifts. However, there are occasions when the requirements of the job interfere with an officer's ability to attend religious services or observe religious holidays. The carrying of firearms may even conflict with an officer's beliefs. In these situations, the employee may be forced to choose between his or her job and religion.

Title VII of the Civil Rights Act of 1964 prohibits religious discrimination in employment. It requires reasonable accommodation of religious beliefs but not to the extent that the employee has complete freedom of religious expression.[69]

Sexual Misconduct

To be blunt, there is ample opportunity for police officers to become involved in adulterous or extramarital affairs. Few other occupations or professions offer the opportunities for sexual misconduct that police work does. Police officers frequently work alone, usually without direct supervision, in activities that involve frequent contact with citizens, usually in relative isolation. The problem seems to be pervasive in police departments of all sizes. Unfortunately, it is also an area of police behavior that is not easily quantified or understood.[70]

Allen Sapp suggested several possible categories of sexually motivated behaviors by police officers (again, the extent to which each occurs is unknown)[71]:

- *Sexually motivated nonsexual contacts.* Officers initiate contacts with female citizens, without probable cause or any legal basis, for the purpose of obtaining names and addresses for possible later contact.
- *Voyeuristic contacts.* Officers seek opportunities to view unsuspecting women partially clad or nude, such as in parked cars on "lovers' lanes."
- *Contacts with crime victims.* A wide variety of behavior can occur, including unnecessary callbacks to homes of female victims, bodily contact with accident victims, and sexual harassment by officers.

- *Contacts with offenders.* Officers may also harass female offenders by conducting body searches and pat-downs or frisks.
- *Sexual shakedowns.* Officers may demand sexual services from prostitutes or other citizens.
- *Citizen-initiated sexual contacts.* "Police groupies"—often young women who are sexually attracted to the uniform, weapons, or power of the police officer—may seek to participate in sexual activities with officers. This category may also include offers of sexual favors in return for preferential treatment or calls to officers from lonely or mentally disturbed women seeking officers' attention.
- *Sex crimes by officers.* Officers may sexually assault jail inmates and citizens.

In a related vein, several federal courts have recently considered whether police agencies have a legitimate interest in the sexual activities of their officers when such activities affect job performance. In one such case, the court held that the dismissal of a married police officer for living with another man's wife was a violation of the officer's privacy and associational rights.[72]

Other courts, however, have found that off-duty sexual activity can affect job performance. When a married city police officer was found to be having consensual sexual relations with unmarried women other than his wife, the department contended that the officer's conduct—which became public—severely damaged public confidence in the department. A Utah court held that adultery was not a fundamental right and refused to strike down a statute criminalizing adultery.[73] In a Texas case, when a male officer's extramarital affair led to his being passed over for promotion, the city civil service commission, the Texas Supreme Court, and the U.S. Supreme Court upheld the denial; they concurred with the city police chief's argument that such a promotion would adversely affect the efficiency and morale of the department and would be disruptive.[74]

Residency Requirements

Many government agencies specify that all or certain members in their employ must live within the geographic limits of their jurisdiction, that is, employees must reside within the county or city of employment. Such residency requirements have been justified on the grounds that officers should become familiar with and be visible in the jurisdiction of employment or that they should reside where they are paid by the taxpayers to work. Perhaps the strongest rationale given by employing agencies is that criminal justice employees must live near their work so they can respond quickly in the event of an emergency.

Moonlighting

The term *moonlight* means to hold a second job in addition to one's normal full-time occupation. The courts have traditionally supported the limitations police agencies have placed on the amount and kind of outside work their employees can perform.[75] For example, police restrictions on moonlighting range from a complete ban on outside employment to permission to engage in certain forms of work, such as investigations, private security, and police science education. The rationale for agency limitations is that "out-side employment seriously interferes with keeping the [police and fire] departments fit and ready for action at all times."[76]

Misuse of Firearms

As noted above, the use of firearms by police, whether justified or not, can have drastic consequences on both the officer(s) involved and the community. Police agencies typically attempt to restrain the use of firearms through written policies and frequent training of a "shoot/don't shoot" nature. Still, a broad range of potential and actual problems remains with respect to the use and possible misuse of firearms. Police agencies generally have policies regulating the use of handguns and other firearms by their officers, both on and off duty. The courts have held that such regulations need only be reasonable and that the burden rests with the disciplined police officer to show that the regulation was arbitrary and unreasonable.[77]

Police firearms regulations may address several basic topics: shooting in defense of life, shooting to stop fleeing felons, identifying juveniles, shooting at or from vehicles, firing warning shots, shooting animals, carrying secondary weapons, carrying weapons off duty, and registering weapons.[78] Next we briefly discuss each of these topics.

Following the 1985 *Tennessee* v. *Garner* decision (discussed earlier), firearms policies are likely to be written from the "defense of life" perspective, which permits shooting only to defeat an imminent threat to an officer's life or to another person's life (as opposed to previous policies which included and allowed for the killing of fleeing felons).[79] Regarding juveniles, agencies generally do not instruct their officers to make a distinction between adults and juveniles when using deadly force, based on the pragmatic view that an armed juvenile can kill as well as an adult and that it is often impossible to tell if an offender is a juvenile or an adult.[80]

Shooting at or from moving vehicles has been severely limited in recent years. Some of the reasons include difficulty in hitting the target, ricochets striking innocent bystanders, difficulty in penetrating the automobile body and tires, and injuries and damages that might result should the vehicle go out of control.[81] A general consensus among police administrators is that warning shots should be prohibited, as they might strike an innocent person.[82] From a safety standpoint, "what goes up must come down," so firing a warning shot into the ground or into a tree, if allowed at all, is restricted to only a few kinds of situations.

Police agencies generally allow their officers to kill animals in self-defense, for prevention of substantial harm to others, or for relief from suffering when the animal is injured so badly that humaneness requires its killing.[83] Secondary, or backup, weapons are generally permitted so that officers who are disarmed during a confrontation have a second weapon and so that they can less conspicuously be prepared to protect themselves during routine citizen stops. A concern is that backup weapons may be used as "throwaways" in the event that an officer shoots an unarmed suspect, but the practice is generally accepted as long as the weapons are registered.[84] Similarly, carrying weapons off duty has also been controversial; however, given that while in their jurisdictions they are viewed as being on duty twenty-four hours a day, officers are generally allowed to carry such weapons, provided the weapons are registered and officers qualify on the pistol range regularly with them.[85]

Finally, most agencies require their officers to use only department-approved weapons on and off duty and may require that the weapons be inspected, fired, and certified by the department's armorer. In addition, some agencies require that the firearms be registered by make, model, serial number, and even ballistics sample.[86]

Courts and juries are increasingly becoming harsher in dealing with police officers who misuse their firearms. The current tendency is to investigate police shootings to determine whether the officer acted negligently or whether the employing agency was negligent in training and supervising the officer.

Alcohol and Drug Abuse

Alcoholism and drug abuse problems are much more acute when they involve police employees. It is obvious, given the law of most jurisdictions and the nature of their work, that police officers must not be walking time bombs; they must be able to perform their work with a clear head that is unbefuddled by alcohol or drugs.[87] Police departments typically specify in their policy manual that no alcoholic beverages may be consumed within a specified period prior to reporting for duty. Such regulations have uniformly been upheld as rational because of the hazards of police work.

Enforcing such regulations occasionally means that police employees are ordered to submit to drug or alcohol tests. In 1989, the U.S. Supreme Court issued a major decision on drug testing: *National Treasury Employees Union* v. *Von Raab*,[88] which dealt with drug-testing plans for U.S. customs workers. This decision addressed all three of the most controversial drug-testing issues: whether testing should be permitted when there is no indication of a drug problem in the workplace, whether the testing methods are reliable, and whether a positive test proves there was on-the-job impairment.[89]

The Supreme Court held that although only a few customs employees tested positive, drug use is such a serious problem that the program was warranted. Second, the Court found nothing wrong with the testing protocol. Finally, while tests may punish and stigmatize a worker for extracurricular drug usage that may have no effect on his or her on-the-job performance, the Court indicated that this dilemma is still no impediment to testing.

DISCIPLINARY POLICIES AND PRACTICES

Maintenance of Public Trust

Clearly, the public's trust and respect are precious commodities, quickly lost through improper behavior by police employees and the improper handling of an allegation of misconduct. Serving communities with professionalism and integrity should be the goal of every police agency and its employees in order to ensure that trust and respect are maintained. The public expects that police agencies will make every effort to identify and correct problems and respond to citizens' complaints in a judicious, consistent, fair, equitable manner.

Employee misconduct and violations of departmental policy are the two principal areas in which discipline is applied.[90] Employee misconduct includes acts that harm the public, such as corruption, harassment, brutality, and violations of civil rights. Violations of policy may involve a broad range of issues, from substance abuse and insubordination to tardiness or minor violations of dress.

Due Process Requirements

There are well-established minimum due process requirements for discharging public employees:

They must be afforded a public hearing.

They have to be present during the presentation of evidence against them and have an opportunity to cross-examine their superiors.

They have an opportunity to present their own witnesses and other evidence concerning their side of the controversy.

They may be represented by counsel if they so choose.

They must have an impartial referee or hearing officer presiding.

There must be an eventual decision for or against them based on the weight of the evidence introduced during the hearing.

Such protections apply to any disciplinary action that can significantly affect a police employee's reputation or future chances for special assignment or promotion.[91]

At times, police administrators determine that an employee must be disciplined or terminated. Grounds for discipline or discharge can vary widely from agency to agency, and the agency's formal policies and procedures should specify what constitutes proper and improper behavior.

Complaints

ORIGINS   A personnel **complaint** is an allegation of misconduct or illegal behavior against an employee by anyone inside or outside the organization. Internal complaints—those made from within the organization—may involve supervisors who observe officer misconduct, officers who complain about supervisors, civilian personnel who complain about officers, and so on. External complaints originate from outside the organization and usually involve the public.

Every complaint, regardless of the source, must be accepted and investigated in accordance with established policies and procedures. Anonymous complaints are the most difficult to investigate because there is no opportunity to obtain further information or to question the complainant about the allegation. Such complaints can have a negative impact on employee morale, as officers may view them as unjust and frivolous.

TYPES AND CAUSES   Complaints may be handled informally or formally, depending on the seriousness of the allegation and the preference of the complainant. A formal complaint occurs when a written and signed or tape-recorded statement of the allegation is made and the complainant asks to be informed of the investigation's disposition. Figure 9-4 provides an example of a complaint form used to initiate a personnel investigation.

An informal complaint is an allegation of minor misconduct, made for informational purposes, that can usually be resolved without the need for more formal processes. The supervisor may simply discuss the incident with the employee and resolve it through informal counseling as long as more serious problems are not discovered and there is no history of similar complaints.

The majority of complaints against officers fall under the general categories of verbal abuse, discourtesy, harassment, improper attitude, and ethnic slurs.[92] It is clear that the verbal behavior of officers generates a significant number of complaints. Finally, minority citizens and those with less power and fewer resources are more likely to file complaints of misconduct and to allege more serious forms of misconduct than citizens with greater power and more resources.

RECEIPT AND REFERRAL   Administrators must have a process for receiving complaints that is clearly delineated by departmental policy and procedures. Generally, a complaint is made at a police facility and is referred to a senior officer in charge to determine what its seriousness is and whether immediate intervention is needed.

In most cases, the senior officer will determine the nature of the complaint and will identify the employee involved; he or she then refers the matter to the employee's supervisor to conduct an initial investigation. The supervisor completes the investigation, recommends any discipline, and sends the matter to the internal affairs unit (IAU) and the agency head to finalize the disciplinary process. This method of review ensures that consistent and fair standards of discipline are applied.

INVESTIGATIVE PROCESS   Generally, the employee's supervisor will conduct a preliminary inquiry of the complaint, commonly known as "fact-finding." If it is determined that further investigation is necessary, the supervisor may question employees and witnesses, obtain written statements from those who were involved in the incident, and gather any necessary evidence, including photographs. Care must be exercised that the accused employee's rights are not violated. The initial investigation is sent to the appropriate division commander and forwarded to the IAU for review.

DETERMINATION AND DISPOSITION   Once an investigation has been completed, the supervisor or IAU officer must make a determination about the culpability

```
*********************************************************************************************
                                                    Control Number _____
Date & Time Reported   Location of Interview   Interview
_____    _____   _____ Verbal _____ Written _____ Taped
Type of complaint:     ____ Force ____ Procedural  ____ Conduct
                       ____ Other (Specify)
Source of complaint:   ____ In Person  ____ Mail  ____ Telephone
                       ____ Other (Specify)
Complaint originally   ____ Supervisor    ____ On Duty Watch Commander  ____ Chief
received by:           ____ IAU           ____ Other (Specify)
Notifications made:    _____ Division Commander           _____ Chief of Police
received by:           _____ On-Call Command Personnel
                       _____ Watch Commander              _____ Other (Sepcify)
Copy of formal personnel complaint given to complainant?   ____ Yes ____ No
*********************************************************************************************
Complainant's Name:                         Address:
                                                                          Zip _____
Residence Phone:                            Business Phone:
DOB:              Race:                      Sex:                Occupation:
*********************************************************************************************
Location of Occurence:                      Date & Time of Occurrence:
Member(s) Involved:                         Member(s) Involved:
(1)_____         (2) _____
(3)_____         (4) _____
Witness(es) Involved:                       Witness(es) Involved:
(1)_____         (2) _____
(3)_____         (4) _____
*********************************************************************************************
(1) ____ Complainant wishes to make a formal statement and has requested an investigation
         into the matter with a report back to him/her on the findings and actions.
(2) ____ Complainant wishes to advise the Police Department of a problem, understands that
         some type of action will be taken, but does not request a report back to him/her on the
         findings and actions.
*********************************************************************************************
                              CITIZEN ADVISEMENTS
(1)  If you have not yet provided the department with a signed written statement or a tape-
     recorded statement, one may be required in order to pursue the investigation of this matter.
(2)  The complainant(s) and/or witness(es) may be required to take a polygraph examination in
     order to determine the credibility concerning the allegations made.
(3)  Should the allegations prove to be false, the complainant(s) and/or witness(es) may be
     liable for criminal and/or civil prosecution.
                       _____   _____
                       Signature of Complainant           Date & Time

_____
Signature of Member Receiving Complaint
```

FIGURE 9-4
Formal Complaint Form

of the accused employee and report that determination to the administrator. The following categories of dispositions are commonly used:

- *Unfounded.* The alleged act did not occur.
- *Exonerated.* The act occurred but was lawful, proper, justified, or in accordance with departmental policies, procedures, rules, and regulations.

- *Not sustained.* There was insufficient evidence to prove or disprove the allegation made.
- *Misconduct not based on the complaint.* Sustainable misconduct was determined but was not a part of the original complaint. For example, a supervisor investigating an allegation of excessive force may find that the force used was within departmental policy but that the officer made an unlawful arrest.
- *Closed.* An investigation may be halted if the complainant fails to cooperate or if it is determined that the action does not fall within the administrative jurisdiction of the police agency.
- *Sustained.* The act did occur and was a violation of departmental rules and procedures. Sustained allegations include misconduct that falls within the broad outlines of the original allegation.

Once a determination of culpability has been made, the complainant should be notified of the department's findings. Details of the investigation or recommended punishment should not be included in the correspondence. As shown in Figure 9-5, the

---

POLICE DEPARTMENT
3300 Main Street
Downtown Plaza
Anywhere, U.S.A. 99999

June 20, 2007

Mr. John Doe
2200 Main Avenue
Anywhere, U.S.A.

Re: Internal Affairs #000666-98
       Case Closure

Dear Mr. Doe,

Our investigation into your allegations against Officer Smith has been completed. It has been determined that your complaint is SUSTAINED, and the appropriate disciplinary action has been taken.

Our department appreciates your bringing this matter to our attention. It is our position that when a problem is identified, it should be corrected as soon as possible. It is our goal to be responsive to the concerns expressed by citizens so as to provide more efficient and effective services.

Your information regarding this incident was helpful and of value in our efforts to attain that goal. Should you have any further questions about this matter, please contact Sergeant Jane Alexander, Internal Affairs, at 555-9999.

Sincerely,

I.M. Boss
Lieutenant
Internal Affairs Unit

FIGURE 9-5
Citizen's Notification-
of-Discipline Letter

complainant will normally receive only information concerning the outcome of the complaint.

APPEAL OF DISCIPLINARY MEASURES   If an officer disagrees with a supervisor's recommendation for discipline, the first step of an appeal may involve a hearing before the division commander, who usually holds the rank of captain or deputy chief. The accused employee may be allowed labor representation or an attorney to assist in asking questions of the investigating supervisor, clarifying issues, and presenting new or mitigating evidence. If the employee is still not satisfied, an appeal hearing before the chief executive, which is usually the final step in appeals within the agency, is granted. The chief or sheriff communicates a decision to the employee in writing. Depending on labor agreements and civil service rules and regulations, some agencies extend their appeals of discipline beyond the department. For example, employees may bring their issue before the civil service commission or city or county manager for a final review. Employees may also have the right to an independent arbiter's review.

Level of Discipline and Type of Sanction

When an investigation against an employee is sustained, the level of discipline and type of sanction must be decided. Management must be very careful when recommending and imposing discipline because of its impact on the overall morale of the agency's employees. If employees view the recommended discipline as too lenient, it may send the wrong message that the misconduct was insignificant; on the other hand, discipline that is viewed as too harsh may have a demoralizing effect on the officer involved and on other agency employees and may result in allegations that the leadership is unfair.

Listed here, in order of severity, are the seven types of sanctions that police agencies commonly use[93]:

1. *Counseling.* This counseling is usually a conversation between the supervisor and the employee about a specific aspect of the employee's performance or conduct. It is warranted when an employee has committed a relatively minor infraction or when the nature of the offense is such that oral counseling is all that is required. No documentation or report is placed in the employee's personnel file.

2. *Documented oral counseling.* Usually the first step in a progressive disciplinary process, documented oral counseling is intended to address relatively minor infractions. It takes place when the employee has had no previous reprimands or more severe disciplinary action of the same or similar nature.

3. *Letters of reprimand.* These letters are formal written notices regarding significant misconduct, more serious performance violations, or repeated offenses. It is usually the second step in the disciplinary process and is intended to provide the employee and the agency with a written record of the violation of behavior. It identifies what specific corrective action must be taken to avoid subsequent and more serious disciplinary action.

4. *Suspension.* The step of suspension is a severe disciplinary action that results in an employee being relieved of duty, often without pay. It is usually administered when an employee commits a serious violation of established rules or after written reprimands have been given and no change in behavior or performance has resulted.

5. *Demotion.* In a demotion, an employee is placed in a position of lower responsibility and pay. It is normally used when an otherwise good employee is unable to meet the standards required for the higher position or when the employee has committed a serious act requiring that he or she be removed from a position of management or supervision.

6. *Termination.* The most severe disciplinary action that can be taken is termination. It usually occurs when previous serious discipline has been imposed and there has been inadequate or no improvement in behavior or performance, but it may also occur when an employee commits an offense so serious that continued employment would be inappropriate.

7. *Transfer.* Many agencies use the disciplinary transfer to deal with problem officers. Officers can be transferred to a different location or assignment, and this action is often seen as an effective disciplinary tool.

SUMMARY

This chapter has examined ethics as well as several topics that might well be termed the "underbelly" of the field: police use of force, police brutality, bias-based policing, police corruption, and the code of silence. We also considered a number of areas in which federal courts have placed limitations on police behaviors by virtue of the unique role of the police and the necessary higher standard of behavior: freedom of speech, search and seizure, self-incrimination, freedom of religion, sexual misconduct, residency requirements, moonlighting, misuse of firearms, and alcohol and drug abuse. The chapter also examined disciplinary policies and practices.

Clearly, it would be a much better profession—and society—if these unsavory topics could be omitted, but ours is not a perfect world, and nor are the police perfect. This chapter underscored the serious nature of police misbehavior and society's attempts to hold officers accountable. Police behavior is being closely scrutinized today, and the police are held to a much higher standard of behavior than ever before, especially since incidents of misprision of office often harm innocent or undeserving people and receive national attention.

The next chapter, on civil liability, examines the high legal cost of the kinds of failures in policing that were discussed in this chapter. Although liability is a form of accountability, it stands alone because it is a reflection of the standard of accountability being owed to the public and a means of measuring public dissatisfaction with improper police performance.

KEY TERMS

accountability
bias-based policing
code of silence
complaint
contagious shooting
crime-control model
"Dirty Harry problem"
double effect
due process model
ethics
Garrity v. *New Jersey*
Lautenberg Amendment
limitations on officers' constitutional rights
model of circumstantial corruptibility
noble cause corruption
police brutality
police corruption
police firearms regulations
police shooting
police use of force
relative ethics
slippery slope perspective
Tennessee v. *Garner*
use-of-force continuum

REVIEW QUESTIONS

1. What is meant by police ethics, and what are some of the unique ethical problems that community policing can pose?

2. What is meant by noble cause corruption and the "Dirty Harry problem," and how do they each relate to Packer's crime-control and due process models of law enforcement?

3. What are the types of police brutality and use-of-force incidents?

4. What did the Supreme Court recently decide with regard to police use of deadly force in stopping speeding vehicles in high-speed pursuits?

5. What are some factors that contribute to police violence?

6. What is meant by bias-based policing, what do recent studies say about police stops and searches of minorities, and what is the result in relations between minorities and police?

7. How and why does police corruption occur, and what factors within both the community and policing seem to foster and maintain it?

8. Which constitutional limitations have federal courts placed on officers' rights and personal behavior?

9. What is the general process that police agencies use to deal with citizen complaints?

10. What are some factors used to determine the level of discipline and type of sanction for officers who are to be disciplined?

INDEPENDENT STUDENT ACTIVITIES

1. Interview local police administrators or internal affairs investigators to determine their policy and philosophy concerning ethics and police gratuities. In general, how are their officers held accountable for their performance? What precautionary measures are taken to prevent graft and corruption? What policies are in place? What are the penalties for violation of these policies?

2. What process exists within the police department in your community for investigating citizen complaints? Is there a citizen review board? If so, what is its role and function? If not, would such a board be beneficial?

3. Using newspaper editorials or interviews, ascertain the level of citizen satisfaction with the police. What seems to be the greatest area of discontent with the police? Do citizens feel that their police are a part of the community? Why or why not?

RELATED WEB SITES

Amnesty International USA
http://www.amnesty.org

Human Rights Watch
http://www.hrw.org

Institute for Criminal Justice Ethics
http://www.lib.jjay.cuny.edu/cje/html/policeethics.html

CIVIL LIABILITY

FAILING THE PUBLIC TRUST

All men are liable to error; and most men are…under temptation to it.
—*John Locke*

Where laws end, tyranny begins.
—*William Pitt*

LEARNING OBJECTIVES

AS A RESULT OF READING THIS CHAPTER, THE STUDENT WILL:

– BE ABLE TO EXPLAIN THE INCIDENCE, EXPENSE, AND BENEFITS OF LAWSUITS AGAINST THE POLICE

– UNDERSTAND THE LEGAL DEFINITION OF A FRIVOLOUS LAWSUIT

– KNOW SEVERAL FUNDAMENTAL TERMS AND CONCEPTS RELATING TO LIABILITY

– UNDERSTAND THE MEANING AND USES OF U.S. CODE TITLE 42, SECTION 1983, AND TYPES OF POLICE ACTIONS THAT ARE VULNERABLE TO SECTION 1983 CLAIMS

– BE ABLE TO EXPLAIN HOW POLICE OFFICERS MIGHT BE HELD CRIMINALLY LIABLE FOR THEIR MISCONDUCT

– KNOW HOW POLICE FACILITIES MAY BRING ABOUT POLICE LIABILITY

– UNDERSTAND THE AREAS OF POLICE LIABILITY IN VEHICLE PURSUITS

– KNOW HOW POLICE SUPERVISORS MAY BE HELD LIABLE FOR THEIR INACTION OR THEIR OFFICERS' MISCONDUCT

– UNDERSTAND SOME OF THE LIABILITY ISSUES RELATED TO COMPUTER EVIDENCE

INTRODUCTION

A police sergeant once commented to the author, "The decision-making process is not directed by the question 'Is it right or wrong?' but rather 'How much will it cost us if we're sued?'" While that may be a bit overstated or in jest, the specter of lawsuits certainly looms large over police officers, their supervisors, and their unit of government; however, we will see that civil liability has arguably provided a number of benefits to policing. This chapter focuses on this omnipresent facet of contemporary police work, discussing civil liability from a number of perspectives, and it cannot be overstated how important it is for students of criminal justice and in-service police personnel to know and understand this indispensable aspect of policing. To assist in this endeavor, dozens of examples and actual court cases are provided.

Policing is a challenging occupation. The police must enforce the laws, perform welfare tasks, protect the innocent, and attempt to prevent crime. They see people at their worst and participate each year in tens of thousands of arrests, searches, seizures, major incidents (such as hostage situations), and high-speed pursuits. They make split-second decisions, and they function as custodians of offenders in local jails. Perhaps no other occupation, with the exception of medicine, is as vulnerable to legal attack for the actions of its practitioners. Some observers even believe that community-oriented policing and problem solving (COPPS, discussed in Chapter 6) could lead to an increase in civil liability filings because of the greater degree of involvement of police in the lives of citizens.[1]

The chapter begins by discussing the incidence, expense, benefits, and sometimes frivolous nature of lawsuits against the police. Next, with an eye toward helping readers develop a better comprehension of liability, is an overview of a number of basic terms and concepts. We then analyze the legal history of the major tool that is used against the police by citizens who believe the police have violated their constitutional rights: U.S. Code Title 42, Section 1983; included here is a comprehensive discussion, with many examples, of the kinds of police actions that foster liability suits. The liability of supervisors who fail to control their personnel is then reviewed. Finally, other areas of potential liability are examined: duty of care, failure to protect, vehicle pursuits, and computer evidence. The chapter concludes with a chapter summary, key terms, review questions, independent student activities, and related Web sites.

INCIDENCE, EXPENSE, BENEFITS, AND NATURE OF LAWSUITS

The police are not irrationally paranoid when it comes to their being sued—to some, it probably seems to be a contemporary rite of passage or a fact of life for officers that one "isn't really a cop" unless he or she has been sued. There is some basis in fact for this belief: Between 1980 and 2005, federal court decisions involving lawsuits against the police nearly tripled, and according to one study, the police are currently faced with more than thirty thousand civil actions annually.[2] Yet this number might seem small given that the police have millions of interactions with citizens each day.

The cost of civil suits against police can be quite high. For example, according to one study, from 1990 to 1999 Los Angeles paid in excess of $67.8 million in judgments and settlements in eighty lawsuits targeting police use of excessive force as well as police officers involved in sexual assault, sexual abuse, molestation, and domestic violence. This amount does not include the millions of dollars the city spent defending itself against any civil suits or lawsuits stemming from the Rampart Division scandal of the late 1990s,[3] where a former Los Angeles Police Department (LAPD) officer testified that he and other officers routinely lied in court, stole and resold drugs, beat handcuffed suspects in the police station, and killed unarmed people and then planted guns and drugs on them; dozens of lawsuits were filed.[4]

Facing potential judgments amounting to millions of dollars, municipalities are forced to secure liability insurance to protect against civil litigation—insurance that is very expensive. But such expenditures are necessary: The cost of an average jury award of liability against a municipality is reported to be about $2 million.[5] In an attempt to prevent such large judgments, many cities and their insurers have made it a routine practice to settle many claims of police misconduct out of court as opposed to having a jury give the plaintiff(s) a large award. A Justice Department study of Los Angeles County (not including the LAPD) found that county officials, in settling sixty-one police misconduct cases, paid plaintiffs between $20,000 and $1.75 million a case.[6]

Such litigation, although costly in terms of both money and police morale, does have beneficial effects. Proponents of civil liabilities argue that these lawsuits keep the police accountable, give real meaning to citizens' rights, foster better police training, and can force police agencies to correct any deficiencies and review all policies, practices, and customs.[7]

It would be understandable if some officers felt that most (if not all) such lawsuits are frivolous in nature, merely an attempt to gain revenue from the officer(s) or jurisdiction defending against the suit; however, their perception of what constitutes a **frivolous lawsuit** may be very different from the legal definition—that it lacks an arguable basis in law or fact.[8] In fact, frivolous lawsuits against the police are quite rare. A study of published cases by the federal district courts indicates that less than 0.5 percent of those cases resulted in a judicial sanction against plaintiffs for cases that clearly lacked merit.[9]

BASIC TERMS AND CONCEPTS

Laws are enacted in three ways: by legislation, by regulation, and by court decision. Statutes and ordinances are laws passed by legislative bodies, such as the U.S. Congress, state legislatures, county commissions, and city councils. These bodies sometimes create a general outline of the laws they enact, leaving to a particular governmental agency the authority to fill in the details of the law through rules and regulations. During the past two decades, administrative rules and regulations constituted one of the fastest-growing bodies of new law.

When the solution to a legal dispute cannot be found in the existing body of law—statutes, rules, or regulations—judges must rely on prior decisions that their own or other courts have made on similar issues. These judicial decisions are known as *stare decisis* (meaning "let the decision stand"), and the judges who follow them are said to be relying on precedent. Of course, prior court decisions can be overruled or modified by a higher court or by the passage of new legislation. Furthermore, judges sometimes create their own tests to fairly resolve an issue. Statutes, judicial decisions, and tests may differ greatly from state to state; therefore, it is important for lawyers and criminal justice practitioners to read and understand the laws as they apply in their own jurisdictions.

It is also important to have a basic understanding of **tort liability**, a tort being an injury inflicted on one person by another. Three categories of torts generally cover most of the lawsuits filed against criminal justice practitioners: negligence, intentional torts, and constitutional torts.

Negligence arises when a police officer's conduct creates a danger to others; in other words, the officer did not conduct his or her affairs in a manner so as to avoid subjecting others to a risk of harm. The officer will be held liable for the injuries caused to others through his or her negligent acts. The law recognizes various levels or degrees of negligence: simple, gross, and willful or criminal negligence. Simple negligence involves a reasonable act performed by a reasonable officer in the scope of employment but performed without due care; the result is usually a charge of mental pain and anguish, for which an employer or an insurance company will pay damages. Gross negligence involves an unreasonable act for which damages for mental pain and anguish will be paid by either the employer (if the officer's acts were within the scope of employment) or the officer. Willful or criminal negligence involves an intentional act rather than negligence; the plaintiff will receive actual damages, mental pain and anguish damages, and punitive damages. These damages will be paid by the officer involved; neither the employer nor the insurance company will be compelled to pay.[10]

Intentional torts occur when an officer engages in a voluntary act that had a substantial likelihood of resulting in injury to another; examples are assault and battery, false arrest and imprisonment, malicious prosecution, and abuse of process. Constitutional torts involve police officers' duty to recognize and uphold the constitutional rights, privileges, and immunities of others, and violations of these guarantees may subject officers to civil suits, most frequently brought in federal court under 42 U.S. Code Section 1983,[11] which is discussed later.

Allegations of false arrest, false imprisonment, criminal behavior (such as assault and battery), and police misconduct (invasion of privacy, negligence, defamation, and malicious prosecution) are examples of torts that are commonly brought against police officers.[12] False arrest is the arrest of a person without probable cause—an arrest that is made even though an ordinarily prudent person would not have concluded that a crime had been committed or that the person arrested had committed it. False imprisonment is the intentional illegal detention of a person, not only jail but any confinement to a specified area. Most false arrest suits result in a false imprisonment charge as well, but a false imprisonment charge sometimes can follow a valid arrest. For example, the police might fail to release an arrested person after a proper bail or bond has been posted, they might delay the arraignment of an arrested person unreasonably, or they might fail to release a prisoner after they no longer have authority to hold him or her. "Brutality" is not a legal tort action per se; rather, it must be brought as a civil assault and/or battery.

A single act may also be a crime as well as a tort. For example, if Officer Smith, in an unprovoked attack, injures Citizen Jones, the state will attempt to punish Smith in a criminal action by sending him to prison or fining him, or both. The state would have the burden of proof at a criminal trial, having to prove Smith guilty "beyond a reasonable doubt." Furthermore, Jones may sue Smith for money damages in a civil action for the personal injury he suffered. Jones would argue that Smith failed to carry out his duty to act reasonably and prudently and that this failure resulted in Jones's injury. This legal wrong, of course, is a tort; Jones would have the burden of proving Smith's acts were tortious by a "preponderance of the evidence," a lower standard and thus easier to satisfy in civil court.

Our system of government has both federal and state courts. Federal courts are intended to have somewhat limited jurisdiction and tend not to hear cases involving private (as opposed to public) controversies unless federal law is involved or both parties agree to have their dispute settled there. Thus most tort suits are filed in state courts. There are two means by which a federal court may acquire jurisdiction of police misconduct suits. The first is the predominant source of our later discussions, referred to as a "1983 suit," a name that is derived from the fact that the suits are brought under the provisions of Title 42, Section 1983, of the U.S. Code. The significant part of this statute and its legislative history follow.

The second means by which a federal court may assume jurisdiction over a police misconduct suit is to allege what some legal commentators call a ***Bivens* tort**, a name that derives from a 1971 case, *Bivens* v. *Six Unknown Named Agents of the Federal Bureau of Narcotics*.[13] The U.S. Supreme Court held that a civil suit based directly on the Fourth Amendment could be filed. In *Bivens,* federal narcotics agents conducted an illegal search, arrest, and interrogation, but a suit by the plaintiffs could not be filed under Section 1983 because that section covers only police agents acting under state law. Civil suits to recover damages for violations of constitutional rights by federal officers have thus become known as *Bivens* suits.

A suit may also be filed against an employer under the doctrine of ***respondeat superior,*** an old legal maxim meaning "let the master answer"; this doctrine is also termed **vicarious liability**. In sum, an employer is liable in certain instances for the wrongful acts of its employee. It is generally inapplicable if a jury determines that the employee's negligent or malicious acts were outside the legitimate scope of the employer's authority. Although U.S. courts have expanded the extent to which employers can be sued for the torts of their employees, the courts are still reluctant to extend this doctrine to police supervisors (sergeants and lieutenants) and administrators. The courts realize that, first of all, police supervisors have little discretion in hiring decisions. Second, the duties of police officers are largely established by the governmental authority that hired them rather than by their supervisors. However, if a supervisor has abused his or her authority, was present when the misconduct occurred and did nothing to stop it, or otherwise participated in the misconduct, he or she can be held liable for the tortious behavior of his or her officers.[14] This issue is discussed at greater length later in this chapter.

Another issue that involves the question of who may be sued involves immunity and whether police departments and the employing governmental unit can be sued for damages caused by police misconduct. Under common law, the government could not be sued because the king could do no wrong. This doctrine, known as **sovereign immunity**, was also adopted in 1795 in the Eleventh Amendment to the U.S. Constitution, which says: "The judicial power of the United States shall not be construed to extend to any suit in law or equity, commenced or prosecuted against one of the United States by citizens of another state, or by citizens or subjects of any foreign state." This amendment therefore bars suits against states, state agencies, and instrumentalities in federal courts; the Supreme Court has also said it bars suits by citizens of the same state.[15]

Municipal governments, however, do not enjoy the same protection since they are creations of state laws and, as such, are not truly "sovereigns." Thus, they do not enjoy blanket immunity and are only cloaked with immunity to the extent that the state sees fit to do so.[16]

SECTION 1983 LITIGATION

History and Escalation

Prior to discussing specific kinds and examples of civil litigation against the police and their supervisors, it is prudent to first gain an understanding of a major legal instrument that is used by citizens against the police when they feel the police have acted in such a manner as to violate their individual rights: U.S. Code Title 42, **Section 1983**.

In the years following the Civil War, Congress, in reaction to the states' inability to control the Ku Klux Klan's lawlessness, enacted the Ku Klux Klan Act of 1871. This was later codified as Title 42, Section 1983, of the U.S. Code. Its statutory language is as follows:

> Every person who, under color of any statute, ordinance, regulation, custom, or usage of any State or Territory, subjects, or causes to be subjected, any citizen of the United States or any other person within the jurisdiction thereof to the deprivation of any rights, privileges, or immunities secured by the Constitution and laws, shall be liable to the party injured in an action at law, suit in equity, or other proper proceeding for redress.

This legislation was intended to provide civil rights protection to all persons protected under the act when a defendant acted "under color of any statute" (misused power of office). It was also meant to provide an avenue to the federal courts for relief of alleged civil rights violations.

The original intent of the law did not include police misconduct litigation. In fact, the law was virtually ignored for ninety years until the U.S. Supreme Court's 1961 decision in

Monroe v. *Pape*,[17] where thirteen members of the Chicago Police Department broke into a home without a warrant, forced the family out of bed at gunpoint, made them stand naked while the officers ransacked the house, and subjected the family to verbal and physical abuse. The plaintiffs (Monroe and his family) claimed that the officers acted "under color of law" as set forth in Section 1983, thus violating their constitutional rights. The U.S. Supreme Court agreed, holding the officers liable.

There was a virtual boom of Section 1983 suits from 1967 through 1976.[18] Several factors contributed to this surge in Section 1983 actions. First, some lawyers believe that clients receive more competent judges and juries in the federal forum than in state courts because federal judges, who are appointed for life, may be less concerned about the political ramifications of their decisions than locally elected judges often are. Also, federal prosecutors may be more aggressive in arguing to jurors from a multicounty area, whereas local prosecutors must argue to jurors who elected them and who may know the defendant-officer. Furthermore, federal rules of pleading and evidence are uniform, federal procedures of discovery are more liberal, and lawyers have easier access to published case law in assisting them to prepare a federal suit.[19] Just as important, Congress passed Section 1988 of the Civil Rights Act in 1976, which allows attorney's fees to the prevailing party over and above the award for compensatory and punitive damages, meaning that a plaintiff's verdict in a police shooting case can be quite profitable.

Also, in 1978, in *Monell* v. *Department of Social Services*,[20] the Supreme Court held that Congress, in the 1871 act, *did* intend that municipalities and other local governments be included as "persons" to whom Section 1983 applies. Local governing bodies and corporate "persons," therefore, can be sued for damages under Section 1983 if such deprivation was the direct result of an official policy or custom of a local unit of government.

Defenses and immunities against Section 1983 suits exist, however. The states themselves, for example, are granted absolute immunity from Section 1983 suits,[21] as are judges, prosecutors, legislators, and federal officials. Federal officials usually act under color of federal law, as opposed to state law, as specified in the act. Police officers are granted **qualified immunity**, meaning that as long as they acted in good faith and their conduct was reasonable, they have a defense. Over the years, the courts have struggled to develop a test for what is meant by "good faith." In 1975, the Supreme Court developed a test that considered both what the officer's state of mind was at the time of the act in question (the subjective element) and whether the officer's act violated clearly established legal rights (the objective element).[22] Overzealous conduct that is not undertaken in good faith and that occurs without regard for the rights of citizens can and will result in a finding of liability.

Police Actions Leading to Section 1983 Liability

Following are some cases based on Section 1983 liability:

- In 1991, Los Angeles motorist Rodney King was beaten by police officers following a police pursuit, an incident that was captured on an eighty-one-second videotape that captured the nation's attention. He was awarded $3.8 million.[23]

- In 1995, federal law enforcement officers at Ruby Ridge, Idaho, used deadly force to seize two citizens, resulting in the federal government's agreement to pay survivors almost $4 million because of unconstitutional use of deadly force. That same year, a federal jury awarded Ramona Africa, the sole survivor of a bombing of her residence by Philadelphia police, $1.5 million (the police had dropped explosives into the home of a radical group trying to make members leave their home). The bombing destroyed sixty-one other homes and killed eleven people, and the total cost to the city exceeded $59 million.[24]
- A jury acquitted four New York police officers of criminal charges in the shooting death of Amadou Diallo. The officers had mistaken Diallo's wallet for a gun and opened fire, discharging forty-one rounds and striking him nineteen times. His parents were awarded $3 million in a settlement with the city.[25]
- Abner Louima was sexually assaulted with a toilet plunger by New York City police officers, a case that resulted in an $8.8 million settlement.[26]

The common thread in all these highly publicized cases (other than the fact that all involved an unconstitutional use of deadly force by the police) was that they used U.S. Code Title 42, Section 1983.

As suggested above, Section 1983 is an appropriate legal tool for citizens who believe they have been victims of police brutality. In *Jennings* v. *City of Detroit*,[27] a twenty-two-year-old single African-American man was permanently paralyzed following a beating at a police station; the jury award was $8 million (settled for $3.5 million). In *Gilliam* v. *Falbo*,[28] the U.S. District Court for Ohio awarded $72,000 to a young man beaten by two officers, and in *Haygood* v. *City of Detroit*,[29] a thirty-five-year-old plaintiff was awarded $2.5 million in punitive damages and $500,000 in compensatory damages after being subjected to racial slurs, beaten, and chained to a bed for twelve hours (charges against the officers were never filed).

Even off-duty activities may get police officers into serious difficulty for acting "under color of law." Part-time work as security guards often opens the door to legal problems. In *Carmelo* v. *Miller*,[30] two off-duty officers were working security at a baseball game. They received information that someone was displaying a gun and stopped a man who fit the description. The officers searched, arrested, beat, and kicked the suspect and his companion. No gun was found in the area, and one of the beaten men required medical treatment. The officers were found liable. In *Stengel* v. *Belcher*,[31] an off-duty officer entered a bar carrying a .32-caliber handgun (which he was required to carry off duty at all times) and a can of Mace. An altercation broke out, and without identifying himself, the officer got involved, killing two men and seriously wounding another. The plaintiffs recovered $800,000 in compensatory damages.

Clearly, the use of off-duty weapons and policies requiring that they be carried pose a risk of liability. In *Bonsignore* v. *New York*,[32] a mentally unstable twenty-three-year veteran police officer shot his wife five times and then killed himself, using a .32-caliber pistol that departmental policy required him to carry when off duty. Evidence produced at trial demonstrated that Officer Bonsignore's unsuitability for police duties was well known by the department—it had even provided him a limited-duty assignment as station house janitor—yet the police code of silence protected him. The jury awarded Mrs. Bonsignore nearly a half million dollars.

Suits involving **wrongful death** are also becoming more frequent, and the following cases illustrate how the law applies in this regard. In *Prior* v. *Woods,*[33] a twenty-four-year-old man was killed outside his home by police officers who mistook him for a burglar; the jury awarded his estate $5.75 million. In *Burkholder* v. *City of Los Angeles,*[34] a Los Angeles police officer killed a man in his early twenties who, while naked and under the influence of drugs, was climbing a light pole (the man had seized the officer's club but had not struck the officer). The jury awarded $450,000 in damages and $150,000 in attorney's fees to his survivors.

Generally, police officers are not liable for damages under Section 1983 for merely arresting someone, but that protective shroud vanishes if the plaintiff proves the officer was negligent or violated an established law or right (as in cases of false arrest). As an illustration, in *Murray* v. *City of Chicago,*[35] the plaintiff's purse and checkbook were stolen; she reported the theft to the police. Later, some of the stolen checks were cashed and the plaintiff was arrested; she appeared in court and cleared up the matter, all charges being dropped. Several months later, she was arrested again at her home by Chicago officers who used an invalid arrest warrant that was related to the earlier mix-up. Murray was taken to the police station, strip-searched by male officers, and detained for six hours before being released. The federal court ruled that the officers acted in good faith but that if the policy or custom of the city was shown to have encouraged such unwarranted arrests, the city could be held liable.

Search and seizure, an especially complicated area of criminal procedure, is ripe for Section 1983 suits, primarily because of the ambiguous nature of the probable cause doctrine. In *Duncan* v. *Barnes,*[36] police officers obtained a warrant to search a suspect's home for heroin and executed the warrant in early morning hours. With guns drawn, officers entered two bedrooms, forcing the two females and one male inside to stand nude, spread-eagled against a wall, while their rooms were searched. Soon the officers realized that they had entered the wrong apartment, and they left the apartment in total disarray. The occupants, students at a court-reporting school, were so upset that they missed classes for two weeks; as a result, their certification and employment as court reporters were delayed. The court had little difficulty finding that the officers had acted in an unreasonable manner.

Negligence by police officers is another cause of action under Section 1983. Negligence can be found in the supervision and training of personnel, among other things. In *Sager* v. *City of Woodlawn Park,*[37] an officer accidentally killed a person when the shotgun he was pointing at the head of the prisoner discharged while the officer was attempting to handcuff the prisoner with his other hand. At trial, the officer stated that he had seen the technique in a police training film. The training officer, however, testified that the film was intended to show how *not* to handcuff a prisoner; unfortunately, none of the trainers had made that important distinction to the class, so the court ruled that improper training resulted in the prisoner's death. In *Popow* v. *City of Margate,*[38] an innocent bystander was killed on his front porch at night by a police officer engaged in foot pursuit, and the court held the city negligent because the officer had had no training on night firing, shooting at moving targets, or using firearms in a residential area.

POLICE AND CIVIL LIABILITY

SAMUEL G. CHAPMAN

"Sue? Me? For what? Why? What do I do now? Will I lose everything?" Such questions preoccupy police officers when they learn that they have been named as defendants in a civil rights lawsuit. Officers need help and direction at this juncture, including assurance that this isn't the end of the world. But they need to know that being sued is not a parlor game either.

Police departments and their personnel must take civil rights litigation seriously, for such actions have been on the increase over the past three decades. Actually, civil rights lawsuits are seen by many as an occupational hazard in policing. Just when (if ever) this virtual flood tide of litigation will ebb is not clear.

When a lawsuit has been filed, the allegations should be evaluated by the government's attorneys. Fact-finding may disclose that the allegations appear to have little merit. It could be that the plaintiff's counsel has seemingly filed a case of dubious substance, really seeking what is called a "convenience settlement," which occurs when a defendant pays the plaintiff a dollar amount less than what the defendant's costs would be to prepare for trial. But if after fact-finding it appears that the department and its officers are culpable, the defense team should start settlement negotiations early. The defense should make a meaningful offer, keeping it in the range of settlements for cases of a similar sort elsewhere.

At the same time, the defense (government and officer) must get under way with discovery within the context of a game plan aimed at minimizing loss should the case eventually go to trial. Settlements that occur just before trial are invariably costly. The defense team should also evaluate the courtroom record of the plaintiff's law firm, since some firms are more competent than others. Moreover, knowledge about the track record of the opposing attorneys may bear on whether to settle and what amount to offer.

In many instances, fact-finding will reveal that a case is realistically defensible. When this is so, the defense team may decide to reject a convenience settlement and prepare for trial. Such a stance will cause the plaintiff's law firm to evaluate whether to expend resources and time in pursuing a case that they are not likely to win. Clearly, when the defense feels it can be successful and decides to stand up and fight, it establishes the jurisdiction as a "hard target" and sends a message that lawsuits with little merit are going to be stridently defended.

Of course, it is crucial that whoever is named to defend officers and police agencies be skilled in handling civil rights cases. It is a grave mistake for the government to take a "bargain basement" approach to defending civil rights lawsuits by assigning staff attorneys who have little or no experience working with these highly technical types of litigation.

With the upsurge in litigation against police, officers may become demoralized, dispirited, and defensive. They are easy prey for cynical locker-room jockeys who proclaim that the best way to avoid trouble is to slow down, cool it, and do no more police work than one has to. Such advice, which is of the worst sort, poses a special urgent challenge for police supervisors, who must ensure that officers execute their duties faithfully and in accordance with departmental guidelines.

Yes, the police can fight back by suing those who sue them, but this means hiring counsel, which is expensive. And even if the lawsuit is successful and brings a dollar judgment against the defendant, such a defendant is usually poor and hence unable to meet any financial judgment levied against him or her. In short, suing back is not a realistic course of action.

The government's best defense against an adverse judgment in a civil rights lawsuit is to thoroughly train and regularly retrain its police personnel and to supervise them well. In addition, the police department's rules and regulations, as well as its procedures manuals, must be kept current and as complete and practical as possible. The content of these important documents must be understood by all officers. If all these things are in place and if officers perform as trained and execute their roles in accord with departmental guidelines and policies, a persuasive defense can be mounted against any allegations of misconduct.

(Samuel G. Chapman, a police consultant, was a Berkeley, California, police officer and a student at the University of California, Berkeley, where he earned a degree in criminology and studied under August Vollmer. He later taught at Michigan State University, served as chief of the Multnomah County Sheriff's Office [Portland, Oregon], and was assistant director of the President's Commission on Law Enforcement and the Administration of Justice in Washington, D.C. In 1967, he began a twenty-four-year career as professor of political science at the University of Oklahoma, where he authored a number of books and monographs on various aspects of policing and the use of police dogs.)

Criminal Prosecutions for Police Misconduct

Whereas Section 1983 is a civil statute, Title 18, **Section 242**, of the U.S. Code makes it a *criminal* offense for any person acting willfully "under color of law," statute, regulation, or custom to deprive any person of the rights and privileges guaranteed under the Constitution and laws of the United States. This law, like Section 1983, dates from the post–Civil War era and applies to all people regardless of race, color, or national origin. Section 242 applies not only to police officers but also to other public officials; prosecutions of judges, bail-bond agents, public defenders, and even prosecutors are possible under the statute.

An example of the use of Section 242 is the murder of a drug courier by two U.S. customs agents while the agents were assigned to the San Juan International Airport. The courier flew to Puerto Rico to deposit approximately $700,000 in cash and checks into his employer's account. He was last seen being interviewed by the two customs agents in the airport; ten days later, his body was discovered in a Puerto Rican rain forest. An investigation revealed that the agents had lured the victim away from the airport and had murdered him for his money, later disposing of the body. They were convicted under Section 242 and related federal statutes, and each agent was sentenced to a prison term of 120 years.[39]

LIABILITY OF POLICE SUPERVISORS

Negligent supervision and direction of officers involve a breach of a duty to provide effective systems for the evaluation, control, and monitoring of police employees' performance. This breach of duty may come in the form of failure to provide written and verbal directives, to develop adequate policies and guidelines, or to articulate clearly to employees how duties are to be performed. It may also involve a supervisor's direction to an employee to engage in an illegal activity or the supervisor's approval of an illegal activity.[40]

In such cases, Section 1983 allows for a finding of personal liability on the part of police supervisory personnel.

McClelland v. *Facteau,*[41] a Section 1983 suit against a state police agency chief as well as a local police chief, was such a case. McClelland was stopped by Officer Facteau (a state employee) for speeding. He was taken to the city jail; there he was not allowed to make any phone calls, he was questioned but not advised of his rights, and he was beaten and injured by Facteau in the presence of two city police officers. McClelland sued, claiming that the two police chiefs were directly responsible for his treatment and injuries due to their failure to properly train and supervise their subordinates. Evidence was produced of prior misbehavior by Facteau. The court ruled that the chiefs could be held liable if they knew of prior misbehavior yet did nothing about it.

Another related case was that of *Brandon* v. *Allen.*[42] In this case, two teenagers who were parked in a "lovers' lane" were approached by an off-duty police officer, Allen, who showed his police identification and demanded that the boy exit the car. Allen struck the boy with his fist and stabbed him with a knife; then he attempted to break into the car where the girl was seated. The boy was able to reenter the car and manage an escape. As the two teenagers sped off, Allen fired a shot at them with his revolver, and the shattered windshield glass severely injured the youths to the point that they required plastic surgery. Allen was convicted of criminal charges, and the police chief was also sued under Section 1983. The plaintiffs charged that the chief and others knew of Allen's reputation for being mentally unstable (none of the other police officers wanted to ride in a patrol car with him). At least two formal charges of misconduct had been filed previously, yet the chief had failed to take any remedial action or even to review the disciplinary records of officers. The court called this behavior "unjustified inaction," held the police department liable, and allowed the plaintiffs' damages. The U.S. Supreme Court upheld this judgment.[43]

Police supervisors have also been found liable for injuries arising out of an official policy or custom of their department. Injuries resulting from a chief's verbal or written support of heavy-handed behavior resulting in excessive force by officers have resulted in such liability.[44]

Today's police supervisors are definitely in a "need to know" position where the law is concerned. They are caught in the middle—not only can they be sued for improper hiring, training, and supervision of their officers, but there are other civil rights laws that can be used by officers who believe they were improperly disciplined or terminated. Indeed, Section 1983 can also be used by unsuccessful job applicants if they can show that the administrator's tests were not job related, included inherent bias, or were not properly administered or graded. The same holds true if it can be shown that proper testing methods were not used in the promotion or the discipline or firing of personnel. Police supervisors have lost in suits in which they disciplined male and female officers who were having a private relationship,[45] in which they disciplined African-American officers who removed the U.S. flag from their uniforms to protest perceived discriminatory acts by the city,[46] and in which they disciplined officers for "improper" political party membership.[47]

OTHER AREAS OF POTENTIAL LIABILITY

Next we look at several interrelated areas in which liability on the part of the police may be found if they fail to perform their duties properly, perform them in a negligent manner, make poor decisions, or abuse their authority.

Duty of Care

While citizens often speak of the broad police duty to serve and protect their community, their lives, and their property, a legal duty is very specific and more limited. This doctrine of **duty of care** is derived from common law and holds that police have no duty to protect the general public from harm, absent a special kind of relationship (discussed below). The Supreme Court addressed this doctrine in an 1856 decision in *South* v. *Maryland*,[48] where a sheriff was sued for refusing to protect a citizen from injuries inflicted from a violent crowd. The court said that peace officers protect the general public, not specific individuals. Since *South,* the doctrine of duty of care has been adopted at the state and federal levels, with most courts ruling that the state is not required to provide police services.[49] This may come as a surprise to many people, but the legal view is that police can only act once a crime is or has already been committed and that they cannot be held liable for failure to arrive in time to save any particular individual from harm unless the victim has a special relationship with the police, such as a protected witness. There are neither sufficient police nor enough resources to act as personal bodyguards for every citizen, twenty-four hours a day. No duty of care exists unless it is established that the agency owed a special duty to the injured party.

Police legal duties can arise from many sources, including laws, customs, court decisions, and agency policies. As examples, a state statute prohibiting drunk driving might also order the police to arrest any persons operating motor vehicles while under the influence of intoxicants, and a police department policy in the same state may require officers who stop such suspected motor vehicle operators to perform field sobriety tests at the scene of the traffic stop.[50]

SPECIAL RELATIONSHIPS   **Special relationships** are those where the officer knows or has reason to know the likelihood of harm to someone if he or she fails to do his or her duty and are thus defined by the circumstances surrounding an injury or damage. A special relationship can be based on the following three areas:

1. Whether the officer could have foreseen that he or she was expected to take action in a given situation to prevent injury is one consideration.[51] (For example, a police officer failed to remove an intoxicated operator of a motor vehicle from a highway.)
2. Departmental policies or guidelines that prohibit a certain course of action are also examined.[52] (For example, when a drunk driver killed another driver, the court noted that the police department had a standard operating procedure manual that mandated that an intoxicated individual who would likely do physical injury to himself or others "*will* be taken into protective custody.")
3. Spatial and temporal proximity of the defendant-officer's behavior to the injury damage is another factor.[53] (For example, an individual who was arrested for drunk

driving, taken into custody, found to have a 0.166 blood alcohol level, and released three hours later then had a fatal car accident.)

PROXIMATE CAUSE   Related to the duty of care and liabilities of the police is the matter of **proximate cause**. Once a plaintiff has demonstrated the existence of a police duty of care and has shown the officer breached that duty, he or she must still prove that the officer's conduct was the proximate cause of the injury or damage. Proximate cause is established by asking, "But for the officer's conduct, would the plaintiff have sustained the injury or damage?" If the answer to this question is no, then proximate cause is established, and the officer can be held liable for the damage or injury. This requirement of negligence limits liabilities, however, in situations where damage would have occurred regardless of the officer's behavior.[54] For example, an officer is involved in a high-speed chase, and the offending driver strikes an innocent third party. Generally, if the officer was not acting in a negligent fashion and did not cause the injury, there would be no liability on the officer's part.[55]

Proximate cause may be found in such cases as when an officer leaves the scene of an accident aware of dangerous conditions (spilled oil, smoke, vehicle debris, stray animals) without proper warning to motorists.[56] In such a case, Louisiana state troopers responded to a one-car accident caused by an oil spill on a dangerous portion of the roadway. Initially, the troopers asked the state's department of transportation to cover the spill with sand and then ignited flares to warn oncoming motorists of the danger; the troopers then returned to other patrol duties. Soon the oil had absorbed the sand and the flares went out; then an unsuspecting motorcyclist slid on the oil, struck a tree, and died. The court held that the troopers breached their duty to provide warning to drivers of the danger and that this breach was the proximate cause of the motorcyclist's death.[57]

PERSONS IN CUSTODY   Courts generally recognize that police officers have a duty of care to persons in their custody.[58] This means that police officers have a legal responsibility to take reasonable precautions to ensure the health and safety of persons in their custody, keeping detainees free from harm, rendering medical assistance when necessary, and treating detainees humanely.[59] Custody is not restricted to those persons who are incarcerated, however; a duty of care is owed by the police, for example, to persons in their physical custody outside a jail setting, such as when arresting or transporting prisoners and mental patients or when holding persons in booking or interrogation areas regardless of whether they have been formally charged with a crime.[60]

This general duty of care to persons in police custody seldom results in liability for self-inflicted injury or suicide because these acts are normally considered to result from the detainee's own intentional conduct rather than from some form of police negligence.[61] There are exceptions to this rule, however.[62] Most courts, for example, have held that if a prisoner's suicide is "reasonably foreseeable," the jailer owes the prisoner a duty of care to help prevent that suicide. As the court stated in *Joseph* v. *State of Alaska* (where an intoxicated jail inmate hanged himself with a nylon cord not taken from his sweatpants at booking, and the jail's video camera lens had been obscured):

> While a prisoner's mental illness, intoxication, or other impairment may be the reasons why the jailer knows or should know that the prisoner is suicidal, other signs—such as declared intent to commit suicide—are also sufficient.[63]

If the suicidal tendencies of an inmate are known, the duty of care required of the custodian is elevated.[64] In these kinds of special cases, officers must ensure that measures are taken to prevent self-inflicted harm; included here are detainees who suffer from a disturbed state of mind and those who are impaired by drugs or alcohol. Duty of care to an impaired individual may include removing shoes, belts, clothing, and other articles from the detainee.[65]

SAFE FACILITIES   Another area of police liability, one that involves both persons in custody and proximate cause, is the need to provide safe facilities. Courts have even considered the design of detention facilities as a source of negligence, such as in a Detroit case where the construction of a jail's holding cell did not allow officers to observe detainees' movements: The construction of the cell doors hampered detainee supervision, there were no electronic monitoring devices for observing detainees, and there was an absence of detoxification cells required under state department of corrections rules. Therefore, following a suicide in this facility, the court concluded that these conditions constituted building defects and were the proximate cause of the decedent's death.[66]

The need to provide a secure environment for detainees extends beyond the confines of the detention center. In a Delaware case, a constable used his private vehicle to transport mental patients and did not handcuff patients while in transport. One patient, who had declared his intention to kill himself, unfastened his seat belt, jumped out of the vehicle while it was in motion, and died. The court found that because the constable knew his vehicle was inadequate for such transports and did not restrain the patient or heed his intention to commit suicide, his misconduct constituted wantonness.[67]

Failure to Protect

A failure to protect may occur if a police officer neglects to protect a person from a known and foreseeable danger, a claim that most often involves battered women. There are, however, other circumstances that can create a duty to protect people from crime. Informants, witnesses, and other people dependent on the police can be a source of police liability if the police fail to take reasonable action to prevent victimization—officers' conduct cannot place a person in peril or demonstrate deliberate indifference for his or her safety.

For example, one morning Juan Penilla was on the porch of his home and became seriously ill. His neighbors called 911, and two police officers arrived first. They found him to be in grave need of medical care, cancelled the request for paramedics, broke the lock and door jam on the front door of Penilla's residence, moved him inside the house, locked the door, and left. The next day, family members found Penilla dead inside the house as a result of respiratory failure. His mother sued under Section 1983, and the court found that the officers' conduct clearly placed Penilla in a more dangerous position than the one in which they found him.[68] Another example is when the Green Bay Police Department released the tape of a phone call from an informant, which led to the informant's death.[69]

Vehicle Pursuits

In Chapter 9 we discussed a 2007 decision by the U.S. Supreme Court regarding the proper level of deadly force that may be used by officers during vehicle pursuits. Still, the police must act reasonably in such instances or they may be found civilly liable. In this section, we discuss vehicle pursuits in more detail, including the kinds of actions by officers that may lead to their being civilly liable.

First, police officers are afforded no special privileges or immunities in the routine operation of their patrol vehicles.[70] Police officers driving in nonemergency situations do not have immunity for their negligence or recklessness and are held to the same standard of conduct as private citizens. When responding to emergency situations, however, officers are governed by statutes covering emergency vehicles.[71] In such circumstances, most jurisdictions afford the police limited immunity for violations of traffic laws; in other words, they are accorded some protections and privileges not given to private citizens and are permitted to take greater risks that would amount to negligence if undertaken by citizens.[72]

Few operational patrol issues are of greater concern to police leadership than police pursuits because of the tremendous potential for injury, property damage, and liability that accompanies them. As one police procedure manual describes it, "The decision by a police officer to pursue a citizen in a motor vehicle is among the most critical that can be made."[73] Civil litigation arising out of collisions involving police pursuits reveals such pursuits to be high-stakes undertakings with serious and sometimes tragic results.[74] Indeed, several hundred people are killed each year during police pursuits,[75] and many of them are innocent third parties.

Pursuits place the police in a delicate balancing act. On one hand is the need for police to show criminals that flight from the law is no way to freedom. If a police agency completely bans high-speed pursuits, its credibility with both law-abiding citizens and law violators may suffer; public knowledge that the agency has a no-pursuit policy may encourage people to flee, decreasing the probability of apprehension.[76] Still, according to one observer, because of safety and liability concerns, "a growing number of agencies have the position that if the bad guy puts the pedal to the metal, it's a 'freebie.' They will not pursue him."[77]

On the other hand, there is indeed the high-speed threat to everyone within range of the pursuit, including suspects, their passengers, other drivers, and bystanders. One police trainer asks a simple question to help officers determine whether to continue a pursuit: "Is this person a threat to the public safety other than the fact the police are chasing him?" If the officers cannot objectively answer yes, the pursuit should be terminated.[78]

In May 1990, two Sacramento County, California, deputies responded to a call about a fight. At the scene, they observed a motorcycle with two riders approaching their vehicle at high speed. Turning on their red lights, the deputies ordered the driver to stop. The motorcycle operator began to elude the officers, who initiated a pursuit that reached speeds of more than a hundred miles per hour over about 1.3 miles. The pursuit ended when the motorcycle crashed; the deputies' vehicle could not stop in time and struck the bike's passenger, killing him. The passenger's family brought suit, claiming that the pursuit violated the crash victim's due process rights under the Fourteenth Amendment.

In *County of Sacramento* v. *Lewis,*[79] decided in May 1998, the U.S. Supreme Court held that the proper standard to be employed in these cases is whether the officer's conduct during the pursuit "shocks the conscience." (Was the conduct offensive to a reasonable person's sense of moral goodness?) The Court further determined that high-speed chases with no intent to harm suspects do not give rise to liability under the Fourteenth Amendment and therefore closed the door on liability for officers involved in pursuits that do not "shock the conscience." But the Court left unanswered many important questions, such as whether it will allow an innocent third party to file a claim against the police for damages and whether a municipality can be held liable for its failure to train officers in pursuit issues.

In sum, a pursuit is justified only when the necessity of apprehension outweighs the degree of danger created by the pursuit. Agencies generally require field supervisors (sergeants) to discontinue the pursuit when it is unjustified or becomes too dangerous.[80]

Computer Evidence

It is almost impossible to investigate a fraud, embezzlement, or child pornography case today without dealing with some sort of computer evidence. Even evidence in a homicide or narcotics case may be buried deep within a computer's hard drive. As a result, many police agencies have recruited self-taught "experts" to fill the role of computer evidence specialists. These specialists are usually highly motivated and have some knowledge of the rules of evidence and some experience in testifying in court. Other police agencies have enlisted the support of personnel at local universities or computer repair shops to help them with computer evidence.[81]

The increased exposure to computer evidence by people both inside and outside policing brings an increase in potential legal liabilities. For example, if a police agency seizes the computerized records of an ongoing business, there may be negative financial consequences for the business. If it can be shown that the police accidentally destroyed business records through negligence, a criminal investigation might well become the civil suit of the decade. Furthermore, if a seized computer contains a newsletter, a draft of a book, or any computer bulletin board system, there may be liability under the Privacy Protection Act.[82]

The risk of liability in these kinds of cases may be reduced substantially if police investigators follow generally accepted forensic computer evidence procedures. Guidelines approved by the Department of Justice's Computer Crime and Intellectual Property

Section dictate how the police are to search, seize, and analyze computers. It is crucial that the police be trained in the proper procedures for handling computers as well as in the rules of evidence. The federal government has made computer evidence training a priority for federal, state, and local law enforcement officers.[83]

SUMMARY

This chapter examined the incidence, expense, benefits, and sometimes frivolous nature of lawsuits against the police; a number of basic terms and concepts that are ingrained in the area of civil liability; Section 1983, a major litigation tool that is used against the police by citizens who believe the police have violated their constitutional rights; the liability of supervisors who fail to control their personnel; and other areas of potential liability such as duty of care, failure to protect, vehicle pursuits, and computer evidence. Included were many examples of the kinds of police actions that foster liability lawsuits, police actions leading to liability, and new areas of potential police liability such as vehicle pursuits and computer evidence.

The weight and breadth of the chapter's litigated cases and decisions against police officers—and their organizations and cities or counties—speak for themselves. Perhaps what has been shown most unequivocally is that the consequences of failing to properly hire, train, and supervise police personnel can be quite costly, in both human and financial terms. There is a clear and present need for officers to know and understand the law regarding liability, to always project themselves in the best possible light, and to conduct themselves in a manner that demonstrates that their behavior was a good-faith effort to do their job properly.

Americans know the police have a difficult job to do and are likely willing to accept less than perfect behavior from them, but the kinds of improper and illegal actions shown in this chapter simply cannot and will not be tolerated.

KEY TERMS

Bivens tort
duty of care
failure to protect
frivolous lawsuit
negligence
negligent supervision
proximate cause

qualified immunity
respondeat superior
Section 242
Section 1983
sovereign immunity
special relationship
stare decisis
tort liability
vicarious liability
wrongful death

REVIEW QUESTIONS

1. What are the incidence and benefits of lawsuits against the police?

2. What is the legal definition of a frivolous lawsuit?

3. What is meant by negligence and Title 42, Section 1983, of the U.S. Code?

4. What caused an increase in Section 1983 lawsuits?

5. What are some types of police actions that are vulnerable to Section 1983 actions?

6. What is meant by duty of care and failure to protect?

7. How might police facilities and vehicles be involved in police liability?

8. What are the areas of civil liability in the area of police vehicle pursuits?

9. What are some examples of how police supervisors may be held criminally liable for their officers' misconduct?

10. What are some of the liability issues related to computer evidence?

INDEPENDENT STUDENT ACTIVITIES

1. Interview police executives to learn of the challenges they face in trying to provide police services in a litigious society. What are they doing in terms of training and policies to minimize the chances of successful lawsuits against their officers? In which areas are the police most vulnerable to charges of negligence?

2. Interview prosecutors and defense attorneys about police civil liability from their perspectives.

3. In a related vein, determine from discussions with police practitioners the technical areas of their work in which they must constantly be retrained and certified to avoid harming citizens and to avoid being involved in litigation.

RELATED WEB SITES

Association of Trial Lawyers
http://www.atlanet.org

International Perspectives on Justice
http://pap01.adt.jjay.cuny.edu

Labor Relations Information System
http://www.lris.com/index.cfm

National District Attorney Association
http://www.ndaa-apri.org

SPECIAL PROBLEMS, POPULATIONS, AND CHALLENGES

Part IV contains three chapters. Chapter 11 deals with how the police are attempting to cope with three very grave problems: terrorism, street gangs, and drugs. The ensuing one, Chapter 12, continues in that same vein by looking at special populations—those who are illegal aliens, those who belong to organized crime (the mob), those who commit hate crimes, and those youth who commit crimes. Finally, Chapter 13 considers several challenges: three trends in policing (labor relations, hiring of women and minorities, and private policing) and three policing issues (stress, higher education for officers, and homelessness).

ADDRESSING TERRORISM, STREET GANGS, AND DRUGS

You will notice that the plane will stop, then will start to fly again. This is the hour in which you will meet God.

—From the spiritual instruction manual for the suicide attacks on the World Trade Center, found in Muhammad Atta's briefcase

Now that you've met me, what will you do?
Will you try me or not? It's all up to you.
I can bring you more misery than word can tell.
Come, take my hand—let me lead you to hell.
—Anonymous (a late addict who died from methamphetamine use)

LEARNING OBJECTIVES

AS A RESULT OF READING THIS CHAPTER, THE STUDENT WILL:

- KNOW THE DEFINITION OF TERRORISM, AS WELL AS ITS CATEGORIES AND TYPES, AND SOME OF THE BASIC LAW ENFORCEMENT RESPONSES TO TERRORISM

- UNDERSTAND THE BASIC FUNCTIONS OF THE NATIONAL INCIDENT MANAGEMENT SYSTEM

- KNOW THE TYPES AND ORGANIZATION OF STREET GANGS, HOW GANGS AND GRAFFITI AFFECT OUR QUALITY OF LIFE, AND SOME COMMUNITY POLICING EFFORTS THAT ARE BEING MADE TOWARD IDENTIFICATION, PREVENTION, AND SUPPRESSION OF GANG ACTIVITIES

- BE AWARE OF WHAT THE POLICE ARE DOING TO MEET THE CHALLENGES POSED BY THE DRUG PROBLEM IN AMERICA, INCLUDING METHAMPHETAMINE? CLANDESTINE DRUG LABS, OPEN-AIR DRUG MARKETS, AND RAVES

INTRODUCTION

This chapter focuses on three areas of criminality that are particularly troublesome and challenging for today's police and consume a tremendous proportion of their resources: terrorism (the structure and function of the federal Department of Homeland Security [DHS] and other federal agencies that deal with terrorism were examined in Chapter 2), gangs, and drugs. Indeed, it is almost painful to imagine the extent to which our lives would be forever changed if the police failed in their efforts in these areas. What would life be like in the United States if terrorists could radically change our form of government, our freedom of speech and religion, and other protections to be like those of Middle Eastern countries; if people could "earn" their living through wide-open, rampant gang-related activities; or if citizens could engage in unfettered drug use and trafficking? We will look at how the police are attempting to ensure that these kinds of scenarios never come to pass.

First, regarding terrorism, we examine how our nation has been transformed since 9/11. We also define terrorism and its different types, discuss the National Incident Management System that has evolved to deal with it, examine the ways that laws (the USA PATRIOT Act, the Military Commissions Act of 2006) attempt to assist in combating terrorism, and look at the dangers posed by bioterrorism. Next, we consider gangs and graffiti (what they are and how they operate), several programs for addressing them, and the relationship between gangs and terrorism. Finally, we examine the problems caused by drugs, including methamphetamine users, clandestine drug labs, open-air drug markets, and raves. A chapter summary, key terms, review questions, independent student activities, and related Web sites conclude the chapter.

Emphasis for each of these areas is placed on describing the nature of each problem, the extent of its effects on society, and several police responses for coping with each of them. A number of case studies are used to bring a real-world flavor to these problem-solving efforts, particularly through the application of the community-oriented policing and problem solving (COPPS) strategy (which was also discussed in Chapter 6).

TERRORISM

Clearly, nothing has changed the structure and function of federal law enforcement agencies as much as the events of September 11, 2001, and their aftermath. While compelled to become much more knowledgeable about terrorists' methods and how to respond in the event of an attack, at the same time our law enforcement agencies were also given a mandate to become much more strategic in their approach to their work, adopting a long-term view of **homeland security**.

A Nation Changed and Challenged

Unquestionably, historians of the future will maintain that the terrorist attacks of the early twenty-first century changed forever the nature of policing and security efforts in the United States. Words are almost inadequate to describe how the events of September 11, 2001, forever modified and heightened the fears and concerns of all Americans with regard to domestic security and the methods and technologies necessary for securing the general public.

The ongoing conflict between Israel and the Palestinians, the antigovernment narcoterrorists in several South American countries, the spread of radical Islamic fundamentalism, and our own homegrown terrorist groups strongly suggest that North

The horrifying destruction of the World Trade Center in New York City in 2001 and the Alfred P. Murrah Building in Oklahoma City in 1993 demonstrated for all Americans that terrorism is a very real threat to our security at home.

(Courtesy Bob Daemmrich, Getty Images Inc. and Brian Hayes)

Americans will face the threat of terrorism for some time to come[1] and that the local police departments are our first line of defense. Within the fifty states, there are three thousand counties and eighteen thousand cities that must be protected. The job of getting law enforcement, emergency services, public-health agencies, and private enterprises coordinated and working together at local, state, and federal levels is a daunting task.[2]

Definition and Types of Terrorism

The FBI defines **terrorism** as the "unlawful use of force against persons or property to intimidate or coerce a government, the civilian population, or any segment thereof, in furtherance of political or social objectives."[3] Terrorism can take many forms, however, and does not always involve bombs and guns. For example, the Earth Liberation Front (ELF) and a sister organization, the Animal Liberation Front, have been responsible for the majority of terrorist acts committed in the United States for several years. These ecoterrorists have burned greenhouses, tree farms, logging sites, ski resorts, and new housing developments.[4] The FBI considers ELF to be one of the nation's most prolific domestic terrorist organizations, responsible for such acts as a $12 million fire at a ski resort in Vail, Colorado, and the burning of mink farms and auto dealerships that sell sports utility vehicles in Pennsylvania.[5]

The FBI divides the current international terrorist threat into three categories[6]:

1. *Foreign sponsors of international terrorism.* Seven countries—Cuba, Iran, Iraq, Libya, North Korea, Sudan, and Syria—are designated as such sponsors and view terrorism as a tool of foreign policy. They fund, organize, network, and provide other support to formal terrorist groups and extremists.

2. *Formalized terrorist groups.* Autonomous organizations (such as bin Laden's al Qaeda, Afghanistan's Taliban, Iranian-backed Hezbollah, Egyptian Al-Gama'a Al-Islamiyya, and Palestinian HAMAS) have their own infrastructures, personnel, finances, and training facilities. Examples of this type are the al Qaeda terrorists who attacked the World Trade Center towers and the Pentagon in 2001.

3. *Loosely affiliated international radical extremists.* Examples are the persons who bombed the World Trade Center in 1993. They do not represent a particular nation but may pose the most urgent threat to the United States because they remain relatively unknown to law enforcement agencies.

Furthermore, police officers confronting terrorists in the United States now find themselves vulnerable in six types of situations[7]:

1. *Traffic stops.* Law enforcement lacks prior knowledge of the individual they are stopping; the officer may also be isolated and the extremist in a heightened state of suspicion or anger as a result of the stop.

2. *Residence visits.* Officers are on the extremists' home turf, putting the police at a disadvantage. The visit may be routine, but the extremist may not view it as such, and the home may be armed and fortified.

3. *Rallies/marches.* The risk to police usually comes not from the group holding the event but from counterprotestors, often anarchists who hate the police and who also believe the best way to confront the demonstrators is through physical violence.

4. *Confrontations/standoffs.* All types of confrontations and standoffs can arise from the three above situations.

5. *Revenge and retaliation.* A terrorist may be motivated by personal benefit or revenge. For example, a terrorist attempts to blow up an Internal Revenue Service office because he was audited.

6. *Incident responses.* These responses can take many forms depending on the type of incident, ranging from activities of terrorists to acts of nature.

Terrorist attacks in the United States are caused by both foreign and domestic terrorists. Examples of the former are the attacks in September 2001 with hijacked jetliners on the World Trade Center complex in New York City and the Pentagon in Virginia, with more than 3,000 people killed or missing, and the bombing of the World Trade Center in New York City in February 1993, killing 6 and injuring 1,000 people. An example of the latter is the April 1995 bombing of the Alfred P. Murrah Building in Oklahoma City by Timothy McVeigh, killing 168 people and injuring more than 500.[8] (McVeigh was executed in June 2001.)

A Companion Threat: Bioterrorism

The use of anthrax in the United States in late 2001 left no doubt about people's vulnerability to biological weapons and the intention of some people to develop and use them for the purpose of **bioterrorism**. Smallpox, botulism, and plague also constitute major threats, and many experts feel that it is only a matter of time before biological weapons get into the wrong hands and are used like explosives were in the past.[9]

All of this brings to mind the 1971 science fiction movie *Andromeda Strain:* A toxic agent was genetically engineered in large quantities and sprayed into the population; that agent then reproduced itself, killing many people. Today the person who controls this type of toxin could then sell it to terrorists (one has to wonder why international terrorists have not already done so). This form of terrorism can wipe out an entire civilization. All that is required is a toxin that can be cultured and put into a spray form that can be weaponized and disseminated into the population. Fortunately, they *are* extremely difficult for all but specially trained individuals to make in large quantities and in the correct dosage; they are tricky to transport because live organisms are delicate; and they must be dispersed in a proper molecule size to infect the lungs of the target. Like chemical weapons, they are also dependent on the wind and the weather and are difficult to control.[10]

The Practitioner's Perspective by Dr. Kenneth Hunter very expertly lays out the nature of bioterrorism and the role that local police would need to assume if an act of bioterrorism were to occur. Some cities, including the New York City Police Department, have developed a planned response to such a catastrophic attack, with drills and training exercises that attempt to prepare officers for their roles in getting emergency antibiotics to every resident, enforcing a quarantine, and using personal radiation detectors to check vehicles.[11]

National Incident Management System

Police have several possible means of addressing terrorism. On a broad level, there are four major aspects involved in dealing with terrorist organizations[12]:

1. Gathering raw intelligence on the organization's structure, its members, and its plans (or potential for the use of violence)
2. Determining what measures can be taken to counter or thwart terrorist activities
3. Assessing how the damage caused by terrorists can be minimized through rapid response and containment of the damage
4. Apprehending and convicting individual terrorists and dismantling their organizations

Another means of addressing domestic terrorism is military support of law enforcement. The **Posse Comitatus Act of 1878** prohibits using the military to execute the laws domestically; the military may be called on, however, to provide personnel and equipment for certain special support activities, such as domestic terrorist events involving weapons of mass destruction.[13]

Furthermore, in DHS Presidential Directive 5, *Management of Domestic Incidents,* President George W. Bush directed the DHS secretary to develop and administer a **National Incident Management System (NIMS)**. This system is to provide a consistent nationwide approach for federal, state, and local governments to work effectively together to prepare for, prevent, respond to, and recover from domestic incidents. This directive requires all federal departments and agencies to adopt the NIMS and to use it—and to make its adoption and use by state and local agencies a condition for federal preparedness assistance beginning in fiscal year 2005.[14] The NIMS is a lengthy document that cannot be duplicated here in its entirety, so the following discussion is limited to some of its primary components.

BIOTERRORISM: CHALLENGES FOR LOCAL LAW ENFORCEMENT

KENNETH W. HUNTER JR.

The use of biological agents in warfare and terrorism is not new. In 1346 after a protracted siege of Kaffa in the Crimea, the Tartars catapulted bodies of plague victims into the city with the intent of killing their adversaries.[1] During the French and Indian Wars (1754–1763), several American Indian tribes were decimated by smallpox when British troops gave them blankets from smallpox victims.[2] Ironically, these events occurred long before microorganisms were identified as the cause of plague and smallpox. In the 1930s, fleas carrying plague were released into Chinese cities by the Japanese, not to attain a strategic military advantage but to create widespread public panic.[3]

History is replete with examples of the use of biological agents as weapons. Still, few of us (including most law enforcement personnel) understand its complexity. For instance, as bad as the release of anthrax spores upwind of a large city would be, there are bioterrorism scenarios that are even more horrifying.

A wide variety of contagious microorganisms (spread by person-to-person contact) have the potential to be used by terrorists, but those listed in Table 11-1 have been suggested as the most probable.[4] However, sophisticated terrorists may have access to modern molecular biology laboratories, and the bioagents may be genetically engineered to have characteristics even more devastating than naturally occurring microorganisms (see Table 11-2). In bioterrorism with contagious agents, there would be no gunshots, no explosions, and no mass casualties in the streets. Instead, the first evidence of an attack would be increasing numbers of sick and dying individuals transported to local clinics and hospitals with a similar constellation of symptoms. With many of these biological agents, the initial symptoms would look like common illnesses (such as influenza), causing a delay in the recognition of the terrorist microorganism. Once it was recognized that an infectious agent was being transmitted in the local population, public-health officials would be notified; immediate attempts would be made to identify and characterize it, usually with the help of federal laboratories such as the Centers for Disease Control and Prevention.

At that time, local law enforcement agencies would be alerted that a possible bioterrorism attack had occurred. The time frame from initial recognition of the disease to its identification may be several days given present technology, and if the offending organism had been genetically manipulated, identification may be even more protracted. Eventually, local public-health officials working in concert with federal specialists would decide whether this is a natural epidemic or bioterrorism. The critical task for public-health officials would be to quickly identify prophylactic and therapeutic modalities to address the problem, and assistance from local police agencies in the distribution of drugs and vaccines would be needed.

As strange as it may seem, the easier forms of bioterrorism to deal with would involve the release of toxins or spores from noncontagious organisms (such as anthrax spores); spread would be limited by environmental parameters and would be local in distribution. Such terrorist attacks could have grave consequences, however. This would have an effect approaching the magnitude of a nuclear weapon.

Clearly, law enforcement agencies would have to respond to a mass casualty situation with extraordinary public panic. However, the devastation would be limited to the region inundated with the spores, perhaps several kilometers.[5] The principal tasks for law enforcement in the anthrax scenario would be to manage public panic and to prevent

TABLE 11-1

List of Some Contagious Microorganisms That Could Be Used as Bioterrorist Agents

- *Varicella major* (smallpox)
- *Yersinia pestis* (plague)
- *Franciscella tularensis* (tularemia)
- Hemorrhagic Fever Viruses (e.g., Ebola, Marburg, Lassa)

TABLE 11-2

How Bioterrorists Could Use Genetic Engineering to Produce Highly Contagious and Lethal Microorganisms

Microorganisms could be engineered to:

- contain one or more antibiotic resistance plasmids (i.e., multi-drug resistant bacteria)
- lack characteristic molecules that respond to antibodies induced by present vaccines (i.e., vaccine-resistant microorganisms)
- express lethal virulence factors like toxins (e.g., common cold viruses engineered to produce lethal botulinum toxin)
- make them more contagious
- produce disease only after a protracted incubation period, thus assuring widespread dissemination before the first clinical cases are recognized
- more easily disperse by aerosol or water and be much more stable in the environment

uninfected people from coming in contact with residual anthrax spores until the spores were decontaminated or had dissipated to noninfectious levels naturally.

On the other hand, if the terrorist attack employed highly contagious microorganisms, the primary task of law enforcement would switch to containment of the disease. While it might seem that some police resources should be devoted to catching the perpetrators, terrorists wielding biological agents could disperse them in a clandestine fashion, and these attackers could be on the other side of the world before the first signs of illness appear in the public.

Contagious disease containment of infected individuals is called quarantine,[6] a concept that goes back many centuries. Quarantine was used in the late nineteenth century to control relatively small outbreaks of contagious microorganisms, but quarantine has not been used in the United States for nearly a century,[7] and never with a large population. Even some microorganisms that spread from person to person may be of insufficient risk to warrant full-scale quarantine. If it is determined that the microorganism responsible for the initial cases is a potentially lethal terrorist weapon and is highly contagious, a decision to implement quarantine to prevent spread of the disease may be appropriate.

It should be pointed out that a bioterrorist attack with a highly contagious microorganism has the potential of expanding into a worldwide pandemic if infected individuals disperse to other locations. Though quarantine will clearly involve state and federal resources, early quarantine will be implemented at the local level; therefore local law enforcement agencies need to be aware of the array of potentially negative attributes of quarantine that may come into play.

Because there have been no actual bioterrorist attacks for American cities to deal with, there is no direct experience to draw on. Most police departments are only marginally prepared to deal with a highly contagious agent spreading in the community. Terrorist attacks using conventional explosives would probably engage an incident command system with the fire department in charge initially, followed by a command switch to local police and, finally, federal authorities (the FBI). However, the critical need to provide rapid containment of a contagious agent by limiting dispersal of infected persons would require the initial incident command structure to shift to a lead by local police, working closely with public-health officials and being supported rapidly by National Guard and federal military resources.

The first inclination of citizens in a community subjected to the release of a bioterrorist agent would be to flee. Unfortunately, there would be no way for people to know whether they were harboring the microorganism in the preclinical stage, and thus fleeing individuals must be prevented from leaving the quarantine area and infecting others.

Civil disobedience and violence against local officials have resulted from an attempt to implement quarantine in small communities.[8] Imagine how much more problematic it would be for local officials to implement an effective quarantine of a large metropolitan area. Several alternatives may be implemented short of full-scale quarantine, including widespread use of disposable masks, short-term voluntary home curfew, restriction on assembly of groups, and closure of mass transportation. Local law enforcement agencies would also need to work closely with the media, public-health organizations, and other local and state government agencies.

(continued)

During the first few days after a bioterrorist attack with a highly contagious agent, local law enforcement personnel would play a critical role in maintaining order and enforcing quarantine or other measures. Police officers would be just as susceptible to the effects of the biological agent as the public, and many would already have been exposed by the time the problem had been identified; they would justifiably be concerned for their own health. Even if police officers had protective clothing and respirators, they would know that their relatives and friends were unprotected, thus causing extraordinary stress and affecting their performance.

Finally, and most importantly, would police officers be able to use the force necessary to maintain quarantine, knowing that infected individuals leaving the local area could transmit the disease and potentially cause the deaths of millions?

1. V. J. Derbes, "De Mussis and the Great Plague of 1348: A Forgotten Episode of Bacteriological Warfare," *Journal of the American Medical Association* 196 (1996): 59–62.

2. E. A. Fenn, "Biological Warfare in Eighteenth-Century North America: Beyond Jeffrey Amherst," *Journal of American History* 86 (2000): 1552–1580.

3. S. Harris, "Japanese Biological Warfare Research on Humans: A Case Study of Microbiology and Ethics," *Annals of the New York Academy of Science* 666 (1992): 21–52.

4. D. A. Henderson, T. V. Inglesby, and T. O'Toole (eds.), *Bioterrorism: Guidelines for Medical and Public Health Management* (Chicago: American Medical Association Press, 2002).

5. J. Simon, "Biological Terrorism: Preparing to Meet the Threat," *Journal of the American Medical Association* 278 (1997): 428–430.

6. P. S. Sehdev, "The Origin of Quarantine," *Clinical Infectious Diseases* 35 (2002): 1071–1072.

7. H. Cumming, "The United States Quarantine System during the Past 50 Years," in *A Half Century of Public Health*, ed. M. Ravenel (New York: American Public Health Association, 1921), pp. 118–132.

8. W. Eidson, "Confusion, Controversy, and Quarantine: The Muncie Smallpox Epidemic of 1893," *Indiana Magazine of History* 86 (1990): 74–398.

(Kenneth W. Hunter Jr., Sc.D., is a professor of microbiology and immunology at the University of Nevada School of Medicine. Dr. Hunter served for eleven years as vice president for research and as dean of the graduate school at the University of Nevada, Reno. He received a doctor of science degree in immunology from Johns Hopkins University in 1978, and for over twenty years he has done research and published scientific articles on the diagnosis and treatment of exposure to toxic chemicals, biological toxins, and infectious microorganisms. His experience includes research and consultation in chemical and biological warfare for the U.S. Army Medical Research Institute for Chemical Defense [Edgewood Arsenal, MD] and the U.S. Army Medical Research Institute for Infectious Disease [Ft. Detrick, MD].)

COMMAND AND MANAGEMENT: INCIDENT COMMAND SYSTEM (ICS)   The Incident Command System (ICS) was created to coordinate response personnel from more than one agency or teams from more than one jurisdiction and has been adopted to help local police agencies respond to terrorist incidents. A key strength of ICS is its unified command component, which is composed of four sections: operations, planning, logistics, and finance. Under ICS, all agencies go to the same location and establish a unified command post.[15] The most critical period of time for controlling a crisis is those initial moments when first responders arrive at the scene. They must quickly contain the situation, analyze the extent of the crisis, request additional resources and special teams if needed, and communicate available information and intelligence to higher headquarters. Their initial actions provide a vital link to the total police response and will often determine its outcome.

Next we briefly review the five major functions of ICS—command, operations, planning, logistics, and finance/administration:

1. *Command.* The command staff is responsible for overall management of the incident. When an incident occurs within a single jurisdiction without any overlap, a single incident commander should be designated with overall incident management responsibility to develop the objectives on which an actual action plan will be based. The unified command (UC) concept is used in multijurisdictional or multiagency incidents to provide guidelines for agencies with different legal, geographic, and functional responsibilities to coordinate, plan, and interact effectively. The composition of the UC will depend on the location(s) and type of incident.

2. *Operations.* The operations section is responsible for all activities focused on reducing immediate hazards, saving lives and property, establishing control of the situation, and restoring normal operations. Resources for this section might include specially trained single-agency personnel and equipment, and even special task forces and strike teams.

3. *Planning.* The planning section collects, evaluates, and disseminates incident situation information and intelligence to the incident commander or UC, prepares status reports, displays situation information, and maintains status of resources assigned to the incident.

4. *Logistics.* The logistics section is responsible for all support requirements needed to facilitate effective incident management: facilities, transportation, supplies, equipment maintenance and fuel, food services, communications and technology support, and emergency medical services.

5. *Finance/administration.* The finance/administration section is not required at all incidents but will be involved where incident management activities require finance and other administrative support services such as compensation/claims, determination of costs, and procurement. Law enforcement executives should also create budget line-item codes and emergency purchase orders before such an event so that they will be readily available and accessible.

INITIAL DUTIES AND RESPONSIBILITIES   The following checklist provides some of the necessary information for quickly assessing the personnel, equipment, and other resources needed during the initial stages of any critical incident[16]:

1. What is the exact nature and size of the incident?
2. What are the location's characteristics and its surroundings?
3. Are there dangers present to persons and property, such as armed suspects, fires, or hazardous materials?
4. Are there any unusual circumstances, such as snipers, explosives, or broken utilities present?
5. Is there a need to evacuate, and are antilooting measures required?
6. Is traffic control needed?
7. Are additional personnel needed for inner and outer perimeter management, evacuation, rescue, special weapons and tactics (SWAT), and negotiators, and are any other specialists needed?
8. Will a command post (CP) and staging area for additional personnel and emergency support be needed?

9. What emergency equipment and personnel are needed, and what safe routes are available for their response to the staging area?

10. What are the other needs (food and drink for long-term incidents, tactical units, rescue operations, bomb squad, K-9, tow trucks)?

MULTIAGENCY COORDINATION SYSTEMS   A multiagency coordination system is a combination of facilities, equipment, personnel, procedures, and communications integrated into a common system to coordinate and support domestic incident management activities. Multiagency coordination systems may contain emergency operations centers (EOCs), which represent the physical location at which the coordination of information and resources to support incident management activities normally takes place. An incident command post (ICP) located at or in the immediate vicinity of an incident site, although primarily focused on the tactical on-scene response, may perform an EOC-like function in smaller-scale incidents or during the initial phase of the response to larger, more complex events. For complex incidents, EOCs may be staffed by personnel representing multiple jurisdictions and functional disciplines; for example, a bioterrorism incident would likely include a mix of law enforcement, emergency management, public-health, and medical personnel.

PUBLIC INFORMATION SYSTEMS   Public information systems refer to processes, procedures, and systems for communicating timely and accurate information to the public during crisis or emergency situations. The answer to the question "How much do we tell the public?" is a simple one: You tell them everything that does not need to be safeguarded for valid reasons of security. Openness and candor are essential, and keeping the public informed will render good results.[17] Teamwork between personnel of different agencies is also key before and after an incident, especially in those circumstances where there are many radio frequencies and institutional policies in play (the ICS, discussed above, can be of assistance here).[18]

PREPAREDNESS   The issue of preparedness can be divided into six areas:

1. *Plans.* Plans describe how personnel, equipment, and other resources are used to support incident management and incident response activities. They provide mechanisms and systems for setting priorities, integrating multiple entities and functions, and ensuring that communications and other systems are available.

2. *Training.* Training includes standard courses on multiagency incident command and management, organizational structure, and operational procedures, as well as the use of supporting technologies.

3. *Exercises.* Incident management organizations and personnel must participate in realistic exercises—including those of a multijurisdictional nature—to improve integration and interoperability and to optimize resource utilization during incident operations.

4. *Personnel qualifications and certification.* It is important to remember that "experts are called experts for a reason," so a terrorist attack or other critical incident might involve local funeral directors, dentists, physicians, biochemists, bomb experts, crane operators, and many others.[19]

5. *Equipment acquisition and certification.* Incident organizations and personnel at all levels rely on various types of equipment to perform their missions; the acquisition

of equipment that will perform to certain standards as well as operate with similar equipment used by other jurisdictionsis critical.

6. *Mutual aid.* Interagency mutual aid agreements are essential for responding to attacks and disasters. They allow for the sharing of resources among participating agencies and the establishment of clear policies concerning command and control when an attack or a disaster occurs. Few agencies have the capability of handling a major tactical incident alone and must rely on the assistance of larger neighboring metropolitan agencies, county sheriff's departments, state agencies, and federal agencies for assistance.[20]

Legislative Measures

USA PATRIOT ACT   A number of new investigative measures were provided to federal law enforcement agencies through the enactment of the **USA PATRIOT Act** shortly after the 9/11 attacks. The act dramatically expanded the federal government's ability to investigate Americans without establishing probable cause for "intelligence purposes" and to conduct searches if there are "reasonable grounds to believe" there may be national security threats. Federal agencies such as the Federal Bureau of Investigation (FBI) and others are given access to financial, mental health, medical, library, and other records.[21] The act was reauthorized in March 2006, providing additional tools for protecting mass transportation systems and seaports from attack, taking steps to combat the methamphetamine epidemic, closing loopholes in our ability to prevent terrorist financing, and creating a National Security Division at the Department of Justice. Among the new version's more controversial provisions are the "roving wiretap" portion and the "sneak and peek" section. The first allows the government to get a wiretap on every phone a suspect uses, while the second allows federal investigators to get access to library, business, and medical records without a court order.[22]

Using a mobile truck X-ray, a seaport container is checked for contraband.

(Courtesy U.S. Customs and Border Protection, photographer James Tourtellotte)

The USA PATRIOT Act has not been without its critics. Because of the broad language the act contains and because of what it permits federal agents to do, many fear that these new governmental powers will be abused or that the act will become a "permanent fixture" in our legal system.[23] Critics also bemoan the fact that federal agents are using the act in cases that "have nothing to do with terrorism"; an example cited is the act's money-laundering language, which allows the government to search every financial institution in the country for the records of suspected terrorists.[24] Furthermore, the treatment of Arab-Americans since 9/11 has been termed a form of "persecution," as many of those under scrutiny have been fingerprinted, photographed, detained, and deported under the act's mandatory registration program. Tensions have also been raised among Arab-Americans and Muslims because hate crimes against them have increased dramatically after 9/11.[25] Still, Americans seem more willing to sacrifice civil liberties in the interest of homeland security and to allow the government to use "every legal means" at its disposal to prevent further terrorist activity.[26]

MILITARY COMMISSIONS ACT OF 2006   The fight against terrorism was also aided and expanded in October 2006 when President George W. Bush signed Public Law 109-366, the **Military Commissions Act (MCA)** of 2006, which he hailed as "one of the most important pieces of legislation in the War on Terror."[27] Under the MCA, the president is authorized to establish military commissions to try unlawful enemy combatants, the commissions are authorized to sentence defendants to death, and defendants are prevented from invoking the Geneva Conventions as a source of rights during commission proceedings. The law contains a provision stripping detainees of the right to file *habeas corpus* petitions in federal court and also allows hearsay evidence to be admitted during proceedings, so long as the presiding officer determines it to be reliable. This law allows the Central Intelligence Agency (CIA) to continue its program for questioning key terrorist leaders and operatives—a program felt by many to be one of the most successful intelligence efforts in American history. The MCA excludes all statements obtained by use of torture, makes U.S. interrogators subject to only a limited range of "grave breaches," and clarifies what actions would subject interrogators to liability under the existing federal War Crimes Act.[28]

Exhibit 11-1 shows how COPPS can help to address terrorism.

STREET GANGS

Definition and Extent of the Problem

A **street gang** is an association of individuals who have a gang name and recognizable symbols, a geographic territory, a regular meeting pattern, and an organized, continuous course of criminality.[29] Street gang activity was first recognized in the early 1900s in the southern California area. Indeed, a major study of gangs in 1927 found that most gangs were small (six to twenty members), that they formed spontaneously in poor and socially disorganized neighborhoods, and that they were the result of disintegration of family life, inefficiency of schools, formalism and externality of religion, corruption and indifference

EXHIBIT 1 1-1

COPPS and Homeland Defense

When a police officer is responding to a call for service and observes a container with fifty gallons of chlorine in a corner of a garage but no swimming pool in the backyard, would he or she know what to do with that information? When emergency medical services personnel are on a call and observe five passports from different countries all bearing the same photograph on the kitchen table, would they know whom to contact?

Information is the lifeblood of contemporary policing, and homeland security begins with the police collecting information at the neighborhood level. This is critical, so first responders need to know how to cultivate information: what information to look for, how to collect it, and where to send it. Training of first responders in this area reduces the information gap between police and other services and must be embraced by each agency's management in order to be effective.

There are numerous community information sources. Following are some of them as well as the kinds of information they might provide:

- Business owners (information about purchasers of dangerous materials such as torches, propane, and blasting supplies)
- Transportation centers and tourist attractions (information about suspicious persons and activities)
- Sellers of licenses and permits (information about persons seeking licenses and permits for handguns, other firearms, liquor, blasting materials, and so on)

- Delivery services (information from letter carriers, couriers, and delivery drivers who observe suspicious activities and packages)
- Colleges and universities (information about possession of hazardous materials, foreign exchange students, controversial speakers and research, and questionable events)
- Real estate agents (information on suspicious activities and locations of wanted persons and undocumented residents)
- Storage unit managers (information on explosive or hazardous materials that could be connected to terrorist or criminal activity)
- Hotel clerks and security officers (information on suspicious guests)

Furthermore, while traumatic events such as the 9/11 attacks might possibly cause police organizations to revert back to more traditional methods—or even to abandon COPPS for more seemingly pedestrian security-oriented concerns—COPPS should play a central role in the defense of our homeland. Because COPPS helps to build trust between police and their communities, deals more effectively with community concerns, and helps the police to develop knowledge of community activities, the problem-solving model is well suited to the prevention of terrorism. Departments can also use a wide variety of data sources to proactively develop detailed risk management and crisis response plans.

Source: Adapted from Rob Chapman and Matthew C. Scheider, "Community Policing: Now More Than Ever," http://www.cops.usdoj.gov/default.asp?Item=716 (accessed April 29, 2003).

---

in local politics, low wages and monotony in occupational activities, unemployment, and lack of opportunity for wholesome recreation.[30] This explanation of causes of gang affiliation still applies in large measure today.

Gangs are comprised of three types of persons: (1) hardcores (members who commit violent acts and defend the reputation of the gang), (2) associates (members who frequently affiliate with known gang members for status and recognition but who move in and out on the basis of interest in gang functions), and (3) peripherals (persons who are not gang members but who identify with gang members, usually from the dominant gang in their neighborhood, for protection). Most females fall into this latter category.

There are several levels of gun-toting "gang-bangers" wanting to earn their stripes. The "wannabe" begins by having target practice and handling the guns; he or she may shoot but doesn't actually aim. The next level is the gang-involved youth who wants a tough reputation; he or she will eventually kill somebody but is not seen as a hardcore crazy person. When a teenager reaches that level—the crazed killer—he or she doesn't care about him- or herself or the victims; his or her violence is random and cold-blooded. Gang members usually join the gang by either committing a crime or undergoing an initiation procedure. Members use automatic weapons and sawed-off shotguns in violent drive-by shootings, are becoming more sophisticated in their criminal activities, and are becoming wealthier.

According to U.S. Justice Department estimates,[31] there are more than sixteen thousand gangs and over a half million gang members in the United States. Nearly half of all gang members (47.8 percent) are African-American youth, while Hispanic youngsters accounted for 42.7 percent and Asians totaled 5.2 percent.[32] (Specific types of ethnic and racial gangs are discussed below.)

Gangs can have a significantly damaging effect on a community; they play a role in firearms transactions and violence, drug sales and use, home invasions, car thefts, homicides, graffiti (discussed below), and a number of other crime problems. Their members are becoming younger. Most research on youth gangs in the United States has concluded that the most typical age range of gang members has been approximately fourteen to twenty-four; researchers are aware of gang members as young as ten years of age, however, and in some areas (such as southern California, where some Latino gangs originated more than a hundred years ago), one can find several generations in the same family who are gang members, with active members in their thirties. Youngsters generally begin hanging out with gangs at twelve or thirteen years of age, join the gang at thirteen or fourteen, and are first arrested at fourteen.[33]

Crips, Bloods, MS-13, and Public Enemy No. 1

The most prominent African-American gangs are the Crips and the Bloods. The Crips began in Los Angeles in 1969, reportedly on the campus of Washington High School, as *Community Resources for an Independent People*; one of the school's colors was blue, which is now the color of gang identification. Another popular belief is that the name derives from "crypt," from the then-popular *Tales from the Crypt* horror movie. Crips address each other with the nickname "Cuzz." Crips graffiti can be identified by the symbol "B/K," that stands for "Blood Killers." The Bloods are reported to have formed in and near Compton, California, as a means of protection against the Crips. Bloods use the color red and address each other as "Blood." Gang graffiti (discussed more fully below) frequently uses the terms "BS" for "Bloodstone" and "C/K" for "Crips Killers." Both Crips and Bloods refer to fellow gang members as "homeboys" or "homeys."[34]

One of the most rapidly spreading, well-organized, and deadly gangs in the United States is Mara Salvatrucha 13, or MS-13. Named for La Mara (a street in San Salvador) and for the Salvatrucha guerillas who fought in El Salvador's bloody civil war, it was organized in Los Angeles in the late 1980s. Its initial purpose was to defend Salvadoran immigrants from being preyed upon by other Los Angeles street gangs. But like any other street gang that was created to defend a particular ethnic group, MS-13 was quickly perverted until its primary purpose was preying on the Salvadoran community. Gang members sometimes wear blue and white, colors taken from the national flag of El Salvador. However, once the police recognize and confront them, they will change and wear different colors; their MS-13 tattoos may also be changed to 67 or 76, as those numbers equal 13.[35]

This gang plague recently came to Los Angeles from El Salvador and moved eastward to New York where its members united to form affiliated groups up and down the East Coast. The senseless violence of MS-13 has shocked Americans, and the police are trying to find ways to deal with it. This is one characteristic that sets MS-13 apart: While some gangs are only into drugs, MS-13 will do any crime at any time.[36]

Another violent gang whose membership is growing in number and that poses an extraordinary degree of danger for the police is Public Enemy No. 1, whose deeds include compiling a hit list of five California officers and a gang prosecutor. This gang traces its roots to the punk rock subculture in Long Beach, California, in the 1980s; it is very violent and deals in drugs, guns, and identity theft. Public Enemy No. 1 has also forged an alliance with the notorious Aryan Brotherhood, a long-standing, highly violent, and dominant white supremacist gang that operates behind bars. The pact between these two has increased Public Enemy No. 1's wealth and recruiting power. Its identity theft activities include stealing credit profiles with the help of girlfriends and wives who take jobs at banks, mortgage companies, and even state motor vehicle departments. Money from these operations is used to fund its methamphetamine business. Authorities worry that Public Enemy No. 1 is using stolen credit card information to learn the addresses of police and their families; some officers have gone to court to have addresses removed from those records.[37]

Graffiti and Hand Signals

In addition to the aforementioned array of problems caused by gangs, another debilitating problem that is inextricably tied to and flows from gang activities is **graffiti**. In addition to being unsightly and a general source of irritation, graffiti incites gang violence, depreciates property values, adds to the deterioration of neighborhoods, and contributes to economic and urban blight.

In the United States, the annual cost of graffiti is estimated to be between $10 billion and $12 billion. In New York City alone, the average cost of removing graffiti has increased from $300,000 to about $10 million. In a ten-year period, Los Angeles removed 162 million square feet of graffiti. A graffiti-removal worker painting over a wall was fatally shot in Los Angeles in June 2004 by a man who police believe was angry because his gang's tags were being covered.[38]

Like New York and Los Angeles, most cities fight graffiti with their paintbrushes, by quickly dispatching work crews to put on a fresh coat of paint over tagger or gang scribblings. Some experts, however, advocate photographing and filing graffiti markings because they represent actual communication and can be a valuable source of intelligence.

Five types of graffiti communication have been identified by researchers[39]:

1. *Publicity graffiti.* The most frequently found form of graffiti—47 percent—publicizes the name or abbreviation of the gang but does not make a threat or mark territory.

2. *Roll call graffiti.* Roll call graffiti (26 percent) identifies the gang name and a list of gang monikers (member nicknames).
3. *Territorial graffiti.* Territorial graffiti (17 percent) is identified by some sort of marking of a gang's territory, often in the form of an arrow pointing down.
4. *Threatening graffiti.* Threatening graffiti makes up 9 percent and contains some sort of threatening message aimed at a rival gang or perhaps at the police. It can result from a gang member crossing out another gang's graffiti.
5. *Sympathetic graffiti.* The least observed form (1 percent), sympathetic graffiti is used to honor a slain gang member, usually in the form of an RIP (rest in peace) message.

Some cities have also enacted ordinances that require property owners to remove graffiti within a specified period of time. For example, in St. Petersburg, Florida, business owners are required to remove graffiti within 48 hours; in other areas the city will paint over the graffiti for a set fee, usually $50 to $75. Furthermore, five states (Arizona, California, Massachusetts, Rhode Island, and Texas) now have laws that ban spray paint sales to minors, and Chicago bans spray paint sales to the public altogether.[40]

Chicano gangs use a nonverbal communication that has existed for over fifty years. This method, called a placa, allows Chicano gang members to "talk" about themselves, their gang, and other gangs and to direct challenges to others. A full placa expresses the gang's opinion of itself, its control of the area, and a warning that other gangs are helpless to do anything about it. An example of a full placa is given in Figure 11-1, with the translation given at the right (the actual graffiti would be written in unique gang style). Figure 11-2 provides a guide to reading gang graffiti.

FIGURE 11-1
A Full Placa (Chicano Gang Graffiti)

Graffiti	Translation
-EZ	He or She (El or La)
WINO	Moniker (Wino)
DE	From (De)
ZOS CHICOS	The gang name (Los Chicos)
-R-	I'm the best
C/S	There is nothing you can do about it (C/S)
ZOS NEIGHBORHOOD	Gang (Los Neighborhood)
TOTAZ	United (Total)
CONTROZZA	Controls (Controlla)
-R	We're the best

FIGURE 11-2
Guide to Reading Gang Graffiti

1. Barrio or Varrio
   Meaning Neighborhood
   or Group/Clique

   B H G R
   PQS
   -13-
   L's

2. The "HG" Meaning
   Hawaiian Gardens City
   and Gang/Clique

   B H G R
   PQS
   -13-
   L's

3. The Letter "R" Meant to
   Be "RIFA" Meaning Rule,
   Reign, or Control

   B H G R
   PQS
   -13-
   L's

4. The actual gang group
   abbreviation of "PQS"
   "PEQUENOS" from Hawaiian
   Gardens (normally younger
   groups, e.g., Chicos, Midgets, or Tiny's)

   B H G R
   PQS
   -13-
   L's

5. The Number "13"* stands
   for "SUR" meaning
   Southern California

   B H G R
   PQS
   -13-
   L's

6. The letter "L" or "L's"
   is used to mean the Vato
   Locos or the Crazy Ones/
   Brave Ones (not normally
   a separate gang or clique)

   B H G R
   PQS
   -13-
   L's

*The number 13 is sometimes used by younger gang members to mean marijuana.

Hand signals, or "throwing signs," are made by forming letters or numbers with the hands and fingers, depicting the gang symbol or initials. This allows the gang member to show which gang he or she belongs to and issues challenges to other gangs in the vicinity. Figure 11-3 shows some examples of hand signals as they are commonly used in the western United States.

Police agencies in jurisdictions experiencing gang problems must develop expertise in gang movements, activities, and all forms of nonverbal communication. Police have also developed intelligence files on known or suspected gang members.

Obviously something more is needed than police work alone to break the cycle of gang delinquency. In too many communities, gang violence is tolerated as long as gang members victimize each other and do not bother the rest of society.[41] Without community support, the contemporary cycle of youth gang activities will continue; even gang members who are imprisoned join branches of their gang behind bars while replacements are found to take their place on the street.[42]

FIGURE 11-3
Gang Hand Signals

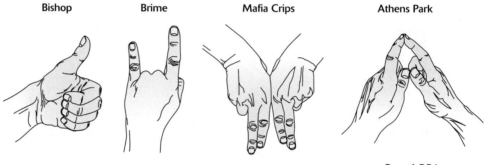

Pird Sign   Kitchen Crip   Bounty Hunters   Crips

"Blood"

Bishop   Brime   Mafia Crips   Athens Park

Boys A.P.B.'s

Across the country, many cities have responded to their gang problems by forming some type of special unit—often suppression oriented—as an initial response to major episodes of gang violence.[43] Today about two-thirds of all large cities in the United States having more than two hundred thousand citizens have a specialized gang intelligence unit (GIU), while about half of all other cities have such a unit.[44] These GIUs identify the core members of the gangs and target them for enforcement. Intelligence is collected by questioning suspected gang members who are arrested and talking with rival gang members and with residents in gang neighborhoods. At the same time, officers collect information on gang activities, monitor graffiti, collect information on assaults and homicides of gang members by rival gangs, and observe disputes involving drug sales. They have also enhanced collaboration with agencies external to the police agency (schools, local code enforcement agencies, probation agencies, community groups, and so on).[45]

Over time, however, many police agencies have shifted from an emphasis on suppression to an emphasis on education. A well-known police response to gangs is the Gang Resistance Education and Training (GREAT) program, which originated in 1991 in Phoenix, Arizona. GREAT emphasizes the acquisition of information and skills needed by students to resist peer pressure and gang influences; the curriculum contains nine-hour lessons offered to middle school students, mostly seventh-graders.

A fundamental question to ask is this: How do we as a society replace the gang's social importance and financial benefits (with children "earning" literally hundreds of dollars a day in drug-related activities) with education or work programs that pay minimum wage? This is a complex issue with no simple answers.

Police Responses

As discussed above, street gangs obviously have a significant damaging effect on a community. Their involvement in firearms transactions and violence, drug sales and use, home invasions, car thefts, homicides, and a number of other crime problems severely affects the quality of life of people in the gangs' neighborhoods and communities.

To address gangs, police agencies must first attempt a problem analysis using the scanning, analysis, response, and assessment (SARA) process (discussed in Chapter 6). This initial step is particularly important because no "cookie-cutter" approach will work. Gangs are unique phenomena, particular to time and place, and failing to undertake a problem analysis of the crime problems at hand and the general gang landscape will likely result in a futile response strategy.[46]

Four Types of Programs

The options available to the police when attempting to address a street gang problem exist on a large spectrum with regard to both goals and tactics. Following are four types of programs that represent the range of activities that exist for this purpose[47]:

1. *Prevention programs.* The prevention programs have the broadest audience of interest and are typically aimed at groups that pose some risk or, more broadly, at general populations. For example, a prevention program may focus on preschool children who reside in gang neighborhoods before they show any symptoms of having joined the gang life. Perhaps the best known of these programs is GREAT. Although evaluation results of GREAT show no long-term impact on gang membership or delinquent behavior, they suggest positive short-term effects on gang-related behavior and attitudes.

2. *Intervention programs.* The intervention programs typically address individuals or places that have manifested some problem. In most cases, such programs attempt to persuade gang members or gang-affiliated youth to abandon their current lifestyle or to reduce gang-related crime. At this stage, defining the type of gang of interest and the level of individual involvement in the gang, as well as the specific problem of focus, becomes extremely important and integral to any success. Interventions may include a gang truce or the use of nonmembers to persuade gang members to leave gang life.

3. *Suppression programs.* The suppression programs also have the aim of reducing gang activities but typically rely on the law as a guide and on criminal justice agencies as the primary (and often only) partner. Deterrence principles often include law enforcement task forces or units and sentencing enhancements. Their success hinges on developing a plan based on a problem analysis to understand the gang problem in the jurisdiction. When operating alone, however, suppression tactics are rarely successful in the long term. Even if a program appears successful in the short term, gangs tend to endure because the police can rarely eradicate them completely, nor do the police have the resources to sustain such an intensive focus over time and across all gangs and gang members. In addition, crime may simply be displaced. Suppression tactics are important but appear to provide the most benefit when part of a larger comprehensive program.

EXHIBIT 11-2

"Designing Out" Gangs

"Designing out" gang homicides and street assaults has been successful in Los Angeles. When a systematic pattern of opportunity was
found—that the majority of drive-by shootings and violent gang
encounters occurred in clusters on the periphery of neighborhoods
linked to major thoroughfares—police closed all major roads leading
to and from the identified hot spots by placing cement freeway
dividers at the ends of streets that led directly to these roads. An evaluation determined that blocking opportunities reduced homicides and
street assaults significantly and that crime was not displaced to other
areas.

Source: Adapted from James Lasley, *"Designing Out" Gang Homicides and Street Assaults* (Washington, DC: U.S. Department of Justice, National Institute of Justice Research in Brief, November 1998), pp. 1–4.

An example of a suppression tactic is shown in Exhibit 11-2.

4. *Comprehensive programs.* The comprehensive programs typically include prevention, intervention, and suppression techniques and hinge on the collaborative work of a variety of agencies, from criminal justice, to social services, to
mental health, to faith-based groups. Though they often require intensive
resources and time, such programs appear to have the most promise in areas that
have an array of problems surrounding a gang problem and fit well within an
existing COPPS philosophy. In addition, should a particular gang pose numerous problems, such as intense gang recruitment in schools, drug sales, and gang-
related homicides, it may require a variety of techniques and partners to address
the issues. Perhaps the best-known comprehensive program is Boston's Operation Ceasefire project (described in Chapter 12, Exhibit 12-2).

Mediation of a Peace Agreement

Another innovative approach to gang behavior was developed in San Mateo, California. When gang violence spread because of seven years of warfare between two opposing gangs that involved shootings, stabbings, car bombings, and murders, a detective
enlisted the support of a local volunteer mediation agency as well as that of the probation department (due to its court-ordered guardianship over many of the seasoned gang
members). The detective also requested a juvenile court judge to waive the nonassoci-
ation clause, which was a condition of most gang members' probation, so that they
could meet without fear of court-ordered sanctions. The mediation service arranged
for separate meetings with the two rival gangs to be held in a neutral place. Three mediators, two probation officers, and the detective also attended. The groups talked about
respect, community racism, and the police; the idea of a truce was raised, but the two
gangs' leaders scoffed at the idea. The mediators met individually with each gang four
more times; both sides seemed tired of the ongoing violence and finally agreed to meet
together again. Each gang selected five members as spokesmen who brought a list of

items to be addressed; respect was at the top of both lists. An agreement for peace was eventually reached and handshakes were exchanged; all agreed to a follow-up meeting, where forty-one gang members agreed to a truce that stated there would be no more violence. They agreed to respect each other; if a confrontation arose, they would try to talk through it as opposed to using weapons. In the four years following implementation of the program, there were no reports of violence between the two gangs.[48]

Gangs and Terrorism

While the relationship between gangs and terrorism is hardly studied and little understood, there are links between the two that demand further investigation. First, some gangs share with terrorists the inclination toward the use of violence to achieve political and economic ends. Some have even suggested that "urban terrorism," in which aggressive gangs dominate the social lives of some American neighborhoods, is a more tangible and daily threat to societal safety than the specter of foreign terrorism. In this sense, then, gang activity could be regarded as a subset of terrorist threats that should be addressed.

Second, there might be physical links between street gangs. For example, there is evidence that Sri Lankan ethnic gangs in Toronto might be funneling funds to terrorist operations[49]; there is also evidence of an intersection between drug and terrorist operations in Latin America and the Middle East. Traffickers might benefit from terrorist organizations' security assurances, while the terrorists can funnel drug money for operations.[50] Third, gang members and terrorists might be drawn from similar ranks of disaffected youths who are either subconsciously or ideologically convinced that the existing social order has betrayed or exploited them and who could see participation in deviant groups as a means to lash out against it.

Still, it is too early to assume a definitive link between gangs and terrorist groups. The most sophisticated terror networks, such as al Qaeda, might not yet find marginalized Westerners to be promising recruits. At this point, it seems that the gang-terrorism connection is one that should not be ignored but should be evaluated and addressed with caution.[51]

OUR NATION'S NIGHTMARE: DRUGS

Societal Conundrum

That the United States is in the throes of a grave drug problem is beyond doubt: About 1.75 million U.S. citizens are arrested for drug violations per year.[52] That amount reflects only the tip of the iceberg in comparison to the actual levels of drug manufacturing, using, and trafficking. The social costs of **drug abuse** are inestimable; however, we know that drug violations have eroded the environment, created undesirable role models for many youth, given rise to a wide variety of related criminal acts, and resulted in innumerable gun-wielding gang members across the United States who are fighting to expand their turf.

Alcohol and drugs together are also major factors in crime and violence, with almost four in ten violent crimes involving alcohol. Half of convicted jail inmates were high on drugs or alcohol at the time of the offense that landed them in jail, and three out of every four convicted jail inmates were somehow involved with alcohol or drugs at the time of their current offense.[53]

Furthermore, as shown in Table 11-3 (the numbers of persons in state prisons by offense, gender, race, and origin) and Table 11-4 (the percentages of those persons), of the 1,256,400 total prisoners in state institutions, 250,900 of them (20 percent) are in prison for drug offenses (19.3 percent of the male prisoners and 29.1 percent of the females). The

TABLE 11-3

Estimated Number of Sentenced Prisoners under State Jurisdiction, by Offense, Gender, Race, and Hispanic Origin

Offense	All Inmates	Male	Female	White[a]	Black[a]	Hispanic
Total	1,256,400	1,173,600	82,800	453,400	562,100	219,200
Violent offenses	650,400	621,600	28,800	227,100	294,000	116,600
Murder[b]	151,500	142,800	8,700	46,900	72,200	28,600
Manslaughter	17,700	15,900	1,800	7,100	7,600	2,600
Rape	61,300	60,800	500	31,500	21,900	6,700
Other sexual assault	87,500	86,300	1,200	49,300	20,000	16,600
Robbery	176,600	169,600	7,000	39,500	106,300	28,300
Assault	124,200	116,900	7,300	40,000	53,400	28,100
Other violent crimes	31,700	29,300	2,400	12,700	12,600	5,600
Property offenses	262,000	237,100	24,900	120,100	100,700	37,200
Burglary	137,600	132,100	5,500	61,000	53,600	21,000
Larceny	49,000	41,200	7,800	21,900	20,400	6,000
Motor vehicle theft	20,600	19,500	1,100	8,200	7,000	4,900
Fraud	30,400	21,700	8,700	16,700	11,100	2,100
Other property crimes	24,400	22,600	1,800	12,300	8,600	3,100
Drug offenses	250,900	226,800	24,100	64,800	133,100	50,100
Public-order offenses[c]	86,400	82,000	4,400	38,500	31,800	14,100
Other/unspecified[d]	6,800	6,200	600	2,900	2,500	1,200

Note: Data are for inmates with a sentence of more than 1 year under the jurisdiction of state correctional authorities. The numbers of inmates by gender were based on jurisdiction counts at year-end (NPS-1); numbers by race and Hispanic origin were based on data from the 2004 Survey of Inmates in State Correctional Facilities; and numbers within each category by offense were estimated using the National Corrections Reporting Program, 2003.

All estimates were rounded to the nearest 100. Detail may not add to total due to rounding.

[a]Excludes Hispanics.

[b]Includes nonnegligent manslaughter.

[c]Includes weapons, drunk driving, court offenses, commercialized vice, morals and decency charges, liquor law violations, and other public-order offenses.

[d]Includes juvenile offenses and unspecified felonies.

Source: U.S. Department of Justice, Bureau of Justice Statistics, *Prisoners in 2005* (Washington, DC: Author, November 2006), p. 9.

TABLE 11-4

Estimated Percent of Sentenced Prisoners under State Jurisdiction, by Offense, Gender, Race, and Hispanic Origin

Offense	All Inmates	Male	Female	White[a]	Black[a]	Hispanic
Total	100%	100%	100%	100%	100%	100%
Violent offenses	51.8%	53.0%	34.8%	50.1%	52.3%	53.2%
Murder[b]	12.1	12.2	10.5	10.4	12.8	13.0
Manslaughter	1.4	1.4	2.2	1.6	1.4	1.2
Rape	4.9	5.2	0.6	7.0	3.9	3.1
Other sexual assault	7.0	7.4	1.4	10.9	3.6	7.6
Robbery	14.1	14.4	8.4	8.7	18.9	12.9
Assault	9.9	10.0	8.8	8.8	9.5	12.8
Other violent crimes	2.5	2.5	2.9	2.8	2.2	2.5
Property offenses	20.9%	20.2%	30.0%	26.5%	17.9%	17.0%
Burglary	11.0	11.3	6.6	13.5	9.5	9.6
Larceny	3.9	3.5	9.4	4.8	3.6	2.7
Motor vehicle theft	1.6	1.7	1.3	1.8	1.3	2.3
Fraud	2.4	1.8	10.5	3.7	2.0	1.0
Other property crimes	1.9	1.9	2.2	2.7	1.5	1.4
Drug offenses	20.0%	19.3%	29.1%	14.3%	23.7%	22.9%
Public-order offenses[c]	6.9%	7.0%	5.3%	8.5%	5.7%	6.4%
Other/unspecified[d]	0.5%	0.5%	0.8%	0.6%	0.4%	0.5%

Note: Data are for inmates with a sentence of more than 1 year under the jurisdiction of state correctional authorities. Detail may not add to total due to rounding.

[a]Excludes Hispanics.

[b]Includes nonnegligent manslaughter.

[c]Includes weapons, drunk driving, court offenses, commercialized vice, morals and decency charges, liquor law violations, and other public-order offenses.

[d]Includes juvenile offenses and unspecified felonies.

Source: U.S. Department of Justice, Bureau of Justice Statistics, *Prisoners in 2005* (Washington, DC: Author, November 2006), p. 9.

figures are even more stark when viewed by race: Drug offenses are the reason that 23.7 percent of blacks, 14.3 percent of whites, and 22.9 percent of Hispanics are in state prisons.[54]

Drugs are clearly related to criminality in multiple ways. Most directly, it is a crime to use, possess, manufacture, or distribute drugs classified as having potential for abuse, but drugs are also related to crime through the effects they have on the user's behavior and because they generate violence and other illegal activity in connection with drug trafficking. Now **methamphetamine (meth)** has exploded onto the scene, with more than 12 million people age 12 and older reporting that they have used this relatively cheap, easy-to-make drug at least once in their lifetime.[55]

Methamphetamine Initiatives

Meth is a central nervous system stimulant often referred to as crank, speed, ice, or crystal. Developed in clandestine laboratories often located in remote areas, meth is cheap and addictive. Its negative effects can include physical addiction, psychotic behavioral episodes, and brain damage; chronic use can cause anxiety, confusion, insomnia, paranoia, and delusions. It is a serious health hazard to anyone who comes in contact with the precursor drugs used to produce meth, including police, medical, and fire personnel. Although meth use is a serious problem across the nation, it has been particularly prevalent in the West and Midwest.

Since 1998, the federal Office of Community Oriented Policing Services has invested more than $385 million nationwide to combat the spread of meth, supporting training, enforcement, and lab cleanup activities.[56] Indeed, training police officers in lab identification and removal is an important first step in any meth initiative. Training public works and hotel/motel staff is also successful for helping to identify meth lab operations. Drug courts are an additional beneficial option for the criminal justice system because they immediately expose meth-addicted individuals to treatment and provide them with a rigid structure with little tolerance for infractions. Another major part of meth initiatives involves establishing the partnerships that are essential for addressing the problem, such as those developed with prosecutors' offices, environmental protection agencies, agencies involved in cleaning up hazardous materials, child welfare and family services agencies, treatment centers, and federal drug enforcement agencies.[57]

Exhibit 11-3 shows some successful initiatives that have been undertaken in several communities to address their growing meth problem. Note the commonalities of the approaches: the reliance on training and the assistance of outside agencies.

Clandestine Drug Labs

A problem that is closely related to meth manufacturing and sales is the clandestine drug labs (meth accounts for 80 to 90 percent of the labs' total drug production). Dealing with clandestine drug labs requires extraordinarily high levels of technical expertise. Responders must understand illicit drug chemistry—how to neutralize the risks of explosions, fires, fumes, and burns and how to handle and dispose of hazardous materials (HAZMAT). They must also know the federal, state, and local laws governing chemical manufacturing and distribution, HAZMAT, and occupational safety. They must collaborate with fire officials, HAZMAT experts, chemists, public-health officials, and social services providers.[58]

Cleaning up clandestine drug labs is an enormously complex, time-consuming, and costly undertaking. Seizing a lab potentially makes a police agency liable for some of the costs of cleaning up on-site hazardous materials. If the lab is in operation when found, it must first be safely neutralized so that it does not contaminate the environment; then the materials must be cleaned up and safely disposed of. The average cost of cleaning up these materials ranges from $2,500 to $10,000.[59]

EXHIBIT 11-3

What Works: Going after Meth

The following communities have begun to address their meth problem:

- The Oklahoma City, Oklahoma, Police Department focused on increased enforcement and training as well as a partnership with a drug court to deal with meth problems. Officers used undercover buys, confidential informants, surveillance, and assistance from patrol officers making traffic stops to apprehend meth users and distributors. A 70 percent increase in meth labs seized occurred in the first year of the initiative. City-wide citizen training in meth use and identification was conducted; part of this training focused on hotel/motel associations and natural gas employees, the latter responding to over 600,000 service calls in the city and having widespread and frequent access to properties and the potential for identifying lab locations.

- In Little Rock, Arkansas, the police also focused on increased enforcement and training of all officers regarding meth identification and response. Other approaches included a telephone hotline for citizens to call if they suspected meth activity, an information campaign for retailers of precursor chemicals (including giving the police license plate numbers of purchasers of large quantities), and interviews with jail detainees regarding meth use and manufacturing to better understand the meth market.

- Salt Lake City, Utah, used enhanced enforcement and prosecution, child endangerment laws, civil remedies to reduce neighborhood impact, public-awareness campaigns, and formation of a meth training team. More than thirty city, county, and federal agencies participated.

- Minneapolis, Minnesota, police first engaged in comprehensive data collection to obtain information about the extent and nature of the meth problem. Interviews with probationers and drug-court clients were conducted (and they confirmed police suspicions that meth users were more likely to be white and employed). The department also developed general training videos on meth lab identification and identification of meth users at traffic stops, and it trained community groups, police officers, and transit, housing, sanitation, and park employees who might come in contact with clandestine meth labs.

Source: Adapted from U.S. Department of Justice, Office of Community Oriented Policing Services, "COPS Innovations: A Closer Look," in *Combating Methamphetamine Laboratories and Abuse: Strategies for Success* (Washington, DC: Author, August 2003), pp. 7–9.

Police responses to the problem of these drug labs involve much more than merely finding and seizing the small "mom and pop" labs. Drug labs are so easy to set up that it seems impossible to find all (or even most) of them. Other responses include the following[60]:

- Using federal and state organized crime and racketeering statutes for dismantling more sophisticated "super labs" run by syndicates
- Searching homes and vehicles of former lab operators who are on probation and parole regularly to determine if they have resumed operating a lab
- Seizing and filing for forfeiture of clandestine drug lab operators' assets (although this strategy is probably not effective with smaller labs)
- Enforcing environmental protection laws because the burden of proof under these laws is typically less than that required for criminal convictions
- Filing civil actions against persons who allow their properties to be used as clandestine drug labs as well as filing nuisance abatement actions and eviction actions
- Monitoring the sale and distribution of essential and precursor chemicals used in such labs, widely considered to be one of the most effective responses, but doing so requires effort at the local, state, national, and international levels

Open-Air Drug Markets

Open-air drug markets represent the lowest level of the drug distribution network. These low-level markets need to be addressed, however, because of the risks posed to market participants and the harm that drug use can inflict on the entire community.

Open markets have several advantages for both buyers and sellers: Buyers know where to go in order to find the drugs they want and can weigh quality against price, and sellers are able to maximize customer access. Open-air markets also generate or contribute to a wide range of problems and disorder in the community, including traffic congestion, noise, disorderly conduct, loitering, prostitution, robberies, burglaries, thefts from motor vehicles, fencing of stolen goods, weapons offenses, assaults, and clandestine drug labs (discussed above).[61]

Dealing with open-air markets presents a considerable challenge for the police. Simply arresting market participants will have little impact on reducing the size of the market or the amount of drugs consumed. However, the nature of open markets means that market participants are vulnerable both to police enforcement and to the dangers of buying from strangers, which may include rip-offs and robberies.

Whichever approach the police choose, it is unlikely that they will be able to eradicate the open-air drug markets completely, and a police crackdown or sweep will only be a deterrent if appropriate sentencing is used. Following are some open-air drug activities that the police have undertaken[62]:

- *Policing the area in a highly visible fashion.* A police presence (including foot patrol) may disrupt the drug market and make it inconvenient for sellers and buyers to engage in drug transactions.
- *Enforcing the law intensively.* The effect of a crackdown is dependent on the drug market that is targeted and the amount of resources available, such as street surveillance and intelligence gathering, a hotline for area residents, and increases in drug-treatment services.
- *Using intelligence-led investigative work.* Information from drug hotlines and local residents can help to identify and analyze a problem. In addition, any arrest may produce information if officers debrief the offender, and drug buyers may lead undercover officers to drug locations.
- *Arresting drug buyers in "reverse stings."* The reverse sting (the sale or purported sale of drugs by a government agent to the target of an investigation) serves to impact the demand side of the market and is most successful against new or occasional drug users. Miami, Florida, police found that the process of being arrested, charged, forced to appear in court, and have a vehicle impounded acted as a deterrent.

Raves

A serious problem that can involve serious drug abuse is **raves**—dance parties that feature fast-paced, repetitive electronic music and light shows. Drug use is intended to enhance ravers' sensations and boost their energy so they can dance for long periods, usually starting late at night and going into the morning hours. Rave party problems are unique: They create a blend of attitudes, drugs, and behaviors not found in other forms of youth culture. Dealing with raves is difficult for police. On the one hand, police often face pressure from society to put an end to raves; on the other hand, raves are enormously popular among teenagers and adults, most of whom are law-abiding and responsible.[63] In addition, raves pose a number of concerns for police, including drug overdoses, drug trafficking, noise, persons driving under the influence, and traffic control. Of particular concern is evidence that suggests the drug most closely associated with rave parties—ecstasy (also known as MDMA or "Eve")—can cause permanent brain damage when used habitually.

In order to understand the extent of the local rave problem, police should conduct an analysis that answers a number of questions concerning rave incidents, locations, and management. Some police responses that have met with success include regulating rave venues to ensure basic health and safety measures are in use, encouraging property owners to exercise control over raves, prohibiting juveniles and adults from being admitted to the same raves, applying nuisance abatement laws where appropriate, prosecuting rave operators and property owners for drug-related offenses, and educating ravers about the risks of drug use and overexertion.[64]

High-Intensity Drug Trafficking Area Program

An initiative that provides additional federal resources to areas most in need of help to reduce or eliminate drug trafficking is the **High-Intensity Drug Trafficking Area (HIDTA) program**. In considering whether to designate an area as a high-intensity drug area, the federal Office of National Drug Control Policy considers the extent to which the area is a center for illegal drug production, manufacturing, importation, or distribution. The priorities of HIDTA are to assess regional drug threats, design strategies to combat those threats, and develop and fund initiatives to implement strategies. The program receives more than $225 million per year to fund its efforts, which are now located in forty-three states and several territories.[65]

This chart shows different types of markings commonly found on ecstasy pills.

(Courtesy U.S. Customs and Border Protection, Fotomaterial: Bundeskriminalamt Wiesbaden)

SUMMARY

This chapter focuses on three areas of criminality that are particularly troublesome and challenging for today's police and that consume a tremendous proportion of their resources: terrorism, gangs, and drugs. Emphasis for each of these areas was placed on describing the nature of each problem, the extent of its effects on society, and several police responses for coping with each of them. A number of case studies were employed to bring a real-world flavor to these problem-solving efforts, particularly through the application of the COPPS strategy (discussed in Chapter 6).

Perhaps a point that needs to be underscored is that these three problems are not found to the same degree or depth from state to state, city to city. Although police work generally tends to be very much the same from region to region and jurisdiction to jurisdiction, the threat of terrorism, gang activities, and drug problems will differ and will require unique approaches in venues that are dissimilar. The potential dangers of terrorist attacks, gangs, and drugs that are posed to a tourist mecca such as Las Vegas will be quite different in kind and scope than those posed for a hub of business and industry such as Chicago. The police, to borrow a phrase, must "put on different faces for different people."

Related to that reality is another fact: The police will be compelled to adapt their training and operations so as to cope with these problems. As society becomes more diverse, the police will continue to face new challenges that rise to the level of the three posed in this chapter and the next. It is important that police officers receive training and education to allow them to be prepared for impending exigencies while ensuring that they maintain a professional approach to such emergencies.

Chapter 12 allows little retreat from societal problems: It covers crimes involving illegal immigrants, organized crime, hate crimes, and crimes by youth. Although perhaps not carrying the potential for societal disasters of the kind discussed in this one, these problems still command a great deal of attention, resources, and training.

KEY TERMS

bioterrorism
drug abuse
graffiti
High-Intensity Drug Trafficking Area (HIDTA) program
homeland security
methamphetamine (meth)
Military Commissions Act (MCA)
National Incident Management System (NIMS)

Posse Comitatus Act
rave
street gang
terrorism
USA PATRIOT Act

REVIEW QUESTIONS

1. What are the three types of terrorism?

2. How has terrorism changed policing, and how do the USA PATRIOT Act and the Military Commissions Act of 2006 attempt to benefit the authorities in their efforts to thwart terrorism?

3. What are the major portions of the National Incident Management System?

4. How could bioterrorism lead to a horrific occurrence in our nation's cities, and what must the police do to prepare for such an attack?

5. What are the nature, causes, and extent of the nation's gang and graffiti problems, and what are some options used by the police to deal with gang members?

6. How would you describe this nation's drug problem and the part that methamphetamine plays in it? How does being designated an HIDTA help a community to combat drug crimes?

7. What is meant by open-air drug markets and raves, and what are the police doing to control these problems?

INDEPENDENT STUDENT ACTIVITIES

1. This chapter is replete with interesting areas of inquiry for inquisitive students. Contact federal and state law enforcement practitioners in your area to determine the methods they are employing in attempting to control the kinds of problems that are addressed in this chapter.

2. Try to learn the extent of local problems with respect to attractiveness for terrorist attack, gangs, and drug trafficking. What are the police doing to combat these problems, and how can COPPS help to address them? Provide examples. What is being done locally with respect to having a prepared plan in the event of a terrorist attack? What kinds of training and education must the police undergo to be able to work these assignments (terrorism or other disaster planning, gang or drug suppression)? What does the future hold for these kinds of problems? If the community has been designated an HIDTA, what benefits for combating

drug trafficking have been realized from such a designation? What new technologies and methodologies exist or should be obtained in the community's ongoing attempts to address them? What appears to be the community's attitude toward these problems?

RELATED WEB SITES

Department of Homeland Security
http://www.whitehouse.gov/homeland

National Institute on Drug Abuse
http://www.nida.nih.gov

National Youth Gang Center
http://www.iir.com/nygc/maininfo.htm

Office of National Drug Control Policy
http://www.whitehousedrugpolicy.gov

U.S. Customs and Border Protection
http://www.customs.gov

CRIMES INVOLVING ILLEGAL IMMIGRANTS, THE MOB, HATE, AND YOUTH

A team is where a boy can prove his courage on his own. A gang is where a coward goes to hide.
—Branch Rickey

People have told me about organized crime in the fashion industry, but I can't talk about that. I'm looking to stay alive.
—Calvin Klein

Attacks upon individuals because of a difference in how they look, pray, or behave have long been a part of human history.
—Federal Bureau of Investigation

LEARNING OBJECTIVES

AS A RESULT OF READING THIS CHAPTER, THE STUDENT WILL:

- KNOW THE FUNCTIONS OF THE FEDERAL CUSTOMS AND BORDER PROTECTION FOR PROTECTING OUR BORDERS

- BE AWARE OF SOME NEW METHODS USED TO CONTROL ILLEGAL BORDER CROSSINGS

- BE ABLE TO LIST SEVERAL FORMS OF ORGANIZED CRIME

- UNDERSTAND HOW THE MAFIA ORIGINATED AND SOME OF THE METHODS THAT HAVE BEEN DEVELOPED TO INVESTIGATE AND PROSECUTE MAFIOSI

- UNDERSTAND HOW HATE CRIMES DIFFER FROM OTHER CRIMES AND SOME POTENTIAL RESPONSES TO THE PROBLEM

- BE ABLE TO EXPLAIN THE NATURE AND EXTENT OF YOUTH CRIME AND VIOLENCE

- KNOW WHY BULLYING IS A PROBLEM AND SOME SUCCESSFUL APPROACHES TO DEALING WITH IT

- UNDERSTAND HOW THE POLICE—WITH THE AID OF COMMUNITY POLICING AND PROBLEM SOLVING—ARE ADDRESSING THE PROBLEM OF YOUTH CRIME, INCLUDING SCHOOL VIOLENCE AND BULLYING, GUN VIOLENCE, DISORDERLY CONDUCT IN PUBLIC PLACES, AND UNDERAGE DRINKING

INTRODUCTION

Continuing with our "extraordinary problems" theme established in Chapter 11, we now know that certain types of people in the United States, through their actions or status, pose unique challenges for the police. A common thread running through the types of offenders who are discussed in this chapter—aliens and others wishing to cross our borders and enter into our country illegally, members of organized crime syndicates, persons who perpetrate crimes because of their hatred for others, and violent and disorderly youth—is that the police are often compelled to engage in clandestine operations in order to arrest or deal with them. Another connecting link for all of these problems is that the police must constantly develop *new* methods and practices for dealing with these individuals.

This chapter examines each of these unique challenges to police and some of the methods used to address them and then concludes with a chapter summary, key terms, questions for review, independent student activities, and related Web sites.

POLICING OUR BORDERS

According to the independent Center for Immigration Studies, in January 2000 there were 7 million **illegal aliens** living in the United States, and the center estimated that number to grow by half a million a year.[1] Therefore, the illegal alien population in 2007 was at least 10 million. Obviously, since 9/11 the need for and the challenge of protecting the borders of the United States are more grave than ever before.

Toward this end, in Chapter 2 we discussed several relatively new federal agencies within the Department of Homeland Security (DHS). One of those agencies in particular, **Customs and Border Protection (CBP)**, was formed in March 2003 to address the problem of illegal entry and now has a workforce of over forty thousand employees. The CBP combined some employees of the Department of Agriculture, personnel from the former U.S. Customs Service, and agents of the U.S. Border Patrol and the Immigration and Naturalization Service. Next we discuss some of the recent law enforcement initiatives that have been undertaken to stem the flow of illegal entries by both terrorists and others.

The CBP is responsible for guarding seven thousand miles of land border the United States shares with Canada and Mexico, as well as two thousand miles of coastal waters surrounding the Florida peninsula and the coast of southern California. To secure this vast terrain, more than eleven thousand CBP agents and eighteen thousand CBP officers stand guard, attempting to prevent terrorists and their weapons from entering the United States while continuing their mission of seizing contraband and apprehending criminals and others who illegally attempt to enter the United States. The CBP secures America's borders by integrating and deploying modern technology, strengthening border infrastructure, and increasing the number of highly trained law enforcement personnel. This strategy is a critical component of the secretary of DHS's Secure Border Initiative (SBI). The CBP continues to implement a national border control strategy that includes a centralized command structure, a rapid response capability, and an in-depth defense, using a layered approach to border security that emphasizes effective personnel, infrastructure, technology, and resources.[2]

Illegal migrants are placed in holding facilities by CBP agents before they are returned to Mexico.

(Courtesy U.S. Customs and Border Protection, photographer Gerald L. Nino)

Following are some recent results achieved and initiatives undertaken[3]:

- Through June 2006, the CBP arrested more than 1.1 million illegal aliens and seized an estimated $1.7 billion worth of illegal drugs.
- The CBP apprehended over 140,000 criminals last year using a recently implemented database, the Integrated Automated Fingerprint Identification System (IAFIS).
- CBP's air officers flew over 11,000 hours in 2005–2006 in missions over the Caribbean, Florida, Texas, and southern California, resulting in the seizure of more than 105 tons of illegal cocaine, marijuana, and heroin.
- DHS's SBI, which is a comprehensive multiyear plan to secure America's borders and reduce illegal migration, was launched.
- The CBP air fleet of fixed-wing aircraft, helicopters, and unmanned aerial vehicles (UAVs, discussed in Chapter 15), with over 500 pilots and 250 aircraft, constitutes the largest civilian law enforcement air force in the world.
- The Arizona Border Control Initiative (ABCI) is an operational initiative aimed at controlling the "weakest link" along the U.S.–Mexico border.
- The Border Patrol Tactical Unit (BORTAC) was continued, with a special operations unit having advanced tactical skills.
- The Border Patrol Search, Trauma, and Rescue (BORSTAR) program is also ongoing, with a highly skilled rescue and emergency care unit.

New Terrorist Watch Program

Early 2004 brought the inception of a new program titled **U.S. Visitor and Immigrant Status Indicator Technology (US-VISIT)**, under which 24 million foreigners are expected to be checked annually at the nation's airports. The program allows customs agents to check passengers instantly against terrorist watch lists and a national database; the database is only available to law enforcement authorities on a need-to-know basis. Foreigners arriving at U.S. airports also have their fingerprints checked by pressing their index fingers onto an inkless scanner and then have their photograph taken as they make their way through customs. The only exceptions are visitors from twenty-seven countries, mostly European nations as well as Canadians and Mexicans coming into the country for a short time and not venturing far from the border.[4]

U.S. Southwestern Border

In September 2006, after several months of debate concerning the illegal immigration issue, Congress sent Americans a message that they are serious about fighting illegal immigration by authorizing a fence along one-third of the U.S.–Mexico border. Although the total cost of the seven-hundred-mile-long fence on the nearly two-thousand-mile-long southern border was not determined, a separate bill made a $1.2 billion down payment on it. (Many people, however, feel the fence is doomed to fail; for example, Senator Edward M. Kennedy called the fence "a bumper sticker solution for a complex problem.") In addition to money for starting work on the fence, a DHS bill that Congress also passed included $380 million to hire 1,500 more CBP agents and money to build detention facilities to hold 6,700 more illegal immigrants until they can be deported.[5]

But will the fence be enough? Each night a drama is played out in many American cities as a hide-and-seek game unfolds at the nation's southwestern border when thousands of people gather to get on American soil and grab their fortune and a new way of life. About 3 million of the 8.5 million Mexican-born people living in the United States are believed to be living here illegally.[6]

Sometimes the simplest border protection methods are effective; here, "dragging" wipes away any footprints or other signs that people are crossing a border road. Later the CBP will check for signs that people have crossed the road illegally, heading into the United States.

(Courtesy U.S. Customs and Border Protection, photographer James Tourtellotte)

Many people do not consider these undocumented immigrants to be a crime problem. In fact, because of their general clandestine lifestyle, they are most likely to avoid contacting the police, even when they are victimized. One crime that has been disproportionately associated with undocumented migrants in the Southwest is drug trafficking. This, too, police officials say, is a false impression. While a few illegal aliens do carry drugs across the border, the typical alien generally comes from a rural area and only wants to work. Most aliens do not trust banks and carry large sums of money in their pockets; therefore, they are prime targets for criminals.[7]

As the United States has fortified the southwestern border, the price and the profits have shot up for the people smugglers, or "coyotes," who will get migrants to Phoenix for a fee of $1,000. The coyotes use several types of employees: a *vendepollo,* or "chicken seller," works the streets in Mexico looking for new clients; a *brincador,* or "fence jumper," guides migrants across the border.[8] While the coyotes are reviled by U.S. authorities, they are hailed as heroes by tens of thousands of migrants. Violence has become rampant at the fortified Arizona border as rival smuggling groups and ripoff gangs, known as *bajadores,* battle over migrants in that sector. For the $1,000 fee, however, the smugglers take migrants to Nogales, Mexico; arrange for a taxi to take them to the border, where more smugglers lift them over the fourteen-foot-high fence; and on the U.S. side of the border, other smugglers drive them to Phoenix.[9]

Because of the violence associated with smuggling in Arizona, in late 2003 federal officials launched Operation Ice Storm, arresting more than five hundred undocumented immigrants in the Phoenix area, prosecuting eighty people on related charges, and seizing $300,000 in smuggling proceeds as well as a large number of weapons.[10]

This border's immigration problem has been termed an "alien invasion" by two civilian patrol groups that have sprung up recently: the Civil Homeland Defense, whose members patrol Arizona's border on foot, and the American Border Patrol (its motto: "The Eyes of America"), which uses surveillance technology. These groups believe they can do the job as well and more cheaply than CBP's agents, and they call Arizona the "last stand" against the migration invasion. The CBP, meanwhile, strongly discourages private parties from taking matters into their own hands.[11]

New Technologies: Rescue Beacons and Border Drones

The deserts and mountains are not friendly to persons wishing to enter the United States from Mexico; indeed, the death toll is so high[12] that the CBP now has a special unit whose only job is to help migrants in trouble. Some wander in the desert for several days, become dehydrated, and lose their ability to think rationally. Therefore, agents have become adept at looking for tracks on the ground, clothing, and even shoes. There are also rescue beacons warning people of the dangers they face and providing them an opportunity to signal for help.

Another pilot program begun in July 2004 targeting illegal immigration uses two UAVs, or **border drones** (discussed more thoroughly in Chapter 15), to monitor illegal activity along the Arizona–Mexico border. The UAVs use thermal and night-vision equipment to spot illegal immigrants and can detect movement from 15 miles of altitude, read a license plate, and even detect weapons. In 39 days of surveillance of the border, the UAVs led to the apprehension of 248 illegal immigrants and the seizure of 518 pounds of marijuana. The vehicles are waist high, weigh about 1,000 pounds, have a 35-foot wingspan, fly faster than 100 miles per hour, and can stay aloft for 20 hours at a time.[13]

POLICING ORGANIZED CRIME

Origin and Organization

Imagine spending an entire police career and only making a few or even no arrests, devoting your career to just the collection and analysis of intelligence information. Visualize yourself investigating crime by watching newspaper obituaries and appearing at funerals to log license plates and take photographs from a safe distance from the mourners and then tracing names to their fifth cousins. Consider spending years to investigate a single case, combing through records and files that go back twenty years. Picture yourself going undercover for several years to investigate a crime organization, never knowing when your cover will be blown and you will be targeted for death (see the Practitioner's Perspective).

Enter the world of organized crime. These are only some of the unusual methods and schemes that are employed by police agents who are assigned to the underworld. **Organized crime** is any group having some manner of formalized structure and whose primary objective is to obtain money through illegal activities. Under this definition, several organized crime syndicates or organizations, such as street youth gangs, prison gangs, gangs from several Asian countries (such as the Chinese Triads, some Vietnamese and

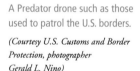

A Predator drone such as those used to patrol the U.S. borders.

(Courtesy U.S. Customs and Border Protection, photographer Gerald L. Nino)

Tong immigrants, and the Japanese Boryokudan), Russian mobsters, Nigerians, bikers, and Gypsies, exist in America. Probably the oldest, most profitable, and most dangerous form of organized crime in the United States is the **Mafia**, also known as "La Cosa Nostra," or "this thing of ours."

Mafia origins can be traced to thirteenth-century Sicily. The history of the Mafia is a confusing hodgepodge of lore and legend, but the one having the most appeal (probably due to its romantic nature) involves the French occupation of Sicily and Italy in 1282. The local people used a form of guerilla warfare to fight the French military, engaging in hit-and-run tactics and using their knowledge of the rugged terrain to fight the superior French army. A legend holds that a young French soldier and an Italian maiden fell in love during this military occupation; unfortunately, one of their trysts was discovered, and they were both assassinated by the French army. Following the deaths of these two young people, a vindictive cry arose among the people: "Morte Alle Francia Italia Anela," meaning "Death to the French is Italy's Cry." The acronym of this cry is MAFIA.

Many Sicilian and Italian mafiosi immigrated to the United States in the late 1800s and early 1900s, maintaining their criminal lifestyle of intimidation and force. It has been argued that organized crime existed even in the Wild West, focusing on the crimes of gambling, prostitution, robbery, and cattle rustling.[14]

Mafia families have a formally organized nature (see Figure 12-1) consisting of the boss, or El Capo, meaning the godfather); underboss (Sotto Capo), consigliere (counselor), lieutenants (caporegimas, or enforcers), and soldiers (or soldiatos). The major obstacle to investigating and apprehending these criminals is that they shun the public spotlight. In fact, their primary centuries-old code of honor is that of *omerta* (silence).

Mafiosi loathe unwelcomed attention for the most part; it has been said that it is almost as if the Mafiosi are products of "parthenogenesis," as if they just rose out of the dust like the mythical phoenix. When confronted by a police officer and asked questions about himself (the Mafia is an all-male organization), he seems to have no roots, parentage, or any other background that the police can maintain as intelligence information.

The Mob Today: Successful Police Offensives

For forty years, Federal Bureau of Investigation (FBI) Director J. Edgar Hoover denied that the Mafia even existed. Until very recently the Mob had a veritable chokehold on America, being involved in killing for hire, extortion, loan-sharking, money laundering, narcotics, prostitution, smuggling, bookmaking, bribery, business infiltration, embezzlement, hijacking, horse-race fixing, racketeering, pornography, bank fraud, and fencing. By the 1960s the Mafia's influence extended from America's largest labor unions into trucking, construction, longshoring, waste disposal, gambling, and garment making; it had grown into a multibillion-dollar syndicate of criminal enterprises run by twenty-six "families" nationwide.[15]

Beginning in the mid-1980s, however, the FBI spearheaded an unprecedented assault on the Mafia, putting away two generations of godfathers on racketeering charges. That initiative continues today and has met with tremendous success in dealing with this very

PRACTITIONER'S PERSPECTIVE

GOING UNDERCOVER: AN FBI AGENT'S TWO-YEAR EXPERIENCE

GEORGE TOGLIATTI

George Togliatti joined the FBI in 1973 and was subsequently assigned to offices in Boise, Detroit, and Las Vegas. He has supervised the White Collar Crime and the Property Crime Programs in the Las Vegas Office, and presently supervises the Organized Crime Investigations and Drug Program in that office. He holds a bachelor's degree in economics from Iona College and a master's in criminal justice administration from the University of Detroit. The following is a case study of his role as a supervisory special agent.

Togliatti is soft-spoken, part Italian and Irish. He flew search and rescue helicopter missions for five years in North Vietnam. He then worked in the computer industry and took graduate accounting courses. Not happy with his career path, he joined the FBI at age twenty-eight. After short assignments in Butte, Montana, and Boise, Idaho, he acquired his first undercover experience in Detroit. But none of that could have prepared Togliatti for his undercover role as "George Dario"—the undercover Mafioso who loved partying and the criminal lifestyle in the Las Vegas underworld.

Information was obtained that mobsters from Detroit and New York were attempting to gain a major foothold in Las Vegas. Wiretaps also revealed serious attempts to skim casino profits before they were counted for tax purposes, some Mafiosi were killing one another, and ties between organized labor and the mob were deepening. The FBI conceived Operation Desert Fox, where Togliatti would operate on the fringe of mob activities and gather information for later prosecutions. Although it was originally intended to be a two-week assignment, Togliatti would be undercover for two years.

"George Dario" sported a Rolex watch, drove a Cadillac Seville and had access to a $500,000 home in a country club addition. He had little trouble assuming his new identity. He was readily accepted by the mob—and he was so readily accepted, in fact, that FBI officials were stunned. He quickly made new friends, his glib, streetwise New York background serving him well. He assumed a phony background as a sales manager for a legitimate New York music company. Cruising casinos, bars and restaurants, he noted criminal activities, such as extortion cases and drug deals. He was once approached by a man with an offer of $10,000 to beat up a girlfriend's ex-husband.

To fit into the underworld, where crime, sex and drugs were easily available, Dario's values were often compromised, as when he would have to fake snorting cocaine. But he realized that one improper move would blow his cover and possibly cost his life. He avoided committing several illegal and unsafe acts by turning ugly, telling associates he preferred alcohol to drugs and saying he wanted a clear head during his crimes. He saw rampant drug addiction among his associates, though, and today many of Dario's former associates who cheated on their wives wonder if that information is still tucked away in some FBI file.

Two close friends—fellow FBI agents—kept Dario informed of developments with the information he had uncovered. The trio often met in hideaway restaurants to discuss goings-on in the bureau office and the other world in general. The friends also performed support work, such as checking license plate numbers or hotel registrations to identify people.

After two years had passed, Dario realized that it was time to become Togliatti again; the mob had learned he was a fake and the telephone lines were abuzz. Operation Desert Fox was a huge success. Would Togliatti do it again? Today he says no; he can never recover the two years lost from his family, and feels it was too high a price to pay. Yet, he says it made him a better special agent; indeed, several promotions came his way in the next five years. He plays down the danger surrounding what he did, saying a lot of people in the FBI could have done the job. And, he says, "Vietnam was tougher, hands down."

(Portions excerpted from the *Reno Gazette-Journal*, November 1, 1987, pp. 1A, 14A. Used with permission.)

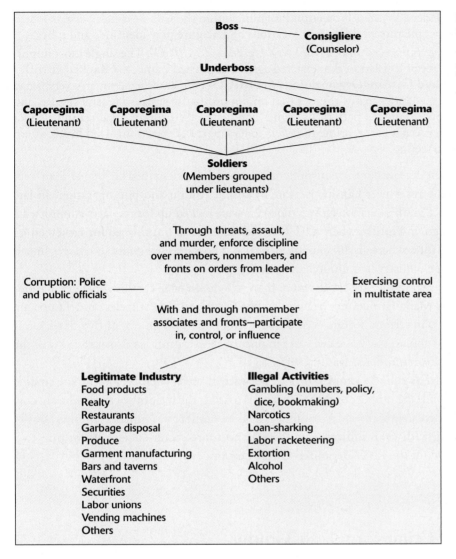

FIGURE 12-1
Organizational Chart for a Crime Family

Source: The President's Commission on Law Enforcement and Administration of Justice, Task Force Report: Organized Crime (Washington, DC: Author, 1967), p. 9.

elusive group. How has this success been obtained? Through tenacity, hard work, and some luck—and for three fundamental, practical reasons:

1. *Expanded use of electronic eavesdropping ("wiretapping").* With federal agents listening in on more conversations each year, mobsters are forced to operate in a climate of constant suspicion. Cooperation between federal and state law enforcement authorities also speeds up convictions. Furthermore, the Internal Revenue Service can legally share information, enabling it to assist in complicated tax cases in almost two-thirds of all organized crime prosecutions.

2. *Use of informants.* A significant tool in the toppling of Mob kingpins has been the use of former gangsters who have proved willing to violate the code of secrecy, or *omerta,* turning state's evidence against their old cronies. More youthful gangsters do not possess the level of loyalty to the family their ancestors did, and government prosecutors have managed to exploit this new less-than-loyal breed of mafiosi. The willingness of some hoodlums to defy the Mafia is also partly due to the existence

of the federal Witness Protection Program, within the U.S. Marshals Service, which helps people move to different locations and acquire new identities and jobs.

3. *Racketeer Influenced and Corrupt Organizations Act (RICO).* The single most important piece of legislation ever enacted against organized crime, the **Racketeer Influenced and Corrupt Organizations Act (RICO)** defines racketeering in a very broad manner, includes many offenses that do not ordinarily violate a federal statute, and attempts to prove a pattern of crimes conducted through an organization. Under RICO, it is a separate crime to *belong* to an enterprise that is involved in a "pattern of racketeering."

For these reasons, in the new millennium the Mafia, described as "bigger than U.S. Steel" by mobster Meyer Lansky, is more of an illicit mom-and-pop operation. In late 2007 in Chicago, three senior-citizen mobsters were locked up for murders committed a generation ago; in Florida, where a 97-year-old mafiosi was imprisoned for racketeering; and in New York, where an 80-something-year-old boss pleaded guilty to charges linked to the garbage industry and union corruption.[16]

At its peak, in the late 1950s, more than two dozen Mob families operated nationwide. Today, Mafia families in strongholds like Cleveland, Los Angeles, and Tampa are gone, and it is in serious decline even in New York City—where two of five crime families are run in absentia by bosses who are in prison. Mob executions also are a thing of the past; the last boss murdered was in 1985.[17]

The Mafia's ruling Commission has not met in years. Membership in key cities is dwindling, while the number of mob turncoats is soaring; the majority of those who are now arrested immediately want to try to cut a deal. The number of "snitches" is enormous—and growing with each indictment; there is no more secret society, according to a spokesperson for the FBI's Organized Crime Section.[18]

POLICING HATE CRIMES

Types of Crimes and Hate Groups

In the past, the police often tended to dismiss the context in which crimes occurred; an assault was simply an assault, and so on. In 1990, however, Congress passed the Hate Crimes Statistics Act, which forced the police to collect statistics on **hate crimes**, and several states have since enacted statutes that place higher penalties on crimes that have a hate motive. Hate crimes and hate incidents—those that are motivated by an offender's bias against an individual's or group's race, religion, ethnic/national origin, gender, age, disability, or sexual orientation[19]—are also major issues for the police because of their unique impact on victims and the community.[20]

The Southern Poverty Law Center (SPLC), founded in 1971 and located in Montgomery, Alabama, has developed expertise in identifying and tracking hate-crime groups and incidents. The SPLC is internationally known for its tolerance education programs, its legal victories against white supremacists, and its tracking of hate groups. The center has become an authority on hate crimes and groups, and its Intelligence Project conducts training for local, state, and federal law enforcement officers on the history, background, leaders, and activities of far-right extremists in the United States. Today the SPLC counts 803 active hate groups in the United States, with California, Florida, Georgia, South Carolina, and Texas each having between 40 and 50 such groups. They include black separatist groups, Christian identity groups, the Ku Klux Klan, neo-Nazis, neo-Confederates, racist skinheads, and dozens of other groups.[21]

Initiatives for Enforcement and Prevention

The rationale for police involvement in hate crimes is that one of their primary roles is the enforcement or reinforcement of community values.[22] Even though a particular hate crime may be relatively minor and unorganized (graffiti, simple assault, or disorderly conduct), it may attack the very fiber of a community and result in special or unusual effects on the victim or the community as a whole.

But preventing and responding to hate crimes can be a daunting task. A recent report by the Federal Bureau of Investigation stated that about 9,650 hate-crime victimizations are reported per year; this number is increasing.[23] About half of these hate-crime incidents (52.1 percent) are motivated by racial bias; in about 15 percent, sexual orientation was described by the victim to have been the basis for the crime. The victim's religion was mentioned in about 18 percent, and the victim's disability in about one percent.[24]

Table 12-1 shows the distribution of hate crimes by victim group.

TABLE 12-1

Motivation and Evidence in Hate Crime

	PERCENT OF HATE CRIME	
	Incidents	Victimizations
Motivation		
Race	55.4%	56.0%
Association	30.7	30.6
Ethnicity	28.7	27.9
Sexual orientation	18.0	17.9
Perceived characteristic	13.7	13.2
Religion	12.9	12.4
Disability	11.2	10.5
Evidence of motivation		
Negative comments, hurtful words, abusive language	98.5%	98.5%
Confirmation by police investigation	7.9	8.4
Hate symbols	7.6	7.8

Note: Detail adds to more than 100% because some respondents included more than one motivation or evidence of motivation.

Source: U.S. Department of Justice, Bureau of Justice Statistics, *Hate Crime Reported by Victims and Police* (Washington, DC: Author, November 2005), p. 3.

Forty-one states and the District of Columbia have crime statutes that enhance the penalties for hate crimes and address hate violence. Furthermore, at the federal level hate crimes are investigated by the FBI's Bias Crimes Unit and church arson and explosives experts of the Bureau of Alcohol, Tobacco, and Firearms.[25]

There is much a law enforcement organization can do with respect to hate crimes: provide victims with a point of contact in the department to whom they can report hate crimes and express concerns, inform victims on case progress, participate in hate-crime training as well as educate the public about these crimes, establish a zero tolerance of prejudice within the department, track the criminal activities of hate groups, and sponsor and participate in community events that promote tolerance and diversity.[26]

A good example of a police agency's effort to fight hate crimes is found in Madison, Connecticut. At a departmental roll call, every officer receives a laminated hate-crime response card that provides officers with important information for responding to hate crimes, working with victims, and pursuing perpetrators. The card includes the definition of a hate crime, questions responding officers should ask, and tips for recognizing signs of organized hate groups. In October 2002, the Anti-Defamation League took the effort further, distributing these cards to more than 7,500 police officers throughout the state of Connecticut.[27]

A final note: One unique problem that exists with hate crimes is that they are difficult to prosecute. Hate-crime charges are the only type where proving motive becomes as important as proving method. Juries often find it too difficult to conclude with any certainty what was going on in a suspect's mind during the crime. Defending a hate crime can also be a daunting task. Defense attorneys argue that a defendant may, for example, dress and talk like a skinhead but not identify with being one, while juries can be prejudiced toward guilt by the mere allegation of affiliation with such a cruel group. Furthermore, attorneys maintain that defending against such allegations can take on the appearance of defending a hate group and that jurors may force a defendant to pay for the sins of a group.[28]

POLICING YOUTH CRIMES

Extent of the Problem

In Chapter 11 we discussed gangs and what the police are doing to try to suppress them. Of course, **youth crimes** are certainly a core feature or outcome of gang activity. But here we take a more expansive view of crimes that are committed by and against youth. Such crimes are as old as crime itself, especially given that "crime is a young person's enterprise" as any police officer, criminologist, or anyone else knows who is employed in the criminal justice system.

Nearly half (46.3 percent) of all persons arrested in the United States are under the age of twenty-four; more than one-fourth (26.2 percent) are under nineteen.[29] Juvenile crime remains one of the nation's most serious problems, particularly as gang activity continues to spread (discussed in Chapter 11). During a recent ten-year period, juveniles ages twelve to fourteen and fifteen to seventeen experienced average annual rates of non-fatal violence that were about 2.5 times higher than the rate for adults. Furthermore, four in five victims of nonfatal violent crime, ages twelve to fourteen, perceived the offender to be a juvenile.[30]

News accounts of serious crimes committed by children and adolescents have encouraged a general belief that young people are increasingly violent and uncontrollable and that the response of the juvenile justice system has been inadequate. Most states have enacted laws that make the juvenile system more punitive and that allow younger children and adolescents to be transferred to the adult system for a greater variety of offenses and in a greater variety of ways. Indeed, at 645 per 100,000, the U.S. incarceration rate of juveniles is second only to that of Russia, at 685 per 100,000 population.[31]

Next we briefly consider several significant problems involving young offenders: school violence and bullying, gun violence, disorderly youth in public places, and underage drinking.

School Violence and Bullying

While school violence has been declining during this millennium (from 1992 to 1999, there were 238 school-associated violent deaths, including the April 1999 massacre of 13 people at Columbine High School in Littleton, Colorado),[32] such violence was shockingly brought back to the public's conscienceness in September 2006 with three such shootings in one week, including one by an adult in a one-room Amish school in Pennsylvania that killed 6 people.[33] There are no simple solutions to this problem. It is neither possible nor tolerable to secure every school or guard every child, nor is it possible or politically tolerable to keep tabs on every gun. But many people see at the root of all this violence an open society threatened by the ubiquity of its weapons.[34]

School safety will certainly always be a concern and require broad-based efforts; those efforts must involve students at an early age and must be reinforced throughout their education.[35] Several strategies have been suggested for police and citizens to help prevent school violence[36]:

- Publicizing the philosophy that a gang presence will not be tolerated, and institutionalizing a code of conduct
- Alerting students and parents about school rules and punishments for infractions
- Creating alternative schools for those students who cannot function in a regular classroom
- Training teachers, parents, and school staff to identify children who are most at risk for violent behavior
- Developing community initiatives focused on breaking family cycles of violence, and providing programs on parenting, conflict resolution, anger management, and recovery from substance abuse
- Establishing peer counseling in schools to give troubled youths the opportunity to talk to someone their own age

Many police agencies now use school resource officers (SROs) for safety planning efforts. SROs can assess the school's structure to determine where potential problems exist and help to address the social environment by such means as explaining what is illegal conduct, employing surveys to measure safety and security concerns of students and staff, and identifying bullies.[37]

A long-standing school problem that may not be declining like school violence is **bullying**. Bullying has two key components: repeated harmful acts and an imbalance of power. It involves repeated physical, verbal, or psychological attacks or intimidation against a victim who is defenseless because of size or strength or who is outnumbered. Between 5 and 9 percent of students bully others with some regularity.[38]

To engage in problem solving regarding bullying, police should determine whether the school has a problem with it and how it is occurring, who the offenders are, how and where they are operating at the school, and who the victims are. Efforts should be made to increase student reporting of bullying; have trained supervisors monitor less supervised and violence-prone areas; consider staggering recess, lunch, and class-release time; and encourage administrators to provide teachers with classroom management training, where necessary.[39]

Exhibit 12-1 discusses an excellent use of the scanning, analysis, response, and assessment (SARA) problem-solving process by SROs for addressing a bullying problem.

EXHIBIT 12-1

SARA Fights Bullying in Ohio

Unchecked disorderly behavior of students in South Euclid, Ohio, led the school resource officer (SRO) to review school data regarding referrals to the principal's office. The SRO found that the high school reported thousands of referrals per year for bullying and the junior high school had experienced a 30 percent increase in such referrals; police data revealed that juvenile complaints about disturbances, bullying, and assaults after school had increased 90 percent in the past 10 years. In the analysis phase, a survey, interviews, and focus groups (with students, teachers, and guidance counselors) conducted by academics from Kent State University's justice studies department provided much more information, and a Geographic Information System mapped hot spots in the schools. The main findings pointed to four areas of concern: the environmental design of school areas, teachers' knowledge and response to the problem, parents' attitudes and responses, and students' perceptions and behaviors.

Responses involved the SRO working closely with other stakeholders to form a planning team, to develop a new school policy on bullying, and to open a new substation within the schools next to a hot spot. Environmental changes included modifying the school bell times and increasing teacher supervision of hot spots; counselors conducting teacher training courses in bullying prevention; [providing] parent education including mailings and information about bullying; and [explaining] new school policy. Finally, student education focused on classroom discussions and assemblies conducted by the SRO.

The assessment found that bullying incidents dropped 60 percent in the hallways and 80 percent in the gym area. Surveys indicated positive attitudinal changes among students about bullying, and greater confidence that teachers would take action.

Source: Center for Problem Oriented Policing, *Excellence in Problem-Oriented Policing: The 2001 Herman Goldstein Award Winners* (Washington, DC: Author, 2002), pp. 55–56.

Gun Violence

Although overall U.S. homicide rates declined in the 1980s and 1990s, youth violence, particularly gun homicide, began increasing dramatically. In urban areas, gun violence takes a particularly heavy toll, as large numbers of young minority males are injured and killed. Research has also linked urban youth gun violence to the gang conflicts over drug markets (discussed above) as well as gun availability.[40]

The numbers speak loudly about the violent nature of our youth: Homicide offending rates for teenagers and young adults increased dramatically in the late 1980s while rates for older age groups declined. Those 18 to 24 years old have historically had the highest homicide offending rates, and their rates nearly doubled from 1985 to 1993. Offending rates of 14- to 17-year-olds increased rapidly after 1985, surpassing the rates of the 25- to 34-year-olds and the 35- to 49-year-olds. Homicide offending rates for the 25- to 34-year-olds fell from 1980 through 1999 but have increased since then.[41] Youth gun violence is related to several other problems, including those of disorderly conduct of youth in public and underage alcohol use (both of which are discussed below).

Perhaps the best-known comprehensive program for addressing the problem of guns and youth is the Boston Gun Project, also known as **Operation Ceasefire**, discussed in Exhibit 12-2, where enlisting community support, convening an interagency working group, involving researchers, developing an effective communication strategy, and having a focused deterrence strategy worked to address a problem involving gang homicides.

EXHIBIT 12-2

Boston's Operation Ceasefire

An innovative and successful gun project, Boston's Operation Ceasefire began as an attempt to address a dramatic increase in local youth violence. The partnerships that formed the base of this strategy included the local, state, and federal criminal justice agencies (police, prosecution, probation) as well as social services agencies, academic researchers, and community groups. After an in-depth analysis of data, the project selected a strategy of focused deterrence that combined suppressive and social intervention techniques. In combination with a focus on shutting down the city's illegal firearms trafficking, a tactic of "pulling levers" was used. When a gang used violence, the relevant partners would pull every potential criminal justice sanction "lever" for that particular gang. At the same time, social services were made available to gang members to support an alternative to life in the gang. The operation resulted in declines in youth homicides, firearm assaults, and shots-fired calls for service. Specifically, the gangs' drug market was disrupted, arrests were made for outstanding warrants, [there was] strict enforcement of probation, and federal sanctions were used. These penalties were borne by the whole gang, not just the shooter, and would be deployed within days of a violent event. Communicating regularly to the gangs served a number of purposes: to ensure that members knew of the new policy and to tell other gangs; to make cause and effect clear—that a particular drug raid, for example, was but a means to an end and was not about drugs but a penalty for violence; and to allow the creation of a fundamental balance of power between the authorities.

Source: David Kennedy, *Pulling the Levers: Getting Deterrence Right* (Washington, DC: National Institute of Justice Journal, July 1998), p. 6.

Disorderly Conduct in Public Places

Disorderly youth in public places constitute one of the most common problems many police agencies must handle, particularly in suburban and rural communities. Disorderly youth are a common source of complaints from urban residents, merchants, and shoppers. Among the kinds of behaviors (some legal and some not) that are associated with youth disorderly conduct are playing loud music; cursing; blocking pedestrians and traffic; using alcohol, tobacco, and drugs; fighting; littering; vandalizing; and spreading graffiti.[42]

Police responses to this problem might include the following[43]:

- Creating alternative legitimate places and activities for youth (such as youth clubs, drop-in centers, and recreation centers), and employing youth at businesses negatively affected by disorderly behavior
- Encouraging youth to gather where they will not disturb others
- Reducing the comfort level, convenience, or attraction of popular gathering places (such as eliminating places to sit or lean, changing the background music)
- Installing and monitoring closed-circuit television cameras
- Establishing and enforcing rules of conduct
- Denying youth anonymity by getting to know the names and faces of young people (without being antagonistic or accusatory)

Underage Drinking

As with the statistics provided for other problems discussed in this chapter, unfortunately the numbers concerning **underage drinking** are not any better: The average age when youth first try alcohol is 11 years for boys and 13 years for girls. The average age at which Americans begin drinking regularly is 15.9 years old, and adolescents who begin drinking before age 15 are four times more likely to develop alcohol dependence than those who begin drinking at age 21. It has been estimated that over 3 million teenagers are out-and-out alcoholics; several million more have a serious drinking problem that they cannot manage on their own. Finally, of the three leading causes of death for 15- to 24-year-olds—automobile crashes, homicides, and suicides—alcohol is a leading factor in all three.[44]

Although underage drinking (alcohol consumption while under the age of 21) is prohibited throughout the nation, young people use alcohol more than any other drug, including tobacco. Many of the harms associated with underage drinking, such as traffic fatalities, driving under the influence, assaults, cruising, street racing, raves, disorderly conduct, acquaintance rape, vandalism, and noise complaints, arise from the overconfidence, recklessness, lack of awareness, aggression, and loss of control that often accompany alcohol abuse.[45] The pressure to drink—whether to experience a rite of passage, to become part of a group, to reduce tension, or to forget worries—also contributes heavily to this problem.[46]

Police have responded in various ways to the problem of underage drinking[47]:

- *Target reduction of the community's overall alcohol consumption.* This may sound impossible to do, but some available means for doing so are discouraging price discounts on alcohol, restricting the hours or days when retailers can sell alcohol, and limiting the number of alcohol outlets.

- *Use a comprehensive approach.* The police can use a combination of examining motivations for drinking, addressing drunken driving, targeting fake IDs, providing counseling or treatment about drinking patterns, enforcing minimum-age purchase laws, conducting undercover "shoulder tap" operations (police have an underage undercover operative ask adult strangers outside a store to purchase alcohol), checking IDs at bars and nightclubs, applying graduated sanctions to retailers that break the law, requiring keg registration (primarily to identify adults who provide alcohol to minors at large house parties or keg parties on college campuses, several states use keg registration to link information about those who purchase a keg to the keg itself), developing house party guidelines and walk-through procedures, and imposing fines for each underage person drinking at a party.

SUMMARY

This chapter has continued the "extraordinary problems" theme established in Chapter 11, and here it was again shown that certain types of people in the United States—illegal aliens, organized crime figures, those responsible for crimes of hate, and youth involved in crimes—pose unique challenges for the police through their actions or status. A number of strategies being employed by the police to address these problems were presented as well.

A common theme running through the types of offenders who are discussed in this chapter is that the police are often compelled to engage in clandestine operations in order to arrest or deal with them. Another connecting link for all these problems is that the police must constantly develop *new* methods, technologies, and practices for dealing with these individuals as well as understand and apply the specific laws (RICO, juvenile law) that are involved. As different crimes and situational problems have arisen, police have also been compelled to adapt their training and operations in order to cope. Still, the unusual policing problems and circumstances discussed in this chapter are not exhaustive. Certainly there are other circumstances that require even further adaptation as the police attempt to guard our borders, keep the Mob at bay, address hate groups, and deal with violence by our youth.

KEY TERMS

bullying
Customs and Border Protection (CBP)
drone
hate crime
illegal alien

Mafia
Operation Ceasefire
organized crime
Racketeer Influenced and Corrupt Organizations Act (RICO)
underage drinking
U.S. Visitor and Immigration Status Indicator Technology (US-VISIT)
youth crime

REVIEW QUESTIONS

1. What are some forms of organized crime besides the Mafia?

2. How did the Mafia originate, and what are some of the more successful police methods that have been developed to investigate and prosecute mafiosi?

3. What are the functions of the federal Customs and Border Protection for protecting our borders?

4. What are some new methods that are available to the police for controlling illegal border crossings?

5. How do hate crimes differ from other crimes, and what are some potential responses to the problem?

6. What is the nature and extent of youth crimes and violence?

7. How and why does bullying occur, and what are some successful approaches to dealing with it?

INDEPENDENT STUDENT ACTIVITIES

1. Interview local police personnel (federal, state, or local) to determine whether or not there is a significant problem with organized crime in your locale, and if so, what measures are being taken for dealing with it. (The very best option is to interview a member of an organization whose full-time assignment is working on organized crime.)

2. Determine from local or state crime data sources how many hate crimes have been reported in your jurisdiction, the types of hate-crime groups that exist, and the outcomes of those cases where arrests were made.

3. Ascertain from crime data or interviews with criminal justice personnel the nature and extent of crime and violence, disorderly conduct, underage drinking, and other related youth crimes in your area.

4. Interview a local school administrator to determine the extent and nature of school violence and bullying in your venue and what is being done to prevent or cope with these problems.

RELATED WEB SITES

Center for Immigration Studies
http://www.cis.org

Criminal Justice Resources: Organized Crime
http://www.lib.msu.edu/harris23/crimjust/orgcrime.htm

Operation Ceasefire
http://ojjdp.ncjrs.org/pubs/gun_violence/profile21.html

RICO Act LLC
http://www.ricoact.com

Southern Poverty Law Center
http://www.splcenter.org/center/about.jsp

U.S. Customs and Border Protection
http://www.cbp.gov

U.S. Visitor and Immigrant Status Indicator Technology
http://www.epic.org/privacy/us-visit/crs_us-visit.pdf

Youth Crime Watch of America
http://www.ycwa.org/world/sl/index.html

POLICING TRENDS AND ISSUES

Debate on public issues should be uninhibited, robust, and wide open.
—*Justice William Brennan*

History has many cunning passages, contrived corridors, and issues.
—*T. S. Eliot*

LEARNING OBJECTIVES

AS A RESULT OF READING THIS CHAPTER, THE STUDENT WILL:

– **UNDERSTAND THE EMPLOYMENT RIGHTS OF POLICE OFFICERS, INCLUDING THE PROVISIONS OF THE PEACE OFFICER BILL OF RIGHTS**

– **BE ABLE TO EXPLAIN THE DEVELOPMENT OF POLICE UNIONS AND THEIR INFLUENCE TODAY**

– **KNOW THE THREE MODELS OF COLLECTIVE BARGAINING**

– **BE ABLE TO DESCRIBE THE FOUR KINDS OF JOB ACTIONS**

– **UNDERSTAND THE FAIR LABOR STANDARDS ACT AND HOW IT OPERATES IN POLICING**

– **BE ABLE TO EXPLAIN THE STATUS OF WOMEN AND MINORITIES AS WELL AS THE DIFFICULTY OF RECRUITING AND RETAINING THEM**

– **UNDERSTAND HOW AND WHY PRIVATE POLICING/SECURITY EVOLVED AND WHAT ITS CURRENT STATUS IS**

– **KNOW THE MAJOR CAUSES OF POLICE STRESS AND SOME MEANS OF COPING WITH IT**

– **BE ABLE TO DELINEATE THE MAJOR ARGUMENTS FOR AND AGAINST POLICE OFFICERS POSSESSING HIGHER EDUCATION**

– **DESCRIBE THE SOCIAL FACTORS THAT CONTRIBUTE TO HOMELESSNESS AND WHAT POLICE AND SOCIETY MIGHT ATTEMPT TO DO IN ORDER TO BREAK THE CYCLE OF PEOPLE LIVING ON THE STREETS**

INTRODUCTION

This chapter addresses a number of important policing matters that could have been included in earlier chapters. But because of their common nature—all represent a substantial degree of change, controversy, and/or influence within the operations of their agencies—they are consolidated and set apart here for discussion.

The chapter is divided into two major sections: contemporary policing trends and contemporary policing issues. In the first (trends) section, we examine labor relations (which include police officers' rights, unionization, and collective bargaining), women and minorities in policing, and the extent and nature of private police/security forces.

Then the issues section consists of three subjects: police stress (which is perhaps not an issue per se but is included because of its myriad causes and physical and emotional effects), the benefits of and arguments against higher education for police, and the significant social problem of homelessness. A chapter summary, key terms, review questions, independent student activities, and related Web sites conclude the chapter.

CONTEMPORARY TRENDS

Labor Relations: Officers' Rights, Unionization, and Collective Bargaining

In an earlier time, police supervisors, middle managers, and chief executives were largely unrestricted and unchallenged in their treatment of rank-and-file officers. Disciplinary action was subjective, and the prevailing theme was often "Do as I say, not as I do." Employees served "at will," or until their employer (for whatever reason) no longer had need of their services. Today the labor-management relationship has changed significantly. First and foremost is the fact that a long line of court cases has established the legal view that public employees have a property interest in their employment. This flies in the face of the old view that employees served at will, until their employer, for whatever reason, no longer had need of their services. The Supreme Court has provided some general guidance on how the question of a constitutionally protected property interest is to be resolved:

> To have a property interest in a benefit, a person…must have a legitimate claim of entitlement to it. It is a purpose of the ancient institution of property to protect those claims upon which people rely in their daily lives, reliance that *must not be arbitrarily undermined* [emphasis added].[1]

Labor relations—a broad term that includes officers' employment rights and the related concepts of unionization and collective bargaining—has become an important issue in policing. This section explores these topics.

POLICE OFFICERS' RIGHTS   Chapter 9 delineated several restrictions on police officers' rights (such as place of residence, religious practices, freedom of speech, and search and seizure). Clearly, because of the nature of their position, police officers may encounter treatment by employers—and federal courts—that is quite different from that received by regular citizens. Officers do give up certain constitutional privileges when they put on a police uniform. In this section, we look at some measures the police have taken to maintain their rights on the job to the extent possible.

In the 1980s and 1990s, police officers began to insist on greater procedural safeguards to protect themselves against what they perceived as arbitrary infringements on their rights. These demands have been reflected in a statute enacted in many states, generally known as the **Peace Officer Bill of Rights**. This legislation confers on police employees a property interest in their position and mandates due process rights for peace officers who are the subject of internal investigations that could lead to disciplinary action. The legislation identifies the type of information that must be provided to the accused officer, the officer's responsibility to cooperate during the investigation, the officer's rights to representation during the process, and the rules and procedures concerning the collection of certain types of evidence. Following are some common provisions of the Peace Officer Bill of Rights:

- *Written notice.* The department must provide the officer with written notice of the nature of the investigation, a summary of the alleged misconduct, and the name of the investigating officer.
- *Right to representation.* The officer may have an attorney or a representative of his or her choosing present during any phase of questioning or any hearing.
- *Polygraph examination.* The officer may refuse to take a polygraph examination unless the complainant submits to an examination and is determined to be telling the truth. In this case, the officer may be ordered to take a polygraph examination or may be subject to disciplinary action.

Officers expect to be treated fairly, honestly, and respectfully during the course of an internal investigation. In turn, the public expects that the agency will develop sound disciplinary policies and will conduct thorough inquiries into allegations of misconduct. It is imperative that supervisors be thoroughly familiar with statutes, contract provisions, and existing rules between employer and employee to ensure that procedural due process requirements are met, particularly in disciplinary cases in which an employee's property interest is affected.

Police officers today are also more likely to file a **grievance** when they believe their rights have been violated. Grievances may cover a broad range of issues, including salaries, overtime, leaves, hours of work, allowances, retirement, opportunities for advancement, performance evaluations, workplace conditions, tenure, disciplinary actions, supervisory methods, and administrative practices. The preferred method for settling an officer's grievance is through informal discussion during which the employee explains his or her grievance to the immediate supervisor, and most complaints can be handled this way. Complaints that cannot be dealt with informally are usually handled through a more formal grievance process, which may involve several different levels of action.

UNIONIZATION   Probably as a result of their often difficult working conditions and traditionally low salary and poor benefits packages, police have often elected for

unionization, banding together to fight for improvement. Another major force in the development and spread of unionization was the aforementioned authoritarian, unilateral "Do as I say, not as I do" management style that characterized many police administrators of the past.

The first campaign to organize the police started shortly after World War I when the American Federation of Labor (AFL) reversed a long-standing policy and issued charters to police unions in Boston, Washington, D.C., and about thirty other cities. Many police officers were suffering from the rapid inflation following the outbreak of the war and believed that if their chiefs could not get them long-overdue pay raises, then perhaps unions could. Capitalizing on their sentiments, the fledgling unions signed about 75 percent of all officers in Boston, 60 percent in Washington, D.C., and a similar proportion in other cities.[2]

The unions' success was short-lived, however. The Boston police commissioner refused to recognize the union, forbade officers to join it, and filed charges against several union officials. Shortly thereafter, on September 9, 1919, the Boston police initiated a famous strike of three days' duration, causing major riots and a furor against the police all across the nation; nine rioters were killed, and twenty-three were seriously injured. During the strike, Massachusetts Governor Calvin Coolidge uttered his now-famous statement: "There is no right to strike against the public safety by anybody, anywhere, anytime." Then, during World War II, the unionization effort was reignited. Unions issued charters to a few dozen locals all over the country even though most police chiefs continued speaking out against unionization. But in a series of rulings, the courts upheld the right of police authorities to ban police unions. Then in the early 1950s, many benevolent and fraternal organizations of police were formed in cities such as Chicago, New York, and Washington, D.C.; others were fraternal orders of police (FOPs). Soon a new group of highly vocal rank-and-file association leaders came into power, supporting higher salaries and pensions, free legal aid, low-cost insurance, and other benefits.[3]

Since the 1970s, the unionization of the police has continued to flourish. Today the majority of U.S. police officers belong to unions.[4] The International Brotherhood of Police Officers touts itself as the largest police union, but it is rivaled by the American Federation of State, County, and Municipal Employees union, which represents about 1.4 million workers and one hundred affiliated associations.[5] This dramatic rise in union membership was fomented by several factors: the job dissatisfaction that was experienced by police officers, the belief that the public was hostile to police needs, and an influx of younger officers who held less traditional views on relations between officers and the department hierarchy.[6]

COLLECTIVE BARGAINING   In this section, different models, relationships, negotiations, and impasses associated with **collective bargaining** (the process of negotiations between employer and employees) are covered.

Three Models.   Each state is free to decide which public-sector employees (if any) will have collective-bargaining rights and under what terms, so there is considerable variety in collective-bargaining arrangements across the nation. In states with comprehensive public-sector bargaining laws, the administration of the statute is the responsibility of a state agency, such as a public employee relations board (PERB) or a public employee relations commission (PERC). Three basic models are used in the states: (1) binding arbitration, (2) meet and confer, and (3) bargaining not required.[7]

Under the binding-arbitration model, used in twenty-five states, public employees are given the right to bargain with their employers. If the bargaining reaches an impasse, the matter is submitted to a neutral arbiter, who decides what the terms and conditions of the new collective-bargaining agreement will be.[8]

Only three states use the meet-and-confer model, which grants very few rights to public employees. As with the binding-arbitration model, police employees in meet-and-confer states have the right to organize and to select their own bargaining representatives.[9] However, when an impasse is reached, employees are at a distinct disadvantage: Their only legal choices are to accept the employer's best offer, try to influence the offer through political tactics (such as appeals for public support), or take some permissible job action.[10]

The twenty-two states that follow the bargaining-not-required model have statutes that either do not require or do not allow collective bargaining by public employees.[11] In the majority of these states, laws permitting public employees to engage in collective bargaining have not been passed.

Bargaining Relationships.   In those states and agencies seeking to organize for collective bargaining, the process goes as follows. First, a union will begin an organizing drive, trying to get a majority of the classes of employees it seeks to represent to sign authorization cards; at this point, agency administrators may attempt to convince employees that they are better off without the union. Questions may also arise, such as whether certain employees (for example, police lieutenants) are part of management and therefore ineligible for union representation.

Once a majority of the eligible employees have signed cards, the union notifies the criminal justice agency. If management believes that the union has obtained a majority legitimately, it will recognize the union as the bargaining agent of the employees it seeks to represent. Once recognized by the employer, the union will petition the PERB or another body responsible for administering the legislation for certification.

Negotiations.   Figure 13-1 depicts a typical configuration of the union and management bargaining teams. Positions shown in dashed boxes typically serve in a support role and may or may not actually partake in the bargaining. The management's labor relations manager (lead negotiator) is often an attorney assigned to the human resources department who reports to the city manager or assistant city manager and represents the city in grievances and arbitration matters. The union's chief negotiator will normally not be a member of the bargaining unit; rather, he or she will be a specialist brought in to represent the union's position and to provide greater experience, expertise, objectivity, and autonomy. The union's chief negotiator may be accompanied by individuals who have conducted surveys on wages and benefits, trends in the consumer price index, and so on.[12]

FIGURE 13-1
Union and Management Collective Bargaining Teams

Source: Reno, Nevada, Police Department.

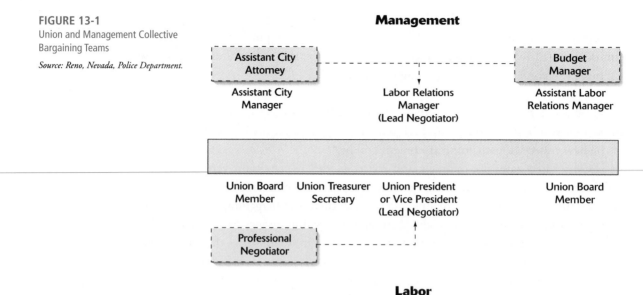

Management

| Assistant City Attorney | | Budget Manager |
| Assistant City Manager | Labor Relations Manager (Lead Negotiator) | Assistant Labor Relations Manager |

| Union Board Member | Union Treasurer Secretary | Union President or Vice President (Lead Negotiator) | Union Board Member |

Professional Negotiator

Labor

Management's chief negotiator may be the director of labor relations or the human resources director for the unit of government involved or a professional labor relations specialist. The agency's chief executive should not appear at the table personally—it is extremely delicate for the chief to represent management one day and then return to work among the employees the next. Management is represented by a key member of the command staff who has the executive's confidence.

Impasses. The purpose of bargaining is to produce a bilateral written agreement to which both parties will bind themselves during the lifetime of the agreement. Even parties bargaining in good faith may not be able to resolve their differences by themselves, and an **impasse** may result. In such cases, a neutral third party may be appointed to facilitate, suggest, or compel an agreement. Three major forms of impasse resolution are mediation, fact-finding, and arbitration:

1. *Mediation.* Mediation occurs when a third party, called the mediator, comes in to help the adversaries with the negotiations.[13] This person may be a professional mediator or someone in whom both parties have confidence. In most states, mediation may be requested by either labor or management. The mediator's task is to build agreement about the issues involved by reopening communication between the two sides. The mediator has no way to compel an agreement, so an advantage of the process is that it preserves the nature of collective bargaining by maintaining the decision-making power in the hands of the parties involved.[14]

2. *Fact-finding.* Fact-finding primarily involves the interpretation of facts and the determination of what weight to attach to them. Appointed in the same way as mediators, fact-finders also do not have a way to impose a settlement of the dispute. Fact-finders may sit alone or as part of a panel, which normally consists of three people. The fact-finding hearing is quasi-judicial, although less strict rules of evidence are applied. Both labor and management may be represented by legal counsel, and

verbatim transcripts are commonly made. In most cases, the fact-finder's recommendations are made public at some point.[15]

3. *Arbitration.* Arbitration parallels fact-finding but differs in that the "end product of arbitration is a final and binding decision that sets the terms of the settlement and with which the parties are legally required to comply."[16] Arbitration may be compulsory or voluntary: It is compulsory when mandated by state law and binding on the parties even if one of them is unwilling to comply; it is voluntary when the parties undertake of their own volition to use the procedure. Even when entered into voluntarily, arbitration is binding on the parties who have agreed to it.

Grievances. The establishment of a working agreement between labor and management does not mean that the possibility for conflict no longer exists; the day-to-day administration of the agreement may also be the basis for strife. Questions can arise about the interpretation and application of the document and its various clauses. Grievances—complaints or expressions of dissatisfaction by an employee concerning some aspect of employment—may arise. The grievance procedure is a formal process that involves the seeking of redress of the complaints through progressively higher channels within the organization. The sequence of the grievance process will be spelled out in the collective-bargaining agreement and will typically include the following steps: The employee presents the grievance to his or her immediate supervisor; if the employee does not receive satisfaction, a written grievance is presented to the division commander, then to the chief executive officer, then to the city or county manager, and finally to an arbiter, who is selected according to the rules of the American Arbitration Association.[17]

The burden of proof is on the grieving party except in disciplinary cases, in which it is always on the employer. The parties may be represented by counsel at the hearing, and the format will include opening statements by each side, examination and cross-examination of any witnesses, and closing arguments in the reverse order in which opening arguments were made.[18]

Job Actions. A **job action** is an activity in which employees engage to express their dissatisfaction with a particular person, event, or condition or to attempt to influence the outcome of some matter pending before decision makers.[19] Job actions are of four types: vote of confidence, work slowdown, work speedup, and work stoppage.

1. *Vote of confidence.* The vote of confidence is used sparingly. A vote of no confidence signals employees' collective displeasure with the chief administrator of the agency. Although such votes have no legal standing, they may have high impact due to the resulting publicity.
2. *Work slowdown.* In work slowdowns, employees continue to work, but they do so at a leisurely pace, causing productivity to fall. As productivity declines, the government is pressured to resume normal work production (for example, a police department may urge officers to issue more citations so revenues are not lost).[20]
3. *Work speedup.* A work speedup involves accelerated activity in the level of services. For example, a police department may conduct a "ticket blizzard" to protest a low pay increase or to pressure government leaders either to make more concessions at the bargaining table or to abandon some policy change that affects their working conditions.

4. *Work stoppage.* Work stoppages constitute the most severe job action. The ultimate work stoppage is the strike, or the withholding of all employee services. This tactic is most often used by labor to force management back to the bargaining table when negotiations have reached an impasse. However, criminal justice employee strikes are now rare. Briefer work stoppages, which do not involve all employees and are known in policing as "blue flu," last only a few days.

Fair Labor Standards Act. An area of policing that is at the heart of management-labor relations is the **Fair Labor Standards Act (FLSA)**. For some police administrators, the FLSA has become a budgetary and operational nightmare. Indeed, one observer referred to the FLSA as the criminal justice administrator's "worst nightmare come true."[21] The act provides minimum pay and overtime provisions covering both public- and private-sector employees and contains special provisions for firefighters and police officers. Although there is currently some discussion in Congress concerning the repeal or modification of the act, at the present time it is still a legislative force that administrators, mid-level managers, and supervisors must reckon with.

The act was passed in 1938 to protect the rights and working conditions of employees in the private sector. During that time, long hours, poor wages, and substandard work conditions plagued most businesses, and the FLSA placed a number of restrictions on employers to improve these conditions. In 1985, the U.S. Supreme Court brought local police employees under the coverage of the FLSA. In this major (and very costly) decision, *Garcia* v. *San Antonio Transit Authority,*[22] the Court held, 5 to 4, that Congress imposed the requirements of the FLSA on state and local governments.

Police operations, which take place twenty-four hours a day, seven days a week, often require overtime and participation in off-duty activities such as court appearances and training sessions. The FLSA comes into play when overtime salaries must be paid. It provides that an employer must generally pay employees time and a half for all hours worked over 40 per week; overtime must also be paid to personnel for all work in excess of 43 hours in a seven-day cycle or 171 hours in a twenty-eight-day period. Public-safety employees may accrue a maximum of 480 hours of "comp" (compensation) time, which, if not utilized as leave, must be paid off upon separation from employment at each employee's final rate of pay or at the average pay over the last three years, whichever is greater.[23] Furthermore, employers usually cannot require employees to take comp time in lieu of cash. The primary issue with the FLSA is the rigidity of application of what is compensable work because the act prohibits an agency from taking "volunteered time" from employees.

Today an officer who works the night shift must receive pay for attending training or testifying in court during the day. Furthermore, officers who are ordered to remain at home in anticipation of emergency actions must be compensated. Notably, however, FLSA's overtime provisions do not apply to those who are employed in a bona fide executive, administrative, or professional capacity. In criminal justice, the act has generally been held to apply to detectives and sergeants but not to those of the rank of lieutenant and above.

Garcia prompted an onslaught of litigation by police and fire employees of state and local government entities. The issues are broad but may include paying overtime compensation to K-9 and equestrian officers who care for department animals while "off duty," overtime pay for officers who access their work computer and conduct business from home, pay for academy recruits who are given mandatory homework assignments, and standby and on-call pay for supervisors and officers who are assigned to units that require their unscheduled return to work. These are just a few of the many FLSA issues that are being litigated in courts across the nation.

Bringing Down the Walls: More Women and Minorities Wearing the Badge

KEY CHALLENGES FOR WOMEN   Over the past thirty years, the proportion of female police officers has grown steadily. During the 1970s, some formal barriers to hiring women such as height requirements were eliminated, and subjective physical agility tests and oral interviews were modified.[24] Some job discrimination suits further expanded women's opportunities. A 1980 lawsuit by a Los Angeles police officer, Fanchon Blake, opened up the ranks above sergeant to women; the case of a New York City detective, Kathleen Burke, who in May 1991 won a settlement and a promotion to detective first grade, broadened their possibilities even more.[25]

AGENCY AND CHIEF EXECUTIVE REPRESENTATION   As noted in Chapter 3, women now represent 11.3 percent of sworn personnel in municipal police agencies and 12.9 percent of sworn personnel in county sheriff's offices.[26] State agencies overall have a

Today women in law enforcement have a variety of assignments, including SWAT and motorcycle patrol.

(Courtesy Monica Geddry)

much lower percentage of female officers (6.8 percent) than local agencies,[27] while women are more highly represented (16.1 percent) in federal agencies[28] (see Chapter 2, Table 2-1, for a thorough breakdown of female and minority representation in federal agencies).

Although the representation of female officers is low compared to their overall population, underrepresentation is even more evident in the leadership ranks, where women constitute only 1 percent of the police chiefs in the United States.[29] The number of women serving as chiefs has expanded considerably, however, since Penny Harrington took over as chief in Portland, Oregon (becoming the first woman chief in a large agency), in 1985 and Elizabeth (Betsy) Watson assumed the helm in Houston (becoming the first in a city of more than 1 million population) in 1990. As examples, in early 2004 newly appointed women were serving as chiefs of police in Boston, Detroit, Milwaukee, and San Francisco, providing further evidence that today "mayors are looking for sophisticated CEOs who can oversee large budgets, negotiate thorny management problems, and set sound departmentwide policy."[30]

A recent survey identified 157 women serving as chiefs of police and 25 who were sheriffs; 96 of these chiefs participated in a survey intended to establish a demographic profile of the women.[31] Of these chief executives, 48 (49 percent) were in charge of municipal police departments, while 40 (42 percent) led college and university police departments. Only 6 of the respondents led agencies with at least a hundred sworn officers (5 being municipal, 1 a campus police agency, and 1 a tribal agency). Conversely, 23 (25.8 percent) were in agencies with 10 or fewer officers. These female CEOs reflect the increasing levels of education achieved by today's chiefs, with three-fourths having either a bachelor's or a master's degree. About a third had a partner who was also in policing.[32]

Certainly a large enough proportion of women have now been employed in policing long enough to be considered for promotion. A number of researchers question the commitment of police agencies and their male administrators in promoting women and have made recommendations for changing the evaluation and promotion process.[33]

KEY ISSUES   Peter Horne identified several key issues that need to be addressed[34]:

- *Recruitment.* Unfocused, random recruiting is unlikely to attract diversity. Literature such as fliers, posters, and brochures should feature female officers working in all areas of policing. Furthermore, agencies should go anywhere (local colleges, women's groups, female community leaders, gyms, martial arts schools) and use all types of media to attract qualified applicants.

- *Preemployment physical testing.* Historically, women have been screened out disproportionately in the preemployment screening physical testing used by many agencies. Tests that include such components as scaling a six-foot wall, bench-pressing one's own weight, and throwing medicine balls are likely to have an adverse impact on female applicants, so agencies should examine their physical tests to determine the reasons women are disproportionately screened out. Also, agencies should permit all candidates to practice for the preemployment physical exam.

- *Academy training.* Recruits must be trained in sexually integrated academy classes to ensure full integration between female and male officers. Female instructors are especially important during academy training because they are positive role models and help female rookies develop skills and confidence. Involving female instructors in firearms and physical/self-defense training will send a message that trained veteran female officers can effectively handle the physical aspects of policing.

- *Field training.* Field training officers (FTOs) play a crucial role in transforming the academy graduate to a competent field officer. FTOs (or police training officers [PTOs], discussed in Chapter 4) should be both support systems for female rookies and effective evaluators of their competence. Females should also serve as FTOs/PTOs.

- *Assignments.* Agencies should routinely review the daily assignments of all probationary officers to ensure they have equal opportunity to become effective patrol officers. If women are removed from patrol early in their careers (for any reason), they will miss vital field patrol experience. The majority of supervisory positions exist in the patrol division, and departments generally believe that field supervisors must have adequate field experience in order to be effective and respected by subordinates.

- *Promotions.* The so-called glass ceiling continues to restrict women's progress through the ranks. Performance evaluations and the overall promotional system utilized by agencies should be scrutinized for gender bias. For example, studies show that the more subjective the promotion process, the less likely women are to pass it. To provide more objectivity (in terms of ability to measure aptitude), the process may include more hands-on (practical, applied) tasks and the selection of board members who represent both sexes.

- *Sexual discrimination and harassment.* Where they exist, sexual discrimination and harassment exact a human cost from the women involved, including a negative impact on their performance and careers (and probably a negative impact on the recruitment of other women into policing). A Police Foundation study found that "most women officers have experienced both sex discrimination and harassment on the job."[35] Departments need to have policies in place concerning gender discrimination and harassment—and they need to enforce them.

- *Mentoring.* The employee's experience as he or she transitions into the organization can be a deciding factor in whether or not the employee remains with the organization. Formal mentoring programs—which can begin even before the rookie enters the academy—have helped some agencies raise their retention rates for women; such programs can include having a veteran employee provide new hires with information concerning what to expect at the academy and beyond during field training and the probationary period.

- *Career and family.* Police work can create a considerable amount of conflict between one's work life and one's family life. Police agencies should have a leave policy covering pregnancy and maternity leave. Light- or limited-duty assignments (desk, communications, records) can be made available to female officers when reassignment is necessary. Other issues include the availability of quality child care and shift rotation (which can more heavily burden single parents) as well as the provision of uniforms, body armor, and firearms that fit women.

As the community-oriented policing and problem solving (COPPS) concept (examined in Chapter 6) continues to expand, female officers can likewise play an increasingly vital role. Experts maintain that the verbal skills many women possess often have a calming effect that defuses sensitive or potentially explosive situations—such as rape and domestic violence calls[36]—which can lead to what one person termed "a kinder, gentler organization."[37]

Still, this clearly remains an area in which law enforcement must change. For women to serve effectively as police officers, executives must see the value of utilizing and vigorously recruiting, hiring, and retaining them. A basic task for the chief executive is to consider how departmental policies impact female officers with respect to selection, training, promotion, sexual harassment, and family leave. Most important, executives must set a tone of welcoming women into the department.

SIMILAR CHALLENGES FOR MINORITIES   As with women, racial and ethnic **minority officers** have made dramatic gains in their representation in local police agencies. In 1987 they represented only 14.5 percent of sworn full-time municipal police officers and 13.4 percent of sworn personnel in sheriff's offices.[38] Today, however, they represent 23.6 percent of such personnel in municipal police departments and 18.8 percent in sheriff's offices.[39]

Several developments of the early 1970s spurred the growth of African-Americans in policing and included federal reports (such as that from the U.S. Commission on Civil Rights[40]), the Supreme Court's decision in *Griggs* v. *Duke Power Company* (1971) banning the use of intelligence tests and other artificial barriers that were not job related,[41] and federal legislation such as the Equal Employment Opportunities Act of 1972. The mid-1970s witnessed the advent of the National Black Police Association and the National

Police departments must strive to enhance diversification in their ranks.

(Courtesy Michael Newman/PhotoEdit)

Organization of Black Law Enforcement Executives (NOBLE), which advocated increased hiring of minority officers and improvement of community relations. In the 1980s, several lawsuits successfully challenged such requirements as height, age, weight, and sex as well as a clean arrest record.[42]

Recruitment of minority officers remains a difficult task. Probably the single most difficult barrier has to do with the image that minority communities have of police officers: Unfortunately, police officers have been seen as symbols of oppression and have been charged with using excessive brutality; they are often seen as an army of occupation. Many minorities view African-American police officers as people who have "sold out." For many of those African-Americans in uniforms, a so-called **double marginality** has existed, whereby the African-American officers feel accepted neither by their own minority group nor by the white officers. However, many African-Americans view police work as an opportunity to leave the ghetto and enter the middle class. As one officer put it, "There were two ways to get out of my neighborhood and not end up dead or in prison. You either became a minister or a cop. I always fell asleep in church so I decided to become a cop."[43]

African-American police officers face problems similar to those of women who attempt to enter and prosper in police work. Until more African-American officers are promoted and can affect police policy and serve as role models, they are likely to be treated unequally and have difficulty being promoted—a classic catch-22 situation. African-Americans considering a police career may be encouraged by a survey of African-American officers, which found that most thought their jobs were satisfying and offered opportunities for advancement.[44]

Interestingly, a study of African-American high school students found that although negative experiences with the police increased negative attitudes toward the police, these attitudes did not in themselves reduce interest in police work. The findings suggested that police recruiters need not expend a lot of effort trying to neutralize perceptions that African-American people are treated unfairly by the police. A greater concern among the students was the danger of the job itself, so it may be more important for police departments to educate the parents of potential African-American recruits about the benefits and objectives of police work rather than focus excessively on dealing with negative attitudes.[45]

NOBLE, an influential coalition of blacks, was founded in 1976 and has fifty-seven chapters in the United States. Its purposes are to unify black law enforcement officers at executive and command levels, to conduct research in relevant areas of law enforcement, to recommend legislation relating to the criminal justice process, to establish means and strategies for dealing with racism in the field of criminal justice, to sensitize people to the problems of the black community, to facilitate the exchange of information among black police executives, and to articulate the concerns of black executives in law enforcement.[46]

On Guard: Private Police

A burgeoning industry in this country, which is both a trend and an issue, is the **private police**, those provide protective services for profit.

HISTORICAL OVERVIEW   Since prehistoric times, people have sought security from enemies and from beasts of prey by developing weapons, building and fortifying caves, and using fire, stone, hemp, and water to punish and control their fellow humans. We have always sought to protect ourselves from a hostile environment.[47]

In the early nineteenth century in England, private police were hired as watchmen by shipping docks, industrial firms, and railroad companies. In the mid-nineteenth century, America's western frontier was awash with train robbers, pickpockets, bootleggers, and common outlaws; as a result, railroad companies were allowed to establish their own in-house proprietary security forces. This was also the beginning of the contract (fee-for-service) security system for private concerns.[48]

In 1851, a pioneer in the private-security industry, Allan Pinkerton, initiated the Pinkerton National Detective Agency, which specialized in railroad security. Pinkerton established the first private-security contract operation in the United States. His motto was "We Never Sleep," and his logo, an open eye, was probably the genesis of the term *private eye;* Pinkerton also established a code of ethics for his agents. Other pioneers in the security industry were Henry Wells and William Fargo, who in 1853 formed a contract security company, Wells Fargo, which provided private detectives and shotgun riders on stagecoaches west of the Missouri River. Later, in 1909, William J. Burns, a former head of the forerunner agency of the Federal Bureau of Investigation (FBI), founded a detective agency. (Pinkerton and Burns had the only national investigative agencies until the formation of the FBI in 1924.) In 1917, the Brinks armored car was unveiled. In 1954, George R. Wackenhut and three other former FBI agents formed the Wackenhut Corporation, another large contract guard and investigative firm in the United States.[49]

William A. Pinkerton, principal of the western branch of Pinkerton's National Detective Agency.

(Reprinted from The Bue and the Brass: American Policing 1890–1910, 1976. Copyright held by the International Association of Chiefs of Police, 515 North Washington Street, Alexandria, VA 22314. Further reproduction without express written permission for IACP is strictly prohibited.)

TODAY: "A NATION OF THIEVES"　　The late loss-prevention expert Saul Astor said, "We are a nation of thieves."[50] It might be added that we are a nation that needs to be protected against would-be terrorists, rapists, robbers, and other dangerous people. There are about 23 million violent and property crime victimizations each year in this nation.[51] As a result (and especially since 9/11), this nation has become highly security minded concerning its computers, lotteries, celebrities, college campuses, casinos, nuclear plants, airports, shopping centers, mass transit systems, hospitals, and railroads. Such businesses, industries, and institutions have recognized the need to conscientiously protect their assets against threats of crime and other disasters (and the limited capabilities of the nation's full-time sworn officers and agents to protect them and their assets) and have increasingly turned to the "other police"—those of the private sector— for protection.

Although there are no recent governmental studies on the numbers of individuals engaged in private policing, estimates are that there are now more than ten thousand private security companies in the United States, employing over seven hundred thousand uniformed officers as well as about one hundred thousand managers and store detectives.[52] If accurate, the private policing field is larger in both personnel and resources than the federal, state, and local forces combined.[53]

In-house security services, directly hired and controlled by the company or organization, are called **proprietary services**; **contract services** are those outside firms or individuals who are hired by the individual or company to provide security services for a fee. The most common security services provided include contract guards, alarm services, private investigators, locksmith services, armored-car services, and security consultants.

Although some of the duties of the security officer are similar to those of the public police officer, their overall powers are entirely different. First, because security officers are not police officers, court decisions have stated that security officers are not bound by the *Miranda* decision concerning suspects' rights. Furthermore, security officers generally possess only the same authority to effect an arrest as does the common citizen (the exact extent of a citizen's arrest power varies, however, depending on the type of crime, the jurisdiction, and the status of the citizen). In most states, warrantless arrests by private citizens are allowed when a felony has been committed and reasonable grounds exist for believing that the person arrested committed it. Most states also allow citizen's arrests for misdemeanors committed in the arrester's presence.

The tasks of the private police are very similar to those of their public counterparts: protecting executives and employees, tracking and forecasting security threats, monitoring alarms, preventing and detecting fraud, conducting investigations, providing crisis management and prevention, and responding to substance abuse.[54] Still, the security industry and security officers are not always portrayed in a positive manner in popular culture; movies often cast them as poorly trained, incompetent individuals. Indeed, one study found that security officers and their work are viewed significantly less positively by males, whites, and the middle class and by those who have had an encounter with a security officer.[55]

RECRUITMENT, TRAINING, AND WEAPONS   Certainly higher-level security positions can be lucrative, often drawing from the ranks of college graduates who perhaps have studied further in such subjects as security administration, business management, and computer science. These individuals will find private-sector positions to be challenging, rewarding, varied, and often complex in nature; furthermore, they may also gain corporate benefits, stock options, and other perquisites.

In contrast to the boom of the industry in terms of both numbers of employees and dollars spent, there have been problems and concerns at the lower levels. As one author noted, "Of those individuals involved in private security, some are uniformed, some are not; some carry guns, some are unarmed; some guard nuclear energy instal-lations, some guard golf courses; some are trained, some are not; some have college degrees, some are virtually uneducated."[56] Studies have shown that security officer recruits often have minimal education and training; because the pay is usually quite low, the jobs often attract only those people who cannot find other jobs or who seek temporary work. Thus much of the work is done by the young and the retired,[57] and the recruitment and training of lower-level private-security personnel can present a real concern.[58] Clearly, today's security officer needs to be taught more than the basics: the chain of command, ways to use a radio, and uniform dress standards. For these rea-sons, security training has been an issue in court cases involving claims of negligent security.

Another issue that arises is whether the private police should be armed. When an employer decides to arm security personnel, the type and level of firearms training that is provided are justifiably given closer scrutiny. In the past, much has been made about secu-rity officers who have received little or no prior training or have undergone no checks on their criminal history records but are carrying a weapon. There are certainly some roles in which security officers must be armed, such as protecting high-risk or high-value assets, including nuclear power plants and money transported in armored cars. Twenty-three hours of firearms instruction is recommended for all security personnel, as well as another twenty-four hours on general matters and proper legal training.[59]

PUBLIC OFFICERS AS PRIVATE POLICE   One additional issue concerns the impact of public officers and their departments when officers are hired to perform private-security work. Several models have been developed to manage off-duty employment of officers. First, the **department contract model** permits close control of off-duty work because firms must apply to the department to have officers assigned to them. Officers are paid by the department, which is reimbursed by the private firm. Departments can screen employers to ensure that the proposed use of officers will not conflict with the department's needs or standards (for example, a department will often ban officers from moonlighting for bail-bond companies, establishments with gambling, bars, bill collectors, and tow truck companies).

Second, the **officer contract model** allows each officer to find off-duty employment and to enter into a direct relationship with the private firm. The officer must apply to the department for permission, however, so the agency retains control over the standards listed above. Finally, under the **union brokerage model**, the police union or association finds off-duty employment for its members. The union sets the standards for the work and bargains with the department over the pay and conditions of the employment.[60]

SAN FRANCISCO'S PATROL SPECIAL POLICE   An interesting departure from the standard forms of private policing is San Francisco's Patrol Special Police, a nonsworn group that was formed in 1847 by merchants to combat the insurgence of Barbary Coast outlaws. The organization was incorporated into the city's charter in 1935. The Patrol Special officers provide neighborhoods with supplementary police patrol, under the supervision of the San Francisco Police Department (SFPD). Patrol Special officers are appointed by the San Francisco Police Commission and are governed by rules and procedures set by the commission. Officers wear uniforms approved by the commission, carry a firearm, and use two-way SFPD radios. For business and home owners, they check the interior and exterior of their property; conduct thorough searches of their premises for fire, open windows, and unlocked doors; respond to alarm calls; and provide escort services for the transport of valuables, deposit of funds, or other protective needs.[61]

CONTEMPORARY ISSUES

Stress: Sources, Effects, and Management

There is a side of policing that many people would prefer to ignore: job-related **stress**. Indeed, Sir W. S. Gilbert observed that "when constabulary duty's to be done, the policeman's lot is not a happy one."[62]

Stress can be defined as a force that is external in nature that causes strain upon the body, both physical and emotional, from its normal process. The late Hans Selye, who is known as the "father of stress research," defined stress as a nonspecific response of a body to demands placed on it.

William Westley observed more than thirty years ago that "the policeman's world is spawned of degradation, corruption and insecurity. He walks alone, a pedestrian in Hell."[63] Being a cop today has been described as a "stop-and-go nightmare."[64] As noted in Chapter 5, the job of policing has never been easy, but the danger, frustration, and family disruption of the past have been made worse by the drug war and by violent criminals who are heavily armed and hold more contempt for the police than ever before.

SOURCES   There are several potential sources of stress for police officers:

I. **Stressors Originating within the Organization**
   A. Intra-Agency Practices and Characteristics
      1. *Poor supervision.* Stress can be fostered by supervisors who go by the book and issue a constant flurry of memos, won't back up their subordinates, or fail to

Dr. Hans Selye, the "father of stress research."

(Courtesy Edward Donovan)

attend to their basic needs. These behaviors can contribute substantially to the stress levels of subordinates.

2. *Absence of career development opportunities.* The vast majority of police officers will begin and end their careers as patrol officers. Promotional opportunities are limited, and the promotion process can lack fairness and generate frustration.

3. *Inadequate reward systems.* Recognition and compensation are limited for work that is well done. A lot of negative reinforcement exists in police work. Punishment—demotion, reprimand, suspension, termination, reassignment—is commonly meted out when things go wrong.

4. *Offensive policies.* Police organizations possess numerous policies and guidelines that officers find offensive, such as locking and unlocking municipal parking lots, emptying parking meters, and running all kinds of errands.

5. *Offensive paperwork.* The volume of paperwork that police officers must complete is incredible. Computerization has generally created more paperwork for police officers because management now wants additional kinds of information.

6. *Poor equipment.* In policing, inadequate vehicles, communication equipment, and safety equipment (for example, flares) can become sources of frustration.

II. **Stressors External to the Organization.**   Stressors that come from outside the organization can cause a great deal of tension; with few exceptions, the individual officer or agency normally has little or no control over them.

A. Interorganizational Practices and Characteristics

1. *Absence of career development opportunities.* Few chances for mobility exist in police work; rank and seniority are seldom transferable to another agency, so opportunities for lateral moves are limited. Thus the officer must remain with the same agency unless he or she retires or is willing to start anew.

2. *Jurisdictional isolationism.* Police agencies are not always the tight, congenial fraternity that the public often imagines. Jurisdictional boundaries can be guarded

zealously. Some police agencies are notorious for withholding information or for grabbing credit for good arrests.

B. Criminal Justice System Practices and Characteristics

    1. *Seemingly ineffective corrections system.* The police often see corrections agencies (for example, probation and parole agencies and prisons) as a revolving door for criminals; attempts to rehabilitate offenders at these agencies often fail.

    2. *The courts.* Unfavorable court decisions and misunderstood judicial procedures (for example, plea bargaining) lead to considerable frustration for the police.

C. Distorted Press Accounts of Police Incidents. Reporters sometimes distort the news because they gather the facts hastily to meet deadlines, do not understand the facts, or simply do not care enough to report them accurately. Overzealous reporters can interfere with investigations.

D. Unfavorable Civilian Attitudes. Minorities often accuse police of over- or under-policing their neighborhoods or being brutal and racist. Similarly, the majority often complain about police response time and argue that the police should be out trying to catch bank robbers instead of issuing traffic citations.

E. Derogatory Remarks by Neighbors and Others. In a sense, police officers are never completely off duty; they are always cops, accosted both at home and at social functions by people who want to complain about the police or who want legal advice.

F. Adverse Government Actions Units of government often make decisions, including decisions about budgeting, recruiting, hiring, firing, and downsizing, without consulting police officers or managers. Public officials may monitor and chase police calls, make and enforce policy, check on officers, and seek to "fix" arrests of friends or family members.

III. Stressors Connected with the Performance of Police Duties

A. Police Work Itself

    1. *Role conflict.* Police must determine when to maintain a crime fighter image and when to portray an order-maintenance role. The public expects officers to be all things to all people—social worker, minister, physician, babysitter, psychologist, and so forth.

    2. *Adverse work scheduling.* Shift work, especially the graveyard shift and a rotating shift schedule, can adversely affect an officer's health as well as family and social life,[65] causing constant adjustment to new sleeping and eating patterns.

    3. *Fear and danger.* As was shown in Chapter 5, danger is a constant companion of police officers, so officers need to keep their survival instincts honed. An annual FBI publication, *Law Enforcement Officers Killed and Assaulted,* regularly reveals an unsettling fact: Police officers often are overpowered, outmuscled, disarmed, and murdered by offenders whom they try to arrest. Different types of assignments can bring greater stress; for example, undercover work[66] and homicide investigation[67] have been identified as particularly stressful. Also, many times officers are simply in poorer physical condition than the criminals they chase. Today more than ever, officers need to be in good physical shape. In addition, they must also properly maintain their equipment; use deescalation techniques (sometimes termed "verbal judo"); employ physical defense, approach, and positioning tactics; properly use backup personnel; deploy proper weapon and driving skills; use safe techniques when searching buildings; and handle prisoners with care.[68]

4. *Sense of uselessness and inefficiency of referral agencies.* Many officers entered the police service to help people. However, in many jurisdictions few agencies are available to which the police can refer people with problems. Police see first-hand the outcomes of the absence of such social services—suicides, murders, spousal or child abuse, and so on.

5. *Absence of closure.* Police can seldom close their cases through disposition; furthermore, plea bargaining affects much of what they did in the first place (what is believed to be a "righteous" arrest is often reduced down by the prosecutor).

6. *People in pain.* The police see firsthand the gamut of violence humans employ against one another, and they witness both crime victims and offenders at their worst. Police deal constantly with people in pain and are expected to remain calm and collected during the entire affair.

IV. Stressors Particular to the Individual Officer

A. The Police Officer Himself or Herself

1. *The fear-ridden officer.* Some (although not many) police officers are overcome by the fear and danger of the job; they are in constant fear for their physical well-being. These officers generally leave the force well before retirement.

2. *The nonconformist officer.* Police work demands a certain amount of conformity and adherence to a chain of command, allowing little room for individualism or freedom of expression. Court decisions have allowed police administrators to have residency requirements, a dress code, and so on. Pressures to conform can be severe, and some noncomforming officers cannot endure such pressure.

An Orlando, Florida, police officer cries after telling a mother that her child died in a house fire.

(Courtesy Orlando Sentinel*)*

An NYPD scuba diver is overwhelmed by what he has just seen at the bottom of a body of water.

(Courtesy NYPD Photo Unit)

3. *The minority officer.* Both African-American and female police officers suffer discrimination by virtue of entering a predominantly white male occupation.

V. **Effects of Critical Incidents.**   Several stressful repercussions can follow a police shooting. The officer is generally suspended from work pending a full investigation. He or she is secluded from work and peers, and the officer's gun, badge, and other trappings of the job are taken away.[69] Relationships with family may become strained, and the officer may experience time distortion, emotional numbing, a feeling of isolation, denial, flashbacks, sleep disturbances, legal problems, and guilt.[70] A high percentage of police officers who kill another person leave the force within five years.[71]

EFFECTS AND MANAGEMENT   It has been estimated that at any one time 15 percent of a department's officers will be in a burnout phase. These officers account for 70 to 80 percent of all the complaints against their department, including physical abuse, verbal abuse, and misuse of firearms.[72] If they do not relieve the pressure, they may eventually suffer heart attacks, nervous breakdowns, back problems, headaches, psychosomatic illnesses, and alcoholism.[73] They may also manifest excessive weight gain or loss; combativeness or irritability; excessive perspiration; excessive use of sick leave; excessive use of alcohol, tobacco, or drugs; marital or family disorders; inability to complete an assignment; loss of interest in work, hobbies, and people in general; more than the usual number of "accidents," including vehicular and other types; and more shooting incidents.[74] An extreme reaction to stress is suicide (see Exhibit 13-1). Police are at a higher risk for committing suicide because of their access to firearms, continuous exposure to human misery, shift work, social strain and marital difficulties, physical illnesses, and alcohol problems. Police are eight times more likely to commit suicide than to be killed in a homicide and three times more likely to kill themselves than to die in a job-related accident.[75]

EXHIBIT 13-1

The Blue Plague of American Policing

Cops kill themselves three times more often than other Americans. They suffer more depression, divorce more, and drink more—as many as one in four police officers have alcohol abuse problems. Cops are unhappy. They feel estranged from their departments and from a public eager to find a scapegoat for their own social, economic and political woes. This problem should give pause to everyone, to supporters and critics of the police department alike. Society needs police officers, and we need them to be happy and healthy.

The numbers are staggering. Researchers at the University of Buffalo have found that police officers are eight times more likely to commit suicide than to be killed in a homicide. The most recent U.S. Census estimates that police officers divorce twice as often as the national average. The respected researchers J. J. Hurrell and W. H. Kroes say that as many as 25 percent of police officers have alcohol abuse problems. This evidence cannot be ignored. Police officers are suffering from anomie; they believe that society is turning its back on them.

So what's going wrong? Why do cops feel unappreciated even as their performance improves? The truth is that the most common and debilitating source of stress in law enforcement comes from within the agency itself. Cops don't complain about the added complexity of their jobs nearly as much as they do about the agency for which they work. Ask cops what they don't like about their jobs and they cite internal politics, favoritism and impersonal treatment as their most common criticisms of their work environment. Internal surveys reveal that cops rate personal stress management as their most pressing need. Working in a

paramilitary structure depersonalizes and marginalizes people from top to bottom. Decision-making structures that deprive them of input embitter officers and breed cynicism. They resent supervisors who treat them as numbers, who have no consideration for their personal or family lives, who play favorites in terms of choice assignments, shifts, and recognition. They doubt whether or not they will be backed up by their superiors in times of trouble.

Police officers have an incredible capacity to deal with incidental stress. What police cannot deal with is the chronic stress of a system that marginalizes them. So what do we do? We need to create a non-toxic work environment for the men and women [who] protect us. The training and education a police officer receives [offer] little or nothing to prepare the future police officer to successfully adjust to the new and very different working environment of law enforcement. Along with body armor, every man and woman entering this profession deserves a "stress vest" that provides them with the knowledge, skills and ongoing services to combat the deadly consequences of stress.

Like any problem, the solution begins with awareness and education. Beginning with the police academy experience, future police officers (cadets) need to learn about working in a complex bureaucracy. They need to learn how to deal with human tragedy and separate it from the way they interact with their own families and loved ones. Police officers need ongoing services in stress management to maintain their identities as human beings first and understand that law enforcement is a job and career, not who they are.

Source: Robert A. Fox, "The Blue Plague of American Policing," *Law Enforcement News,* May 15/31, 2003, p. 9. John Jay College of Criminal Justice, CUNY, 899 Tenth Avenue, New York, NY 10019.

No human being can exist in a continuous state of alarm. The body, striving to maintain its normal state (homeostasis) and adapt to the alarm, can actually develop a disease in the process. Often, however, the problem of stress is exacerbated by the reluctance of police to admit they have problems. They often avoid seeking professional psychological help; officers fear being placed on limited duty or being labeled "psychos" by their peers.[76] As they start to acknowledge the problem, many police departments are attempting to improve their recruit screening and provide better counseling programs.

It is imperative that officers learn to manage their stress before it causes deep physical or emotional harm. One means is to view the mind as a "mental bucket" and strive to keep it full through hobbies or activities that provide relaxation. Exercise, proper nutrition, and positive lifestyle choices (such as not smoking or abusing alcohol) are also essential for good health.

The federal government has taken official notice of the problem of police stress. In 1997, the National Institute of Justice awarded grants to eight police agencies and organizations for devising effective stress-reduction programs.[77]

Higher Education

AN ENDURING CONTROVERSY   Today a relatively small proportion of police officers have (or are required to have) a college degree. Indeed, of all local police agencies, only 8 percent require officers to have some college; 9 percent require a two-year college degree, and only 1 percent require a four-year degree[78] (a statistic that becomes more poignant when one considers that 28 percent of U.S. adults age twenty-five and older hold at least a bachelor's degree).[79] These low percentages are certainly surprising in light of the reports of numerous studies, courts, and national commissions (some of which are discussed below) that have concluded that higher education is essential for police officers. As will be seen, this remains one of policing's most enduring and controversial issues.

Efforts to involve college-educated personnel in police work were first made by August Vollmer (discussed in Chapter 1) in 1917 when he recruited University of California students as part-time police officers in Berkeley.[80] However, few departments elsewhere in the country took any immediate steps to follow Vollmer's example. Rank-and-file officers strongly resisted the concept of college-level studies for police, and officers with a college education remained very much an exception; they were often referred to disparagingly as "college cops."[81]

However, the movement toward higher education for police continued to spread: By 1975, there were 729 community college programs and 376 four-year programs.[82] The Law Enforcement Education Program (LEEP) provided tuition assistance for in-service police officers and preservice students. In 1973, ninety-five thousand college and university students were receiving LEEP assistance—unquestionably the "glory days" of higher education in criminal justice.[83] Many patrol officers who otherwise could not have afforded it received quality higher education.

RATIONALES IN FAVOR OF HIGHER EDUCATION FOR POLICE   As indicated above, the issue of higher education for police officers has been addressed by a number of notable entities, going back more than forty years. First, the President's Commission on Law Enforcement and the Administration of Justice made this statement in 1967:

> It is nonsense to state or assume that the enforcement of law is so simple that it can be done by those unencumbered by the study of liberal arts. Officers of any department should certainly be conversant with the structure of government, [and] be well grounded in sociology, criminology, and human relations in order to understand the ramifications of the problems which confront them daily.[84]

Shortly afterward, in 1972, the American Bar Association provided more accolades for higher education for police:

> Police need personnel in their ranks who have the characteristics a college education seeks to foster: intellectual curiosity, analytical ability, articulateness, and a capacity to relate the events of the day to the social, political, and historical context in which they occur.[85]

In 1973, the National Advisory Commission on Criminal Justice Standards and Goals, concurring that college-educated officers were needed, recommended that all police officers have a four-year college education by 1982,[86] a goal that obviously went unmet. Nevertheless, from 1967 to 1986, every national commission that studied crime, violence, and policing in America came to the conclusion that a college education could help the police do their jobs better.[87] Advocates of higher education for the police maintain that it will improve the quality of policing by making officers more tolerant of people who are different from themselves; in this view, college-educated officers are more professional, communicate better with citizens, are better decision makers, and have better written and verbal skills than less educated officers.

A ringing endorsement for higher education for the police also came in 1985 when a lawsuit challenged the Dallas, Texas, Police Department's requirement that all applicants for police officer positions possess forty-five credit hours and at least a C average at an accredited college or university. The Fifth Circuit Court of Appeals, and eventually the U.S. Supreme Court, upheld the educational requirement. The circuit court said:

> Even a rookie police officer must have the ability to handle tough situations. A significant part of a police officer's function involves his ability to function effectively as a crisis intervenor, in family fights, teen-age rumbles, bar brawls, street corner altercations, racial disturbances, riots and similar situations. Few professionals are so peculiarly charged with individual responsibilities as police officers. Mistakes of judgment could cause irreparable harm to citizens or even to the community. The educational requirement bears a manifest relationship to the position of police officer. We conclude that the district court's findings …are not erroneous.[88]

Many proponents of higher education requirements in policing (including many police executives and sheriffs themselves) bemoan the fact that local police have the lowest standards for education and training in the criminal justice system. They find it incomprehensible that in more than 80 percent of all agencies someone can enter policing with only a General Education Diploma (GED) or a high school diploma. Then, after attending a training academy of less than six months' duration followed by field training, the officers are expected to "guide people through complex, life-threatening situations far beyond their abilities and training" and interact daily with highly educated people in the community.[89] They also wonder how policing can thus be deemed a profession when a hallmark of professionalism is high educational requirements, at the expense of the candidate.[90]

Abundant empirical evidence also indicates that college-educated police officers are better officers. Compared to less educated officers, they have significantly fewer founded citizen complaints[91]; have better peer relationships[92]; are likelier to take a leadership role in the organization[93]; tend to be more flexible[94]; are less dogmatic and less authoritarian[95]; take fewer leave days, receive fewer injuries, have less injury time, have lower rates of absenteeism, use fewer sick days, and are involved in fewer traffic accidents[96]; have greater ability to analyze situations and make judicious decisions; and have a more desirable system of personal values.[97] Furthermore, college graduates are significantly less likely to violate their department's internal regulations regarding insubordination, negligent use of a firearm, and absenteeism than officers who lack a college degree.[98]

RATIONALES AGAINST HIGHER EDUCATION FOR POLICE (AND REBUTTALS)   A major argument by police administrators against requiring a college degree for entry-level officers is that the recruitment of minorities will greatly suffer, which is particularly problematic at a time when agencies seek to diversify their ranks. However, a number of jurisdictions argue just as strongly that this is not a problem and offer evidence (albeit anecdotal) that the reverse is actually true and that maintaining the college requirement has a number of benefits[99]:

- The Arlington, Texas, Police Department (APD) has required police officers to have bachelor's degrees since about 1983 and has successfully recruited officers, even protected-class officers. In fact, people from these protected classes have made up about two-thirds of each of its recruit classes since 1986. Colleges with higher minority and female enrollment, directors of female athletic programs, community referrals—all are sources for college-educated recruits and are heavily targeted.

- Dover Township, New Jersey, has required a two-year associate's degree since 1978 and a four-year degree since 1994; it also recruits heavily on college campuses and advertises widely in the mainstream media, including cable television. Dover has also found that many applicants are from other departments who are seeking the opportunity to work in the professional atmosphere of a college-educated agency.

- The Lakewood, Colorado, Police Department (LPD) had required bachelor's degrees for its officers (known as agents) since 1970, and today many agents have graduate degrees, including law degrees. LPD street officers are generalists, and the LPD feels they amass more experience in a few years than officers in other departments obtain in their entire careers; officers are given the authority to take creative approaches in their daily assignments and are among the highest paid officers in the state. Sixty of their agents have become chiefs of police and sheriffs in other agencies across the nation.

- The Tulsa, Oklahoma, Police Department (TPD) instituted a bachelor's degree requirement in 1996. Uniquely, if a young black man or woman met all the criteria for employment except for education, the TPD would lend him or her the money for books and tuition (with donated funds); then, after meeting the educational requirement, he or she would be employed as an apprentice police officer and enter the academy, later becoming a full-fledged officer. (This program was very successful, but claims of reverse discrimination caused it to be terminated.) Educational incentives are offered today, and the higher education requirement has not made recruiting more difficult. The TPD has also found that its educated officers maintain a much higher degree of community involvement—coaching, mentoring, teaching, volunteering, serving on boards and committees, and having a lifelong learning mentality.

- Redlands, California, requires sixty credit hours upon hiring, but most officers have bachelor's degrees; educational requirements become higher as officers are promoted up through the ranks. To make it easier for officers to complete their education, the department offers flexible schedules and will pay for the officers' education.
- Charleston, South Carolina, and Burnsville, Minnesota, have a surplus of well-qualified applicants with bachelor's degrees and higher; attracting college-educated personnel has meant retooling the traditional recruiting techniques through extensive outreach to all colleges in the southeastern United States.

Some studies, however, have found negative effects of higher education. Critics believe that educated officers are more likely to become frustrated with their work and that their limited opportunities for advancement will cause them to leave the force early. Furthermore, they argue that police tasks that require mostly common sense or street sense are not performed better by officers with higher education.[100]

These studies found that it had no positive effect on officers' public-service orientation (those with a degree displayed less orientation toward public service than those without a degree)[101] and that college-educated officers attach less value on obedience to supervisors than officers without a college education.[102]

It seems paradoxical—given the research, the increase in educational level of society in general, and the need for police agencies to recruit the best people—that in this new millennium, our society still does not require higher educational standards for police officers. No true profession requires less than a college degree, and police, in their quest for greater professionalism, should take notice.

An Ongoing Problem: Homelessness

Although **homelessness** has been a substantial problem in American society since the early 1980s, it seems that quite a lot less is written or spoken about this population today than during the 1980s and 1990s. However, while the dialogue in the media about homelessness may not be as robust as it once was, this problem is probably never very far from the top of the list of priorities of most governmental entities.

SIGNIFICANT SOCIAL PROBLEM   Homelessness is a condition of people who lack regular legal access to adequate housing. A first-of-its-kind "groundbreaking" count of the homeless announced in February 2007 by the U.S. Department of Housing and Urban Development found that 704,000 people nationwide had sought emergency shelter in a three-month period. Families with children accounted for one-third of those seeking shelter; the rest were individuals, mostly adult men (about half of them black).[103] About one-third of the adult homeless are chronically mentally ill; about half are alcoholic

A homeless man lives on a steam grate in Washington, D.C.

or abuse drugs.[104] To provide some indication of the extent of the problem, each night there are 80,000 homeless people in Los Angeles County,[105] and Las Vegas, known for its open lifestyle and relatively inexpensive food and beverage industries, has more than 50,000 people experiencing homelessness per year.[106] It remains a serious concern for all Americans, especially when so many families are forced to live on the streets and in shelters.

CAUSES AND COSTS   The causes of homelessness are several: poverty, declining supply of low-income housing, lack of available public housing, and increases in welfare payments not keeping pace with inflation. Other factors implicated in the trend are changes in the treatment of the chronically mentally ill, drug use, inability of some families to support dependent adult members, and increasing rates of violence against women.[107] The lack of affordable housing looms large here—it does not require a doctorate in economics to realize that if a person must earn about $14 per hour just to afford a one-bedroom apartment in a community where the median wage is only $11 per hour, there will be a homelessness problem. Other issues that impact the homeless are the closing of mobile home parks and the condominium conversions in cities and rural areas.[108]

Another way of looking at the economic impact of homelessness is by costing out police calls for service for the homeless. If a city spends $1 million per year helping the homeless on the streets and another $5 million handling calls at low-budget motels where many homeless find temporary refuge from the streets, then spending a few million dollars for shelters and transitional housing does not sound so expensive after all. Cost estimates for daily jail stays must also be taken into account. Calculate $80 to $175 per night in a jail, $300 per day for substance abuse detoxification, $3,700 per night in an emergency room, $4,500 for a typical three-day hospital stay, and $215 per ambulance ride, and the costs become staggering.[109]

WHAT CAN BE DONE?   What can be done nationally to stop the cycle of homelessness? Certainly far better and more economical solutions exist than frequent trips to police stations, jails, and emergency rooms—transitional housing and support services are two options. Clearly, the state legislatures and city and county commissions must help to break the cycle of homelessness by appropriating adequate funds to social services. There must be enough money allocated to help the police not be the initial or sole point of contact for how society helps the homeless or someone else in crisis. The police argue that rather than trying to cope with the homeless population, they must instead be allowed to focus their fight against genuine criminals, particularly those who are truly violent.[110]

The police are often caught in the middle, being pressured by merchants, public officials, and private citizens to do something about the homeless population but not having the power to arrest the homeless because of limits in court rulings, local ordinances, or state statutes. Still, the police can enforce local ordinances if extant in their jurisdiction; as importantly, police can work with mental health agencies and shelters and make referrals for this population. They can also conduct a census to assess the extent of homelessness in their jurisdiction, have record-keeping procedures put in place, and generally consider the special needs of this population, particularly during winter months. A well-planned response to homeless populations, with emphasis on the COPPS approach, would allow police departments to manage significant social problems while making efficient use of police resources.

To raise awareness, in early 2007 the police in Reno, Nevada, gave 40 homeless people disposable cameras and asked them to document their life through pictures; 15 homeless people turned in 240 pictures that captured the life of isolation and limited resources. Many of those photos were then put on display in the state's legislative building in Carson City, where 200 homeless advocates slept in cardboard boxes and tents on the legislature's lawn to bring awareness to the problem.[111]

SUMMARY

This chapter has examined several contemporary trends and issues in policing. Despite its 180-year history and many advances, policing still has many issues that have not been resolved. Certainly the section on collective bargaining and the discussion of officers' rights would be completely foreign to the major figures (Peel, Vollmer, Parker, and so on) who were instrumental in the development and maintenance of the reform era of policing (discussed in Chapter 1).

Women and minorities have yet to be accepted in this occupation, even though studies have shown their tremendous value to the field. The argument seems compelling that until there are enough women and minorities at all levels of a police force, policy decisions about hiring and promoting them will be ineffective or nonexistent. It was shown that the low numbers of women and minorities in policing result in a need for role models for others who might consider such a career. Higher education also remains a questionable element of policing for many people—notwithstanding that several major national commissions and court decisions as well as other entities and police executives have been advocating this requirement for nearly three decades. The major argument against having a college education requirement, that it greatly diminishes the minority hiring pool, was also brought into question in this chapter. Very low percentages of women, minorities, and college-educated police officers indicate there is much work remaining to be done in those areas, particularly when one compares those percentages with our society at large.

The two concepts of private policing and police stress (which in their own ways, some good and some bad, are related to public policing) are probably going to remain a part of the fabric of policing forever. The problem of homelessness has been very acute for nearly three decades, and it shows little sign of abating in spite of data on its causes and costs.

In sum, this chapter lays bare some elements of policing that have vastly changed, some that have largely remained the same, and some that are likely going to be around for a long time. Whether or not they prove to be a blessing or a curse for the police largely remains to be seen—and remains to some degree, large or small, to be decided by the police themselves.

KEY TERMS

collective bargaining
contract services
department contract model
double marginality
Fair Labor Standards Act (FLSA)
grievance
homelessness
impasse
job action
labor relations
minority officer
officer contract model
Peace Officer Bill of Rights
private police
proprietary services
stress
union brokerage model
unionization

REVIEW QUESTIONS

1. What employment rights do today's police officers possess, and what are some of the common provisions of the Peace Officer Bill of Rights?

2. What are the major reasons for the development and expansion of police unions, and what is their impact today?

3. What are the three models of collective bargaining, and what happens under each model when there is an impasse?

4. What are the four kinds of job actions?

5. How would you describe the Fair Labor Standards Act and the way it operates in policing?

6. What are some difficulties in recruiting and retaining women and minorities in policing, and what are some issues facing those who are employed in the field?

7. How did private policing evolve, and what is its status today?

8. Describe the unique nature and functions of San Francisco's Patrol Special Police.

9. What are the three models under which public police officers may work as private police/security officers?

10. What are some of the major causes of stress, and how can officers reduce or manage it?

11. Why is the possession of higher education by police officers controversial, and what are some rationales given for and against officers having such education?

12. What factors contribute to homelessness, what are some of the hidden costs involved with this social problem, and what can the police and social services organizations do to try and stop the cycle of homelessness?

INDEPENDENT STUDENT ACTIVITIES

1. Inquire of your local police department or sheriff's office about whether or not a labor agreement exists in their agency. If so, find out its advantages, disadvantages, length and provisions of the labor agreement or contract, methods by which collective bargaining takes place, the state's enabling legislation, some of the major contractual provisions (salary structure; special consideration and pay for promotion, longevity, holiday work and overtime, college or university credits and degrees, and so on).

2. Try to determine the extent to which there are women and minorities working in your area's law enforcement agencies. Perhaps you can interview such an individual to determine the challenges or difficulties he or she confronted upon entering law enforcement as well as at present.

3. Interview local police practitioners about the kinds of calls for service that create the most stress for them. What lifestyle changes (if any) have they adopted to manage their stress?

You might also probe into other possible contributors of stress, such as working the night shift or seeing crime victims at their worst.

4. Interview officers from different area agencies to determine whether or not their organizations provide educational incentives and tuition reimbursement for their officers.

5. Determine the extent of the homeless problem in your city and county and what your local agencies are doing about it, including shelters, treatment programs, ordinances, and enforcement policies.

RELATED WEB SITES

American Society for Industrial Security
http://www.securitymanagement.com

Commission on Accreditation for Law Enforcement Agencies
http://www.calea.org

National Labor Relations Board
http://www.nlrb.gov/nlrb/home/default.asp

National Organization of Black Law Enforcement Executives
http://www.noblenational.org

Police Association for College Education
http://www.police-association.org

Police-Stress.Com
http://police-stress.com

U.S. Interagency Council on Homelessness
http://www.ich.gov

OTHER CHALLENGES TODAY AND BEYOND

This part's two chapters have a futuristic theme. Chapter 14 provides information concerning the kinds of technologies that exist or are in development for use by the police. With the aid of computers, this chapter demonstrates that this rapidly developing area is hindered only by our imagination and available funding. Finally, Chapter 15 focuses specifically on the future, including some means available for making predictions and some contemporary best guesses concerning what the future holds in several areas for both the police and society.

TECHNOLOGY REVIEW

TOOLS FOR THE TASKS

Give us the tools, and we will finish the job.
—*Winston Churchill*

LEARNING OBJECTIVES

AS A RESULT OF READING THIS CHAPTER, THE STUDENT WILL:

- SEE HOW NEW USES FOR SOFTWARE ARE BEING APPLIED TO OLD PROBLEMS OF CRIME AND NATIONAL SECURITY

- UNDERSTAND SOME OF THE MAJOR DISCOVERIES IN LESS-LETHAL WEAPONS

- BE AWARE OF HOW WIRELESS TECHNOLOGY, MAPPING, AND PROFILING SYSTEMS HAVE BENEFITED THE POLICE

- UNDERSTAND HOW TECHNOLOGY ASSISTS THE POLICE IN THEIR TRAFFIC- AND GANG-SUPPRESSION FUNCTIONS

- KNOW SOME OF THE RECENT DEVELOPMENTS IN FIREARMS TRAINING AND INVESTIGATION

- BE ABLE TO EXPLAIN HOW POLICE TRAINING AND COMMUNICATIONS FUNCTIONS ARE ENHANCED BY TECHNOLOGY

- HAVE AN UNDERSTANDING OF THE PURPOSES FOR WHICH ROBOTS ARE BEING USED IN POLICING

INTRODUCTION

Probably nowhere in society does technology have more potential and impact than in criminal justice. Certainly the rapidly expanding use of technology in the forensics laboratories is a good example of this progress, but there are innumerable applications for technologies for the work of policing on the streets as well. Several photographs and some discussions in Chapter 7 demonstrated the kinds of technologies now available for forensic analyses. This chapter reviews more broadly the kinds of technologies that are either currently available to the police or on the horizon.

The new millennium brings ongoing exciting opportunities for policing with regard to technology. As will be seen below, since the advent of computers we are limited only by our collective imagination and willingness to provide the funding necessary for technology to evolve. It is not surprising that most technological innovations in criminal justice were developed for and involve the police, given the nature of their work, tools, and problems.

This chapter begins by showcasing ten new uses of technologies for addressing old crime and security problems. Then we consider some fundamental problems that exist in the area of policing and technology, particularly the need for better-trained personnel who understand computer hardware and software. Next we discuss technologies that are being developed to combat terrorism; then we look at the development and status of less-lethal weapons, followed by a consideration of wireless technology for use in databases, in crime mapping, and in analyses of serial offenders and gunshots. Then we examine how electronic capabilities are being applied to several traffic functions. Following a brief look at technological advances with DNA, we review developments with fingerprints and mug shots. New uses of technologies in the area of crime-scene investigations are presented, and we then consider how computers are assisting with regard to firearms, particularly in training officers and in solving cases involving guns. Following short commentaries on intelligence systems of gangs and expanding uses of robots in policing, the chapter concludes with a summary, key terms, review questions, independent student activities, and related Web sites.

Several of the technologies discussed in this chapter may be—and are being—applied to community-oriented policing and problem solving (COPPS, examined in Chapter 6). Some crime-analysis methods and tools (such as computer mapping) that were briefly mentioned in Chapter 6 are examined in more detail in this chapter. Chapter 15 will discuss future technologies in more detail as they relate to policing. Three technologies in particular are still "out there" in terms of research and development: nanotechnology, augmented reality, and unmanned aerial vehicles.

SELECTED EXAMPLES: NEW TECHNOLOGIES FOR OLD PROBLEMS

Following are ten examples of new uses of software now being deployed by criminal justice agencies to combat problems of crime and to enhance the nation's security. Note that some of them are in the early stages of development, are still controversial and as yet unproven for scientific accuracy, and may be quite expensive to obtain. Nonetheless, these vignettes demonstrate the unlimited potential for applying computer technologies for policing:

1. Finding a suspected stolen vehicle has been made easier for the Ohio State Police (OSP) with new technology for reading license plates. This technology scans both moving and parked cars, reads and matches the license plates with stolen or wanted plate numbers in a database, and notifies the officer via an alarm—all within seconds. The OSP recovered more than seventy vehicles in two years using this capability, which involves a central processing unit placed in the trunks of patrol cars.[1]

2. Handheld voice-translation devices are being tested by several police agencies. The units contain interchangeable computer chips loaded with more than one thousand phrases from different languages, including Spanish, Arabic, Vietnamese, Cantonese, and Mandarin. The translators offer a menu from which users select a phrase and language with a stylus, and the device then speaks in the chosen language.[2]

3. With a wireless mesh networking system, officers in Ripon, California, can literally watch each other's back from anywhere in the city. Linked to more than fifty video cameras placed strategically around the eight-square-mile city and in all police cars, the $500,000 mesh network provides real-time video to officers in the field and in the office. A supervisor can sit in an office and see how an officer's traffic stop is going.[3]

4. For decades the Breathalyzer has served police agencies well for indicating blood alcohol levels, but it is not longer manufactured and replacement parts are becoming difficult to find once they wear out. New Jersey police are experimenting with a new blood alcohol level test that is quicker and provides printouts of the levels. The instrument does not rely on the operator's ability to read the device properly. Court challenges are still looming, however, to determine the product's scientific reliability.[4]

5. With more than 500,000 registered sex offenders in the United States, 100,000 of which are "lost" by disappearing into society without properly notifying authorities, keeping track of them has proven difficult for the police. To help the police keep tabs on the offenders, a Web-based application has been developed that includes a database of registered sex offenders accessible to local police agencies. A Massachusetts-based firm purchases data from sources around the country and strings a range of information together in the database. For example, a previously known address of a wanted felon may yield the names of others who have lived at that address; the police can then know the names of people who have been in contact with the offender and go talk to them to try to learn the missing offender's whereabouts.[5]

6. An academic researcher at Columbia University has applied a geographic information system (GIS) to protect citizens against domestic violence. GIS has been adapted to study patterns of domestic violence throughout New York City, analyze the effectiveness of domestic violence outreach programs, and offer presentations to city agencies and nonprofit organizations. The number and time of occurrence of domestic violence reports filed and geographic information—data on streets, boundaries, congressional districts—are obtained and help the mayor's domestic violence office plan its activities.[6]

7. A tool for **voice-stress analysis** is gaining popularity among police agencies for use with suspects and in prisons for use with inmates. At least 1,500 such agencies are using voice-stress analysis software when questioning subjects. The software (which costs about $10,000) is typically loaded onto a laptop. During an interrogation, the

subject talks into a microphone, and the words are translated on screen into graphs that measure speech with algorithms and formulas, showing patterns indicative of confusion and cognitive dissonance. Critics, however, say no studies show the system works. They point to several anecdotal accounts where persons being questioned made false confessions and argue that such people confess because they are afraid of the analyzer. Clearly, more studies are needed to determine whether voice-stress analysis is, as one writer stated, "good science, or just bunk."[7]

8. Homicide detectives in Alabama are putting case files of up to eight hundred pages in length on a single compact disk. There are no more reams of paper, lost case files, audiotapes, or expensive costs involving copying, clerical time, or mailing of voluminous case files. An entire case—including the arrest report, audiotapes and videotapes of witnesses and suspects, phone records, and any other pieces of evidence obtained during an investigation—is collected and presented to the district attorney on a CD. This also makes it easier to hand over evidence to the defense. When a lot of CDs are accumulated, a server is used to house the archives, and all case files may later be easily called up by case number, type of crime, or suspect or victim name.[8]

9. Under recent legislation, Arizona law enforcement officials can investigate profits from alleged immigrant smuggling across the 389-mile Arizona-Mexico border. People who smuggle immigrants across the border—and who collect an average of $1,000 for each person they assist—prefer Western Union transfers because they are not easily traced. Special software is now used to analyze data documenting Western Union financial transfers of amounts greater than $750, looking for evidence of smuggling. Investigators, armed with a court subpoena, request data relating to persons sending and receiving wire transactions of $750 or more during a certain time period. Computers sift through the data looking for suspicious patterns. If a person can prove no illegal activity is involved, the money is released. Money found to be associated with trafficking is seized and deposited into a revolving account that helps fund the operation.[9]

10. The Department of Homeland Security has completed installation of next-generation **biometrics** to assess entries at 104 land border ports, as mandated by Congress. The program verifies each visitor's identity and compares his or her biometric and biographical information against watch lists of terrorists, criminals, and immigration violators. Federal penitentiary escapees, convicted rapists, drug traffickers, and others have also been nabbed at the borders using biometrics.[10]

POLICE AND TECHNOLOGY OF THE FUTURE: PROBLEMS AND PROSPECTS

First, the good news: It is anticipated that police officers of the future will function in very different ways and on very different terms than officers of the past. There will be few time and space constraints because all officers will be equipped with a pager, a cellular phone, and a laptop computer with software that includes encryption programs and sophisticated databases and search engines. Officers will have software that allows them to have real-time chats with officers from other agencies, in other states, or even in other countries. Before going on the streets, every rookie will be an expert at using computers and

A CBP officer looks at an X-ray of an entire truck for potential contraband.

(Courtesy U.S. Customs and Border Protection, photographer James Tourtellotte)

will be able to use crime-analysis software.[11] Exhibit 14-1 describes how one form of handheld technology—the handheld minicomputer—already allows officers to be away from their patrol car laptops.[12]

As the saying goes, however, "The fleas come with the dog." Aspects of the alliance between police and technology presage problems for the foreseeable future. From 1995 to 1998 (the last year of the program), the federal Office of Community Oriented Policing Services poured hundreds of millions of dollars into police agencies for new equipment.[13] But this federal largesse brought problems: Many departments lacked the in-house computer expertise to install or run the software and equipment—even today, many police executives believe that they hire people to be police officers, not computer programmers or database experts. But the nature of the policing business is changing, and officers with such problem-solving skills are not only desirable and valuable but also increasingly and rapidly a necessity.

In many police agencies, information technology staff are often civilians who are generally kept away from the operational side of the organization. They understand what computers do but not necessarily how that capability supports the operational needs of the police officer on the street. This is in addition to other technology-related shortcomings. For example, the police are also playing catch-up to counter a host of evasive criminal schemes, such as digital compression, remote storage, audit disabling, anonymous remailers, digital cash, computer penetration and looping, and cloning of cellular phones and phone cards.[14]

In this chapter, we examine the kinds of advances that are rapidly being made in the field. It should be emphasized that several of the systems described here are extremely expensive and too costly for most agencies. Furthermore, these systems are not a panacea and cannot replace the traditional forms of police work; rather, they are simply a way of managing information and focusing an investigation or search in a small area.

EXHIBIT 14-1

The Power of Information, in a Palm-Sized Package

What the newest hand-held minicomputers lack in heft, they more than make up for in the wealth of information they can supply to police in those crucial moments before they approach a suspect. The devices, which tip the scales at a mere four ounces or so, are finding their way onto the equipment belts of law enforcement officers in a steadily growing number of jurisdictions, including New York City, Charleston, S.C., and Franklin County, Ohio....

New York is the first city in the nation with officers using the devices during routine street patrols. Worn on the officers' gun belts, they come with small keyboards that can be used to enter license numbers, names and other data. What sets them apart from existing NYPD computers that can provide the same information, however, is their speed and stealth.

Said Ari Wax, the NYPD's deputy commissioner for technology and development: "It can be just like the cop on the street is checking his e-mail."

In April, two housing officers demonstrated how effective the hand-helds could be when police are faced with quality-of-life crimes. Confronting a man drinking beer on a Harlem stoop, the officers entered his name into a device they were testing. It turned out that the subject, Adrian Bowman, was wanted for a triple homicide in St. Louis....

[Detective] Chris Floyd noted that in the past, when suspects are detained, deputies might use a walkie-talkie to call the dispatcher for arrest information. Those results, transmitted over the radio, could then be heard by the suspect. "Now this guy knows I know who he is," said Floyd. "It's giving this guy a warning to run or fight."

While it is the portability of hand-held computers that has garnered the greatest appreciation thus far from police, they also cost much less than laptops, noted Sgt. Robert Flynn, director of computer services for the Charleston Police Department. The agency handed out 25 minicomputers last month to its traffic officers as part of a 60-day trial. It is the only department in the state to try out the devices so far, according to the *Charleston Post and Courier*....

"It's tremendous in that respect," he said, "but the cost can't be ignored." To install a laptop in a vehicle costs approximately $7,100; the hand-held computers, with software and network data time through a provider, cost approximately $1,900. "It's substantial. We can do everything a laptop was doing for us in the palm of the officer's hand for less money."

Source: "The Power of Information, in a Palm-Sized Package," *Law Enforcement News*, May 31, 2001, p. 11. John Jay College of Criminal Justice, CUNY, 899 Tenth Avenue, New York, NY 10019.

TECHNOLOGY VERSUS TERRORISTS

The terrorist attacks on September 11, 2001, not only changed the way federal, state, and local law enforcement agencies approach their mission (in essence, they now also protect citizens against attack from the outside rather than only from within the United States) but also set in motion research and development of new technologies for protecting against terrorist acts. And Americans seem accepting of more surveillance and screening technologies even if it means giving up some of their privacy: Polls conducted immediately after the September 11 attacks revealed that an overwhelming majority of Americans—about 75 percent—thought it necessary to give up some personal freedoms for the sake of security.[15] Following are some technologies that have been or are being developed to supplement luggage scanners and metal detectors to assist in detecting and foiling terrorists.

A low-dose X-ray imager can see through garments to detect stashed weapons, drugs, or other contraband. (The September 11 terrorists slipped through checkpoints with box cutters.) Surveillance cameras can scan faces and feed the images to a computer that scours a database of digital mug shots for a match. These devices were used during the 2001

Super Bowl in Tampa, Florida, and identified several petty criminals in the crowd. Soon after that, however, many Floridians and the state's civil liberties union protested their use.[16] Better bomb-detecting technology is also being developed, including machines that perform a cross-sectional X-ray scan of checked baggage, and ion-detecting swabs can find bomb residue on hand luggage. Also being considered for limited use are "smart cards"—IDs equipped with memory chips that store personal data and that can track movements and transactions.[17]

DEVELOPMENT OF LESS-LETHAL WEAPONS

Overview

Our recorded history is full of accounts of the need to protect ourselves from a hostile environment.[18] Certainly, international police forces have attempted to employ many means to protect themselves and the public at large. Next we briefly consider how **less-lethal weapons** developed since professional policing first appeared with London bobbies. Some of these weapons seem a bit archaic and even humorous, but it will be shown that the police and those who are engaged in research and development have long sought—and are still seeking—the perfect tool that can be deployed safely and efficiently.

Note that although the term *nonlethal weapon* is often used to describe these tools, this term is inappropriate because any tool or weapon can be lethal if it is used in an improper or unintended manner. For this reason, the term *less-lethal weapon* is more properly used to designate a weapon designed to produce only a temporary effect and minimal medical consequences for healthy people.[19]

1829: THE UNVEILING   When London's new bobbies began patrolling the streets in September 1829, they were armed with a baton, or truncheon, that still is a standard-issue weapon. Traditionally, it was made of hardwood, and it was two to four centimeters in diameter and thirty to sixty-five centimeters in length.[20]

Social turmoil in America between 1840 and 1870 brought increased use of force by the police, who themselves were frequent victims of assault. The New York City police and other departments were armed with thirty-three-inch clubs, which officers were not reluctant to use. Charges of police brutality were common in the mid-nineteenth century, when officers allegedly clubbed "respectable" citizens with frequency.[21]

Until the end of the nineteenth century, the baton remained a staple tool among American police. As late as 1900, when the Chicago Police Department numbered 3,225 officers, the only tools given the new patrolmen were "a brief speech from a high-ranking officer, a hickory stick, whistle, and a key to the call box."[22] Charges of police brutality continued.

1860s–1950s: CHEMICAL WEAPONS   From 1860 to 1959, there was only one major addition to the small array of less-lethal police tools: chemical weapons. CN gas (**chloroacetophenone**) was synthesized by German chemists in 1869 and was the first tear gas; it produced a burning sensation in the throat, eyes, and nose. It became available for use in aerosol cans in 1965. Chemical Mace was the most well-known brand. By 1912, chemical weapons were increasingly used for quelling riots and subduing criminals.[23]

CS gas (**2-chlorobenzalmalononitrile**) was first synthesized in 1928 as a white powder that stored well. It was adopted by many police forces because it had a greater effect than CN, causing a very strong burning sensation in the eyes that often caused them to close involuntarily. Severe pain in the nose, throat, and chest; vomiting; and nausea are also associated with its use.[24]

1960s: A TECHNOLOGICAL EXPLOSION The 1960s witnessed major technological advances in less-lethal weaponry. This was the age of rioting, on both domestic and foreign soil. Aerosol chemical agents, developed to provide alternatives to police batons and firearms, became the most popular less-lethal weapons for police use. Mace seemed like "manna from heaven."[25]

CR gas (**dibenzoxazepine**) appeared in 1962; six times more potent than CS and twenty times more potent than CN, it caused extreme eye pressure and occasionally hysteria. CS gas cartridges, which were fired by shotguns at a range of 125 meters, were used in the United States and Britain as early as 1968.

In 1967, alternatives to lethal lead bullets were first used in Hong Kong. Wooden rounds, fired from a signal pistol with a range of twenty to thirty meters, were designed to be ricocheted off the ground, striking the victim in the legs. The wooden rounds proved to be fatal, however, and direct fire broke legs at forty-six meters. Rubber bullets were developed and issued to British troops and police officers in 1967, only a few months after the wooden rounds appeared. Intended to deliver a force equivalent to a hard punch at twenty-five meters, the rubber bullets caused severe bruising and shock. Also intended to be ricocheted off the ground, the rubber bullet was designed so that riot police could outrange stone throwers.[26] Rubber bullets were employed by Seattle police officers in December 1999 during protests against the World Trade Organization meeting.[27]

During the 1960s, British riot police began employing water cannons, which were designed to fire large jets of water at demonstrators. Resembling armored fire engines, water cannons were also used in Belgium, France, Germany, and the United States. Non-toxic blue dye was added to the water for marking the offenders. For a time, the firing of a CR solution was contemplated.[28]

In 1968, another unique riot-oriented weapon was unveiled in America: the Sound Curdler, which consisted of amplified speakers that produced loud shrieking noises at irregular intervals. Attached to vehicles or helicopters, the device was first used at campus disturbances.

1970s: BEANBAG GUNS, STROBE LIGHTS, AND "NEW AGE" BATONS Another unique tool was introduced in 1970: a gun that shot beanbags rather than bullets. The apparatus fired a pellet-loaded bag that unfurled into a spinning pancake and was capable of knocking down a two-hundred-pound person at a range of three hundred feet. Although its manufacturer warned that it had potentially lethal capabilities, it quickly became popular in several countries, including Saudi Arabia and South Africa.[29]

Several other inventions were added to the less-lethal arsenal in the 1970s. The Photic Driver, first used by police in South Africa, produced a strobe effect; its light caused giddiness, fainting, and nausea. A British firm developed a strobe gun that operated at five flickers per second. Another apparatus, known as the Squawk Box, had two high-energy ultrasound generators operating at slightly different frequencies that produced sounds and caused nausea and giddiness.[30]

Other inventions of the early 1970s included an electrified water jet; a baton that carried a six-thousand-volt shock; shotgun shells filled with plastic pellets; plastic bubbles that immobilized rioters; a chemical that created slippery street surfaces for combating rioters; and an instant "cocoon," an adhesive substance that, when sprayed over crowds, made people stick together.[31]

Two new types of projectiles were developed in 1974: the plastic bullet and the TASER Electronic Control Device (ECD). The "softer" plastic bullets could be fired from a variety of riot weapons at a speed of 160 miles per hour and a range of thirty to seventy meters, making them attractive to riot police. Like wooden bullets, however, these new plastic bullets could be fatal, and several people died in Northern Ireland during the early 1980s after being struck in the head by these bullets.[32]

The TASER ECD resembled a flashlight and shot two tiny darts into its victim. Attached to the darts were fine wires through which a transformer delivered a fifty-thousand-volt electrical shock, which would incapacitate a person at a distance of fifteen feet. Police officers in every state except Hawaii, Massachusetts, Michigan, and New Jersey had tried the device by 1985, but its use was not widespread because it had range limitations and because it was not always effective on people under the influence of drugs; heavy clothing could also render it ineffective.[33] The stun gun, also introduced in the mid-1970s, initially competed with the TASER as the police tool of choice. Slightly larger than an electric razor, it also delivered a fifty-thousand-volt shock when its two electrodes were pressed directly against the body. Like the TASER, its amperage was so small that it did not provide a lethal electrical jolt. It would apply a localized electrical application to cause pain compliance but not incapacitation.[34]

As reported by the Bureau of Justice Statistics in 2006, today about one-fourth (23 percent) of all municipal police agencies and 30 percent of sheriff's offices authorize their personnel to use a TASER or stun gun[35]; these percentages will likely increase rapidly in the near future because the units have become easier to carry (now as small as six inches by three inches in size and seven ounces in weight) and more effective to use (including a range of up to thirty-five feet; data port storage of date, time, and duration of deployment; a red-dot laser light; and enhanced accountability). TASER devices can also disperse tiny unique coded tags, allowing a complete trace on the serial number of the unit that was deployed. Recently the new TASER Cam was introduced, which offers increased protection for officers because the suspect's behavior prior to the TASER's deployment can be recorded with full audio and video, even in zero light conditions.[36]

By late 2004, more than 100,000 police officers in 5,500 police agencies were carrying a TASER.

(Courtesy TASER International, Inc., Scottsdale, AZ)

As with any less-lethal tool, however, the TASER is not without controversy. In some parts of the country, strong emotions have been stirred among civilians due to the use of the TASER to control offenders who were children or elderly (in Florida, the device was used against a six-year-old and a twelve-year-old, and in South Carolina, it was used against a seventy-five-year-old woman in a nursing home). Amnesty International, the activist human rights organization, maintains that at least ninety people have died after being shocked with TASERS and has called for a ban on its use until its true risk can be thoroughly researched.[37]

A study announced in late 2007 by the Wake Forest University School of Medicine, however—touted as "the first large, independent study to review every TASER deployment and to reliably assess the overall risk and severity of injuries in real world conditions"—reported that 99.7 percent of nearly 1,000 cases of TASER use resulted in only mild injuries, such as scrapes and bruises, or no injuries at all; only three subjects (0.3 percent) suffered injuries severe enough to need hospitalization.[38]

The Continuing Quest

Obviously, the quest continues today for completely noncontroversial and effective alternatives to lethal force. As the foregoing discussions show, the innovations of the past were sometimes deadly or ineffective, so the search for the "perfect" less-lethal weapon continues. The TASER has probably developed more rapidly than any other tool and arguably carries the most promise. In 2008, TASER will debut wireless technology designed to be launched from a 12-gauge shotgun and provide similar incapacitation effects as the TASER X26. Still, police nationwide—some in cities that have witnessed loud public outcries in the aftermath of fatal police shootings—continue to seek a weapon that offers a less-lethal alternative, one that stops short of the deadly firearm. One has to wonder if there can ever be a less-lethal weapon developed that can truly and completely replace the firearm.

Since 1986, the National Institute of Justice (NIJ) has maintained a Less-Lethal Technologies Program, which serves as the research, development, and evaluation arm of the U.S. Department of Justice and provides funds to identify, develop, and evaluate new or improved

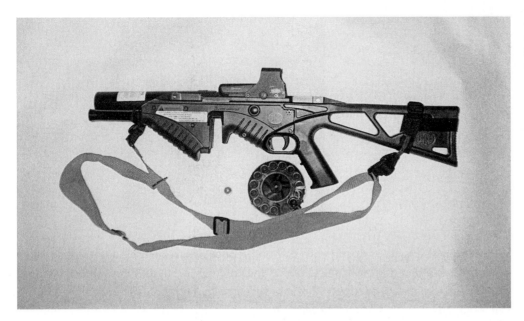

A relatively new less-lethal tool is a compressed-air gun that fires small pellets filled with oleocapsicum or other gases.

(Courtesy Sparks, Nevada, Police Department)

technologies that will minimize the risk of injury and death to law enforcement officers, suspects, prisoners, and the general public. As part of this effort, in 2004 the NIJ prepared a comprehensive review to inform police agencies of equipment that the U.S. Department of Defense is developing as part of its Joint Nonlethal Weapons Program.[39]

As was also stated in Chapter 3, pepper spray (oleoresin capsicum) is a popular less-lethal tool now in use by 97 percent of municipal police and sheriff's departments.[40] This spray inflames the mucous membranes of the eyes, nose, and mouth, causing a severe burning sensation for twenty minutes or less.[41] The spray is highly effective in subduing suspects without causing undue harm or long-term aftereffects.[42] A related innovation is the Option, which offers lethal and less-lethal capabilities in a single unit; the weapon has a cylinder of pepper spray that is mounted to the barrel of a pistol or shoulder weapon.[43]

USE OF WIRELESS TECHNOLOGY

Instant Access to Information

Mobile data systems have been available since the 1970s, but the first-generation systems were based on large proprietary computers that were very costly and were often beyond the reach of many small- and medium-sized police agencies. The first digital data were not transmitted from police headquarters to a cruiser until the mid-1980s. Today, armed with a notebook computer and a radio modem, police officers can have almost instant access to information in numerous federal, state, and local databases. Even small agencies can now afford a network and mobile data terminals (MDTs).[44]

A growing number of American police departments, including small agencies, are using laptop computers with wireless connections to crime and motor vehicle databases. These systems are believed to pay for themselves in increased fines and officer safety.

Police officers are using new handheld pocket computers.

(Courtesy of Motorola)

Officers can access court documents, in-house police department records, and a system of **computer-aided dispatching (CAD)** as well as enter license numbers into their computers. Through a national network of motor vehicle and criminal history databases, they can locate drivers with outstanding warrants, expired or suspended licenses, and so on. Furthermore, rather than using open radio communications, police officers use their computers to communicate with one another via e-mail.[45]

Integrated Databases

In 1999, a "railroad killer" was engaged in a rampage across the southwest. U.S. Border Patrol agents in Texas unknowingly picked up the killer near the Mexican border and dutifully checked the agency's database for any outstanding warrants. Finding none, they released him, and within a few days he struck again, killing two women. Several federal and local law enforcement agencies wanted the suspect for questioning, but the Border Patrol had no way of searching those agencies' databases; had it been able to do so, the killing spree might have ended sooner.[46]

Agencies will be able to cross-search databases when the U.S. Department of Justice builds its proposed Global Justice Information Network to link crime networks—including police, courts, and corrections agencies—at the local, state, national, and international levels. This is being termed a new course for the criminal justice community, which is at a historic turning point with these integration efforts. Such systems will improve the quality of information and decisions made by criminal justice officials.[47]

We will discuss integrating DNA databases later in this chapter.

Crime Mapping

Conclusive evidence from clay tablets found in Iraq proves that maps have been around for several thousand years—perhaps tens of millennia.[48] A relatively recent development in policing is computerized **crime mapping**, which has become increasingly popular among law enforcement agencies.[49] In fact, a federal study found that departments with one hundred or more officers used computer crime mapping 35 percent of the time.[50] Computerized crime mapping combines geographic information from global positioning satellites with crime statistics gathered by the department's CAD system and demographic data provided by private companies or the U.S. Census Bureau. (Some agencies acquire information from the Census Bureau's Internet site.) The result is a picture that combines disparate sets of data for a whole new perspective on crime. For example, maps of crimes can be overlaid with maps or layers of causative data: unemployment rates in the areas of high crime, locations of abandoned houses, population density, reports of drug activity, or geographic features (such as alleys, canals, or open fields) that might be contributing factors.[51] Furthermore, the hardware and software are now available to nearly all police agencies for a few thousand dollars.

The importance of crime mapping is evidenced by the fact that in 1997 the NIJ established the Crime Mapping Research Center (CMRC) to promote research, evaluation, development, and dissemination of geographic information systems technology for criminal justice research and practice. The CMRC holds annual conferences on crime mapping to give researchers and practitioners an opportunity to gain both practical and state-of-the-art information on the use and utility of computerized crime mapping.[52]

Exhibit 14-2 discusses the use of interactive crime mapping on the Internet, and Exhibit 14-3 describes the use of process mapping by an Illinois police department. Figure 14-1 is the initial screen that appears when the user chooses "vehicle and traffic incidents" from the San Diego County Web site. The screen provides information about auto thefts and burglaries as well as traffic accidents.

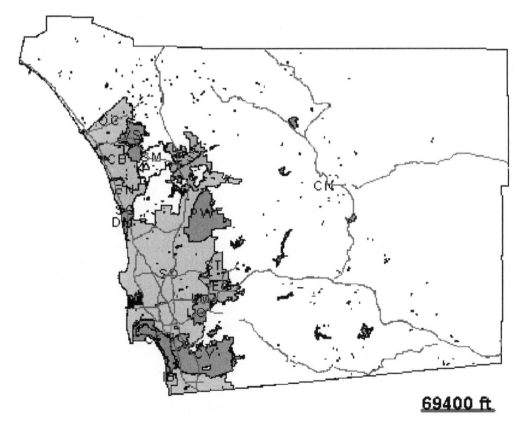

69400 ft

FIGURE 14-1
San Diego County's "Automated Regional Justice Information System" (ARJIS) vehicle and traffic map.

Source: Automated Regional Justice Information System.

An excellent example of mapping success is the New York Police Department's Compstat program(discussed in Chapter 12) which provides up-to-the-minute statistics, maps, and patterns and establishes causal relationships among crime categories. Compstat also puts supervisors in constant communication with the department's administration, provides updates to headquarters every week, and makes supervisors responsible for responding to crime in their assigned areas.[53]

Locating of Serial Offenders

Most offenders operate close to home and tend to operate in target-rich environments to "hunt" for their prey. **Geographic profiling**—a relatively new development in the field of environmental criminology—analyzes the geography of such locations and the sites of the victim encounter, the attack, the murder, and the body dump and maps the most probable location of the suspect's home.[54]

Geographic profiling is most effective when used in conjunction with linkage analysis. For example, the Washington State Attorney General's office uses a **homicide investigation and tracking system (HITS)** that includes crime-related databases and links to vice and gang files, sex offender registries, corrections and parole records, and department of motor vehicle databases. HITS can scan these databases simultaneously. When an agency in the state has a major crime in its jurisdiction, the case is loaded into a central system, which scans every database and linking file for connections by comparing eyewitness descriptions of a suspect and vehicle. It then builds a data set containing profiles of the offender, the victims, and the incidents. The data set then goes into a GIS, where the program selects and maps the names and addresses of those suspects whose method of operation fits the crimes being investigated.[55]

EXHIBIT 14-2

Interactive Crime Mapping on the Internet

Recently San Diego County's Automated Regional Justice Information System (ARJIS) developed the first multiagency interactive crime-mapping Web site in the nation, making interactive crime maps available to the public on the Internet. These systems not only enable citizens to obtain much more information than was previously available but also preclude their having to make formal requests for information while freeing crime analysts to devote more time to analyzing crime instead of providing reports to the public. Now anyone in the world can query and view certain crime, arrest, call, and traffic data for the county. Searches can be geographic (by street, neighborhood, police beat, or city) as well as by time of day or day of week. People access ARJIS for a variety of purposes, including information about crime in their area, for a grant proposal, for evidence for a debate on an issue, for citizen patrol, and even for real estate information.

Source: Adapted from Julie Wartell, "Evaluating a Crime Mapping Website" in *Crime Mapping News,* a Police Foundation newsletter, Vol. 3 (summer 2001): 1–6.

EXHIBIT 14-3

Twenty-First-Century Police Department

Naperville, Illinois

Over the last decade, companies in the manufacturing, entertainment, and defense industries have used a tool called "process mapping" to help them describe, analyze, and ultimately improve how their organizations operate. Members of the Naperville, Illinois, Police Department and twenty-three other police agencies were invited to attend training in process mapping, which involves the development of three different flowcharts that visually depict the series of activities involved in carrying out one of the organization's major functions:

1. *As-is map.* The as-is map describes the organization as it currently exists. This map is based on interviews and observations of people and is used to diagnose waste, duplication of effort, coordination of problems, or breakdowns in the flow of information.

2. *Should-be map.* The should-be map makes short-term changes to reduce waste, remove duplication, and improve coordination and flow of information. This map is based on management analysis of the as-is map and suggestions gathered from field personnel during interviews.

3. *Could-be map.* The could-be map describes the ideal process for the future. This map is based on the organization's vision and highlights the long-term changes that are needed to get there.

For example, Naperville is focusing on "crime solving" as the major function to be mapped and is focusing on one crime type: burglary. Process mapping allows the agency to increase the clearance rate for crimes by identifying areas where new work methods or organizational changes might improve police ability to investigate crimes and arrest offenders, and it makes more widespread and effective use of automation and technology by identifying areas where work processes can be improved, such as automated case reporting.

Source: Adapted from City of Naperville, Illinois, Web page, "Twenty-First-Century Police Department," 1997, pp. 1–2 (Accessed November 16, 2003).

Gunshot Locator System

A primary difficulty for the police is determining the location of gunshots. Technology is now being tested that is similar to that used to determine the strength and epicenter of earthquakes. Known as a "gunshot locator system," it uses microphone-like sensors placed on rooftops and telephone poles to record and transmit the sound of gunshots by radio waves or telephone lines. Software is then used to alert a dispatcher and to pinpoint the origin of gunshots via a flashing icon on a computerized map. Ideally, the system, which triangulates based on how long it takes the sound to reach the sensors, would greatly reduce police response time to crime scenes, meaning quicker aid for victims and a greater likelihood of arrests.[56]

In Chicago, technology is being tested that recognizes the sound of a gunshot within a two-block radius, pinpoints the location of the shot with a surveillance camera, focuses on the location, and places a 911 call in less than one second. A microphone surveillance system, located twenty feet above the ground, contains an acoustic sensor that recognizes a sound as a gunshot and sends range and bearing data to a camera, which starts out with a wide angle, tilts, and zooms in on the area; it then sends a 911 message to a call center.[57]

A related use of geographic technology—used extensively with military tanks and in the private sector (such as in taxicab firms, car rental franchises, and express delivery companies)—is the Global Positioning System (GPS, discussed more below), which plots locations

In addition to traditional functions such as capturing offenders, conducting building searches, hunting offenders, and looking for lost people, today's police dogs also sniff for bombs, narcotics, dead bodies, illegal currency, and smuggled agricultural products.

(Courtesy U.S. Customs and Border Protection, photographer Gerald L. Nino)

of vehicles and even people with remarkable accuracy. The police, for example, have adapted GPS for the problem of knowing exactly where search-and-rescue dogs are and how effective they have been in their search efforts. A small specially designed backpack containing software is attached to the dog; after a search for lost persons, data from the backpack are downloaded to show where the dog has searched as well as areas that may need to be searched further.[58]

ELECTRONICS IN TRAFFIC FUNCTIONS

Accident Investigations

A multicar accident can turn a street or highway into a parking lot for many hours, sometimes even days. The police must collect evidence relating to the accident, including measurements and sketches of the scene, vehicle and body positions, skid marks, street or highway elevations, intersections, and curves. These tasks typically involve a measuring wheel, steel tape, pad, and pencil. The cost of traffic delays—especially for commercial truck operators—is substantial.

Some police agencies have begun using GPS to determine such details as vehicle location and damage, elevation, grade, radii of curves, and critical speed. A transmitter takes a series of "shots" to find the exact locations and measurements of accident details like skid marks, area of impact, and debris. That information is then downloaded into the system, and the coordinates are plotted on an aerial shot of the intersection or roadway. Using computer technology, the details are then superimposed on the aerial shot, thus re-creating the accident scene to scale. Finally, digital photos of the accident are incorporated into the final product, resulting in a highly accurate depiction of the accident. Furthermore, with a fatal accident or one with major injuries, what once required up to eighteen hours' time for several officers is reduced to mere minutes.[59]

Similarly, other agencies use a version of a surveyor's "total station," electronically measuring and recording distances, angles, and elevations as well as the names and features of

Some agencies use a Global Positioning System to accurately draw accident scenes. Here, police and technical personnel employ the system at a fatal accident scene.

(Courtesy Sparks, Nevada, City Works Department)

objects. Data from the system can be downloaded into a computer for display or printed out on a plotter. The system consists of four components: a base station, a data collector, a tripod, and a prism (which reflects an infrared laser beam back to the tripod-mounted base station). With this device, officers can get measurements in an hour or so at major traffic accidents, push a button, and have lines drawn for them to scale; this process enables officers to get 40 percent more measurements in about 40 percent less time, allowing the traffic flow to resume much more quickly. This system is also being used at major crime scenes, such as murders.[60]

Arrests of Impaired Drivers

During a vehicle stop for driving under the influence (DUI), officers might spend a long time questioning the driver and conducting a barrage of screening tests. Then, if an arrest is made, the officer necessarily devotes a lot of time transporting and processing the arrestee at the jail before beginning formal testing of urine or blood. This delay in formal testing can skew test results because the alcohol has had time to metabolize.

New instruments now help automate the DUI arrest process. One tool used routinely during a drunk-driving stop is a breath-screening device—a small portable machine that resembles a video game cartridge. The DUI suspect blows into the device, and the officer gets a reading of the amount of alcohol in the suspect's system. It is hoped that this device can be adapted in such a way that the test can be used in court. Fewer hours would then be spent transporting DUI suspects and testing them, only to find that they were below the legal limit and thus cannot be prosecuted for DUI.

The revamped instrument would be attached to a notebook or a laptop computer that officers would use to help speed them through the process; an officer would simply run a magnetic-strip driver's license through a reader on the computer to bring up all of the driver's information. The computer would prompt the officer to start the test and would supply a readout of the results on the screen. The officer would then transmit the test results over telecommunications lines to a central location for recording.[61]

Prevention of High-Speed Pursuits

Chapter 10 discussed the current controversy over the tremendous potential for injury, property damage, and liability that accompanies high-speed pursuits by police—this is such a concern that some agency policies completely prohibit such pursuits by officers. Such techniques as bumping, crowding, employing the three-cruiser rolling roadblock, and using tire spikes can all result in personal injuries and significant damage to vehicles.

Tire spikes can be deployed when a fleeing vehicle is approaching and then retracted so that other vehicles and police cars can pass safely. However, tire spikes often do not work effectively, or they result in the suspect losing control of the vehicle (although some spike devices are designed to prevent loss of control by breaking off in the tires and thus deflating them slowly).[62] Furthermore, use of the spikes is limited to times and places where other traffic can be diverted.

One new device stops the suspect's vehicle with a short pulse of electric current that disrupts the vehicle's ignition system. Once pulsed, the vehicle rolls to a controlled stop, similar to running out of fuel, and will not restart until the affected parts are replaced. Since this device requires near-direct contact with the suspect vehicle, other nearby vehicles and people are not affected. This device, which is still being refined and miniaturized, is now being demonstrated for federal, state, and local law enforcement agencies across the country, as well as for transportation officials.[63]

DNA

New success stories involving the use of DNA in criminal justice are reported nearly each day. Here's an example:

> A case file in the rape of a twelve-year-old Englewood, Colorado, girl was starting to yellow. A sketch of the suspect had not produced anything concrete. Then the Colorado Bureau of Investigation linked a DNA "fingerprint" from the evidence file to a man recently imprisoned for another sexual assault.[64]

Today, some of the nation's most effective crime fighters wear white lab coats instead of blue uniforms and study DNA fingerprinting. Unfortunately, successes such as the Colorado case are severely limited by the scarcity of DNA fingerprints on file.

When integrated databases were discussed earlier, it was shown that today's police are exchanging information quickly and with good results, and there have certainly been successful outcomes in the area of DNA databases as well. For example, in the late 1980s, states began passing laws mandating that DNA samples be collected from people convicted of sexual assault or other violent crimes. These data could then be used to solve existing cases and to identify the felons if they committed further crimes after they were released. All fifty states now have such laws, and by the end of 1999 they had gathered nearly 750,000 DNA samples and made the data accessible to police agencies. The downside, however, is that this figure represents less than 5 percent of the total number of DNA samples that need to be analyzed for thirteen genetic markers.[65]

The U.S. Department of Justice has stepped in to help the states process their backlog of more than 700,000 DNA samples. The government has funded a private firm to develop and use a process called "laser desorption mass spectrometry" in conjunction with robots; this process enables a sample to be analyzed in a matter of seconds. Once this process becomes available, states will be able to clear their backlogs in a matter of months, enabling DNA to be used much more broadly in identifying, apprehending, and prosecuting criminals.[66]

DATABASES FOR FINGERPRINTS AND MUG SHOTS

Though perhaps not as exotic as DNA identification, fingerprints are still a reliable means of positively identifying someone. Throughout the country, filing cabinets are filled with ink-smeared cards that hold the keys to countless unsolved crimes if only the data could be located. An **automated fingerprint identification system (AFIS)** allows this legacy of data to be rapidly shared throughout the nation. One such system is the Western Identification Network (www.winid.org), established by nine states as a way to share their 17 million fingerprint records. These states were later joined by local agencies and the Federal Bureau of Investigation (FBI), the Internal Revenue Service, the Secret Service, and the Drug Enforcement Administration. The system can generally provide a match within a few hours and has helped solve more than five thousand crimes. A digital photo exchange facility known as WINPHO is now being added to supplement fingerprint data.[67]

Major advances are being made toward development of a national automated fingerprint identification system connecting hundreds of police agencies in the United States and abroad.

(Courtesy NYPD Photo Unit)

The Boston Police Department, like most others in the country, was devoting tremendous resources to identifying prisoners with mug shots and fingerprints. Then the department replaced all of its mug shots and inked fingerprints with a citywide integrated electronic imaging identification system—the first system of its kind in North America. The Boston Police Department is also the first city to receive the FBI's certification for electronic fingerprint submission.

Instead of transporting prisoners to a central booking facility in downtown Boston—a task that took forty thousand hours of officers' time per year—officers at the eleven district police stations can electronically scan a prisoner's fingerprints, take digital photographs, and then route the images to a central server for easy storage and access. This network gives investigators timely access to information and mug shot lineups and is saving the police department $1 million per year in labor and transportation costs while freeing officers from prisoner transportation duties.[68]

Technology involving mug shots and imaging systems can be useful in a variety of situations. For example, as a police officer responds to a domestic violence call, the CAD system searches the address and finds a restraining order against the ex-husband or boyfriend; moments later, a street map and digital mug shot of the suspect appear on the officer's laptop computer monitor. The officer is thus aided with an image of the suspect and his criminal history before arriving at the scene.[69]

New Technologies for Crime Scenes

Several technologies exist or are being developed that are relevant to crime-scene investigations. Three-dimensional CAD (3-D CAD) software is now available and can be purchased for a few hundred dollars. Working in 3-D, CAD users create scenes that can be viewed from any angle, so nontechnical people can visualize very technical evidence. Juries can "view" crime scenes and see the location of evidence; they can view just what the witness says he or she saw. Police give the CAD system the exact dimensions and get a scaled drawing. A five-day, forty-hour course teaches 3-D CAD to police investigators, traffic accident reconstructionists, and evidence technicians.[70]

Often, crime-scene evidence is too sketchy to yield an obvious explanation of what happened. New software called Maya has been developed for the field of forensic animation; this software helps experts determine what probably occurred. Maya is so packed with scientific calculations that it can create a virtual house from old police photos and can replicate the effects of several types of forces, including gravity, indicating how a fall could or could not have produced massive injuries, how flames would spread in a house fire, or how smoke might have cut a pilot's visibility in a plane crash.[71]

The federal Department of Energy is testing a prototype laptop computer equipped with digital video and still cameras, laser range finders, and GPS. A detective using it can "beam" information from a crime scene back to a laboratory to get input from experts. Researchers are also working on a so-called lab-on-a-chip that would give police the ability to process more evidence—including DNA samples—at the crime scene, eliminating the risk of contamination en route to the lab.[72]

DEVELOPMENTS WITH FIREARMS

Handguns are, and nearly always have been, the weapon of choice for violent criminals, especially murderers. Handguns are also used with greatest frequency—in about seven of every ten incidents—when police officers are murdered.[73] It is therefore important that everything that is technologically possible be done to train the police to use lethal force against citizens, to identify those who would use lethal force against others, and to keep out of harm's way.

Computer-Assisted Training

A device known as FATS (for firearms training system) is said to be "as close to real life as you can get."[74] Recruits and in-service officers alike use the system. They are given a high-tech lesson in firearms and can be shown a wide variety of computer-generated scenarios on a movie screen, with an instructor at a console controlling the scene. Using laser-firing replicas of their actual weapons, they learn not only sharpshooting but also judgment—when to shoot and when not to shoot. The system, consisting of a container about the size of a large baby buggy with a computer, a laser disk player, a projector, and a hit-detect camera, can be transported to sites throughout the state. Some sites combine FATS with a driving simulator and have recruits drive to the scene of a bank robbery and then bail out of their car into a FATS scenario.[75]

Recent developments have made firearms simulators even more realistic than the basic FATS system just described. One new version has a synchronized "shootback cannon." If an individual on a projection screen pulls a gun and fires toward the trainee, a cannon, which hangs above the screen, pelts the trainee with painful .68-caliber nylon balls. This newest generation of firearms training systems—which are getting more realistic and better at breaking down how the trainee reacted under stress—now cost between $25,000 for a small system and $200,000 for a trailer that police departments can haul from station to station.[76]

Use of Gun "Fingerprints" to Solve Cases

Every gun leaves a unique pattern of minute markings on ammunition. If gun makers test-fire their weapons before the guns leave their factories, the police can use spent ammunition recovered from crime scenes to trace a gun, even when the gun itself is not recovered. This technology could even be taken to the next level: creating an automated database of the fingerprints of new guns. A $45 million multiyear contract was recently awarded to a Montreal, Canada, firm by the U.S. Bureau of Alcohol, Tobacco, Firearms, and Explosives to help fund the development of such technology.[77]

Several problems need to be resolved, however: (1) Criminals can easily use a nail file to scratch a new gun's firing pin; (2) even if the system worked and turned up a serial number, the number could be used to trace the gun to its initial owner and not necessarily to the criminal; (3) the database would not include the estimated 200 million weapons already in circulation; and (4) gun lobbies would undoubtedly oppose the system as being "suspiciously like a national gun registry."[78]

GANG INTELLIGENCE SYSTEMS

Often a witness to gang violence has only a brief view of the incident—a glimpse of the offenders and their distinguishing characteristics and their vehicles and license plate numbers. Police are now armed with laptop computers and cellular phones to assist in solving gang-related crimes. Recently, for example, the California Department of Justice began installing CAL-GANG (known as GangNet outside California), an intranet software package linked to nine other sites throughout the state. It is essentially a clearinghouse for information about individual gang members, the places they frequent or live, and the cars they drive. Within a few minutes, a police officer in the field can be linked to CALGANG through a laptop and cellular phone, type in information, and wait for matches. Other officers can be moving to make the arrest even before the crime laboratory technicians have dusted the scene for fingerprints.[79]

ROBOTICS

Recent advances in **robotics** ("bots" in tech-speak) have allowed policing (and soldiering) to become safer. Robots are now fitted with video capability, including night vision; a camera (also useful for photographing crime scenes); a TASER; and even the ability to engage in two-way communications.[80] Robotics researchers at Carnegie-Mellon University recently developed a small throwable remote-controlled prototype robot with a top speed of twenty miles per hour designed for surveillance in urban settings; it can see around corners and deliver information from locations where human access is dangerous.[81]

Although bomb-handling robots have been in use for several years, recently the military employed a robot that can sniff explosive devices. Such robots—with seven-foot arms (that scan the inside and undercarriage of vehicles for bombs), lights, video cameras (that zoom and swivel), obstacle-hurling flippers, and jointed arms (that have hand-like grippers to disable or destroy bombs)—were sent to Iraq in early 2007 to give soldiers the ability to better detect and deal with roadside bombs.[82] Their use in policing cannot be far behind; for example, they would be very helpful if programmed to sniff for methamphetamine ingredients.

A major constraint for police use of robotics is the cost of acquisition. The bomb-sniffing robot described above costs $165,000, and one with elongated tracked wheels that can act like legs to climb over obstacles, making it useful for search-and-rescue activities, can run more than $100,000. Even a robot that is used only for under-vehicle inspections can cost up to $15,000.[83] Many jurisdictions will have to either go without or wait until the price of robots declines before they can be deployed.

EXHIBIT 14-4

The Technology Gateway: Los Angeles County's Technology Exploration Program

Some of the technologies with the best chance to be developed for law enforcement use are those that detect contraband, stop fleeing vehicles, and help officers intervene with less-lethal force; such new technologies are being tested under live conditions in the Technology Exploration Program (TEP) of the Los Angeles County Sheriff's Department. Some have privacy and legal obstacles issues that must be addressed prior to marketing, such as a three-dimensional scanner that now allows jail and prison officials to detect contraband on inmates. Several unmanned aerial vehicles (UAV) are being tested, some that are extremely lightweight and can fly as high as 8,000 feet. Included are a UAV that weighs four pounds and fits in the trunk of a police car for surveilling suspects, and another that is five-feet long and weighs about 12 pounds that can also serve in police search-and-rescue missions (e.g., to replace helicopters during heavy storms, observing levees that might rupture or leak). TEP also tests such innovations as the Magnetic Acoustic Devise (MAD), which can broadcast a voice message up to 1,000 feet and, with a flip of a switch, allow the sender to hear a voice response from that same distance; it would be invaluable for locating someone who is stranded in the wilderness or in a collapsed building. MAD can also replace bullhorns and other such devices: it artificially broadcasts creepy sounds like fingernails on a chalkboard, to possibly flush perpetrators out of hiding. Also being tested is the so-called "Dragon Egg," a small wireless video system that can be thrown through windows or around corners to act as an extra set of eyes; it contains four cameras that provide 360-degree viewing.

Source: Adapted from Government Technology, "Inspector Gadget," http://www.govtech.com/gt/159406?topic=117680 http://www.govtech.com/gt/159406?topic=117680> (accessed January 8, 2008).

SUMMARY

This chapter examined the exciting high-technology developments in policing (and some with applications in corrections as well), including those in the areas of less-lethal weapons, wireless technology, electronics, imaging systems, firearms, and communications. This is an exciting time for the police—more new technologies than ever are being made available to aid them in their efforts to analyze and address crimes. This chapter has shown the breadth of research and development that is under way.

The rapid expansion in computer technology, while certainly a strong advantage for society overall, bodes ill as well. The first problem lies in adapting the computer technologies to the needs of policing. While this nation's air force can drop a smart bomb down a smokestack and our army is rapidly moving toward the electronic battlefield, modern-day crooks and hackers engage in a variety of cybercrimes and (even though the technology exists) the police are still unable to halt a high-speed chase that threatens the lives of officers and citizens.[84]

Obviously, many challenges remain. For example, we must continue to seek a weapon with less-lethal stopping power that can effectively and safely be employed. We must also strive to enhance police effectiveness and efficiency through electronic means. As has been noted, "It is not enough to shovel faster. Criminal justice must enter the Information Age by incorporating technology as a tool to make the system run efficiently and effectively."[85]

KEY TERMS

automated fingerprint identification system (AFIS)
biometrics
computer-aided dispatching (CAD)
chemical weapons
crime mapping
DNA
FATS
geographic profiling
gunshot locator system
homicide investigation and tracking system (HITS)
less-lethal weapon
mobile data system
robotics
TASER
voice-stress analysis

REVIEW QUESTIONS

1. What are some of the major discoveries in less-lethal weapons for use by the police?

2. What are four new uses of software that are being applied to old problems of crime and national security?

3. How has the development of wireless technology benefited the police?

4. How can mapping and profiling systems aid the police, and what do these systems specifically provide?

5. How does technology assist the police traffic function? How has it affected gang intelligence?

6. What are some recent developments in the area of firearms training and investigation?

7. How are the police training and communications functions enhanced by technology?

8. What new developments have recently occurred in the use of robots by the police?

INDEPENDENT STUDENT ACTIVITIES

1. Using the Internet or interviews, identify a few major corporations that sell technological products for police use to learn of their current efforts in terms of product research and development.

2. Interview local police administrators to determine what kinds of technologies are in use and are planned for the future, especially for addressing computer-related, identity-theft, financial, and other complicated types of crimes. Also, what type of less-lethal weapon do they feel is most promising? If money were no object, what kinds of technologies would they find most helpful?

3. For comparative purposes, consult some old issues of police trade magazines (for example, *Police Chief* or *Law and Order*) and examine the product advertisements. What tools were available to the police in the "olden days"?

RELATED WEB SITES

Crime Mapping Research Center (CMRC)
http://www.ojp.usdoj.gov/cmrc

Government Technology
http://www.govtech.net

Justice Technology Information Network (JUSTNET) (a component of the National Law Enforcement and Corrections Technology Center)
http://www.nlectc.org

PoliceOne.com
http://www.policeone.com

FOCUS ON THE FUTURE

The confrontation that we are calling for...knows the dialog of bullets, the ideals of assassination, bombing, and destruction, and diplomacy of the cannon and machinegun.
—Terrorist manual

Trying to plan for the future without knowing the past is like trying to plant cut flowers.
—Daniel Boorstin

LEARNING OBJECTIVES

AS A RESULT OF READING THIS CHAPTER, THE STUDENT WILL:

– KNOW WHY IT IS IMPORTANT FOR CHIEF LAW ENFORCEMENT EXECUTIVES TO STUDY THE FUTURE

– DESCRIBE TWO GROUPS THAT CAN ASSIST THE POLICE IN STUDYING AND PREDICTING THE FUTURE

– DEMONSTRATE HOW ENVIRONMENTAL SCANNING AND SCENARIO WRITING ARE TOOLS FOR PREDICTING THE FUTURE

– BE ABLE TO DESCRIBE THE MAJOR FUTURE CHALLENGES IN CRIME INVOLVING DRUGS, ALCOHOL, GUNS, AND COMPUTERS

– UNDERSTAND HOW HIGH TECHNOLOGY, INCLUDING AUGMENTED REALITY, UNMANNED AERIAL VEHICLES, AND NANOTECHNOLOGY, MIGHT BENEFIT LAW ENFORCEMENT IN THE FUTURE

– BE ABLE TO DELINEATE HOW COMMUNITY POLICING AND PROBLEM SOLVING WILL FIT INTO THE FUTURE CRIME PICTURE

– UNDERSTAND WHICH CHANGES MIGHT EVOLVE IN THE ROLE OF BEAT POLICE OFFICERS

– KNOW SOME PROBLEMATIC POLICE PERSONNEL ISSUES THAT LOOM IN THE FUTURE

INTRODUCTION

As William Tafoya observed, "For 45,000 years humankind huddled in the darkness of caves, afraid to take that first step into the light of day. Police leadership must now be out in front, pointing the way for others to follow, not waiting for someone else to set the pace."[1] Perhaps more than anything, the preceding chapters of this book demonstrated that policing is a dynamic field, existing in a society and a world in which problems and challenges are constantly changing. Undoubtedly, our lives will continue to be drastically altered as the world continues to change.

Given all that, the question that looms largely is, What will the future bring? That troublesome question becomes even more important and ominous as we consider our present state of affairs, and the many challenges for policing are discussed below. It will also be shown that peering into the future is not easy. Many variables—such as war, technology, and economic upheaval—can greatly affect otherwise sound predictions and trends. Indeed, much of our planning and predictive efforts revolve around the unstable future of finance. As the saying goes, "There's a lot of crime prevention in a T-bone steak." While all predictions are grounded in past trends and future likelihoods, unforeseen variables and major events can and do change the course of the future in ways that no one could have anticipated, so the best we can possibly do is render an educated guess.

The chapter begins with a brief explanation of why the police (and, indeed, all of us) must take an examination of the future seriously; included here are mentions of several groups that have been created to assist the police in this endeavor. Then we consider two means by which the police may perform their predictive work: environmental scanning and scenario writing. Next is a discussion of some major challenges facing the police with respect to the nature and types of crime, with an overview of the impact of violence, drugs, alcohol, guns, and cybercrime. Then we shift to three possible "coming attractions" in the area of high technology—augmented reality, unmanned aerial vehicles, and nanotechnology—and what they might contribute to the future of policing. We next view community-oriented policing and problem solving (COPPS) and what it needs in the future to succeed and also consider the future role of the beat officer and the necessity for the police to change. A chapter summary, key terms, review questions, independent student activities, and related Web sites conclude the chapter.

WHY TAKE THE FUTURE SERIOUSLY?

Principles of Futures Research: Probable, Possible, and Preferable Outcomes

Because change is inevitable, law enforcement professionals must understand the importance of futures research so as to have the capacity not only to manage change but also to thrive on it. This research provides the tools to analyze, forecast, and plan in ways rarely seen in policing in the past.

Because of the reactive nature that has always been a part of the field of policing (responding to and taking reports at crime scenes after offenses have been committed), in past decades police officials tended not to be overly concerned about the future. Even those chief executives who were engaged in looking at the future usually concentrated on the next budget year rather than on a five- or ten-year strategic plan for their agencies.[2] But the future is here—and is probably changing faster than anyone could envision—and the choice is either to ignore the future until it is upon us or to try to anticipate what the future holds and gear our resources to cope with it. As Sandy Boyd, Alberto Melis, and Richard Myers pointed out:

> A world exists beyond traditional police exercises of annual budgeting, strategic planning for 3- to 5- year periods, and critical incident debriefings. Futures research leads to the examination of the probable, possible, and preferable outcomes of the future and provides a basis for decision making today that will lead to a preferable future.[3]

Therefore, planning for the future is essential. As an example, today it is difficult for us to imagine a world without computers or cellular phones, yet in the relatively short time they have been available, those same items have greatly changed and are contributing to today's nature and extent of crime.[4]

Society existed for ten thousand years with a foundation that was primarily agricultural in nature. Then, little more than one hundred years ago, industry replaced agriculture as the dominant means of producing wealth. Later, mass production began to give way to the information society. Given these trends, one must ask, What will society be like in *another* ten, fifty, or one hundred years? Today's police administrator must also attempt to determine what future legal, economic, and sociological developments can be logically inferred from today's trends.

To accomplish this, the principles of futures research that are utilized include (1) the unity or interconnectedness of reality, (2) the crucial importance of time, and (3) the significance of ideas. Futurists do not view the world as a hodgepodge of unconnected entities acting in arbitrary or random fashion, coincidentally interacting without purpose or meaning. Futurists generally are not preoccupied with immediate concerns, although they do not discount them; rather, they tend to focus on time frames of five years and beyond, believing that in most organizations a time lag of three to five years occurs between making a decision and its impact on the organization. Futurists also believe that virtually anything can be changed in society's organizations, given a lead time of two decades. Furthermore, futurists subscribe to six time frames: immediate present (two years), short term (two to five years), mid-level (five to ten years), long range (ten to twenty years), extended (twenty to fifty years), and distant (fifty years and beyond).[5]

Guiding Groups

To help the police in their futures research and to build a stronger partnership between all facets of law enforcement and the Federal Bureau of Investigation (FBI), the **Futures Working Group** was formed in April 2002. It represents a partnership between the FBI and **Police Futurists International (PFI)**, which was founded in 1991 and is based at Sam Houston State University, Huntsville, Texas (see Exhibit 15-1). The goals of the partnership include the development of forecasts and strategies to maximize the effectiveness of all law enforcement entities as they strive to maintain peace and security. Breakthrough technologies such as nanotechnology, artificial intelligence, and genetic engineering; changing demographic and cultural conditions; and the threat of international crime and

EXHIBIT 15-1

Police Futurists International

Police Futurists International (PFI) is an organization of law enforcement practitioners, educators, researchers, private-security specialists, technology experts, and other professionals dedicated to improving criminal and social justice through the professionalization of policing. Futures research (long-range planning and forecasting) is the pivotal discipline that constitutes the philosophical underpinnings of PFI. The tools and techniques of this field are applied in order to more accurately anticipate and prepare for the evolution of law enforcement ten, twenty, and even fifty years into the future. Futures research offers both philosophical and methodological tools to analyze, forecast, and plan in ways rarely seen in policing in the past. PFI conducts conferences and other activities and publishes a newsletter.

Source: Adapted from Society of Police Futurists International Web site, http://www.policefuturists.org/about_pfi.htm (accessed November 16, 2007).

terrorism will provide tremendous challenges for the members of these groups, who represent some of the best and brightest in policing.[6]

An adjunct to both the Futures Working Group and the PFI is the **World Future Society**, which was founded in 1966 and is a nonprofit educational and scientific organization in Washington, D.C. The World Future Society's members are interested in how social and technological developments are shaping the future.[7]

PREDICTING THE FUTURE: ENVIRONMENTAL SCANNING AND SCENARIO WRITING

Contemporary futures research has two major aspects: environmental scanning and scenario writing. **Environmental scanning** is an effort to put a social problem under a microscope, with an eye toward the future. In other words, we look at the current situation, perhaps reviewing the literature and looking for theories to aid in understanding the subject. We may also consult experts, particularly demographers, social scientists, technologists, and economists. Then we try to put together all this information and glean from it an idea of what will happen in the future. Environmental scanning thus allows us the capability to identify, track, and assess the prospects of emerging changes in the environment, changes that could improve or adversely affect society in important ways.[8]

Through scanning, crime and justice researchers can examine the factors that seem likely to "drive" the environment. "Drivers" are factors or variables—economic conditions, demographic shifts, governmental policies, social attitudes, technological advances, and so on—that will have a bearing on future conditions.[9] Three categories of drivers will serve to identify possible trends and impacts on the American criminal justice system beyond the year 2007: (1) social and economic conditions (including the size and age of the population, their immigration patterns, the nature of employment, and lifestyle characteristics); (2) shifts in the amounts and types of crimes (including the potential both for new types of criminality and for technological advances that might be used for illegal behaviors); and (3) possible developments in the criminal justice system itself (including changes in the way the police, courts, and corrections subsystems operate) as well as important innovations.[10]

Scenario writing is simply the application of drivers to three primary situations or elements: tolerance for crime, amount of crime, and capacity of the criminal justice system to deal with crime. An important consideration is whether each will occur in high or low degrees. For example, drivers may be analyzed in a scenario of *low* public tolerance for crime, a *high* amount of crime, and a *high* capacity of the criminal justice system to deal with crime; conversely, a scenario may include a view of the future where there is a *high* tolerance for crime, a *low* amount of crime, and a *low* capacity for the system to cope with crime. Of course, the resources required and philosophies employed to attack crime will vary for each scenario.

Environmental scanning and scenario writing together provide a method of systematically surveying the prospects for change in the environment and exploring the value of potential policies, given such prospects. The goal is to conjecture within reason while allowing our minds to range freely so that we take into account even what initially may seem farfetched.[11] It should be noted, however, that many people and organizations do not want to allow their minds to range freely, who resist change to some degree, for either personal or organizational reasons. People and organizations may simply suffer from rigidity.[12]

What changes are anticipated to occur in the future with respect to demographics and crime in America? As we have seen, this is a very important question that has a strong bearing on the future role of criminal justice practitioners. Following are the experts' best indications of what will occur.

Defining solutions to the problems that police will face in the future is difficult at best. Factors such as locale, political environment, and economics determine how an agency and its employees will view and react to future events. For some police leaders, the future is next Friday, and their goal is to survive without a crisis until their next day off. As Sheldon Greenberg has noted, for some police leaders the future is the next fiscal year; they subscribe to the notion expressed by Albert Einstein, who said "I never think of the future. It comes soon enough."[13] For others, however, the future is a three- to five-year span of time toward which they have set into motion a strategic planning process. Any discussion of the future must include the short term as well as the long term and must give attention to operational issues, administrative issues, and the community as well as the basic philosophy of policing.[14]

MAJOR CHALLENGES IN THE NATURE AND TYPES OF CRIME

One of the most highly respected of all prognosticators is Alvin Toffler, whose books *Future Shock, The Third Wave,* and *Power Shift*[15] have become internationally renowned. Toffler has been speaking and writing on police futures for the FBI since 1982. He believes the future in America will be anything but tranquil; indeed, he predicts that we are moving into some of the most turbulent years in our history. This turbulence will put enormous new strains on our police system, making the field much more complex, dangerous, and different.

Toffler believes that almost all of the major systems on which our society depends, from transportation and health care to the postal and educational systems, are in simultaneous crisis. There is currently a breakdown of America as we knew it in the 1950s. That was a simpler time, a time Toffler calls "Smokestack America," with the industrial boom, nuclear families, and blue-collar workers. This country has been battered by the most accelerated technological revolution in history, Toffler adds, with computers, robots, satellites, space travel, and expert systems. Our economy is based on knowledge, and today more and more jobs demand skills, training, and education, so fewer jobs remain for those on the bottom rung, and the results are clear in our inner cities.[16]

Toffler states that it is simple-minded to blame crime solely on poverty when there are plenty of societies in which poverty does not produce crime. But it is equally witless, he adds, to assume that millions of poor, jobless young people "are going to stay off the streets and join knitting clubs."[17] The collapse of the traditional nuclear family, and its replacement by two-career couples, childless couples, and much-married couples, has had a massive impact on policing.

Victimization and Violence

As noted in Chapter 13, there are about 23 million violent and property crimes each year in this nation.[18] A number of factors contribute to the high number of victimizations: immediate access to firearms, alcohol and substance abuse, drug trafficking, poverty, racial discrimination, and cultural acceptance of violent behavior.[19] While that figure is certainly massive, the good news is that the U.S. crime rate fell from 1992 through 2004 to its lowest point in a generation, although it increased somewhat in 2005 and the first half of 2006. Certainly, the robust economy that preceded the September 11, 2001, terrorist attacks and the overall aging of the population contributed in large fashion to the decline.

Other factors have certainly contributed to this lengthy overall decline in crime. First, state legislators imposed tougher sentences on violent criminals; second, local officials implemented aggressive and intelligent methods of COPPS. The effectiveness of good police work and the extended incarceration of hardened criminals are beyond dispute.[20]

Still, there are serious problems with respect to violence in the United States. In both the immediate and distant future, police will continue to deal with the "new violence" that has emerged over the past ten to fifteen years. In the past, violence was a means to an end, with revenge, robbery, and jealousy among the many reasons that people resorted to violence. Today an entire culture has emerged that sees the use of violence as an end in itself. The people who make up this culture (gangs, pseudo-gangs, well-armed young people, and others) are not going to change their way of thinking or reduce their hostility and aggression, and for these people, many of whom are fueled by drugs, the wanton use of violence—aggression for the sake of aggression—is not abhorrent behavior. Taken in combination, these factors present challenges for police leaders. Police will need training and education far beyond what they are given today to understand such violent behavior.[21]

Furthermore, the reduction in crime has had a minimal effect on reducing the public's fear of crime. Reducing fear, not simply reducing crime statistics, will be a major challenge facing police leaders in the future. Few police leaders and officers know anything about fear. What is it? How does it work? What is the cycle of fear? How can the police intervene to break the cycle? Why is fear contagious? Do problem solving, partnering, and the implementation of crime-control strategies and tactics reduce fear? Officers should be trained to assess causes and levels of individual, neighborhood, and community fear.[22]

Drugs, Alcohol, and Guns

As noted in Chapter 11, substance abuse (in which we include both drugs and alcohol) is a major factor in crime and violence. Nearly four in ten violent crimes involve alcohol, half of convicted jail inmates were under the influence of drugs or alcohol at the time of the offense, and three out of every four convicted jail inmates were alcohol- or drug-involved at the time of their current offense.[23]

Most police agencies remain reactive to the drug trade. They sweep street corners, arrest users and low-level dealers, rely on specialists (narcotics units) to assume primary responsibility for drug-law enforcement, and participate in regional task forces (generally when funded by the federal government). Police leaders will have to "think outside the box" in the future in response to a changing drug market. All agencies will need excellent problem-solving skills and a well-planned strategic approach to deal with the drug trade. More agencies must become involved in teaching employees about market analysis and forecasting in the drug trade.

In addition to drugs and alcohol, another crime **accelerator**—guns—might still increase the risk of victimization and a general fear of crime. This is a well-armed nation: While estimates vary widely, one source estimated that 250 million guns are legally owned in the United States, and with roughly 83 to 96 guns per 100 people, we are approaching a statistical level of a gun for each person.[24] Consequently, gun violence in the United States has become both a criminal justice and a public-health problem; firearms are still the weapons most frequently used for murder and are the weapons of choice in nearly two-thirds of all murders. Strategies and programs to reduce gun violence include interrupting sources of illegal guns, deterring illegal possession and carrying of guns, and responding to illegal gun use.[25]

Cybercrime

Cybercrime will also greatly challenge the police through such activities as data manipulation, software piracy, industrial espionage, bank card counterfeiting, and embezzlement. Hackers of all ages are breaking into computer systems of major corporations and obtaining credit card, telephone, and account information; some entice children for sexual purposes.

We may not have yet seen the worst that can happen: cyberterrorism. Imagine a world where the information superhighway could be used to remotely access the processing control systems of a cereal manufacturer, changing the levels of iron supplement and thereby sickening and killing children who eat it; disrupt banks, international financial transactions, and stock exchanges, causing our citizens to lose faith in their economic system; or attack air traffic control systems and aircraft in-cockpit sensors, causing large civilian aircraft to collide. These are the domain of the serious, determined cyberterrorist, and the future of terrorism involves much more than planting a relatively harmless virus in a computer system or hacking into a major corporation's voicemail system.[26] These types of crimes require the development of new investigative techniques, specialized training for police investigators, and employment of individuals with specialized, highly technological backgrounds. If the police are not prepared, these crimes could become the Achilles' heel of our society. As Special Agent Edward J. Tully of the FBI sees it, "The specter of a Three Mile Island in the banking industry must cause all of us serious concern."[27]

Another Challenge: An Aging America

Certainly we now live in a "graying" country, with 12.4 percent of the total population being at least sixty-five years old.[28] The good news is the elderly are less likely than younger people to become victims of violence and less likely to be injured during a violent crime—only about 2.1 violent crimes per 1,000 are committed against persons over sixty-five years of age.[29] However, elderly victims are more likely to be killed during the commission of a felony; because of brittle bones, they have more severe injuries, so their victimization can be permanently disabling; and being on a fixed income, they cannot receive the best medical care. The elderly have a high fear of crime but are less likely to take protective measures than younger people but are more likely to report a crime. They can also be victimized in nursing homes and hospitals, and their relative isolation can lead to a high percentage of victimization occurring in their homes. The elderly are targeted more often for financial fraud than other people, which can lead to severe depression and other serious health problems.[30]

Certainly now and in the future, the police must become more adept at preventing and investigating those types of crimes that tend to target our seniors. Their susceptibility to fraudulent schemes, purse snatchings, theft of checks from the mail, and crimes in long-term-care settings pose unique challenges for investigative personnel, as do other financial and computer-related crimes.

HIGH TECHNOLOGY: COMING ATTRACTIONS

In Chapter 14, we discussed a number of contemporary technologies that are (or soon will be) available to the police. Here we discuss three technologies that are still far removed from day-to-day use but that promise to greatly alter police methods in the future.

Augmented Reality

One of the most powerful technologies that is emerging, **augmented reality (AR)**, uses wearable components to overlay virtual (computer-generated) information onto a real-world view in a way that improves and enhances the ability to accomplish a variety of missions and tasks. Still in the early stages of research and development, AR combines the real and the virtual, displaying information in real time.[31] AR is already here: If you watch televised sports, you may have noticed the yellow first-down lines superimposed on a football field or the driver and speed information tagged to race cars speeding around a track. At a more advanced level, today's military fighter pilots can observe critical information superimposed on the cockpit canopy.[32]

Fundamentally, an AR system consists of a wearable computer, a head-mounted display, and tracking and sensing devices along with advanced software and virtual three-dimensional (3-D) applications. It is a mobile technology designed to improve situational awareness and to speed human decision making. Among the many possible uses in the future of policing are the following (some of which have already been developed but need to be refined for street use and, oftentimes, made more affordable for purchase) [33]:

- Real-time language translation, along with data on cultural customs and traditions
- Real-time intelligence about crimes and criminals in the patrol area
- Facial, voiceprint, and other biometric recognition data of known criminals
- Integration of chemical, biological, and explosives sensors that denote local contamination
- Accessibility of scalable 3-D maps (with building floor plans, utilities systems, and so forth)

Similarly, special weapons and tactics (SWAT) officers could be provided with advanced optics that provide zoom, thermal, and infrared imaging for locating fleeing criminals, as well as a friend-or-foe indicator that could reduce or eliminate friendly-fire casualties. Investigative personnel could use speaker-recognition technology for accurately matching voices against known criminals and for lip reading from a distance; thermal imaging might improve interrogations by indicating the truthfulness of suspects' statements. Supervisors could use video feed from their personnel on the street to determine what their officers are seeing in real time and to monitor their physical status during critical incidents.[34] Certainly a number of issues would accompany the planned adoption of AR. Acceptance by officers themselves may prove problematic, given the bulk and mobility issues associated with additional equipment, and the public (including the courts) may be uncomfortable with the constitutional issues and legal ramifications that AR abilities might raise.

Would AR bring us dangerously close to a real-life "Robo-Cop" scenario? The answer to that question is in the eye of the beholder. It cannot be questioned, however, that AR technology and the uses described above will soon be available and could provide the police with a new degree of efficiency and effectiveness never seen before. The question is whether or not the public—and the police—will be willing to accept this "virtual intrusion" in their daily lives.

In a similar vein, technology will also be available soon to allow realistic simulated humans to be used as a tool for training in decision making. Law enforcement personnel need experience making decisions in which other people—whether suspects, bystanders, or team members—are involved. A 3-D computer graphic would represent a variety of settings; the trainee would have the ability to move about, look around, and direct actions toward a variety of computer representations of human figures that move naturally, display appropriate gestures and expressions, and exhibit realistic patterns of speech. Such simulation technology, which should be available and affordable within the next five to ten years, will have a very positive impact on police training.[35]

Unmanned Aerial Vehicles

Another technology that warrants close attention is that of the **unmanned aerial vehicle (UAV)** (discussed briefly in Chapter 12 in relation to border security). UAVs are powered aerial vehicles that do not carry human operators and are designed to carry nonlethal payloads for missions such as reconnaissance, command and control, and deception. UAVs, which are directed by a ground or airborne controller, come in a variety of designs, from one that fits into a backpack to one with a longer wingspan than a Boeing 747. More than two dozen companies in the United States are currently involved in production of prototype UAV products.[36]

While UAV research and development is almost totally focused on military applications at present, the potential uses for law enforcement should not be ignored. For example, a low-flying UAV could patrol a given stretch of road, on vigil for speeders; images could be piped to a monitor in a patrol car along with rate of speed, direction of travel, and Global Positioning System (GPS) coordinates, which can be overlaid on a map for the officer on the ground.[37] UAVs could also provide real-time reconnaissance, surveillance, and target spotting in a variety of situations.[38]

Sandy Boyd and colleagues[39] argue that, overall, government and law enforcement seem to lag behind the private sector in both the use of new technologies and the development of expertise in such applications. A common theme among members of the Society of Police Futurists International is the fear that the law enforcement profession will never catch up with the necessary computer-based investigative skills to keep pace with criminals who use computer technology. But technology involves much more than using computers to hack into systems or to commit identity theft. Whether through nanotechnology, AR, or biometrics, criminals will always attempt to steal, misuse, or exploit others. If law enforcement does not anticipate such illicit uses, the victims of these crimes will eventually rely on private sources for relief.

Nanotechnology

The term **nanotechnology** is based on the root *nanos,* meaning "one billionth." It is the engineering of components that have at least one physical dimension the size of one hundred nanometers or less. (For perspective, a human hair is gigantic in the realm of nanotechnology.) This technology allows for "getting small," which means making objects smarter, more powerful, and more economical (for example, the computers of the 1940s were the size of a room, compared to those of today). Nanotechnology allows for revolutionary new products using new materials and substances that are not accessible with other technologies. Such products, ranging from knives never needing sharpening to better spaceships and computers, will be stronger, lighter, and even interactive—and may possibly mean the end of disease as we know it.[40] Imagine, for example, a chip strategically placed in the brain that could prevent epileptic seizures or allow someone to control an artificial limb just by thinking about it. It may sound like science fiction, but University of Florida researchers are developing devices that can interpret signals in the brain and stimulate neurons to perform correctly, advances that might someday make it possible for a tiny computer to fix diseases or even allow a paralyzed person to control a prosthetic device with his thoughts.[41]

COMMUNITY-ORIENTED POLICING AND PROBLEM SOLVING

As noted in Chapter 6, the conventional style of reactive, incident-driven policing employed during the professional era had several drawbacks. That type of police department was hierarchical, impersonal, and rule based, and most importantly policy decisions were made at the top; line officers made few decisions on their own. In this section, we analyze where the current policing era—that of **community-oriented policing and problem solving (COPPS)**—fits into the challenges of the future.

Many fundamental questions remain concerning COPPS. For example, how many police agencies have made a commitment to community policing? How many agencies have demonstrated the link between community policing and the quality of the communities they serve? How many have embraced community policing just to gain a share of available federal dollars? Will community policing endure without federal funding?[42]

From 1994 to 2001, the federal Office of Community Oriented Policing Services (COPS), created by the Violent Crime Control and Law Enforcement Act of 1994, spent about $9 billion to help police agencies implement COPPS, adding officers to the beat and providing technical assistance, technology, equipment, and training. By mid-2000, COPS had provided funding to 82 percent of America's police departments by awarding more than thirty thousand grants to more than twelve thousand departments. This included funding more than 105,000 community policing officers and training more than 90,000 officers and citizens.[43] However, the future remains uncertain for COPS.[44] Any police agency that is currently hanging its COPPS efforts on federal funds may find itself in desperate straits in the years ahead.

Another central issue with respect to COPPS concerns community partnerships. Much of society—including the police—has come to realize that the police cannot function independently to address crime and disorder. The challenge to leaders, now and in the future, is to develop meaningful and lasting partnerships rather than the superficial relationships that exist in many communities. For many police officers, the concept of partnership means simply attending occasional neighborhood association meetings or periodically visiting neighborhood leaders who live on their beat. Partnerships for the sake of partnership do not endure; they will work only when the mutual benefits to the parties involved are well defined, well understood, and attainable.

Several other issues for the future must be addressed if COPPS is to survive and thrive. These include whether police chief executives will change the culture of their agencies, implement the concept, decentralize their departments (pushing decision making downward), invest in the necessary technology to locate hot spots, and develop the necessary mechanisms to support COPPS; recruitment, selection, training, performance appraisals, and reward and promotions systems are additional challenges. Police unions must work with administrators to effect the kinds of changes that are needed for COPPS. The answers to these issues could be critical, not only to the future of COPPS but also to policing and society.

In a related vein, some authors point to what they believe are several unfavorable social forces that could militate against the future spread and application of the COPPS strategy: local governments being pushed toward a more legalistic crime-control model of policing, the public being less willing to pay more taxes to address fundamental social problems, and public policy not allowing the police to focus on the root causes of crime but only on their symptoms—such as criminal conduct—through aggressive strategies rather than through COPPS.[45] Indeed, the landscape of policing is littered with the skeletons of strategies and approaches that died after the departure of a dedicated COPPS chief or sheriff. One would hope that such a fate would not befall COPPS, as history has shown it to be a boon to addressing crime and disorder.

In sum, several questions for the future remain concerning COPPS:

1. Will *all* police organizations come to believe that they cannot control crime alone and truly enlist the aid of their communities in this endeavor?
2. Will *all* police chief executives acquire the innovative drive necessary to change the culture of their departments, implement COPPS, flatten the organizational structure of their departments, and see that officers' work is properly evaluated?
3. Will *all* police executives enjoy sufficient job security to accommodate COPPS, or will the at-will employment of chiefs place COPPS at risk?
4. Will *all* police departments work with their communities, other city agencies, businesses, elected officials, and the media to sustain COPPS?
5. Will *all* police unions work with administrators to effect the changes needed for COPPS?
6. Will *all* police employees (from top to bottom, sworn and civilian) who have not yet done so realize that the traditional reactive mode of policing has obviously not been successful and cannot work in the future?
7. Can *all* police organizations (from top to bottom) become more customer and value oriented?
8. Will *all* police executives and supervisors come to develop the necessary policies and mechanisms, including recruitment, selection, training, performance appraisal, and reward and promotion systems, to support COPPS?

9. Will *all* police executives and supervisors begin viewing the patrol officer as a problem-solving specialist, and will they give street officers enough free time and latitude to engage in proactive policing?

10. Will *all* police organizations come to view COPPS as a departmentwide and city-wide strategy, and will they invest in technology to support problem-oriented policing?

11. Will *all* those agencies attempt to bring diversity into their ranks to reflect the changing demographics and cultural customs of our society?

ROLE OF BEAT OFFICERS

Changes in Philosophy

The changing role of rank-and-file officers also looms large in future police philosophy and service. The good news is that future generations of police officers will have been raised to be at ease and fluent with information technologies, which bodes well for recruiting, hiring, and developing officers who possess the skills needed in the future and who are familiar with the kinds of technologies that both police and offenders will use (such as those described earlier).

Another area of interest for the future of policing concerns the attitudes and cognitive abilities of the recruits as they relate to the management styles they will confront. In the past—particularly under the professional model of policing—while undergoing the academy phase of their training, recruits adopted a new identity and a system of discipline in which they learned to take orders and to not question authority; they learned that loyalty to fellow officers, a professional demeanor and bearing, and respect for authority, are highly valued qualities. That kind of philosophy—and the police executive's set of expectations for recruits—must change. Only those candidates who can think critically, plan, and evaluate will be hired. At the same time, chiefs, sheriffs, commanders, and even sergeants will wield less power and control and will filter less information; instead, they will move into enhanced roles as coaches, supporters, and resource developers.[46]

People entering police service in the future will probably not have military experience and its inherent obedience to authority but will have higher levels of education and will tend to be more independent and less responsive to traditional authoritarian leadership styles. These recruits will have been exposed to more participative, supportive, and humanistic approaches and will want more opportunities to provide input into their work and to address the challenges posed by problem solving. The autocratic leader of the past will not work for patrol officers now or in the future. The watchwords of the new leadership philosophy and paradigm are *coach, inspire, gain commitment, empower, affirm, flex, respond, self-manage,* and *share power.* Therefore, a major need for police leadership will be the surrendering of power to lower organizational employees, creating a flattened hierarchy.

Other Personnel Issues

Some traditional police personnel problems are not likely to go away. Such matters as the need for more women and minorities in policing, unionization and job actions, contract and consolidated policing, civilianization, accreditation, higher education, and stress recognition and management will not be resolved in the near future. Furthermore, changing societal values, court decisions about the rights of employees, and the Peace Officers' Bill of Rights will make police leadership increasingly challenging. Nor will opportunities decline for officers to engage in graft and corruption, so administrators must develop personnel policies that will protect the integrity of the profession.

Furthermore, because of the increasingly diverse and aging nature of this country, one area where the police must begin planning for the future of human resources is recruiting. Shifts toward older workers, fewer qualified entry-level workers, and more women, minorities, and immigrants in the population will require the police both to devise new strategies for and to become more flexible in competing with the private sector for qualified applicants. Departments looking only at recent high school graduates as a principal source of candidates will likely face a shortage of qualified workers and will need to offer better wage and benefits packages, especially in order to attract women. With many young single mothers heading households, the police must offer them not only attractive salaries and benefits but other workplace accommodations as well, such as day care, flexible hours, time and place for nursing their infants, and paid maternity leave.

Finally, a major need will be for the police to be able to communicate with non-English-speaking communities.[47]

Other Predicted Changes

Some futurists believe that policing in general will undergo other metamorphoses in the near future such as the following:

- Ethics will be woven into everything the police do: the hiring process, the field training officer (FTO) program, the decision-making processes. There will be increased emphasis on accountability and integrity within police agencies as policing is elevated to a higher standing and reaches more toward being a true profession. Concomitantly, the majority of officers will be required to possess a college degree.
- Formal awards ceremonies will recognize officers who have improved citizens' quality of life as well as those who have made felony arrests or engaged in other high-risk activities.
- Communications will be greatly improved through internal intranets that contain local and agency operational data, phone books, maps, calendars, calls for service, crime data sheets, speeches, newsletters, news releases, and so on.[48]
- Major cities will no longer require that the chief police executive have prior policing experience; instead, they may begin to recruit from private industry. The future heads of police agencies will essentially be recognized as CEOs who need good business sense as a trend toward the privatization of certain services expands. Knowledge will continue to increase at lightning speed, forcing the police CEO to be involved in trend analysis and forecasting in order to keep ahead of the curve.

- The rigid paramilitary style of police organizations currently in effect will become obsolete, replaced by work teams consisting of line officers, community members, and business and corporation employees.
- The current squad structure will give way to more productive, creative teams of officers who, empowered with more autonomy, will become efficient problem solvers, thus strengthening ties between the police and the citizenry.
- Neighborhoods will more actively participate in the identification, location, and capture of criminals.

IN SUM: ORGANIZATIONS AND CHANGE

History has shown that police innovation is not simple. There are political and economic elements in policing that have a strong bearing on change, that pull toward tradition, and that create resistance, the latter perhaps being the police agency's strongest obstacle to change. Most police organizations remain paramilitary, bureaucratic, and reactive. Yet major change has been occurring in many of these organizations, where the chief executive has motivated (and possibly even manipulated) departmental personnel into accepting desired innovations, but some officers will continue to cling to the old ideals and must be brought along with the new methods of thinking and operation. Public support is also essential for innovation.[49]

Alvin and Heidi Toffler[50] feel strongly that every arm of policing should immediately assign some of its best thinkers to the task of probing the future, plugging their findings into their decision-making process. What should be the police agency's budget? How should police personnel be trained? What skills will be needed? What new technologies will the police face? How should forces be deployed? The Tofflers think that if the police are to continue to help guarantee the survival of the democratic system in America, it is essential that all of its agencies should rethink their assumptions, ask the right questions, and shake people out of their mental lethargy.[51]

Indeed, police organizations do typically engage in some degree of planning for change, either by design (such as the initiation of the aforementioned COPPS strategy) or by happenstance. In "The Future Policeman," James Q. Wilson identified three types of change that police undergo[52]:

1. *Unplanned near-term changes.* Many important changes are the result of unplanned and unseen events, such as the riots of the 1960s and the economic crisis of the early 1980s and 1990s.
2. *Planned near-term changes.* Many short-term changes are consciously planned. The educational levels of police recruits, for example, rose dramatically from the early 1960s to the mid-1970s as the result of a planned effort to raise personnel standards.
3. *Fundamental long-term changes.* The police are highly dependent on the social and political environments in which they exist. The future of the police, consequently, will be shaped by fundamental long-term changes in the social structure and in the American political system. For example, social and political pressures to criminalize or decriminalize certain behaviors have a profound effect on the police. Changing attitudes toward crime and the police are other important factors.

SUMMARY

This chapter explained why the police must seriously examine the future and provided several means by which they may perform their predictive work. Also under discussion were some of the major challenges facing the police with respect to the future nature and types of crime, followed by some "coming attractions" in the area of high technology. We also considered COPPS and what it needs in the future to succeed and then considered the future role of the beat officer.

No one knows for certain what the future holds, but one thing is certain: Our society is changing. Police administrators must anticipate and plan for the future; they certainly cannot drive into the twenty-first century with their eyes fixed firmly on the rearview mirror.

This is a very exciting and challenging time in the history of police service. No matter what issues lie ahead, the public will continue to expect a high degree of service from its police. Today's leaders and those who follow must plan for dealing with unforeseen problems caused by new drugs, small but hostile groups of extremists, young people raised in an environment of violence, and more. The police have the opportunity to deal with these issues supported by advanced technology, highly evolved information resources, better-trained officers and deputies, and a heightened commitment to interjurisdictional cooperation.

There is no indication that a significant abatement of today's social problems is looming on the horizon. The police will be affected in many ways by the social and economic changes to come, so they can no longer be resistant to change or unmindful of the future.

Hopefully at some point in the future, Americans can reflect back on the challenges of today and say, "The police profession today is the intellectual leadership of the criminal justice profession in the United States. The police are in the lead. They're showing the world how things might better be done."[53]

KEY TERMS

accelerator
augmented reality (AR)
community-oriented policing and problem solving (COPPS)
cybercrime
environmental scanning
Futures Working Group
nanotechnology
Police Futurists International (PFI)
scenario writing
unmanned aerial vehicle (UAV)
World Future Society

REVIEW QUESTIONS

1. Why it is important for law enforcement administrators to study the future, and which two prominent groups have recently been formed for this purpose?

2. How do environmental scanning and scenario writing serve as helpful tools for predicting the future?

3. What specific challenges relating to crime and violence are predicted for the future, and what role will computers play?

4. What are augmented reality, unmanned aerial vehicles, and nanotechnology, and how might these technologies benefit law enforcement?

5. How will COPPS fit into the future crime picture?

6. How will the role of beat officers change in the future?

7. What are some problematic police personnel issues that loom on the horizon?

INDEPENDENT STUDENT ACTIVITIES

1. Assume that you have unlimited financial resources and a favorable political climate. Engage in an environmental scanning and scenario writing exercise for your jurisdiction, designing a police organization for 2025 that would attempt to prevent crime while upholding the constitutional rights of all citizens. What kinds of people would be recruited for your agency, and how would they be educated, trained, uniformed, and equipped? What would be their primary mission and their day-to-day tasks? What kinds of equipment would these officers need? What role would women and minorities fill in this futuristic police force? What classes of crimes and criminals must you guard against?

2. Interview local law enforcement administrators to determine how they are engaged in strategic planning, what methods they use to make projections and predictions, and what current strategic-planning activities they are using to prepare for the future.

RELATED WEB SITES

Futures Working Group
http://www.fbi.gov/hq/td/fwg/workhome.htm

Police Futurists International
http://www.policefuturists.org

World Future Society
http://www.wfs.org

WHAT WORKS

POLICE PROBLEM-ORIENTED APPROACHES TO COMMUNITY PROBLEMS

Beginning in 2002, the federal Office of Community Oriented Policing Services (COPS), U.S. Department of Justice, began publishing *Problem-Oriented Guides for Police* on a variety of subjects; the number of guides available now exceeds fifty. These guides, which are relatively brief (about fifty to sixty pages in length), are available at http://www.cops.usdoj.gov/default.asp?Item=248, as well as on CD or paper copy; they describe how the police can reduce the harms caused by specific crime and disorder problems. They are guides for improving the overall response to incidents, are most helpful to people who understand basic problem-oriented policing principles and methods (described in Chapter 6 of this book), and are designed to help police decide how best to analyze and address problems they have already identified.

The COPS Office emphasizes that certain responses to problems may not work in all jurisdictions, that is, what works in one place may not work everywhere. The guides describe responses that other police departments have used or that researchers have tested. It is also emphasized that in order for these approaches to work, the police must be willing to work with other community agencies to find effective solutions to the problem. The police alone cannot implement many of the responses discussed in the guides and must use them in partnership with other responsible private and public entities. An effective problem solver must know how to forge genuine partnerships with others and be prepared to invest considerable effort in making these partnerships work.

Below we discuss three problems of crime and disorder that challenge today's police and that have been addressed in three different COPS *Problem-Oriented Guides for Police:* child pornography on the Internet, identity theft, and street racing.

CHILD PORNOGRAPHY ON THE INTERNET

The Problem

The treatment of children as sexual objects has existed through the ages, and so too has the production of erotic literature and drawings involving children, beginning with the invention of the camera in the early nineteenth century. However, the advent of the Internet in the 1980s dramatically changed the scale and nature of the child pornography problem, necessitating new approaches to investigation and control.

Internet child pornography is unlike most crimes that local police departments handle. Local citizens may access child pornography images that were produced and/or stored in another city or on another continent; alternatively, they may produce or distribute images that are downloaded by people thousands of miles away. An investigation that begins in one police district will almost certainly cross jurisdictional boundaries, so most of the major investigations of Internet child pornography have involved cooperation among jurisdictions, often at an international level. However, within this broader scheme, local police departments have a crucial role to play. By concentrating on components of the problem that occur within their local jurisdictions, they may uncover evidence that initiates a wider investigation, or they may receive information from other jurisdictions about offenders in their districts. Therefore, it is important that all police departments develop strategies for dealing with the problem. Larger departments or districts may have their own dedicated Internet child pornography teams, but most smaller agencies do not, so the responsibility for day-to-day investigations will fall to general-duties officers.

Specific Police Responses

The police role in combating child pornography certainly involves working in cooperation with other groups or acting as educators. However, a number of strategies and responses are the primary responsibility of the police alone:

- Police agencies may scan the Internet to locate and remove illegal child pornography sites. Many areas of the Internet are not accessible via the usual commercial search engines, so investigators need to be skilled at conducting sophisticated searches of the "hidden net." Police may issue warnings to Internet service providers (ISPs) that are carrying illegal content.

- Law enforcement agents may enter pedophile newsgroups, chat rooms, or other networks posing as pedophiles and request e-mailed child pornography images from others in the group. They may also enter child or teen groups posing as children and engage predatory pedophiles lurking in the group who may send pornography or suggest a meeting. A variation of the sting operation is to place ads on the Internet offering child pornography for sale and wait for replies. Recently Microsoft announced the development of the Child Exploitation Tracking System to help link information such as credit card purchases, Internet chat room messages, and conviction histories.

- Police might establish "honey sites," purported to contain child pornography but in fact designed to capture the personal or credit card details of visitors trying to download images. These can be considered a type of sting operation and have resulted in numerous arrests. However, their primary purpose is to create uncertainty in the minds of those seeking child pornography on the Internet, thus reducing the sense of freedom and anonymity they feel.

- Many police departments have learned to use the media to good effect to publicize crackdowns on Internet child pornography. Coverage of crackdowns in the mass media increases the perception among potential offenders that the Internet is an unsafe environment in which to access child pornography.

- Although most media attention is often given to technological aspects of controlling Internet child pornography, in fact many arrests in this area arise from traditional investigative police work. Investigations may involve information from the following five sources:

   1. *The public.* The public may contact police directly, or information may be received on one of the various child pornography hotlines.
   2. *Computer repairers/technicians.* Some states mandate computer personnel to report illegal images. There are cases where computer repairers have found child pornography images on an offender's hard drive and notified police. Police may establish relationships with local computer repairers/technicians to encourage reporting.
   3. *Victims.* A point of vulnerability for producers of child pornography is the child who appears in the pornographic images. If the child informs others of his or her victimization, then the offender's activities may be exposed.
   4. *Known traders.* The arrest of one offender can lead to the arrest of other offenders with whom he or she has had dealings, producing a cascading effect. In some cases the arrested offender's computer and Internet logs may provide evidence of associates.
   5. *Unrelated investigations.* There is increasing evidence that many sex offenders are criminally versatile and may commit a variety of other offenses. Police may find evidence of Internet child pornography while investigating unrelated crimes such as drug offenses.

Source: Richard Wortley and Stephen Smallbone, *Child Pornography on the Internet* (Washington, DC: Office of Community Oriented Policing Services, Problem-Oriented Guides for Police, May 2006). It is also available at http://www.cops.usdoj.gov/mime/open.pdf?Item=1729.

IDENTITY THEFT

The Problem

Identity theft is a relatively new crime, facilitated through underlying established crimes such as forgery, counterfeiting, check and credit card fraud, computer fraud, impersonation, pickpocketing, and even terrorism. It became a federal crime in the United States in 1998, with the passage of the Identity Theft Assumption and Deterrence Act, which identifies offenders as follows:

> [An offender] knowingly transfers or uses, without lawful authority, any name or number that may be used, alone or in conjunction with any other information, to identify a specific individual with the intent to commit, or to aid or abet any unlawful activity that constitutes a violation of Federal law, or that constitutes a felony under any applicable State or local law.

A significant feature of identity theft is the offender's repeated victimization of a single person. This may include repeatedly using a stolen credit card, taking over a card account, or using stolen personal information to open new accounts.

The longer it takes to discover the theft, the greater the victim's loss and suffering. Identity thieves steal wallets or purses from shopping bags, from cars, or by pickpocketing. They steal mail by several means, including taking it from insecure mailboxes, submitting a false change-of-address form to the post office to direct someone's mail to themselves, or colluding with a postal employee to steal mail that contains personal information. Other forms of theft committed by identity thieves to further their aims include stealing preapproved credit card applications, energy or telephone bills, and bank or credit card statements; rummaging through residential trash cans or through business dumpsters ("dumpster diving"); obtaining people's credit reports by posing as someone who is legally permitted to do so, such as a landlord or employer; colluding with or bribing employees of businesses, government agencies, or service organizations, such as hospitals and HMOs, to obtain personnel or client records; breaking into homes to find personal information on paper or on personal computers; hacking into corporate computers and stealing customer and employee databases and then selling them on the black market or extorting money from the database owners for their return; calling credit card issuers and changing the billing address for an account; buying on the street identities or credit cards that may be either counterfeit or stolen; and/or buying counterfeit documents such as birth certificates, visas, or passports.

Specific Police Responses

Some possible police responses to the problem of identity theft might include the following scenarios:

- Offenders steal many identities from inadequately protected business records. There are many commonsense low-tech ways to protect databases. Police may work through local business associations or establish working relationships with local businesses. Mindful of businesses' reasonable concern for profits, police should also try to convince businesses that the costs of losing data, in terms of both their reputation with clients and possible lawsuits by victims, are much higher than those of following the many simple procedures to protect private information. Businesses should also be encouraged to conduct regular staff training, new-employee orientations, and spot checks on proper information care; support and participate in multiagency financial-crimes task forces; limit data collection to the minimum information needed (for example, requests for Social Security numbers); restrict data access to only those employees with a legitimate need to know; audit electronic trails; impose strict penalties for browsing and illegitimate access; and conduct employee background checks.

- The Internet has an enormous amount of information on how to avoid becoming an identity theft victim. Some police departments include special sections on identity theft on their Web sites, all with information on how to protect one's identity. If the budget permits, police can print out information brochures to hand out at department meetings.

- Police agencies need to support efforts to reduce the use of Social Security numbers as identifiers (very common on health insurance cards, for example), and local agency personnel may need to be constantly reminded of the risks involved in lax use of private information.

- The major credit card companies have national and international reach, so it is unlikely that local efforts will directly influence their security policies. However, local banks often have agreements with the major credit card companies, especially as many ATM (or debit) cards also serve as credit cards. Thus, police must work with local banks to have some influence on their card-issuing policies.

- Police must work with victims to prevent them from being liable for unauthorized charges, withdrawals, or other unlawful activities of identity thieves. Police need to understand how consumers are protected and provide victims with educational resources that explain their rights and the steps they need to take to assert them.

- Police should prepare a plan to prevent or minimize the harm of identity theft when large identity databases have been breached. When a business or government agency reports that its employee records or client databases have been violated, police and others must act quickly to reduce the amount of time the thief has to use the stolen identities. The following three steps can be taken:

  1. Set up dedicated toll-free phone lines for employees to call the three major credit bureaus to warn of the theft.
  2. Give employees information packets on what to do to protect their identities and reduce damage, how to read credit reports, how a fraud alert on a credit file works, and so on.
  3. Hold statewide workshops for employees, distribute videos, and launch a Web page with helpful information.

Source: Graeme Newman, *Identity Theft* (Washington, DC: Office of Community Oriented Services, Problem-Oriented Guides for Police, June 2004). It is also available at http://www.cops.usdoj.gov/mime/open.pdf?Item=1271.

STREET RACING

The Problem

The American street-racing tradition dates back to the 1950s and has long been a staple of Hollywood movies. But no movie did more to boost the popularity of street racing than the 2001 surprise hit *The Fast and the Furious,* which includes spectacular racing scenes and daring stunts. At the root of the problem is the fact that youth have always had a profound need for speed.

Street races typically involve racers and spectators meeting at a popular gathering place, often on a relatively remote street in an industrial area. Here they decide where to race; they then convoy to the site, where a one-eighth- or one-quarter-mile track is marked off. Cars line up at the starting line, where a starter stands between them and drops his or her hands to begin the race while up to several hundred spectators may be watching. These illegal street races encourage spectators to stand near possibly inexperienced drivers and poorly maintained vehicles—a combination that can be deadly for onlookers. Racers and spectators also participate in what are termed "sideshows," where they engage in 360-degree burnouts, and "centipedes," where they form a convoy of vehicles and play a game of follow the leader, darting in and around normal traffic at high speeds.

Street racing can also be unorganized and sporadic in nature, involving impromptu one-time races between persons who do not know one another. The police generally have little means for dealing with these types of racers other than utilizing the media to make it very clear that if they are caught, violators will be severely prosecuted.

Specific Police Responses

Some possible police responses to the problem of organized street racing might include the following scenarios:

- The involvement and support of public officials, citizens, and business owners are essential for the success of most (if not all) of the specific responses and might include using members of a police explorers post, a citizens' police academy, senior citizens' groups, merchant associations, and so on to report racers' activities to police. Community support might also come from those who provide racers with their equipment, including shops selling high-performance car parts, and those who are at risk for being burglarized for these parts.

- Street racers can be informed about the dangers and legal consequences of racing as well as police enforcement intentions. Street-racing Web sites (on which they commonly announce past and future events, host chat rooms, and have message boards), police agency Web sites, newspapers, television, radio, and personal contacts with street racers might be employed. A publicity campaign about the problem and enforcement actions has been central to many efforts to combat street-racing problems. Performance shop owners also might be asked to provide customers with information about existing laws and potential penalties for racing.

- Unmarked police vehicles, plainclothes officers, and video equipment may be covertly used to observe racers' movements and methods and to determine the problems they create, where they live, the kinds of cars they drive, what their license plate numbers are, and so on. This allows for prerace intervention, access to race areas to be closed off, and participants to later be charged. Racers' use of police scanners can be thwarted by using radio code words, in-car computers, and specially programmed cell phones. During undercover surveillances, police can videotape illegal street races and participants; later crime reports can be written for each race and used to prepare arrest warrants for drivers and court orders for vehicle seizures. Street-racing Web sites can also be monitored for tracking racers' activities and communications.

- Police should review existing ordinances and statutes to determine whether they have adequate enforcement authority. Laws likely to be enforced against drivers include racing/reckless driving, driving under the influence of alcohol or drugs, and driving with suspended/revoked licenses. Police officers and vehicle-emission enforcement agents might jointly conduct smog equipment inspections on street-racing vehicles, issue the owner a citation if the equipment was disconnected or modified, and even order the vehicle removed from the street until it is brought into compliance with the law. Drivers should be checked for proof of insurance and vehicle registration. Officers can work with automotive experts to identify street-racing vehicles that have been illegally enhanced or altered or that have mechanical defects. Enforcement against nondrivers might include violations for trespassing on private property of adjacent businesses, obstructing traffic (if standing in the roadway), or aiding in a speed contest (for people acting as starters for races). Enforcement of curfew laws might also reduce the numbers of juveniles present at racing venues.

- A vehicle may be impounded and a fee assessed in order for the owner to retrieve the vehicle under an ordinance when the driver is arrested for engaging in a speed contest, for driving recklessly, or for demonstrating speed exhibitions (peeling or screeching tires due to hard acceleration). A vehicle forfeiture ordinance may be enacted to declare a vehicle a nuisance so that it can be permanently seized if it was used in a race or exhibition of speed and the driver has a prior conviction for certain serious driving offenses (such as reckless driving or evading officers).

- Owners and managers of private businesses at popular street-racing gathering places must be enlisted in efforts to discourage street-racing activity. Among the helpful measures are posting "no trespassing" signs and authorizing police to enforce them, limiting after-hours access, employing private security during weekends, and closing earlier.

- Some jurisdictions have installed speed humps, barricades, "k-railings" (concrete barricades), and freeway message signs and billboards (both permanent and temporary) to control, warn, and inform racers; others authorize police to erect barricades and close streets when racing becomes a problem. Parking can be prohibited on public properties and roadways in the race area to discourage spectators from congregating along roadsides during prime racing hours; offenders' vehicles can be towed.

- Several cities and counties have successfully addressed their illegal street-racing problem by creating, either on their own or in collaboration with other organizations, a legal racing venue. This is intended to divert people to a safer racing environment, which allows racers to experience some of the positive aspects of legal drag racing—fun, camaraderie, and excitement. Police can either align with an existing national program that encourages safe, legal on-track racing or implement their own local program.

Source: Kenneth J. Peak and Ronald W. Glensor, *Street Racing* (Washington, DC: Office of Community Oriented Policing Services, Problem-Oriented Guides for Police, December 2004). It is also available at http://www.cops.usdoj.gov/mime/open.pdf?Item=1418.

Career Information

This book has examined policing from many perspectives. If you are not yet working in the field but have made the decision to consider a career in local policing or federal or state law enforcement, you will find this appendix helpful in that regard. It discusses some realities of career selection and methods for preparing for career opportunities at the federal, state, and local levels.

First Things First: Preparation for Job Hunting

As a preliminary matter, a question often posed by police recruiters to interviewees asks what they have done to prepare for a policing career. In actuality, there are several means available for you to prepare for a prospective career in policing. For example, it is helpful if you can point to studying criminal justice, participating in a police ride-along program or having auxiliary police service, having a clean criminal record, staying in good physical shape, volunteering in such agencies, and so on.

Also, you may wish to read about the federal, state, and local law enforcement agencies that are described in Chapters 2 and 3; furthermore, Chapter 4 discusses police screening, recruitment, hiring, and training processes. Those chapters will serve as a good resource in your job search. You should consider and be prepared to respond to the kinds of oral interview questions that are presented as examples in Chapter 4.

Then you can more objectively determine your areas of interest and possible suitability for such employment. Remember, too, that we all have some limitations on our ability to secure employment in a particular field: mobility (ability to relocate to where the job is), personal appearance, character, physical abilities, prior academic performance, related experience, quality and content of a résumé, and interviewing skills.

Therefore, you should try to determine whether or not you possess all these qualities— the "right stuff"—to successfully pass the entry-level examinations and handle the challenges of police work. Also, do you work well under pressure? Do you write well? Are you action oriented when necessary? Do you accept cultural differences found in others? Can you enroll in an internship experience at a college or university? (See Chapter 13 for rationales for higher education for police.) And you must generally have the patience of Job. Remember the old adage that "Rome wasn't built in a day"; neither will you be hired for a law enforcement position in a day.

Also bear in mind that college and university career planning and placement offices may be contacted for job announcements, assistance in preparing résumés and developing interviewing skills, dates when law enforcement organizations are coming to campus to conduct job interviews, and so on. There are also private for-profit organizations that assist with preparing your résumé and developing your interviewing skills. Do not underestimate the value of a good résumé.

HELPFUL DOSE OF REALITY

After getting a professional degree, teaching and working in criminal justice for a good number of years, and interacting with hundreds of students about their career goals, it has become very clear to me that there are many misperceptions surrounding how to get into certain related fields. This is largely due to the many television programs and movies that often portray law enforcement functions, such as those that involve investigative, forensic (DNA), and profiling work, in unrealistic terms. So I would first like to emphasize the following three things:

1. A person does not become a detective by merely obtaining a college degree and then getting hired by a local agency and indicating a preference for that type of work. The rank of detective or investigator is normally obtained by going through the conventional hiring process (see Chapter 4), getting hired by a police agency, working for a prescribed (minimum) length of time as a rank-and-file police officer, and then applying and testing for a detective's assignment. The only exceptions to this rule are if one is hired by a state or federal agency that is investigative in nature, such as a state bureau of investigation, the Federal Bureau of Investigation (FBI), the Drug Enforcement Administration (DEA), the Bureau of Alcohol, Tobacco, Firearms, and Explosives (ATF), and so on. In that case, the agency will send the hiree to a specialized school (normally of several months' duration) to be trained specifically in its type of investigative work.

2. The odds of one becoming a *profiler,* in the words of a special agent of the FBI, are probably about one in a million—even if that person has been hired by the FBI. Again, television programs and movies about serial killers and profiling have caused great levels of interest in profiling among criminal justice students, but as with the aforementioned detective position, the reality does not match the perception.

3. One does not become a forensic (DNA) specialist by possessing a degree in criminal justice. Again, some high-profile celebrity criminal cases have heightened interest in this area, but the proper place to major or minor is in the hard sciences (the field of chemistry) in order to work with DNA and other laboratory-related evidence.

Careers in Local Policing

Most of this book's chapters have examined the roles and functions of local police departments and sheriff's offices. The 17,000 municipal police agencies constitute the largest segment of police personnel (with 452,000 sworn police and 174,000 sworn sheriff's personnel) in the nation, and these organizations offer a broad spectrum of specialized assignments. Normally, however, the smaller the agency is, the fewer the opportunities for such assignments; even a medium-sized municipal police department or county sheriff's office will normally have many more opportunities for specialized assignments than an agency serving a smaller community. For example, the opportunities for working as a detective (such as in the homicide, drugs, robbery, burglary, or juvenile divisions); as a member of a gang, drug, or K-9 unit; on motorcycle, horse, or bicycle patrol; or many other such assignments will be found in larger agencies, whereas smaller agencies do not have such specialization and their officers are more generalist in nature.

The same kinds of specialized assignments may be found in larger county sheriff's offices. As shown in Chapter 2, these agencies often lean heavily toward the detention (jail) functions and provide court security, prisoner transport, and related functions; county prosecutors also often use sheriff's personnel as investigators. Counties may have other specialized personnel, such as county park deputies.

If you are interested in local police employment, you should contact the relevant human resources department for the city or county agency in which you are interested or contact the agency directly (many smaller agencies do not have a human resources department or advertise position vacancies). You should also be alert for hiring notices on television, in the newspapers, or on the radio.

Careers with State Agencies

As noted in Chapter 2, nearly all states (except Hawaii) have two general types of law enforcement organizations: the general law enforcement agencies, which are engaged in patrol and related functions, and state bureaus of investigation (SBIs), which are the state's equivalent to the FBI. The SBIs may have a number of specialized units, such as organized crime, major crimes, even livestock brand inspection in more rural states. They are plainclothes agencies that usually investigate both criminal and civil cases and provide technical support to local agencies in the form of laboratory or record services, while often assisting smaller jurisdictions with major crimes.

State police organizations, conversely, perform general law enforcement duties. While seen primarily in the role of patrolling state highways, the state's statutes may authorize these troopers to perform a variety of nontraffic functions as well, such as special weapons and tactics (SWAT), search and rescue, and even special drug units.

Nearly all of the state police, highway patrol, and investigative agencies require a high school degree or its equivalent as a minimal educational requirement for trooper, investigator, and agent positions. As an applicant, you should also be aware that persons in these positions normally may be transferred by their state agency to work and live in any part of the state for as long as the agency deems it best for the organization.

If you are interested in state employment, you should watch for hiring notices online or in the media or for hiring announcements at state employment offices. You may also contact a state personnel office and ask for information concerning a particular state agency.

Careers in Federal Law Enforcement

Chapter 2 showed and discussed the organizational structures of most major traditional federal law enforcement agencies in the United States. In addition, with the relatively new addition of the Department of Homeland Security and its many subcomponent agencies (Immigration and Customs Enforcement, Customs and Border Protection, Transportation Security Administration, and so on), there has probably never been a better time to consider a career in federal enforcement. Each of these agencies has Web sites, and you should certainly go online to learn more about each of these agencies and others in which you have an employment interest.

Several methods may be employed for learning about position openings in federal law enforcement agencies. Undoubtedly the foremost (and official) job finder for the federal government is USAJOBS, available at http://www.usajobs.opm.gov/. This Web site contains information about 22,500 federal positions, forms to fill out for applying, and instructions for developing and online posting of a résumé.

Also, many federal law enforcement agencies have agents in-house who are assigned specifically as recruitment coordinators; they may be contacted for information about the application process and the hiring outlook. You can also look for hiring announcements in your campus career office.

Before considering a career in any federal law enforcement agency, an applicant must first complete and submit an application form—the SF-171 form—for federal employment. The federal Office of Personnel Management (OPM) coordinates the testing of most federal law enforcement agencies, although requirements for federal positions are determined by the individual agencies (the FBI and some other agencies do not utilize the OPM). Once the applicant has tested and passed, he or she receives an employment rating for the particular agency. The applicant must pass the test with a minimum score of seventy; the recruiting agency can then proceed to interview the best candidates, after which a background investigation is initiated.

The minimum salary and grade of hiring depend on the applicant's education, experience, and training, although some agencies do not hire above a specific level (generally General Schedule [GS] 5, 7, or 9).

Here in particular, it is important for you, as a career seeker, to be patient and to be prepared for a very thorough and lengthy hiring procedure. The federal and state agencies described in Chapter 2 will leave no rock unturned in vetting their applicants.

Chapter 1 Historical Development: Coming to America

1. Samuel Walker, *The Police in America: An Introduction* (New York: McGraw-Hill, 1983), p. 2.
2. Bruce Smith, *Rural Crime Control* (New York: Columbia University, 1933), p. 40.
3. Ibid., pp. 42–44.
4. Ibid.
5. Ibid.
6. Ibid., pp. 182–84.
7. Ibid., pp. 188–89.
8. Ibid., p. 192.
9. Ibid., pp. 218–22.
10. Ibid., pp. 245–46.
11. Ibid.
12. Craig Uchida, "The Development of American Police: An Historical Overview," in *Critical Issues in Policing: Contemporary Readings,* eds. Roger G. Dunham and Geoffrey P. Alpert (Prospect Heights, IL: Waveland Press, 1989), p. 14.
13. Charles Reith, *A New Study of Police History* (London: Oliver and Boyd, 1956).
14. Carl Klockars, *The Idea of Police* (Beverly Hills, CA: Sage, 1985).
15. Ibid., pp. 45–46.
16. Ibid., p. 46.
17. David R. Johnson, *American Law Enforcement History* (St. Louis: Forum Press, 1981), p. 4.
18. Ibid., p. 5.
19. Ibid.
20. Ibid., p. 6.
21. Ibid., p. 1.
22. Ibid., pp. 8–10.
23. Ibid., p. 11.
24. Ibid., p. 13.
25. David A. Jones, *History of Criminology: A Philosophical Perspective* (Westport, CT: Greenwood Press, 1986), p. 64.
26. Johnson, *American Law Enforcement History,* pp. 14–15.
27. Ibid., pp. 17–18.
28. Ibid., pp. 18–19.
29. Leon Radzinowicz, *A History of English Criminal Law and Its Administration from 1750,* vol. IV: *Grappling for Control* (London: Stevens and Son, 1968), p. 163.
30. Johnson, *American Law Enforcement History,* p. 19.
31. Ibid., pp. 19–20.
32. Ibid., pp. 20–21.
33. A. C. Germann, Frank D. Day, and Robert R. J. Gallati, *Introduction to Law Enforcement and Criminal Justice* (Springfield, IL: Charles C. Thomas, 1962), p. 63.
34. Clive Emsley, *Policing and Its Context, 1750–1870* (New York: Schocken, 1983), p. 37.
35. Pamela D. Mayhall, *Police-Community Relations and the Administration of Justice,* 3rd ed. (New York: John Wiley and Sons, 1985), p. 425.
36. Johnson, *American Law Enforcement History,* p. 26.
37. Ibid., pp. 26–27.
38. Ibid., p. 27.
39. Ibid.
40. Ibid., pp. 28–29.
41. Ibid., pp. 30–31.
42. James F. Richardson, *Urban Policing in the United States* (London: Kennikat Press, 1974), pp. 47–48.

43. James F. Richardson, *The New York Police: Colonial Times to 1901* (New York: Oxford Press, 1970), p. 259.

44. Richardson, *Urban Policing in the United States,* p. 48.

45. Richardson, *The New York Police,* pp. 195–201.

46. Richardson, *Urban Policing in the United States,* p. 51.

47. Ibid.

48. Ibid., pp. 53–54.

49. Ibid., pp. 55–56.

50. Ibid., pp. 59–60.

51. Johnson, *American Law Enforcement History,* p. 92.

52. Ibid.

53. Ibid., pp. 96–97.

54. Ibid., p. 98.

55. U.S. Department of Justice, "The Marshals Service Turns 215," http://www.usmarshals.gov/monitor/mon215.pdf (accessed February 1, 2007).

56. Johnson, *American Law Enforcement History,* pp. 100–101.

57. Eric H. Monkkonen, *Police in Urban America, 1860–1920* (New York: Cambridge University Press, 1981), p. 158.

58. John E. Eck, *The Investigation of Burglary and Robbery* (Washington, DC: Police Executive Research Forum, 1984).

59. George L. Kelling, "Juveniles and Police: The End of the Nightstick," in *From Children to Citizens,* vol. II: *The Role of the Juvenile Court,* ed. Francis X. Hartmann (New York: Springer-Verlag, 1987).

60. Herman Goldstein, *Policing a Free Society* (Cambridge, MA: Ballinger, 1977).

61. August Vollmer, "Police Progress in the Past Twenty-Five Years," *Journal of Criminal Law and Criminology* 24 (1933): 161–75.

62. Alfred E. Parker, *Crime Fighter: August Vollmer* (New York: Macmillan, 1961).

63. Douthit, "August Vollmer," in *Thinking about Police: Contemporary Readings,* ed. Carl B. Klockars (New York: McGraw-Hill, 1983), p. 102.

64. Ibid.

65. Paul Jacobs, *Prelude to Riot: A View of Urban America from the Bottom* (New York: Random House, 1966), pp. 13–60.

66. Ibid.

67. Samuel Walker, *A Critical History of Police Reform: The Emergence of Professionalism* (Lexington, MA: Lexington Books, 1977), p. 81.

68. Ibid., pp. 80–83.

69. See Gene E. Carte and Elaine H. Carte, *Police Reform in the United States: The Era of August Vollmer, 1905–1932* (Berkeley: University of California Press, 1975), for a chronology of Vollmer's career and a listing of his publications.

70. Orlando Wilson, *Police Administration* (New York: McGraw-Hill, 1950).

71. Mark H. Moore and George L. Kelling, "'To Serve and Protect': Learning from Police History," *The Public Interest* 70 (winter 1983): 49–65.

72. Johnson, *American Law Enforcement History,* pp. 119–20.

73. Ibid., pp. 120–21.

74. Richardson, *Urban Policing in the United States,* pp. 139–43.

75. Peter K. Manning, "The Researcher: An Alien in the Police World," in *The Ambivalent Force: Perspectives on the Police,* 2nd ed. (Hinsdale, IL: Dryden Press, 1976), pp. 103–21.

76. Herman Goldstein, *Problem-Oriented Policing* (New York: McGraw-Hill, 1990), p. 9.

77. William G. Doerner, *Introduction to Law Enforcement: An Insider's View* (Englewood Cliffs, NJ: Prentice Hall, 1992), pp. 21–23.

78. Samuel Walker, "'Broken Windows' and Fractured History: The Use and Misuse of History in Recent Police Patrol Analysis," in *Classics in Policing,* ed. Steven G. Brandl and David E. Barlow (Cincinnati: Anderson, 1996), pp. 97–110.

79. Thomas J. Baker, "Designing the Job to Motivate," *FBI Law Enforcement Bulletin* 45 (1976): 3–7.

80. Police Foundation, *The Newark Foot Patrol Experiment* (Washington, DC: Author, 1981).

81. Ibid., p. 71.

82. George Gallup, *Community Policing Survey* (Wilmington, NY: Scholarly Resources, 1996).

83. Willard M. Oliver, "The Third Generation of Community Policing: Moving through Innovation, Diffusion, and Institutionalization," *Police Quarterly* 3 (December 2000): 367–88.

84. Herman Goldstein, "Improving Policing: A Problem-Oriented Approach," *Crime and Delinquency* 25 (1979): 236–58.

85. James Q. Wilson and George L. Kelling, "Broken Windows: The Police and Neighborhood Safety," *Atlantic Monthly,* March 1982, pp. 29–38.

86. Samuel Walker, *The Police in America: An Introduction* (New York: McGraw-Hill, 1985).

87. T. McEwen, *National Assessment Program: 1994 Survey Results* (Washington, DC: National Institute of Justice, 1995).

88. U.S. Department of Justice, Bureau of Justice Statistics, *Law Enforcement Management and Administrative Statistics: Local Police Departments 2000* (Washington, DC: Author, January 2003), p. iii.

Chapter 2 Federal and State Agencies: Protecting Our Borders

1. "DHS Organization," http://www.dhs.gov/dhspublic/display?theme=10 (accessed October 8, 2006).

2. U.S. Department of Homeland Security, "Department Components and Subagencies," http://www.dhs.gov/xabout/structure/index.shtm (accessed October 20, 2006).

3. "U.S. Customs and Border Protection, 'On a Typical Day,'" http://www.cbp.gov/linkhandler/cgov/toolbox/about/organization/orgcha1.ctt/orgcha1.pdf (accessed October 9, 2006).

4. "FAQ—Commonly Asked Questions about ICE," http://www.ice.gov/about/faq.htm (accessed October 9, 2006).

5. "TSA Law Enforcement," http://www.tsa.gov/lawenforcement/index.shtm (accessed October 9, 2006).

6. "Welcome to FLETC," http://www.fletc.gov/ (accessed October 9, 2006).

7. United States Secret Service, "Frequently Asked Questions," http://www.secretservice.gov/faq.shtml#employees (accessed October 9, 2006).

8. David R. Johnson, *American Law Enforcement History* (St. Louis: Forum Press, 1981), pp. 166–70.

9. Ibid.

10. U.S. Department of Justice, Federal Bureau of Investigation, "About Us—Quick Facts," http://www.fbi.gov/quickfacts.htm (accessed February 1, 2007).

11. Personal communication, Edward Duffer, September 23, 2003.

12. Chitra Ragavan, "Muller's Mandate," *U.S. News and World Report,* May 26, 2003, pp. 19–29.

13. "FBI Agents Get Sweeping New Powers," Associated Press, May 31, 2002.

14. "FBI Agents Still Lacking Arabic Skills," http://www.washingtonpost.com/wp-yn/content/article/2006/10/10/AR2006101001388.html (accessed February 7, 2007).

15. Jeff Glasser, "In Demand for Fifty Years: The FBI's 'Most Wanted' List—Good Publicity, and a History of Success," *U.S. News and World Report,* March 20, 2000, p. 60.

16. Bureau of Alcohol, Tobacco, Firearms, and Explosives, "Changes in ATF Resulting from the Signing of the Homeland Security Bill: Two Separate Bureaus Created" (press release), http://www.atf/gov/press/fy03press/112702homelandatf.htm (accessed September 7, 2004).

17. For an excellent overview of the duties of federal law enforcement agents as well as other state and local personnel, see, for example, Department of Labor, Bureau of Labor Statistics, "Occupational Outlook Handbook: Police and Detectives," http://www.bls.gov/oco/ocos160.htm (accessed January 13, 2005); and James Stinchcomb, *Opportunities in Law Enforcement and Criminal Justice Careers,* rev. ed. (New York: McGraw-Hill, 2003).

18. See, for example, Patrick G. O'Brien and Kenneth J. Peak, *Kansas Bootleggers* (Manhattan, KS: Sunflower University Press, 1991); Joseph E. Dabney, *Mountain Spirits* (New York: Charles Scribner's Sons, 1974); and Jess Carr, *The Second Oldest Profession: An Informal History of Moonshining in America* (Englewood Cliffs, NJ: Prentice-Hall, 1972).

19. Bureau of Alcohol, Tobacco, Firearms, and Explosives, "ATF Snapshot 2004," http://www.atf.gov/about/snap2004.htm (accessed September 13, 2004).

20. Ibid.

21. Ibid.

22. Ibid.

23. Ibid.

24. Ibid.
25. U.S. Department of Justice, Drug Enforcement Administration, "DEA Mission Statement," http://www.usdoj.gov.dea/agency/mission.htm (accessed January 6, 2004).
26. U.S. Department of Justice, Drug Enforcement Administration, "Factsheet: DEA Data," July 1995, pp. 1–2.
27. U.S. Department of Justice, "Federal Law Enforcement Officers, 1996," *Bureau of Justice Statistics Bulletin,* December 1997, p. 3.
28. U.S. Department of Justice, U.S. Marshals Office, *The FY 1993 Report to the U.S. Marshals* (Washington, DC: Author, 1994), pp. 188–89.
29. Central Intelligence Agency, "CIA Vision, Mission, and Values," http://www.cia.gov/cia/information/mission.html (accessed January 4, 2005).
30. Central Intelligence Agency, "About the CIA," http://www.cia.gov/cia/information/info.html (accessed January 5, 2005).
31. "Central Intelligence Agency," *U.S. News and World Report,* October 30, 2006, p. 59; "CIA Career Opportunities," https://www.cia.gov/careers/index.html (accessed October 29, 2006).
32. Ibid.
33. U.S. Department of Justice, "Federal Law Enforcement Officers, 1996," p. 3.
34. Ludovic Kennedy, "The Airman and the Carpenter: The Lindbergh Kidnapping and the Framing of Richard Hauptmann," *Seton Hall Law Review* 14, 574–98.
35. Don Vogel, quoted in Department of the Treasury, Internal Revenue Service, *CI Digest,* pub. no. 1827, June 1994, p. 12.
36. See the Internal Revenue Service Web site, "Criminal Investigation Special Agent," http://www.jobs.irs.gov/mn-LawEnforcement.html (accessed January 4, 2004).
37. Department of the Treasury, Federal Law Enforcement Training Center, *Catalog of Training Programs* (Washington, DC: Author, 1995), p. 1.
38. General Accounting Office, *Federal Law Enforcement Training Center: Capacity Planning and Management Oversight Need Improvement,* Report to Congressional Requesters (Washington, DC: Author, July 2003), p. 7.
39. "State Bureau of Investigation: Encyclopedia," http://experts.about.com/e/s/st/State_Bureau_of_Investigation.htm (accessed October 17, 2006).
40. U.S. Department of Justice, Bureau of Justice Statistics, *Law Enforcement Management and Administrative Statistics, 2000: Data for Individual State and Local Agencies with 100 or More Officers* (Washington, DC: Author, April 2004), pp. 247–49.
41. U.S. Department of Justice, "Sourcebook of Criminal Justice Statistics Online, Table 1.0001.2003," http://www.albany.edu/sourcebook/pdf/t100012003.pdf (accessed October 17, 2006).
42. Missouri State Highway Patrol, "Missouri State Trooper," http://www.theblueline.com/feature/MOstatehwypatrol.htm (accessed January 15, 2007).
43. U.S. Department of Justice, Bureau of Justice Statistics, *Law Enforcement Management and Administrative Statistics, 2000,* pp. 247–49.
44. Ibid.
45. U.S. Department of Justice, Bureau of Justice Statistics, *Traffic Stop Data Collection Policies for State Police, 2004* (Washington, DC: Author, June 2005), p. 1.

Chapter 3 Police in Society: Organization and Administration of Municipal and County Agencies

1. Steven Levy, "Working in Dilbert's World," *Newsweek,* August 12, 1996, pp. 52–57.
2. David A. Tansik and James F. Elliott, *Managing Police Organizations* (Monterey, CA: Duxbury, 1981), p. 1.
3. Larry K. Gaines, Mittie D. Southerland, and John E. Angell, *Police Administration* (New York: McGraw-Hill, 1991), p. 9.
4. Ibid.
5. Samuel Walker, *The Police in America: An Introduction,* 2nd ed. (New York: McGraw-Hill, 1992), pp. 356–59.

6. Ibid., p. 77.

7. Ibid., p. 86.

8. *Interpersonal Communication: A Guide for Staff Development* (Athens: University of Georgia, Institute of Government, August 1974), p. 15.

9. Wayne W. Bennett and Karen Hess, *Management and Supervision in Law Enforcement,* 2nd ed. (St. Paul, MN: West, 1996), p. 85.

10. See R. C. Huseman, quoted in Bennett and Hess, *Management and Supervision in Law Enforcement,* pp. 21–27. Material for this section was also drawn from Charles R. Swanson, Leonard Territo, and Robert W. Taylor, *Police Administration: Structures, Processes, and Behavior,* 6th ed. (Upper Saddle River, NJ: Prentice Hall, 2005), pp. 309–11.

11. D. Katz and R. L. Kahn, *The Social Psychology of Organizations* (New York: John Wiley and Sons, 1966), p. 239; as cited in P. V. Lewis, *Organizational Communication: The Essence of Effective Management* (Columbus, OH: Grid, 1975), p. 36.

12. See R. K. Allen, *Organizational Management through Communication* (New York: Harper and Row, 1977), pp. 77–79.

13. Alex Markels, "Managers Aren't Always Able to Get the Right Message Across with E-mail," *Wall Street Journal,* August 6, 1996, p. 2.

14. Connie Glaser, "Take Grandma's Advice: Quiet Down and Listen Up," *Atlanta Business Chronicle* http://www.connieglaser.com/monthly_march2002.html (accessed February 1, 2007).

15. Bennett and Hess, *Management and Supervision in Law Enforcement*, p. 101.

16. See George D. Eastman and Esther M. Eastman, eds., *Municipal Police Administration,* 7th ed. (Washington, DC: International City Management Association, 1971), p. 17.

17. Ibid., p. 18.

18. "Chicago: Population Profile," http://www.city-data.com/us-cities/The-Midwest/Chicago-Population-Profile.html (accessed October 23, 2006).

19. "The Chicago Police Department: Annual Report 2005 Year in Review," http://egov.cityofchicago. org/webportal/COCWebPortal/COC_EDITORIAL/04AR.pdf (accessed October 23, 2006).

20. President's Commission on Law Enforcement and Administration of Justice, *Task Force Report: The Police* (Washington, DC: Government Printing Office, 1967), p. 46.

21. U.S. Department of Justice, Bureau of Justice Statistics, *Police Departments in Large Cities, 1987* (Washington, DC: Author, 1989), p. 5, Table 10 (Special Report NCJ-119220).

22. M. D. Iannone and Nathan F. Iannone, *Supervision of Police Personnel,* 6th ed. (Upper Saddle River, NJ: Prentice Hall, 2000).

23. Michael Carpenter, "Put It in Writing: The Police Policy Manual," *FBI Law Enforcement Bulletin* (October 2000): 1.

24. Robert Sheehan and Gary W. Cordner, *Introduction to Police Administration,* 2nd ed. (Cincinnati: Anderson, 1989), pp. 446–47.

25. Charles R. Swanson, Leonard Territo, and Robert W. Taylor, *Police Administration: Structures, Processes, and Behavior,* 5th ed. (Upper Saddle River, NJ: Prentice Hall, 2001), p. 248.

26. Stephen W. Mastrofski, "Police Agency Accreditation: The Prospects of Reform," *American Journal of Police* 5, no. 3 (1986): 45–81.

27. U.S. Department of Justice, "Census of State and Local Law Enforcement Agencies, 1996," *Bureau of Justice Statistics Bulletin,* June 1998, p. 1.

28. U.S. Department of Justice, Bureau of Justice Statistics, *Local Police Departments, 2003* (Washington, DC: Author, 2006), p. iii.

29. U.S. Department of Justice, Bureau of Justice Statistics, *Sheriff's Offices, 2003* (Washington, DC: Author, 2006), p. iii.

30. U.S. Department of Justice, Bureau of Justice Statistics, *Local Police Departments, 2003,* p. iii.

31. U.S. Department of Justice, Bureau of Justice Statistics, *Sheriff's Offices, 2003,* p. iii.

32. U.S. Department of Justice, Bureau of Justice Statistics, *Local Police Departments, 2003,* p. iii.

33. U.S. Department of Justice, Bureau of Justice Statistics, *Sheriff's Offices, 2003,* p. iii.

34. Data contained in Tables 3-1 through 3-7 are adapted from: U.S. Department of Justice, Bureau of Justice Statistics, *Local Police Departments, 2003* (Washington, DC: Author, 2006), and U.S. Department of Justice, Bureau of Justice Statistics, *Sheriff's Offices, 2003* (Washington, DC: Author, 2006).

35. Gaines, Southerland, and Angell, *Police Administration,* pp. 10–11.

36. Ibid., p. 42.

37. Janice Penegor and Ken Peak, "Police Chief Acquisitions: A Comparison of Internal and External Selections," *American Journal of Police* 11, no. 1 (1992): 17–32.

38. Richard B. Weinblatt, "The Shifting Landscape of Chiefs' Jobs," *Law and Order,* October 1999, p. 50.

39. "Survey Says Big-City Chiefs Are Better-Educated Outsiders," *Law Enforcement News,* April 30, 1998, p. 7.

40. R. J. Filer, "Assessment Centers in Police Selection," in *Proceedings of the National Working Conference on the Selection of Law Enforcement Officers*, ed. C. D. Spielberger and H. C. Spaulding (Tampa: University of South Florida, March 1977), p. 103.

41. National Advisory Commission on Criminal Justice Standards and Goals, *Police Chief Executive* (Washington, DC: Government Printing Office, 1976), p. 7.

42. Weinblatt, "The Shifting Landscape of Chiefs' Jobs," p. 51.

43. R. Simpson and H. Miller, "Social Status and Anomia," *Social Problems* 10, no. 3 (1963): 256–64.

44. Kraig L. Hayes, Robert M. Regoli, and John D. Hewitt, "Police Chiefs, Anomia, and Leadership," *Police Quarterly* 10, no. 1 (March 2007): 3–40.

45. L. Srole, "Social Integration and Certain Corollaries: An Exploratory Study," *American Sociological Review* 21 (1956): 709–16.

46. Hayes, Regoli, and Hewitt, "Police Chiefs, Anomia, and Leadership," pp. 14–15.

47. National Advisory Commission on Criminal Justice Standards and Goals, *Police Chief Executive,* p. 7.

48. Clemens Bartollas, Stuart J. Miller, and Paul B. Wice, *Participants in American Criminal Justice: The Promise and the Performance* (Englewood Cliffs, NJ: Prentice Hall, 1983), pp. 51–52.

49. Ronald G. Lynch, *The Police Manager: Professional Leadership Skills,* 3rd ed. (New York: Random House, 1986), p. 1.

50. Henry Mintzberg, "The Manager's Job: Folklore and Fact," *Harvard Business Review* 53 (July–August 1975): 49–61.

51. Donald C. Witham, *The American Law Enforcement Chief Executive: A Management Profile* (Washington, DC: Police Executive Research Forum, 1985), p. xii.

52. Peter C. Dodenhoff, "LEN Salutes Its 1996 People of the Year, the NYPD and Its Compstat Process," *Law Enforcement News,* December 31, 1996, pp. 1, 4–5.

53. Ibid., p. 4.

54. Ibid.

55. Eli B. Silverman, "Mapping Change: How the New York City Police Department Re-engineered Itself to Drive Down Crime," *Law Enforcement News,* December 15, 1996, p. 10.

56. Dodenhoff, "LEN Salutes Its 1996 People of the Year, the NYPD and Its Compstat Process," p. 4.

57. Bennett and Hess, *Management and Supervision in Law Enforcement,* pp. 44–45.

58. Richard N. Holden, *Modern Police Management* (Englewood Cliffs, NJ: Prentice Hall, 1986), pp. 294–95.

59. Ibid., p. 295.

60. Thomas J. Peters and Robert H. Waterman Jr., *In Search of Excellence* (New York: Warner, 1982), pp. 306–17.

61. John Van Maanen, "Making Rank: Becoming an American Police Sergeant," in *Critical Issues in Policing: Contemporary Readings,* ed. Roger G. Dunham and Geoffrey P. Alpert (Prospect Heights, IL: Waveland Press, 1989), pp. 146–61.

62. Kenneth J. Peak, Larry K. Gaines, and Ronald W. Glensor, *Police Supervision and Management: In an Era of Community Policing,* 2nd ed. (Upper Saddle River, NJ: Prentice Hall, 2004), pp. 33–34.

63. R. S. Engel, "Supervisory Styles of Patrol Sergeants and Lieutenants," *Journal of Criminal Justice* 29 (2001): 341–55.

64. Norm Stamper, *Breaking Rank: A Top Cop's Exposé of the Dark Side of American Policing* (New York: Nation Books, 2005), p. 185.

65. *Webster's Ninth New Collegiate Dictionary* (Springfield, MA: Merriam-Webster, 1983), p. 910.

66. Richard Brzeczek, "Chief-Mayor Relations: The View from the Chief's Chair," in *Police Leadership in America: Crisis and Opportunity,* ed. William A. Geller (New York: Praeger, 1985), pp. 48–55.

67. George F. Cole and Christopher Smith, *The American System of Criminal Justice,* 9th ed. (Belmont, CA: West/Wadsworth, 2001), p. 237.

68. James F. Richardson, *Urban Police in the United States* (Port Washington, NY: Kennikat Press, 1974), pp. 55–58.

69. Bartollas, Miller, and Wice, *Participants in American Criminal Justice,* p. 35.

70. Ibid., pp. 39–40.

71. Ibid., pp. 49–50.

72. The Museum of Broadcast Communications, "Police Programs," http://www.museum.tv/archives/etv/P/htmlP/policeprogra/policeprogra.htm (accessed January 4, 2007).

73. Ibid.

74. "Be Careful What You Say," *Law Enforcement News,* December 15, 1997, p. 1.

75. U.S. Department of Justice, Bureau of Justice Statistics, *Law Enforcement Management and Administrative Statistics: Local Police Departments, 2003* (Washington, DC: Author, May 2006), p. 2.

76. National Advisory Commission on Criminal Justice Standards and Goals, *Police* (Washington, DC: Government Printing Office, 1973), p. 108.

77. Samuel Walker and Charles M. Katz, *The Police in America: An Introduction* (New York: McGraw-Hill, 2002).

78. Jerome H. Skolnick and James J. Fyfe, *Above the Law: Police and the Excessive Use of Force* (New York: Free Press, 1993).

79. Steven M. Cox, *Police: Practices, Perspectives, Problems* (Boston: Allyn and Bacon, 1996), p. 90.

80. Personal communication, CALEA, October 25, 2006; also see the CALEA Web site, http://www.calea.org.

81. Cox, *Police,* p. 90.

82. Fulton County, Georgia, Sheriff's Office, "CALEA Law Enforcement Accreditation," p. 2.

83. Kimberly A. McCabe and Robin G. Fajardo, "Law Enforcement Accreditation: A National Comparison of Accredited versus Nonaccredited Agencies," *Journal of Criminal Justice* 29 (2001): 127–31.

84. Ibid., pp. 129–30.

Chapter 4 From Citizen to Officer: Preparing for the Street

1. William A. Westley, *Violence and the Police* (Cambridge, MA: MIT Press, 1970).

2. Geoffrey P. Alpert and Roger G. Dunham, *Policing Urban America,* 2nd ed. (Prospect Heights, IL: Waveland Press, 1992), p. 80; for an excellent description of the evolving police role, also see Roger G. Dunham and Geoffrey P. Alpert, *Critical Issues in Policing: Contemporary Readings,* 5th ed. (Long Grove, IL: Waveland Press, 2005), pp. 1–9.

3. Quoted in V. A. Leonard and Harry W. More, *Police Organization and Management,* 3rd ed. (Mineola, NY: Foundation Press, 1971), p. 128.

4. Joel Lefkowitz, "Industrial-Organizational Psychology and the Police," *American Psychologist* (May 1977): 346–64.

5. R. B. Mills, "Use of Diagnostic Small Groups in Police Recruit Selection and Training," *Journal of Criminal Law, Criminology and Police Science* 60 (1969): 238–41; John Van Maanen, "Police Socialization: A Longitudinal Examination of Job Attitudes in an Urban Police Department," *Administrative Science Quarterly* 20 (1975): 207–28.

6. C. Gorer, "Modification of National Character: The Role of the Police in England," *Journal of Social Issues* 11 (1955): 24–32; Arthur Niederhoffer, *Behind the Shield: The Police in Urban Society* (New York: Anchor, 1967), p. 140.

7. M. Steven Meagher and Nancy A. Yentes, "Choosing a Career in Policing: A Comparison of Male and Female Perceptions," *Journal of Police Science and Administration* 14 (1986): 320–27.

8. Lefkowitz, "Industrial-Organizational Psychology and the Police."

9. J. D. Matarazzo, B. V. Allen, G. Saslow, and A. N. Wiens, "Characteristics of Successful Policemen and Firemen Applicants," *Journal of Applied Psychology* 48 (1964): 123–33.

10. Bruce N. Carpenter and Susan M. Raza, "Personality Characteristics of Police Applicants: Comparisons across Subgroups and with Other Populations," *Journal of Police Science and Administration* 15 (1987): 10–17.

11. Carpenter and Raza also compared police applicants with other similar occupational groups and found that police applicants appear to be most like nuclear submariners and least like air force trainees and security guards.

12. Lawrence S. Wrightsman, *Psychology and the Legal System* (Monterey, CA: Brooks/Cole, 1987), pp. 85–86.

13. Al Seedman and P. Hellman, *Chief!* (New York: Arthur Fields, 1974), pp. 4–5.

14. Jennifer Nislow, "Is Anyone Out There?" *Law Enforcement News,* October 31, 1999, p. 1.

15. Nicole Ziegler Dizon, "Searching for Police," Associated Press, June 3, 2000.

16. Marc Lifsher, "State Strains to Recruit New Police," *Wall Street Journal,* November 10, 1999, p. CA1.

17. Dizon, "Searching for Police."

18. "Plenty of Talk, Not Much Action," *Law Enforcement News,* January 15/31, 1999, p. 1.

19. "Hiring Problem? What Hiring Problem? NYSP Has Answers to Recruiting Slump," *Law Enforcement News,* November 30, 2000, p. 1.

20. "Police Chiefs Try Many Recruiting Strategies to Boost Applicant Pool," *Crime Control Digest,* February 2, 2001, pp. 1–2.

21. U.S. Department of Justice, Bureau of Justice Statistics, *Local Police Departments, 2003* (Washington, DC: Author, May 2006), p. 8.

22. Alfred Stone and Stuart DeLuca, *Police Administration* (New York: John Wiley and Sons, 1985).

23. Hans Toch, *Psychology of Crime and Criminal Justice* (Prospect Heights, IL: Waveland Press, 1999), p. 44.

24. Philip Ash, Karen B. Slora, and Cynthia F. Britton, "Police Agency Officer Selection Practices," *Journal of Police Science and Administration* 17 (December 1990): 259–64.

25. S. H. Marsh, "Validating the Selection of Deputy Sheriffs," *Public Personnel Review* 23 (1962): 41–44.

26. William H. Thweatt, "A Vocational Counseling Approach to Police Selection" (unpublished dissertation, University of Arizona).

27. W. Clinton Terry III, *Policing Society* (New York: John Wiley and Sons, 1985), p. 194.

28. George E. Hargrave, "Using the MMPI and CPI to Screen Law Enforcement Applicants: A Study of Reliability and Validity of Clinicians' Decisions," *Journal of Police Science and Administration* 13 (1985): 221–24.

29. Roger G. Dunham and Geoffrey P. Alpert, *Critical Issues in Policing: Contemporary Readings* (Prospect Heights, IL: Waveland Press, 1989), p. 80.

30. For a complete discussion of the Sparks Police Officers Physical Abilities Test (POPAT), see Ken Peak, Douglas Farenholtz, and George Coxey, "Physical Abilities Testing for Police Officers: A Flexible, Job Related Approach," *Police Chief* (January 1992): 51–56.

31. Terry Eisenberg, D. A. Kent, and C. R. Wall, *Police Personnel Practices in State and Local Governments* (Gaithersburg, MD: International Association of Chiefs of Police, 1973), p. 15.

32. George E. Hargrave and Deirdre Hiatt, "Law Enforcement Selection with the Interview, MMPI, and CPI: A Study of Reliability and Validity," *Journal of Police Science and Administration* 15(2) (1987): 110–17.

33. U.S. Department of Justice, Bureau of Justice Statistics, *Local Police Departments, 2003,* p. 8

34. Quoted in Charles R. Swanson, Leonard Territo, and Robert W. Taylor, *Police Administration,* 2nd ed. (New York: Macmillan, 1988), pp. 202–203.

35. Terry, *Policing Society,* p. 196.

36. See, for example, David Bradford and Joan E. Pynes, "Police Academy Training: Why Hasn't It Kept Up with Practice?" *Police Quarterly* 2 (September 1999): 283–301; N. Marion, "Police Academy Training: Are We Teaching Recruits What They Need to Know?" *Policing: An International Journal of Police Strategies and Management* 21 (1998): 54–79; Richard F. Brand and Ken Peak, "Assessing Police Training Curriculums: 'Consumer Reports,'" *Justice Professional* 9, no. 1 (winter 1995): 45–58.

37. John J. Broderick, *Police in a Time of Change,* 2nd ed. (Prospect Heights, IL: Waveland Press, 1987), p. 215.
38. Quoted in John M. Violanti, "What Does High Stress Police Training Teach Recruits? An Analysis of Coping," *Journal of Criminal Justice* 21 (1993): 411–17.
39. Ibid., p. 416.
40. John Van Maanen, "On the Making of Policemen," in *Thinking about Police,* ed. Carl Klockars (New York: McGraw-Hill, 1983), pp. 388–400.
41. Quoted in Bradford and Pynes, "Police Academy Training," p. 289.
42. Ibid., pp. 292, 297.
43. Ibid., p. 298.
44. Alpert and Dunham, *Policing Urban America,* p. 50.
45. Lois Pilant, "Enhancing the Patrol Image," *Police Chief* (August 1992): 55–61.
46. Wrightsman, *Psychology and the Legal System,* p. 86.
47. Quoted in Jerome Skolnick, "A Sketch of the Policeman's Working Personality," in *The Police Community,* ed. Jack Goldsmith and Sharon S. Goldsmith (Pacific Palisades, CA: Palisades Publishers, 1974), p. 106.
48. Thomas F. Adams, "Field Interrogation," *Police* (March–April 1963): 1–8.
49. Jonathan Rubenstein, "Cop's Rules," in *Police Behavior: A Sociological Perspective,* ed. Richard J. Lundman (New York: Oxford University Press, 1980), pp. 68–78.
50. Bruce Catton, "Eyewitness Reports on the Assassination of Abraham Lincoln," in *Criminal Justice: Allies and Adversaries,* ed. John R. Snortum and Ilana Hader (Pacific Palisades, CA: Palisades Publishers, 1978), pp. 155–57.
51. Tom Wilkenson and John Chattin-McNichols, "The Effectiveness of Computer-Assisted Instruction for Police Officers," *Journal of Police Science and Administration* 13 (1985): 230–35.
52. Niederhoffer, *Behind the Shield,* p. 51.
53. Dunham and Alpert, *Critical Issues in Policing,* p. 112.
54. Ibid., p. 111.
55. Ibid., pp. 112–15.
56. Alpert and Dunham, *Policing Urban America,* p. 58.
57. Kenneth J. Peak, Steven Pitts, and Ronald W. Glensor, "From 'FTO' to 'PTO': A Contemporary Approach to Post-Academy Recruit Training" (paper presented at the annual conference of the Academy of Criminal Justice Sciences, Seattle, March 22, 2007).
58. "Field Trainers Have Reports Well in Hand," *Law Enforcement News,* November 15, 2000, p. 5.
59. "Pursuit Simulation Training Is No Ordinary Crash Course," *Law Enforcement News,* November 15, 2000, p. 6.
60. Jerome Skolnick, "A Sketch of the Policeman's Working Personality," quoted in *The Police Community,* eds. Jack Goldsmith and Sharon S. Goldsmith (Pacific Palisades, CA: Palisades Publishers, 1974), p. 106.
61. William Westley, *Violence and the Police* (Cambridge, MA: MIT Press, 1970), p. 56.
62. Elizabeth Burbeck and Adrian Furnham, "Police Officer Selection: A Critical Review of the Literature," *Journal of Police Science and Administration* 13 (1985): 58–69.
63. Joseph Matarazzo, B. V. Allen, George Saslow, and Arthur N. Wiens, "Characteristics of Successful Policemen and Firemen Applicants," *Journal of Applied Psychology* 48 (1964): 123–33.
64. George E. Hargrave, Deirdre Hiatt, and Tim W. Gaffney, "A Comparison of MMPI and CPI Profiles for Traffic Officers," *Journal of Police Science and Administration* 14 (1986): 250–58.
65. Quoted in Seymour M. Lipset, "Why Cops Hate Liberals—and Vice Versa," *Atlantic Monthly* 223 (March 1969): 76.
66. Niederhoffer, *Behind the Shield,* p. 140.
67. John J. Broderick, *Police in a Time of Change* (Prospect Heights, IL: Waveland Press, 1987), p. 215.
68. Adapted from Dennis Nowicki, "Twelve Traits of Highly Effective Police Officers," *Law and Order,* October 1999, pp. 45–46.
69. Samuel Walker, *The Police in America: An Introduction,* 2nd ed. (New York: McGraw-Hill, 1992), p. 61.
70. Herman Goldstein, *Policing a Free Society* (Cambridge, MA: Ballinger, 1977), p. 21.
71. Steven M. Cox, *Police: Practices, Perspectives, Problems* (Boston: Allyn and Bacon, 1996), pp. 18–19.
72. Ibid., p. 61.

73. See Albert Reiss, *The Police and the Public* (New Haven, CT: Yale University Press, 1971), p. 96.

74. Jerome H. Skolnick and David H. Bayley, *The New Blue Line: Police Innovation in Six American Cities* (New York: Free Press, 1986), p. 4.

75. Patrick V. Murphy and Thomas Plate, *Commissioner: A View from the Top of American Law Enforcement* (New York: Simon and Schuster, 1977). Also see Samuel Walker, *The Police in America,* pp. 55–56.

76. Cox, *Police,* pp. 18–19.

77. James Q. Wilson, *Varieties of Police Behavior* (Cambridge, MA: Harvard University Press, 1968), pp. 140–226.

78. Cox, *Police,* pp. 18–19.

79. Wilson, *Varieties of Police Behavior,* pp. 140–226.

Chapter 5 Policing as Work: Patrolling, Problem Solving, Detecting

1. Quoted in John A. Webster, "Patrol Tasks," in *Policing Society: An Occupational View,* ed. W. Clinton Terry III (New York: John Wiley and Sons, 1985), pp. 263–313.

2. American Bar Association, *Standards Relating to Urban Police Function* (New York: Institute of Judicial Administration, 1974), Standard 2.2.

3. W. Clinton Terry III, ed., *Policing Society: An Occupational View* (New York: John Wiley and Sons, 1985), pp. 259–60.

4. Anthony V. Bouza, *The Police Mystique: An Insider's Look at Cops, Crime, and the Criminal Justice System* (New York: Plenum, 1990), p. 27.

5. See U.S. Department of Justice, Office of Community Oriented Policing Services, *311 for Non-Emergencies* (August 2006).

6. Elizabeth Reuss-Ianni, *Two Cultures of Policing: Street Cops and Management Cops* (New Brunswick, NJ: Transaction Books, 1983).

7. Lauren Frayer, "12,000 Iraqi Police Killed since 2003," Associated Press, December 25, 2006.

8. Federal Bureau of Investigation, Uniform Crime Reports, "Law Enforcement Officers Killed and Assaulted, 2006," http://www.fbi.gov/ucr/killed/2006 (accessed January 2, 2008).

9. CNNMoney.com, "America's Most Dangerous Jobs," http://money.cnn.com/2006/08/16/pf/2005_most_dangerous_jobs/index.htm (accessed January 3, 2007).

10. Personal communication, National Law Enforcement Memorial Fund, March 30, 2007.

11. Associated Press, "More Police Dying in Traffic Accidents," http://www.msnbc.msn.com/id/16362182/ (accessed December 27, 2006).

12. Anthony J. Pinizzotto, Edward F. Davis, and Charles E. Miller III, "Suicide by Cop Defining a Devastating Dilemma," *FBI Law Enforcement Bulletin* 74, no. 2 (February 2005), http://www.fbi.gov/publications/leb/2005/feb2005/feb2005.htm#page8 (accessed January 8, 2007).

13. H. Range Huston and Diedre Anglin, "Suicide by Cop," *Annals of Emergency Medicine* 32, no. 6 (December 1998).

14. Adapted from Pinizzotto, Davis, and Miller, "Suicide by Cop Defining a Devastating Dilemma."

15. Ibid.

16. Jerome H. Skolnick and David H. Bayley, *The New Blue Line: Police Innovation in Six American Cities* (New York: Free Press, 1986), pp. 141–42.

17. John P. Crank, *Understanding Police Culture* (Cincinnati: Anderson, 1998), p. 83.

18. Ibid., p. 254.

19. Quoted in Mark Baker, *Cops: Their Lives in Their Own Words* (New York: Pocket Books, 1985), p. 298.

20. Bouza, *The Police Mystique,* p. 74.

21. See the full text of the law at http://www.sdsos.gov/adminservices/adminpdfs/h218enr.pdf (accessed April 30, 2007).

22. Law Enforcement Alliance of America, "President Bush Signs Historic 'National Concealed Carry for Cops' into Law," http://www.leaa.org/218/218release0722.html (accessed April 30, 2007).

23. U.S. Department of Justice, Federal Bureau of Investigation, *Law Enforcement Officers Killed and Assaulted, 2003* (Washington, DC: Author, November 2004), p. 15

24. Luke Dawson, "The Evolution of the Cop Car," *Gear* (n.d.), p. 70.

25. Ibid.

26. Ibid., p. 71.

27. Ibid.

28. Ibid.

29. George P. Blumberg, "Detroit's High-Speed Pursuit of the Police Car Market," *New York Times,* July 7, 2002, p. 12-1.

30. John L. Bellah, "Performance Review: Police Cars," http://www.policeone.com/writers/columnists/PoliceMagazine/articles/77189/ (accessed February 1, 2007).

31. Dawson, "The Evolution of the Cop Car," p. 72.

32. Jim McKay, "Balancing Act: Segway Scooters Have Become a Favorite Tool among Some Cops and Medics," *Government Technology* (December 2006): 52.

33. Joel Samaha, *Criminal Justice,* 2nd ed. (St. Paul, MN: West, 1991), pp. 163–64.

34. Police Foundation, *The Newark Foot Patrol Experiment* (Washington, DC: Author, 1981), p. 9.

35. Quoted in Kevin Krajick, "Does Patrol Prevent Crime?" *Police Magazine* 1 (September 1978): 4–16.

36. T. J. Baker, "Designing the Job to Motivate," *FBI Law Enforcement Bulletin* 45 (1976): 3–7.

37. Krajick, "Does Patrol Prevent Crime?" p. 10.

38. Ibid., pp. 11–13.

39. Robert C. Trojanowicz and Dennis W. Banas, *Job Satisfaction: A Comparison of Foot Patrol versus Motor Patrol Officers* (East Lansing: Michigan State University, 1985).

40. Ibid.

41. Ibid., p. 235.

42. Skolnick and Bayley, *The New Blue Line,* p. 4.

43. Carl B. Klockars and Stephen D. Mastrofski, "Police Discretion: The Case of Selective Enforcement," in *Thinking about Police: Contemporary Readings,* 2nd ed., ed. Carl B. Klockars and Stephen D. Mastrofski (Boston: McGraw-Hill, 1991), p. 330.

44. James Q. Wilson and George L. Kelling, "'Broken Windows': The Police and Neighborhood Safety," *Atlantic Monthly,* March 1982, pp. 28–29.

45. David H. Bayley and Egon Bittner, "Learning the Skills of Policing," in *Critical Issues in Policing: Contemporary Readings,* ed. Roger G. Dunham and Geoffrey P. Alpert (Prospect Heights, IL: Waveland Press, 1989), pp. 87–110.

46. Kenneth Culp Davis, *Police Discretion* (St. Paul, MN: West, 1975), p. 73.

47. Kenneth Culp Davis, *Discretionary Justice* (Urbana: University of Illinois Press, 1969), p. 222.

48. Klockars and Mastrofski, "Police Discretion," p. 331.

49. Ibid.

50. Richard J. Lundman, "Routine Police Arrest Practices: A Commonweal Perspective," *Social Problems* 22 (1974): 127–41; Donald Petersen, "Informal Norms and Police Practices: The Traffic Quota System," *Sociology and Social Research* 55 (1971): 354–61.

51. Lawrence W. Sherman, "Experiments in Police Discretion: Scientific Boon or Dangerous Knowledge?" *Law and Contemporary Problems* 47 (1984): 61–82.

52. For a thorough discussion, see Gregory Howard Williams, "The Politics of Police Discretion," in *Discretion, Justice and Democracy: A Public Policy Perspective,* ed. Carl F. Pinkele and William C. Louthau (Ames: Iowa State University, 1985), pp. 19–30.

53. Davis, *Police Discretion,* p. 22.

54. See James F. Doyle, "Police Discretion, Legality, and Morality," in *Police Ethics: Hard Choices in Law Enforcement,* ed. William C. Heffernan and Timothy Stroup (New York: John Jay Press, 1985), pp. 47–68.

55. *Tennessee* v. *Garner,* 471 U.S. 1 (1985).

56. U.S. Department of Justice, Bureau of Justice Statistics, *Characteristics of Drivers Stopped by Police, 2002* (Washington, DC: Author, 2006), pp. 1–2, 5.

57. Ibid.

58. See, for example, Terry C. Cox and Mervin F. White, "Traffic Citations and Student Attitudes toward the Police: An Examination of Selected Interaction Dynamics," *Journal of Police Science and Administration* 16, no. 2 (fall 1988): 105–21.

59. Adam F. Carr, John F. Schnelle, and John F. Kirchner, "Police Crackdowns and Slowdowns:

A Naturalistic Evaluation of Changes in Police Traffic Enforcement," *Behavioral Assessment* 2 (spring 1980): 33–41; Tom Robinson, "Extinction Rate Measurement of the Mobile Radar Display Trailer" (unpublished manuscript, Department of Political Science, University of Nevada, Reno, 1993).

60. Richard J. Lundman, "Working Traffic Violations," in *Policing Society: An Occupational View,* ed. W. Clinton Terry III (New York: John Wiley and Sons), pp. 327–33.

61. City of Berkeley City Council, "Agenda: June 27, 2000," http://www.ci.berkeley.ca.us/citycouncil/ 2000citycouncil/agenda/062700A.html (accessed January 4, 2007).

Chapter 6 Community-Oriented Policing and Problem Solving: Addressing Crime and Disorder

1. W. L. Melville Lee, *A History of Police in England* (London: Methuen, 1901), ch. 12.

2. Robert Trojanowicz and Bonnie Bucqueroux, *Community Policing: A Contemporary Perspective* (Cincinnati: Anderson, 1990), p. 154.

3. Mark H. Moore and Robert C. Trojanowicz, *Corporate Strategies for Policing* (Washington, DC: Government Printing Office, 1988), pp. 8–9.

4. Sheila Muto, "Arresting Design: Police Stations Get a Lift," *The Wall Street Journal*, January 5, 2005, p. B-1.

5. Herman Goldstein, "Problem-Oriented Policing" (paper presented at the Conference on Policing: State of the Art III, National Institute of Justice, Phoenix, June 12, 1987).

6. Ibid., pp. 43–52.

7. Noah Fritz, *Crime Analysis* (Tempe, AZ: Tempe Police Department, n.d.), p. 9.

8. John Eck, *A Dissertation Prospectus for the Study of Characteristics of Drug Dealing Places* (College Park: University of Maryland, November 1992).

9. Barbara Webster and Edward F. Connors, *Community Policing: Identifying Problems* (Alexandria, VA: Institute for Law and Justice, March 1991), p. 9.

10. See Lawrence W. Sherman, Patrick R. Gartin, and Michael E. Buerger, "Hot Spots of Predatory Crime: Routine Activities and the Criminology of Place," *Criminology* 27 (1989): 27.

11. Ibid., p. 36.

12. William Spelman, *Beyond Bean Counting: New Approaches for Managing Crime Data* (Washington, DC: Police Executive Research Forum, January 1988).

13. Webster and Connors, *Community Policing,* p. 11.

14. For an example of this type of survey process, see William H. Lindsey and Bruce Quint, *The Oasis Technique* (Fort Lauderdale: Florida Atlantic University/Florida International University Joint Center for Environmental and Urban Problems, 1986).

15. Rana Sampson, "Problem Solving," in *Neighborhood-Oriented Policing in Rural Communities: A Program Planning Guide* (Washington, DC: U.S. Department of Justice, Office of Justice Programs, Bureau of Justice Assistance, 1994), p. 4.

16. Darrel Stephens, "Community Problem-Oriented Policing: Measuring Impacts," in *Quantifying Quality in Policing,* ed. Larry T. Hoover (Washington, DC: Police Executive Research Forum, 1995).

17. U.S. Department of Justice, Office of Community Oriented Policing Services, *Problem-Solving Tips: A Guide to Reducing Crime and Disorder through Problem-Solving Partnerships* (Washington, DC: Author, 2002), p. 20.

18. Moore and Trojanowicz, *Corporate Strategies for Policing,* p. 11.

19. Kenneth J. Peak and Ronald W. Glensor, *Community Policing and Problem Solving: Strategies and Practices,* 5th ed. (Upper Saddle River, NJ: Prentice Hall, 2008), p. 85.

20. Ibid.

21. Herman Goldstein, *Problem-Oriented Policing* (New York: McGraw-Hill, 1990), p. 172.

22. Gregory Saville and D. Kim Rossmo, "Striking a Balance: Lessons from Community-Oriented Policing in British Columbia, Canada" (unpublished manuscript, June 1993), pp. 29–30.

23. Ronald W. Glensor and Kenneth J. Peak, "Implementing Change: Community-Oriented Policing and Problem Solving," *FBI Law Enforcement Bulletin* 7 (July 1996): 14–20.

24. John E. Eck and William Spelman, *Problem-Solving: Problem-Oriented Policing in Newport News* (Washington, DC: Police Executive Research Forum, 1987), pp. 100–101.

25. Ibid., p. 9.

26. Herman Goldstein, "Toward Community-Oriented Policing," *Crime and Delinquency* 33 (1987): 6–30.

27. Ibid., p. 21.

28. Ibid.

29. John E. Eck, *Assessing Responses to Problems: An Introductory Guide for Police Problem-Solvers* (Washington, DC: U.S. Department of Justice, Office of Community Oriented Policing Services, 2002), p. 6.

30. Community Policing Advisory Committee, *Community Policing Advisory Committee Report* (Victoria, British Columbia: Author, 1993), p. 61.

31. U.S. Department of Justice, Bureau of Justice Assistance, Community Policing Consortium, *Understanding Community Policing: A Framework for Action* (Washington, DC: Author, 1993), p. 86.

32. California Department of Justice, Attorney General's Office, Crime Prevention Center, *COPPS: Community Oriented Policing and Problem Solving* (Sacramento: Author, November 1992), pp. 90–91.

33. Ibid., pp. 4–5.

34. Jim Jordan, "Shifting the Mission: Seeing Prevention as the Strategic Goal, Not a Set of Programs," in *Subject to Debate* (Washington, DC: Police Executive Research Forum, December 1999), pp. 1–2.

35. Ibid., p. 8.

36. C. R. Jeffrey, *Crime Prevention through Environmental Design* (Beverly Hills, CA: Sage, 1971).

37. National Crime Prevention Council, *Designing Safer Communities: A Crime Prevention through Environmental Design Handbook* (Washington, DC: Author, 1997), pp. 7–8.

38. Ibid., p. 3.

39. G. Farrell and W. Sousa, "Repeat Victimization in the United States and Ten Other Industrialized Countries" (paper presented at the National Conference on Preventing Crime, Washington, DC, October 13, 1997).

40. Ibid.

41. Ibid.

42. G. Farrell, "Preventing Repeat Victimization," in *Building a Safer Society,* ed. M. Tonry and D. P. Farrington (Chicago: University of Chicago Press, 1995), pp. 469–534.

43. Rocky Anderson, quoted in Claudia Kalb, "DARE Checks into Rehab," *Newsweek,* February 26, 2001, p. 56.

44. Ibid.

45. Ibid.

46. Adapted from Police Executive Research Forum, *Excellence in Problem-Oriented Policing: The 2002 Herman Goldstein Award Winners* (Washington, DC: Author, November 2002), pp. 19–26.

47. U.S. Department of Justice, Bureau of Justice Assistance, *Problem-Oriented Drug Enforcement: A Community-Based Approach for Effective Policing* (Washington, DC: Police Executive Research Forum, October 1993), pp. 27–28.

Chapter 7 Criminal Investigation: The Science of Detection

1. Quoted in Leonard Roy Frank, ed., *Random House Webster's Quotationary* (New York: Random House, 1999), p. 761.

2. Marc H. Caplan and Joe Holt Anderson, *Forensic: When Science Bears Witness* (Washington, DC: Government Printing Office, 1984), p. 2.

3. Charles R. Swanson, Neil C. Chamelin, Leonard Territo, and Robert W. Taylor, *Criminal Investigation,* 9th ed. (Boston: McGraw-Hill, 2006), p. 10.

4. Paul L. Kirk, "The Ontogeny of Criminalistics," *Journal of Criminology and Police Science* 54 (1963): 238.

5. Peter R. DeForest, R. E. Gaensslen, and Henry C. Lee, *Forensic Science: An Introduction to Criminalistics* (New York: McGraw-Hill, 1983), p. 29.

6. U.S. Department of Justice, National Institute of Justice, *Crime Scene Investigation: A Reference for Law Enforcement Training* (Washington, DC: Author, 2004).

7. Richard Saferstein, *Criminalistics: An Introduction to Forensic Science,* 9th ed. (Upper Saddle River, NJ: Prentice Hall, 2007), p. 8.

8. Jurgen Thorwald, *Crime and Science* (New York: Harcourt, Brace and World, 1967), p. 4.

9. Jurgen Thorwald, *The Century of the Detective* (New York: Harcourt, Brace and World, 1965), p. 7.

10. Ibid., pp. 9–10.

11. Ibid., p. 12.

12. Swanson, Chamelin, Territo, and Taylor, *Criminal Investigation,* p. 12.

13. Ibid., pp. 12–13.

14. Ibid., p. 12.

15. Anthony L. Califana and Jerome S. Levkov, *Criminalistics for the Law Enforcement Officer* (New York: McGraw-Hill, 1978), p. 20.

16. Frederick R. Cherrill, *The Finger Print System of Scotland Yard* (London: Her Majesty's Stationery Office, 1954), p. 3.

17. Thorwald, *The Century of the Detective,* p. 18.

18. Ibid., p. 33.

19. Saferstein, *Criminalistics,* p. 6.

20. Jurgen Thorwald, *The Marks of Cain* (London: Thames and Hudson, 1965), p. 81.

21. Thorwald, *The Century of the Detective,* p. 62.

22. Thorwald, *The Marks of Cain,* pp. 78–79.

23. U.S. Department of Justice, Bureau of Justice Statistics, "Firearms and Crime Statistics," http://www.ojp.usdoj.gov/bjs/guns.htm#findings (accessed January 14, 2007).

24. Reported in *Newsweek,* September 30, 1991, p. 10.

25. Thorwald, *The Marks of Cain,* pp. 87–88.

26. Thorwald, *The Century of the Detective,* pp. 418–19.

27. Thorwald, *The Marks of Cain,* p. 164.

28. DeForest, Gaensslen, and Lee, *Forensic Science,* p. 14.

29. Swanson, Chamelin, Territo, and Taylor, *Criminal Investigation,* p. 17.

30. Saferstein, *Criminalistics,* pp. 460–461.

31. DeForest, Gaensslen, and Lee, *Forensic Science,* pp. 13–14.

32. Ibid., p. 19.

33. Augustine E. Costello, *Our Police Protectors* (1885; reprint, Montclair, NJ: A. Patterson Smith, 1972), p. 402.

34. James F. Richardson, *The New York Police* (New York: Oxford, 1970), p. 37.

35. Swanson, Chamelin, Territo, and Taylor, *Criminal Investigation,* p. 7.

36. William J. Bopp and Donald Shultz, *Principles of American Law Enforcement and Criminal Justice* (Springfield, IL: Charles C. Thomas, 1972), pp. 70–71.

37. William J. Mathias and Stuart Anderson, *Horse to Helicopter* (Atlanta: Community Life Publications, Georgia State University, 1973), p. 22.

38. Thorwald, *The Marks of Cain,* p. 136.

39. Ibid.

40. Ibid., p. 137.

41. Reppetto, *The Blue Parade,* p. 26.

42. Ibid., p. 267.

43. Swanson, Chamelin, Territo, and Taylor, *Criminal Investigation,* p. 8.

44. Ibid., pp. 8–9.

45. President's Commission on Law Enforcement and the Administration of Justice, *Task Force Report: Science and Technology* (Washington, DC: Government Printing Office, 1967), pp. 7–18.

46. Paul B. Weston and Kenneth M. Wells, *Criminal Investigation: Basic Perspectives,* 4th ed. (Englewood Cliffs, NJ: Prentice Hall, 1986), pp. 5–10.

47. Ibid., p. 207.

48. Ibid., pp. 207–209.

49. Ibid., p. 214.

50. Peter W. Greenwood and Joan Petersilia, *The Criminal Investigation Process,* vol. 1: *Summary and Policy Implications* (Santa Monica, CA: RAND, 1975). The entire report is found in Peter W. Greenwood, Jan M. Chaiken, and Joan Petersilia, *The Criminal Investigation Process* (Lexington, MA: D. C. Heath, 1977).

51. Ibid.

52. Ibid., p. 19.

53. Weston and Wells, *Criminal Investigation,* p. 5.

54. DeForest, Gaensslen, and Lee, *Forensic Science,* p. 11.

55. Mark R. Pogrebin and Eric D. Poole, "Vice Isn't Nice: A Look at the Effects of Working Undercover," *Journal of Criminal Justice* 21 (1993): 383–94.

56. Ibid., pp. 383–84.

57. Peter K. Manning, *The Narc's Game: Organizational and Informational Limits on Drug Enforcement* (Cambridge, MA: MIT Press, 1980).

58. M. Girodo, "Drug Corruption in Undercover Agents: Measuring the Risk," *Behavioral Sciences and the Law* 3 (1991): 299–308; also see David L. Carter, "An Overview of Drug-Related Conduct of Police Officers: Drug Abuse and Narcotics Corruption," in *Drugs, Crime, and the Criminal Justice System,* ed. Ralph Weisheit (Cincinnati: Anderson, 1990).

59. U.S. Department of Justice, Federal Bureau of Investigation, *The Special Agent in Undercover Investigations* (Washington, DC: Author, 1978).

60. A. L. Strauss, "Turning Points in Identity," in *Social Interaction,* ed. C. Clark and H. Robboy (New York: St. Martin's, 1988).

61. Gary T. Marx, "Who Really Gets Stung? Some Issues Raised by the New Police Undercover Work," in *Moral Issues in Police Work,* ed. F. Ellison and M. Feldberg (Totowa, NJ: Bowman and Allanheld, 1988), pp. 99–128.

62. G. Farkas, "Stress in Undercover Policing," in *Psychological Services for Law Enforcement,* ed. J. T. Reese and H. A. Goldstein (Washington, DC: Government Printing Office, 1986).

63. Frank Horvath, "Polygraph," in *The Encyclopedia of Police Science,* 2nd ed., ed. William G. Bailey (New York: Garland, 1995), pp. 640–42.

64. Ibid., p. 643.

65. Ibid., p. 642.

66. Richard Willing, "DNA to Clear 200th Person," http://www.usatoday.com/news/nation/2007-04-22-dna-exoneration_N.htm (accessed April 23, 2007).

67. John S. Dempsey and Linda S. Forst, *An Introduction to Policing,* 3rd ed. (Belmont, CA: Wadsworth, 2005), p. 373.

68. Julia Preston, "U.S. Set to Begin a Vast Expansion of DNA Sampling," *New York Times,* February 5, 2007, p. A15.

69. Richard Saferstein, *Criminalistics,* pp. 382–83.

70. Judith Martin, "The Power of DNA," *Law and Order,* May 2001, pp. 31–35.

71. Federal Bureau of Investigation, "DNA Analysis Unit," http://www.fbi.gov/hq/lab/org/dnau.htm (accessed March 3, 2007).

72. Terry L. Knowles, "Meeting the Challenges of the 21st Century," *Police Chief* (June 1997), pp. 39–43.

73. Federal Bureau of Investigation, "Combined DNA Index System (CODIS)," http://www.fbi.gov/hq/lab/org/systems.htm (accessed March 3, 2007).

74. National Conference of State Legislatures, "Postconviction DNA Motions," http://www.ncsl.org/programs/health/genetics/dnamotions.htm (accessed March 3, 2007).

75. Preston, "U.S. Set to Begin a Vast Expansion of DNA Sampling," pp. A1, A15.

76. Ibid., p. A15.

77. Patrick E. Cook and Dayle L. Hinman, "Criminal Profiling: Science and Art," *Journal of Contemporary Criminal Justice* 15 (August 1999): 230.

78. Ibid., p. 232.

79. Steven A. Egger, "Psychological Profiling," *Journal of Contemporary Criminal Justice* 15 (August 1999): 243.

80. Ibid., p. 242.

81. Walter C. Langer, *The Mind of Adolph Hitler* (New York: World, 1978).

82. Swanson, Chamelin, and Territo, *Criminal Investigation,* 4th ed., pp. 601–602.

83. Brad Darrach and Joel Norris, "An American Tragedy," *Life,* August 1984, p. 58.

84. Swanson, Chamelin, and Territo, *Criminal Investigation,* pp. 606–607.

85. Cook and Hinman, "Criminal Profiling," p. 234.

86. Martin Reiser, Louise Ludwig, Susan Saxe, and Clare Wagner, "An Evaluation of the Use of Psychics in the Investigation of Major Crimes," *Journal of Police Science and Administration* 7 (1979): 18–25.

87. Joseph Deladurantey and Daniel Sullivan, *Criminal Investigation Standards* (New York: Harper and Row, 1980), p. 72.

88. *People* v. *Quaglino*, Cal. Ct. App., 2d Dist., 1977; cert. denied, 439 U.S. 875, 99 S. Ct. 212 (1978).

89. Bill O'Driscoll, "Hypnotist Keeping Busy Since Law Let His Evidence into State Courts," *Reno Gazette Journal,* June 21, 1999, p. 1C.

90. M. Lee Goff, *A Fly for the Prosecution: How Insect Evidence Helps Solve Crimes* (Cambridge, MA: Harvard University Press, 2000), p. 9. An excellent source of information concerning forensic entomology, this book contains not only the effects of insects but also the consequences of predators, air, fire, and water and provides a number of related case studies.

91. Ibid., p. 10.

92. Ibid., p. 11.

93. Ibid., pp. 12–13.

94. Joannie M. Schrof, "Murder, They Chirped," *U.S. News and World Report,* October 14, 1991, pp. 67–68.

95. Goff, *A Fly for the Prosecution*, p. 14.

96. Daniel Pedersen, "Down on the Body Farm," *Newsweek,* October 23, 2000, pp. 50–52.

97. Ibid., p. 67.

98. Ibid., p. 68.

99. BBC: "Crime Fighters: Police Dog Units," http://www.bbc.co.uk/crime/fighters/policedogunit.shtml (accessed September 27, 2006).

100. Harvey Wallace, *Victimology: Legal, Psychological, and Social Perspectives* (Boston: Allyn and Bacon, 1998), p. 333.

101. Ibid.

102. U.S. Department of Justice, Violence Against Women Office, *Stalking and Domestic Violence: Report to Congress* (Washington, DC: Author, May 2001), p. 26.

103. Harvey Wallace, *Victimology,* pp. 333–34.

104. George E. Wattendorf, "Stalking: Investigation Strategies," *FBI Law Enforcement Bulletin* (March 2000): 10–15.

105. NUA Archives, "How Many Online?" http://www.nua.ie/surveys/how_many_online/ (accessed January 20, 2005).

106. Ibid., p. 45.

107. D. Pettinari, "Are We There Yet? The Future of Policing/Sheriffing in Pueblo—Or in Anywhere, America," http://www.policefuturists.org/files/yet.html (accessed February 13, 2001).

108. Janis Wolak, Kimberly Mitchell, and David Finkelhor, *Internet Sex Crimes against Minors: The Response of Law Enforcement* (Alexandria, VA: National Center for Missing and Exploited Children, November 2003), p. 17.

109. Ibid.

110. Crimes against Children Research Center, "Fact Sheet: Overall Crime Victimization of Juveniles," http://www.unh.edu.ccrc/factsheet/overallcrime.htm (accessed August 17, 2004).

111. Andrea J. Sedlak, David Finkelhor, Heather Hammer, and Dana J. Schultz, *National Estimates of Missing Children: An Overview* (Washington, DC: Office of Juvenile Justice and Delinquency Prevention, National Incidence Studies of Missing, Abducted, Runaway, and Throwaway Children [NISMART], October 2002), p. 6.

112. National Center for Missing and Exploited Children, http://www.missingkids.com (accessed February 7, 2007), p. 1.

113. Ryan Turner and Rachel Kosa, *Cold Case Squads: Leaving No Stone Unturned* (Washington, DC: U.S. Department of Justice, Bureau of Justice Assistance, July 2003), pp. 2–4.

114. Robert Tanner, "States Stalled on Probing Lab Problems," http://news.yahoo.com/s/ap/forensic_flaws (accessed March 27, 2007).

115. Richard Willing, "Local DNA Labs Avoid State and U.S. Laws to Nab Criminals," http://www.usatoday.com/news/nation/2007-03-25-dna-databases_N.htm (accessed March 27, 2007).

Chapter 8 Rule of Law: Expounding the Constitution

1. Albert Venn Dicey, *Introduction to the Study of the Law of the Constitution,* 10th ed. (London: Macmillan, 1959), p. 187.

2. David Neubauer, *America's Courts and the Criminal Justice System,* 9th ed. (Belmont, CA: Wadsworth, 2008), pp. 294–300.

3. *Draper* v. *United States,* 358 U.S. 307 (1959).

4. *Illinois* v. *Gates,* 462 U.S. 213 (1983).

5. *United States* v. *Sokolow,* 109 S.Ct. 1581 (1989).

6. *Hunter* v. *Bryant,* 112 S.Ct. 534 (1991).

7. *People* v. *Defore,* 242 N.Y. 214, 150 N.E. 585 (1926).

8. *Weeks* v. *United States,* 232 U.S. 383 (1914).

9. This doctrine was overruled by the Supreme Court in *Elkins* v. *United States,* 364 U.S. 206 (1960).

10. *People* v. *Defore,* 242 N.Y. 214, 150 N.E. 585 (1926).

11. *Olmstead* v. *United States,* 277 U.S. 438, 48 S.Ct. 564 (1928).

12. *Mapp* v. *Ohio,* 367 U.S. 643 (1961).

13. John Kaplan, Jerome H. Skolnick, and Malcolm M. Feeley, *Criminal Justice: Introductory Cases and Materials,* 5th ed. (Westbury, NY: Foundation Press, 1991), pp. 258–59, 269.

14. *Rochin* v. *California,* 342 U.S. 165 (1952).

15. In *New York* v. *Quarles,* 467 U.S. 649 (1984).

16. *Nix* v. *Williams,* 52 LW 4732 (1984). This case began as *Brewer* v. *Williams,* 430 U.S. 387 (1977).

17. *United States* v. *Leon,* 82 L.Ed.2d 677 (1984).

18. *Murray* v. *United States,* 487 U.S. 533 (1988).

19. Kaplan, Skolnick, and Feeley, *Criminal Justice,* p. 269.

20. *California* v. *Minjares,* 443 U.S. 916 (1979).

21. Alexander B. Smith and Harriet Pollack, *Criminal Justice: An Overview* (New York: Holt, Rinehart and Winston, 1980), pp. 154–55.

22. *Payton* v. *New York,* 445 U.S. 573 (1980).

23. *Dunaway* v. *New York,* 442 U.S. 200 (1979).

24. *Delaware* v. *Prouse,* 440 U.S. 648 (1979).

25. *Michigan Department of State Police* v. *Sitz,* 110 S.Ct. 2481, 110 L.Ed.2d 412 (1990).

26. *Pennsylvania* v. *Muniz,* 110 S.Ct. 2638, 110 L.Ed.2d 528 (1990).

27. *Maryland* v. *Pringle,* 124 S.Ct. 795 (2004).

28. *Illinois* v. *Lidster,* 124 S.Ct. 885 (2004).

29. *Riverside County, Calif.* v. *McLaughlin,* 59 LW 4413 (May 13, 1991).

30. *U.S.* v. *Banks,* 124 S.Ct. 521 (2003).

31. *Pennsylvania* v. *Bull,* 63 LW 3695 (1995).

32. *Wilson* v. *Arkansas,* 115 S.Ct. 1914 (1995).

33. *Muehler* v. *Mena,* 125 S.Ct. 1465 (2005).

34. *Zurcher* v. *Stanford Daily,* 436 U.S. 547 (1978).

35. *Maryland* v. *Garrison,* 480 U.S. 79 (1987).

36. *California* v. *Greenwood,* 486 U.S. 35 (1988).

37. Rolando V. Del Carmen and Jeffrey T. Walker, *Briefs of One Hundred Leading Cases in Law Enforcement* (Cincinnati: Anderson, 1991), p. 49.

38. *Brower* v. *County of Inyo,* 109 U.S. 1378 (1989).

39. *Florida* v. *Bostick,* 59 LW 4708 (June 20, 1991).

40. *U.S.* v. *Drayton,* 536 U.S. 194, 231 F.3d 787 (2002).

41. *California* v. *Hodari D.,* 59 LW 4335 (April 23, 1991).

42. *Schmerber* v. *California,* 384 U.S. 757 (1966).

43. *Winston* v. *Lee,* 470 U.S. 753 (1985).

44. *United States* v. *Robinson,* 414 U.S. 218 (1973).

45. *Chimel* v. *California,* 395 U.S. 752 (1969).

46. *United States* v. *Edwards,* 415 U.S. 800 (1974).

47. *Maryland* v. *Buie,* 58 LW 4281 (1990).

48. Smith and Pollack, *Criminal Justice,* p. 161.

49. *Adams* v. *Williams,* 407 U.S. 143 (1972).

50. *United States* v. *Hensley,* 469 U.S. 221 (1985).

51. Smith and Pollack, *Criminal Justice,* p. 162.

52. *Minnesota* v. *Dickerson,* 113 S.Ct. 2130 (1993).

53. *Illinois* v. *Wardlow,* 120 S.Ct. 673 (2000).

54. Ibid., at 673.

55. *Maryland* v. *Wilson,* 117 S.Ct. 882 (1997).

56. *Carroll* v. *United States,* 267 U.S. 132 (1925).

57. *Preston* v. *United States,* 376 U.S. 364 (1964).

58. *Harris* v. *United States,* 390 U.S. 234 (1968).

59. *Chambers* v. *Maroney,* 399 U.S. 42 (1970).

60. *Cardwell* v. *Lewis,* 417 U.S. 583 (1974).

61. *South Dakota* v. *Opperman,* 428 U.S. 364 (1976).

62. *New York* v. *Belton,* 453 U.S. 454 (1981).

63. *United States* v. *Ross,* 456 U.S. 798 (1982).

64. *Michigan* v. *Long,* 463 U.S. 1032 (1983).

65. *Colorado* v. *Bertine,* 479 U.S. 367 (1987).

66. *Florida* v. *Jimeno,* 59 LW 4471 (May 23, 1991).

67. *California* v. *Acevedo,* 59 LW 4559 (May 30, 1991).

68. *Wyoming* v. *Houghton,* 119 S.Ct. 1297 (1999).

69. *Illinois* v. *Caballes,* 543 U.S. _____ (2005).

70. *Texas* v. *Brown,* 460 U.S. 730 (1983).

71. *Oliver* v. *United States,* 466 U.S. 170 (1984).

72. *California* v. *Ciraolo,* 476 U.S. 207 (1986).

73. *New York* v. *Class,* 54 LW 4178 (1986).

74. *Arizona* v. *Hicks,* 55 LW 4258 (1987).

75. *Schneckloth* v. *Bustamonte,* 412 U.S. 218 (1973).

76. *Bumper* v. *North Carolina,* 391 U.S. 543 (1968).

77. *Stoner* v. *California,* 376 U.S. 483 (1964).

78. *Georgia* v. *Randolph,* 126 S.Ct. 1515 (2006).

79. *Olmstead* v. *United States,* 277 U.S. 438 (1928).

80. *Katz* v. *United States,* 389 U.S. 347 (1967).

81. *Berger* v. *New York,* 388 U.S. 41 (1967).

82. *Lee* v. *United States,* 343 U.S. 747 (1952).

83. *United States* v. *Karo,* 468 U.S. 705 (1984).

84. *United States* v. *Wade,* 388 U.S. 218 (1967).

85. *Kirby* v. *Illinois,* 406 U.S. 682 (1972).

86. *Foster* v. *California,* 394 U.S. 440 (1969).

87. *United States* v. *Dionisio,* 410 U.S. 1 (1973).

88. Kaplan, Skolnick, and Feeley, *Criminal Justice,* pp. 219–20.

89. Ibid., pp. 220–21.

90. *Spano* v. *New York,* 360 U.S. 315 (1959).

91. *Escobedo* v. *Illinois,* 378 U.S. 478 (1964).

92. *Miranda* v. *Arizona,* 384 U.S. 436 (1966).

93. *Berkemer* v. *McCarty,* 468 U.S. 420 (1984).

94. *Arizona* v. *Roberson,* 486 U.S. 675 (1988).

95. *Edwards* v. *Arizona,* 451 U.S. 477 (1981).

96. *Michigan* v. *Mosley,* 423 U.S. 93 (1975).

97. *Colorado* v. *Connelly,* 479 U.S. 157 (1986).

98. *Colorado* v. *Spring,* 479 U.S. 564 (1987).

99. *Connecticut* v. *Barrett,* 479 U.S. 523 (1987).

100. *Duckworth* v. *Eagan,* 109 S.Ct. 2875 (1989).

101. *Davis* v. *United States,* 114 S.Ct. 2350 (1994).

102. *Sherman* v. *United States,* 356 U.S. 369 (1958).

103. *United States* v. *Russell,* 411 U.S. 423 (1973).

104. *Hampton* v. *United States,* 425 U.S. 484 (1976).

105. Ibid., at 1540.

106. *Powell* v. *Alabama,* 287 U.S. 45 (1932).

107. *Gideon* v. *Wainwright,* 372 U.S. 335 (1963).

108. *Argersinger* v. *Hamlin,* 407 U.S. 25 (1973).

109. *Escobedo* v. *Illinois,* 378 U.S. 478 (1964).

110. Smith and Pollack, *Criminal Justice,* p. 177.

111. *Rhode Island* v. *Innis,* 446 U.S. 291 (1980).

112. *Arizona* v. *Mauro,* 481 U.S. 520 (1987).

113. *McNeil* v. *Wisconsin,* 59 LW 4636 (June 13, 1991).

114. *Minnick* v. *Mississippi,* 59 LW 4037 (1990).

115. Arnold Binder, Gilbert Geis, and Dickson Bruce, *Juvenile Delinquency: Historical, Cultural, Legal Perspectives* (New York: Macmillan, 1988), pp. 6–9.

116. *Kent* v. *United States,* 383 U.S. 541 (1966).

117. *In Re Gault,* 387 U.S. 9 (1967).

118. *In Re Winship,* 397 U.S. 358 (1970).

119. *McKeiver* v. *Pennsylvania,* 403 U.S. 528 (1971).

120. *Breed* v. *Jones,* 421 U.S. 519 (1975).

121. *Roper* v. *Simmons,* 543 U.S. 551 (2005).

Chapter 9 Accountability: Ethics, Use of Force, Corruption, and Discipline

1. See Carl Klockars, "The Dirty Harry Problem," in *Police and Society: Touchstone Readings,* 2nd ed., ed. Victor E. Kappeler (Prospect Heights, IL: Waveland Press, 1999), pp. 329–46.

2. Herbert Packer, *The Limits of the Criminal Sanction* (Stanford, CA: Stanford University Press, 1968).

3. Jocelyn M. Pollack, "Ethics and Law Enforcement," in *Critical Issues in Policing: Contemporary Readings,* 5th ed., ed. Roger G. Dunham and Geoffrey P. Alpert (Long Grove, IL: Waveland Press, 2005), pp. 280–303.

4. Brian Withrow and Jeffrey D. Dailey, "When Strings Are Attached: Understanding the Role of Gratuities in Police Corruptibility," in *Contemporary Policing Controversies, Challenges, and Solutions: An Anthology,* ed. Quint Thurman and Jihong Zhao (Los Angeles: Roxbury, 2004), pp. 319–26.

5. "No Free (or Discounted) Lunch for Bradenton Cops," *Law Enforcement News,* October 15, 2000, p. 6.

6. Kenneth J. Peak, B. Grant Stitt, and Ronald W. Glensor, "Ethics in Community Policing and Problem Solving," *Police Quarterly* 1 (1998): 30–31.

7. L. Morris, *Incredible New York* (New York: Bonanza, 1951).

8. James A. Inciardi, *Criminal Justice,* 5th ed. (Orlando, FL: Harcourt Brace, 1996).

9. Egon Bittner, "The Functions of the Police in Modern Society," in *Policing: A View from the Street,* ed. Peter K. Manning and John Van Maanen (Santa Monica, CA: Goodyear, 1978), pp. 32–50.

10. Ibid., p. 36.

11. Adapted from Lorie A. Fridell, "Improving Use-of-Force Policy: Policy Enforcement and Training," in *Chief Concerns: Exploring the Challenges of Police Use of Force,* ed. Joshua A. Ederheimer and Lorie A. Fridell (Washington, DC: Police Executive Research Form, April 2005), p. 48.

12. "LAPD Shooting Blamed on Poor Supervision," http://www.latimes.com/news/local/los_angeles_metro/la-me-pena6dec06,0,5058221,print.story?coll=la-commun-los_angeles_metro (accessed January 12, 2007).

13. Pat Milton, "Grand Jury Indicts 3 in NYPD Shooting," http://abcnews.go.com/US/wireStory?id=2957956 (accessed April 19, 2007).

14. Michael Wilson, "50 Shots Fired, and the Experts Offer a Theory," http://www.nytimes.com/2006/11/27/nyregion/27fire.html?ei=5088&en=357cf73362b1de61&ex=1322283600&partner=rs&pagewanted=print (accessed January 10, 2007).

15. "L.A. Police Corruption Case Continues to Grow," *Washington Post,* February 13, 2000, p. 1A.

16. Human Rights Watch, *Shielded from Justice: Police Brutality and Accountability in the United States* (New York: Author, 1998).

17. Ibid.

18. *New York Times,* April 29, 2001, p. A1.

19. Ibid.

20. Kit R. Roane, "Policing the Police Is a Dicey Business: But the Feds Have a Plan to Root Out Racial Bias," *U.S. News and World Report,* April 30, 2001, p. 28.

21. James J. Fyfe, Jack R. Greene, William F. Walsh, et al., *Police Administration,* 5th ed. (New York: McGraw-Hill, 1997), pp. 197–98.

22. *Tennessee* v. *Garner,* 471 U.S. 1, 105 S.Ct. 1694, 85 L.Ed.2d 1 (1985).

23. George F. Cole and Christopher E. Smith, *The American System of Criminal Justice,* 8th ed. (Belmont, CA: West/Wadsworth, 1998), p. 228.

24. A. C. Germann, Frank D. Day, and Robert R. J. Gallati, *Introduction to Law Enforcement and Criminal Justice* (Springfield, IL: Charles C. Thomas, 1976), p. 225.

25. Albert J. Reiss Jr., "Police Brutality: Answers to Key Questions," *Transaction* (July–August 1968): 10–19.

26. Ibid.

27. Germann, Day, and Gallati, *Introduction to Law Enforcement and Criminal Justice,* p. 225.

28. *Scott* v. *Harris,* 550 U.S. _____ (2007), at p. 13.

29. Bureau of Justice Statistics, "Police Stop White, Black, and Hispanic Drivers at Similar Rates According to Department of Justice Report," http://www.ojp.usdoj.gov/bjs/pub/press/cpp05pr.htm (accessed May 1, 2007).

30. Randall Kennedy, "Suspect Policy," *New Republic,* September 13, 1999, pp. 30–35.

31. Donald Black, *Manners and Customs of the Police* (New York: Academic Press, 1980), p. 117; Richard J. Lundman, "Domestic Police-Citizen Encounters," *Journal of Police Science and Administration* 2 (March 1974): 25.

32. Jerome Skolnick, *The Police and the Urban Ghetto* (Chicago: American Bar Foundation, 1968).

33. Samuel Walker, *The Police in America: An Introduction* (New York: McGraw-Hill, 1983), p. 234.

34. Ibid., p. 235.

35. Robert Friedrich, "Racial Prejudice and Police Treatment of Blacks," in *Evaluating Alternative Law Enforcement Policies,* ed. Ralph Baker and Fred A. Meyers (Lexington, MA: Lexington Books, 1979), pp. 160–61.

36. Douglas A. Smith and Christy A. Visher, "Street-Level Justice: Situational Determinants of Police Arrest Decisions," *Social Problems* 29 (December 1981): 167–87.

37. Albert J. Reiss, *The Police and the Public* (New Haven, CT: Yale University Press, 1971), p. 151.

38. "Beat Your Spouse, Lose Your Job," *Law Enforcement News,* December 31, 1997, p. 9.

39. Ibid.

40. Adapted from Jerry Hoover, "Brady Bill Unfair in Broad Approach to Police Officers," *Reno Gazette Journal,* September 25, 1998, p. 11A.

41. "Denver Cop's Case Galvanizes Opponents of Lautenberg Gun Ban," *Law Enforcement News,* February 14, 1999, p. 1.

42. Lawrence W. Sherman, ed., *Police Corruption: A Sociological Perspective* (Garden City, NY: Anchor, 1974), p. 1.

43. See Peter Maas, *Serpico* (New York: Viking, 1973).

44. Herman Goldstein, *Policing a Free Society* (Cambridge, MA: Ballinger, 1977), p. 188.

45. Ibid.

46. Gordon Witkin, "When the Bad Guys Are Cops," *Newsweek,* September 11, 1995, p. 20.

47. Ibid., p. 22.

48. Lawrence W. Sherman, "Becoming Bent," in *Moral Issues in Police Work,* ed. F. A. Elliston and M. Feldberg (Totowa, NJ: Rowan and Allanheld, 1985), pp. 253–65.

49. Christian P. Potholm and Richard E. Morgan, eds., *Focus on Police: Police in American Society* (New York: Schenkman, 1976), p. 140.

50. Ellwyn R. Stoddard, "Blue Coat Crime," in *Thinking about Police: Contemporary Readings,* ed. Carl B. Klockars (New York: McGraw-Hill, 1983), pp. 338–50.

51. Walker, *The Police in America,* p. 175.

52. "Police Aides Told to Rid Commands of All Dishonesty," *New York Times,* October 29, 1970.

53. Brian L. Withrow and Jeffrey D. Dailey, "When Strings Are Attached," in *Contemporary Policing: Controversies, Challenges, and Solutions*, ed. Quint C. Thurman and Jihong Zhao, (Los Angeles: Roxbury, 2004), pp. 319–26.

54. David L. Carter, "Drug Use and Drug-Related Corruption of Police Officers," in *Policing Perspectives: An Anthology,* ed. Larry K. Gaines and Gary W. Cordner (Los Angeles: Roxbury, 1999), pp. 311–23.

55. Patrick V. Murphy and Thomas Plate, *Commissioner: A View from the Top of American Law Enforcement* (New York: Simon and Schuster, 1977), p. 226.

56. William A. Westley, *Violence and the Police* (Cambridge, MA: MIT Press, 1970), pp. 113–14.

57. Thomas E. Wren, "Whistle-Blowing and Loyalty to One's Friends," in *Police Ethics: Hard Choices in Law Enforcement,* ed. William C. Heffernan (New York: John Jay Press, 1985), pp. 25–43.

58. David Weisburd and Rosanne Greenspan, *Police Attitudes toward Abuse of Authority: Findings from a National Study* (Washington, DC: U.S. Department of Justice, National Institute of Justice, Research in Brief, May 2000), p. 5.

59. See, for example, *United States* v. *Hyde,* 448 F.2d 815 (5th Cir. 1971), cert. den., 404 U.S. 1058 (1972); *United States* v. *Addonizia,* 451 F.2d 49 (3d Cir.), cert. den., 405 U.S. 936 (1972); and *United States* v. *Kenney,* 462 F.2d 1205 (3d Cir.), as amended, 462 F.2d 1230 (3d Cir.), cert. den., 409 U.S. 914 (1972).

60. Herbert Beigel, "The Investigation and Prosecution of Police Corruption," in *Focus on Police,* ed. Christian P. Potholm and Richard E. Morgan (New York: Schenkman, 1976), pp. 139–66.

61. "Artificial Intelligence Tackles a Very Real Problem—Police Misconduct Control," *Law Enforcement News,* September 30, 1994, p. 1.

62. *Pickering* v. *Board Of Education,* 391 U.S. 563 (1968), p. 568.

63. *Muller* v. *Conlisk,* 429 F.2d 901 (7th Cir. 1970).

64. *Kelley* v. *Johnston,* 425 U.S. 238 (1976).

65. See *People* v. *Tidwell,* 266 N.E.2d 787 (Ill. 1971).

66. *McDonell* v. *Hunter,* 611 F. Supp. 1122 (SD Iowa 1985), aff'd. as mod., 809 F.2d 1302 (8th Cir. 1987).

67. *Garrity* v. *New Jersey,* 385 U.S. 483 (1967).

68. See *Gabrilowitz* v. *Newman,* 582 F.2d 100 (1st Cir. 1978).

69. *United States* v. *City Of Albuquerque,* 12 EPD 11, 244 (10th Cir.); also see *Trans World Airlines* v. *Hardison,* 97 S.Ct. 2264 (1977).

70. Allen D. Sapp, "Police Officer Sexual Misconduct: A Field Research Study," in *Crime and Justice in America: Present Realities and Future Prospects,* ed. Paul F. Cromwell and Roger G. Dunham (Upper Saddle River, NJ: Prentice Hall, 1997), pp. 139–51.

71. Ibid.

72. See *Briggs* v. *North Muskegon Police Department,* 563 F. Supp. 585 (W.D. Mich. 1983), aff'd. 746 F.2d 1475 (6th Cir. 1984).

73. *Oliverson* v. *West Valley City,* 875 F. Supp. 1465 (D. Utah 1995).

74. *Henery* v. *City Of Sherman,* 928 S.W.2d 464 (Sup. Ct. Texas), cert. den., 17 S.Ct. 1098 (1997).

75. See, for example, *Cox* v. *McNamara,* 493 P.2d 54 (Ore. 1972); *Brenckle* v. *Township Of Shaler,* 281 A.2d 920 (Pa. 1972); *Flood* v. *Kennedy,* 239

N.Y.S.2d 665 (1963); and *Hopwood* v. *City Of Paducah,* 424 S.W.2d 134 (Ky. 1968).

76. Richard N. Williams, *Legal Aspects of Discipline by Police Administrators,* Traffic Institute Publication 2705 (Evanston, IL: Northwestern University, 1975), p. 4.

77. See *Lally* v. *Department Of Police,* 306 So.2d 65 (La. 1974).

78. Charles R. Swanson, Leonard Territo, and Robert W. Taylor, *Police Administration*, 5th ed. (Upper Saddle River, NJ: Prentice Hall, 2005), p. 586.

79. Ibid.

80. Ibid.

81. Kenneth James Matulia, *A Balance of Forces: Model Deadly Force and Policy Procedure* (Alexandria, VA: International Association of Chiefs of Police, 1985), pp. 23–24.

82. Catherin H. Milton, Jeanne Wahl Halleck, James Larndew, et al., *Police Use of Deadly Force* (Washington, DC: Police Foundation, 1977), p. 52.

83. Matulia, *A Balance of Forces*, p. 52.

84. Ibid., p. 177.

85. Ibid.

86. Ibid., p. 78.

87. See *Krolick* v. *Lowery,* 302 N.Y.S.2d 109 (1969), p. 115; and *Hester* v. *Milledgeville,* 598 F. Supp. 1456, 1457 (M.D. Ga. 1984).

88. *National Treasury Employees Union* v. *Von Raab,* 489 U.S. 656 (1989).

89. Robert J. Alberts and Harvey W. Rubin, "Court's Rulings on Testing Crack Down on Drug Abuse," *Risk Management* 38 (March 1991): 36–41.

90. V. McLaughlin and R. Bing, "Law Enforcement Personnel Selection," *Journal of Police Science and Administration* 15 (1987): 271–76.

91. Ibid.

92. Allen E. Wagner and Scott H. Decker, "Evaluating Citizen Complaints against the Police," in *Critical Issues in Policing: Contemporary Readings,* 3rd ed., ed. Roger G. Dunham and Geoffrey P. Alpert, (Prospect Heights, IL: Waveland Press, 1989), pp. 302–18.

93. Kenneth J. Peak, Larry K. Gaines, and Ronald W. Glensor, *Police Supervision and Management: In an Era of Community Policing*, 2nd ed. (Upper Saddle River, NJ: Prentice Hall, 2004), pp. 271–72.

Chapter 10 Civil Liability: Failing the Public Trust

1. See, for example, John L. Worrall and Otwin Marenin, "Emerging Liability Issues in the Implementation and Adoption of Community Oriented Policing," *Policing: An International Journal of Police Strategies and Management* 22 (1998): 121–36.

2. Isidore Silver, *Police Civil Liability* (New York: Matthew Bender, 2005), p. 4.

3. The Feminist Majority Foundation and the National Center for Women & Policing, "Gender Differences in the Cost of Police Brutality and Misconduct: A Content Analysis of LAPD Civil Liability Cases: 1990–1999," http://www.womenandpolicing.org/ExcessiveForce.asp?id=4516 (accessed April 4, 2007).

4. "LAPD Officers Take Stand in Rampart Scandal Trial," http://archives.cnn.com/2000/LAW/10/16/lapd.corruption.tria/ (accessed April 4, 2007).

5. Victor E. Kappeler, *Critical Issues in Police Civil Liability,* 4th ed. (Long Grove, IL: Waveland Press, 2005), p. 4.

6. Ibid., p. 11.

7. G. P. Alpert, R. G. Dunham, and M. S. Stroshine, *Policing: Continuity and Change* (Long Grove, IL: Waveland Press, 2006).

8. *Harper* v. *Showers,* 174 F.3d 716, 718 (5th Cir. 1999).

9. S. F. Kappeler and V. E. Kappeler, "A Research Note on Section 1983 Claims against the Police: Cases before the Federal District Courts in 1990," *American Journal of Police* 11, no. 1: 65–73.

10. H. E. Barrineau III, *Civil Liability in Criminal Justice* (Cincinnati: Pilgrimage, 1987), p. 58.

11. Ibid., p. 5.

12. Charles R. Swanson, Leonard Territo, and Robert W. Taylor, *Police Administration: Structures,*

Processes, and Behavior, 6th ed. (Upper Saddle River, NJ: Prentice Hall, 2005), p. 549.

13. *Bivens* v. *Six Unknown Named Agents of the Federal Bureau of Narcotics,* 403 U.S. 388, 29 L.Ed.2d 619, 91 S.Ct. 1999 (1971).

14. Swanson, Territo, and Taylor, *Police Administration,* pp. 438–39.

15. *Hans* v. *Louisiana,* 134 U.S. 1 (1890); also see "Sovereign Immunity," http://touchngo.com/lglcntr/usdc/bnkrptcy/briefs/bnk21.htm (accessed January 28, 2005).

16. Ibid.

17. *Monroe* v. *Pape,* 365 U.S. 167, 81 S.Ct. 473 (1961).

18. Wayne W. Schmidt, "Section 1983 and the Changing Face of Police Management," in *Police Leadership in America,* ed. William A. Geller (Chicago: American Bar Foundation, 1985), p. 228.

19. Ibid., p. 227.

20. *Monell* v. *Department of Social Services,* 436 U.S. 6587 (1978).

21. *Alabama* v. *Pugh,* 438 U.S. 781 (1978).

22. Swanson, Territo, and Taylor, *Police Administration,* p. 558.

23. Kappeler, *Critical Issues in Police Civil Liability,* p. 2.

24. J. R. Daughen, "Potential Cost of Philadelphia House-Bombing Incident up to $59 Million," *Philadelphia Daily News,* April 14, 2005, p. B8.

25. Ibid.

26. T. Mauro, *The Legal Intelligencer,* 230, no. 5 (2000): 4.

27. *Jennings* v. *City of Detroit,* Wayne County Circuit Court, Michigan (August 1979).

28. *Gilliam* v. *Falbo,* U.S. District Court, Southern District of Ohio (April 1982).

29. *Haygood* v. *City of Detroit,* Wayne County Circuit Court, Michigan, No. 77-728013 (December 29, 1980).

30. *Carmelo* v. *Miller,* 569 S.W. 365 (1978).

31. *Stengel* v. *Belcher,* 522 F.2d 438 (6th Cir. 1975).

32. *Bonsignore* v. *New York,* 521 F. Supp. 394, aff'd., 683 F.2d 635 (2d Cir. 1982).

33. *Prior* v. *Woods,* U.S. District Court, (E.D. Michigan) (October 1981).

34. *Burkholder* v. *City of Los Angeles,* L.A. County Superior Court, California (October 1982).

35. *Murray* v. *City of Chicago,* 634 F.2d 365 (1980).

36. *Duncan* v. *Barnes,* 592 F.2d 1336 (1979).

37. *Sager* v. *City of Woodlawn Park,* 543 F. Supp. 282 (D. Colo. 1982).

38. *Popow* v. *City of Margate,* 476 F. Supp. 1237 (1979).

39. On appeal, the Section 242 convictions were vacated, as the victim was not an inhabitant of Puerto Rico; therefore, he enjoyed no protection under the U.S. Constitution. On resentencing, in January 1991, the agents each received fifty years in prison for convictions of several other federal crimes under Title 18.

40. Kappeler, *Critical Issues in Police Civil Liability,* p. 29.

41. *McClelland* v. *Facteau,* 610 F.2d 693 (10th Cir. 1979).

42. *Brandon* v. *Allen,* 516 F. Supp. 1355 (W.D. Tenn. 1981).

43. *Brandon* v. *Holt,* 469 U.S. 464, 105 S.Ct. 873 (1985).

44. See, for example, *Black* v. *Stephens,* 662 F.2d 181 (1991).

45. *Swope* v. *Bratton,* 541 F. Supp. 99 (W.D. Ark. 1982).

46. *Leonard* v. *City of Columbus,* 705 F.2d 1299 (11th Cir. 1983).

47. *Elrod* v. *Burns,* 427 U.S. 347 (1975).

48. *South* v. *Maryland,* 59 U.S. (18 How.) 396 (1856).

49. *Reiff* v. *City of Philadelphia,* 477 F. Supp. 1262 (E.D. Pa. 1979).

50. Kappeler, *Critical Issues in Police Civil Liability,* pp. 25–26.

51. *Irwin* v. *Ware,* 467 N.E.2d 1292 (1984).

52. *Fudge* v. *City of Kansas City,* 239 Kan. 369, 720 P.2d 1093 (1986), at 373.

53. *Kendrick* v. *City of Lake Charles,* 500 So.2d 866 (La. App. 1 Cir.1986).

54. Kappeler, *Critical Issues in Police Civil Liability,* p. 27.

55. *Fielder* v. *Jenkins,* 833 A.2d 906 (N.J. Super. A.D. 1993).

56. Silver, *Police Civil Liability,* p. 4; also see *Coco* v. *State,* 474 N.Y.S.2d 397 (Ct.Cl. 1984); and *Duvernay* v. *State,* 433 So.2d 254 (La. App. 1983).

57. *Naylor* v. *Louisiana Dept. of Public Highways,* 423 So.2d 674 (La. App. 1982).

58. *Joseph* v. *State of Alaska,* 26 P.3d 459 (2001).

59. *Thomas* v. *Williams,* 124 S.E.2d 409 (Ga. App. 1962).

60. *Morris* v. *Blake,* 552 A.2d 844 (Del. Super. 1988).

61. *Guice* v. *Enfinger,* 389 So.2d 270 (Fla. App. 1980).

62. *Manuel* v. *City of Jeanerette,* 702 So.2d 709 (La. App. 3 Cir. 1997).

63. *Joseph* v. *State of Alaska,* 26 P.3d 459 (2001), at 474.

64. *Saunders* v. *County of Steuben,* 693 N.E.2d 16 (Ind. 1998).

65. *Manuel* v. *City of Jeanerette,* 702 So.2d 709 (La. App. 3 Cir. 1997).

66. *Davis* v. *City of Detroit,* 386 N.W.2d 169 (Mich. App. 1986).

67. *Morris* v. *Blake,* 552 A.2d 844 (De. Super. 1988).

68. *Penilla* v. *City of Huntington Park,* 115 F.3d 707 (9th Cir., 1997).

69. *Monfils* v. *Taylor,* 165 F.3d 511 (7th Cir. 1998), cert. den., 528 U.S. 810 (1999).

70. *Seide* v. *State of Rhode Island,* 875 A.2d 1259 (2005).

71. Silver, *Police Civil Liability,* p. 8.

72. *Seide* v. *State of Rhode Island,* 875 A.2d 1259 (2005).

73. Tulsa, Oklahoma, Police Department, Procedure Manual (Ronald Palmer, chief of police), June 10, 1998, p. 1.

74. John Hill, "High-Speed Police Pursuits: Dangers, Dynamics, and Risk Reduction," *FBI Law Enforcement Bulletin* (July 2002): 14–18.

75. National Highway Traffic Safety Administration, *National Highway Traffic Safety Administration Statistics* (Washington, DC: Author, 1995).

76. C. B. Eisenberg, "Pursuit Management," *Law and Order,* March 1999, pp. 73–77.

77. A. Belotto, "Supervisors Govern Pursuits," *Law and Order,* January 1999, p. 86.

78. G. T. Williams, "When Do We Keep Pursuing? Justifying High-Speed Pursuits," *Police Chief* (March 1997): 24–27.

79. *County of Sacramento* v. *Lewis,* 118 S.Ct. 1708 (1998).

80. Oklahoma County Sheriff John Whetsel, quoted in Nicole Marshall, "Hot Pursuit," *Tulsa World,* June 15, 1998, p. A11.

81. Michael R. Anderson, "Reducing Computer Evidence Liability," *Government Technology* (February 1997): 24, 36.

82. Ibid.

83. Ibid.

Chapter 11 Terrorism, Gangs, and Drugs

1. E. J. Tully and E. L. Willoughby, "Terrorism: The Role of Local and State Police Agencies," http://www.neiassociates.org/state-local.htm (accessed July 31, 2002).

2. J. Meisler, "The New Frontier of Homeland Security," *Government Technology's Tech Trends 2002: Combined Effort* (August 2002): 26–30.

3. Quoted in M. K. Rehm and W. R. Rehm, "Terrorism Preparedness Calls for Proactive Approach," *Police Chief* (December 2000): 38–43.

4. D. Westneat, "Terrorists Go Green," *U.S. News and World Report,* June 4, 2001, p. 28.

5. "SUVs Torched in Pennsylvania," *Reno Gazette Journal,* January 5, 2003, p. 4A.

6. J. F. Lewis, Jr., "Fighting Terrorism in the 21st Century," *FBI Law Enforcement Bulletin* (March 1999): 3.

7. K. Garrett, "Terrorism on the Homefront," *Law Enforcement Technology* (July 2002): 22–26.

8. Lewis, "Fighting Terrorism in the 21st Century," p. 3.

9. K. Strandberg, "Bioterrorism: A Real or Imagined Threat?" *Law Enforcement Technology* (June 2001): 88–97.

10. D. Rogers, "A Nation Tested: What Is the Terrorist Threat We Face and How Can We Train for It?" *Law Enforcement Technology* (November 2001): 16–21.

11. "With Biochem Terror No Longer 'Unthinkable,' NYPD Gets Ready," *Law Enforcement News,* spring 2004, pp. 1, 13.

12. Tully and Willoughby, "Terrorism."

13. D. G. Bolgiano, "Military Support of Domestic Law Enforcement Operations: Working within Posse Comitatus," *FBI Law Enforcement Bulletin* (December 2001): 16–24.

14. U.S. Department of Homeland Security, *National Incident Management System* (Washington, DC: Author, March 2004), pp. viii, ix.

15. J. Buntin, "Disaster Master," *Governing* (December 2001): 34–38.

16. N. F. Iannone and M. P. Iannone, *Supervision of Police Personnel,* 6th ed. (Englewood Cliffs, NJ: Prentice Hall, 2001).

17. Frank Keating, "Catastrophic Terrorism: Local Response to a National Threat," *Journal of Homeland Security* (August 2001); also available at http://www.homelandsecurity.org/journal/Articles/Keating.htm (accessed November 1, 2004).

18. Ibid.

19. Ibid.

20. Buntin, "Disaster Master," p. 38.

21. Gary Peck and Laura Mijanovich, "Give Us Security While Retaining Freedoms," *Reno Gazette Journal,* August 28, 2003, p. 9A.

22. "House Approves Patriot Act Renewal," http://www.cnn.com/2006/POLITICS/03/07/patriot.act/ (accessed January 3, 2007).

23. Peck and Mijanovich, "Give Us Security While Retaining Freedoms," p. 9A.

24. Michael Isikoff, "Show Me the Money," *Newsweek,* December 1, 2003, p. 36.

25. Lorraine Ali, " 'We Love This Country,' " *Newsweek,* April 7, 2003.

26. John Ashcroft, quoted in Begley, "What Price Security?" p. 58.

27. Jurist: Legal News and Research, "Bush Signs Military Commissions Act," http://jurist.law.pitt.edu/paperchase/2006/10/bush-signs-military-commissions-act.php (accessed January 2, 2007).

28. Ibid.

29. Carolyn R. Block and Richard Block, *Street Gang Crime in Chicago* (Washington, DC: National Institute of Justice, Research in Brief, 1993), p. 2.

30. Frederic M. Thrasher, *The Gang* (Chicago: University of Chicago Press, 1927), pp. 33, 339, 346.

31. See G. David Curry, Richard A. Ball, and Scott H. Decker, *Estimating the National Scope of Gang Crime from Law Enforcement Data* (Washington, DC: National Institute of Justice, Research in Brief, 1996).

32. Scott H. Decker and G. David Curry, "Responding to Gangs: Comparing Gang Member, Police, and Task Force Perspectives," *Journal of Criminal Justice* 28 (2000): 129–37.

33. Ronald C. Huff, *Comparing the Criminal Behavior of Youth Gangs and At-Risk Youths* (Washington, DC: National Institute of Justice, Research in Brief, 1998).

34. Gregory Vistica, " 'Gangstas' in the Ranks," *Newsweek*, July 24, 1995, p. 48.

35. Shelley Feuer Domash, "America's Most Dangerous Gang," http://www.policemag.com/t_cipick.cfm?rank=90876 (accessed March 8, 2007).

36. Ibid.

37. CBS News, "White Supremacist Gang Gains Clout," http://www.cbsnews.com/stories/2007/03/05/national/main2535231.shtml?source=RSS attr=HOME_2535231 (accessed March 8, 2007).

38. Douglas Page, "Taggers Beware: The Writing Is on the Wall," *Law Enforcement Technology* (September 2005): 194, 196.

39. Ibid., p. 196.

40. Bob Hills, "Officials Looking for Regional Solution to Problem," *Reno Gazette Journal,* December 1, 2003, p. 5A.

41. Ruth Horowitz, "Community Tolerance of Gang Violence," *Social Problems* 34 (December 1987): 437–450.

42. James B. Jacobs, *New Perspectives on Prisons and Imprisonment* (Ithaca, NY: Cornell University Press, 1983).

43. D. L. Weisel and E. Painter, *The Police Response to Gangs: Case Studies of Five Cities* (Washington, DC: Police Executive Research Forum, 1997).

44. Ibid.

45. Ibid.

46. "Parolees, Recruits Fuel Increase in Gang Crimes," *Reno Gazette Journal,* April 10, 2003, p. 2B; Jean M. McGloin, *Street Gangs and Interventions: Innovative Problem Solving with Network Analysis* (Washington, DC: U.S. Department of Justice, Office of Community Oriented Policing Services, September 2005), p. 2.

47. Ibid., pp. 1–4.

48. Rana Sampson and Michael S. Scott, *Tackling Crime and Other Public Safety Problems: Case Studies in Problem Solving* (Washington, DC: U.S. Department of Justice, Office of Community Policing Services, 2000), p. 67.

49. High Commission of Sri Lanka, "Street Gangs in Toronto Fund Terrorism in Sri Lanka" (press release), http://203.115.21.154/news/press/27th_march_2000.html (accessed November 27, 2002).

50. Neil A. Pollard, *Terrorism and Transnational Organized Crime: Implications of Convergence* (n.p.: Terrorism Research Center, 1996).

51. Kenneth J. Peak and Timothy Griffin, "Gangs: Origin, Status, Community Responses, and Policy Implications," in *Visions for Change: Crime and Justice in the Twenty-First Century,* 4th ed., ed. Roslyn A. Muraskin and Albert R. Roberts (Upper Saddle River, NJ: Prentice Hall, 2005), p. 49.

52. U.S. Department of Justice, Bureau of Justice Statistics, "Drug and Crime Facts," http://www.ojp.usdoj.gov/bjs/dcf/tables/arrtot.htm (accessed April 28, 2006).

53. U.S. Department of Justice, Bureau of Justice Statistics, "Criminal Offenders Statistics," http://www.ojp.usdoj.gov/bjs/crimoff.htm#inmates (accessed January 15, 2007).

54. U.S. Department of Justice, Bureau of Justice Statistics, *Prisoners in 2005* (Washington, DC: Author, November 2006), p. 9.

55. Office of National Drug Control Policy, http://www.whitehousedrugpolicy.gov/publications/factsht/methamph/#background (accessed February 27, 2006).

56. U.S. Department of Justice, Office of Community Oriented Policing Services, "COPS Innovations: A Closer Look," in *Combating Methamphetamine Laboratories and Abuse* (Washington, DC: Author), pp. 3–5.

57. U.S. Department of Justice, Office of Community Oriented Policing Services, "Methamphetamine Initiative," http://www.cops.usdoj.gov/mime/open.pdf?Item=1356 (accessed April 28, 2006).

58. Michael S. Scott, *Clandestine Drug Labs* (Washington, DC: U.S. Department of Justice, Office of Community Oriented Policing Services, 2002), p. 1.

59. Ibid., pp. 14–15.

60. Ibid., pp. 24–26.

61. Alex Harocopos and Mike Hough, *Drug Dealing in Open-Air Markets* (Washington, DC: U.S. Department of Justice, Office of Community Oriented Policing Services, January 2005), p. 1.

62. Ibid., pp. 24–26.

63. Michael S. Scott, *Rave Parties* (Washington, DC: U.S. Department of Justice, Office of Community Oriented Policing Services, 2002), p. 1.

64. Ibid., pp. 1–2, 13–14.

65. Office of National Drug Control Policy, "The High-Intensity Drug Trafficking Area Program: An Overview," http://www.whitehousedrugpolicy.gov/hidta/overview.html (accessed April 29, 2007).

Chapter 12 Crimes Involving Illegal Immigrants, the Mob, Hate, and Youth

1. Center for Immigration Studies, "Illegal Immigration," http://www.cis.org/topics/illegalimmigration.html (accessed October 9, 2006).

2. U.S. Customs and Border Protection, "Securing America's Borders by Land, Air, and Sea," http://www.cbp.gov/linkhandler/cgov/newsroom/fact_sheets/press_kit/sbi_press.ctt/sbi_press.pdf (accessed October 9, 2006).

3. Ibid.

4. "U.S. Airports Boost Security," *Reno Gazette Journal,* January 6, 2004, p. 2A.

5. "Congress OKs 700 Miles of Fence on Border with Mexico," http://www.cnn.com/2006/POLITICS/09/29/fence.congress.ap/index.html?section=cnn_world (accessed October 9, 2006).

6. Reed Karaim, "South of the Border: Illegal Crossings Dip," *U.S. News and World Report,* February 26, 2001, p. 28.

7. Ibid., p. 8.

8. Alan Zarembo, "People Smugglers Inc.," *Newsweek,* September 13, 1999, p. 36.

9. Daniel Gonzalez and Sergio Bustos, "U.S. Reviles Border Smugglers; Migrants Hail 'Coyote' Heroes," *Reno Gazette Journal,* November 29, 2003, p. 9C.

10. Ibid.

11. Bay Fang, "Between Two Lands," *U.S. News and World Report,* August 4, 2003, pp. 18–23.

12. See, for example, "In Quest for Living Wage, Many Immigrants Make Ultimate Sacrifice," http://newstandardnews.net/content/index.cfm/items/1443 (accessed December 18, 2006).

13. Amanda Lee Myers, "Officials Say Border Drones Producing Positive Results," *Reno Gazette Journal,* August 34, 2004, p. 4C.

14. James N. Gilbert, "Organized Crime on the Western Frontier" (paper presented at the annual conference of the Western Social Science Association, Oakland, California, April 27, 1995), p. 1.

15. David E. Kaplan, "Getting It Right: The FBI and the Mob," *U.S. News and World Report,* June 18, 2001, p. 20.

16. Larry McShane, "Italian Mobsters in Widespread Decline," ABCNews, Associated Press, October 25, 2007, http://abcnews.go.com/US/wireStory?id=3776988 (accessed November 15, 2007).

17. Ibid.

18. Ibid.

19. International Association of Chiefs of Police, *Responding to Hate Crimes: A Police Officer's Guide to Investigation and Prevention* (Arlington, VA: Author, 2000), p. 27.

20. Michael Lieberman, "Responding to Hate Crimes," *Community Policing Exchange* (Washington, DC: Community Policing Consortium, January/February 2000), p. 3.

21. Southern Poverty Law Center, "Active U.S. Hate Groups in 2005," http://www.splcenter.org/intel/map/hate.jsp (accessed January 4, 2007).

22. J. Garofalo and S. Martin, "The Law Enforcement Response to Bias-Motivated Crimes," in *Bias Crime: American Law Enforcement and Legal Responses,* ed. R. Kelly (Chicago: University of Illinois at Chicago).

23. Federal Bureau of Investigation, "Hate Crime Statistics, 2006," http://www.fbi.gov/ucr/hc2006/victims.html (accessed November 21, 2007).

24. Ibid.

25. U.S. Department of Justice, Federal Bureau of Investigation, "Hate Crime Statistics, 2003," http://www.fbi.gov/ucr/03hc.pdf (accessed January 23, 2005).

26. International Association of Chiefs of Police, "Responding to Hate Crimes: A Police Officer's Guide to Investigation and Prevention," http://www.theiacp.org/documents (accessed April 28, 2003).

27. Madison, Connecticut, Police Department, "Special Programs: ADL and Police Launch Statewide Effort to Fight Hate Crimes," http://www.madisonct.org/pdspcprog.htm (accessed April 28, 2003).

28. Sean Webby, "Hate-Crime Prosecutions Have Proved to Be Difficult," *Reno Gazette Journal,* October 25, 2002, p. 8C.

29. U.S. Department of Justice, "Crime in the United States, 2004," http://www.fbi.gov/ucr/cius_04/persons_arrested/table_38-43.html (accessed February 27, 2006).

30. U.S. Department of Justice, Bureau of Justice Statistics, *Juvenile Victimization and Offending, 1993–2003* (Washington, DC: Author, August 2005), p. 1.

31. Joan McCord, Cathy Spatz Widom, and Nancy A Crowell, eds., *Juvenile Crime, Juvenile Justice: Panel on Juvenile Crime, Prevention, Treatment, and Control* (Washington, DC: National Academy Press, 2001), p. 25.

32. Gene Marlin and Barbara Vogt, "Violence in the Schools," *Police Chief* (April 1999): 169.

33. "Three School Shootings," http://www.nytimes.com/2006/10/03/opinion/03tue4.html (accessed October 9, 2006).

34. Ibid.

35. Ira Pollack and Carlos Sundermann, "Creating Safe Schools: A Comprehensive Approach," *Journal of the Office of Juvenile Justice and*

Delinquency Prevention 8, no. 1 (June 2001): 13–20.

36. Marlin and Vogt, "Violence in the Schools," p. 169.

37. Center for the Prevention of School Violence, "School Resource Officers and Safe School Planning," http://www.ncsu.edu/cpsv/srossp.htm (accessed May 27, 2003).

38. Rana Sampson, *Bullying in Schools* (Washington, DC: U.S. Department of Justice, Office of Community Oriented Policing Services, March 2002), pp. 1–2.

39. Ibid.

40. Anthony A. Braga, *Gun Violence among Serious Young Offenders* (Washington, DC: U.S. Department of Justice, Office of Community Oriented Policing Services, June 2003), pp. 1–2.

41. U.S. Department of Justice, Bureau of Justice Statistics, "Homicide Trends in the U.S.: Age Trends," http://www.ojp.usdoj.gov/bjs/homicide/teens.htm (accessed April 28, 2006).

42. Michael S. Scott, *Disorderly Youth in Public Places* (Washington, DC: U.S. Department of Justice, Office of Community Oriented Policing Services, June 2002), pp. 2–5.

43. Ibid., pp. 14–21.

44. Focus Adolescent Services, "Teen Drinking," http://www.focusas.com/Alcohol.html (accessed April 28, 2006).

45. Kelly Dedel Johnson, *Underage Drinking* (Washington, DC: U.S. Department of Justice, Office of Community Oriented Policing Services, September 2004), pp. 1, 4.

46. Ibid., p. 5.

47. Ibid., pp. 23–39.

Chapter 13 Policing Trends and Issues

1. *Board of Regents* v. *Roth,* 408 U.S. 577, 92 S.Ct. 2709 (1972).

2. W. Clinton Terry III, *Policing Society: An Occupational View* (New York: John Wiley and Sons, 1985), p. 168.

3. Ibid., pp. 170–71.

4. Samuel Walker, *The Police in America: An Introduction,* 3rd ed. (Boston: McGraw-Hill, 1999), p. 368.

5. American Federation of State, County and Municipal Employees, "About AFSME," http://www.afscme.org/about/officers.htm (accessed January 30, 2005).

6. Ibid., p. 318.

7. Will Aitchison, *The Rights of Police Officers,* 3rd ed. (Portland, OR: Labor Relations Information System, 1996), p. 7.

8. Ibid.

9. Ibid.

10. Ibid., p. 8.

11. Ibid., p. 9.

12. Charles R. Swanson, Leonard Territo, and Robert W. Taylor, *Police Administration: Structures, Processes, and Behavior,* 6th ed. (Upper Saddle River, NJ: Prentice Hall, 2005), p. 517.

13. Arnold Zack, *Understanding Fact-Finding and Arbitration in the Public Sector* (Washington, DC: U.S. Government Printing Office, 1974), p. 1.

14. Thomas P. Gilroy and Anthony V. Sinicropi, "Impasse Resolution in Public Employment," *Industrial and Labor Relations Review* 25 (July 1971): 499.

15. Robert G. Howlett, "Fact Finding: Its Values and Limitations—Comment," in *Arbitration and the Expanded Role of Neutrals* (Proceedings of the twenty-third annual meeting of the National Academy of Arbitrators) (Washington, DC: Bureau of National Affairs, 1970), p. 156.

16. Zack, *Understanding Fact-Finding and Arbitration in the Public Sector,* p. 1.

17. Charles W. Maddox, *Collective Bargaining in Law Enforcement* (Springfield, IL: Charles C. Thomas, 1975), p. 54.

18. Swanson, Territo, and Taylor, *Police Administration,* p. 530.

19. Ibid., p. 423.

20. Ibid.

21. L. Lund, "The 'Ten Commandments' of Risk Management for Jail Administrators," *Detention Reporter* 4 (June 1991): 4.

22. *Garcia* v. *San Antonio Transit Authority,* 469 U.S. 528 (1985).

23. Swanson, Territo, and Taylor, *Police Administration,* p. 392.

24. Barbara Raffel Price, "Sexual Integration in American Law Enforcement," in *Police Ethics: Hard Choices in Law Enforcement,* ed. William C. Heffernan and Timothy Stroup (New York: John Jay Press, 1985), pp. 205–14.

25. Jeanne McDowell, "Are Women Better Cops?" *Time,* February 17, 1992, p. 71.

26. U.S. Department of Justice, Bureau of Justice Statistics, *Local Police Departments, 2003* (Washington, D.C.: Author, 2006), p. iii; U.S. Department of Justice, Bureau of Justice Statistics, *Sheriff's Offices, 2003* (Washington, DC: Author, 2006), p. iii.

27. National Center for Women and Policing, *Equality Denied: The Status of Women in Policing* (Washington, DC: Feminist Majority Foundation, 2001), p. 5.

28. U.S. Department of Justice, Bureau of Justice Statistics, *Federal Law Enforcement Officers, 2004* (Washington, DC: Author, July 2006), p. 6.

29. Dorothy Moses Schulz, "Women Police Chiefs: A Statistical Profile," *Police Quarterly* 6, no. 3 (September 2003): 330–45.

30. Peg Tyre, "Ms. Top Cop," *Newsweek,* April 12, 2004, p. 49.

31. Schulz, "Women Police Chiefs," p. 333.

32. Ibid.

33. Ibid.

34. Peter Horne, "Policewomen: 2000 A.D. Redux," *Law and Order,* November 1999, p. 53.

35. Quoted in Horne, "Policewomen," p. 59.

36. McDowell, "Are Women Better Cops?" p. 71.

37. Quoted in McDowell, "Are Women Better Cops?" p. 72

38. U.S. Department of Justice, Bureau of Justice Statistics, "State and Local Law Enforcement Statistics," http://www.ojp.usdoj.gov/bjs/sandlle.htm (accessed January 21, 2004).

39. U.S. Department of Justice, Bureau of Justice Statistics, *Local Police Departments, 2003,* p. iii; U.S. Department of Justice, Bureau of Justice Statistics, *Sheriff's Offices, 2003,* p. 3.

40. Richard Margolis, *Who Will Wear the Badge? A Study of Minority Recruitment Efforts in Protective Services: A Report of the United States Commission on Civil Rights* (Washington, DC: U.S. Government Printing Office, n.d.).

41. *Griggs* v. *Duke Power Company,* 401 U.S. 424 (1971).

42. Robert Pursley, *Introduction to Criminal Justice* (Encino, CA: Glencoe Press, 1977).

43. Quoted in Peggy S. Sullivan, "Minority Officers: Current Issues," in *Critical Issues in Policing: Contemporary Readings,* ed. Roger G. Dunham and Geoffrey P. Alpert (Prospect Heights, IL: Waveland Press, 1989), p. 338.

44. Lena Williams, "Police Officers Tell of Strains of Living as a 'Black in Blue,'" *New York Times,* February 14, 1988, pp. 1, 26.

45. Robert J. Kaminski, "Police Minority Recruitment: Predicting Who Will Say Yes to an Offer for a Job as a Cop," *Journal of Criminal Justice* 21 (1993): 395–409.

46. National Organization of Black Law Enforcement Executives, "About NOBLE," http://www.noblenational.org/displaycommon.cfm?an=1&sub articlenbr=211 (accessed January 3, 2007).

47. Kenneth Peak, "The Quest for Alternatives to Lethal Force: A Heuristic View," *Journal of Contemporary Criminal Justice* 6 (1990): 8–22.

48. Ibid.

49. Ibid.

50. Saul D. Astor, "A Nation of Thieves," *Security World* 15 (September 1978).

51. U.S. Department of Justice, Bureau of Justice Statistics, "Criminal Victimizations, 2005," http://www.ojp.usdoj.gov/bjs/cvictgen.htm (accessed January 18, 2007).

52. Mahesh K. Nalla and Cedrick G. Heraux, "Assessing Goals and Functions of Private Police," *Journal of Criminal Justice* 31 (2003): 237.

53. Ibid.

54. Ibid., p. 238.

55. Ibid., pp. 243–44.

56. Lawrence J. Fennelly, ed., *Handbook of Loss Prevention and Crime Prevention,* 2nd ed. (Boston: Butterworths, 1989), foreword.

57. George F. Cole and Christopher E. Smith, *The American System of Criminal Justice,* 11th ed.

(Belmont, CA: Thomson Wadsworth, 2007), p. 253.

58. Ibid.

59. National Advisory Commission on Criminal Justice Standards and Goals, *Private Security* (Washington, DC: Government Printing Office, 1976), p. 99.

60. Cole and Smith, *The American System of Criminal Justice,* pp. 251–52.

61. San Francisco Patrol Special Police, "About Us," http://www.sfpatrolspecpolice.com/mission.htm (accessed January 6, 2007).

62. John Bartlett, ed., *Familiar Quotations,* 16th ed. (Boston: Little, Brown, 1992), p. 529.

63. William A. Westley, *Violence and the Police* (Cambridge, MA: MIT Press, 1970), p. 3.

64. Gordon Witkin, Ted Gest, and Dorian Friedman, "Cops under Fire," *U.S. News and World Report,* December 3, 1990, pp. 32–44.

65. Michelle Ingrassia and Karen Springen, "Living on Dracula Time," *Newsweek,* July 12, 1993, pp. 68–69.

66. See, for example, Stephen R. Band and Donald C. Sheehan, "Managing Undercover Stress: The Supervisor's Role," *FBI Law Enforcement Bulletin* (February 1999): 1–6.

67. See, for example, J. Sewell, "The Stress of Homicide Investigations," *Death Studies* 18 (1994): 565–82.

68. Adapted from Gerald W. Garner, "Prepare to Survive," *Police* (January 1994): 18–19, 90.

69. Anne Cohen, "I've Killed That Man Ten Thousand Times," in *Annual Editions: Criminal Justice, 88/89,* ed. John J. Sullivan and Joseph L. Victor (Guilford, CT: Dushkin, 1988), pp. 86–90.

70. John G. Stratton, *Police Passages* (Manhattan Beach, CA: Glennon, 1984), pp. 235–36.

71. James M. Horn and Roger M. Solomon, "Peer Support: A Key Element for Coping with Trauma," *Police Stress* 9 (winter 1989): 25–27.

72. Ben Daviss, "Burnout," *Police Magazine,* May 1982, p. 10.

73. Ibid., p. 50.

74. Gerald L. Fishkin, *Police Burnout: Signs, Symptoms and Solutions* (Gardena, CA: Harcourt Brace Jovanovich, 1988), pp. 233–39.

75. "What's Killing America's Cops?" *Law Enforcement News,* November 15, 1996, p. 1.

76. Ibid.

77. "Stressed Out? Help May Be on the Way," *Law Enforcement News,* January 31, 1997, p. 5.

78. U.S. Department of Justice, Bureau of Justice Statistics, *Local Police Departments, 2003* (Washington, DC: Author, 2006), p. 9.

79. "U.S. Census Bureau News," http://www.census.gov/PressRelease/www/releases/archives/education/009749.html (accessed April 24, 2007).

80. Albert Deutsch, *The Trouble with Cops* (New York: Crown, 1955), p. 122.

81. Herman Goldstein, *Policing a Free Society* (Cambridge, MA: Ballinger, 1977), pp. 283–84.

82. Deutsch, *The Trouble with Cops,* p. 213; *Law Enforcement and Criminal Justice Education: Directory, 1975–76* (Gaithersburg, MD: International Association of Chiefs of Police, 1975), p. 3.

83. Law Enforcement Assistance Administration, *Fifth Annual Report, Fiscal Year 1973* (Washington, DC: Government Printing Office, 1973), p. 119.

84. President's Commission on Law Enforcement and the Administration of Justice, *The Police* (Task Force Report) (Washington, DC: Government Printing Office, 1973), p. 155.

85. American Bar Association, *Standards Relating to the Urban Police Function* (Chicago: Institute of Judicial Administration, 1972).

86. National Advisory Commission on Criminal Justice Standards and Goals, *Police* (Washington, DC: Government Printing Office, 1973), p. 369.

87. Gerald W. Lynch, "Why Officers Need a College Education," *Higher Education and National Affairs* (September 20, 1986): 11.

88. *Davis* v. *City of Dallas,* 777 F.2d 205 (5th Cir. 1985).

89. Reuben M. Greenberg, Police Chief (Ret'd.), Charleston, South Carolina, quoted in Louis Mayo, "College Education and Policing" Proceedings of the 110th Annual Conference of the International Association of Chiefs of Police, October 18–23, 2003.

90. Ibid.
91. Victor E. Kappeler, Allen D. Sapp, and David L. Carter, "Police Officer Higher Education, Citizen Complaints and Departmental Rule Violations," *American Journal of Police* 11 (1992): 37–54. Also see Mayo, "College Education and Policing."
92. Charles L. Weirman, "Variances of Ability Measurement Scores Obtained by College and Non-College Educated Troopers," *Police Chief* 45 (August 1978): 34–36.
93. Ibid.
94. Robert Trojanowicz and T. Nicholson, "A Comparison of Behavioral Styles of College Graduate Police Officers versus Non-College Going Police Officers," *Police Chief* 43 (August 1976): 56–59.
95. A. F. Dalley, "University and Non-University Graduated Policemen: A Study of Police Attitudes," *Journal of Police Science and Administration* 3 (1975): 458–68.
96. Wayne F. Cascio, "Formal Education and Police Officer Performance," *Journal of Police Science and Administration* 5 (1977): 89–96; Bernard Cohen and Jan M. Chaiken, *Police Background Characteristics and Performance* (New York: RAND, 1972); B. E. Sanderson, "Police Officers: The Relationship of College Education to Job Performance," *Police Chief* (August 1977): 62–63.
97. James W. Sterling, "The College Level Entry Requirement: A Real or Imagined Cure-All?" *Police Chief* 41 (April 1974): 28–31.
98. Gerald W. Lynch, "Cops and College," *America,* April 4, 1987, pp. 274–75.
99. Mayo, "College Education and Policing," n.p.
100. Robert E. Worden, "A Badge and a Baccalaureate: Policies, Hypotheses, and Further Evidence," *Justice Quarterly* 7 (September 1990): 565–92.
101. Jon Miller and Lincoln Fry, "Reexamining Assumptions about Education and Professionalism in Law Enforcement," *Journal of Police Science and Administration* 4 (1976): 187–98.
102. John K. Hudzik, "College Education for Police: Problems in Measuring Component and Extraneous Variables," *Journal of Criminal Justice* 6 (1978): 69–81.
103. Wendy Koch, "HUD Gets New View of Who's Homeless," http://www.usatoday.com/news/nation/2007-02-27-hud-homeless_x.htm (accessed March 1, 2007).
104. "Homelessness," http://encarta.msn.com/encyclopedia_761579476/Homelessness.html#s3 (accessed February 22, 2007).
105. Institute for the Study of Homelessness and Poverty, "Homelessness in Los Angeles," http://www.weingart.org/institute/research/facts/pdf/JusttheFactsHomelessnessLA.pdf (accessed April 3, 2007).
106. "Las Vegas Averages 11,639 Homeless," *Reno Gazette Journal,* April 23, 2007, p. 4A.
107. Ibid.
108. Jaclyn O'Malley, "Assembly Tackles Homeless Problem," *Reno Gazette Journal,* February 20, 2007, p. 5A.
109. Ibid.
110. Ibid.
111. Ibid.

Chapter 14 Technology Review: Tools for the Tasks

1. Jim McKay, "Eyeing Auto Thieves," *Government Technology* (August 2006): 50–52.
2. Jim McKay, "Lost in Translation," *Government Technology* (July 2005): 56.
3. Jim McKay, "Military Mesh," *Government Technology* (October 2005): 50.
4. Jim McKay, "Eyeing Auto Thieves, *Government Technology* (January 2006): 38.
5. Jim McKay, "Keeping Tabs," *Government Technology* (August 2005): 58.
6. Merrill Douglas, "Putting Violence on the Map," *Government Technology* (June 2006): 50.
7. Jim McKay, "Good Science or Just Bunk," *Government Technology* (June 2006): 46–48.
8. Jim McKay, "Going Digital," *Government Technology* (June 2005): 40.
9. Leslie Friesen "On the Wire," *Government Technology* (September 2005): 62.

10. "DHS Completes Foundation of Biometric Entry System," http://www.govtech.net/magazine/channel_story.php/97728 (accessed January 6, 2007).

11. Dave Pettinari, "Are We There Yet? The Future of Policing/Sheriffing in Pueblo—Or in Anywhere, America," http://www.policefuturists.org/files/yet.html (accessed February 13, 2001).

12. Ibid.

13. Jennifer Nislow, "Big Benefits, Huge Headaches," *Law Enforcement News,* May 15/31, 2000, p. 1.

14. "Cybergame for the Millennium: Cops 'n' Robbers Playin' Hide 'n' Seek on the Net," *Police Futurist* 8, no. 1 (spring 2000): 4.

15. "Polls: Trade Some Freedom for Security," *Law Enforcement News*, September 15, 2001, p. 1.

16. "Surveillance Cameras Stir Up Static," *Law Enforcement News,* July–August 2001, p. 13.

17. Dana Hawkins and David LaGesse, "Tech versus Terrorists," *U.S. News and World Report,* October 8, 2001, pp. 16–17.

18. Kenneth J. Peak, "The Quest for Alternatives to Lethal Force: A Heuristic View," *Journal of Contemporary Criminal Justice* 6, no. 1 (1990): 8–22.

19. S. Sweetman, *Report on the Attorney General's Conference on Less Than Lethal Weapons* (Washington, DC: U.S. Department of Justice, National Institute of Justice, 1987).

20. Peak, "The Quest for Alternatives to Lethal Force," p. 10.

21. Ibid.

22. Ibid.

23. T. S. Crockett, "Riot Control Agents," *Police Chief* (November 1968): 8–18.

24. M. H. Haller, "Historical Roots of Police Behavior: Chicago, 1890–1925," *Law and Society Review* 13, no. 2 (1976): 303–23.

25. T. F. Coon, "A Maze of Confusion over Amazing Mace," *Police* (November–December 1968): 46.

26. Sarah Manwaring-White, *The Policing Revolution: Police Technology, Democracy, and Liberty in Britain* (Brighton, Sussex: Harvester Press, 1983).

27. Luis Cabrera, "Police Explore 'Less-Than-Lethal' Weapons," Associated Press, June 19, 2000.

28. Manwaring-White, *The Policing Revolution,* pp. 141–42.

29. Peak, "The Quest for Alternatives to Lethal Force," pp. 15–16.

30. Ibid., p. 16.

31. Manwaring-White, *The Policing Revolution,* pp. 145–46.

32. Ibid., pp. 142–43.

33. Sweetman, *Report on the Attorney General's Conference on Less Than Lethal Weapons,* pp. 4–5.

34. M. S. Serrill, "ZAP! Stun Guns: Hot But Getting Heat," *Time,* May 1985, p. 59.

35. U.S. Department of Justice, Bureau of Justice Statistics, *Local Police Departments, 2003* (Washington, DC: Author, 2006), p. iii; U.S. Department of Justice, Bureau of Justice Statistics, *Sheriff's Offices, 2003* (Washington, DC: Author, 2006), p. iii.

36. TASER International, "TASER Cam: The Truth Is Undeniable," http://www.TASER.com/TASERcam/index.htm (accessed January 10, 2007).

37. Amnesty International, "Aftershock," http://www.amnestyusa.org/magazine/spring_2005/aftershocks/has (accessed January 5, 2007).

38. Medical News Today, "Study Suggests Taser Use by U.S. Police Is Safe," October 9, 2007, http://www.medicalnewstoday.com/articles/84955.php (accessed November 16, 2007).

39. U.S. Department of Justice, National Institute of Justice, *Department of Defense Nonlethal Weapons and Equipment Review: A Research Guide for Civil Law Enforcement and Corrections* (Washington, DC: Author, October 2004); also available at http://www.ncjrs.gov/pdffiles1/nij/205293.pdf (accessed January 12, 2007).

40. U.S. Department of Justice, Bureau of Justice Statistics, *Local Police Departments, 2003,* p. iii; U.S. Department of Justice, Bureau of Justice Statistics, *Sheriff's Offices, 2003,* p. iii.

41. "Effectiveness Times Three," *Law Enforcement News,* May 15, 1993, p. 1.

42. Ibid., p. 6.

43. "Rethinking Stopping Power," pp. 1, 9.

44. Blake Harris, "Goin' Mobile," *Government Technology* 10 (August 1997): 1.

45. Kaveh Ghaemian, "Small-Town Cops Wield Big-City Data," *Government Technology* 9 (September 1996): 38.

46. Tod Newcombe, "Combined Forces," *Government Technology* (April 2001): 15.

47. Ibid.

48. U.S. Department of Justice, National Institute of Justice, *Crime Mapping and Analysis by Community Organizations in Hartford, Connecticut* (Washington, DC: Author, March 2001), p. 1.

49. Donna Rogers, "Getting Crime Analysis on the Map," *Law Enforcement Technology* (November 1999): 76–79.

50. U.S. Department of Justice, National Institute of Justice, *Crime Mapping Research Center* (Washington, DC: Author, 2000), pp. 1–3.

51. Lois Pilant, "Computerized Crime Mapping," *Police Chief* (December 1997): 58.

52. U.S. Department of Justice, *Crime Mapping Research Center*, pp. 1–3; the CMRC Web site address is http://www.ojp.usdoj.gov/cmrc.

53. Pilant, "Computerized Crime Mapping," pp. 64–65.

54. Bill McGarigle, "Crime Profilers Gain New Weapons," *Government Technology* (December 1997): 28–29.

55. Ibid.

56. Justine Kavanaugh, "Locator System Targets Shooters," *Government Technology* (June 1996): 14–15.

57. Jim McKay, "Triggered Response," *Government Technology* (December 2005): 62.

58. "GPS-Loaded Dogs to the Rescue," *Government Technology* (April 1997): 24.

59. Alison Bath, "Accident Scene Investigation Is High Tech," *Reno Gazette Journal* (Sparks Today section), November 18, 2003, p. 4.

60. Bill McGarigle, "Electronic Mapping Speeds Crime and Traffic Investigations," *Government Technology* (February 1996): 20–21.

61. Justine Kavanaugh, "Drunk Drivers Get a Shot of Technology," *Government Technology* (March 1996): 26.

62. Ibid.

63. "Freshnews.com: Less-Than-Lethal Technologies," http://www.jaycor.com/jaycor_main/web-content/eme_ltlt.html (accessed February 1, 2005).

64. Rutt Bridges, "Catching More Criminals in the DNA Web," *Law Enforcement News,* September 15, 2000, p. 9.

65. Drew Robb, "The Long New Arm of the Law," in *Crime and the Tech Effect* (Folsom, CA: Government Technology, April 2001), pp. 44–46.

66. Ibid.

67. Ibid., p. 46.

68. Tod Newcombe, "Imaged Prints Go Online, Cops Return to Streets," *Government Technology* (April 1996): 1, 31.

69. Corey Grice, "Technologies, Agencies Converge," *Government Technology* (April 1998): 24, 61.

70. Tod Newcombe, "Adding a New Dimension to Crime Reconstruction," *Government Technology* (August 1996): 32.

71. John McCormick, "Scene of the Crime," *Newsweek,* February 28, 2000, p. 60.

72. Joan Raymond, "Forget the Pipe, Sherlock: Gear for Tomorrow's Detectives," *Newsweek,* June 22, 1998, p. 12.

73. Samuel G. Chapman, *Murdered on Duty: The Killing of Police Officers in America,* 2nd ed. (Springfield, IL: Charles C. Thomas, 1998), p. 33.

74. Patrick Joyce, "Firearms Training: As Close to Real As It Gets," *Government Technology* (July 1995): 14–15.

75. Ibid.

76. John McCormick, "On a High-Tech Firing Line," *Newsweek*, December 6, 1999, p. 64.

77. Vanessa O'Connell, "The Next Big Idea: Using 'Fingerprints' of Guns to Solve Cases," *The Wall Street Journal*, February 10, 2000, p. A1.

78. Ibid.

79. Ray Dussault, "GangNet: A New Tool in the War on Gangs," *Government Technology* (January 1998): 34–35.

80. Brian Huber, "Wisconsin Police Get Robo-Cop's Help," http://www.policeone.com/police-technology/robots/articles/1190983/ (accessed April 2, 2007).

81. "Remote-Controlled Throwable Robot Developed by Carnegie Mellon with Marines Sent to Iraq for Testing," http://www.policeone.com/police-technology/robots/articles/91534/ (accessed April 2, 2007).

82. James Hannah, "New Robot Line Will Improve Bomb Detection," Associated Press, April 2, 2007; also available at http://www.dailybreeze.com/business/articles/6807622.html (accessed April 2, 2007).

83. Ibid.

84. Pettinari, "Are We There Yet?" p. 2.

85. George Nicholson and Jeffrey Hogge, "Retooling Criminal Justice: Interbranch Cooperation Needed," *Government Technology* 9 (February 1996): 32.

Chapter 15 Focus on the Future

1. William L. Tafoya, "The Changing Nature of the Police: Approaching the 21st Century," *Vital Speeches of the Day* 56 (February 1990): 244–46.

2. Sandy Boyd, Alberto Melis, and Richard Myers, "Preparing for the Challenges Ahead: Practical Applications of Futures Research," *FBI Law Enforcement Bulletin* (January 1, 2004): 2–3.

3. Quoted in Ibid., p. 3.

4. Ibid.

5. Police Futures International, "Futures Research," http://www.policefuturists.org/futures/index.htm (accessed December 13, 2006).

6. "Focus on the Future: A Look Forward," *FBI Law Enforcement Bulletin* 73(1) (January 2004): 1.

7. World Future Society, "Frequently Asked Questions," http://www.wfs.org/faq.htm (accessed December 13, 2006).

8. Thomas Cowper and Carl Jensen, "Emerging Technology," *Law and Order,* June 2003, pp. 124–27.

9. Ibid.

10. Ibid.

11. Ibid.

12. R. M. Steers, *Organizational Effectiveness: A Behavioral View* (Santa Monica, CA: Goodyear, 1977), p. 167.

13. Quoted in Boyd, Melis, and Myers, "Preparing for the Challenges Ahead," p. 2.

14. Sheldon Greenberg, "Future Issues in Policing: Challenges for Leaders," in *Policing Communities: Understanding Crime and Solving Problems*, ed. Ronald W. Glensor, Mark E. Correia, and Kenneth J. Peak (Los Angeles: Roxbury, 2000), p. 315.

15. See Alvin Toffler, *Future Shock* (New York: Random House, 1970); *The Third Wave* (New York: Bantam, 1981); and *Powershift: Knowledge, Wealth, and Violence at the Edge of the 21st Century* (Bantam Books, New York, 1990).

16. Alvin Toffler and Heidi Toffler, "The Future of Law Enforcement: Dangerous and Different," *FBI Law Enforcement Bulletin* (January 1990): 2–5.

17. Ibid., p. 3.

18. Department of Justice, Bureau of Justice Statistics, "Criminal Victimizations, 2005," http://www.ojp.usdoj.gov/bjs/cvictgen.htm (accessed January 18, 2007).

19. Lee P. Brown, "Violent Crime and Community Involvement," *FBI Law Enforcement Bulletin* (May 1992): 2–5.

20. Ibid., p. 3.

21. Greenberg, "Future Issues in Policing," pp. 315–21.

22. Ibid.

23. U.S. Department of Justice, Bureau of Justice Statistics, "Criminal Offenders Statistics," http://www.ojp.usdoj.gov/bjs/crimoff.htm#inmates (accessed January 15, 2007).

24. Edith M. Lederer, "Americans Have Far More Guns Than Any Other Population," Associated Press, July 8, 2003.

25. David Sheppard, "Strategies to Reduce Gun Violence" (Fact sheet no. 93) (Washington, DC: U.S. Department of Justice, Office of Juvenile Justice and Delinquency Prevention, February 1999), p. 1.

26. Stanford University, "Computers, Ethics, and Social Responsibility," http://cse.stanford.edu/class/cs201/projects-98-99/computer-crime/future.html (accessed December 20, 2006).

27. Edward J. Tully, "The Near Future: Implications for Law Enforcement," *FBI Law Enforcement Bulletin*, 55 (July 1986): 1–9.

28. U.S. Census Bureau, "USA Statistics in Brief: Population by Sex, Age, and Region," http://www.census.gov/statab/www/pop.html (accessed February 22, 2006).

29. U.S. Department of Justice, Bureau of Justice Statistics, "Violent Victimization Rates by Age, 1973–2004," http://www.ojp.usdoj.gov/bjs/

glance/tables/vagetab.htm (accessed February 25, 2006).

30. Andrew Karmen, *Crime Victims: An Introduction to Victimology,* 6th ed. (Belmont, CA: Wadsworth, 2006), p. 228.

31. Thomas Cowper, "Improving the View of the World: Law Enforcement and Augmented Reality Technology," *FBI Law Enforcement Bulletin* (January 2004): 13.

32. Ibid.

33. Ibid., p. 15.

34. Ibid., p. 16.

35. Chris Forsythe, "The Future of Simulation Technology for Law Enforcement: Diverse Experience with Realistic Simulated Humans," *FBI Law Enforcement Bulletin* (January 2004): 19–21.

36. Brian P. Tice, "Unmanned Aerial Vehicles: The Force Multiplier of the 1990s," http://www.airpower.maxwell.af.mil/airchronicles/apj/4spr91.html (accessed January 17, 2004).

37. SPI CORP., "UAV ONE–The Unmanned Aerial Vehicle Source," http://www.uav1.com (accessed February 2, 2005).

38. Tice, "Unmanned Aerial Vehicles."

39. Boyd, Melis, and Myers, "Preparing for the Challenges Ahead," p. 5.

40. Nanoink, Inc., "What Is Nanotechnology?" http://www.nanoink.net/4100_whatis.html (accessed February 2, 2005).

41. Nanowerk, "The Future of Medicine: Insert Chip, Cure Disease?" http://www.nanowerk.com/news/newsid=2276.php (accessed November 16, 2007).

42. Greenberg, "Future Issues in Policing," pp. 318–19.

43. Thomas C. Frazier, "Community Policing Efforts Offer Hope for the Future," *Police Chief* (August 2000): 11.

44. Ibid.

45. Roy Roberg, John Crank, and Jack Kuykendall, *Police and Society*, 2nd ed. (Los Angeles: Roxbury, 2000), pp. 522–23.

46. Dave Pettinari, "Are We There Yet? The Future of Policing/Sheriffing in Pueblo—Or Anywhere, in America," http://www.policefuturists.org/files/yet.html (accessed February 2, 2005).

47. Rob McCord and Elaine Wicker, "Tomorrow's America," p. 31.

48. Pettinari, "Are We There Yet?" p. 2.

49. Jerome H. Skolnick and David H. Bayley, *The New Blue Line* (New York: Free Press, 1989), pp. 220–24.

50. Alvin Toffler and Heidi Toffler, "The Future of Law Enforcement," p. 3.

51. Ibid.

52. James Q. Wilson, "The Future Policeman," in *Issues in Police Patrol,* ed. Thomas J. Sweeney and William Ellingsworth, (Kansas City, KS: Kansas City Police Department, 1973), pp. 207–221.

53. James Q. Wilson, "Six Things Police Leaders Can Do about Juvenile Crime," *Subject to Debate* (newsletter of the Police Executive Research Forum), September/October 1997, p. 1.

U

Underage drinking, 356–357
Undercover work, 200–201
Uniform Crime Reports (UCR), 51–52
Uniforms, police, 19–20
   academy training and, 115
Union brokerage model, 377
Unionization, 363–364
United States v. *Robinson,* 233
Unity of command, 74
Unmanned aerial vehicles (UAVs), 343, 345–346, 430
Upward communication, 69
U.S. Marshals Service (USMS), 55
U.S. Visitor and Immigrant Status Indicator Technology (US-VISIT), 343–344
USA PATRIOT Act, 322
Use of force. *See* Force, use of
Use-of-force continuums, 259–260

V

Van Maanen, John, 114
Vehicle pursuits, 263, 265
   liability of police and, 304
   prevention of high-speed pursuits, 412
Verbal abuse, 266
Verbal direction, 259
Vicarious liability, 293
Victimization
   false victimization syndrome, 211
   future of policing and, 426–427
   repeat (RV), 181
Vigilante committees, 23–24
Violent Crime Control and Law Enforcement Act of 1994, 35, 36, 431
Violent crimes, future of, 426–427
Virtual reality, as training method, 117
Vollmer, August, 27–31, 383
   criminalistics and, 195
Vote of confidence, 367

W

Wackenhut Corporation, 374
Wake Forest University School of Medicine, 404
Warrantless arrests, 229
Warrants, searches and seizures with and without, 232–239
Wartell, Julie, 408
Watchman style of policing, 127–128
Water cannons, 402
Watson, Elizabeth (Betsy), 370
Wells, Kenneth, 197, 199
Wells Fargo, 374
West case, fingerprints and, 194
Westley, William, 100, 122, 271, 377
Weston, Paul, 197, 199
Wickersham Commission, 30–31
Wilmington, Delaware, 152
Wilson, James Q., 36, 127, 435
Wilson, O. W., 30, 156
Wilson v. *Arkansas,* 230
Wireless technology, 405–406
Witness Protection Program, 55
Women. *See* Domestic violence; Female police officers
Working personality, 115, 122–125
Work slowdowns, 367
Work speedups, 367
Work stoppages, 368
World Future Society, 424
Wrightsman, Lawrence, 101
Written communication, 70
Written examinations, 106
Wrongful death suits, 297

Y

Youth crimes, 352–357